First published in 1940, R. M. Jackson's *Machinery of Justice in England* has long been established as the classic text on the subject. For this new edition J. R. Spencer has undertaken a further full-scale revision, incorporating such major recent innovations as the Police and Criminal Evidence Act of 1984 and the Prosecution of Offences Act 1985.

JACKSON'S MACHINERY OF JUSTICE

Edited by
J. R. SPENCER

University Lecturer in Law
Fellow of Selwyn College, Cambridge

The right of the
University of Cambridge
to print and sell
all manner of books
was granted by
Henry VIII in 1534.
The University has printed
and published continuously
since 1584.

Cambridge University Press

Cambridge

New York   New Rochelle   Melbourne   Sydney

Published by the Press Syndicate of the University of Cambridge
The Pitt Building, Trumpington Street, Cambridge CB2 1RP
32 East 57th Street, New York, NY 10022, USA
10 Stamford Road, Oakleigh, Melbourne 3166, Australia

Jackson's Machinery of Justice succeeds and replaces
the seventh edition of *The Machinery of Justice in England*,
by R. M. Jackson, first published in 1940

First published 1989

Printed in Great Britain at the University Press, Cambridge

British Library cataloguing in publication data

Jackson, R. M. (Richard Meredith), *1903–1986*
Jackson's machinery of justice.–8th edn
1. England. Legal system
I. Title   II. Spencer, J. R.   III. Jackson,
R. M. (Richard Meredith), *1903–1986*
Machinery of justice in England
344.207

Library of Congress cataloguing in publication data

Jackson, R. M. (Richard Meredith), 1903–1986
[Machinery of justice]
Jackson's machinery of justice / edited by J. R. Spencer.
p.   cm.
"Eighth edition" – Pref.
Rev. ed. of: The machinery of justice in England. 7th ed. 1977.
Includes bibliographical references and index.
ISBN 0 521 36257 1.   ISBN 0 521 31767 3 (pbk.)
1. Courts – Great Britain.   2. Justice, Administration of – Great
Britain.   I. Spencer, J. R.   II. Jackson, R. M. (Richard Meredith),
1903–1986 Machinery of Justice in England.   III. Title.
KD7100.J3   1989
347.41'01 – dc 19   88–23208   CIP
[344.1071]

ISBN 0 521 36257 1 hard covers
ISBN 0 521 31767 3 paperback

Contents

v

Contents

III Tribunals

IV Criminal jurisdiction

Contents

V The personnel of the law

VI The European dimension

VII The cost of the law

VIII Law reform

Acknowledgements

A number of friends and colleagues were generous with their time in reading parts of the text and making suggestions. In particular I would like to thank Patrick Halnan, John Hall, Brian Napier, Helen Napier, Clive Lewis, Andrew Grubb, John Tiley, Kenneth Polack, Stephen Tromans, Donald Rattee, and Philip Brown. I would also like to thank four students who worked hard for me as research assistants: Nicholas O'Neill, Michael Rollason, Paul Tucker and Robert Webb. (The mistakes in the book, however, are entirely my responsibility.)

I am grateful to Her Majesty's Stationery Office for permission to reproduce copyright material for figures 4 and 9 and tables 6, 7 and 12, and for permission to make use of copyright material in compiling figures 5, 7 and 8, and tables 1, 2, 3, 4, 5, 8 and 9.

Figures

Tables

Preface

I agreed to help Professor Jackson with the eighth edition of his book in 1984. Sadly, he was already in failing health and in 1986 he died, having been unable to do any more than read my preliminary attempt to edit the first two chapters and to offer his comments on my draft. Thus the changes in this edition are almost all my own.

Producing this new edition turned out to be an enormous task. The Police and Criminal Evidence Act 1984, the Prosecution of Offences Act 1985 and a number of other very important developments have taken place since the seventh edition appeared in 1977. As a result it has been necessary to rewrite about a third of the book. Much of what was not rewritten has been heavily revised. Since the first edition appeared the book had more than doubled in length and the time had come, I felt, to cut out or condense a lot of detailed material which had been added when it was topical, but was now of only passing historical interest. I have indicated where this has been done, referring readers to the earlier editions. Clearly, there was also a need for a section on the influence of the EEC and other matters European. Rather than simply expanding the book, I decided that something must give way to these matters; I therefore deleted the short chapter on habeas corpus and contempt of court. Perhaps some readers will be disappointed that I did not add a discussion of yet other matters: the prison service, for example, or the various theories about the purpose of the criminal justice system. To them I can only give a rather lame answer: that there are limits to how far I could go when editing an existing book without being accused of passing off one product as another.

I inherited from Professor Jackson a series of files relating to each of the previous editions. In these he had collected the various letters people had written pointing out errors which he had made; some were sorrowful, others showed undisguised glee, and one, from a solicitor, actually demanded that by some magical means he get hold of everyone who had bought a copy and give them a correction. Somewhat daunted, yet fortified by the knowledge that even a polymath like Professor Jackson could sometimes make mistakes, I proclaim that I have tried to make this edition accurate up to early January 1988.

The text contains a number of references to the work of the Lord Chancellor's Department's Civil Justice Review, and to the work of the Marre Committee.

Neither body had reported when the typescript was submitted to the publishers in January 1988. Both reported while the proofs were in my hands. It was not possible to re-write the body of the text to deal with their recommendations, but I have added a short Appendix to cover them. Certain other developments since January 1988 are mentioned in additional footnotes.

Cambridge   J. R. Spencer

Preface to the first edition of
The Machinery of Justice in England

The object of this book is to explain the system of law courts and allied matters relating to the administration of justice. In the past the administration of justice has hardly been considered a 'subject'. Writers on constitutional law have included the system of the courts, but necessarily cannot give it much space; other law books are apt to assume that the reader is acquainted with the subject. Thought about law has changed a good deal in the last twenty years. The attempt to treat law as a pure science, isolated from the society it serves, is succumbing to a more sociological approach. To some extent this means that the lawyer must come down from his high perch and look at law in the light of its effects upon individuals and society. The best introduction to law is a study of the institutions and environment in which lawyers work. It is prescribed, under the title of 'The English Legal System', for the first year study in some law schools, although academic tradition has there succeeded in imposing a mass of historical study to satisfy the idea that it is cultural to know what happened in the middle ages and not cultural to know what happens in the twentieth century. My own impression, and I have been teaching this subject for some years, is that the needs of the law student and the needs of those interested in public affairs are here exactly the same – to know the present system for administering justice, how it really works, and what criticisms and suggestions have been made.

As this book is far from being an exhaustive treatise I have omitted a full documentation. References are confined to indicating further reading of a complementary nature, or to giving my sources for subjects that are not well known or statements that would otherwise appear merely dogmatic.

I give my grateful thanks to many people including practising lawyers and teachers of law, who have helped me by discussion or by reading and criticising sections where their knowledge far exceeded mine.

Cambridge   R.M.J.
February 1939

Abbreviations

AC	*Law Reports, Appeal Cases*
All ER	*All England Law Reports*
Camb. LJ	*Cambridge Law Journal*
CB(NS)	*Common Bench* (New Series)
Ch.	*Law Reports, Chancery Division*
Ch. D	*Law Reports, Chancery Division*
CMLR	*Common Market Law Reports*
C, Cd, Cmd, Cmnd, Cm	Command Paper
Cr. Ap. R	*Criminal Appeal Reports*
Cr. Ap. R(S)	*Criminal Appeal Reports (Sentencing)*
Crim. LR	*Criminal Law Review*
DPP	*Director of Public Prosecutions*
ECR	*European Court Reports*
EHRR	*European Human Rights Reports*
HC	House of Commons
HL	House of Lords
HMSO	Her Majesty's Stationery Office
HO Circ.	Home Office Circular
ICR	*Industrial Court Reports*
ITR	*Industrial Tribunal Reports*
Journal SPTL	*Journal of the Society of Public Teachers of Law*
JP	*Justice of the Peace Law Report*
JPN	*Justice of the Peace Newspaper*
KB	*Law Reports, King's Bench Division*
KIR	*Knight's Industrial Reports*
Law Com.	Law Commission
Law Soc. Gaz.	*Law Society's Gazette*
LGR	*Local Government Reports*
LJ	*Law Journal*
Lloyd's Rep.	*Lloyd's Reports*
LQR	*Law Quarterly Review*
Mod LR	*Modern Law Review*

NLJ	*New Law Journal*
P	*Law Reports, Probate Division* (Probate, Divorce, Admiralty)
Parl. Deb.	*Parliamentary Debates (Hansard)*
QB	*Law Reports, Queen's Bench Division*
RSC Ord.	Rules of the Supreme Court, Order Number
SI	Statutory Instrument
St. Tr.	*State Trials*
TLR	*Times Law Reports*
U of Chicago LR	*University of Chicago Law Review*
U of Michigan LR	*University of Michigan Law Review*
WLR	*Weekly Law Reports*

I

HISTORICAL
INTRODUCTION

1

THE COURTS

The present system of courts of law in England and Wales depends almost entirely on legislation passed during the last 150 years. Yet it is difficult to describe the present system without referring to older courts, because the functions of some of the newer courts have been defined in terms of the older institutions; the legislative changes did not so much sweep away the debris of centuries as take materials that were to hand and from them fashion a new design. When our superior courts were rehoused in the Strand, in 1882, they were given a huge neo-Gothic building. It would have symbolised our legal institutions much better if the architect had made a building out of all the styles and dates to be found in the country. The past history of our courts is also responsible for a curious distinction being made between courts of law (often called 'ordinary courts') and special tribunals. This is not a distinction of function, but a distinction of age. During the last century, Parliament entrusted some judicial and quasi-judicial functions to various persons or bodies; if this process had occurred at a more remote time, these tribunals would now be 'ordinary' courts. To ignore these tribunals would lead to a lop-sided view of the administration of justice. However, there are advantages in discussing the system of 'ordinary' courts first, for they occupy a key position in our system. Furthermore, it is largely the limitations of 'ordinary' judicial process that have led to the creation of tribunals. These limitations are discussed in part II.

Today we generally assume that the administration of justice is a function of government to be exercised by the State. We express this in terms of the Sovereign, and speak of the Queen's judges, the Queen's courts, and Her Majesty's prisons, just as we speak of Her Majesty's ships of war. But if we consider the early history of our courts, we find that they used to be viewed quite differently. In the Norman period, the King's Court was merely one of the many courts, including the old local courts surviving from Anglo-Saxon times. These were the courts of the County – not to be confused with the present-day county court, on which see chapter 5 – and the courts of the Hundred which was a subdivision of the County. The ancient County and Hundred Courts had a wide jurisdiction over both civil and criminal offences. The Church claimed jurisdiction over laymen in a multitude of matters, and exercised it through a country-wide network of courts. Feudal courts arose from the principle that any overlord who had tenants enough could hold a court for his tenants. In theory the feudal courts had no criminal jurisdiction, but in practice they dealt with minor offences. The King also had his court. All these courts were concerned with a great deal of business other than the trying of cases. In fact, the early King's Court was far more concerned with non-litigious matters than with litigation, for it was in effect the machinery of central government: it was composed of the great officers of State and such other men as the King chose to summon, and that assembly, sometimes large and sometimes small, legislated and administered and judged. The right to hold a court, and take the profit to be made, was more in the nature of private property. It was on the same footing as the right to run a ferry and exclude anyone else from running a ferry in competition. These were called franchises, which always signified the exclusive right of a private person to exercise functions which we now consider should be in public hands. Privately run jurisdiction no more shocked the conscience of the Norman period than privately owned land shocks our conscience today.

The early development of the judicial machinery centred round one process: the King's Court gradually ousted most of the other courts and took over their work. This was not a sudden process. No frontal attack could be made, because the issues were those of property. A decree that feudal courts or franchise courts were to be abolished would have been an expropriation of property, hardly distinguishable from seizing rents due from other people's tenants. The success of the King's Court was due to the fact that the King offered better justice – his courts were selling a better and more reliable commodity. The first great steps were taken under Henry II (1154–89), and the system he devised was good enough to withstand the upheavals under King John. The Magna Carta was, on the whole, an attempt to safeguard the rights of the propertied classes in the kingdom. It included one clause designed to stop the King from taking work from feudal courts, but apart from this it accepted the existing judicial system. During the thirteenth century the King's Court steadily increased its jurisdiction, partly by inventing judicial remedies that no other court was able to offer. Royal justice was the most popular justice. The increase in business led to institutional changes. The old King's Court or Council split into several different institutions, with far more specialised functions. These divisions, or the germs of them, can all be seen in the thirteenth century, but it is easier to take stock of the changes at their completion in the late fourteenth century.

The judicial activities of the 'King's Court' were separated from the general governmental activities, and this separation led to a change in nomenclature. 'King's Court' then signified judicial institutions, and 'King's Council' was applied to the assemblies which the King held for carrying on his government: the large council of important people, sometimes fortified with representatives of the commons, which evolved into Parliament, and the small council of advisors and officials, which unlike the large council was almost permanently in session. 'The Council' from the fourteenth century onwards was the small group of

4

advisors and officials. The judicial work had originally been a council activity, but gradually it came to be exercised in definite institutions which lost touch with the council and emerged as three independent law courts. There was overlapping of the jurisdiction of these courts, but the main line was that disputes between subject and subject should be brought in the Court of Common Pleas. Cases in which the King was particularly concerned (such as control over inferior courts and tribunals and royal officials) went to the court of King's Bench and revenue cases went to the Court of Exchequer. These three were central courts sitting at Westminster, and by the end of the fourteenth century, they were staffed by professional judges appointed by the King from the ranks of the practising bar. They were known as the *common law* courts, to distinguish them from the ecclesiastical courts and other tribunals with special jurisdiction. The expression *common law* is discussed in the next section.

The common law system also included the Assize Courts. From early Norman times the King had sent trusted persons to visit the counties for various purposes. The Domesday Book was compiled from the answers to inquiries made by itinerant commissioners. The purpose of such a visitation depended on the terms of the royal commission. At first these commissioners exercised very little judicial authority, being far more concerned with making inquiries into matters where the King might have a fiscal interest, but eventually their judicial activities became the main purpose of their visits: they became itinerant justices, and each county was visited three or four times a year. The commission usually instructed the itinerant to hear and determine allegations of serious crime, while lesser offences were dealt with locally by the sheriff and later by justices of the peace. Thus virtually all criminal trials took place in the King's Courts in the county where the crime was committed. Civil trials in the King's Courts, however, at first usually went on in one of the common law courts at Westminster. With the growth of jury trial this became highly inconvenient. Since early juries were essentially neighbour witnesses, both the jurors and the parties to the suit had to travel to Westminster, which could be a grievous burden upon them. The comparative excellence of the central courts was thus somewhat undermined by the distance that might separate a litigant from the fountain of justice. To meet this it was provided in 1285 that an action could be begun in one of the common law courts at Westminster and would be sent down to be tried there, unless first – *nisi prius* – a justice of Assize should visit the county. The practical working was that the action was started at Westminster, the actual hearing took place in the county before the itinerant justice – who was usually a judge of one of the common law courts, but who might be an eminent practising barrister sent as a commissioner – and the formal judgment was made at Westminster. The proceedings at Westminster could be conducted by attorneys and counsel, so that the parties, witnesses and jurymen would have to attend only at the Assize Court in the county town. Hence, when the itinerant justices visited the counties they had to do both criminal and civil work. After 1875 the whole of a civil case (that is, commencement and judgment as well as the hearing) took place in the Assize town, and we talk of the 'civil side' instead of '*nisi prius*'. The system of itinerant justice was extremely durable and lasted until modern times. It was not until 1 January 1972 that Assizes were abolished: the criminal side was replaced by a network of permanent Crown Courts, and the civil side was replaced by an arrangement whereby the High Court – the modernised version of the courts at Westminster – distributes justice from a number of permanent locations outside London.

It thus appears that in the fourteenth century, England had a fairly comprehensive judicial system, as the Assize Courts were a happy compromise between centralisation and decentralisation. The best available justice was brought to the counties, points of law were chiefly argued at Westminster, and the common law courts were therefore able to develop a law which was uniform for the whole realm. Unfortunately, however, the law gradually lost its flexibility as it developed. Our thirteenth-century judges considered that they were empowered to do what justice demanded, but after the early fourteenth century, judges considered that their duty was to apply the law as their predecessors had laid it down. Common law became narrow and dominated by technicality; the merits of a case might be totally obscured by a fog of procedure. Furthermore, especially in the fifteenth century, a litigant might be deprived of remedies at common law through the activities of 'over-mighty subjects'; juries and even judges were often intimidated by powerful men. Many would-be litigants thought that common law would not or could not give them justice, and in such cases they adopted the expedient of petitioning the King. Since the King acted through his Council, the petition might be addressed to the King, or Council, or to individual councillors. The Council was the government of the country and was generally disinclined to waste its time considering petitions. Some petitions raised points in which the Council felt a real interest: piracy might have led to disputes with a foreign prince, and certain kinds of disorder might have directly affected the government. But most of the petitions were disposed of by telling the petitioner to go to common law, or by handing the petition over to the Lord Chancellor – who was then the general secretary of state – to investigate. At first the Chancellor investigated it with the help of a few councillors. Later he did it alone and reported his conclusion to the Council, who then made such decree as they saw fit. By the late fifteenth century, petitioners frequently sent their petitions direct to the Chancellor, and he investigated the case and made the decree himself. When this stage was reached it becomes proper to speak of the Court of Chancery. We do not know very much about the methods of the Chancellor in the earlier days, but in the sixteenth century there was a regular Chancery Court and its practice is fairly well known. The guiding principle of Chancery was 'conscience'. This was of course no precise guide, but it meant that relief would be given to a petitioner if the Chancellor thought that good conscience entitled him to a remedy. Within that vague limit, the work of Chancery was supplemental to that of the common law. There were occasional unseemly wrangles, but the relationship beween Chancery and the common law courts was mainly quite harmonious. Fifteenth-century judges accepted the need for a mechanism to bypass the usual procedures in cases of emergency, just as modern judges accept the need for the Home Secretary's discretion to release persons wrongly sent to prison when the usual safeguards have failed.

During the sixteenth century the Council was reorganised. Some councillors were assigned to attendance on the King, and these formed what was later called the Privy Council. Others were to stay at Westminster to do routine work. Most of the routine work was of a judicial nature, being a continuation of the judicial activities of the Council: this became known as the Court of Star Chamber. Other courts closely connected with the Star Chamber were also set up. The political conflicts of the seventeenth century brought all courts connected with the Council into disrepute. In 1641 the Star Chamber and allied courts were abolished though the Court of Chancery survived.

A review of the law courts in the later seventeenth century shows that the old three common law courts, Assizes, and the Court of Chancery dominated the scene.[1] The common lawyers, siding with the successful parliamentarians, had got rid of serious competition from the Council courts, captured the commercial work previously done in the Court of Admiralty, and prevented any extension of ecclesiastical courts. The old division of work between the Exchequer, Common Pleas and King's Bench had broken down; by ingenious fictions litigants could bring ordinary actions in whichever court they preferred. The King's Bench benefited most by this change and became the most important of the common law courts. The Court of Chancery was accepted and thoroughly taken over by the common lawyers. The old idea of 'conscience' was gradually eclipsed. Chancery was still said to be a court of 'equity', but equity ceased to be a fluid thing and became a set of rules. This is shown very clearly by the use of decided cases. Up until 1700 there were over a hundred volumes of reports of common law cases and only eighteen volumes of Chancery cases, and few of these contain decisions earlier than 1660. In the eighteenth century there were almost as many Chancery reports as common law reports. Eighteenth-century Chancellors had received the same training as common lawyers and they ran their court in much the same way, looking for definite rules to be found in and deduced from previous decisions. In fact, common law and equity (using this term in its technical sense of the rules applied in the Court of Chancery) were approaching each other so fast that Blackstone[2] saw little difference between them. By the early nineteenth century a working partnership was well established. Equity became a gloss on the common law; it was a set of rules which could be invoked to supplement the deficiencies of common law or to ease the clumsy working of common law actions and remedies.

[1] The courts of justices of the peace are discussed in chapter 19 (ii).
[2] *Commentaries on the laws of England* (1768), III, 429ff.

During the nineteenth century other superior courts were set up. In 1857 the jurisdiction of ecclesiastical courts over wills and intestacies and matrimonial cases was abolished and a Probate Court and a Divorce Court were established. Special provision was made for bankruptcy proceedings. Further, the elaborate and exceedingly inefficient system of appeal courts was mended piecemeal. There was no lack of superior courts: the trouble was mostly one of overlapping jurisdictions, varying procedure and lack of coordination. A complete reorganisation was made by the Judicature Acts 1873–75. The courts numbered 1 to 12 in figure 1 were abolished. A Supreme Court of Judicature was established, divided into the High Court and the Court of Appeal. The jurisdiction formerly possessed by courts here numbered 1 to 8 was conferred on the High Court and the former jurisdiction of courts 9 to 12 was (with modifications and additions) conferred upon the Court of Appeal. The High Court was at first divided into five divisions and Assizes. The five divisions were consolidated into three divisions: Queen's Bench Division,[1] Chancery Division and Probate Divorce and Admiralty Division in 1881. In 1972 the divisions were further rearranged with the abolition of Assizes and the Probate Divorce and Admiralty Division being replaced by a new Family Division. The Apellate Jurisdiction Act 1876 provided salaried professional judges for the House of Lords so that the House in its judicial capacity became an adequate final court. The Judicature Acts also ended the separation of 'law' and 'equity'. The High Court succeeded to the jurisdiction of the old common law courts and the old Court of Chancery, so it can do anything that any of those could have done. The rules of common law and the rules of equity were not fused: the provision made was that *all* courts should apply and use both sets of rules and that in case of conflict between the rules, the rules of equity should prevail.

The growth and expansion of the King's Courts was doubtless an excellent thing for the building of a uniform law and standard of justice in the country, but it was achieved at the expense of competing courts which were perhaps more suitable for poor litigants and small cases. The greatest number of disputes relate to small sums of money and most of the inhabitants of this country were – and are – not wealthy. The King's Courts offered trial at Westminster or at Assizes held at most four times a year; neither proceeding was cheap. In Tudor times there had been an attempt to deal with small cases and poor litigants by the creation of a Court of Requests, but it was too close to the King's Council to survive the political storms of the seventeenth century. In many of the ancient towns there were local courts which survived and some of these were improved by statutes of the eighteenth and early nineteenth centuries. There was no system at all, but this was largely remedied by the creation of county courts by statute in 1846. The passing of this Act was not easy. Lord Brougham's propaganda had to overcome an opposition which included most of the legal profession. The County Courts

---

[1] Which automatically becomes the King's Bench Division when the sovereign is a King.

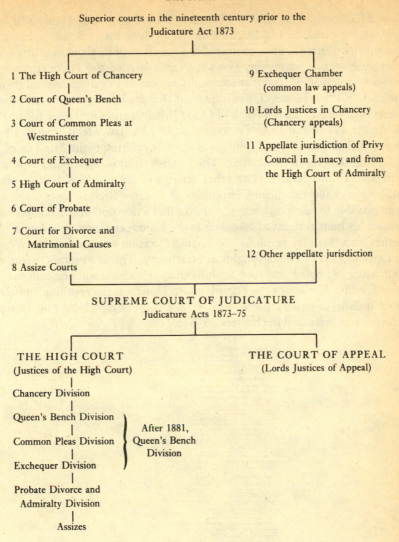

Superior courts in the nineteenth century prior to the
Judicature Act 1873

1 The High Court of Chancery

2 Court of Queen's Bench

3 Court of Common Pleas at
Westminster

4 Court of Exchequer

5 High Court of Admiralty

6 Court of Probate

7 Court for Divorce and
Matrimonial Causes

8 Assize Courts

9 Exchequer Chamber
(common law appeals)

10 Lords Justices in Chancery
(Chancery appeals)

11 Appellate jurisdiction of Privy
Council in Lunacy and from
the High Court of Admiralty

12 Other appellate jurisdiction

SUPREME COURT OF JUDICATURE
Judicature Acts 1873–75

THE HIGH COURT
(Justices of the High Court)

Chancery Division

Queen's Bench Division

Common Pleas Division

Exchequer Division

Probate Divorce and
Admiralty Division

Assizes

After 1881,
Queen's Bench
Division

THE COURT OF APPEAL
(Lords Justices of Appeal)

HOUSE OF LORDS. Final Court of Appeal for Great Britain and (now
Northern) Ireland. (Lords of Appeal in Ordinary) Appellate Jurisdiction Act 1876

Figure 1 Reorganisation of the superior courts of law in the nineteenth century

Act 1846 set up a network of local courts to deal with small claims and with
various minor changes the original scheme survives intact today. The organisation of county courts is explained in chapter 5.

Until recently, the system of courts in England and Wales was self-contained,
in that the courts' decisions were not open to scrutiny in any tribunal outside the

United Kingdom. This state of affairs had existed ever since Henry VIII broke with the Pope and thereby put an end to appeals to the ecclesiastical courts in Rome, after which any attempt to challenge the laws of England in courts abroad was condemned as *praemunire*. This was a vague offence: the Tudor equivalent of 'anti-soviet activities', and it theoretically remained in existence until its quiet abolition in 1967. However, two important changes have come about in the last twenty-five years. One is a result of Great Britain's entry into the EEC in 1973. By Article 177 of the EEC Treaty, points of EEC law which arise in English litigation always may be and sometimes must be referred to the European Court at Luxembourg for determination. The English court is then bound by what the European Court decides. The other change is the result of Great Britain's ratification of the European Convention on Human Rights. Since 1966 it has been possible for an individual who thinks that a decision of the English courts violates his human rights to complain to the European Commission on Human Rights, and this may result in the English decision being condemned by the European Court of Human Rights at Strasbourg. This is a moral censure only. As a matter of English law, such a condemnation does not automatically overturn the offending decision of the English court. However, the resulting embarrassment usually causes Parliament to change the relevant law. The European dimension is discussed in chapters 35–37.

2

THE COMMON LAW

The expression *common law* originally came into use through the canonists. 'They use it to distinguish the general and ordinary law of the universal church both from any rules peculiar to this or that provincial church, and from those papal *privilegia* which are always giving rise to ecclesiastical litigation.'[1] The phrase passed from the canonists to the lay lawyers. The emergence of the three courts of Common Pleas, King's Bench and Exchequer gave England a system of courts with wide jurisdiction. The judges were appointed to administer the 'law and custom into the realm', which meant that (apart from the small amount of law enacted by the King and Council or, later, Parliament) the judges built up their own set of principles and rules. Their material consisted of general and local custom and the juridical ideas of an age in which theology and law shared the hegemony of intellectual effort. The different 'laws' that had governed various parts of England tended to disappear. There emerged a general body of principles and rules that were applied in the King's Courts at Westminster and carried through the realm by the Assize judges on their circuits. This part of the law was 'common', and was to be contrasted with anything that was particular, extraordinary or special, such as surviving local custom, canon law or Roman law. The essence of common law was that it grew through judicial decisions recorded by lawyers.

The use of reports of decisions in past cases is not a phenomenon peculiar to English lawyers, although the actual technique they have developed is highly specialised. The tendency to look to past practice for guidance is prevalent in meetings and other organised activities. The appeal to the past minutes of clubs and societies is a familiar proceeding, and one would, for example, expect a local Jubilee Celebration Committee to begin its work by looking over the records of previous celebrations. The judicial use of precedents is a more formalised method of following what is really a widespread habit of mind. What is peculiar about the English courts in this respect is that they generally consider themselves *bound* to follow their previous decisions. This was not always so. The older view was

'that precedent is evidence, the best possible evidence, of rules of law, but *not more than*

---

[1] Pollock and Maitland, *History of English law* (2nd ed. 1898), p. 176.

11

that; and that if the law which precedent purports to embody is erroneous, unreasonable, or even intolerably inconvenient, the precedent may be disregarded'.[1]

This attitude lasted until about the middle of the last century, when a further hardening took place and our courts adopted a theory of 'absolutely binding' precedent. In the modern theory, the decisions of a court bind all inferior tribunals.[2] In 1898, the House of Lords finally decided[3] that it could not reverse its own prior decisions. Thereafter, a House of Lords' decision stood and was binding on every court in our system (of which that House is the apex), however inappropriate this might become with the passage of time. Although the ingenuity of various judges contrived to make that rigid system more flexible than it appeared to be, the absolutely binding character of the House of Lords' decisions was a nuisance and there was a general welcome when, in a Practice Direction in 1966, the Lord Chancellor announced that in future the House of Lords would occasionally be prepared to depart from its previous decisions.[4]

In this practice statement, the Chancellor stressed that this alteration was not to affect 'the use of precedent elsewhere than in this House', meaning in the Court of Appeal and at the Court of Criminal Appeal, which was merged in the Court of Appeal to become the Court of Appeal (Criminal Division) in 1966. The detailed rules governing precedent in these courts are a complicated playground for academic-minded lawyers, but the main outlines are clear enough. The rules differ according to whether the case is civil or criminal.

The Court of Appeal, dealing solely with civil cases, decided in *Young* v. *Bristol Aeroplane Co.* in 1944[5] that it is bound by its own decisions except in three instances, namely: (1) it can choose between conflicting decisions of its own; (2) it should refuse to follow decisions of its own which, though not expressly over-ruled by the House of Lords, are inconsistent with a decision of the House of Lords; and (3) it is not bound to follow a decision of its own given *per incuriam* (which is legal language for inadvertence, mistake or ignorance of relevant authority). Naturally this self-imposed straitjacket has been irksome to members of the court who would like to have a more activist role, but clearly there is a difference of opinion among the Lords Justices as to how far, if at all, its members should have an activist role.[6] It does not seem that the announcement about the use of precedent in the House of Lords has so far affected the Court of Appeal in civil cases.

[1] C. K. Allen, 'Case law: an unwarrantable intervention', (1935) 51 LQR 333.
[2] The working of precedents is such an important part of our legal system and of legal systems derived from the English that the published material is extensive. For a general account see Rupert Cross, *Precedent in English law* (1961); a student willing to cope with more detail and stronger assertions of opinion may well add C. K. Allen, *Law in the making* (1958).
[3] *London Street Tramways* v. *London County Council* [1898] AC 375.
[4] Practice statement [1966] 1 WLR 1234.
[5] [1944] KB 718. We speak of the Court of Appeal in terms of it being a single court, but it sits in divisions, and one 'court' may not be aware of what another 'court' is doing.
[6] See G. Drewry, 'Precedent and per incuriam', (1971) 121 NLJ 277; J. K. Bentil, 'The Court of Appeal's adherence to its jurisprudence', (1974) 124 NLJ 733.

In the days of the Court of Criminal Appeal it was never finally decided how far that court was bound by its previous decisions and doubts remain now that it has become the Court of Appeal (Criminal Division). The Court of Appeal (Criminal Division) is generally bound, but it is readier to overrule previous decisions than is the Civil Division. In addition to the situations described in *Young* v. *Bristol Aeroplane Co.*, the Court of Appeal (Criminal Division) usually holds itself free to overrule any decision of law which it later considers to be unduly harsh to the accused. It also freely departs from precedent when giving guidance on sentencing and when dealing with points of criminal procedure rather than of substantive law. Matters are complicated, however, because the court normally sits with three judges but may occasionally be a 'full court', which means five or a larger uneven number of judges sit. The extent to which a full court might have wider power than an ordinary court has never been entirely clear.[1]

The history of the doctrine of precedent is closely connected with the history of law reporting and necessarily so, because it is impossible for a judge to follow the reasoning of his predecessor if he is unable to discover what his reasoning was. From the earliest days our superior courts have had an official 'record', but that contains merely the bare bones of the case and usually reveals little or nothing of the reasoning in the case. Unlike the record, however, a report contains the facts as found by the court, the arguments put forward, and the reasons given by the judge for coming to his decision. From the late thirteenth to the mid sixteenth centuries, the only reports which existed were a series of jottings known as the Year Books. These were compiled anonymously and originally were circulated among the legal profession in manuscript form. They do not contain reports of cases as we understand the term, but are more notes of points that would be of use to practitioners. No hard and fast system of precedent was possible in Year Book days, although even then judges were concerned to be consistent, and a barrister who could point to a course of judicial conduct would generally be able to convince a judge that he ought to follow it. In the sixteenth century, the anonymous Year Books gave way to printed collections of reports which appeared under the author's name. These volumes were published either because the author felt certain that if he did not publish the work someone would pirate the manuscript, or because there was a market for such books. The following two centuries saw little change in these methods. Lawyers, learned or otherwise, collected accounts of cases and published them as they saw fit. Some of the reports are excellent, others are intolerably bad. It was during this period that the doctrine of precedent began to develop, but naturally the judges were not prepared to hold themselves firmly bound by cases which they knew might be inaccurately or incompletely reported. The modern doctrine evolved with the availability of full and reliable reports, coupled with the creation of a clear

[1] Useful articles are G. Zellick, 'Precedent in the Court of Appeal, Criminal Division' [1974] Crim. LR 222, and R. Pattenden, 'The power of the Criminal Division of the Court of Appeal to depart from its own precedents' [1984] Crim. LR 592.

hierarchy of courts by the Judicature Acts. Towards the end of the eighteenth century, a firm of publishers began to issue reports at regular intervals and during the nineteenth century the proprietors of legal periodicals began to issue series of reports. From 1866 onwards we have what are known simply as 'The Law Reports': these are produced by a cooperative and non-profit-making system set up by the legal profession. They carry most cases that are of real importance, and print in full a version of the judgment which has been vetted for publication by the judge. Since 1953 the same organisation has also run a supplementary series called the 'Weekly Law Reports', which produces unvetted versions of earlier judgments. It was with the Law Reports at their elbows that the higher courts decided they were bound by their previous decisions.

The new cooperative system did not displace the older method of publishing for profit. After 1866 several new private systems of general reports appeared, one of which survives today. There is also a seemingly endless array of specialist law reports (such as the Building Law Reports) which mainly publish cases not considered worthy of publication in the Law Reports. Published reports are expensive to buy and store and take valuable time to read, yet there seems to be an almost unlimited market for them. In theory, all decisions are binding precedents, so every lawyer hopes to find buried in the Law Report (which he would perhaps really rather not buy) the very precedent which will explode his opponent's case. As his opponent hopes the same, a kind of bibliographical arms-race seems to be unstoppable. A Committee was appointed in 1939 to investigate the problem but could suggest no cure.[1] Since then, problems have got worse. In the past, judgments which were not reported simply vanished into thin air. Since 1951, however, most judgments have been taken down in short-hand by court officials and their transcriptions stored in various libraries associated with the courts in London. Thus the texts of many unreported judgments have been preserved. It is permissible to cite these unreported cases if you can find them, but the problem of access to the transcripts and the difficulty of browsing has meant that, until recently, only limited use of unreported cases could be made. This changed in 1980, however, when enterprising law publishers arranged for the texts of many decisions to be stored in a vast computer. This included all decisions of the House of Lords and of the Court of Appeal and many unreported decisions at first instance. Lawyers are now able to search this material on a computer terminal and conjure up the text in their offices as easily as Aladdin used to summon the slave of the lamp. The computer searches the material by looking for key words and phrases which the lawyer types in on his terminal; judgments in which these words and phrases appear may then be read on the video display screen. This has led to the Court of Appeal transcripts prior to 1980 being made available on microfiche.[2] These developments caused a sudden increase of unreported cases, many of them not very important, being cited to the

---

[1] Report of the Law Reportation Committee, 1940.
[2] See Tunkel, 'Available at last: the Court of Appeal transcripts', (1986) 137 NLJ, 1045.

courts. The resulting protraction of cases displeased the Court of Appeal and the House of Lords, which in 1983 issued statements condemning the general use of unreported cases.[1] This is understandable, but also quite illogical, given the current theory of binding precedent. A decision of the court is a decision of the court, and equally binding whether or not anyone has bothered to print a report of it. Yet there is clearly a limit to the amount of case-law which the courts can be expected to cope with. Just as few and inaccurate reports prevented a rigid doctrine of precedent developing, so reports which are too many and too full look like making the rigid system practically unworkable. This problem is further discussed in chapter 42.

In a narrow sense common law is the result of the system of precedent used in the common law courts: that is, the old courts of Common Pleas, King's Bench and Exchequer and, in more modern times, the King's Bench Division of the High Court. However, the place of statute law must be considered. Our earliest enacted law was made by the King with the concurrence of his Council and then, as Parliament became the accepted institution, by statute. The earliest form of statutes was amorphous, and the judges could query the existence of a statute or its exact terms. By Tudor times, statutes had taken the form in which they are still cast: that is, an enactment by the King with the advice and consent of the Lords and Commons and by authority of the same. In practice, judges accepted the authority of statute law, although as late as Blackstone in the eighteenth century it was still customary to suggest that judges might disregard a statute that infringed natural or divine law. However, the Stuart political controversies finally settled the question of the highest authority in the State: the common law judges finally accepted the political fact of the dominant position of Parliament. It thus became an indisputable dogma that anything Parliament enacts will be accepted as law by our courts. Until after the Reform Act of 1832 the part played by statutes was not very great. The judges took the view that the law built up from precedents was the real body of the law, and that statutes were a kind of excrescence that, however useful, disturbed the otherwise harmonious form of their system. Statutes were construed to be in conformity with the common law whenever that was possible. The older statutes had been so construed and had become surrounded with such a mass of case-law that lawyers usually thought of the case-law and not of the statute. The legislation of the last 150 years, and of this century particularly, has raised a difficult problem; this is discussed in chapter 42. The phrase 'common law' may be used to include statute, or to exclude it, according to context; it depends upon whether we are thinking of the whole body of law administered by the common law courts, or of the principles and rules that rest entirely upon precedent.

The growth of the Chancery Court has been mentioned in the last section.

---

[1] *Roberts Petroleum* v. *Bernard Kenny Ltd.* [1983] 2 AC 192; *Stanley* v. *International Harvester Co.*, *The Times* 7 February 1983. See also R. J. C. Munday, 'The limits of citation determined', (1983) 80 Law Soc. Gaz. 1337.

When the early nebulous character of this jurisdiction suffered a metamorphosis in the eighteenth century, it came to look much like common law. 'Equity' came to mean the principles and rules acted upon in the Chancery Court; the essence of equity came to be a precedent, although precedents in equity were worked in a more flexible way, since it was never possible to suppose that they were anything but relatively recent creations. The men who worked the Chancery system received training at the Inns of Court, alongside those who practised in common law and the Lord Chancellor was frequently a man whose practice had been in common law. Since equity was a system complementary to the common law, and chiefly to be distinguished because it gave different remedies, the antithesis of 'law' and 'equity' is frequently used. When lawyers say that a remedy is 'legal' or 'equitable', they mean that the remedy in question has certain characteristics derived from the court in which it was devised.

Whatever court we turn to in our system, the authoritative sources of the law are confined to statutory provisions and reported decisions. The works of jurists, ancient or modern, may be of great assistance, and in practice a text writer of great standing may influence the court more than some obscure and ill-reported case, but in theory there is a definite line between the authoritative and the unauthoritative. Of course, the primary duty of a judge is to dispose of the case before him, and to do this he proceeds upon the supposition that the authoritative legal sources enable him to state the law. In most cases this is true, but when new points arise, that supposition becomes a fiction. In theory the judge then deduces some rule from the accepted material; in reality he consciously or unconsciously invents a rule that appears to be not inconsistent with accepted doctrine and announces that that is the law of England, thus implying that the judges merely declare the law and do not make it. This habit of mind is so ingrained that the common law is often thought of as a comprehensive body of law that has always existed, although in searching precedents, every practitioner is actually engaged upon tracing the growth of some part of the law.

In a wide sense the expression 'common law' is used to mean the legal system and habits of legal thought that Englishmen have evolved. In this sense it is contrasted with systems of law derived from Roman law. It has been a principle of our law that when new lands have been settled by colonisation the settlers carry with them the law of England as far as it is applicable to the new conditions, whereas in territories acquired from a civilised power, the existing law remains in force until the new sovereign alters the law. Hence in the Commonwealth, the common law of England is the basis of the system where colonisation occurred, but where there was an existing system (as French law in Lower Canada and Roman-Dutch law in South Africa) the basis of the law is generally that of our predecessors, France, Holland or Spain. This principle led to the North American colonies having the common law, a heritage that was undisturbed when they became the United States. In the British Isles, the English system has dominated Wales and Ireland, but not Scotland, which retains a separate system of law in the Roman tradition and a separate system of courts. The Irish courts, although following the English pattern, are a separate system. The subject of this book is the English system in the narrow sense of that which applies to England and Wales, but since it is part of a wider conception it is relevant to consider the differences that exist between the common law systems and those founded on Roman law.

The common law or Roman law is the basis of most modern systems, at least in the West. The Roman law would, of course, be barely recognisable to a Roman. The Romans made up their laws as they went along, much as the English did a thousand years later, and Roman law reached a highly developed state in the second century AD. In the sixth century, it was codified under the emperor Justinian. In those parts of Europe where the Roman influence remained, Justinian's code was overlaid with gloss and comment and comment on the comment until it sometimes had no apparent connection with the original texts. Roman law in this form was then recodified in France after the French Revolution and in Germany in the late nineteenth century. The tradition of codification has been largely responsible for the spread of modern Romanesque law. For instance, in the desire to modernise her law, Japan would have preferred to adapt English law, but it was impracticable to import a system of law that could not be found in any concise form. The codes of France and Germany offered intelligible material in accessible form, and so the Far East and the countries of South America turned to these Romanesque codes for study and adaptation. The division of countries into common law and Romanesque law is easy to make, but rather more difficult to substantiate. A distinguished jurist has explained that

there is indubitably something which enables English and Irish and American and Canadian and Australian lawyers to read each other's books and understand each other's arguments and apply each other's judicial decisions and adapt each other's legislation as surely as they are unable to understand the arguments and read effectively the books and apply the authoritative texts of the non-English speaking world. This is something we call the common law. But what is it?[1]

To some extent it is a matter of vocabulary. Technical legal terms can rarely be translated into a foreign language. Our word 'freehold' can be explained in French in a page or so of type, but it cannot be translated, for French law has no legal concept that is exactly equivalent. Many of our terms are Norman-French and Latin, but the same difficulties arise. On the other hand, the Roman law terms provide the Romanesque systems with a common basis of reference. For instance, suppose that when your neighbour is away a storm damages his roof; unable to get in touch with him, you act as a good neighbour and instruct a builder to make emergency repairs, after which your neighbour refuses to pay the bill. English law says that generally there is no obligation to indemnify a person who has voluntarily incurred expense in protecting the interests of another in his

---

[1] Roscoe Pound in *The future of the common law* (1936).

absence. Roman law recognised an obligation, called *negotiorum gestio*. So that, if we wished to make a symposium of foreign law on the matter, we could simply ask foreign jurists if their law recognises *negotiorum gestio* and thereby avoid the pitfalls of rendering 'obligation', 'indemnify', 'voluntary' and 'interests' into several foreign languages. The problem of language must not be overlooked, but it does not supply a complete explanation of the differences between the Roman and common law systems.

The function of case-law in common law is another suggested difference, but the Romanesque systems also make considerable use of precedent. French case-law is voluminous and essential to the working of their courts. Again, jury-trial has been singled out, but jury trial has spread widely in the Romanesque system – and has also been ditched to a greater extent than is often generally recognised in the countries of the common law. The 'rule of law' is often instanced. If this means merely public order and civil liberties, we can claim no monopoly; if it means the constitutional position of our Parliaments and courts, it does not exist in the United States; if it means that the powers of the government are derived from law, then it is characteristic of every state.[1] It is a pity that such a high-sounding phrase, suggestive of a decent international and social order, should have acquired too many meanings to be of much use.

There is one distinction between the common law and the Romanesque systems that perhaps provides a key to the differences. It is the position of the judge. Where the Roman law tradition holds, a lawyer must choose at an early age whether he will practice before the courts or whether he will go on the bench. The judiciary is part of the administrative hierarchy; a young lawyer starts as an assistant in a very inferior court and slowly works up to more exalted judicial status. This does not mean that he is a civil servant acting under the orders of his government department in all matters, but it does mean that the judiciary is a separate profession from that of practising lawyers.[2] The English tradition, examined more fully in part V, is that the legal profession is practically an autonomous body from which the judges are drawn when they are not less than middle-aged. The theory is that the best practising lawyers are ultimately elevated to the judiciary, where the terms of their appointment ensure that they shall be independent of administrative interference. Hence for the common lawyer the revered figure and the oracle is the judge. We should therefore seek for the nature of English law not in its substantive rules but in its machinery of justice.

[1] The 'rule of law' as a characteristic of our system is principally associated with Dicey, *Law of the Constitution*, first published in 1885.
[2] That does not prevent some judicial appointments from being practising lawyers or academic lawyers. England academic lawyers may have the formal qualifications, but have never been given judicial appointments except at the very lowest level.

3

TRIAL AT COMMON LAW

It is generally accepted that there have been two main systems of trial in civilised law, the accusatorial and the inquisitorial. At the time of the foundation of our legal system in the twelfth and thirteenth centuries, common law procedure was accusatorial; the parties came before the court upon an equal footing and the court gave no help to either of them. It was the duty of one party to formulate his grievance and the duty of the other party to deny it. The mode of trial was some type of ordeal, which was *judicium dei*: the judgment was that of God, not that of the president of the court. A dislike of such proceedings was manifested by the Church. When, for instance, it was alleged that a priest was not conducting himself properly the ecclesiastical superiors showed little enthusiasm for a trial by *judicium dei*; the twelfth-century technique was to send a trusted person along to inquire into the allegations. This founded the inquisitorial concept of a trial, whereby the judge was expected to find out for himself what had happened, and he was to do this by examining all persons, including the accused or suspected person, who might have been able to enlighten him. In the thirteenth century the inquisitorial system represented the cause of progress and eventually became the accepted theory on the Continent. The English kept to the accusatorial theory, partly because of an insular dislike for things foreign and partly because of the emergence of jury trial. Jury trial simply replaced trial by ordeal; the verdict of the jury having the same finality and the same inscrutability as the judgment of God. With a workable method of trial there was no need to import foreign or ecclesiastical ideas and, when in the inquisitorial system the use of torture became institutionalised, the English lawyer could feel that his system was superior.[1] The emergence of the Chancery Court in the fifteenth century introduced the ideas of the inquisitorial system, for the Chancellor adopted the canon law theory of a trial. The Chancellors considered that their function was to get to the bottom of the cases submitted to them and to do this they must interrogate those concerned, either by oral examination or by compelling one party to answer on oath a string of written questions. Further, a party could be compelled to give 'discovery', which meant that he had to disclose all documents

---

[1] In England, suspects were sometimes tortured in state cases, but torture never became an official part of the justice system as it did elsewhere in Europe. See J. H. Langbein, *Torture and the law of proof* (1977).

he had that related to the case. The Chancellor eventually came to deal exclusively with civil actions and here his notions prevailed. Before the Judicature Acts of 1873–75, a litigant at common law could seek assistance from the Chancery in such matters as discovery and, under our present system, all civil courts can order a party to answer interrogatories or make discovery of his documents. The Chancellor did not have occasion to touch our criminal law and so in criminal trials there is none of this compulsory interrogation. English civil proceedings therefore must be classed as inquisitorial while English criminal proceedings are accusatorial, whereas the Romanesque countries that invented the inquisitorial process use it for their criminal proceedings but retain a rigid accusatorial theory for civil litigation.

The distinction between the accusatorial and the inquisitorial system is one that has been made for centuries and as a historical fact it has great importance, but it is perhaps of less use today than the distinction between what may be called the 'contest' theory and the inquisitorial theory of a trial. The interrogation of the defendant is the outward sign of the inquisitorial system, but it is historically no more than an incident in the performance of the judicial office. The fundamental idea of inquisitorial proceedings is that the judge himself must investigate a complaint, find out the facts for himself and then do what ought to be done according to law. Early English Chancery proceedings show this; the petitions were often little more than an allegation that the defendant was a 'bad lot', with very sketchy accounts of his ill-doings. The request in the petition was that the Chancellor would investigate and do right in the matter. At common law we find a different conception. The judge was thought of as an umpire who must see fair play between two contesting parties. Whether the case was civil or criminal, it was the complainant who selected the precise ground of his complaint. The common law system of 'pleading' was designed to reduce a case to one issue, either of fact or of law, so that when the case came before the court for trial the parties had already formulated the question that was to be answered. If the point was one of law it would be decided by the judges, whilst if it was one of fact it would go to the jury. The judges could, of course, see that the process of the court was not abused, but otherwise their function was confined to the issue that was before them. If the parties had selected the wrong issue, then the judge might point out what would have been the correct issue, but it was no part of the judicial duty to see that the court got to the bottom of a case and dealt with the true grounds of the dispute. Following the analogy of the judge as umpire, we can say that the parties selected the game that was to be played and the umpire saw that the game was properly played. The idea of a contest eventually prevailed in Chancery, where the form of pleading gradually changed, so that by the early nineteenth century, proceedings in Chancery had come to resemble common law actions in many respects. Since then, the contest theory has been watered down in some respects. The modern law of pleading in civil cases gives considerable scope for amending pleadings so that the right issue is eventually raised. In criminal cases, the basic rule is still that the defendant must be charged with a definite offence and must be acquitted if that offence is not proved, even if it appears that he has committed some other offence, but this rule has been modified significantly as far as trials in the Crown Court are concerned. Nowadays, where the allegations in an indictment charging offence X amount to or expressly or impliedly include allegations of offence Y, the jury may convict of Y instead of X.[1] The old rule survives intact as far as trials in Magistrates' Courts are concerned, however, and throughout both civil and criminal law the contest theory still holds true to the extent that it is up to the parties, not the judge, to decide what issues shall go before the court. If a motorist runs someone over in circumstances amounting to manslaughter or even murder, the prosecution is free to undercharge by prosecuting for careless driving only, and the court must try the case as presented.[2] At a civil trial, a defendant is at liberty to avoid a particular line of defence which would unquestionably succeed, but might be commercially embarrassing; if the defendant does not raise it, nor will the judge. The judge is not an inquisitor who must find out whether the defendant has broken the law, but an umpire who is limited to the issue raised between the parties.

It was implicit in the common law conception of a trial that it was a culmination; the day comes when the issues that have been settled and defined by pleadings come before the court. Under an inquisitorial system, the judge will collect evidence and material from the time when he becomes seized of the case and hearings and final trial are essentially to make sure that the file or dossier is completed by representations on fact or law from those who are involved. In contrast, the common law process was geared to jury trial. Once the pleadings showed an issue for a jury, the case had to be presented as a whole, at one hearing. That was the 'day in court' which in a criminal case decided guilt or innocence and sentence and in a civil case decided liability and amount of damages. It was a public process and it could hardly have been otherwise; the jury was traditionally the neighbours, and they were supposed to know about the facts. That slowly changed until juries were expected to decide on the evidence put before them, but the jury was still a man's 'country' to whose verdict he committed himself, and Assizes and Quarter Sessions were the periodical assemblies for the most important kinds of public business. A man might be hanged, or cast in damages, by the same process that could determine liability to remove an obstruction of the highway or repair a bridge. Open court was not derived from liberal thought but was an almost inevitable consequence of our system of courts and the use of juries.

By contrast, courts which used different procedures did not find it necessary to

---

[1] Thus where a man is indicted for rape, for example, the jury can convict of attempted rape or indecent assault or any other offences which are normally committed in the course of a rape.

[2] Criminal Law Act 1967 s.6. The scope of the section was considerably extended by the House of Lords decision in *Wilson* [1984] AC 242, which discards the technical interpretation which the courts had previously put upon it.

operate with permanently open doors. Matrimonial affairs were originally the province of the ecclesiastical courts, where evidence was taken in private by examiners, who reported to the court, which gave judgment in public. Matrimonial jurisdiction was transferred to a lay court in 1857. The lay court was amalgamated with the other superior courts in 1873 and the practice of private hearings went on. The common law rule of open court eventually triumphed, however, because in *Scott* v. *Scott* the House of Lords ruled that the principle of open court was fundamental and the courts were bound to sit in public.[1] They held that unless statute provided for a private hearing, the court could only sit *in camera* where justice could not be done in public. Examples given were of litigation about secret processes where the court could not do justice if it sat in public and thereby destroyed the subject-matter, and circumstances of tumult or disorder that would make a public hearing impossible. The interests of public decency, said the House of Lords, would not affect the ability of a court to administer justice, and therefore a hearing in camera could not be ordered on those grounds. They were divided on what the position was when a woman was too embarrassed to be able to give evidence in open court; later courts held that even this did not justify a private hearing.[2]

The list of cases where there may be a private hearing outside the principles laid down in *Scott* v. *Scott* has steadily lengthened. Many concern family law. Wardship applications and proceedings for the guardianship of lunatics and custody of their property have always been heard privately in chambers – a special exception recognised by the House of Lords in *Scott* v. *Scott*. By statute the public is excluded from domestic proceedings in magistrates' courts and adoption proceedings. In 1935 a statute permitted certain types of nullity proceedings to be heard privately[3] and a statute of 1968, which was enacted in response to a particular case which had caused some concern, did the same for proceedings to legitimate children.[4] Another group of exceptions to open court concerns juveniles. The public are excluded from juvenile courts as from domestic courts, and may be excluded from any court if children are called to give evidence against adults accused of indecency. There are other exceptions on grounds of national security, notably a provision for trials in camera where persons are prosecuted under the Official Secrets Acts. The courts have developed the practice of excluding the public when allegedly pornographic films are shown in obscenity

---

[1] [1913] AC 417. A woman was held in contempt of court for obligingly sending to her husband's relatives the medical evidence of his impotence, called at a nullity suit which had been heard in camera. The House of Lords held that as the proceedings should have been held in public it was no contempt to publish the evidence.

[2] *Greenway* v. *A-G* (1927) 44 TLR 124; *B (otherwise P)* v. *A-G* [1967] P 119.

[3] Matrimonial Causes Act 1973 s.48(3), originally enacted by the Supreme Court of Judicature (Amendment) Act 1935.

[4] Domestic and Appellate Proceedings (Restriction of Publicity) Act 1968, passed to implement the recommendations of the Law Commission in their Report on Powers of Appeal Courts to Sit in Private and the Restriction upon Publicity in Domestic Proceedings (1966) Cmnd 3149. The provision about legitimacy proceedings is now the Matrimonial Causes Act 1973 s.45(a).

prosecutions. When sentencing, the judges frequently act on detailed reports about the convicted person which are not read out in open court. The biggest exception is in the County Court, where, in order to encourage litigants to appear in person, small claims are usually tried by an arbitration procedure which is always private.

Newspapers were allowed in court on the same footing as members of the public: press reporters had no greater right than other members of the public to be present, but if present they were free to repeat all that went on. It is still true that law courts (unlike meetings of local authorities) are not required to provide special accommodation and facilities for the press and it is only by courtesy that some space is saved for reporters, but otherwise things are now more complicated. The press is privileged in that newspaper reporters, unlike members of the general public, are permitted at juvenile and domestic courts – although they are severely restricted in what they may print about the proceedings. On the other hand, the press is now considerably restricted in what it may print about court proceedings to which the general public is admitted. The Judicial Proceedings (Regulation of Reports) Act 1926 prohibits the publication of 'indecent matter or indecent medical, surgical or physiological details being matter or details the publication of which would be calculated to injure public morals'. This was enacted to end the field-day the popular press was having with the Russell divorce[1] and similar sordid cases. The Children and Young Persons Act 1933 s.39 protects juveniles against newspaper reports which would reveal their names or their school, whether they are the defendant, the victim or a witness. Since 1967 there have been severe restrictions on the reporting of committal proceedings;[2] these were enacted to prevent matters coming out which might unfairly prejudice potential jurors against the defendant. The Sexual Offences (Amendment) Act 1976 prevents the publication of the name of the alleged victim in a rape trial and the name of the defendant as well unless he is convicted. The Contempt of Court Act 1981 adds further restrictions. It empowers the court to order the press to wait before they publish, so that where, for example, a person pleads guilty to nineteen burglaries and not guilty to the twentieth, the court may embargo a report of the guilty pleas until the contested case is over. And where as in a blackmail trial a witness appears as 'Mr X', the court may now validly ban the press from saying who X really is. In 1970 there was an attempt to give the Commercial Court power to sit in camera, but this was defeated in Parliament; see chapter 6 (i).

The argument for open court is that it discourages abuse of judicial process. 'Publicity is the very soul of justice. It is the keenest spur to exertion and the surest of all guards against improbity. It keeps the judge himself while trying under trial.'[3] On this entirely disinterested ground it is vigorously defended by

---

[1] *Russell* v. *Russell* [1924] AC 687.
[2] They are now contained in the Magistrates' Courts Act 1980 s.5.
[3] Bentham, 'Draft for the Organization of Judicial Establishments', *Works* ed. Bowring (1843) 316.

the newspapers. But that all hearings should be in public is not universally accepted. If a person is injured in an accident and claims damages, negotiation is private and the press has no access to medical reports, financial reckonings and other personal matters; go to arbitration and it stays private; go to court and the more gruesome bits of any 'revelation' of private affairs may be reported. The business community prefers arbitration in private to the Commercial Court in public. It may seem obvious that the trial of criminal charges should be in public and be reported, but there are drawbacks even here. A person may be reluctant to give evidence if he has a bad record which may be dragged out in public after he reckons that he has lived it down, and if police informers have to give evidence in open court everyone discovers who they are and their future usefulness is destroyed.[1] As elsewhere, there are advantages and disadvantages, and they need to be balanced against each other.

These matters of the nature of a trial at common law have been followed because the machinery of justice in England has to be seen in its peculiar historical setting. It must not be regarded as a logical structure designed round basic principles. Procedures and practices led to a 'contest' conception of a trial, in open court, but this gives neither any special sanctity. We have to see how these ideas work out in the courts and processes of our own day.

[1] The report of inquiry by Mr A. E. (later Lord Justice) James into Detective Sergeant Challenor's continuing on duty after he had become mentally ill, (1965) Cmnd 2735 p. 6, illustrates the kind of problem which arises. The submissions by Mr Park (later Mr Justice Park) on the matter of public or private sittings are given in *The Times* 27 November 1964.

II

CIVIL JURISDICTION

4

CIVIL LAW AND
CRIMINAL LAW

The division of the law into civil and criminal gives us the only two categories that are sharply distinguished for the administration of justice, for as a general rule civil cases are dealt with by one hierarchy of courts and criminal cases by another. The word 'civil' is unfortunate, since in connection with law it has four meanings. To those in the Armed Forces 'civil' generally denotes everything that is not peculiar to the Services; a civil court as contrasted with a court-martial then means a non-service tribunal irrespective of whether it has civil or criminal jurisdiction. To lawyers, the term 'civil' is sometimes used to mean the whole law of some particular state in contrast to international law. It may also signify Roman law: this comes from the medieval contrast between Justinian's compilation known as the *corpus iuris civilis* and ecclesiastical law known as the *corpus iuris canonici*. In this sense 'civilian' means a person learned in Roman law. The fourth sense, in which the word is generally used today, means that part of a country's law that is not criminal. The dichotomy here is really criminal and non-criminal, so that civil cases must be distinguished by settling the boundary of the criminal law.

Any attempt to define a crime in terms of acts or omissions leads to considerable difficulty. If, for instance, the driver of an omnibus drives recklessly and comes into collision with a private car, damaging that car and some of his own passengers, we find that the one act of reckless driving is at once a crime and a tort (civil wrong) to his passengers and the owner of the private car *and* a breach of contract with the passengers in not using due care and skill in carrying them. The distinction is not between acts, but between the legal proceedings that are brought. If proceedings against the driver are aimed at punishing him, then those proceedings are criminal, whereas proceedings that aim at compensating the injured persons are civil. Most criminal acts are also civil wrongs, but some crimes (such as treason and sedition) do not injure any particular person and many civil wrongs (such as the majority of breaches of contract) do not amount to criminal acts. When the act is both a crime and a civil wrong, there is in general no reason why both a prosecution and a civil action should not be brought: the proceedings will be quite separate, coming before different courts. The Civil Evidence Act 1968 provides that if a person is criminally convicted, he is presumed in later civil proceedings to have been guilty – a presumption which is

27

irrebuttable in a civil action for defamation – but outside the scope of this Act each court will normally hear the whole of the relevant evidence and decide independently of the other. In practice, it is harder to get a conviction in a criminal court than to get judgment in a civil court in several types of case, so that it often happens that a motorist is acquitted of criminal charges arising out of his driving, whilst a civil court holds that he drove negligently and so must compensate the injured plaintiff. Assault is anomalous; the person assaulted must choose between criminal and civil proceedings. Libel is an instance where in theory both proceedings lie, but criminal proceedings are nowadays extremely rare, and it is possible that they will soon be largely abolished.[1]

Unfortunately it is impossible for several reasons to draw a clear line between civil and criminal proceedings on the basis of 'compensation' and 'punishment'. First, since 1973 the criminal courts have had a wide power, outside motoring cases, to order convicted persons to pay compensation to the victims of their crimes. Compensation orders were originally an 'optional extra' to some purely penal measure, but in 1982 the law was changed to allow a criminal court to deal with an offender simply by ordering him to pay compensation, and to require the court to give preference to a compensation order when dealing with an offender who could afford to pay either a fine or a compensation order, but not both.[2] As a result, prosecutions are now occasionally instituted with the sole aim of getting compensation for the victim. Secondly, although damages in civil actions are usually assessed at a figure based on the loss which the plaintiff has suffered, so satisfying the notion that they are compensation, there are a few cases where 'exemplary' or 'punitive' damages may be given.[3] 'Compensation' and 'punishment' nevertheless remain useful for marking the difference between civil and criminal proceedings and in practice there is no difficulty whatever in distinguishing one from the other.[4]

The customary divisions of the law, such as the law of contract, tort and property, are thought of as subdivisions of civil law, although it is obvious that much of the criminal law exists for the protection of property. Constitutional law, as generally understood, is partly civil, partly criminal, and partly not law at all as far as the courts are concerned. The division into civil and criminal is vital for an appreciation of the working of the courts, but it cannot form the basis of all classifications of law.

[1] Law Commission Report No. 149 on Criminal Libel (1985).
[2] Powers of Criminal Courts Act 1973 s.35, amended by the Criminal Justice Act 1982.
[3] A further cause of confusion was a class of case called a 'penal action', in which by various statutes conduct was prohibited under a penalty of a fixed sum which a private person, called a 'common informer', could recover as a civil debt. These are nowadays obsolete. For details, see the seventh edition of this book, pp. 25–26.
[4] For further discussion, see Smith and Hogan, *Criminal law* (5th ed. 1983) chapter 2; Winfield, *Province of the law of tort* (1931) chapter VIII; Allen, 'The nature of a crime', (1931) 13 (3rd series) *Journal of the Society of Comparative Legislation* 1, reprinted in Allen, *Legal duties* (1931); Williams, 'The definition of crime', (1955) 8 *Current Legal Problems* 107; Hughes, 'The concept of crime: an American view' [1959] Crim. LR 331.

In outline, the system of courts for civil matters is relatively simple. Small cases go to the County Courts, and large cases go to the High Court. There were formerly a number of ancient local courts like the Norwich Guildhall Court and the Salford Hundred Court, which also had civil jurisdiction, but the Courts Act 1971 swept them away – except for the Mayor's and City of London Court, which now functions as a County Court, although keeping its ancient name. The only remaining complication in the scheme is that certain domestic matters like maintenance orders for deserted spouses are brought in the magistrates' courts, together with liquor licensing and a few other odds and ends of civil business.

5

COUNTY COURTS

The ancient county court became a court for small cases and then virtually died away. When in 1849 Parliament set up a system of courts for small civil cases it was thought to be a good thing to continue with such a hallowed name, and the new courts were named county courts. It was an unfortunate choice of name because from their beginning down to this day they have nothing whatever to do with counties. The legislation establishing county courts was inspired by the rationalising spirit of Bentham and the organisation of these courts has been guided by convenience and not tradition. They are entirely creatures of statute. Their constitutional document is now the County Courts Act 1984.

County courts are distributed around the country on the same principle as post-offices: the idea is to make sure that in all parts of the country there is a county court within reasonable distance. To achieve this, the Lord Chancellor can alter the number and boundaries of county court districts and places where the courts are held. At one time there were over 400 county courts, but the advent of the motor-car has made it possible to concentrate the work in fewer centres, and in 1986 the number stood at 267. The volume of work varies as between courts. In the Metropolitan districts, the work is so heavy that the courts are in more or less constant session and some courts have to be staffed by two or three judges. In less heavily populated areas a single judge may suffice for a court, or a court may not need the full-time service of a judge. In such areas, courts are grouped so that a judge may have his main court and two or three or more adjacent courts. Each court must be held at least once every month, but it is possible for one judge to manage this because in the smaller towns a few days a month are sufficient to cope with the business. The judges are Circuit Judges and Recorders, who also try criminal cases in the Crown Court; the Lord Chancellor assigns them to particular courts and types of work, and moves them around as business requires. (Their qualifications and terms of employment are discussed in part V.) Each court also has a registrar, appointed and removable by the Lord Chancellor. The registrar is a solicitor and the Lord Chancellor decides in each case whether it is to be a full-time appointment or whether the registrar may also engage in private practice and what salary is to be paid: these decisions depend upon the amount of business in the particular court. The registrar is the head of the office staff of the court and he also acts as a lesser judge.

The jurisdiction of county courts is strictly limited, for they may hear only those kinds of cases assigned to them by statute. They have no criminal jurisdiction. The jurisdiction which they exercise is largely over matters which are also dealt with by the High Court. This is called *general jurisdiction*. General jurisdiction is unlimited in all matters which could be brought in the Queen's Bench Division and in most Chancery and Admiralty matters, provided the parties agree that the county court should deal with it. When, as is usual, they do not agree, general jurisdiction is limited both as to subject and monetary amount of claim. Where the limit relates to the amount claimed, the plaintiff can limit his claim. Thus, if the amount owed is £5,500, for example, a plaintiff can sue for £5,000 and so bring the case in the county court, but he cannot divide his claim and bring two actions that add up to the whole amount. Where the money claim is expressed differently, as in annual rateable value of property or the paid up capital of a company, the plaintiff has to abide by those limits. In all these matters a plaintiff may go to the High Court if he wishes, but the rules governing costs are designed to encourage him to make use of the county court general jurisdiction if he can. The most important matters of general jurisdiction come under these headings:

1   Claims for debt or damages. The county court may deal with actions founded on contract or tort or for money due under a statute (such as recovery of a penalty or expenses, contribution or other such claim) where the sum claimed does not exceed £5,000. Libel and slander actions are excluded, however.

2   Actions concerning land, which includes houses and other buildings, where the net annual value for rating does not exceed £1,000. Most of these are by landlords to recover possession after serving a notice to quit, and the jurisdiction is commonly called a possession action.

3   Equity matters such as trusts, mortgages and dissolution of partnership and certain contentious probate matters, where the amount of the fund or value of the property involved does not exceed £30,000.

4   Some courts have limited Admiralty jurisdiction. Where such jurisdiction exists, it is limited to claims not exceeding £5,000, except in the case of a claim for salvage, where the limitation is that the value of the property saved must not exceed £15,000.

5   Bankruptcies are dealt with in certain courts outside the London Bankruptcy District and there is also jurisdiction in the winding up of companies with paid-up capital not exceeding £120,000.

6   Matrimonial causes: the great majority of these are petitions for divorce. This jurisdiction is so closely linked with the matrimonial jurisdiction of the Family Division of the High Court that both jurisdictions are dealt with together: see chapter 6 (iii) below.

7   Proceedings transferred from the High Court. This is discussed later; see chapter 6 below.

The rest of the jurisdiction of the county court is called its *special jurisdiction*. This mainly comprises matters over which the county court and the county court alone has jurisdiction. For example, by statute, a tenant of a shop whose lease

Table 1. *The work of the county court in 1986*

Proceedings begun	
Total	2,534,864
'Money plaints'	2,296,440
under £100	667,280
£100–£500	873,280
£500–£1,000	261,220
£1,000–£2,000	202,340
over £2,000	147,740
Other proceedings (including divorce and bankruptcy)	238,424
Judgments entered by default or with consent	1,147,271
Cases decided after	
– formal trial	25,323
– arbitration	44,634
Days sat by judges	28,474
by registrars	39,676
by deputy registrars	8,245

expires and whose landlord wishes to put him out, can ask the county court to override the landlord's wishes and grant him a new tenancy. Special jurisdiction arises under statutes dealing with so many different subjects that there is no method of classification that helps in understanding it. The customary exposition is by arranging the subjects in alphabetical order and treating each of them separately. Fifty-nine such topics are listed in the *County Court Practice* for 1987. Some of them are comparatively unimportant, others – such as applications by business tenants for new leases – represent large amounts of litigation. Most areas of special jurisdiction receive some explanation in the *County Court Practice*, but some are too large to be intelligently treated in an omnibus work. For these – which include company law and matrimonial cases – practitioners use special textbooks.[1]

The hearing of cases is divided between the judge and the registrar. It is possible in many matters for there to be a jury, but as a matter of practice, litigants rarely ask for one. The registrar is in effect an assistant judge taking the lesser cases. These include cases where the defendant does not appear, or admits the claim, and defended cases in which less than £1,000 is involved, or more if the parties agree and the judge gives leave.

The volume of work handled by the county courts is enormous. Over two and a

---

[1] An interesting position arises over adoption. This, in its sense of a full process that extinguishes the rights of the natural parents and puts the adopted person into virtually the same legal position as a child born in wedlock to the adopter, takes place after an order of a court made after procedure under the Adoption Act 1958. The legislation allows an applicant to choose whether to apply to the High Court or to a county court: for obvious reasons, the jurisdiction is not split according to a monetary limit. For good measure, it allows adoption proceedings to take place in the magistrates' courts as well. In practice, the county court has most of the business.

32

half million proceedings were instituted in 1986, not far short of ten times the number begun in the High Court in the same year. The general shape of the business is shown in table 1. The great bulk of the work consists of 'money plaints' – claims for debts and damages – and of these most are for relatively small sums. In 1986, 29 per cent were for less than £100, 67 per cent were for less than £500, and only just over 6 per cent were for over £2,000. Table 1 also shows that there are far more proceedings entered than there are judgments given. This is because a large number of cases are struck out or withdrawn, usually because the defendant has paid up. The table also shows that in the proceedings which are not withdrawn, the defendant puts up no fight in most of them. Fought cases result in judgment after a trial or arbitration, and the number of judgments after trial or arbitration is only a fraction of the total number of judgments, the rest of which are given against defendants who enter no defence, or simply ignore the proceedings and lose by default. In these cases, if there is an issue it is usually only whether or not the defendant shall be allowed to pay the sum by instalments. Despite the increase in jurisdiction, the bulk of county court work continues to be a vast amount of relatively small claims brought against a large number of comparatively poor people. If we consider that, from a social point of view, the importance of a court is the number of *persons* whose affairs it deals with, there can be no doubt that county courts are the most important civil courts in the country. Except for a small section of the community, civil litigation means creditors, tradesmen and landlords pursuing their actions, or more rarely being pursued, in county courts.

Over the years county court jurisdiction has been greatly extended. When county courts were set up in 1846 they were limited to cases involving less than £20, a figure which had crept up to £100 before the Second World War. After several extensions by Acts of Parliament after the war, the Administration of Justice Act 1969 raised the ordinary limit to £750 and for the future gave the Lord Chancellor power to extend the limits further by Order in Council. They were so raised to £1,000 in 1974, £2,000 in 1977, and to the present £5,000 figure in 1981. The total rise is real and considerably outstrips the fall in the value of money. Since the Second World War the county court has also acquired an important jurisdiction over divorce (see chapter 6(iii)). In the past, the question of extending county court jurisdiction has usually been contentious. Solicitors have the right of audience in county courts, which are spread over the country in places large and small as are the offices of solicitors. The Bar has a virtual monopoly of advocacy in the higher courts and barristers, like the High Court, are based in London and a few other large cities. Hence, in the past, pressure to extend county court jurisdiction has usually come from solicitors and extension has taken place in the face of opposition from the Bar. The pressure for the latest large extension in 1981 came not from solicitors, however; indeed, they generally complained about it. The pressure came from the Lord Chancellor's Department, which felt the High Court was overburdened, and wished to shift some of its work elsewhere.[1] There are signs that this will lead to further extensions in the future.

However, when county court jurisdiction was extended in 1981, solicitors were uneasy about the proposal because many of them felt that in a number of respects the county court lacked teeth enough to cope with the larger and more important cases. Most of their criticisms centred on the enforcement of judgments, which is discussed later (chapter 9). Others concerned various aspects of county court procedure, which was less convenient for plaintiffs than the High Court equivalent, particularly against knowledgeable and unscrupulous defendants. For example, under county court procedure it was easy for someone with no real defence to an action to play for time, and he could do so painlessly because the county court, unlike the High Court, could not award interest for the period the plaintiff had been kept waiting. Some of these complaints were easily solved by a rewriting of the County Court Rules which took place in 1981. Others, particularly those relating to the enforcement of judgments, are more intractable problems.

A more fundamental complaint about the county court was made by the Consumer Council in 1970. In a report entitled *Justice Out of Reach*, it showed that many consumers with sound legal claims were not having them adjudicated. County court procedure was too abstruse and complicated for most persons to be able to present their own cases. Where small sums were at issue, the costs of instructing a solicitor to appear in court were disproportionate to the size of the claim. Legal aid was of little use in these cases because the legally aided person usually has to pay a contribution. And although the plaintiff might expect to recover the costs of legal representation from the defendant if the claim was made out, this was more than counterbalanced by the risk of having to pay the costs of the defendant's legal representation if he failed. These were very serious criticisms. What they amounted to was that the county court had failed in its original purpose, which was to be a readily accessible court for small claims. There were various views on what should be done. One was that a new system of small claims courts should be set up. As an experiment, two independent small claims courts, one in Manchester and one in Westminster, were established in 1971–73 with the support of local solicitors and the help of various grants. These had no statutory basis and thus their jurisdiction rested on the agreement of the parties to accept the 'court' as arbitrator. The Lord Chancellor rejected the idea of a new system of small claims courts, however, and following a conference of county court judges, registrars and clerks, a new and simpler form of county court procedure was devised for small claims. The Administration of Justice Act 1973 and some new County Court Rules made under it provided for small claims to be referred to an arbitrator. The usual arbitrator was to be the county court registrar, who, in his capacity as arbitrator rather than deputy judge, would hear the case in

[1] The Lord Chancellor's Consultative Paper is printed in (1980) 130 NLJ 827.

a sufficiently informal way to enable litigants to present and defend their cases in person. Table 1 shows the wide extent to which the arbitration procedure is used. Its use increased nearly ten-fold between 1974 and 1982 and arbitrations are now more common in the county court than formal trials. It was originally available only in claims for up to £75 and where one party asked for it, but now all claims not exceeding £500 are referred to the registrar for arbitration automatically. The procedure on a county court arbitration is discussed later (chapter 7).

6

THE HIGH COURT

The High Court was created by the Judicature Acts 1873–75, the general plan of which was given in chapter 1. Today its constitution is contained in the Supreme Court Act 1981, which consolidates the Judicature Acts and later amendments to them.

Its jurisdiction in civil matters is almost unlimited. Apart from a few special matters which by statute *must* be brought in a county court, the High Court can hear any case great or small, and can take any case that can come before a county court as well as everything that is outside county court limits. In practice, however, litigants are discouraged from taking small cases to the High Court and in practice it is only the weightier matters which are heard there. If, for instance, an action is begun in the High Court when it could have been brought in the county court, such as an ordinary trade debt, two things may happen. First, a High Court registrar or master may order the case to be transferred to a county court. This may occur if the sum in dispute is within the £5,000 limit for starting county court proceedings and, under a rule introduced in 1981 in an attempt to shift more business to county courts, it may also occur in cases with larger sums at stake if the issues of law or fact are simple.[1]

Alternatively, the case may continue in the High Court, subject to special rules as to costs. For example, if the plaintiff recovers less than £600 he is not entitled to any costs and when the sum eventually recovered is between £600 and £3,000, recoverable costs do not exceed those which would have been recoverable if the action had been instituted in the county court. Whilst the sum in dispute is the normal criterion for choice of court, it does not always represent the real issue. If one of a group of underwriters of an insurance policy is sued for his contribution towards an alleged loss, the action may well be for a few pounds. It is known that all the other underwriters will abide by the decision and hence the action may be well within county court limits, yet still be a very proper case for the High Court. Test actions are brought in a considerable variety of cases where one decision will, in fact, govern the settlement of several claims. Cases relating to civil liberties may also involve a nominal or small money claim: if pamphlets and posters are said to have been illegally seized by the police it may be desirable to

---

[1] County Courts Act 1984 s.40(1)(d), originally enacted by the Supreme Court Act 1981, Schedule 3.

36

seek the decision of a High Court judge irrespective of the money value of the 'literature'. Hence, if the action is a proper one for the High Court it will not be remitted to a county court and it is provided by statute that the plaintiff will not be penalised in costs if there was 'sufficient reason' for bringing the action in the High Court.[1] It may happen that a plaintiff chooses to sue in a county court but the defendant deems that the real importance of the action merits High Court proceedings: in such a case the defendant can apply to have the action transferred to the High Court.

These rules are based upon good sense, and generally work well, but they do present problems. Where a person claims for general damages, as for pain and suffering, rather than for a specific sum like a trade debt, he may hope to get over £5,000, but may know there is a risk that he will be awarded less. The rules as to costs give him a little leeway: provided he recovers at least £3,000 he is entitled to costs on the High Court scale; but if he is awarded less than this he should be penalised in costs. In this situation he is reduced to trying to argue that he really had 'sufficient reason' for suing in the High Court. It is partly because of diffi-culties like this that proposals are sometimes made to amalgamate the High Court and the county court into one single institution. This was proposed in the first edition of this book in 1940. The idea has recently been put forward again in a Consultative paper by the Lord Chancellor's Department's Civil Justice Review.[2]

In practice the distribution of work between the High Court and the county courts does not always proceed according to the principles given in the last para-graph. Table 3 (p.43) shows that the bulk of proceedings begun in the High Court are for sums within the county court limit. In many cases an action is commenced without any expectation that the defendant will contest the matter. When instructed to take proceedings for recovery of a debt of a substantial sum (though less than £5,000), most solicitors go to the High Court rather than the county court. The chance of the case being referred to a county court, or of it being heard in the High Court but of costs being awarded on the county court scale, is not a discouragement when a case is not likely to be contested. In an undefended case the difference in costs is small, and in some ways procedure is less troublesome and more efficacious in the High Court. There is also the very important fact that debtors are more scared of a High Court writ than they are of a county court summons.

We speak of *the* High Court as if it were a single body like the House of Commons. Actually it consists of between eighty and ninety High Court judges who normally sit singly, proceedings before each of them being proceedings in the High Court. The High Court is divided into three Divisions, each of which does different kinds of work. The idea of Divisions is to secure some measure of specialisation among the judges who are to try civil actions where there are large sums at stake. For all practical purposes we can regard each Division as having a

[1] County Courts Act 1984 s.19(3).
[2] Consultation Paper No. 6 – General Issues (1987). See chapter 8 below, and Appendix A. In its final Report the Civil Justice Review rejected the idea.

separate jurisdiction and the judges as being judges of a particular Division, although strictly speaking the jurisdiction is that of the High Court and the judges are justices of the High Court. It is merely a matter of convenience that a judge usually does more or less the kind of work with which he is acquainted, and to ensure this, actions in a number of matters must be brought in the appropriate Division. The Divisions were originally created to reflect the split of business between the earlier courts which the High Court replaced, and the outlines of the old courts are still partly visible in the Divisions today. The Queen's Bench Division was the successor of the old common law courts of King's Bench, Common Pleas and Exchequer, and the Chancery Division was the successor of the old Chancery Court. Until 1971 the third Division was the Probate Divorce and Admiralty Division, which represented the jurisdiction of the separate courts which used to handle those topics: a hilarious combination which led A. P. Herbert to suggest that the connecting factor was wrecks – wrecks of wills, marriages and ships. The reason why these diverse topics were lumped together was that they were all once dealt with in courts which applied Roman law rather than the native common law, and the same body of practitioners – known as 'civilians' – used to handle all three types of work.[1]

This pattern of professional specialisation ceased a great many years ago and it then became inconvenient for the same Division to deal with three subjects so disparate. When few barristers learned in Admiralty matters knew or cared about divorce, and fewer barristers learned in divorce knew or cared about maritime law, it became difficult to appoint judges to the Division who understood all aspects of its work. Furthermore, Admiralty work has much affinity with commercial litigation, in which a number of Queen's Bench Division judges are highly specialised; it seemed undesirable to divide and duplicate one body of professional expertise between the two Divisions. Probate work was closely connected with some matters within the jurisdiction of the Chancery Division and the same argument applied here too. A rearrangement of the Divisions was therefore proposed in 1933,[2] but it took thirty-seven years and a great deal of discussion[3] before this came about. In 1971 the Probate Divorce and Admiralty

[1] The ecclesiastical courts originally dealt with probate and divorce, to which they applied canon law, which owes much to Roman law. The Admiralty Court, which formerly dealt with nautical matters, applied a general European maritime law which had a Roman law basis. The advocates in these courts were once a separate profession. Their society, called Doctors' Commons, was disbanded in the later nineteenth century. See G. D. Squibb, *Doctors' Commons* (1977).

[2] Second Interim Report of the Business of Courts Committee (Hanworth Committee), (1933) Cmnd 4471.

[3] The proposal was examined again by the Committee on Supreme Court Practice and Procedure (Evershed Committee) in its Second Interim Report (1951) Cmd 8176, which reached the timid conclusion that whereas change was desirable, the benefits would not justify the disruption involved. The Committee on the Age of Majority (Latey Committee) recommended a single Division of the High Court for all family matters and this was brought about by the Administration of Justice Act 1970. Future changes should be easier to make, because the Supreme Court Act 1981 permits the Divisions to be rearranged and work to be redistributed between them by Order in Council rather than Act of Parliament.

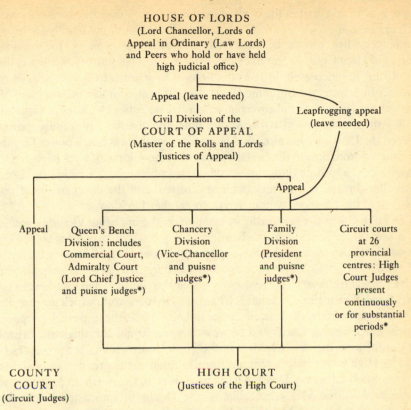

HOUSE OF LORDS
(Lord Chancellor, Lords of
Appeal in Ordinary (Law Lords)
and Peers who hold or have held
high judicial office)

Appeal (leave needed)

Civil Division of the
COURT OF APPEAL
(Master of the Rolls and Lords
Justices of Appeal)

Leapfrogging appeal
(leave needed)

Appeal

Appeal

| Queen's Bench Division: includes Commercial Court, Admiralty Court (Lord Chief Justice and puisne judges*) | Chancery Division (Vice-Chancellor and puisne judges*) | Family Division (President and puisne judges*) | Circuit courts at 26 provincial centres: High Court Judges present continuously or for substantial periods* |

COUNTY
COURT
(Circuit Judges)

HIGH COURT
(Justices of the High Court)

* Judges may, in accordance with Practice Directions, release a particular case to be
tried by a Circuit Judge or a Recorder: these remain High Court cases.

Figure 2 System of courts exercising civil jurisdiction after reorganisation in 1971–72

Division was renamed the Family Division. Its Admiralty work was sent to the
Queen's Bench Division and its probate jurisdiction was sent to the Chancery
Division. In recent years people have begun to question whether there is any real
need for separate Divisions in the High Court at all. In a case in 1987 Sir John
Donaldson, Master of the Rolls, said 'The existence of Divisions in the High
Court, once created as an aid to efficiency, was now an obstacle. In that situation
consideration would no doubt be given to their abolition, thereby creating a
unified High Court, or to their redefinition.'[1] For the present, however, the
Divisions are with us. The structure of the High Court, and its relation to the
other courts which administer civil justice, is given in figure 2.

Each Division has its head, namely the Lord Chief Justice for the Queen's
Bench Division, the Lord Chancellor for the Chancery Division – though he has

[1] *Barclays Bank plc* v *Bemister, The Times* 15 December 1987.

long ceased to take part in the work of the Division and the effective head since 1970 has been the Vice-Chancellor – and the President of the Family Division. The judges other than the heads of Divisions are known as *puisne*[1] judges. The number of High Court judges has steadily risen as the volume of litigation in the High Court has increased. In 1925 it was fixed by statute at 17; after a series of increases by statute, the Supreme Court Act 1981 raised it to a maximum of 80 and conferred power on the government to raise it further by Order in Council. In 1986 the number stood at 79. At one time, the distribution of judge-power between the Divisions was also fixed by statute, but there is now a power for this to be altered from time to time to take account of the volume of work in each. On appointment, a puisne judge is attached to whichever Division the Lord Chancellor directs, and he may (with his consent and the concurrence of the president of the Division) be transferred to another Division.

The High Court sits principally in London, in the imposing Victorian gothic law courts in the Strand and the less forbidding modern structures tacked on behind. But it also conducts business at 26 centres outside London (see Figure 9 at the end of the book). These centres operate as fully-fledged departments of the High Court, and almost all the cases which could be conducted in London can be heard there. The major exception is Chancery Division work, which is normally heard only at certain designated centres. Until 1982 these were Liverpool, Manchester, Preston, Leeds and Newcastle upon Tyne; Birmingham, Bristol and Cardiff were then added. Most of the High Court work in the provinces is heard by High Court judges sent out from London as the pressure of business requires. Such Chancery Division work as is done in the northern provinces is mainly tried by the Vice-Chancellor of the Duchy of Lancaster (not to be confused with the Vice-Chancellor who is acting head of the Chancery Division). He is a Circuit Judge, but sits with the status of a High Court judge for Chancery cases at the request of the Lord Chancellor.

The High Court centres in the provinces are part of a unified system of court administration established by the Courts Act 1971, under which the High Court, the Crown Court and the county courts are all under the direction of the Lord Chancellor, who is advised by a Court Service Board. For this purpose, England and Wales are divided into six circuits, each with an administrative headquarters, a full-time administrator and staff appointed by the Lord Chancellor. The administrator is a civil servant, whose job is to exercise managerial control. In order to make sure that it is the judges who keep the upper hand, however, the Lord Chancellor also appoints for each circuit two presiding judges. Within each circuit, there is a pattern of court centres. In ascending order of importance, there are 'third tier' centres, where the Crown Court is served by Circuit Judges and Recorders for the trial of the less serious indictable offences; 'second tier' centres, where the Crown Court is also served by High Court judges, who

---

[1] Pronounced 'puny'. It is the same word, which originally meant 'junior' rather than insignificantly small.

conduct the trials of the most serious criminal offences; and 'first tier' centres, where in addition to all this, the High Court also operates to conduct civil business. The integrated system permits a useful degree of flexibility in that when business is particularly heavy, simple High Court cases can, subject to principles laid down in Practice Directions, be 'released' for trial by a Circuit Judge.

High Court jurisdiction is divided between the Divisions according to the type of case, but there are no geographical limits. In theory there is a single High Court which operates in various places, and any branch of it may try a case no matter where the cause of action arose. Where the trial takes place depends on the wishes of the parties and the balance of convenience. Most High Court actions which are likely to be suitable for trial in the provinces are begun by writ,[1] and the plaintiff can obtain a writ by paying the appropriate fee either at the Central Office at the Law Courts, or any of the offices of the High Court (District Registries) that are established in 133 provincial towns. The writ is 'served' by delivering to the defendant (or more commonly his solicitors) a sealed copy of the writ together with a form upon which he is required to 'acknowledge service', which means telling the court office that the writ has been received. If the defendant fails to acknowledge service the plaintiff can proceed straight to judgment. Soon afterwards, the respective solicitors go before an official, a 'master'[2] if the case was commenced in London or a registrar if the case was commenced in a district registry, on a 'summons for directions'. After hearing what the parties have to say, the master or registrar makes an order about various preliminary matters, including the place and mode of trial.

For example, if a resident of Oxford and a resident of Cambridge have a car collision in the Lake District, trial in London is likely to be equally convenient to both parties and to suit them better than trial in Preston, Leeds or Carlisle, but this may have to be balanced against the convenience of witnesses, all of whom may live in the north. (In a criminal case it is different; prosecutions usually take place in the appropriate court for the area where the crime was committed.)

The present simple arrangements for conducting High Court business in the provinces replace a much more complex system. Chancery Division work was generally restricted to London. This was inconvenient for people in the north of England, and would have been more inconvenient if there had not existed ancient courts in the Counties Palatine of Lancaster and Durham which had some Chancery jurisdiction. (The special arrangements for Chancery work at High Court centres in the north partly reflect the existence of these old courts, which were abolished by the Courts Act 1971.) Ordinary Queen's Bench Division cases – and latterly divorce – could be heard in the provinces at Assizes, the origins of which were explained in chapter 1. The details of Assize arrangements and why they were inadequate are now a matter of legal history, for which students should

[1] Most Chancery business is begun by an alternative process called an Originating Summons. Divorce is begun by filing a Petition and this is done in the office of the county court.
[2] The office is described by Diamond, 'The Queen's Bench Master', (1960) 76 LQR 504.

consult earlier editions of this book and the report of the Royal Commission on Assizes and Quarter Sessions[1] which recommended their abolition and replacement in the Courts Act 1971. In brief, the problems were three. First, unlike the present system of permanent High Court centres in 26 provincial towns, Assizes were a temporary court which trailed around the countryside visiting 61 Assize towns for a specified number of days each. For the big cities, periodic visits were insufficient to get through the business that originated there, whilst valuable judicial time was often wasted visiting ancient and now comparatively small towns like Beaumaris and Dorchester where there might be only a little business, all of which could easily go elsewhere. Secondly, Assizes were courts for the conduct of criminal as well as civil cases. For obvious reasons the criminal work had to be given precedence, and so increasingly it crowded the civil work out. This is no longer the case, because each provincial High Court centre is now separate from the Crown Court which also sits there. And thirdly, the administrative arrangements for Assizes were usually bad, because responsibility for different matters was split between local and central government, and no one was in overall control. From the First World War onwards there was a history of mounting delays on both the civil and criminal side, and tinkering reforms which at best slowed the speed at which things were getting worse. In 1967 the government took matters in hand by appointing a Royal Commission with its Chairman Lord Beeching, a prominent industrialist who had recently been responsible for a drastic reorganisation of the railway network. His Commission worked quickly, and in 1969 recommended root and branch reforms: the abolition of Assizes and Quarter Sessions, their replacement by permanent High Court centres in the provinces and a network of permanent Crown Courts for criminal cases. Remarkably the radical changes he proposed for the courts system proved acceptable to all parties concerned and were quickly enacted in the Courts Act 1971. Nobody doubts that they are a great improvement on what was there before. The only thing which some people regret about the abolition of Assizes is the ceremonial which went with them. This dated from when the purpose of Assizes was partly to act as a manifestation of Royal authority in the provinces. As well as processions, Assizes were accompanied by a considerable round of eating and drinking, and although the ceremonial is gone for ever, High Court Judges and barristers still talk about 'going on circuit' and the gastronomic traditions live on.

Further consideration of the High Court requires discussion of the Divisions.

Table 2. *Distribution of business between the Divisions of the High Court: Number of days sat by judges in 1986*

Queen's Bench Division	Chancery Division	Family Division
9,006	4,440	3,224

Note: In addition, 1,540 days were sat by official referees.
Source: Judicial Statistics 1986.

[1] (1969) Cmnd 4153.

i The Queen's Bench Division

The judicial strength of the Queen's Bench Division consists of the Lord Chief Justice of England and some fifty puisne judges. The number of judges exceeds that of the other two Divisions, partly because (as table 2 shows) the Queen's Bench Division has the largest volume of work and partly because the judges are required to do work besides that of their Division. As the successor of the old common law courts of King's Bench, Common Pleas and Exchequer, the Queen's Bench Division has a varied jurisdiction.

Table 3. *Analysis of Queen's Bench Division business in 1986*

Proceedings commenced (total)		234,782
Sums involved:	under £5,000	125,222
	over £5,000	61,560
	unliquidated claims	48,000
Matters involved:	debt	183,199
	breach of contract	9,150
	personal injury and death	24,183
	recovery of land	5,190
	other	13,060
Judgments given without trial		100,967
Judgments after trial (contested cases)		3,540
	personal injury and death	4,890
	other cases	2,170

Source: Judicial Statistics 1986.

Ordinary civil actions

The bulk of the work, as in the county courts, consists of actions between private persons (including limited companies) who are suing one another for debts, or damages for civil wrongs such as breach of contract, personal injuries, defamation, and false imprisonment. Some idea of the range of work may be gained from table 3. In many of these cases, there is a choice between the Queen's Bench and the Chancery Divisions; this will be discussed later.

It will be noticed that actions for damages for personal injury and death form a very large part of the work. They represent some 20% of the proceedings which are begun, and are disproportionately time-consuming because they represent some 70% of the cases which are tried. Indeed, a judge sitting in the Queen's Bench Division will spend most of his time trying personal injury actions. It is generally accepted that the number of personal injury actions has increased hugely since the Second World War. This, together with the rising rates of crime and divorce, explains why it has been necessary for the number of High Court judges to be more than doubled in the last fifty years; but it is difficult to produce figures for the increase of personal injury actions, because until recently the annual judicial statistics did not identify the different types of action in the Queen's Bench Division.[1] A study in 1978 concluded that 40% of all personal injury actions stem from road accidents, 46% are the result of injuries sustained at work, and claims against negligent manufacturers, doctors, occupiers and so forth account for the rest.[2]

In the United Kingdom, motor-vehicles kill some 6,000 people and seriously injure around 20,000 every year. Each one of these accidents is a potential law-suit as the driver is liable if he was negligent, and it was the introduction of compulsory third-party insurance in the 1930s and more generous legal aid in the 1940s which made suing him both possible and worth-while. Industrial accidents kill substantially fewer people, but injure many more. At one time the law discouraged actions by injured workers in a number of ways, notably by requiring them to choose between suing for damages and accepting statutory compensation payments under the Workmen's Compensation Acts: a relic of this thinking survived until recently in the rule which precluded members of the armed forces from suing the Crown over accidents at 'work'.[3] Since the Second World War, however, injured workers have been allowed to claim damages whilst taking their industrial injuries benefits, and the courts have grown more sympathetic to their claims against their employers. Each favourable decision on a point of principle has added to the number of claims. For example, it was for a long time imagined that industrial deafness was just something which workmen had to put up with, but a case in 1971 held that an employer could be liable for negligence for failing to protect his workforce against it, and this gave rise to 8,661 claims against one big employer alone.[4]

As in the county court, only a small proportion of High Court actions for debt and damages get as far as a trial. Most writs result in a settlement, or where there is no possible defence to the claim, in summary judgment without trial.

Commercial cases: the Commercial Court

This section of the Queen's Bench Division exists for commercial litigation.[5] Some commercial law is highly specialised, the sums of money involved are often

---

[1] The judicial statistics contained elaborate details until their size was reduced as an economy measure in 1922. These details were not reinstated in the judicial statistics 1974.

[2] Royal Commission on Civil Liability and Compensation for Personal Injury (Pearson Commission) (1978) Cmnd 7054–II 19.

[3] Abolished by section 1 of the Crown Proceedings (Armed Forces) Act 1987. However, section 2 allows the Home Secretary to revive the rule during an emergency if he considers it expeditious to do so.

[4] *Berry* v. *Stone Manganese & Marine Ltd* (1972) 12 KIR 13; subsequent developments described in *Kirkup* v. *British Rail Engineering Ltd* [1983] 3 WLR 1165.

[5] A. Colman, *The practice and procedure of the Commercial Court* (1982), gives an interesting account of the history of the Commercial Court as well as of its present business. See also the Lord Chancellor's Department's Civil Justice Review, Consultation Paper No. 3, *The Commercial Court* (November 1986).

large, and many commercial disputes must be dealt with quickly if at all. Accordingly, special provision is made for 'commercial actions', which the Rules of the Supreme Court define as 'any cause arising out of the ordinary transactions of merchants and traders, and . . . any cause relating to the construction of a mercantile document, the export or import of merchandise, affreightment, insurance, banking, mercantile agency and mercantile usage'.[1]

At one time these cases were listed and heard with the general business of the Queen's Bench Division, but this caused dissatisfaction in the commercial world[2] and from 1895 they were put in a special 'Commercial List' before judges with appropriate knowledge and experience. In 1970, the Commercial List was raised to the status of a special court, which operates under the wing of the Queen's Bench Division.[3]

A case goes to the Commercial Court either because the plaintiff specifies this when he starts the action, or because one of the parties later applies for it to be transferred there. If no application is made the case will be tried as an ordinary Queen's Bench Division action. The Commercial Court sits only in London. It is staffed with Queen's Bench Division judges knowledgeable in commercial matters nominated by the Lord Chancellor, which ensures that the court has the necessary specialist knowledge. Speed is secured in a number of ways. There are separate lists for short urgent matters and for cases that are substantial; thus the weighty cases do not crowd out the urgent matters. For the heavier cases there is a system of fixed dates, with a waiting-list for cases which can be fitted in when a fixed-date case is settled. In order to keep the workload to a size which can be handled quickly, attempts to smuggle non-commercial cases into the Commercial Court are rigorously suppressed. In recent years, the Commercial Court has also invented ways of making its proceedings more effective. The *Mareva* injunction – a court order freezing the assets of a defendant to stop him spending all his money while the plaintiff is still suing him – was invented by the commercial judges. (See chapter 9 below.) All this activity has led to a steady increase in work. In 1963 one judge handled the Commercial List: at the time of writing the Commercial Court has five judges. Most of the business consists of short, urgent applications made in the course of current disputes, and the number of full trials taking place in the aftermath of commercial difficulties now past are few. In 1982 there were less than 200 trials in the Commercial Court, out of between two and three thousand assorted applications.[4] The Commercial

---

[1] RSC Ord. 72 (2).

[2] As described by Lord Justice Mackinnon in (1944) 60 LQR 324, the precipitating event was a case which was expected to decide a point on general average of great commercial interest. It came before Mr Justice Lawrence who 'knew as much about the principles of general average as a Hindoo about figure-skating'. Failing to understand any of the issues, he pronounced judgment for the plaintiff without giving any reasons. More about the history of the Commercial List will be found in (1970) 86 LQR 313.

[3] Administration of Justice Act 1970; now contained in the Supreme Court Act 1981 s.6.

[4] The annual judicial statistics no longer give figures for the Commercial Court, and these are taken from Colman, *The practice and procedure of the Commercial Court* (1982).

Court regularly sits in the Long Vacation when most of the High Court is closed. The Commercial Court has also broken new ground with the Commercial Court Committee, through which it listens to the views of its users on its procedures. Behind this unusual responsiveness there are economic pressures. Businessmen, unlike would-be divorcees and people run down by motor-cars, have an alternative tribunal to the law courts for many of their disputes in the form of commercial arbitration. The Bar is anxious to keep the weightier commercial work in the law courts because it is well-paid and interesting, and the judges are traditionally sensitive to the interests of the Bar. For some years there have been repeated claims that the Commercial Court is under-resourced. The Civil Justice Review (see chapter 8) produced a Consultation Document on the Commercial Court and this confirmed that it was seriously overworked, and recommended an increase in the number of judges assigned to it.

The Admiralty Court

The Admiralty Court is of ancient origin. It began as a separate court in the mid-fourteenth century. Under the Judicature Acts it became part of the Probate Divorce and Admiralty Division of the High Court; since 1970, like the Commercial Court, it has been part of the Queen's Bench Division. In Tudor times the Admiralty Court was a general commercial court, but the King's Bench, jealous of its thriving rival, poached much of its business by using its supervisory jurisdiction (see below) to forbid the Admiralty to hear all but a narrow range of purely maritime matters. There are still signs of this piece of history in the jurisdiction of the Admiralty Court today. The Admiralty Court hears disputes about the ownership of ships, maritime collisions, and recondite matters like salvage and bottomry. Charter-parties, in which a ship is hired, and a number of other matters with a distinctly salty smell about them may be heard in the Admiralty Court, but are normally heard in the Commercial Court or as ordinary Queen's Bench Division actions. When aircraft and then hovercraft made their appearance earlier this century, the Admiralty Court was given a jurisdiction over them equivalent to that which it has over ships.

Admiralty law is highly specialised. In one sense the court is international, since it is frequently trying cases where foreign ships are concerned, and a high standard of judicial ability is needed. This is reinforced by the system of nautical assessors. When the judge requires assistance in matters of nautical skill he is assisted by two Brethren of Trinity House, who sit on the Bench with the judge. A jury is never used. The system of a judge with technically qualified and disinterested assessors is alien to the common law, but it appears to work very well in Admiralty; it certainly appears to be far better than the common law technique of listening to expert witnesses called by the parties at great expense to assert contradictory views. The procedure in Admiralty has several peculiarities when compared with other courts. The most noticeable difference is that some proceedings are *in rem* ('against the thing'). In all other courts, proceedings are necessarily *in personam*, that is, they are against some person or body – such as a corporation, which is regarded as a fictitious person. If you have been run down by a motor-car you can sue the driver or his employer but you cannot sue the car itself. In Admiralty it is possible to sue a ship or a cargo. The writ may be served on the ship if in British waters by nailing it to the mainmast (or tying it on with string or wire if the mast is of metal), whereupon the ship is not allowed to leave port unless security is given. Normally, of course, the owners defend the action. The purpose of this is to make sure that the plaintiff will recover damages if he wins, for the owners (particularly if they are foreign owners) may have no assets within the jurisdiction. Proceedings *in rem* mean that either security is given or the ship is still in port, in which case she can be sold by order of the court and the judgment satisfied out of the proceeds.

The volume of work in Admiralty is not large; in 1986, 754 writs were issued, of which only 44 reached trial. The amount of money involved is often considerable. Since proceedings may mean that a ship is detained, and under modern conditions this may mean an expenditure of thousands of pounds a day, the court has to keep abreast of the work. In most of the cases both parties (or their insurers) can afford the costs; the problem of litigation by poor people or those of modest means, which has been such a difficulty in most of our courts, hardly affects Admiralty. Also when a substantial sum is in dispute the amounts of costs incurred may appear reasonable. If my £1,000 motor-car is destroyed in a collision, it could easily cost as much as the car is worth to decide who is liable to pay for it. A minor collision may cause tens or even hundreds of thousands of pounds of damage to a ship and the odd thousand pounds of costs is more proportionate to the importance of the issue. It is perhaps for these reasons, as well as the nature of the court and its proceedings, that make the Admiralty Court the least criticised tribunal.

At one time almost all Admiralty work was done in London, where the work was in the hands of a few firms of solicitors and a few barristers. This is less so today. In 1983, eight Admiralty actions were tried in London and the remaining 21 were tried at High Court centres in the provinces. In time of war, the law of prize comes into operation and the Court then sits as a Prize Court.

Appellate jurisdiction

The Court of King's Bench was originally created to look after the King's interests. When dispensing justice was a source of profit to the King, one function of the King's Bench was to ensure that the various inferior courts from which he took no fees did not poach within the jurisdiction of his courts. From this the King's Bench acquired the task of ensuring that inferior tribunals generally behaved themselves, and in particular that they correctly applied the law. The Judicature Acts transferred this jurisdiction to the Queen's Bench

Division, which to this day hears appeals on points of law from magistrates courts, either directly or after initial appeal to the Crown Court. (See chapter 21.) For this purpose several judges sit together and constitute what is called a *Divisional Court*. Traditionally, the Divisional Court consisted of three judges; in order to save judicial time and so speed up justice, the usual number has been reduced to two in recent years. Modern statutes that impose duties upon individuals and companies commonly provide for some administrative process or tribunal to deal with disputes and give a right of appeal on point of law to the courts. Some, such as appeals by solicitors who have been punished for professional misbehaviour, go to the Divisional Court; others are directed to a single judge, such as appeals from V.A.T. tribunals; others, such as appeals on point of law under the Town and Country Planning Act 1962, may go to either the Divisional Court or a single judge.

Supervisory jurisdiction

The Queen's Bench Division also continues the task of seeing that inferior tribunals keep to their appointed jurisdiction, follow their appointed procedures, and conform to a minimum standard of fairness known as 'the rules of natural justice'. Thus, for example, when a prison disciplinary body punished a prisoner without allowing him to call evidence in his defence the Queen's Bench Division quashed their proceedings.[1] The Queen's Bench Division does the same when by statute some official person rather than some administrative body is given powers to regulate or control another. For example, the Home Secretary has power to cancel a TV licence. When a number of people, who had heard that the price of a licence was about to go up, bought new licences early and the Home Secretary threatened to cancel the new licences in order to make them buy again at the increased rate, they challenged his decision in the Queen's Bench Division.[2] During this century, and particularly since the Second World War, officials and administrative bodies have been given an ever-increasing range of powers over the citizens of this country and their affairs. Whether this is a matter for regret or a welcome development is a political matter beyond the scope of this book. But what is beyond question is that the more such powers there are, the more examples there will be of their oppressive use, and the more people there will be who wish to challenge their exercise. At one time the courts were comparatively shy about interfering with the exercise of such powers, particularly when they were exercised by some manifestation of central rather than local government, but in the 1960s and 1970s they became increasingly bold. As a result, Administrative Law has become a subject of major importance.

This supervisory jurisdiction was originally administered by prerogative writs;

[1] *R* v. *Board of Visitors of Hull Prison, ex pte. St Germain* (No. 2) [1979] 1 WLR 1401.
[2] *Congreve* v. *Home Office* [1976] QB 629. The challenge failed in the Queen's Bench Division, but succeeded in the Court of Appeal.

we still talk of them as 'writs', although they were (except for the writ of *habeas corpus*) renamed 'prerogative orders' when the procedure relating to them was simplified in 1938.[1] They were originally peculiarly royal machinery, intended for use by the Crown in the interests of the Crown; in the course of time they became available for use by ordinary citizens, even against servants of the Crown. The best known (albeit the least used) is the writ of *habeas corpus* whereby the courts can inquire into the legality of imprisonment or private detention and secure the release of any person unlawfully detained. *Mandamus* and proceedings of a like nature lie to command the performance of the public duties of persons, bodies and inferior courts. For instance, a local council may be commanded to levy rates required by other authorities and justices may be commanded to hear a case that they have declined to hear. *Prohibition* lies against an inferior tribunal and a party to proceedings therein to prevent the hearing or further hearing of a case which it has no jurisdiction to hear. *Certiorari* also lies against inferior tribunals, the object being to bring the proceedings of the inferior tribunal before the High Court for review; if the original proceedings were in excess of jurisdiction, or proceeded upon an error of law, they may be quashed.[2]

In more modern times the courts supplemented the ancient prerogative writs and orders with other remedies. If an ordinary private action was begun against a public authority they would sometimes grant a *declaration*, which means they would make an official statement that a certain piece of behaviour was or was not legal. Likewise they would sometimes grant an *injunction*, which is an order to refrain from doing something (or, more rarely, an order to do something) on pain of being imprisoned for contempt of court. And they would sometimes entertain an action for damages against the body or official where the alleged misbehaviour had caused loss. So wide did the range of remedies become that it became an embarrassment for litigants. They had to decide at the outset which remedy they wanted, but it was not always clear at that stage which remedy was appropriate, and meritorious cases were sometimes thrown out because the applicant should have asked for a different remedy. These problems were referred to the Law Commission, which in 1976 recommended a number of changes.[3] What they proposed was a single unified procedure for setting the supervisory jurisdiction in motion, the applicant being allowed to make his choice of remedies in the course of the proceedings, and the court being empowered to give him a remedy different from the one he originally sought. The Law Commission assumed that this change would need an Act of Parliament; but the judges decided it could be achieved without this. Thus in 1977 they amended the Rules of the Supreme

---

[1] Administration of Justice (Miscellaneous Provisions) Act 1938. The procedure before 1938 is described in the seventh edition of this book, pp. 43–44.

[2] There was a further and less commonly used procedure called *quo warranto*, for challenging the authority by which a person holds a public office. The 1938 Act replaced it with a power to issue an injunction to restrain the person improperly appointed from acting. See the Supreme Court Act 1981 s.30.

[3] Law Com. No. 73, *Remedies in Administrative Law*, Cmnd 6407.

Court by promulgating a new Order 53, under which a person applies not for this remedy or that, but for 'Judicial Review'. On an application for judicial review the court can grant mandamus, prohibition, certiorari, a declaration, an injunction or damages. To quell doubts as to whether such a drastic change could properly be achieved merely by amending the Rules of Court, section 31 of the Supreme Court Act 1981 confirms what had taken place.

Challenging the decisions of the government in the law-courts is a favourite sport of cranks. Thus it has always been necessary to have some kind of preliminary filter for applications for Judicial Review in order to prevent government officials wasting much of their time preparing their defence to quite hopeless actions. This is done by dividing the procedure into two stages. First, the person seeking Judicial Review applies to the court *ex parte*; that is to say he alone is heard, and the defendant is not troubled. If the court thinks the application is hopeless the case ends there. If it thinks the application is plausible, the defendant is summoned to a further hearing *inter partes* in which the applicant and the defendant argue the merits of the case. For many years, both stages in the process took place in open court before a Divisional Court of three judges, usually with the Lord Chief Justice presiding. This worked well enough up to the 1960s when there were only about a couple of hundred applications annually. The system was creaking badly by the end of the 1970s when applications were running at some 500 per annum, and the illness and consequent disability of Lord Widgery, the then Lord Chief Justice, made matters worse; by 1980 there was a backlog of some 700 cases and it was taking up to two years for a case in the Divisional Court to be heard. After Lord Widgery's retirement in 1980, Lord Justice Donaldson was temporarily put in charge, and sitting in a two-judge court he succeeded in clearing the arrears within six months – a truly remarkable effort. However, the number of applications continued to rise to the point where even this sort of judicial heroism could not cope within the existing system, and in 1980 the Rules of Court were further revised. The first *ex parte* stage now takes place before a single judge, who decides whether there is a prima facie case on the papers without an oral hearing unless the applicant requests one. This decision is usually made quickly, within a matter of days of the plaintiff filing the papers. The second *inter partes* stage does involve a hearing, but now this takes place before a single judge, except when the case arises from the criminal courts or is a criminal matter; then it is heard by a Divisional Court of two.[1] The number of applications continues to rise; in 1986 they totalled 1,169. Since 1981 a special group of nine judges with experience in various areas of administrative law has been detailed by the Lord Chief Justice to hear these cases, and the Lord Chief Justice has removed himself from hearing judicial review cases at first instance and sits in the

[1] The right of appeal is restricted if the matter is criminal, which is why a Divisional Court is retained for Judicial Review in criminal cases. In 1985 the government attempted to remove the right of appeal in civil cases, but withdrew the proposal in the face of opposition in Parliament and from the judges.

Court of Appeal to hear them on appeal. Thus in practice if not in name there now exists within the Queen's Bench Division a specialist Administrative Court. Within a decade the law and practice in this area has changed almost beyond recognition.[1]

At one time, the Queen's Bench Division was also a court for the first-instance trial of criminal cases. The old court of King's Bench was where the King's major political enemies were tried for treason, and after the abolition of the Star Chamber it was also the place for trials for such lesser political offences as sedition and blasphemous libel. It was also the practice for other criminal cases of great difficulty or importance to be removed to the King's Bench for trial, usually before the Lord Chief Justice. This criminal jurisdiction was transferred to the Queen's Bench Division by the Judicature Acts, and was occasionally exercised until the early years of this century. Mylius was tried there in 1910 for libelling King George V by accusing him of bigamy, and so were a number of First World War traitors, notably Roger Casement. The jurisdiction then fell into disuse, and was finally abolished by the Courts Act 1971.[2]

Queen's Bench Division judges perform various other duties. Procedural matters have to be settled. Appeals from masters are heard by a judge sitting in his room; this is known as 'in chambers', and takes up a substantial amount of time. A person who has been refused bail may apply to a judge in chambers (see chapter 22(iv) below). There are several other special matters, some of importance to civil liberties. For example, a newspaper cannot be prosecuted for a criminal libel without the leave of the judge in chambers.[3] It is also predominantly the judges of the Queen's Bench Division who try major criminal cases in the Crown Court. Queen's Bench Division judges also help in the work of the Criminal Division of the Court of Appeal and the courts martial appeal court, and perform a number of similar tasks. (See chapter 21 below.) In recent years, a Queen's Bench Division judge has been chairman of the Law Commission.

ii The Chancery Division

In 1986 there were 12 puisne judges in this Division. The Lord Chancellor is the President, but as he is too busy elsewhere to take any active part in this work, it was provided in 1970 that he may nominate one of the puisne judges to be Vice-

[1] A good account is given by Louis Blom-Cooper, QC, 'The new face of judicial review', [1982] *Public Law* 250.
[2] Abolition was done in a roundabout way. Criminal proceedings were begun in the Queen's Bench Division either by indictment in the usual way, or by a streamlined process known as *criminal information*. Criminal informations were finally abolished in 1967, and the Courts Act 1971 s.6 (now contained in the Supreme Court Act 1981) provides that indictments shall be tried only in the Crown Court. A fuller account of the Queen's Bench criminal jurisdiction is given in the seventh edition of this book, pp. 185–86.
[3] Law of Libel Amendment Act 1888 s.8.

Table 4. *Chancery Division business in 1986*

Total actions and matters commenced	26,156
Writs and other originating processes commenced:	
in London	7,225
outside London	2,515
Companies' proceedings (mostly petitions to wind up)	11,762
Bankruptcy petitions	4,672
Matters re. land (sales, mortages etc.)	3,767
Trusts	415
Contentious probate actions	128
Inheritance (family provisions)	138
Partnership	170
Copyright and patents	867
Cases disposed of after trial or hearing	838

Source: Judicial Statistics.

Chancellor.[1] The Chancery Division inherited the jurisdiction of the Old Chancery Court. As was explained in chapter 1, the genesis of the Chancery Court was the need for a set of remedies to supplement the common law. For this reason the jurisdiction of both the old and the new court has always appeared somewhat heterogeneous, being in effect a list of matters in which the common law either gave no remedy (or did not give an adequate remedy) or required some assistance of a procedural nature. The modern jurisdiction is set out in the Supreme Court Act 1981 s.61 and Schedule 1 in a manner too detailed to be given here; the broad outlines will be gathered from table 4, which gives the matters which generate the bulk of the work. At the risk of oversimplification we may say that whereas the Queen's Bench Division is largely concerned with obligations – claims in contract and tort for debt and damages – the Chancery Division is largely concerned with matters of property: its ownership, control, transfer, distribution and, in such matters as patents and copyright, its creation and destruction as well.

A sizeable part of Chancery Division business is litigation arising from the sale of land. This found its way into the old Chancery Court because it offered to the disappointed vendor or purchaser of land a superior remedy to that which the common law courts provided. Whereas the most he could expect at common law was damages, the Chancellor would give him a decree of 'specific performance': a command to the defendant to keep his promise on pain of imprisonment for contempt of court. Nowadays any Division of the High Court can order specific performance, but cases involving the sale, exchange or partition of land still go to the Chancery Division.

Another important invention of the Chancellor was the trust. As far as the common law courts were concerned, property belonged either to A or to B; they

[1] The title 'Vice-Chancellor' has stood for different things at different times. There is an account of them, and a description of the present office, by Vice-Chancellor Megarry in (1982) 98 LQR 370.

would not accept the idea that A might own property but be under an obligation to use it for the benefit of B, although there are many situations where such an arrangement is convenient. Where A and B tried to create such an arrangement and A went back on his word it was the Chancellor who gave a remedy to B. He thus brought the legal notion of a trust into being, and trusts remain to this day a matter for the Chancery Division. The executor or administrator of a deceased person's estate is in a position analogous to that of a trustee in that property is vested in him subject to a duty to deal with it for the benefit of others: he must wind up the estate and pay the balance remaining after payment of debts to those entitled under the will or intestacy. Disputes arising from the administration of estates are also dealt with in the Chancery Division.

Because the Chancery Division already had jurisdiction to control the behaviour of executors and administrators it was given jurisdiction over contested wills – 'contentious probate' – when the Probate Divorce and Admiralty Division was abolished in 1971. The main function of probate jurisdiction is to ensure that the right people are validly appointed as executors or administrators. If the deceased made a will, the court has to decide whether the document, or which of several documents, is a valid will, and whether there is under that will an executor to carry it out; the court 'grants probate' to executors, who may then take the necessary steps to deal with the estate. If the deceased died intestate, or left a will but there is no executor, then the court has to determine who should be appointed to wind up the estate. Such a person is called an administrator and is authorised by 'letters of administration'. In the great majority of cases there is no dispute and the functions of the court are performed by officials as a matter of administrative routine. Persons named as executors in wills, or near relations in the case of intestacies, apply to the Registry at Somerset House or to their local District Probate Registry, and by producing the necessary sworn statements receive probate or letters of administration. Over 250,000 grants are made in this way each year. Occasionally there is a dispute, however: in 1986 128 people wished to challenge the validity of a will. In such a case there must be a trial in court before a judge to determine the issue. When the Probate, Divorce and Admiralty Division was broken up in 1971, it was originally intended to transfer all probate jurisdiction, contentious and non-contentious, to the Chancery Division, but there was an administrative difficulty. Non-contentious probate is done by officials in 13 District Probate Registries and in the principal Registry in London, and whilst the District Registries deal only with probate, the principal Registry is also the divorce registry. It was felt that to divide up the principal registry between the Chancery Division and the Family Division would cause unjustifiable work and expense. So the compromise was that only contentious probate passed to the Chancery Division. The principal probate registry was renamed the principal registry of the Family Division, and all probate matters are first dealt with either there or in the district registries as before; but if a writ is issued challenging the validity of the will the case comes within the Chancery

Division. As an alternative to challenging the validity of the will, disgruntled relatives who think they are unfairly cut out may petition for a share of the estate under the Inheritance (Provision for Family and Dependants) Act 1975, and this may be heard either in the Family Division or in the Chancery Division. There were 138 such applications in the Chancery Division in 1986.

Because they were too busy to handle all the business themselves, the Chancellors took to delegating the hearing of certain points to court officials known as masters, on whose reports the Chancellor then acted. This proved to be a useful technique in dealing with trusts and related matters, which offer considerable field for investigation and report by a skilled official. This Chancery technique of taking accounts proved useful in disputes arising from the dissolution of partnerships, and was the origin of the present Chancery Division jurisdiction over partnership matters. Because the Chancery dealt with partnership matters, it was the obvious place to send business relating to the affairs of limited companies when they were invented by statute in the nineteenth century, and nowadays company cases amount to a big slice of its work. Much of this work consists of petitions to wind companies up, and this is handled by a special department within the Chancery Division known as the 'Companies Court'. This court does not have a separate legal existence and an exclusive jurisdiction as does the Admiralty Court, but is an administrative arrangement. The Chancery judges take it in turns to sit there, and business taken there can also be taken elsewhere in the Chancery Division.[1]

The Chancery Division also has an important jurisdiction in bankruptcy. Bankruptcy law, which begins with a statute of 1542 and has remained a creature of statute, originally treated bankruptcy as virtually a crime. The modern conception is that bankruptcy serves the two purposes of securing an equitable distribution of the assets amongst the creditors of an insolvent debtor and of enabling the bankrupt to get quit of the burden of debt. A petition may be filed by a creditor or by the debtor himself. If an act of bankruptcy is proved, a receiving order is made. The investigation is peculiar in that it is partly administrative and partly judicial. The official receivers are officials of the Department of Trade and also officers of the court. In due course the bankrupt's property will be distributed and he will receive his discharge, the date of the latter depending upon the circumstances. Statutes in the mid-nineteenth century created a special Bankruptcy Court for London and a series of District Bankruptcy Registries for the provinces. After a series of statutory metamorphoses, the London Bankruptcy Court merged with the High Court and bankruptcy jurisdiction for the London area ended up in the Chancery Division. Outside London, the District Bankruptcy Registries were eventually merged with the larger county courts, where provincial bankruptcies are still handled. In 1987, following a boom in bankruptcy work and some new pieces of legislation, an Insolvency Court User's Committee was set up on similar lines to the Commercial Court Committee.

[1] *Fabric Sales Ltd* v. *Eratex Ltd* [1984] 1 WLR 863.

The Chancery Division also handles litigation about copyright and patents. This is a highly specialised topic, and since 1977 a Patents Court has existed within the Division to ensure the necessary expertise.[1] Two Chancery judges are assigned to it. There is at present insufficient work to fill all their time, the rest of which they spend on general Chancery Division business. Revenue cases used to go to the King's Bench Division as heir to the old Exchequer Court, but as tax law nowadays is associated with companies, partnerships, settlements and so forth, the Revenue List is nowadays taken by a Chancery judge.

To appreciate the nature of much of the work peculiar to the Chancery Division, it is helpful to notice a small point of language; for the Queen's Bench Division we usually talk about 'actions', denoting the idea of litigants who have a dispute to be determined, whilst in the Chancery Division we are more apt to speak of 'actions and matters'. Some of the causes in the Chancery Division are normal litigation between contesting parties, but 'matters' do not necessarily mean that there is a dispute. It often happens that trustees or executors under a will are in genuine doubt about their duties, and so, whether or not this had led to a dispute among themselves or with some beneficiary, the method is to get the matter before the Chancery Division. It does not matter particularly who commences proceedings, provided that all those concerned are represented. The trustees or executors may take the line that they do not mind what happens because their sole desire is to do whatever the court says they ought to do. Many of the applications under the Companies Acts are for 'leave' for a company to do something, such as to reduce its share capital, or for the court to 'sanction a scheme' of reorganisation. Hence in the Chancery Division we may find bitter opponents fighting to the best of their counsel's ability, or we may find a friendly atmosphere in which the common desire is that the judge shall approve of some proposal put forward by agreement among those concerned.

A number of actions, particularly in contract and tort, can be brought either in the Chancery or the Queen's Bench Division. At one time the choice would have depended upon the remedy the plaintiff wanted, because the Court of Queen's Bench could only give damages, whereas the Chancery could only grant equitable remedies, consisting of orders for people to do or refrain from doing things on pain of imprisonment for contempt of court. Now that all remedies, legal and equitable, are available in all courts this reason no longer applies. More recently the decisive factor might have been the desire for jury trial, which was more readily available in the Queen's Bench Division. Since the decline of jury trial in civil cases this reason is also obsolete, and it is hard to say what nowadays influences practitioners when they have a choice of Division. The elusive factor is probably a difference of 'atmosphere'. Traditionally the notions of a trial were different and although law and equity learned to walk in harmony there are differences of outlook which remain. The Chancery judges, and counsel

[1] Supreme Court Act 1981 s.62, re-enacting Patents Act 1977 s.96. The work of the Court is described in the government White Paper on *Intellectual Property and Innovation*, (1986) Cmnd 9712.

appearing before them, are concerned with the elucidation of facts and the determination of the correct principle to be applied, working in a quiet and somewhat academic manner to build up their system. The common law judges are, of course, also concerned with facts and principles, but historically the determination of the facts has been a matter for the jury, and the law applicable has to be stated so that a jury could at least appear to understand it. Since the distinctions might be called temperamental, we may say that the practitioner often feels that the Chancery or the Queen's Bench Division, as the case may be, will be more sympathetic, and in accordance with this estimate he selects his Division. One solid practical reason for choosing one Division concerns publicity: motions for injunctions are heard in open court in the Chancery Division, but are taken discreetly in chambers in the Queen's Bench Division.

Like the Queen's Bench Division judges, the judges of the Chancery Division are available for various other duties. One of these is to act as judges of the Court of Protection. If a person goes insane he is frequently incapable of managing his property. When this occurs his relatives can apply to the Court of Protection, which is empowered to remove it from his control and to vest it in a receiver who is required to apply it for his benefit. In the last century this was done by proceedings which were very legal and highly formal. The modern procedure is low-key and largely administrative. Most of the decisions are taken on the papers without an oral hearing by a group of officials called Masters of the Court of Protection, but some awkward questions can be referred for a more formal decision to the judges of the Court of Protection, who by statute are the judges of the Chancery Division. The Court of Protection does an important job, and its importance is increasing as doctors get daily better at keeping people's bodies living longer than their minds. Many of those whose affairs come before it have survived to a great age and then become senile, and another large group are hitherto poor people who have survived terrible accidents which have left them with severe brain damage, for which they have received large sums in compensation. In 1982 the Court of Protection controlled the affairs of some 23,000 people, with assets amounting to £450,000,000.[1] Chancery judges could be sent out to try criminal cases on circuit, but by tradition they are not.[2]

iii The Family Division

This Division has a President and 16 puisne judges. Under the Administration of Justice Act 1970 there was allocated to this new Division all the High Court

[1] A readable and constructively critical account is Larry Gostin, *The Court of Protection* (1983).
[2] After the Judicature Acts there was an attempt to train Chancery lawyers for common law work. Sir Frederick North, who had been a leading Chancery practitioner, was made a judge of the Queen's Bench Division, but he made such a mess of the much-publicised trial of Ramsey and Foote at the Old Bailey for blasphemy that he had to be quietly transferred to the Chancery Division, and the experiment seems to have been abandoned. In recent years, however, several leading Chancery practitioners have demonstrated their versatility on being assigned on their appointment as judges to the Family Division.

business which concerns marriage, family property and children; there is thus jurisdiction in wardship of minors, adoption, guardianship, financial relief, property disputes between spouses, occupation of the matrimonial home and other proceedings. Like the Queen's Bench Division and the Chancery Division, the Family Division shares jurisdiction over many (but not all) of its matters with the county court; although, as will be explained later, the work is divided between the courts on rather different lines. The core of the work is divorce and matters consequent upon divorce. Most proceedings are commenced by filing a petition praying for the remedy required. The following remedies might be sought:

(1) *A decree of dissolution of marriage*, otherwise known as divorce. This presupposes that the parties are bound by a valid and subsisting marriage. In 1986, 179,844 divorce petitions were filed; 8,031 in the Principal Registry of the Family Division in London and 171,813 in the registries of the various county courts. Between them, the Family Division and the county courts produced 152,073 decrees nisi of divorce.

(2) *A decree of nullity*: this differs from divorce in that the principle here is that for some reason the apparent marriage is declared to be void or thereby avoided. In the case of a marriage void for lack of capacity, as where both parties are within the prohibited degrees of relationship or are both of the same sex, the theory is that there never has been a marriage. In such a case a decree is merely a safeguard. In other cases the marriage may be declared to be no marriage, but until the matter has been before the court the marriage is still existing. A husband whose wife refuses to consummate the marriage is still her husband, and remains her husband until a nullity decree is pronounced. A party to a voidable marriage who marries again without obtaining a nullity decree contracts a void marriage and can be prosecuted for bigamy, whereas if the original marriage was void he can contract a valid and non-bigamous marriage without obtaining a decree. Whether the original marriage was void or voidable used at one time to determine other matters, including whether any children born to the union were legitimate or illegitimate, but by statute the same rules generally govern these matters whether the marriage was voidable or void. In 1986, 554 nullity decrees were granted; 53 were dealt with by the Family Division and the rest were processed by the county courts.

(3) *A decree of judicial separation*: this decree does not entitle the parties to remarry; in effect it says that one party has behaved in such a way that the other party can refuse to cohabit without thereby breaking the obligations of matrimony. The usual result of a decree is that if a wife petitions she will be enabled to live apart from her husband and at the same time get assured financial provision from him. There were some 3,430 petitions for judicial separation in 1986, 480 by husbands and 2,950 by wives. In the same year 1,768 decrees were granted of which 56 were dealt with by the Family Division and the remainder through the county courts.

(4) *An order concerning the matrimonial home*: one spouse – usually the husband

– may turn the other spouse out of the house or behave so badly towards him or her that they are forced to quit; the unfortunate spouse may be left with no roof over his or her head, and so may the children. This sort of behaviour usually results in a divorce, at the end of which the divorce court is likely to award the matrimonial home to the spouse who most needs and deserves it. Whether or not there is a petition for divorce, however, under the Matrimonial Homes Act 1983 either spouse may apply to the court for an order to be allowed to occupy the matrimonial home, which may be accompanied by an order that the other spouse leave it. In addition the court has power to make orders restraining one spouse from molesting the other spouse or the children, breach of which is punishable with imprisonment.[1] There were 3,274 applications of this sort in total in 1986.

(5) *A decree of presumption of death and of dissolution of marriage may be sought.* The court will presume death from evidence that shows that death is the only reasonable supposition, as when a person falls overboard from a ship at sea and is not rescued. The petitioner's task is made easier by the rule that a person's continual absence for seven years without reason to believe that person is still alive raises a presumption of death that holds good unless the contrary is proved. Two such decrees were granted in 1983.[2]

(6) *Other remedies*: there is a wide range of other remedies which are much more rarely sought. The Family Division hears a number of petitions for a declaration of the validity in England of a foreign decree of divorce. Another matter that comes up occasionally are petitions for a declaration of legitimacy. If it is thought that the legitimacy of some person can be proved now but may be difficult to prove at a later date, the court may be asked to make a declaration. Such a step may well be taken when rights to property are involved, for then the expense of putting evidence into safe storage may be justified. In theory, there was until recently the possibility of a suit for *jactitation of marriage*, under which A asks the court to order B to cease publicly claiming to be his or her spouse; this was rarely used and was abolished by the Family Law Act 1986.

The great bulk of the work of the Family Division either consists of or involves divorce. This is an area in which a revolution in public attitudes has taken place over the last fifty years, accompanied by an almost complete transformation of the law. In the 1930s divorce was comparatively rare and widely disapproved of. Involvement in a divorce in any capacity other than that of judge carried considerable social stigma, and often brought the sort of prurient newspaper attention which is nowadays reserved for the trial of sexual offenders in the criminal courts. In those days the law took the attitude that divorce, being thoroughly unsavoury, should be discouraged by being made as difficult as

---

[1] Some of these powers are duplicated in the Domestic Violence and Matrimonial Proceedings Act 1976 which, contrary to the usual pattern, applies to the county courts but not the Family Division of the High Court.

[2] These figures are not regularly published; the editor obtained them from the Lord Chancellor's Department.

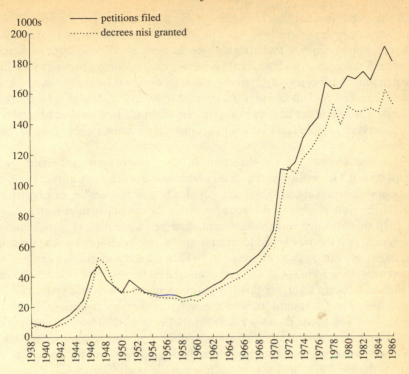

Figure 3 Divorce rates in England and Wales 1938–86

possible. It was therefore permitted, as a regrettable necessity, in favour of the innocent, and then only against the provedly guilty. Thus the only way in which a married couple could become divorced was for the petitioner – that is, the party who starts the proceedings – to show in open court by a process akin to a private prosecution that the other spouse, the respondent, had committed some misbehaviour amounting to what was called a 'matrimonial offence'. The petition was liable to fail if it came out that the petitioner was also guilty, because the petitioner's misconduct gave the court a discretion to refuse to grant the divorce.[1] If divorce was difficult when both parties misbehaved, where they were in agreement it was nearly impossible: attempts by the parties to be divorced by arrangement were called 'collusion', which was an absolute bar to a divorce.

---

[1] 'Perhaps it is not vouchsafed to everybody, whether in Holy Orders or out of them, to appreciate the full sublimity and beauty of the doctrine that if one of two married persons is guilty of misconduct there may properly be divorce, while if both are guilty they must continue to abide in the holy estate of matrimony.' Lord Hewart CJ, writing in the *Daily Telegraph* 21 October 1935.

Since then the position has changed out of all recognition, as figure 3 shows. Nowadays divorce is exceedingly common: 179,844 petitions were filed in 1986, a figure which suggests that roughly one in three of all marriages ends in a divorce. A divorce carries little if any social stigma. It no longer bars a divorce that the petitioner has been guilty of misbehaviour. Divorce is frequently available by mutual consent. And instead of being granted at the end of a trial in open court, in practice if not in theory divorce is now usually obtained by a routine administrative process little more complicated than conveying a house or obtaining probate of a will.

The first changes in the direction of the present state of affairs were jurisdictional. Originally divorce was available only in the High Court in London. This put divorce beyond the reach, physically and financially, of many poor people who were eligible for divorce even under the restrictive rules then in force. In 1920 this injustice was partially remedied by giving Assizes jurisdiction in divorce. At first this was available only for uncontested petitions by poor persons, but Assize jurisdiction was extended in 1943 to meet the increasing demand for divorce resulting from social dislocation caused by the outbreak of war. The end of the war brought a further flood of petitions under which this system all but broke down, and a committee was appointed under the chairmanship of Mr Justice Denning (as he then was) to look into the matter.[1] The obvious solution would have been to confer jurisdiction in divorce upon the county courts, but there was strong resistance to this within the legal profession, particularly at the Bar. As the Bar has a monopoly of audience in the High Court which it does not have in the county court, barristers feared that if divorce went to the county court they would lose a considerable part of their business. For public consumption this problem was usually presented entwined with the further argument that to make divorce a county court matter would trivialise it and so undermine the institution of marriage. To meet these objections, the solution was adopted of appointing a number of county court judges as *Commissioners*; that is to say, they were elevated to the status of High Court judges for the limited purpose of hearing divorce. By giving county court judges different robes and extra fees, divorce was made more widely available without undermining either the sanctity of marriage or the financial position of the Bar. Of course a side-effect of dressing up the county court judge in High Court robes was to make divorce more expensive than it need have been, because it obliged petitioners to engage a barrister as well as a solicitor and also to pay costs on the more expensive High Court scale. As the divorce rate continued to rise, and more and more divorce was done on legal aid, the government eventually became concerned at what it saw as a needless waste of public money, and in 1967 a Matrimonial Causes Act was passed which officially handed over a large slice of jurisdiction in matrimonial causes – divorce, nullity, judicial separation and jactitation of

[1] Committee on Procedure in Matrimonial Causes. First Interim Report, (1946) Cmnd 6881; Second Interim Report, (1946) Cmnd 6945; Final Report, (1947) Cmnd 7024.

marriage – to the county courts. The position now is that a number of county courts (at present 174) are designated *divorce county courts*.[1]

At first, their jurisdiction was limited to undefended cases: if the respondent entered a defence the proceedings were automatically transferred to the Family Division. In practice, however, the defended cases were frequently tried by a circuit judge sitting in the capacity of a High Court Judge, and the Matrimonial and Family Proceedings Act 1984 made defended as well as undefended proceedings triable in divorce county courts.

These jurisdictional changes enabled more people to obtain a divorce, but this alone did not satisfy public discontent with the divorce laws. In 1966 Mr Justice Scarman described the position thus

By and large, English divorce law as it stands meets the demand of the public for dissolution of marriage. That is to say, most people who seek divorce get the relief they seek and do so without undue delay. But it does not necessarily follow that the law as it stands is satisfactory. On the contrary, I think there are good grounds for believing that the law achieves a high productivity level of divorce by artificialities which most of us deplore, and sometimes at a price of suffering inflicted upon the innocent which no humane society should tolerate.[2]

It was increasingly felt that the basis upon which divorce was granted – as relief to the innocent and punishment for the guilty – was artificial. It ignored the notorious fact that marriages usually fail because of faults on both sides, and that it is often equally in the interest of both parties that the marriage should be dissolved. In the 1960s there was a growing body of opinion that the divorce laws should be reframed so as to base divorce on irretrievable breakdown of marriage instead of on matrimonial offences. Following an influential report by a Church of England study group in 1966[3] and a report by the Law Commission[4] in the same year, the substantive law of divorce was completely refashioned on approximately these lines in the Divorce Reform Act 1969 – which is now incorporated in the Matrimonial Causes Act 1973. The difficulty with the proposal to make irretrievable breakdown of marriage the basis of divorce was that if the courts were literally required to make a thorough investigation of many tens of thousands of marriages each year to see if they had irretrievably broken down the legal system would have become a hopeless traffic jam. Consequently some compromise was essential, and a compromise is enshrined in the Act. Section 4 provides that the sole ground on which a petition for divorce may be presented shall be that the marriage has broken down irretrievably, but goes on to provide that irretrievable breakdown of marriage may only be established by the

---

[1] The original scheme was for a few county courts to be designated 'trial courts' where matrimonial causes could be tried, and a larger number to be divorce county courts for the limited purpose of instituting proceedings and filing papers in the case; but the Lord Chancellor has now designated all divorce county courts as courts of trial.

[2] In a lecture in the University of Bristol.

[3] *Putting asunder: the report of a group appointed by the Archbishop of Canterbury.*

[4] *Reform of the grounds of divorce: the field of choice* (1966) Cmnd 3123.

petitioner satisfying the court of one or more of a list of specified facts, and that on proof of any of those facts the marriage shall be presumed to have irretrievably broken down unless the contrary is shown. These facts are five: that the respondent has committed adultery and the petitioner finds it intolerable to live with him or her; behaviour such that the petitioner cannot reasonably be expected to live with the respondent; respondent has deserted the petitioner for at least two years; five years' separation; or two years' separation where the respondent consents to a decree being granted. The first three in this list are rather similar to what were already recognised as matrimonial offences giving grounds for divorce, but the last two were new and made divorce much more widely available.[1]

Section 1(3) provides that 'on a petition for divorce it shall be the duty of the court to enquire, so far as it reasonably can, into the facts alleged by the petitioner and into any facts alleged by the respondent'. This was intended to continue the rule that divorce jurisdiction is inquisitorial, derived from its origin in ecclesiastical law. It shows that when the Divorce Reform Act was passed everyone assumed that a divorce would continue to require a judicial hearing, as had always been the case. Indeed, some people imagined that this provision, together with the requirement that the marriage had irretrievably broken down, might actually make divorce harder to obtain than before. In fact, the judicial hearing was rapidly abandoned in most cases. In 1973 a 'special procedure', without a formal hearing, was introduced for petitions based on two years' separation where there were no children of the family under 16 (or 18 if in full time education) and the respondent consented to the divorce, and a few years later this 'special procedure' was extended to cover virtually all undefended cases, whatever the basis of the petition, and whether or not there were children. The essence of this procedure is that the petitioner fills in forms, and swears an affidavit, and these (together with other affidavit evidence in support if desired) are lodged in the appropriate Registry or county court office, where they are scrutinised by the Registrar. If the case appears to be proved from the documents, the Registrar grants his certificate and they are placed before the judge, who pronounces the decree of divorce without either party having to attend. By law the decree is supposed to be pronounced in open court, but if (as often happens) the courtroom is empty the judge often marks the petition 'decree nisi granted' in his chambers and does not bother with this rather empty formality. Although it is still called 'special procedure', this informal method is now the usual procedure, being used in well over 90 per cent of all cases. There is a court hearing only in the few undefended cases where the Registrar declines to give his certificate, and in the tiny minority – around 1 per cent – of cases where the respondent defends the petition. Thus for all practical purposes the dissolution of marriage has become an administrative routine, like obtaining probate of a will.

These changes were made not so much to ease the travail of petitioners as to

---

[1] Further changes in the grounds of divorce are advocated by the Law Commission in *Facing the Future – A Discussion paper on the Grounds of Divorce* (June 1988).

save money, particularly public money. 'Special procedure' divorces are quick for the courts to process and have enabled the court system to cope with a sharply rising divorce rate without the need for a large number of extra judges and new court buildings. Furthermore, the absence of a court hearing automatically spares the parties the expense of paying lawyers to attend it. As a result, a decree nisi is obtained in an undefended divorce case for the cost of the court fee, and a solicitor's advice and assistance in filling up the necessary forms – a total outlay of between £100 and £200. It would cost perhaps four times that amount if the solicitor had to attend a court hearing. It is even possible to do it without the help of a solicitor, a course encouraged by the Lord Chancellor's Department which has produced an instruction booklet for those with a taste for legal do-it-yourself; where this is done a decree nisi can be obtained for little more than the court fee, or even more cheaply, since this fee is waived in favour of those who are unable to afford it. All this has saved public money, because it enabled legal aid[1] to be withdrawn from undefended divorce – although it remains available if the divorce is defended – and for ancillary matters like determining who has custody of the children and who shall have the matrimonial home.

One strange thing is left over from the old inquisitorial procedure, and this is the division of divorce into two stages. The decree which is pronounced at the end of the process which has just been described is called the 'decree nisi'[2] and is only provisional; the marriage is not dissolved for all legal purposes until, following an interval of at least six weeks, there has been a further application to the court and a 'decree absolute' has been granted. This dates from when it was public policy to make divorce as difficult as possible. The idea was partly to give the respondent the chance to appeal before the petitioner remarried, and partly to give busy-bodies the chance to tell the Queen's Proctor[3] of collusion or misconduct or other bars to divorce which the parties were keeping quiet about, so that he could intervene to have the decree set aside before it was made absolute. This can still happen, but there are so few bars to a divorce nowadays that it is extremely rare,[4] and the existence of two stages does little except confuse the parties.

The divorce courts have an important ancillary jurisdiction under which they

[1] Legal *aid* is state help to pay for a lawyer to conduct a case. There is also legal *advice and assistance*, the 'green form scheme' under which the state pays for a consultation with a solicitor. This is still available for undefended divorce, and enables a would-be petitioner to have up to £90-worth of free advice and help in filling in the forms. Legal aid is discussed in chapter 40.

[2] *Nisi* is Latin for 'unless'; the decree is good unless someone raises an objection before it is made final.

[3] A *proctor* was the lawyer who filled the role equivalent to that of a solicitor in the ancient courts which eventually became the Probate, Divorce and Admiralty Division of the High Court. The Queen's Proctor is the state official who looks after Crown interests in certain divorce and maritime matters. The post is now held by the Treasury Solicitor.

[4] On 19 February 1985 the newspapers carried an account of an intervention by the Queen's Proctor where a woman had obtained a decree nisi against her husband because his behaviour made him intolerable to live with, and was then discovered to be still living with him 15 months afterwards.

make decisions about the custody of children of the family, the extent to which one spouse (usually the husband) must continue to maintain the other, and the division of the house or other matrimonial property. The hearings take place in chambers, not in open court.

By section 41 of the Matrimonial Causes Act 1973, a judge is forbidden to make a divorce decree absolute unless he is satisfied that the arrangements for the children 'are satisfactory or the best that can be devised in the circumstances'. The judge actually looks into these arrangements, even where the parties reached them by agreement, and this is the one remaining thing of real substance which a judge still does in a 'special procedure' divorce. Where there are children, a 'children's appointment' is usually made for later in the day upon which the decree nisi is expected to be pronounced. At least one of the parties attends and the judge asks them questions: if he does not approve of the proposed arrangements, or has doubts about them, he may refer the case to a welfare officer who is attached to the court, or take various other steps. If the parties are at loggerheads about who shall have the children there will be a contested hearing at which the parties may be legally represented, usually at the cost of much money, time and bitterness. They are therefore officially encouraged to reach agreement as far as possible. For several years there has been a pilot scheme in operation in some courts where in cases of dispute about custody and access the parties are first summoned with their children to a 'conciliation appointment' before the registrar, who tries to compose their differences. In Bristol a group of public-spirited volunteers set up a private conciliation scheme designed to offer the same service away from the courtroom atmosphere, and this experiment is now being copied in Cambridge and elsewhere. If they produce agreement these schemes clearly deserve official encouragement, not only because anything which takes the bitterness out of these disputes is good, but because they are likely to lead to considerable savings in court time and public money in the form of legal aid. It is therefore unfortunate that at present the government is reluctant to give these schemes financial support, although in 1985 it did go as far as to fund a unit to study the working of conciliation. In the same year a further voluntary conciliation service was launched by the Family Law Bar Association, with what success it is still too early to say.

Decisions about financial provision are made by the registrar, from whose orders an appeal lies to the judge. If the parties are able to reach agreement the registrar may well make an order by consent in the absence of the parties and, unlike what happens over custody, no hearing is required. If they cannot agree then there is a hearing in chambers and the registrar decides who is to pay and how much. The factors which he is required to take into account are laid down by statute, and include such things as the parties' relative wealth, age, obligation to care for others, behaviour, and so on. Until recently the ultimate objective was supposed to be 'to place the parties, so far as it is practicable and, having regard to their conduct, just to do so, in the financial position in which they would have been if the marriage had not broken down and each had properly discharged his or her financial obligations and responsibilities towards the other'. This prescribed for the court an impossible task, except where the parties were extremely wealthy; for there is no getting around the basic fact that income that may suffice for a married couple will rarely suffice if they become two households. Even if it does, it is inconceivable that it will enable them to live as comfortably as they did before. It was also open to criticism in that it encouraged ex-wives to look to their ex-husbands for an income for life, which was not sensible when they were free to and capable of working. In 1984, following a Law Commission report, the law was changed by the Matrimonial and Family Proceedings Act 1984.[1] The dominant criterion has now become the welfare of the children, and the courts are supposed to encourage those spouses capable of fending for themselves to do so.

It is also the registrar who decides how matrimonial property, if any, shall be divided. Unlike that in many other countries, English law has no highly developed conception of family assets. Until recently, on the dissolution of a marriage each spouse was in principle entitled to take away all the assets which he or she owned, and there was room for much expensive and fruitless litigation as to who, as a matter of law, owned what item. The solution adopted in 1970 was to give the court granting a divorce the widest power to override individual property rights, and to do 'palm-tree justice' by taking property away from one spouse and giving it to the other. Even where the matrimonial home belongs entirely to one spouse, the registrar is fully empowered to give half or even all of it to the other as part of the settlement on divorce.

The system of Matrimonial Causes in the High Court and the county court is only part of what the law has to offer those with domestic problems, for there is also the matrimonial jurisdiction of the magistrates' courts. This depends so much on other aspects of magisterial jurisdiction that it is dealt with later in chapter 26. In some cases appeals lie from the magistrates in family matters to the Crown Court, and it is therefore true to say that all regular law courts, civil and criminal, have a hand in some part or another of family law. This is not satisfactory. In the first place, it can mean that what is essentially the same dispute ends up being litigated in a whole series of courts. For example, suppose that W, the wife of H, commits adultery, and H leaves; and suppose further that one of their children, C, reacts by behaving in a wildly anti-social way. In such a case W may go to the magistrates' Domestic Court to seek maintenance; the divorce petition may be filed in the county court and could then be transferred to the Family Division; and the local authority may seek to take C into care, when proceedings will take place in the Juvenile Court. This quagmire for the potential family law litigant is well illustrated by Professor Hoggett in a hypothetical example involving five different types of court, and including three separate

[1] Law Commission Report No. 112, The Financial Consequences of Divorce (1981).

juvenile courts, the High Court (twice), the Crown Court, and three separate county courts.[1]

The second problem is that the law is not coherent, because the different types of court sometimes apply different rules to similar sets of facts and produce conflicting results. The most striking example was in the period before 1978, when the rules which magistrates' courts operated to determine liability to a separated spouse still turned on the notion of a 'matrimonial offence', although this idea has been largely abandoned for the purpose of divorce and ancillary jurisdiction in the High Court and the county court. This anomaly was eventually cured by an Act of Parliament – but others remain. For example, there is one set of tests and criteria for making a child a ward of court in the High Court, and another for depriving his parents of custody in the magistrates' courts.

These considerations have led many people to suggest that what is needed is a simple unified 'family court' for the determination of all these matters. A further consideration which points in the same direction is the need to develop an informal and non-adversarial method for handling family disputes. This, it is said, could best be done in a set of courts separate from the rest of the system. Such a system already operates in Commonwealth jurisdictions in Australia, New Zealand and Canada. Perhaps the most relevant of the three is the New Zealand experience, since before the creation of a family court as a separate division of every district court, family law jurisdiction in New Zealand was, like ours, spread over three court systems.

The family court in New Zealand is designed to be as informal as possible and wholly separate from the criminal courts. Great emphasis is placed on counselling and mediation. Counselling is mandatory for all applicants involved in family law matters and aims to promote reconciliation (that is bringing the spouses together again) and, more realistically, conciliation (negotiating a friendly separation). Mediation is available for all separation, maintenance, custody and access cases and is free as well as voluntary. A 'mediation conference' is chaired by a family court judge to enable the parties to discuss the points of agreement and dispute and aims to find a solution to the latter without the need for litigation. Children can be represented by counsel, but lawyers employed by the parents (if any) are obliged not to play an active role in proceedings. The scheme is said to have been very successful.[2]

In England the idea of a family court was first put forward by the Finer Committee on One Parent Families in 1974.[3] Since then, the idea has gained a large measure of support. A pressure group called the Family Courts Campaign has been formed to fight for it, and all the political parties seem sympathetic.

---

[1] 'Family courts or family law reform – which should come first?', Brenda Hoggett, (1986) 6 *Legal Studies* 1.

[2] A more detailed account of the New Zealand family court structure is to be found in 'Family Courts in New Zealand' by Yvonne Craig, (1987) 151 JPN 26.

[3] Cmnd 5629.

66

Lord Hailsham was well disposed to the idea at the end of his period as Lord Chancellor. In 1986 things had progressed to the point at which the Lord Chancellor's Department issued a Consultative Paper to 're-examine the idea of a unified family court'. This suggests three possible outlines of a family court. First, a rationalisation of the present system, reallocating business and removing all anomalies; secondly, a family court as a distinct part of the High Court and county court system assuming the roles of the magistrates' courts and domestic courts in care proceedings; and thirdly, an entirely separate court structure with its own accommodation, staff and trained bench.

In its response to the Consultative Paper, the Law Commission rejects the first option.[1] The Commission points out that the problem is not duplication at all, but rather a lack of an extensive overlap between the jurisdictions of the three tiers which prevents all aspects of one issue being decided by one court. The Commission favours a cross between the other two options: a separate division of the High Court and county courts, presided over by a panel of one lawyer and three trained lay members who may also be magistrates and based on an informal inquisitorial and not a formal adversarial system. The second option, which is nearer to those of the Commonwealth jurisdictions, is thus probably the most likely to be adopted. The third of these options has already been rejected by the Lord Chancellor as 'not one which any government would consider affordable'.

The main opponent of family courts is the Treasury, on grounds of cost. It was cost that prevented the Labour Government from implementing the recommendations of the Finer Committee in 1975 for a unified family court. Again, it was the Lord Chancellor's inability to give a firm figure for the cost of the scheme that prevented its appearance in the Conservative Party's manifesto in the 1987 General Election.

What would it cost? In Parliament it has been said that the scheme would cost somewhere in the region of £40 million; but clearly the size of the bill would be very much affected by whether a wholly new system was to be implemented, or existing resources redeployed in a new way. Also there is the possibility of compensating savings. In a Parliamentary debate it was estimated that £20 million could be saved by establishing a family court.[2] This, it is said, would be partly by rationalisation and the elimination of duplication, but mostly because far fewer cases would be litigated (as witness what has happened in New Zealand and Australia). The Family Courts Campaign estimates that £40 million per year could be saved by a mere 1 per cent drop in the number of applications for care orders under the Children and Young Persons Act 1969.[3] Unfortunately, much of the argument on cost so far, by the Treasury as well as by supporters of family courts, looks as if it is based on guesswork.

---

[1] This has not so far been published.

[2] Lord MacGregor of Durris in Parl. Deb. (HL) vol. 488 col. 1395, referring to a paper: 'A Unified Court – The Cost Factor', by Her Honour Judge Jean Graham Hall and Douglas Martin.

[3] Referred to by Baroness Faithful in Parl. Deb. (HL) vol. 488 col. 1408.

Proponents of the family court usually stress the need to set up a system which – unlike the Domestic Court in the magistrates' court system – has no overtones of crime. Thus most people, including the Law Commission, do not wish to see a family court take over the criminal jurisdiction of the Juvenile Courts. For this reason, some people would also like to see magistrates play no part in the new family court whatever. But magistrates surely have something useful to offer the family court. They are people who live locally, unlike High Court Judges and some Circuit Judges. They are also more likely than professional judges to have up-to-date personal knowledge of the way in which those whose disputes appear before them live their lives. Whatever their backgrounds originally, professional judges belong to the fee-earning upper middle classes, and among magistrates there is a much greater social spread. Professional judges are almost always men, whereas there are many women magistrates; if it is thought desirable for the family court to sit as a panel on which both sexes are represented this will require the use of laymen, and the laymen might as well be lay magistrates. There is also the point that magistrates on domestic panels are now a source of experience and expertise, and the further point that magistrates – unlike professional judges – give their services free. Hence any benefit gained by dispensing with the services of magistrates would almost certainly be outweighed by the disadvantages. An increased use of conciliation and mediation and less emphasis on blame would, one hopes, remove any overtones of blame or guilt.

In a public lecture in London on 27 April 1988 the Lord Chancellor, Lord Mackay, made sympathetic remarks about the need for a family court. However, he stressed that in his view an overhaul of the substance of the law was a step which should come first. It is widely expected that the Government will introduce legislation to alter child-care law in the near future, and proposals for a family court may follow.

7

THE MODE OF TRIAL

Matters of procedure are governed almost exclusively by Rules of Court made under powers given by statute. The High Court and the Court of Appeal are governed by the Rules of the Supreme Court, which are made by a Rule Committee that consists of: the Lord Chancellor, the Lord Chief Justice, the Master of the Rolls, the President of the Family Division, the Vice-Chancellor and three judges of the Supreme Court, two practising barristers and two practising solicitors. The three judges and the barristers and solicitors are appointed by the Lord Chancellor. The Rules that are made must be published and laid before Parliament. County court Rules are made by a committee of five county court judges, two barristers, two registrars of county courts, and two solicitors, all appointed by the Lord Chancellor. The Rules then have to be submitted to the Lord Chancellor, who may allow, disallow or alter them. In all cases the Rules are subject to the limitation that, being delegated legislation, they can be valid only within the scope of the powers given by Parliament, but since the rule-making power is so largely vested in judges, it is unlikely that judges will find that the statutory power has been exceeded. The Rules of the Supreme Court are bulky: at present they consist of 114 main sections, which are called *Orders*, each divided into a number of subsections called *Rules*. Following a comprehensive revision in 1965, they were issued by Her Majesty's Stationery Office in loose-leaf form. In fact, practitioners generally use a two-volume, 3,000-page commercial publication called the *Supreme Court Practice* – usually known from its cover as the 'White Book' – which is published every three years, with supplements in between. This contains the rules together with a commentary. For the county courts the equivalent is the 'Green Book', officially called the *County Court Practice*, an annual one-volume publication of a mere 2,000 pages. In addition to the Rules of the Supreme Court and the county court Rules there is a separate code, the Matrimonial Causes Rules, which regulates procedure in divorce and related matters.[1]

---

[1] The present set were made in 1977. The Committee which makes them is constituted by the Matrimonial Causes Act 1973 s.50. The Crown Court also has its own Rules and Rules Committee, and procedure in the House of Lords is regulated by Standing Orders which are issued by the House of Lords itself.

It is impossible to describe procedure in detail within a short compass,[1] and here it is proposed to deal only with certain salient points.

It is customary to think of 'procedure' as governing the steps that must be taken from the commencement of a case down to the trial itself, and subsequent steps for enforcing the judgment or order of the court, together with the bringing or defending of any appeal that may be made to a higher court. The centre of this picture is the trial, which means the hearing of the case before a judge or a judge and jury. In practice only a small number of the actions commenced ever result in a trial. A case will not reach trial unless it is contested. This is clearly shown in table 1 for county courts, and table 3 for the Queen's Bench Division, where we see that more than nine judgments out of ten are given without a trial. In most of these cases the proceedings are started without any expectation that they will reach trial because it is obvious from the start that there is no defence to the case. Special provision is made by the Rules of the Supreme Court for obtaining speedy judgment where a case is unlikely to be contested. Order 13 provides that where a writ is indorsed for a claim for a liquidated sum and the defendant fails to give notice of his intention to defend within a prescribed time (usually fourteen days) the plaintiff may enter final judgment for the sums claimed and costs. Under Order 14, where the defendant does give notice of his intention to defend the case, the plaintiff may then apply for what is called *summary judgment*; the plaintiff swears an affidavit to show that he has an unanswerable case, and unless the defendant then shows cause against the application the plaintiff gets judgment without trial. These cases are taken by officials called masters (with a right of appeal to a judge, to the Court of Appeal and with leave to the House of Lords). Order 14 procedure is available in the High Court for most (but not all) types of action, and both Order 14 and Order 13 have their equivalents in county court procedure. The Judicial Statistics suggest that of the actions that do not follow either of these short-cuts to judgment, only about one-sixth are set down for trial, and of these rather under half are actually tried. The main reason for so many of these proceedings being withdrawn is the prevalence of settlements: this will be explained at p. 81 in connection with personal injury cases but it occurs in all kinds of actions. The high cost of litigation and the uncertainties make a tolerable settlement more attractive than a fight. The rules of procedure also encourage settlement in various ways. If the plaintiff insists upon claiming what is thought to be too much, the defendant may 'pay into court' what he thinks is a reasonable sum. The plaintiff must then choose between accepting that sum and ending the action, or continuing the action on the terms that if he is awarded more than that sum he will get his costs in the ordinary way, but if he is awarded

---

[1] A readable introduction is David Barnard, *The civil court in action* (2nd ed. 1985). Fuller accounts are Langan and Henderson, *Civil procedure* (3rd ed. 1983), and Odgers, *Pleading and practice* (22nd ed. 1981). However, Professor Jackson remembered Mr Weldon (of the firm of law coaches) impressing upon his class of students that procedure can never be learned from books alone, and that students could not expect to know all the stages of a lengthy chancery action because none of them had lived long enough.

less then he must pay his own costs and the costs of the defendant since the date of the payment into court. It is thus wrong to think of legal proceedings being synonymous with the trial of cases: the great bulk of the actions brought are settled or terminated by judgment without trial. In the background to all actions there is, of course, the possibility of a trial, and the nature of this necessarily conditions much of our system.

Confining ourselves here to civil cases, the purpose of proceedings prior to the trial is to clarify the dispute. The steps are usually taken by the solicitors to the parties, often in consultation with a barrister who drafts the documents required, but for convenience these will be referred to as if the parties themselves were acting. The first step is to issue a writ: the plaintiff draws up a document in appropriate legal form and on payment of a fee a court official validates it by applying the official court stamp.[1] The writ is then served on the defendant; he is given a copy, together with a form which he must return to acknowledge service, also indicating whether or not he intends to contest the case. The plaintiff then sends to the defendant a Statement of Claim setting out the allegations that he makes. The reply to this is a document called the Defence. Neither of these documents deals with the evidence upon which the allegations will be supported. For instance, in a libel action the Statement of Claim will allege that the defendant published certain matter concerning the plaintiff and that the words bear a defamatory meaning. The Defence may deny the publication, or admit the publication but deny that the words were defamatory, or plead that the words were fair comment on matters of public interest, or that the words were true. The general idea is that each party should know with some precision the case that he has to meet, and that this process must be complete before the parties go into court. The process of pleadings is under the control of the officers of the court, with an appeal to a judge, and appropriate orders are made to see that each party has adequate information. Thus, if the defendant has published a 'life-story' of the plaintiff in which the plaintiff is described as having lived 'a life of crime', in a libel action the defendant may plead in defence that those words are true. This will enable him to produce any evidence of the criminal activities of the plaintiff, and unless the plaintiff is further informed he will have no idea what charges he may have to meet. Hence an order will be made that the defendant produce Particulars, or Further and Better Particulars, which means that he must give adequate information of the matters he proposes to prove so that the plaintiff can prepare to meet such allegations. An order may be made for a party to answer certain questions in advance (*interrogatories*), or to produce for inspection any relevant documents he may possess. Eventually the pleadings are closed, and the case is ready for trial. In the course of these preliminary proceedings the place and the mode of trial will have been determined. The place of trial has already been discussed (chapter 6); the mode of trial is determined in the same way, that

---

[1] County court procedure is basically similar, but there are some differences, especially of terminology. The county court issues 'summonses', not writs.

is, by an official of the courts subject to an appeal to a judge. The most important distinction as to mode of trial is between trial before a judge alone or before a judge and jury.

The sort of case in which there is usually jury trial is the happy hunting-ground of newspaper reporters, so that the public accustomed to reading accounts in newspapers probably still believes that juries are commonly used in civil cases. In fact, their use is now very rare.[1] Trial by judge and jury was the required method of trial in the common law courts, and it remained usual there even after 1854 when it first became possible for litigants in those courts to elect trial by judge alone. In Chancery juries were never used, and the Judicature Acts 1973–75, in fusing the administration of law and equity, may be regarded as the triumph of Chancery ideas in civil suits. From this point onwards, litigants at common law increasingly began to choose trial by judge alone. From 1885 to 1917, roughly half the cases heard in the King's Bench Division were before a judge alone. The shortage of manpower during the First World War led to restrictive measures, which brought jury trial to a low ebb. A small measure of recovery took place after the war was over, aided by the repeal of the restrictions in 1925, but the popularity of jury trial again declined. So there was little opposition in 1933 when Parliament, in the hope of making justice quicker and cheaper, imposed on jury trial in the Queen's Bench Division the severe restrictions which remain in force today by the Supreme Court Act 1981. By section 69 of this Act jury trial is to be ordered in the Queen's Bench Division when there is a charge of fraud, or the case is one of libel, slander, malicious prosecution or false imprisonment,[2] unless the court is of opinion that the trial requires any prolonged examination of documents or accounts or any scientific or local investigation which cannot conveniently be made with a jury.[3] In other cases, there is to be trial in the Queen's Bench Division by judge alone unless the court in its discretion decides otherwise; litigants rarely ask for one, and still more rarely obtain it. Juries are never used in the Admiralty Court or in the Chancery Division. In the earlier years of this century they were considerably used in defended divorce cases, but the Matrimonial Causes Rules now provide that trial is to be by judge alone unless the court orders otherwise, and in practice juries are now unheard of in the Family Division. Juries have never been popular in the county courts, and changes in the right to jury trial were made on the same lines as for the Queen's

---

[1] In previous editions of this book, this point was illustrated with a table, but jury actions in the High Court are now no longer published in the *Judicial statistics*.

[2] Under the Administration of Justice Act 1933, actions for seduction or breach of promise of marriage were also included, but these types of claim have now been abolished. The Supreme Court Act 1981 empowers the Rules Committee to add other classes of case as fit for jury trial, but it has not done so.

[3] In response to a libel action which had lasted from October 1980 to March 1981, it was proposed in the Supreme Court Bill 1981 to add to this list cases which are likely to last a long time, but this was defeated in Parliament.

Bench. The rules governing county courts were enacted in the County Courts Act 1934.[1]

The result was a virtual end to jury trials in county courts. A case prominently reported in the newspapers in September 1983 was said to be the first in York County Court for over forty years.[2] The decline in the use of juries in civil cases is not due entirely to lack of faith in this mode of trial. It is partly a matter of cost. Also, the effectiveness of jury trial depends largely upon the type of juror, the selection of matters that are left to juries and the measure of control over the quantum of damages; these problems are examined later.[3]

The pleadings and the other formal steps in the preparation of a case represent merely part of the work that has to be done. Often the most difficult part of the preparation is the securing of the necessary evidence. The solicitors to the parties interview all the possible witnesses and make a full written note of what they will say. This may involve some travelling. In some cases it is necessary to submit a question to an expert; the extent of personal injuries may be more skilfully assessed by a specialist than by a general practitioner. The solicitor then prepares the 'brief' for the barrister[4] (more often referred to as 'counsel'). This is a bundle of papers which includes a chronicle of the case made by the solicitor, together with copies of all documents and of the statements made by witnesses. Counsel usually indicates which of the witnesses should be called, whereupon the solicitor must make arrangements for the witnesses to attend the trial. Some witnesses attend voluntarily, subject to their expenses being paid, whilst other witnesses are summoned by a *subpoena* which compels their attendance on threat of punishment for contempt of court.

In English practice the trial, or 'day in court', is a climax at which the whole case must be presented. In the now typical case of a trial before a judge alone, the plaintiff's counsel 'opens the case' by giving an account of the facts and referring to any documents. The plaintiff's witnesses are then called, and give their evidence orally by being 'examined' by plaintiff's counsel. They may then be 'cross-examined' by defendant's counsel, and, if this leaves ambiguities, 're-examined' by plaintiff's counsel. If the defendant is going to call witnesses, the case for the defendant is then taken in the same way, defence counsel opening his case, calling witnesses, and then summarising the evidence and presenting his arguments. Plaintiff's counsel then has the last say, because he may reply by

---

[1] Now contained in the County Courts Act 1984 s.66.

[2] *White* v. *Brown*, *The Times* 30 September 1983. Possibly this well-publicised case has led to a minor revival of juries in county courts: see Nolan, 'The jury in the county court', (1988) 85 Law. Soc. Gaz. 19.

[3] See chapter 32 below. There is a fuller account of the decline in the use of civil juries by R. M. Jackson in (1937) 1 Mod. LR 132.

[4] In the American legal system 'briefs' are written statements prepared by lawyers and handed in to an apellate court to show the contentions that are being put forward – a practice which is discussed in chapter 10 below.

comparing the evidence for the plaintiff with that for the defendant. He also presents his arguments. If the defendant does not propose to call any witnesses, then the final speech for the plaintiff is made after the plaintiff's witnesses have been called. The defendant's counsel will then comment on the evidence for the plaintiff and deal with any relevant points. When the case is tried by judge alone it is now time for the judge to announce his decision. Unlike a jury, he is required to state briefly the basis upon which he has reached it; in a difficult case he may reserve judgment, which means that he will consider his notes and consult legal works, finally writing a judgment which he will read in court. In the case of a trial by jury there will be some differences. The openings must be longer, the final speeches must be fuller, and the evidence will be taken less speedily because counsel will want to make sure that the jury have grasped certain points. At the end the judge must sum up to the jury, after which the jury will be asked to consider their verdict. They may be asked for a general verdict for the plaintiff or defendant, or – less commonly – the judge may put specific questions to the jury, their answers to which are called a 'special verdict'. In the latter case there may be legal argument as to the meaning of the verdict. The jury decide not only who has won, but if it is the plaintiff, how much damages he is to receive. After their verdict there is therefore little for the judge to do in giving judgment except to direct judgment in accordance with the verdict of the jury and make an order as to costs.

A number of points arise on this type of trial. First, the responsibility of the parties is not confined to settling the issue to be decided, but extends to the preparation of the evidence and its presentation. There is no rule in civil cases that all the available evidence must be put before the court. If the plaintiff has statements from several witnesses, he may select those witnesses whose evidence appears favourable to him and he need not tell the defendant or the court about evidence that he has discarded, and the defendant may act in the same way. Whereas documents must be revealed in the interlocutory stage, and counsel must exchange notes of cases that they propose to cite, there is no obligation to reveal anything about witnesses.[1] Thus there may be a measure of 'trial by ambush':[2] a defendant may, for example, produce at the trial persons who testify that they saw the road accident, and although it may seem odd that this is the first occasion on which the existence of these witnesses becomes known to the plaintiff, one party is quite entitled to spring a surprise on the other. In the past, this led to such abuse in the case of expert witnesses, whose evidence it is difficult for anyone to probe effectively unless he has had time to digest it, that in 1971 the law was changed to require pre-trial disclosure of expert evidence in civil cases. Section 81 of the Police and Criminal Evidence Act 1984 makes similar provision for criminal trials in the Crown Court.

[1] The position is otherwise in criminal cases; see chapter 23 below.
[2] See the Report of the Committee on Personal Injuries Litigation (Winn Committee), (1968) Cmnd 3691 para. 131. For 'cards on the table', see paras. 132–37.

This leads to the second major point, which is that our 'contest' theory of trial has a number of drawbacks when technical questions are involved. Medical questions are a case in point. In the last few years judges have been inclined to urge litigants to submit agreed medical reports, but if the doctors do not agree the technique is to call the doctors for each party. One set of professionals, paid by the plaintiff, says one thing, and another set of professionals, paid by the defendant, says another thing. The same thing regularly happens with almost every other type of expert evidence. Under the inquisitorial system the judge would have been compiling a dossier on the case long before the trial, and he would himself have appointed some medical or other expert to make a report for the use of the court. In the same way, inspection of vehicles, plans of the scene of accidents, and other matters would be investigated and reported upon. The 'trial' would be far from a comprehensive review of everything in issue, for the court would want to hear evidence primarily on points not already covered by the dossier, which often means that the trial is no more than a completion of the dossier upon which the judges – for when the inquisitorial system is used there are usually more than one – will come to a decision. In our system it is usually necessary to counter the other party's experts by producing equally weighty (and equally expensive) experts. The professions in England are so organised that there should be no difficulty in avoiding these troubles by a system of reports made at the request of judges. Indeed, since 1934 it has been possible for a court expert to be appointed on the application of either of the parties, but little use is made of this. This is because lawyers bred in our contest system want to keep control over evidence: one does not know whether a court expert is going to be for or against one, and it is safer to provide the expert oneself, for by shopping around one can usually find an apparently well-qualified expert who will give favourable evidence.

Expert evidence is not only a problem in terms of getting experts. Indeed, the whole position when legal proceedings involving technical or specialist matters that can fairly be regarded as outside the knowledge and experience of a judge is problematic. In England various different methods have been tried of coping with the problem. In olden days, it was sometimes the practice to summon a special jury composed of people with particular experience. A method still current is to have specialist assessors sitting with the judge. This is a well-established practice in Admiralty and it is possible, though somewhat rare, in other Divisions.[1]

Under the old Workmen's Compensation legislation, which existed before there was state compensation for industrial injuries under the social security system which was operated by the county courts, there was a provision for medical assessors to sit with county court judges. In some appeals to Crown

[1] An assessor helped the judge in *Southport Corporation* v. *Esso Petroleum Co. Ltd* [1953] 3 WLR 773, a Queen's Bench Division action on nuisance, trespass and negligence when oil escaped from a stranded ship and polluted the foreshore. A. Dickey, 'The Province and Functions of Assessors in English Courts', (1970) 33 Mod. LR 494, contains much useful material.

Courts the court must consist of a judge sitting with justices who have special experience (see chapter 21 below), and under the Race Relations Act 1976 a county court judge must be assisted by two race relations assessors. In the Patents Court there is power to appoint an official scientific advisor to the case. Unlike an assessor, he appears for the part of the case where he is needed, and does not have to sit with the judge throughout the whole case. Another approach to the problem is to have the case tried by an Official Referee. Cases which involve prolonged examination of documents or accounts, or a technical or scientific or local investigation may be listed as what is called 'Official Referee's business'. A body of circuit judges – four in London and two in each of the provincial circuits – are designated to handle these cases and have developed their own specialist techniques for dealing with them. Whereas in ordinary trials the interlocutory stages come before separate officials called masters, an Official Referee handles the entire case himself and therefore controls the shape of the case which he will eventually try. Official Referees make greater use of the power to appoint court experts, and through regularly trying certain types of case they themselves acquire a measure of expert knowledge. Complicated building disputes are generally heard this way, and as these have increased in number recently so the work of the Official Referees has increased: 3,015 cases were designated Official Referees' business in 1986, a 10 per cent increase on the previous year, and this led to serious delays in the hearing of this type of case.

These special methods of dealing with the problems of expert evidence are almost entirely confined to civil cases. In criminal trials technical questions often create severe difficulties. A recurrent problem is said to be fraud trials, in which lay juries (and occasionally judges with little skill at figures) sometimes have great difficulty in understanding complicated questions of accounting. An official committee under Lord Roskill was appointed in 1984 to examine this problem; it recommended the abolition of juries in complex fraud trials in 1986,[1] but the government rejected the idea in the face of some public outcry. Even in the civil law, furthermore, the general solution has been to cut out the ordinary courts and to provide for adjudication by a tribunal which is hand-tailored for coping with the particular technicalities and issues that arise within the special field. This is a major factor in considering the operation of administrative or special tribunals, discussed in part III below.

A third major point in the practical working of the contest system of trial is that evidence is presented in such a way that it imposes a considerable strain upon those who listen to it, which is particularly important in jury trials. The cross-examination of the plaintiff's witnesses is the only thing that gives any indication of the extent to which the defendant is going to contradict what is said for the plaintiff. The method of 'confrontation', which is not used in trials in our courts, allows the immediate contradiction of evidence. Thus, if witness A says that he

[1] Fraud Trials Committee Report, HMSO (1986) (but not a Command Paper).

was not at a given place at a given time, confrontation allows A's evidence to be interrupted so that witness X may testify that A was at that place. Under our method the evidence of A may be contradicted by X some hours or days later; the jury, aided by counsel, is expected to remember what A said. The method of confrontation has its own drawbacks, and it is mentioned here simply to show that our method is not inevitable. The trained lawyer may make light of the burden of marshalling many apparently unconnected pieces of evidence, weighing them against similar fragments, and producing an ordered whole, but to most minds a decision is facilitated by an early statement of both points of view so that there can be the least possible doubt about the bearing and relevance of the evidence. But we have a contest theory of trial, witnesses appear for one side or the other, and each side must have its go in turn. Traditionally the people who decided the contest were a jury of lay people, and this was responsible for the growth of a very complicated law of evidence. Until comparatively recently, the jury were of course too illiterate to deal with documents, and this gave rise to a general rule that the court would only receive oral testimony. If evidence is crucial and likely to be disputed it is essential that the witness should come to court and be orally examined; but if both sides accept what he has to say, or if the witness is someone like a meteorologist who has merely kept a written record of details which are no longer present in his mind, bringing him to court for oral examination is only an expensive way of prolonging the trial and making it more complicated that it need be. Furthermore, because jurors are unlikely to have trained minds and may even be prejudiced or dim-witted, it was also found necessary to create a set of complicated exclusionary rules to prevent them from hearing evidence which was unfairly prejudicial or dubiously relevant. The result was a law of evidence which was both technical and expensive to operate. In civil cases the decline of jury trial has been rapidly followed by a great relaxation of the old stringent rules of evidence, culminating in the Civil Evidence Act 1968; but in criminal cases, where jury trial is still dominant, the old law of evidence survives largely intact.

Discussion of the law of evidence leads to a final point about the mode of trial at common law. This is that it is far too difficult for anyone but a trained lawyer to operate it. Laymen may admire the extraordinary Colonel Wintle, who as a litigant in person sued a lawyer and won his case in the House of Lords,[1] but few would be able to copy him. It is far beyond the powers of most laymen to present a case, produce witnesses, coax legally admissible evidence out of them, and then aptly cross-examine the witnesses for the other side. Most laymen can only manage if the judge takes over the job and investigates their case – which is the inquisitorial system, alien to our tradition. At one time this meant that there was a failure of justice in most small claims in which the cost of briefing a barrister or solicitor to represent the parties was disproportionate to the sums of money involved. As mentioned in chapter 5, all claims not in excess of £500 are now

[1] *Wintle* v. *Nye* [1959] 1 WLR 284.

referred to the county court registrar to hear as an arbitrator, and larger claims can be so dealt with when the parties agree. The idea is to provide a method of trial simple enough for the litigant in person. The parties are discouraged from employing lawyers to represent them by a rule that they must pay any costs of legal representation they may incur, and can recover from their opponent only witness expenses and the court fee if they win; despite this, however, lawyers are quite often used. When acting as arbitrator the registrar, like any other arbitrator, is required to apply the law of the land, but he is free to disregard the more refined rules of procedure and evidence in determining the facts. County court arbitrations are invariably heard in private, usually in a small room with everyone sitting around a table: beyond this the method of trial is impossible to describe because there is no set form and it is left to each registrar to decide how he goes about it. He generally holds a pre-trial review which takes the form of a preliminary conference attended by both parties. Here he tries to find out what matters are in dispute, and tells them what evidence he will need to hear in order to decide the case. Often this is the first time that the parties have spoken face to face since the incident which gave rise to the law-suit, and a good many cases are promptly settled. If the case is not settled there is a further hearing to determine the case. Where either or both parties are unrepresented, most registrars play an inquisitorial role and question the parties and their witnesses in an attempt to get to the bottom of the case; but this is much harder work than sitting back and listening, and not all registrars are willing to do this. It is possible for a county court arbitration to be conducted entirely in writing, which is quicker and cheaper than an oral hearing. Although it is on offer litigants very rarely use it: even at this level the Englishman values his day in court. How good a method of trial the county court arbitration is obviously depends to a large extent on how far the registrar in question is willing to enter into the spirit of the proceedings; but table 1 (page 32 above) shows the extent of their use, and all in all they can be reckoned one of the modest successes of law reform in recent years.

A survey commissioned by the Civil Justice Review (see page 83 below) reported that over 80 per cent of plaintiffs thought they would happily use the scheme again if similar circumstances arose. Sixty-seven per cent of plaintiffs were successful; 73 per cent of plaintiffs and 58 per cent of defendants thought the proceedings fair.

8

COMPLAINTS ABOUT THE CIVIL COURTS

Complaints about law courts have a long history. We can feel satisfaction that 'our one great judicial scandal'[1] happened in the reign of Edward I, but we have had a steady stream of lesser troubles. There has never been a time when law courts have been free from complaints: complaints have been about delay, costs, vexatious elements in procedure, incompetent administration and a generally inconvenient and inefficient arrangement of courts. These charges are difficult to examine because the incidence shifts and because there is apt to be a confusion between cause and effect. Nevertheless, there can be no doubt that the service given to the public by law courts has not satisfied consumers other than those charged with criminal offences who have a vested interest in being acquitted through the inefficiency of judicial process. Delay and costs have been particularly stressed in recent years.[2]

Part of the trouble in the past has stemmed from an addiction to out-of-date ways of conducting business. In the early middle ages, when the law courts began, there was no post and no telephone and the way in which one did business with the King or with a high official was to 'wait upon him': the citizen went to where he held court and hung about patiently until the great man was pleased to give him an audience. This remained the method of doing business with the High Court office until long after the Second World War. To carry out even the most routine steps in a High Court action it was necessary to go in person to see the relevant official. Virtually nothing could be done by post, nor could one telephone to make an appointment in advance because until the 1960s the officials resolutely refused to have telephones. To some this seemed a quaint and amusing anachronism, but it was less than funny for the litigant anywhere outside London who had to pay his solicitor to engage a London agent to send someone from his office to waste half a day conducting business which could equally well have been done by letter. In the middle ages it was also the custom for all men of substance to leave London for the summer in order to supervise the harvest on their estates and to escape the plagues and smells of the city, which got worse in hot weather. Consequently the whole public administration shut down, law-courts included. Most public business now carries on as usual during the

[1] Maitland, in Selden Society edition of *Mirror of justices* (1893), p. xxiv.
[2] Costs are discussed in chapter 39.

79

summer, but the High Court closes for the months of August and September (although there is nowadays a skeleton service for urgent cases). Inconveniences of this sort were particularly prevalent in the Chancery Division[1] where for many years it seemed quite impossible to get any of these practices changed: they were roundly condemned by an official committee which reported in 1960,[2] but in 1981 another committee was expressing regret that nobody had taken any notice.[3] This time, however, notice was taken; a major overhaul of Chancery Division procedure took place in 1982, producing a number of considerable improvements.

Even after these reforms most people would hardly call Chancery a cheap or speedy court;[4] but it is the Queen's Bench Division, particularly in relation to the personal injury claims which comprise some 70 per cent of its work, which is nowadays the main focus for complaints about cost and delay. The report of the Pearson Commission in 1978 contains a wealth of information on this,[5] including extracts from sad interviews with a number of disgruntled plaintiffs, some of whom described their worry and frustration vividly. It seems that the time which elapses between an injury and the case being disposed of by the court is very rarely less than a year, usually around three years, and in a quarter of all cases four years or more. Part of the delay is caused by the fact that when a case is ready for trial it must take its place in the queue for a trial date. In 1986 trials in the Queen's Bench Division in London were being fixed for twelve months ahead, and in 1987 the diary was booked up for the next twenty months. There are also substantial waiting-lists in the Provincial High Court Centres (although county court waiting times are generally much less). Not all of this is directly attributable to the courts, however. Many injured people do not make a claim immediately

[1] The following charming story appeared in (1967) 64 Law Soc. Gaz. 263. 'Recently when filing an affidavit in a Chancery matter I presented with it a xerox copy which was stapled down the left side. I was told that this was not acceptable and that the copy must be either stuck together with Sellotape or sewn up with green silk . . . I went out and bought green tape, needle and thimble and did the job there and then. I did not plump for Sellotape as I have previously lost many an unequal battle with that stuff. My needlework was accepted by Her Majesty's Court . . . You may feel this medieval story of slight interest, but it is typical of the thousand and one petty time-wasting nonsenses that go on in Chancery.'

[2] Report of the Committee on Chancery Chambers and Chancery Registrars' Office (Harman Committee), Cmnd 967.

[3] Report of the Review Body on the Chancery Division of the High Court (Oliver Committee), (1981) Cmnd 8205.

[4] Although a recently retired Chancery Master said in its defence that 'the practice is probably the most efficient in the country, if not in the world . . . it must not be subjected to ill-thought-out tinkerings masquerading as reform' (1981) 78 Law Soc. Gaz. 729.

[5] Royal Commission on Civil Liability and Compensation for Personal Injury (Pearson Committee) Cmnd 7054–I, 7054–II and 7054–III, especially 7054–II. A certain amount of further information is also contained in the Report of the Committee on Personal Injuries Litigation (Winn Committee), (1968) Cmnd 3691 and in the report in 1966 by a Committee of *Justice* on *Trial of motor accident cases*, the Report of the Personal Injuries Litigation Procedure Working Party (Cantley Committee) (1979) Cmnd 7476, the study by D. Harris and others *Compensation and support for illness and injury* (1984), and The Civil Justice Review Consultation Paper on Personal Injuries Litigation (1985, Lord Chancellor's Department).

after an accident occurs, and when they do get round to taking some action they may accept the services of a claims negotiator or report their accident to their trade union (see chapter 41). If no settlement is negotiated, the case goes to a solicitor, and he may move slowly, or send the papers to counsel, so creating further delay. The defendant's insurers, of course, have no incentive to dispose of the case quickly. There may be sloth in the way some of these matters are handled, but the whole atmosphere of dealing with personal injury claims is governed by the expectation that the claim is going to be settled, and when the plaintiff's solicitor goes on negotiating instead of issuing a writ he is often acting in his client's best interests. According to the Pearson Commission, some 86 per cent of personal injury claims are settled without starting any legal proceedings, and even here the process of negotiation usually spins out for two years after the accident. Starting legal proceedings is usually no more than a further tactical move, because little more than 10 per cent of those cases in which a writ is issued will reach the doors of the court, and even half of these will be settled just before the trial is due to begin. Hence if 'delay' means the elapsed time between accident and settlement of a claim, the most frequent cause of 'delay' is the time spent on negotiations and not the time spent awaiting trial. That conclusion does not, however, give a clean bill of health to the judicial process, for the efficiency or otherwise of the judicial process has an effect on the negotiating process as well as on the cases that do in the end go for trial.

The preference for getting a settlement rather than fighting a case to judgment is very pronounced: it can be explained as being an instance of our national preference for compromises: better take what you certainly can get than hold out for a lot more. But this process is enormously affected by attitudes towards litigation, and here there seems to be an important factor in that people in this country have a reluctance to go to law. This is noticeable in various ways, notably in the preference in many fields for having special tribunals rather than law courts. Some of the causes can be seen in a consideration of how injured persons fare if their case does proceed to trial.

An injured person commonly has plenty of worries; he will receive hospital and medical treatment on the National Health Service, but in most cases his earnings cease. If he was injured at work he will ordinarily receive National Insurance payments. The social security system should see that he and his family have the basic necessities, and legal aid should look after his professional assistance to pursue his claim. Nevertheless, an injured person does commonly have a financial set-back, for building society mortgage payments, hire-purchase and other outgoings have to be met, and an upset of domestic arrangements often means extra expense. It comes to this: that of all litigants, or potential litigants, a person unable to work because of personal injuries has the greatest need of speedy justice: and yet he has to wait as long as anyone else and often far longer.

Over the last 80 years committee after committee has made proposals to speed up the process of litigation in personal injury cases, many of which have been adopted, and yet the length of time the injured person must wait to get his money never seems to get appreciably shorter. This is a matter of serious concern, and in the early 1970s gave rise to the radical proposal that the whole business of compensation for personal injury be taken away from the ordinary courts and covered by some extended form of social security, as was done in New Zealand in 1972.[1]

Each year the public directly or indirectly pays huge sums in premiums for third-party insurance of various kinds, out of which insurance companies take their overheads and profits, and lawyers and courts take their fees, before what is left is distributed to injured plaintiffs in the form of damages for personal injury several years later. If this money were paid to the state as a tax instead, it could be distributed to the injured as social security benefits much more quickly. It is also said that so much would be saved in overheads that there would be enough money left over to compensate even those who are injured where no defendant is actually to blame; under the present system, such people can usually claim no damages at all. In 1973, a Royal Commission was set up with Lord Pearson (a retired Lord of Appeal) as chairman to look into this proposal, and a three-volume report was produced in 1978.[2]

Unfortunately the Pearson Commission was deeply divided on whether or not it was proper and moral to abolish civil liability for accidental personal injury. It produced a compromise proposal under which the existing system would be retained and an extended social security system would be created to supplement it. This had the obvious drawback of being certain to cost the public a lot of extra money in the form of taxes without any corresponding savings in insurance premiums. Like many compromises, it satisfied nobody and the idea now seems to have been quietly shelved.

So it looks as if the best that reformers can hope for in the short term is some better method of dealing with personal injury cases within the existing court structure and framework of legal rules. This century has seen a long procession of committees and commissions which have deplored the delay in the legal process.[3] The efforts of these committees have produced various sensible reforms – for example, the introduction of a trial date booked in advance instead of the old system under which all cases had to wait their turn in an erratically-moving queue – but never any really large or radical changes. This probably has much to do with the fact that these committees have mainly consisted of judges

---

[1] The main advocate of this idea in the United Kingdom is Professor P. S. Atiyah, whose influential book *Accidents, compensation and the law* first appeared in 1970.

[2] Report of the Royal Commission on Civil Liability and Compensation for Personal Injury, (1978) Cmnd 7054–I, II, III.

[3] Royal Commission on Delay in the King's Bench Division, (1913) Cd 6761, (1914) Cd 7177; Business of the Courts Committee, (1933) Cmd 4265, (1933) Cmd 4471, (1936) Cmd 5066; Royal Commission on Despatch of Business at Common Law, (1936) Cmd 5065; Committee on Supreme Court Practice and Procedure, (1949) Cmd 7764, (1951) Cmd 8176, (1952) Cmd 8617, (1953) Cmd 8878; Committee on Personal Injuries Litigation, (1968) Cmnd 3691.

and eminent practising lawyers who, like other mortals, find it difficult to think radically about an organisation of which they are part and in which they have achieved success.

One committee in recent times which had a predominantly non-legal membership, the Beeching Commission, did produce truly radical reforms in the court structure.[1] This precedent gave cause for cautious optimism when in 1985 the Lord Chancellor, Lord Hailsham, set up a Civil Justice Review, with an industrialist as its chairman and a majority of members who are neither judges nor practising lawyers (although both these categories are represented on it). The idea is that it should study civil litigation type by type, rather than by looking at the work court by court. Moving rapidly, it has commissioned several studies by firms of management consultants, and has produced a series of Consultation Papers on different aspects of civil justice, the first of which in 1986 was on personal injury litigation.[2] Among the thoughts contained in this paper is the idea that the traditional process of having an oral trial is simply too complicated and expensive for determining the smaller kinds of personal injury claim, and that it would be better if they were determined by someone who simply read the papers; this is further discussed later in this book. At present these and the other proposals are only tentative. The purpose of the Consultation Papers is to stimulate public discussion, and it is hoped that eventually the process will lead to firm proposals for change which are widely acceptable to the public and to the legal profession.

The Civil Justice Review has produced a number of other radical ideas. One is that the courts themselves should take a much more active part in the conduct of litigation in order to prevent delays. At present Court Rules lay down time limits for taking various steps, but it is left to the parties themselves to comply with them. When a procedural step is due nobody in the court administration reminds the litigant that he should take it, and if he fails to take it or takes it late no official sanction is applied unless his opponent complains. The Civil Justice Review suggests that the courts should assume responsibility for seeing that cases follow the schedule laid down in the Rules, which need to be 'policed (and not just refereed)'.[3]

In the county courts there is a system of 'performance indicators' under which each Circuit sets objectives for the dispatch of its work, and continuous checks are made to see if the objectives are being met, and if not why not. It is suggested that this should be extended to the High Court. More radical is the idea that the High Court and the county court should be amalgamated to form one single organisation. The case for this is that having two separate systems causes

[1] Royal Commission on Assizes and Quarter Sessions, (1969) Cmnd. 4153; see chapter 6 above.
[2] (1) Personal Injuries Litigation (1986); (2) Small Claims in the County Court (1986); (3) The Commercial Court (1986); (4) The Enforcement of Debt (1987); (5) Housing Cases (1987); (6) General Issues (1987). These are available from the Lord Chancellor's Department, as are the studies upon which these are based. Among their many virtues is the fact that they are extremely cheap.
[3] Consultation Paper on General Issues (1987) p. 63.

needless and sometimes expensive complications in practice, and causes uneconomical use of judicial manpower, which is in turn the cause of delays. What is tentatively proposed is that all civil cases should start in what is now the local county court office, with a decision then being taken as to the level of judge who is appropriate to try it – much as happens when criminal cases are sent for trial in the Crown Court.

So far the reaction from the legal profession to these proposals has been mixed. On behalf of solicitors, the Law Society has welcomed the proposal to amalgamate the courts. The Bar opposes the scheme as 'contrary to the overall interests of civil justice'.[1] Interpreted, this probably means that it is contrary to the financial interests of the Bar, which has a virtual monopoly of audience in the High Court, and might lose it in a single integrated civil court. The higher judiciary are firmly opposed to many of the proposals, and some of them, including the Lord Chief Justice, have spoken out against them. The case for a single civil court seems almost overwhelming, and in family work it is almost what we have already. What have the higher judges against it? A number of matters have probably coloured their reaction to the whole of the Civil Justice Review. At present there is an important difference of status between High Court Judges and Circuit Judges, and some High Court Judges probably feel that an amalgamation of courts would undermine their position. But there are other factors which are less unworthy. Government public spending squeezes have affected the civil justice system. An important cause of the present delays in civil justice is the fact that the amount of work has increased in recent years whilst the government has been reluctant to increase the number of superior judges. The Civil Justice Review was instituted by Lord Hailsham, a Lord Chancellor who was thought not to have pressed an obvious case for a larger number of superior judges as strongly as he should have done, and was generally thought to have been anxious to help the Treasury to avoid spending public money on the administration of justice. Consequently, the Review is easily seen as a covert scheme to cut public spending rather than to improve the service the courts offer to consumers. Almost immediately after Lord Mackay became Lord Chancellor in October 1987 an increase in the number of superior judges was announced, and this may reduce judicial suspicions. The superior judges were also very irritated by the suggestion in one of the Consultation Papers that if the long vacation was abolished it would be possible to make High Court judges sit for more days in the year and generally work harder. There may be a good case for abolishing the long vacation, but the implicit suggestion that High Court judges do not work except when they are sitting in court is very foolish, because it ignores the fact that they need time to read papers, write judgments in difficult cases and to do a large number of other chores such as reading applications for leave for judicial review and applications for leave to appeal in criminal cases. The superior judges, and

[1] (1987) 137 NLJ 726.

particularly the Heads of Divisions and the Lords Justices of Appeal, are exceptionally hard-working people, and it is quite understandable that they are furious at the suggestion that court delays occur because they are slacking. The real root of the trouble is probably that there was a failure of tact and diplomacy in the way in which the Civil Justice Review was set up, apparently over the heads of the superior judges. It is quite understandable if in consequence all the ideas that come from the Review, whether good or bad, get an equally hostile reception; but it is a pity nevertheless.[1]

---

[1] The Civil Justice Review published its Report in June 1988, too late for its recommendations to be discussed in the text. They are discussed in Appendix A below.

9

THE ENFORCEMENT OF JUDGMENTS AND ORDERS

Some judgments are merely declaratory and need no enforcement – like a decree of divorce, for example.[1] Generally, however, a judgment against a defendant requires him to do or refrain from doing something, and if he fails to comply the plaintiff has to take further legal action to make him do so – a process rather dramatically known as 'proceeding to execution'. If the court has granted the plaintiff one of the equitable remedies, such as an injunction restraining the defendant from molesting the plaintiff or forbidding him to publish a defamatory statement, or an order of specific performance requiring the defendant to perform his contract, the defendant's refusal to obey is a contempt of court for which he may, on the application of the plaintiff, be committed to prison until he 'purges his contempt'. Usually the court directs committal to prison, suspending the operation for a short time so that the party in default may have an opportunity of obeying the directions of the court. As an alternative to prison, such a defendant may be fined for contempt, or the court may order sequestrators to seize his property until he obeys. Injunctions, orders for specific performance and so forth are exceptional, however, and most judgments are money judgments, under which the defendant is ordered to pay a sum of money in damages or to meet a debt. In the days of Charles Dickens this type of judgment was also enforceable by having the defendant committed to prison, where he stayed until he paid. Originally he could be imprisoned whether or not he had the money to pay, and many a penniless judgment debtor spent long years in prison at the hands of creditors who were vindictive, or who hoped to blackmail the debtor's friends or relations to pay the debt and so secure his release. The Debtors Act 1869 severely curtailed imprisonment for debt by introducing the principle that a man should not be imprisoned for debt unless his default was wilful; a committal to prison was not to be made unless a judge was satisfied that the defendant had or had had, since the date of the judgment, the means to pay the sum.[2]

Practice did not always accord with the theory, however, and people not

---

[1] A short account of the system is contained in the Civil Justice Review's Consultation Paper No. 4 *Enforcement of debt* (1987); for the Civil Justice Review, see chapter 8 above.

[2] The power to imprison for debt is said to have been retained at the instance of the county court judges, who at the time had little to do except debt-collecting cases, and feared that if committal orders were abolished the work of their courts would decline and their jobs would disappear.

infrequently ended up in prison for debt who could not, rather than would not pay.[1] With a steep rise in committals for debt in the 1960s, public disquiet was eventually aroused and a committee under Mr Justice Payne was appointed to consider the matter. The committee recommended that imprisonment for the enforcement of ordinary judgment debts be completely abolished.[2] Not without some opposition, this was enacted in the Administration of Justice Act 1970.[3] It was felt that non-payment of taxes and maintenance orders deserved special treatment, however. Tradesmen take a calculated risk when they extend credit, and they do so because on balance it helps their trade to do so. Whilst they should have some remedies against those who fail to pay, it seems excessive to enable them to turn their bad risks into good risks by resorting to imprisonment at public expense. The same argument obviously does not apply either to deserted wives and children or to the Inland Revenue. Furthermore, the public in general suffers when people fail to pay their taxes. It also suffers when maintenance orders are left unpaid, because the destitute wife and children almost invariably end up as a charge on the public purse. Therefore the possibility of imprisonment for wilful refusal to pay a judgment debt was retained, and is still retained, in these two cases.

The primary method of enforcing a judgment debt is to have the property of the defendant seized and sold. Moveable property is seized by the appropriate officer and sold. For High Court judgments this work is done by sheriff's officers, who are independent contractors licensed to do it in return for fees which are calculated according to their success, and they usually act vigorously. In the county court the job is done by court bailiffs, who are usually retired policemen of advancing years and who receive fixed salaries to do this together with a number of other less dangerous and unpleasant tasks. Their lack of enthusiasm for this part of their work is a source of bitter complaint from solicitors, and led to a provision allowing county court judgments for over £2,000 to be transferred to the High Court for enforcement when county court jurisdiction was widely extended in 1981; but solicitors' complaints may not be justified, because a study of enforcement procedures by the Civil Justice Review showed little difference between sheriffs and bailiffs in terms of the results produced. The defendant's land may also be taken, but the complicated nature of our land law requires a further order of the court before it can be sold. Debts due to the defendant (which includes any credit balance he may have at his bank) cannot be physically seized, but the court may order the money to be paid to the plaintiff; the process is called *attachment* and the order is called a *garnishee order*. Similarly stocks and

---

[1] See the article 'In gaol for debt' by Sir Artemus Jones, (1939) *Quarterly Review*, and Henry Cecil, *Not such an ass* (1961). Both authors were county court judges.

[2] Report of the Committee on the Enforcement of Judgment Debts (Payne Committee), (1969) Cmnd 3909.

[3] A Conservative Member of Parliament described the proposal as 'typical of the soft treatment now given to wrong-doers of all kinds'; he later became a Circuit Judge, and on being convicted of smuggling became the first Circuit Judge to be removed from office for wrong-doing!

shares belonging to the defendant require special provisions. Where the defendant has an income-yielding asset that cannot be taken it is possible to get a receiver appointed to take the income and apply it to the judgment debt. The general effect of all this is that all the assets a man has may be taken away by the appropriate process for the satisfaction of the judgment. Of course, if the defendant has no assets, then by these means the plaintiff will get nothing. A sensible plaintiff therefore makes sure before he begins the action that there is a fair chance of the defendant's being able to meet any judgment that might be given. Even then, there is the risk that once the defendant gets wind of the impending action he will dissipate his assets or transfer them out of the jurisdiction. To meet this particular problem the courts in the 1970s invented a procedure called the *Mareva* injunction.[1] On starting a High Court action, the plaintiff may apply in secret to the court which, on the plaintiff's undertaking to compensate the defendant if the action is unsuccessful, issues an injunction forbidding him to dissipate his assets pending trial.

If the defendant has no assets it may still be possible to enforce a money judgment against him by a procedure called attachment of earnings, which was made available to the civil courts in 1970 in an attempt to fill the gap left by the virtual abolition of imprisonment for debt. The judgment creditor then applies to court, which has power to make an order that an employer must deduct so much money from an employee's wages and pay the money to the court.[2] Attachment of earnings is administered by the county courts; the procedure can be used for High Court judgments, but they must be transferred to the county court for the purpose. It is widely used for enforcing all sorts of judgment debts, in the region of 40,000 orders being made in civil cases each year, but like other methods of enforcement it has its special drawbacks. The first is that bad payers are apt to be men who change employment faster than the legal machine can catch up with them, and the second and more basic problem is that if the defendant has no job then he has no earnings to attach. Unemployment has risen sharply in the recent years, and with this the use of attachment of earnings has noticeably declined. Nor is attachment of earnings available against a defendant who is self-employed. The only available method of enforcing a judgment against a self-employed person without assets is to make him bankrupt. Against a person who is in trade the mere threat of this is often effective to make him pay, because if he is made bankrupt he is forced to close his business. To make someone bankrupt is a serious matter, however, and at present it is official policy to discourage it as a means of enforcing any but the larger debts; in 1984 the minimum debt upon which bankruptcy proceedings may be started was raised from £200 to £750.

---

[1] So called from the case in which it originated: *Mareva Compania Naviera S.A.* v. *International Bulk Carriers S.A.* [1975] 2 Lloyd's Rep. 509.
[2] Attachment of earnings has long existed in Scotland. It became available to magistrates' courts in England for maintenance orders in 1958 and for fines in 1967, and became generally available in the civil courts in 1970. It is now regulated by the Attachment of Earnings Act 1971.

The system of enforcing court judgments is not very efficient: according to the Civil Justice Review[1] it fails to recover more than about fifty per cent of money due. It has been suggested that part of the reason for this is that the creditor must operate in the dark as to the debtor's assets and hence the best means of attacking them. In 1969 the Payne Committee recommended that all enforcement should be transferred to a specialist Enforcement Office, which would collect information about the debtor and co-ordinate the fragmented efforts of creditors. This has been tried in Northern Ireland: but apparently without increasing the success-rate.

If someone who is convicted of a criminal offence fails to pay his fine, he is traced and made to pay without any further trouble or expense on the part of the prosecutor, and the same is true if instead of a fine he defaults on a compensation order which the criminal court has imposed in favour of the victim of his offence. The beneficiary of a compensation order is therefore better off in some ways than a civil judgment creditor. Indeed, for this reason people who have a choice between civil and criminal proceedings sometimes elect to prosecute rather than to sue in the civil courts. Laymen are often surprised to learn that if they wish to enforce the civil judgment which they have obtained with trouble and expense, it is necessary for them to incur yet further trouble and expense. Some critics of the system of justice argue that there should be a system of automatic enforcement for civil judgments, on the lines of what takes place with fines and compensation orders in the criminal courts.

[1] See note 1 p. 86 above.

10

THE CIVIL DIVISION OF THE COURT OF APPEAL AND THE HOUSE OF LORDS

From the county courts and the High Court there may be an appeal to the Court of Appeal.[1] Appeal lies as of right from most decisions of the High Court, but county court appeals are restricted. From a county court appeal lies as of right where an injunction has been granted, where the case concerns custody of or access to a child, or where in financial terms the case is over half the maximum size that may be brought in a county court; otherwise there may be an appeal only if the county court judge or a single judge of the Court of Appeal grants leave. Since the Court of Criminal Appeal was abolished in 1966 the Court of Appeal has also heard criminal appeals from the Crown Court, and it now has a Criminal as well as a Civil Division; the Criminal Division and its work is discussed in chapter 21.

The constitution of the Court of Appeal is governed by the Supreme Court Act 1981. It has as *ex officio* members the Lord Chancellor, any ex-Lord Chancellor, Lords of Appeal in Ordinary, the Lord Chief Justice, the Master of the Rolls, the Vice-Chancellor and the President of the Family Division. In addition there are 22 full-time judges appointed to the staff of the Court of Appeal, who are called Lords Justices of Appeal.[2] Usually at least three judges must sit together to form a court but for certain purposes business may be conducted by two or even one. The president of the Court of Appeal is the Master of the Rolls, and he usually sits as chairman of one of the courts. There is no prescribed limit to the number of courts which may sit at the same time, either in the criminal or the civil division, but of course the number of judges available, along with court-rooms and facilities, limits the number of courts that can be held. Over the years there has been a steady increase in work, which has necessitated a steady increase in the

[1] Further information will be found in D. Karlen, *Appellate courts in the United States and England* (1965), in Lord Evershed MR, *The Court of Appeal in England* (1950), in Lord Cohen, 'Jurisdiction, practice and procedure in the Court of Appeal', (1951) 11 Camb. LJ 3, and in Lord Asquith, 'Some aspects of the work of the Court of Appeal', (1950) 1 (NS) *Journal of the Society of Teachers of Public Law*, 350. More recent information is contained in Blom-Cooper, 'The changing nature of the appellate process', (1984) 3 *Civil Justice Quarterly* 295.
[2] The statutory maximum is 23; it is about to be raised to 28, although not all the new posts will be immediately filled.

number of Lords Justices: in 1938 it was raised from five to eight, and by 1986 it had risen to 22. When there is a temporary need for additional judge-power High Court judges may be required, and retired Lords Justices of Appeal and retired High Court judges may be requested by the Lord Chancellor to sit in the Court of Appeal.[1] The Law Lords, who as we have seen are Court of Appeal judges *ex officio* as well as being the judges in the House of Lords, also help out from time to time if business in the House of Lords is slack. Courts are normally constituted so that the judges will include at least one and preferably two whose experience has been in the part of the law in question. The composition of courts for the Criminal Division is explained in chapter 21.

The notion of an appeal as we understand it, that is, a review of a case on the grounds that the trial court came to the wrong conclusion, is alien to the common law. At common law the most that the discontented litigant could do was to mount an attack on the procedure at the trial with a view to getting it set aside, leaving the possibility of the plaintiff starting new proceedings if he had the money and the determination. To this end there existed a number of cumbrous procedures, including writs of error and motions for a new trial. The simpler idea of going over the case again in order to get the right result was introduced by the Chancery Court, the practices of which prevailed when the Court of Appeal was set up by the Judicature Acts 1873–75. Ever since then it has been expressly provided that 'an appeal to the Court of Appeal shall be by way of rehearing',[2] although 'rehearing' is a slightly misleading term, because the Court of Appeal does not hear the case again in the sense of listening to the witnesses. The evidence is taken from a shorthand note or tape recording made at the trial if the appeal is from the High Court; in county court appeals it is taken from the judge's longhand note, there being no shorthand writers in the county courts. Nowadays an appellant in a civil case will almost invariably be appealing from the decision of a first-instance court consisting of a judge alone, and in such a case he will be asking for the judgment to be reversed. Such an appellant will seek to show with reference to the evidence and the reasons which the judge gave for his decision that he came to the wrong conclusion. Here the notion of 'rehearing' comes in, for the Court of Appeal can make any order that the trial court could have made, which enables the judgment to be reversed or varied and some other judgment substituted for it. Where the appellant in a civil case is challenging the outcome of a jury trial the process is different, however, and the older common law notions of appeal reappear. There is no direct appeal from the verdict of a jury, and hence if the real ground of complaint is that the jury's verdict ought not to stand, the appellant must ask for a new trial. An appellant may contend that the judge misdirected the jury as to the law or as to the evidence, or that the damages are

---

[1] Supreme Court Act 1981 sections 2 and 9. This also empowers the Lord Chancellor to require Lords Justices of Appeal to sit at first instance if it is the High Court or the Crown Court which is under pressure.
[2] Rules of the Supreme Court, Order 59/3.

excessive or inadequate, or that there was no evidence upon which the jury could have come to their decision, and many other grounds. If the Court of Appeal allows the appeal, then the case must be retried before some other jury, or perhaps before a judge alone on a question of damages; assuming the case goes no further, the losing party will have to pay the costs of two trials and one appeal. In the case of a trial before a judge alone, the Court of Appeal is very chary of questioning the facts as found by the judge, but they may, of course, find that he drew wrong inferences from the facts or that his application of law to the facts was incorrect: just as a judge may unfortunately misdirect a jury so he may in the language of the Court of Appeal 'misdirect himself' when sitting without a jury.

The principles upon which the Court of Appeal operates have remained the same since it was created, but there have been some recent upheavals in its methods of day-to-day working. Traditionally it relied very heavily on the oral presentation of cases and the notion of the 'day in court'. There was little advance paper-work for the appellant to do. The expectation was that the appeal court judges would come to the case unprepared, and much time in court would be taken up by counsel for the appellant telling them the general background to the case, describing what had happened at the trial, and only then developing his objections to the decision from which he was appealing. All this was a very uneconomical use of judicial time, because judges like other literate persons can read information much quicker than it can be read aloud to them. For this reason, appeals in other countries usually involve the submission of lengthy statements which the judges read in advance. There were attempts to alter procedure in the Court of Appeal in this direction in the 1960s[1] but there was no great incentive to change since the court was then able to keep abreast of its work despite its inefficient methods. During the 1970s, however, there was a steady increase in the volume of appeals. Whereas in the 1960s less than 1,000 civil appeals were set down for hearing annually and cases would be heard within three to six months, by 1980 the number had risen to over 1,400 and the delay was eighteen months and more. The delays became quite a scandal, and in 1978 a working party under Lord Scarman made a number of recommendations to improve the situation, most of which were carried out.[2]

Many of the changes were purely administrative, but one was the introduction of 'skeleton arguments': instead of opening the case orally the appellant is now expected to give the Court of Appeal and his opponent a short written account of the main facts of the case and an outline of his main arguments.[3] This change is not wholly popular with barristers, who fear that judges are more likely to get hold of the wrong end of the stick from skeleton arguments, and who sometimes feel

---

[1] Following exchange visits between 'teams' of English and American lawyers. Karlen's book, *Appellate courts in the United States and England*, grew out of those visits.

[2] The report of the Working Party was not published. An account of the changes introduced was given by Sir John Donaldson, Master of the Rolls, in (1982) 132 NLJ 959ff.

[3] See Practice Notes, [1982] 1 WLR 1312 and [1983] 1 WLR 1055.

their performance is devalued when their audience knows what they are going to say in advance.[1]

Nevertheless, since the volume of work in the Court of Appeal seems to be rising as fast as new methods can be devised to clear the backlog,[2] even greater use of paper pleading can probably be expected in future. In 1986 the Master of the Rolls suggested that the present limited requirement to obtain leave to appeal should be made a general one. The Court of Appeal handles a substantial load of work. In the course of 1986, 1,489 cases were set down for appeal to the Civil Division of the Court of Appeal. Many appeals are withdrawn, however, and the number of cases actually heard and decided in 1986 was only 894: the appeal succeeded in rather over a third of them. Nearly all the appeals came from the High Court or the county courts, but appeal to the Civil Division of the Court of Appeal also lies from various tribunals, such as the Employment Appeal Tribunal, the Lands Tribunal, the Court of Protection, the Transport Tribunal and so forth. In 1986 the Court of Appeal disposed of 22 appeals from the Employment Appeal Tribunal, 12 from the Lands Tribunal, and 12 appeals from all the other tribunals put together. By contrast the workload of the Criminal Division is very much heavier: in 1986 it received 7,676 applications to appeal, and 3,509 cases resulted in a hearing before a full court.[3]

The survival of the appellate jurisdiction of the House of Lords in the reorganisation of the courts in 1875 was only possible if adequate provision was made for legal strength. A statute of 1876 provided for the appointment of Lords of Appeal in Ordinary, commonly known as Law Lords, who are paid professional judges with life peerages.[4] At first there were two Law Lords, but as with Lords Justices of Appeal the number has been gradually raised. At one time it was necessary to pass an Act of Parliament each time this was done, but under the Supreme Court Act 1981 it may now be done by Order in Council; at the time of writing there are 9 (occasionally assisted by retired law lords), and the maximum permitted number is 11. To do appellate work the House of Lords must consist of at least three persons from among the Law Lords, the Lord Chancellor, and peers who hold or have held high judicial office; for most purposes there is a panel of five. The Law Lords form the normal personnel; in modern times the Lord Chancellor has rarely sat, although recently Lord Hailsham has revived the practice to some extent. Ex-Lord Chancellors are in receipt of a pension and have often done something to earn it by sitting in the

---

[1] Describing a similar procedure which has long been used in hearings of House of Lords Appeal Committees, Robert Megarry QC (later Vice-Chancellor Sir Robert Megarry) said it was like 'trying to tell a long but funny story to an audience which has announced that it has already heard some, if not all, of it, but politely inquires whether you wish to make sure that they have seen the point': *Lawyer and litigant in England* (1962) 170.

[2] Court of Appeal: Civil Division Review of the Legal Year 1983–84, (1984) 134 NLJ 883.

[3] That is to say a full court heard either a renewed application to appeal, or an actual appeal in that number of cases.

[4] R. B. Stevens, 'The Final Appeal: Reform of the House of Lords and Privy Council', in (1969) 80 LQR 343 gives an account of the legal and political manoeuvres that led to the 1876 Act.

House of Lords and the Privy Council.[1] The House of Lords is the final appeal court for England and Northern Ireland in both civil and criminal matters, and for Scotland in civil cases only.

A party who has lost his case in the Court of Appeal could originally appeal to the House of Lords as of right, but is now obliged under the Administration of Justice (Appeals) Act 1934 to obtain leave either from the Court of Appeal or from the House of Lords. This, together with the inevitable extra cost, ensures that the number of cases which reach the House of Lords is never large. In 1980 it heard and determined 60 civil appeals, and 68 in 1986; as in the Court of Appeal the success rate is about one third. The ordinary rule of appeals is that they must follow the hiearchy of courts, that is to say that an appeal from a county court or from the High Court must go to the Court of Appeal, and only if the Court of Appeal has heard an appeal can the case go on to the House of Lords. The Administration of Justice Act 1969 made it possible for an appeal from the High Court to go direct to the House of Lords, thus bypassing or as it is commonly called 'leapfrogging' the Court of Appeal. This procedure is designed for a small number of cases where either or both of the parties wish to have a ruling from the House of Lords and it is severely limited;[2] it must involve a point of law of general public importance, either relating to construction of legislation fully argued and considered by the judge, or be a matter in which the judge is bound by previous decisions of the Court of Appeal or of the House of Lords, but in which there is ground for thinking that the precedents could well be reconsidered. The trial judge must give a certificate and then there must be an application to the House of Lords for leave, this being decided on the papers.

Although the judicial House of Lords is in practice a court of law, it remains in theory the upper House of Parliament, and a certain amount of play-acting and subterfuge is necessary to square the two ideas. An appeal to the House of Lords is by petition, and the hearing is quasi-legislative in form. There is no rule of law that lay lords are excluded, but there is a rigorous convention excluding them; on one occasion in the nineteenth century a lay lord did express an opinion, but he was just ignored when judgments were being delivered. On the other hand Law Lords may sit and vote in the House of Lords in its ordinary sittings; by convention they do not take part in matters of political controversy, but they do regularly contribute to debates on matters of law reform. Originally cases were argued in the House itself, counsel being heard from beyond the Bar. Physically this was about the most inconvenient court-room in the country, and it also precluded hearings when the House was in ordinary session. Since 1948 these problems have been overcome with the device of an Appellate Committee.[3]

---

[1] On Lord Chancellors and on ex-Lord Chancellors, see chapter 31.
[2] The idea was put forward by the Evershed Committee: Final Report of the Committee on Supreme Court Practice and Procedure, (1953) Cmd 8878 paras. 483–530. For procedure on leapfrogging see Practice Direction [1970] 1 WLR 97.
[3] The Appeal Committee, which also can sit in two sessions, must not be confused with an Appellate Committee; an Appellate Committee is the judicial body that hears appeals whereas an Appeal

Arguments are now heard before Law Lords sitting as a Committee of the House of Lords. The Appellate Committee can sit while the House is sitting, and two Appellate Committees can sit simultaneously. Conforming to the theory that it is a Parliamentary Committee and not a law court, however, the Law Lords do not wear judicial robes, and instead of sitting on a bench elevated above the parties they sit on a level with them on the other side of a large oval table. The public may attend but rarely bothers, and the proceedings are rather like a university tutorial, except that there are five somewhat formidable professors arguing with one student instead of the other way round. The separate judgments that may be given are technically speeches (although these days they may be printed and handed down instead of being read aloud), and the matter is finally decided by the 'House' on a vote at a time when the Law Lords are sitting as the House of Lords rather than a Committee.

It will be noted that both the Court of Appeal and the House of Lords are situated in London. This centralisation of appeal work caused some resentment in the 1930s, but this appears to have died away. The Beeching Commission in 1969 thought there was little demand for a decentralised appeal system, and that the present arrangement ensures consistency and the economical use of judge-power.[1]

A further matter that has been much discussed is the duplication of appeals. It is difficult to justify two appeal courts. It may be argued that at any given time either the Court of Appeal or the House of Lords is the better tribunal, or they are both equally good, so that on either hypothesis there is no need for both of them. The result upon litigants is that an appeal to the Court of Appeal is not necessarily final, so that if the case is taken on to the House of Lords the whole of the costs in the Court of Appeal appear wasted. It is sometimes disquieting to find that a litigant may lose a case, although the majority of judges find for him. If the trial judge finds in favour of A and against B, and then B appeals to the Court of Appeal where all three judges uphold the decision in A's favour, B may yet win in the House of Lords because out of the five judges sitting there three may be in his favour and two may be against him; the result is that altogether six judges favour A's case and three judges favour B's case, yet B wins.[2] Since costs normally follow the event, A must pay B's costs in the trial court (where A won) and in the Court of Appeal (where A also won) and in the House of Lords where he lost; and of course he must also pay his own costs in all three courts.[3]

Committee consists of Law Lords sitting to deal with applications for leave to appeal and other preliminary matters.

[1] Report of the Royal Commission on Assizes and Quarter Sessions, (1969) Cmnd 4153 para. 222.

[2] As in the case of Mrs Gillick's celebrated attempt to ban Health Authorities from giving contraceptive advice to girls under 16. Mrs Gillick lost at first instance, won before a unanimous Court of Appeal, and lost by a majority of three to two in the House of Lords. Hence Mrs Gillick lost on the verdict of only three out of eight appeal judges. Whether or not one sympathises with her litigation it is hard not to sympathise with her feeling that she really should have won. The case is reported as *Gillick* v. *W. Norfolk A.H.A.* [1984] QB 581 (CA), [1986] AC 112 (HL).

[3] See chapter 40 below on legal aid, and chapter 39 below on special provision that could be made to cover the costs of appeals.

There is some weighty evidence in favour of having a single appeal court.[1] In discussing this question we have the advantage of the work of Mr Blom-Cooper and Mr Drewry, whose book published in 1972 contains a wealth of material on the actual process of these appeals in the years 1952–68.[2] With many facts and figures they conclusively dispel, at any rate for the period of their study, the common assumption that an appeal to the House of Lords means a long wait and colossal expense. On the time between the Court of Appeal and the House of Lords they found that the median was about 11 months, and that four-fifths were heard in less than 15 months. They also showed that the costs involved in an appeal to the House of Lords were frequently no greater, and sometimes even less than those incurred in a difficult and complicated trial in the High Court. The authors undoubtedly show that the House of Lords is not dilatory, expensive or inefficient when measured against other higher courts, but as they themselves recognise, abolition or retention of this final court cannot depend entirely on assessment of these factors. Higher law courts and especially final appeal courts raise questions about their social utility. To many lawyers, an important part of their function is developing and adapting the law in the light of changing conditions, and if this is accepted as one of the reasons for their existence then it makes sense to keep the House of Lords as a less busy, more fully-staffed appeal court which is able to give particular attention to difficult and developing areas of the law. But a problem arises with the House of Lords as presently constituted if what one is looking for is the ideal expert court. With only nine Law Lords and a few extra helpers, it is not always possible – as it usually is possible in the Court of Appeal – to ensure that a case in the House of Lords is always heard by a panel at least one member of which has expert knowledge of the area of law in question. This, more than anything, probably explains the poor record of the House of Lords in criminal cases over the years.[3]

Ordinary litigants are unlikely to regard courts, whether of first instance or appellate, in any other way than as machinery provided by the State for adjudicating upon particular claims. As an appeal to the House of Lords involves considerable extra expense, it is worth asking what compels disappointed litigants to take their cases to that court. Obviously, like every litigant who takes a case to appeal they hope to gain the victory which has so far eluded them, but is there anything apart from stubborn optimism that makes them press on this far? If we look at the Law Reports we see that in a large proportion of civil appeals to the House of Lords, a government department or national authority was a party. These bodies are engaged in work on lines that they conceive as being authorised or required by legislation; if a judicial decision 'obstructs' them, then their

---

[1] See *Law reform now* (1963), edited by Gerald Gardiner (later Lord Chancellor) and Andrew Martin (later a Law Commissioner).

[2] L. J. Blom-Cooper and G. R. Drewry, *Final appeal: a study of the House of Lords and its judicial capacity* (1972). Another useful study of how the Law Lords operate is Alan Paterson, *The Law Lords* (1982).

[3] See chapter 21 below.

reaction is that the obstruction must be removed; the simplest step is to see what the final appeal court says, for a successful outcome may remove the 'obstruction', whilst if this fails the matter can only be 'put right' by legislation, if the relevant minister can be persuaded to take action. The point is that appeal must be *final* before legislation is considered, and there is no magic in finality coming from a second appeal court rather than from a single appeal court. A good many other civil appeals that reach the House of Lords involve large commercial concerns (or their insurers), and many of these are probably brought in order to get a final ruling on a questionable point, but there can also be a compulsion to go on appealing because of the position as to costs. All in all, one suspects that litigants really press on to the House of Lords for the same reason as mountaineers climb to the summit – because it is there – and whether the summit is high or low its existence is enough to make people try to climb it.

The strongest argument for retaining a second appeal court is the rigidity of the Court of Appeal. So long as the Court of Appeal holds that it is bound by its own decisions, there must from time to time be poor results through attempts to follow previous decisions that have come to be regarded as wrong or seriously inconvenient or conflicting. This deficiency in the Court of Appeal can be tolerated so long as 'there is always the House of Lords to put things right', though adherents of that view omit to say who it is that pays the bills of costs. But this line of argument really amounts to saying that we must retain the House of Lords in order to avoid altering the habits of the Court of Appeal.

Establishment of a single appeal court would not be free of any difficulty. Abolition of the Court of Appeal, so that all appeals would go direct to the House of Lords, would require so much reorganisation to deal with the volume of work that the character of the House of Lords would be lost in the process. Abolition of the appellate jurisdiction of the House of Lords, so that the Court of Appeal would be the final court, would offer less difficulty and to the English lawyer it might seem the simplest step. It must, however, be remembered that the House of Lords is a United Kingdom court. There are always some members appointed from Scotland and from time to time someone from Northern Ireland. Some important parts of law, including much of commercial law and law relating to road traffic, is the same all over the United Kingdom, and it is most desirable that there should be a single appellate court whose decisions are authoritative in every part of the kingdom. And we have gained greatly from having Scots lawyers in the House of Lords, for there is perhaps no better stimulus to legal thought than contact with other systems of law.[1]

[1] Appeals in criminal matters do not come from Scotland, so the Scots have escaped some deplorable decisions that the House of Lords have made in English criminal law (see chapter 21 below).

11

THE JUDICIAL COMMITTEE OF THE PRIVY COUNCIL[1]

The downfall of the conciliar courts as a result of the constitutional conflicts in the Stuart period deprived the King's Council of jurisdiction that it had previously exercised. The position was that the Council had jurisdiction in any matter unless jurisdiction had been taken away or had become vested in some other tribunal. Practically the only jurisdiction left to the Council was the hearing of petitions from the King's dominions beyond the seas. As the British Empire increased, this jurisdiction became substantial. The cases were handled by a committee of the Privy Council, which generally acted judicially. In 1833 the committee was reorganised by statute, the general idea being to reconstitute it as a body drawn from the superior judges. Subsequent statutes broadened the composition, so that it included judges from dominions and British India and some colonies and allowed the Crown to make two special appointments carrying salaries. In fact the judicial personnel of the House of Lords has supplied much of the working judicial strength. A somewhat belated widening of the membership of the Judicial Committee was the appointment in 1962 of nine Commonwealth judges to be Privy Councillors, and there have been other such appointments since. These judges do not all sit regularly, but may attend when they can be spared from their own countries. For many years the greater part of the work of the Judicial Committee was the hearing of appeals from the Dominions and from India, but the general changes that have taken place in the Commonwealth have understandably resulted in most of those countries preferring to keep appeals within their own judicial systems. The Statute of Westminster 1931 and subsequent independence Acts provided a legal basis for countries becoming independent to terminate these appeals from their own courts if they so desire.[2]

Thus these appeals were abolished in India, Pakistan, Sri Lanka, Canada,

[1] An excellent description of the Judicial Committee in its grander days may be found in 'The Judicial Committee of the Privy Council', (1939) 7 Camb. LJ 2 by Sir George Rankin, a member of the Committee. A more recent account is Loren P. Beth, 'The Judicial Committee: Its development, organisation and procedure' [1975] *Public Law* 219.

[2] An independent country's own constitution may restrict this right. Some juggling with words is required if a country becomes a republic or has its own monarchy yet wishes to retain appeals to the Judicial Committee, for an appeal can hardly be described as being to 'Her Majesty in Council' if the Queen is not head of State.

nearly all of what was once British Africa, and in 1986, Australia. The present position is that the Judicial Committee is the ultimate court of appeal from the Channel Islands, Isle of Man, colonies, protectorates and associated states, and from those independent countries of the Commonwealth that have not abolished such appeals, namely New Zealand, Jamaica, Trinidad and Tobago, Malaysia, Singapore, The Gambia, Barbados, Mauritius, Fiji and the Bahamas. In 1986, it dealt with 92 Commonwealth appeals.[1]

There is no *right* of appeal (unless given by statute), the process being a petition to the Crown for leave to appeal. It is in practice much easier to get leave to appeal in civil than in criminal cases. The form of the proceedings is that of a petition to the Crown, the deliberations of the Committee being a prelude to advising the Crown. It used to be said that, since it is unconstitutional for the Crown to receive contradictory advice, the 'judgment' of the Judicial Committee had to be in the form of unanimous advice, which, of course, is always accepted and acted upon by the Crown. However, in 1966 an Order-in-Council provided that a dissenting member 'shall be at liberty to publish his dissent in open court together with his reasons'.

The Judicial Committee has jurisdiction in some matters that arise in the United Kingdom and in respect of these, which are all statutory, the Judicial Committee has a place in the English judicial system. These are:

(1)   In time of war the Admiralty Court has a prize jurisdiction, appeal lying to the Judicial Committee.
(2)   It hears appeals in some matters from ecclesiastical courts (Church of England) and in respect of Schemes as under the Pastoral Measure 1968: one case in 1986.
(3)   It hears appeals from the disciplinary bodies set up by statute for the medical, dental and optical professions and the professions ancillary to medicine: seven cases in 1986.
(4)   It can hear an application for a declaration that a Member of the House of Commons is subject to a statutory disqualification.
(5)   The Crown (that is, the government) may refer any matter to it for an advisory opinion. This process, used from time to time, although little in recent years, is really a method of getting an authoritative legal opinion; it is not an adjudication between parties.

It is hard to say whether the Judicial Committee has been a satisfactory tribunal for Commonwealth countries. When the last Canadian appeal was heard in May 1951 (Canadian legislation having abolished appeals for the future), kind things were said on behalf of the Canadian Bar. Lord Simon, in replying, explained that for many years his view had been that the Judicial Committee should have been partly appointed by dominion governments and should have gone on circuit. 'It

---

[1] Bahamas: 3; Barbados: 1; Bermuda: 1; Cayman Is.: 2; Hong Kong: 18; Isle of Man: 3; Jamaica: 14; Jersey: 3; Malaysia: 21; Mauritius: 8; New South Wales: 4; New Zealand: 3; Queensland: 14; Singapore: 13; St. Lucia: 1; Trinidad and Tobago: 15; Victoria: 2; Virgin Is.: 1; West Indies and Associated States: 2; West Australia: 3.

might have been, if those ideas had prevailed in time, that it would have created a new kind of Supreme Commonwealth tribunal.'[1]

This idea was later discussed at the Commonwealth and Empire Law Conference at Sydney in 1965, and although the United Kingdom government was prepared for almost any change that other Commonwealth governments desired, nothing came of it. There are conflicting views on how far it would have been desirable. It can also be maintained that the very English character of the Committee has been a strength, for it has enabled a steady, consistent body of common law principles to be applied. It seems clear from appeals from some territories that this process is needed; it is best seen in appeals in criminal matters, for these are not allowed unless some important principle of the administration of justice is involved. As one of the major problems of our legal system is to ensure that people can make use of it irrespective of their capacity to pay costs, one cannot help but wonder how accessible the Judicial Committee really is for a poor aggrieved inhabitant of a distant place, but to follow up these questions is to go far beyond the range of this book.[2]

[1] *The Times* 3 May 1951.
[2] New rules came into force in 1958, but they do not go very far in helping a litigant.

12

ARBITRATION

To most laymen, arbitration suggests referring a dispute to a third party to apply palm-tree justice instead of the law of the land.[1] To a lawyer, however, it means referring a case to a person to decide according to law, but untrammelled by the normal rules of court etiquette and legal procedure. Sometimes a law-suit begun in the usual way is referred to a judge or other court official to hear informally as an arbitrator. As we have seen, this is extensively done with small claims in the county court, and the High Court does something similar with its Official Referees' business; it is also possible for a judge of the Commercial Court to sit as an arbitrator. Generally, however, 'arbitration' means a voluntary submission by the parties of their dispute to the judgment of some person who is neither a judge nor an officer of any court. The agreement to arbitrate is generally made in writing, and it may be made either after the dispute has arisen, or in anticipation of any disputes that may arise. Clauses providing for arbitration are common in many commercial contracts and in insurance policies. The agreement, known as the 'submission to arbitration', will normally name the arbitrator or provide for some method of appointing him. The type of arbitrator chosen will depend upon the nature of the case: for some cases a barrister with a commercial practice may be suitable, whilst in others it may be desirable to select an arbitrator who has technical qualifications or knowledge of the conduct of a particular business or trade. In commercial contracts it is often provided that the president of the appropriate trade organisation shall nominate an arbitrator. Although arbitration is an extra-judicial proceeding, the High Court (usually in the Queen's Bench Division) may exercise considerable control either actually or potentially. Thus, if there is no arbitrator because the method of appointment cannot operate, the court will appoint an arbitrator. An arbitrator may be removed by the court if he acts improperly. An important effect of a valid submission to arbitration is that actions in the courts are generally stayed. The court is not bound to refuse to allow an action to be brought, and if it appears to the court that judicial proceedings are desirable the action may be brought, but, as a general rule, a

---

[1] A most useful and very readable short account is by Lord Parker at Waddington LCJ, *The history and development of commercial arbitration*, a lecture given in the Hebrew University of Jerusalem, published in 1959. For further information, see Mustill and Boyd, *Commercial arbitration* (1982), or *Russell on arbitration* (20th ed. 1982).

submission to arbitration precludes the parties from litigation. An arbitrator may obtain the opinion of the court on a point of law that arises during his conduct of the case, and he may frame his award with alternative directions in order that the court may determine a legal point. The parties can insist upon an arbitrator putting proper matters before the court. The award of the arbitrator is binding upon the parties, subject to the possibility of an appeal to the courts on a point of law if the other party consents to this, or the court in its discretion grants leave to appeal. There is also a mechanism for enforcing the award, so that by order of the court it is equivalent to a judgment as far as execution is concerned. It is obvious that with so many ways in which an arbitration may involve application to the court there need be little fear that arbitration may be conducted in an irresponsible manner.

Voluntary arbitration mainly occurs in a commercial setting, but 'commercial setting' covers some widely different situations. Much arbitration involves major disputes between large companies, either or both of which may be multinational concerns. Such arbitrations are big business to lawyers. The top firms of London solicitors usually handle this sort of work; eminent barristers are often engaged as well, and it is all highly profitable. Where multinational firms are concerned the arbitration could usually take place in one of a number of different countries, and the commercial capitals of the world compete to attract this sort of work. In this type of case both parties are usually of equally strong bargaining power, and both are equally anxious to go to arbitration rather than the ordinary law-courts in order to avoid ventilating their business affairs in public. At the other end of the scale many quite small disputes are submitted to arbitration, and in these cases the submission may be less than truly voluntary. The practice of insurance companies may leave the citizen with no option. It is prudent to insure certain risks, and essential to insure others. The insurance of third-party risks for motoring is compulsory. Yet the form of policy that the citizen may take out is, in practice, prescribed by the insurance companies. To drive I must insure, and to insure I must take what policy the various companies offer, and if I find that all the companies insist upon an arbitration clause on disputes on amount, then I must agree to arbitrate or give up the motor-car. In other directions the extensive use of standard form contracts put forward by business interests pursuing a common course of business leaves the citizen with little freedom of contract: accept a service upon the terms that are offered, or do without the service. If the service is virtually essential he may find that, among other things, he is compelled to agree that he will not resort to the law courts. Aware of this – as well as disliking the competition which arbitration provides – the courts produced a series of decisions which in effect invalidated clauses in contracts providing for arbitration with no right to appeal on point of law to the courts. This may have been satisfactory in the sort of case where there was inequality of bargaining power and the submission to arbitration was not really voluntary, but it did not please the big commercial concerns that a dispute arising from a contract containing an

102

arbitration clause could easily end up in a law-court, despite a term purporting to oust the jurisdiction of the courts. Lawyers involved in big multinational arbitrations complained that their former clients were taking their arbitrations to other countries where clauses providing that the decision of the arbitrator was final were upheld, and as a result they were losing valuable work. The result of this was the Arbitration Act 1979, which validates agreements of this sort in a number of cases. Clauses in contracts providing that any dispute arising under it shall be referred to arbitration without the possibility of appeal to the courts are now valid where either party is a foreign resident or a company controlled and managed abroad. In domestic disputes, where both parties are British or are companies controlled by directors resident in Britain, an exclusion agreement may be entered into only after the arbitration has begun.[1]

Arbitration has other advantages besides privacy. It is often cheaper: for example, a solicitor may present a case which, if it were brought in the High Court, would necessitate a barrister in addition to a solicitor. It is also far quicker. In arbitrations it is normal for documents to be put in and oral evidence is not often given, whereas in court, documents have to be proved and witnesses called. The atmosphere of commercial arbitration is friendly. Questions of quality are better decided by someone who is expert. Foreigners prefer arbitration, partly because awards are easier to enforce abroad than judgments. Not all these advantages are always present. Some arbitrations involve complicated issues and disputes about facts. Arbitrators do not usually act for nothing, and the fee of a good arbitrator may be substantial. The service of solicitors and barristers is frequently necessary, and their charges may be as high for an arbitration as for an action. As is explained in chapter 39, a large part of the cost of litigation is the collection of evidence and its presentation in court; if an arbitrator is to have the same evidence that would be required by a judge, then the cost will be much the same. One great advantage of arbitration is that the hearing can be arranged for a time and date and place that suits the parties. In litigation it may be possible to get a date fixed for the trial of a case, but even then the date is primarily fixed by reference to the work of the judge. It is possible for the parties to an arbitration to telephone the arbitrator and make a suitable appointment. Arbitration may take place out of normal courtroom hours: it may be conducted in instalments between 5 p.m. and 7 p.m. on successive days if that happens to be what suits the parties best. Proceedings that can be varied to suit the needs of the parties are bound to have considerable advantages over proceedings that must be shaped to fit a common mould.

There is no doubt that arbitration has grown greatly in popularity during this century, and that it continues to do so. Not only is it widely used in commercial contracts: nowadays it is common to find arbitration clauses in contracts of

---

[1] There is an account of the Arbitration Act 1979 by Staughton, (1979) 129 NLJ 920–23. The problems which the Act was intended to solve are stated in the Report of the Commercial Court Committee on Arbitration, (1978) Cmnd 7284.

employment as well. At one time, many lawyers and judges were inclined to view the trend to arbitration and away from the courts with alarm and despondency.[1] Indeed, as we have seen it was partly fear of competition from arbitration which led to reforms in the Commercial Court. Lawyers nowadays seem generally less worried by the trend. They have woken up to the fact that in substantial cases their services are still likely to be required, whilst at the other end of the scale arbitration relieves them of a lot of small-scale litigation which it is hard to conduct profitably. The position in its broad outline can be summed up thus:

The truth of the matter is that there is a range of problems proper for the courts, and a range proper for arbitration, so that merchants and traders would be well advised to take the most expeditious course open for the disposal of any dispute having regard to its proper intrinsic character.[2]

[1] The Evershed Committee, Final Report, (1953) Cmd 8878 para. 895, were 'much troubled by this trend to arbitration'; their prejudice in favour of law courts not being put out of business was at variance with a halting realisation that perhaps the consumer had grounds for going elsewhere. No such fears are expressed in the Report of the Commercial Court Committee on Arbitration, (1978) Cmnd 7284.
[2] Lord Parker of Waddington, *History and development of commercial arbitration*, (1959) 24.

III

TRIBUNALS

13

THE CREATION OF TRIBUNALS[1]

The courts described in the last chapter are commonly known as the ordinary courts, a phrase that has been used in legislation[2] but has not got a statutory definition: it is assumed that everyone who has to deal with legal affairs is acquainted with the system of county courts, the High Court, the Court of Appeal and the House of Lords for civil matters and magistrates' courts and the Crown Court for criminal matters: they are just 'the courts'. The system covers all the country and all the courts have a wide jurisdiction. In contrast, England for centuries had a number of courts that were local or that dealt with 'special matters'. A 'court' was a place for doing business of a public nature, judicial or otherwise, and wherever we find places with any peculiar standing (Royal Forests, Staple Towns, Cinque Ports) or certain industries (lead mining in the Mendips, tin mining in Devon and Cornwall) or classes of men differentiated from the general population (merchants, soldiers, ecclesiastics) we find historically a special body of law with special courts. The development of the courts described in earlier chapters resulted in most of the special jurisdictions becoming absorbed in the common law system. Courts-martial and ecclesiastical courts are the chief survivors of the ancient special courts. Courts-martial are now entirely governed by statute, the Army Act, with jurisdiction confined to those in military service. A similar system exists for the navy and air force. Ecclesiastical courts are now largely statutory, and their jurisdiction is in practice confined to discipline of the clergy and matters affecting the ornamentation and fabric of churches. The constitutional position of the armed forces of the Crown and of the Church of England can be studied in works on constitutional law. A number of these ancient courts still in theory survive. In 1954 the Court of Chivalry sat again, not having sat for 223 years, to try a complaint by the City of Manchester against a theatre company for unauthorised use of the armorial

[1] The principal modern book is R. E. Wraith and P. G. Hutchesson, *Administrative tribunals* (1973). See also J. F. Garner, *Administrative law* (6th ed. 1985); J. A. Farmer, *Tribunals and government* (1974). Two small books are Kathleen Bell, *Tribunals in the social services* (1969) and Harry Street, *Justice in the welfare state* (2nd ed. 1975). Since 1986 there has been a loose leaf service, *Tribunals practice and procedure* (ed. Bowers). The most important of the earlier books is W. A. Robson, *Justice and administrative law* (first published 1928; 3rd ed. 1951).

[2] Notably in the Tribunals and Inquiries Act 1971 s.15(1) which refers to 'tribunals other than any of the ordinary courts of law'.

bearing of the city.[1] A total of 141 moribund borough courts were quietly abolished by the Local Government Act 1972; a further quiet massacre was achieved by the Administration of Justice Act 1977.

However, the decay and abolition of old local and special courts did not result in the ordinary courts having a monopoly of dealing with all manner of disputes. New special jurisdictions have been created over the years, but it has been an unsystematic development. The explanation is that these procedures and tribunals are part of social history. The period since the middle of the nineteenth century has seen a vast growth in the scope of government activities. In the eighteenth and early nineteenth centuries it was generally thought that the government should maintain order and see to the protection of property and the enforcement of contracts, but that it should do as little else as was possible. Those views slowly changed, until in the modern welfare state we accept a governmental or public responsibility for the general economic condition of the country and the principal social needs of the population.[2]

This transformation has come about piecemeal; social and political pressure has been directed at some practice or state of affairs needing a remedy and legislation has dealt with the particular need. One method is by establishing a system of direct interference between employers and workers, shopkeepers and customers and in other relationships, the classic example being the Factories Acts. Regulation of trade and of employment by statute was no new thing, but the Factories Act 1833 went much further by establishing an inspectorate. The pattern of regulation by law, backed by an administrative system for checking and enforcing, has been applied to other needs for improving working conditions, accuracy of weights and measures, cleanliness of food supplies and many other fields. No new tribunals were created; enforcement was through the magistrates' courts.

A new pattern of adjudication arose from the need for regulating railways. The trend towards monopoly by the railway companies led Parliament in 1854 to compel railway companies to afford reasonable facilities and to prevent them from giving preference to particular traders. Complaints were to be made to the Court of Common Pleas, but this proved unsatisfactory,[3] and a tribunal of Commissioners was set up in 1873. In 1888 the tribunal was re-formed as the Railway and Canal Commission, consisting of two persons (one of whom must be experienced in railway business) appointed by the Home Secretary on the recommendation of the President of the Board of Trade, and a High Court Judge nominated by the Lord Chancellor. The Commission was by statute a court of

[1] *The Times* 22 December 1954, describes the ceremonial of this picturesque affair; the case is in the Law Reports [1955] P 133. Lord Goddard, the then Lord Chief Justice, made it clear that there should be no more cases of this kind.
[2] The classic exposition is A. V. Dicey, *Law and opinion in England*, first published in 1905: the 2nd ed., 1914, has an introduction dealing with legislation up to 1913 and is full of forebodings.
[3] Added to the complaints of traders and railwaymen was that of Lord Campbell, Lord Chief Justice at the time, who complained that Parliament was trying to turn his judges into railway directors.

record, which meant that it had its own seal and that other courts would take cognisance of its proceedings. The judge, who presided, gave a ruling on any point that the Commissioners decided was one of law, and on points of law there was a right of appeal to the Court of Appeal. The Railway and Canal Commission was thus the forerunner of tribunals composed of a lawyer chairman, a member experienced in the subject matter and a member with no prescribed qualifications, all appointed by a Minister of the Crown.

The use of tribunals of this type did not immediately become the universal method of handling disputes which arose under the new social legislation. When a system of workmen's compensation was established in 1897, disputed cases were sent to the county courts, and continued to be handled there until the whole system was replaced in 1947 under the Industrial Injuries Act; and when old age pensions were first introduced, disputes were handled through the machinery of local government. The use of special tribunals became increasingly common, however. The National Insurance Act of 1911 set up a scheme (which in essence we still have) whereby employers, employees and the State contribute to a fund which supports payments to workers in sickness or unemployment. For unemployment pay the Board of Trade appointed Insurance Officers to determine claims, from whom appeal lay to a 'Court of Referees' composed of an employers' representative, a workers' representative, and a chairman appointed by the Board of Trade, from whom further appeal lay to an umpire who was a lawyer appointed by the Crown; in outline, this is the method which is used for determining disputed social security claims to this day. The war of 1914–18 resulted in heavy casualties and tribunals were set up to deal with pensions for those who were disabled and for the dependents of those who had been killed. Local war pension committees made enquiries and made recommendations to the Minister, and from the Minister appeal lay to pensions appeal tribunals appointed by the Lord Chancellor and consisting of a lawyer chairman, a disabled officer or man, and a medical practitioner. These tribunals still exist, although their constitution is now slightly different, and they continue to handle a considerable volume of business.[1]

The years between the wars, 1919–39, were dominated by massive unemployment and troubles over the national economy. The railways had to be reorganised, and the new factor of road transport of passengers and freight led to the creation of new tribunals for their regulation; indeed the regulation of trade and industry went on apace. The common prescription for the national ills was to confer wide powers on ministers, tempered by setting up tribunals for some matters. The war of 1939–45 made necessary yet further government powers, new tribunals, and increased work for those which already existed. Compulsory national service led to appeals for exemption on grounds of hardship, occupation or conscience. War damage involved claims for compensation. The war pensions

[1] There is an account of them at p. 132 in the previous edition of this book.

system had to be extended to include claims by civilians. Price controls and the allocation of commodities were introduced. Agriculture was subjected to a number of controls principally through the War Agricultural Executive Committee. Some of these tribunals became redundant after the war and a number were abolished, but others survived; an example is the Agricultural Lands Tribunal, which was originally set up to deal with appeals from the wartime Agricultural Executive Committees, but now exists to handle certain disputes between landowners and tenant farmers. Yet of far more long-term importance than these new tribunals was the change of attitude towards social matters which took place during the war years, because it was at this time that the idea firmly took hold that food, clothing, housing, medical care, and education should be distributed more equitably than before, and that it was the proper function of the State to bring this redistribution about. The result was a series of post-war statutes which laid the foundations of the modern welfare state. A number of these, like the Family Allowances Act 1945, the National Insurance (Industrial Injuries) Act 1946, the National Insurance Act 1946 and the National Assistance Act 1948, provided for certain benefits which usually take the form of money payments. The system adopted for all of these was to appoint a body of officials to deal with claims, with appeal from this decision to a network of tribunals. The National Health Service Act 1946 provided free medical care for all. This gave rise to a different problem of adjudication, namely the need for examination of complaints about the quality of the service, including the conduct of practitioners in the service. For this again, a system of tribunals was created.

Among the major social problems which this country has had to face since 1945 are a housing shortage, an influx of immigrants and chronic industrial unrest. Governments have tried to tackle each of these with legislation involving the creation of more special tribunals to handle disputed cases. Inflated rents caused by housing shortages first led to statutory rent control during the 1914–18 war; rent control has continued ever since, and in the period since 1945 the method of fixing the maximum rent that may lawfully be charged has been through an official called a Rent Officer and a network of Rent Tribunals and Rent Assessment Committees (chapter 15(vi)). Uncontrolled Commonwealth immigration was checked by the Commonwealth Immigrants Act 1962 and later legislation which gave immigration officers the power to refuse to let would-be immigrants in; in 1969 a two-tier system of appeals was created, with an official Adjudicator as the first tier and an Immigration Appeal Tribunal above him. One attempt to improve industrial relations was the creation of a statutory claim for unfair dismissal by the Industrial Relations Act 1971; claims are handled not by the ordinary courts but by a network of Industrial Tribunals, which now deals with over 30,000 cases every year. New work is found for tribunals irrespective of the political colour of the government. In 1979 a scheme was introduced to compensate children injured by vaccination; a Vaccine Damage Tribunal was set up to handle claims. Mental Health Review Tribunals, which were established in 1959 to review the compulsory detention of patients in mental hospitals, had their work tripled when their powers and duties were increased in 1982; see chapter 15(iii).

14

THE FRANKS
COMMITTEE

After the Second World War much of life was heavily controlled. There were many restrictions left over from the war, whilst new controls had been imposed by the government in the course of creating social change. Many people found that some control or other cut across their expectations: it seemed to them that some power, commonly called 'they', possessed unlimited power to stop them from doing what they reasonably wanted to do. People who were disgruntled, justifiably or otherwise, found plenty of lawyers ready to champion their cause. Lawyers were able to reduce the discontents to apparent order: 'they' were the executive, and the trouble came from 'decisions' which ought to be made by the courts, or at least in accordance with certain basic principles. It was becoming clear that a general inquiry by a Departmental Committee or Royal Commission was needed[1] when a special impetus came from the affair of Crichel Down in 1954.[2]

In 1955 the Lord Chancellor appointed a Committee on Administrative Tribunals and Enquiries under the Chairmanship of Sir Oliver Franks, and the Committee reported in 1957.[3] Most of the recommendations were accepted by the government and they were carried out by the Tribunals and Inquiries Acts in 1958 and 1966, consolidated with other provisions in the Tribunals and Inquiries Act 1971, and by regulations.

Thirty years afterwards, there seems to have been a curious failure in the logic of all this. Public discontent was mainly with the executive powers of local and central government, not with the workings of tribunals. The Crichel Down affair

---

[1] There was an earlier inquiry which produced the Report of the Committee on Ministers' Powers, (1932) Cmd 4060, often called the Donoughmore Committee after its Chairman, though he resigned for reasons of ill health and Sir Leslie Scott (who became Lord Justice in 1935) was Chairman when the Report was being drafted.

[2] Report of the Inquiry held by Sir Andrew Clark, (1954), Cmd 9176 and Report on whether civil servants should be transferred, (1954) Cmd 9220. J. A. G. Griffith, 'The Crichel Down Affair', (1955) 18 Mod. LR 557, is a most useful account.

[3] (1957) Cmnd 218. The evidence was taken in public and published, along with memoranda from departments. See also E. C. S. Wade, 'Administration under the Law', (1957), 73 LQR 470; W. A. Robson, 'The Franks Report', [1958] *Public Law* 12; G. Marshall, 'The Franks Report', (1957) 35 *Public Administration*; 'Tribunals and Inquiries: Developments since the Franks Report', (1958) 36 *Public Administration* 261; J. A. G. Griffith, 'Tribunals and Inquiries', (1959) 22 Mod. LR 125. There is a useful note by H. W. R. Wade on the Tribunals and Inquiries Act in [1958] Camb. LJ 129.

was a story of muddle, arrogance and deviousness by civil servants engaged in disposing of a piece of land which had been compulsorily acquired as a bombing range and was no longer needed: no tribunal had anything to do with it. Furthermore, the terms of reference of the Franks Committee were limited to looking at the 'constitution and working' of tribunals, and the 'working' of ministers' decisions *where a formal procedure had been prescribed by statute.* Ministers' powers which had no formal procedure laid down for their exercise were outside the Committee's terms of reference, so that what had happened at Crichel Down, for example, could not be considered because no statutory procedure was applicable to it. At the time this was all less obvious, however. Although nowadays everyone can see that tribunals are special courts designed for particular functions for which the ordinary courts are ill-equipped, and that they are quite distinct from the executive powers of central and local government, at that time many people were unable to perceive the difference between them. Many lawyers were unshakably convinced that only the ordinary courts are courts, and that tribunals are an extra arm of the executive and an infringement of the doctrine of separation of powers. Thus a public inquiry which was mainly concerned with tribunals was publicly acceptable as a response to the Crichel Down affair, and no doubt one which was preferable to the government than any general inquiry into ministers' powers.

The Franks Committee grasped the distinction between tribunals and ministers' powers without difficulty. It said that they were related in that both tribunals and decision-making by ministers should follow procedures which have certain characteristics:

We call these characteristics openness, fairness and impartiality ... Take openness. If these procedures were wholly secret, the basis of confidence and acceptability would be lacking. Next take fairness. If the objector were not allowed to state his case, there would be nothing to stop oppression. Thirdly, there is impartiality. How can the citizen be satisfied unless he feels that those who decide his case come to their decision with open minds?[1]

But the Report went on to explain that the method of adjudication by tribunals is the application of rules, and that they are thereby distinguished from ministers' decisions. They 'are not ordinary courts but neither are they appendages of Government Departments'. Tribunals should properly be regarded as machinery provided by Parliament for adjudication rather than as part of the machinery of administration.[2] Hence the Committee dealt with tribunals and ministers' decisions separately, but applied to each the principles of openness, fairness and impartiality. The greater part of the Report is accordingly concerned with improvements and safeguards within the existing structure. The principal recommendations, with the action that has subsequently been taken, fall under the following headings:

[1] Franks Report, paras. 23, 24.   [2] Franks Report, paras. 37, 40.

113

The Council on Tribunals[1]

This is a permanent body of up to 16 members appointed by the Lord Chancellor and the Lord Advocate under the Tribunals and Inquiries Act 1971. It is similar in many ways to a Departmental Committee; its members serve in their spare time as a form of voluntary public work, meeting monthly and of course making visits and doing home-work; there is an official full-time secretariat, and the functions are advisory. It is required to keep the tribunals specified in the Act and the new ones that may be added to the list under review, to report on any matters referred to it concerning tribunals or statutory inquiries, or to report of its own initiative if the Council thinks that something is sufficiently important. The Tribunals and Inquiries Act 1966 (now consolidated in the 1971 Act) extended the supervisory powers of the Council, which must now be consulted before procedural rules are made. The Council makes an annual Report on its work, and that is published. It was intended to be a consumers' watchdog. The whole matter of tribunals has expanded greatly and the position of the Council (and certainly of its resources) needs reviewing. This is considered in chapter 16.

The members and chairmen of tribunals

There was criticism of the general position whereby the minister concerned with the subject-matter of a tribunal appointed the chairman and members and could dismiss them. It is essentially a question of appearances: there is no evidence that ministers want members of tribunals to be subservient or that any attempt has been made to exercise any kind of influence. Nevertheless, when a tribunal sits to adjudicate between a citizen and a minister it is possible that the citizen may doubt the impartiality of the tribunal if it is appointed and liable to be dismissed by the minister. On the other hand, members have to be appointed by someone, and in theory all ministers are part of the same institution: a prisoner tried by a magistrates' court for an alleged offence against the Crown is brought before a bench appointed and dismissible by the Crown. The Committee thought that members should be appointed by the Council on Tribunals, but the government could not accept this, and the Act leaves appointment of members to be made as hitherto with, however, a right for the Council to make general recommendations. Dismissal, however, is now restricted: no member or member of a panel can be dismissed except with the concurrence of the Lord Chancellor, and also

[1] See 'The Council on Tribunals' by H. W. R. Wade in [1960] *Public Law* 351; Professor Wade advocated such a body in his evidence to the Franks Committee, and he was an original member of the Council. J. F. Garner, 'The Council on Tribunals', (1965) 43 *Public Administration* 321 is an excellent account written from direct observation. 'The Council on Tribunals – the first twenty-five years' by D. G. T. Williams [1985] *Public Law* 73 is another account written from first-hand knowledge by a member. See also chapter 8 of R. E. Wraith and P. G. Hutchesson, *Administrative tribunals* (1973), and the Council's own report, The Functions of the Council on Tribunals (1980) Cmnd 7805.

with that of the Lord President of the Court of Session and of the Lord Chief Justice of Northern Ireland for tribunals that sit in all parts of the United Kingdom.

The Committee recommended that all chairmen should be appointed by the Lord Chancellor, but the Act does not so provide; for an important group of tribunals the Act requires the Lord Chancellor to appoint a panel and then the appropriate minister selects a chairman from that panel. There is some extension of requiring legal qualifications in chairmen, but no general rule.

Reasons are to be given for decisions

The Act provides that tribunals and ministers who make decisions after statutory inquiries shall, if requested, give reasons for their decisions. The reasons may be given orally or in writing, and they then form part of the record. There are a number of exceptions, but the general effect is to introduce a requirement that is regarded as essential to sound methods of adjudication. Judges are always required to give reasons – although juries, paradoxically, are not, and it is actually a criminal offence to try to discover what a jury's reasons were, assuming that it had any (see chapter 32). The interest of lawyers in making tribunals and ministers give reasons is twofold. First, there is a belief that people will accept decisions against them if they are told the reasons why they have lost their case. There is some truth in that, but it is somewhat naive to suppose that people are always so easily satisfied. Secondly, if reasons are given, then the High Court can look at the record and decide whether the reasons are good reasons; this has to be considered in connection with other grounds for judicial review.

Representation before tribunals

In some tribunals legal representation was not allowed but, following the Franks Committee's recommendations, such restrictions have been removed. Nevertheless legal representation does not occur at all often in most tribunals. The common explanation is that this is due to the cost and because legal aid is not available for representation in tribunals, other than the Lands Tribunal, the Commons Commissioners and before Mental Health Review Tribunals. The litigant before a tribunal can get legal advice under the 'Green Form Scheme', see chapter 40(i), but when it comes to the hearing he must either pay for his legal representative or argue the case himself. Lawyers are apt to think that if a person is to be represented then legal representation is the best that he can have. That is perhaps not surprising since lawyers can make some claim to expertise in advocacy. It is true that for cases in the ordinary law courts the advocacy developed by lawyers is the best that is available, but that does not mean that it is absolutely good: it is good in relation to the courts constituted as they are and dealing with their present kind of business. But the fact that lawyers are the best people to have in law courts does not mean that they are the best people to have for all kinds of tribunals. Some issues between workers and employers may be better handled by trade-union officials and representatives of the employers' side. In tribunals dealing with taxation, revenue officials often appear on one side and accountants on the other. Surveyors and valuers may be the most help before a Rating Valuation Court of a Rent Assessment Committee, though in the Lands Tribunal legal issues may suggest that surveyors and valuers are more use as witnesses called by lawyer advocates. If, however, we turn to tribunals concerned with social services and allied matters, there is no obvious course. The general effect of a lawyer appearing as an advocate is often that the tribunal begins to function badly because the lawyer will try to conduct his case as if he were in a law court. The tedious and inefficient method of dealing with witnesses and the repetitions and the stilted language compare unfavourably with the common-sense way in which such tribunals commonly handle their work. Further, lawyers are often insufficiently acquainted with the whole setting of the tribunal and its role in the services or matters that are outside ordinary legal practice: though this would presumably change if they did this sort of work regularly, as they might if legal aid was available and they could be paid. There is a widely held view amongst those who are concerned with such tribunals that many people appearing before them do need some help, but not necessarily legal representation. Figures which the Department of Health and Social Security published concerning the success-rate in appeals to Supplementary Benefit Appeal Tribunals show that solicitors representing claimants succeeded in 41.2 per cent of cases, but the success-rate of social workers was 46.6 per cent.[1]

But whether solicitors are the best or the worst representatives for cases before any kind of tribunal is only one of the factors. A social worker may have all the experience and qualities needed, but some 'clients' may feel that they are 'up against the establishment' and they want someone who cannot possibly be identified with those in authority, and a practising lawyer gets a clean bill of health on that score. Also, there is no obvious basis for creating a service that would provide representation by social workers, trade unions and others, whereas the legal aid service is well established. The Lord Chancellor's Advisory Committee on Legal Aid has repeatedly recommended that legal aid should be extended to all statutory tribunals at present within the supervision of the Council on Tribunals in which representation is permitted. The problem, of course, is what the cost would be to public funds. The open-ended commitment for criminal and civil legal aid is already sufficiently disturbing to the custodians of the public purse. An open-ended commitment to provide legal aid for proceedings in tribunals is something which they are bound to resist, particularly since one of the main arguments in favour of tribunals has traditionally been that they can evolve simple procedures which enable the citizen to present his case himself. And yet

[1] DHSS Social Security Statistics 1984, table 34.21.

116

the uncomfortable fact remains that before almost any kind of tribunal, the citizen who has some kind of expert help or representation has a much greater chance of success than the one who does not. We have seen that before Supplementary Benefit Appeal Tribunals the success-rate where solicitors and social workers were involved was 41.2 per cent and 46.6 per cent: it is only 21.2 per cent where he is unrepresented and presents the case himself.

Public hearings

The Committee considered that tribunals should, in general, sit in public, but recognised that there are certain types of case where justice may be better done and the interests of the citizen better served by privacy. Public security is an obvious instance, though such issues can hardly arise in most tribunals. The major reasons for sitting in private are cases in which intimate personal and financial circumstances have to be disclosed: war pensions which depend on physical or mental disability, mental health and hearings by tax commissioners come within this category. Another occasion for privacy is in preliminary hearings involving professional conduct, such as tribunals under the National Health Service which deal with questions of whether doctors, dentists and others are carrying out their obligations.[1]

Inquiries and ministers' decisions

The second half of the terms of reference of the Franks Committee was: 'The working of such administrative procedures as include the holding of an inquiry or hearing by or on behalf of a minister on an appeal or as the result of objections or representations, and in particular the procedure for the compulsory acquisition of land.' The Committee discussed the allocation of decisions to tribunals and ministers in paragraphs 26 to 32 of their Report. It is misleading to try and pinpoint the distinction, but paragraph 31 comes near to doing so:

We observe that the methods of adjudication by tribunals are in general not the same as those of adjudication by Ministers. All, or nearly all, tribunals apply rules. No ministerial decision denoted by the second part of our terms of reference is reached in this way.

Hence the Report separated the two subjects, dealing with Tribunals in parts II and III and administrative procedures in parts IV and V.

Despite this clear indication of the distinction between tribunals and administrative procedures, the Tribunals and Inquiries Acts have included both subjects, and the Council on Tribunals is charged with supervision of both of them. Nevertheless they must be kept apart. Tribunals are part of the machinery of justice and the next chapter deals with tribunals as they are today.

---

[1] H. Street, *Justice in the welfare state* (2nd ed. 1975) 57, argues strongly against these procedures. Removal from the register is a very different matter; see chapter 15(ix) below.

15

TRIBUNALS TODAY

The previous chapter has already given some idea of the number, range and scope of special tribunals. Many of them, like the Immigration Appeal Tribunal and the tribunals in the social security system, exist to decide disputed matters between the individual and the State. But there are other important tribunals which handle disputes between citizen and citizen: Rent Tribunals, Rent Assessment Committees and Industrial Tribunals are obvious examples. The number of special tribunals has grown and goes on growing. The number of tribunals under the supervision of the Council on Tribunals now stands at well in excess of 50. The number of cases heard by tribunals has also increased. The days when tribunals could be described as a kind of appendix or addendum to the ordinary law courts have gone. A high proportion of adjudications dealing with the affairs of ordinary people, namely social security, housing and jobs are made by tribunals, not by the ordinary courts. Table 5 shows the number of cases which were heard in the county courts before judges and registrars and in some of the more important tribunals in 1985. This shows that the tribunals handled nearly three times as many as the county courts. Many of these are small cases, which is also characteristic of county courts, but a number of cases are substantial, notably in Industrial Tribunals on questions of unfair dismissal and redundancy which commonly need a whole day or more for a case.

County courts, the High Court and the Court of Appeal are the 'ordinary' civil courts in the sense that at each level in the hierarchy they deal with many different kinds of cases: there is a measure of specialisation in the Divisions of the High Court but it is all one court and if an action is begun in the wrong Division it can be moved into the right Division.[1] There is a *system* of courts, so that if Parliament creates new rights the statute can refer to 'the court' and in its interpretation section provide that 'the court' means the High Court; there is no need to say anything more because the legal provisions about the composition of the court, procedures and so on are standard and apply automatically. It is otherwise with

---

[1] An important exception occurs if a writ is issued when there should have been an application for Judicial Review. As the law stands at present there is no alternative for the litigant but to start all over again (by which time his claim may be blocked by some time limit): see *O'Reilly* v. *Mackman* [1984] 2 AC 237.

Table 5. *Caseload of the major tribunals in 1985*

Immigration appeals	
by adjudicators	6,120
Immigration Appeal Tribunal	737
Industrial Tribunals	
cases begun	34,249
hearings	10,722
Family Practitioner Committees	2,123
Rent Assessment Committees[a]	13,053
Rent Tribunals	2,447
Tribunals in the Social Security field: National Insurance Local Tribunals and Social Security Appeal Tribunals (1983)[b]	77,503
County courts	
proceedings commenced	2,296,440
judgments	25,624

[a]Includes cases withdrawn and cases settled
[b]Figures for 1985 (and 1984) unavailable because of a strike

tribunals, for there is no system. Each tribunal is established by Parliament;[1] the statute has to say what matters are to be decided and lay down the composition of the tribunal, how it is to be appointed and to confer sufficient powers to enable the jurisdiction to be exercised. It is of course possible for statute to add a new kind of work to an existing tribunal, and that has happened for the Lands Tribunal (section vii) and for Industrial Tribunals (section iv) but there is no standard pattern. When it is decided that some new matters are to be decided by a tribunal, as for example by a Mental Health Review Tribunal (section iii), it is designed and created for that special purpose. Hence it is difficult to study tribunals because of their number, their differences and the need to know sufficient about the matters with which they deal.

The following tribunals give a general view of the field but it must be remembered that tribunals are a very mixed bag and that one cannot take a sample that is representative of the whole. Even the nomenclature has no recognisable pattern. The Restrictive Practices Court (section x) has High Court Judges and lay members and ranks alongside the High Court, and yet the Employment Appeal Tribunal (section iv) also has High Court Judges and lay members and the same judicial status but is called a 'Tribunal'.

i Adjudication under the social security system

Under the social security system there are two complementary schemes. First, there are the contributory schemes which originated in the National Insurance and the National Insurance (Industrial Injuries) Acts. Contributions are paid by

[1] Sometimes there is not even an Act of Parliament. The Criminal Injuries Compensation Board was originally set up merely by administrative action.

employed earners, employers, self-employed earners and in respect of profits of a trade, profession or vocation. These payments, together with Treasury supplements, make up the National Insurance Fund. From this fund payments are made on the occurrence of certain specified events like unemployment, sickness and invalidity, maternity, widowhood, and reaching the appropriate age for an old age pension; they are made only to those who have contributed to the scheme, and, broadly speaking, whether or not the applicant is in need. The amount of the contributions and of the benefits is fixed by the legislation; contributions may be altered by an Order after a draft has been approved by each House of Parliament and benefits may be increased by the same process. It is of the essence of the scheme that there is a legal obligation to pay the appropriate contribution and that there is a legal right to receive the appropriate benefit. Secondly, there is what was until recently called Supplementary Benefit, and various associated benefits. These are the successors of the old Poor Relief, which became Public Assistance in 1929 and was reconstructed as National Assistance in 1946. In 1966 they were recast as Supplementary Benefit and related benefits; in 1986 there was another upheaval when these were replaced by three new benefits: Income Support, Family Credit and Housing Benefit.[1]

To be eligible for such payments as these the claimant need not have contributed to any fund; payments are made solely on grounds of financial need. The largest number of cases arise from national insurance or similar benefits together with a person's own resources not being sufficient. But there are also many claimants who for a variety of reasons do not qualify for national insurance benefits (including unmarried mothers, separated wives, unemployed men who have exhausted their entitlement to unemployment benefit), and who are wholly or mainly dependent on such payments for their income. Originally these non-contributory benefits were purely discretionary, but in 1966 the theoretical basis was changed and it became possible to claim most of them as of right. Formerly there was one mechanism for determining disputed claims under the National Insurance legislation and a separate system for disputed claims to Supplementary Benefit as it then was. Then the Health and Social Services and Social Security Adjudication Act 1983 amalgamated the two systems. In order to explain the new system and why it was introduced it is necessary to give a short account of the systems which it replaces. Because they no longer exist, the past tense will be used when describing the old tribunals; but the procedures followed continue to be in essence the same before the new unified tribunal.

Claims under the National Insurance scheme were made to a local office of the Department, the staff of which was responsible for interviewing the applicant and compiling a dossier of all the information relevant to the claim. This was then passed to an official called an *insurance officer* whose function it was to adjudicate upon the claim. These were civil servants appointed by the Secretary of State and

---

[1] Social Security Act 1986.

whose position was more or less independent of the Department; their job was to grant or refuse the benefit on the basis of the dossier put before them, not to investigate the claim. If the insurance officer rejected the claim an appeal lay from his decision to a *National Insurance Local Tribunal* (NILT). These consisted of a chairman and two other members. The chairman was usually a barrister or solicitor and had to be appointed from the Lord Chancellor's panel for legal chairmen. The other members were drawn from panels appointed by the Secretary of State, one representative of employers and insured persons other than employers and the other panel representative of employed persons. The insurance officer who gave the adverse decision had to prepare written submissions with copies of the evidence and information on which his decision was based, which were available to the claimant and the tribunal members in advance. The tribunal sat in public (although it was rare for anyone to come and watch). The appeal would be defended by an insurance officer, usually a different one from the one whose decision was the subject of the appeal. The claimant might be represented at the tribunal hearing by a lawyer or by any other person of his choice, but legal aid was not available; the proceedings were informal, and designed on the assumption that the claimant would represent himself. In fact it was quite usual for claimants not to appear, and sometimes no insurance officer would appear either, in which case the tribunal would proceed to determine the appeal on the basis of the papers before it. From a NILT appeal lay to a group of 13 *National Insurance Commissioners*.[1] These were appointed by the Crown with a statutory qualification of barrister or advocate (in Scotland) of at least ten years' standing. There was a Chief Commissioner, and he had the standing of a High Court Judge. The Commissioners might sit separately, or for determining a point of law there could be a tribunal of three who would decide by a majority vote. Their decisions, which were reported and published by HMSO, formed a body of case-law for the guidance of Insurance Officers and NILTs.

The same officers, tribunals and Commissioners decided claims arising out of industrial disease or injury. There is a variation in the procedure here, however, because 'disablement questions' arise. It must be decided whether the accident or disease has resulted in a loss of faculty, what is the extent of the disablement and for what length of time. For industrial injury cases these questions were (and still are) determined by a *Medical Board* or a *Medical Appeal Tribunal*. Industrial diseases raise questions for specialists, and are handled by *Special Medical Boards*.

The system of adjudication was similar for Supplementary Benefit and similar claims, but there were significant differences. Before 1980 the initial decision to grant or withhold benefit was taken by an anonymous official of the Department acting in the name of the Supplementary Benefit Commission; in 1980 the Supplementary Benefit Commission was abolished and the officials who made the decision were called *benefit officers* in the case of Supplementary Benefit and

---

[1] Sir Robert Micklethwaite, formerly Chief National Insurance Commissioner, *The National Insurance Commissioner* (1976).

supplement officers in the case of Family Income Supplement. Appeal from their decisions lay to a network of Supplementary Benefit Appeal Tribunals (SBATs). SBATs were similar to NILTs in that they consisted of three members, a chairman and two others, and in that their procedure was informal and inquisitorial, designed on the assumption that claimants would present their cases in person. They were dissimilar in that the chairman was not usually a lawyer, in that they sat in private, and in that there was no further appeal from their decisions.

NILTs were generally reckoned to be among the best of the various tribunals. The members knew their job, their chairmen understood their judicial function, there was an adequate system of appeals if they made a mistake, and the Commissioners' reported decisions ensured that 150 or so tribunals approached similar issues in a consistent way. SBATs on the other hand were a source of much discontent. Part of the trouble lay in the nature of rules which they were supposed to apply. Although Supplementary Benefit was theoretically available as of right, the rules were very vague leaving much room for discretion, and although administrative directions were issued to the officials as to how they should exercise their discretion, these were never published. This obviously made it difficult for claimants to appeal: it is always hard to challenge the exercise of a discretion, and almost impossible when the other side knows the rules governing its exercise and you do not. But much of the discontent was with the way in which SBATs were constituted and how they behaved. The departmental officials who argued against the appeal were often those involved in making the initial decision and were sometimes too enthusiastic opposing the appeal; the unqualified tribunal chairman were said to be unable or unwilling to see fair play; and the absence of any further appeal not only made it impossible for mistakes by SBATs to be corrected, but prevented a consistent approach being taken to recurrent problems. In 1975 an influential study by Professor Kathleen Bell was published.[1]

This highlighted all these problems, and led rapidly to change.[2] Published rules were issued to regulate the grant of Supplementary Benefit in place of the previous secret administrative directions. Administrative measures were immediately taken to increase the number of legally qualified chairmen. A right of appeal from SBATs was created, at first to the High Court, and after 1980 to the National Insurance Commissioners who were renamed the *Social Security Commissioners*. Then by the Health and Social Services and Social Security Adjudication Act 1983 the two systems of adjudication and appeal were merged. Insurance officers, benefit officers and supplement officers all became adjudication officers; NILTs and SBATs were merged to become *Social Security Appeal Tribunals* (SSATs); as before there is a right of appeal (with leave and on point of

---

[1] *Research study on Supplementary Benefit Appeal Tribunals* (1975) HMSO.
[2] See N. Harris, 'The reform of the Supplementary Benefit appeal system', [1983] *Journal of Social Work and Law* 212.

law only) to the Social Security Commissioners, and thence to the Court of Appeal and the House of Lords. The new tribunals, like NILTs, consist of a legally qualified chairman sitting with two lay members. The lay members are now drawn from a single panel, the membership of which is no longer restricted to representatives of employers and representatives of the employed. Another important change is the creation of a new office of President of Social Security Appeal Tribunals; unlike the tribunals which are replaced, SSATs are organised under the direction of a President, who is charged with a number of functions, including organising the training for tribunal members.

It remains the case that there is no legal aid for representation, and SSATs like their predecessors continue to operate on the basis that the claimant will come in person to present his case. Claimants are well advised to have someone to represent them if they can get them, however, because as has already been mentioned, expert assistance greatly increases an appellant's chance of success.

It has long been possible for a citizen to claim a one-off payment in the event of a sudden emergency, such as when his house is burnt down leaving him with nothing. In 1986 a new regime was introduced for these various one-off payments, which are now called 'Social Fund Payments'. Where someone is refused a Social Fund Payment he no longer has a right of appeal to a SSAT; instead there is a special system of review by a team of inspectors. This is likely to reduce the work of the SSATs considerably.

ii The National Health Service

People sometimes have complaints about the standard of service which they have received from the National Health Service. The machinery for dealing with these complaints at first instance is through the Family Practitioner Committees, which are the bodies through which the day-to-day administration of the National Health Service is carried out within each Area Health Authority. A Family Practitioner Committee consists of 30 members, 11 appointed by the Area Health Authority, 4 by the local authority and the remaining 15 being representative of the local doctors, dentists, chemists and opticians. A complaint that a practitioner working for the National Health Service has not carried out his duties properly goes first to a Service Committee of the Family Practitioner Committee. A Service Committee consists of equal numbers of lay and professional members, with a lay chairman, and the Committee investigates and reports to the Family Practitioner Committee its finding of facts and its recommendation. If the Family Practitioner Committee considers that no action should be taken, or that the practitioner was at fault but some penalty less than removal is called for, both the complainant and the practitioner have a right of appeal to the minister, whose decision is final. If, however, the Family Practitioner Committee considers that the practitioner should be removed from the service, the Family Practitioner Committee makes representations to the

National Health Service Tribunal, which then hears the case. The chairman of the tribunal must be a practising barrister or solicitor of not less than ten years' standing, and is appointed by the Lord Chancellor. The two other members, appointed by the minister, are a layman appointed after consultation with the National Association of Family Practitioner Committees, and a professional man belonging to the same profession as the person whose case is being investigated. The 'practitioner members' are appointed after consultation with the appropriate professional organisations. If the tribunal finds in favour of the professional that decision is final; if, however, the tribunal finds against him, he can appeal to the minister. The minister can thus override the tribunal in favour of a professional but never against him. In 1985 Family Practitioner Committees decided 2,123 cases; only a handful of cases reach the tribunal, which in 1985 dealt with only five cases.

If a patient is injured by the bad treatment he receives he may of course sue the practitioner for negligence in the ordinary courts; and a National Health Service practitioner who fails to perform his duties properly may also be disciplined by the General Medical Council or other professional body.

The National Health Service Act 1977 also provides for one Health Service Commissioner for England and one for Wales to conduct investigations, commonly called the Health Service Ombudsman. The Act lays down the matters that he may investigate, which are primarily those of administration, and also specifies the matters which are not within his field: these include diagnosis of illness or the care or treatment of a patient taken in consequence of a clinical judgment, and any actions in respect of which a person aggrieved has or had a remedy through a law court or tribunal. The institution is analogous to that of the Parliamentary Commissioner discussed in chapter 18.

iii Mental Health Review Tribunals[1]

Most of the inhabitants of mental hospitals are voluntary patients, but there are a number of ways in which a person can be detained in a mental hospital against his wishes. He may be civilly committed under one of a number of compulsory powers contained in sections 2, 3 and 4 of the Mental Health Act 1983: in 1983 some 15,800 patients were 'sectioned', as this process is luridly named. Alternatively, a person may be compulsorily detained by order of the criminal courts after they have been accused of a criminal offence. This is what happens when a person who is put on trial is found unfit to plead, and also when he is found not guilty by reason of insanity. Insanity as a defence to a criminal charge is very limited, and the mentally disturbed are usually convicted despite their mental state. Where this happens, the court when sentencing may make a hospital order against them if it finds that they are suffering from one of a list of specified mental

---

[1] See Brenda Hoggett, *Mental health law* (2nd ed. 1984). Unless otherwise stated, the figures quoted in this section are taken from her book.

disorders and thinks this is the most suitable way of dealing with them. A person subject to a hospital order is compulsorily admitted and detained, but may be released at any time by the medical authorities unless the court adds a *restriction order*, when (subject to what is said below) he may be released only with the consent of the Home Secretary. In 1981, some 1,200 people were compulsorily admitted to mental hospitals via the criminal courts.

An obvious conflict arises when the compulsorily detained patient or his relatives think that this is unnecessary because he is now cured or because he was committed on incorrect information and that he ought to be released. A person who receives a hospital order following a criminal conviction can of course appeal against his conviction and sentence like any other convicted person, but this procedure does not cater for the person who was properly given a hospital order and is now cured, or for the majority of compulsory patients who were 'sectioned' and were not sent to mental hospital via the criminal courts. Accordingly Mental Health Review Tribunals (MHRTs) were set up by the Mental Health Act 1959 to review compulsory detention in mental hospitals. At first their scope was severely limited. They could only review when the patient or his relatives asked for a review, which in the overwhelming majority of cases they did not. And although they could order the discharge of any patient who had been 'sectioned', their power to discharge hospital order patients was limited to those who were not also subject to restriction orders. As far as restricted patients were concerned they could only advise the Home Secretary to let them out, and he was free to ignore their advice.[1]

In 1981 the European Court of Human Rights condemned these rules as too restrictive to comply with the European Convention on Human Rights[2] and in 1982 Parliament responded by amending the law so that the functions and powers of MHRTs were greatly extended; the present law is now contained in the Mental Health Act 1983. The changes were as follows. The interval which had to elapse between a patient or his relative's successive applications for review was halved, thereby doubling their opportunities to apply; they can now apply once within the first six months of detention and annually after that. In addition there is now an automatic review of all cases after six months of committal, and thereafter at three-yearly intervals, whether the patient or his relatives applies or not. And MHRTs are now empowered to release any patient, even those subject to restriction orders, whether the Home Secretary wishes them to be released or not. Consequently these tribunals now carry out a considerably more important function than they did before, and their work-load has been greatly increased. In year 1981 they disposed of just over 700 cases, a figure which had risen to over 2,316 in 1985.

---

[1] According to Jill Peay in [1982] Crim. LR 794, 795, the Home Secretary rejected the advice of the MHRT in 56% of all cases.
[2] *X.* v. *U.K.* (1981) 4 EHRR 181. For the European Convention on Human Rights see chapter 35 below.

There is one tribunal for each regional health authority: 14 in England and one in Wales. Each is under the general direction of a regional chairman who has a regional office and a small staff of full-time civil servants. For a hearing the tribunal must consist of at least three members, one a doctor, one a lawyer and one a layman. The regional chairman chooses the people who are to compose the tribunal for each sitting from panels of possible members appointed by the Lord Chancellor. The legal member usually, but not invariably presides. When MHRTs were given the power to release restricted patients the government was concerned at the prospect of over-kindly tribunals letting dangerous criminal lunatics loose upon society, and special provision was made for the membership of the tribunals when reviewing the detention of restricted patients.[1]

For these cases the chair must be taken by a legal member who is specially approved by the Lord Chancellor; this usually means a Recorder or Circuit Judge. The hearing is private unless the patient asks for it to be in public and the tribunal is satisfied that this would not be harmful to the patient; this is sensible, because mental patients sometimes make wild and very offensive assertions about other patients, hospital staff and their own relatives. It normally takes place at the hospital where the patient is detained, and shortly before the hearing the medical member of the tribunal will examine the patient and go through his medical records. If the tribunal then finds that he is not mentally disordered, or that his disorder is not of a nature or degree to warrant his compulsory detention, or that his detention is not justified in the interests of his own health or safety or in order to protect others, they must order his release; and they have a discretion to release unrestricted patients even where these criteria are not met. There is no general right of appeal on the merits, but the tribunal is subject to judicial review, and there is also a statutory procedure similar to the case stated procedure in magistrates' courts[2] for challenging the decision of the tribunal on point of law.

It is normally axiomatic that a court must permit the litigant to present a case, and that the litigant must know the case against him. Severe problems exist in applying either of these principles to mental patients. Many of them are incapable of presenting a reasoned case. Telling a mental patient the full story behind his compulsory detention can also be problematical. It may further upset his mental balance to know what is the matter with him; if he was committed partly because his family said they could not cope with him, this information may sour any personal relationship that still exists between him and them; if the patient is dangerous, telling him what others have said about him may even put them in physical danger. The first problem has been partly solved by providing mental

---

[1] And perhaps rightly, in view of the two well-publicised cases in 1986: one where a MHRT released a sexual psychopath who was subject to a restriction order, and six months later he carried out two further offences; and another where a MHRT released a restricted patient against medical advice, and a year later he terrorised shoppers in Woolworths with a knife. *The Times* 15 April 1986, 29 July 1986.

[2] See chapter 21 below. It has not been much used. The procedure has been available since 1959 and *Bone* v. *Mental Health Review Tribunal* [1985] 3 All ER 330 is said to have been the first case.

patients with free legal advice and assistance. Since 1972 they have been entitled to legal advice under the 'green form scheme' and since 1983 this may be freely converted into representation at the tribunal hearing. However, the difficulty remains that at present not many lawyers have experience in the area of mental health, and there is no means of providing public funds to pay fees or expenses of any experienced laymen who might be more suitable. The problem of information which may harm the patient is handled by giving the tribunal power to withhold information from him if it would 'adversely affect the health or welfare of the patient or of others'. Information so withheld must be disclosed to his legal advisor, however, which makes it all the more important if the appeal system is to work that he should have one.

A general verdict on Mental Health Review Tribunals must be that they have done their work fairly well. Some criticism in the past was directed at their limited powers, criticism which was taken fully into account when their powers were extended. They have also been criticised for operating more like medical case-conferences than legal tribunals concerned with vital questions of personal liberty.[1] Such criticism ignores the fact that special tribunals were created to do this job precisely because the ordinary courts and ordinary legal procedures were ill-suited to do it; because of the very nature of the problems they have to deal with it is difficult to see how they could behave differently. As long as Mental Health Review Tribunals look with fresh eyes at the evidence upon which the patient was compulsorily committed, and obtain further reliable evidence if its reliability is questioned, there seems no reason to criticise them for taking a paternalistic approach.

iv Industrial tribunals and the Employment Appeal Tribunal[2]

These were established under the Industrial Training Act 1964; that Act established training boards and empowered the boards to impose a levy on employers and tribunals were set up to give employers who were assessed to the levy a body to whom they could appeal. That would not of itself have made industrial tribunals at all important, but subsequent statutes have greatly extended their jurisdiction.[3] In 1965 the Redundancy Payments Act gave the large and important matter of redundancy payments as well as compensation questions arising from loss of employment as a result of statutory changes and some questions arising from the Contracts of Employment Act 1963 to industrial tribunals. In 1966 they were given some tax questions under the Selective Employment Tax (since abolished) and some matters under the dock labour

[1] See P. W. H. Fennell, 'The Mental Health Review Tribunal: a question of imbalance', (1977) 4 *British Journal of Law and Society* 186.

[2] A number of criticisms of industrial tribunals are contained in the report by *Justice, Industrial Tribunals*, (1987); reviewed by Hepple, (1988) 138 NLJ 11.

[3] A good account is L. Dickens, M. Jones, B. Weeks and M. Hart, *Dismissed* (1985).

scheme. But the big increase in jurisdiction came with the Industrial Relations Act in 1971, which gave employees a remedy for 'unfair dismissal', and provided that it should lie not in the ordinary courts but in the industrial tribunals. The Employment Protection Act 1975 created many new statutory rights for employees (e.g. maternity leave), and these are implemented through industrial tribunals. The Industrial Relations Act was also the legislation which set up the National Industrial Relations Court (NIRC); that was a superior court of record, which means that it was of equal rank to the High Court though not part of the Supreme Court. There were judicial members nominated by the Lord Chancellor and the Lord President, and lay members appointed by the Crown. The idea was to build a separate system of industrial courts, with the industrial tribunals as the lower layer and NIRC as the upper; collective issues were to go to NIRC and issues concerning an individual to a tribunal. The NIRC was bitterly opposed by the trades unions and when the Labour Party came to power in 1974 it promptly passed the Trades Union and Labour Relations Act which repealed the Industrial Relations Act and abolished the NIRC. The provisions giving a remedy in an Industrial Tribunal for unfair dismissal were retained, however, and are still with us: they are now contained in the Employment Protection (Consolidation) Act 1978. The Industrial Relations Act had also given a parallel remedy to workers unreasonably excluded or expelled from a trades union. This like NIRC was highly charged politically, and was abolished in 1974. It was then recreated by the Employment Act 1980, but only in cases where there is a 'closed shop' in operation and union membership is essential to obtain work. New powers contained in the Employment Act 1988 extend the jurisdiction of industrial tribunals to complaints made by union members against their union.

When industrial tribunals were set up a presidential system was adopted. The Lord Chancellor appoints the president, a barrister or solicitor of at least seven years' standing; it is a full-time pensionable position comparable with that of a Circuit Judge. There are 16 regions, each with a full-time regional chairman who is a lawyer, appointed by the Lord Chancellor. The president has a general responsibility for the organisation though the regional chairmen arrange sittings and select a chairman and members for the individual sittings. The lay members are appointed to a panel by the Secretary of State from persons who have knowledge or experience in industry or commerce after consultation with bodies representing employers and employees. Two lay members selected from a rota sit with a legal chairman to form a tribunal. Booklets are available at government and tribunal offices which explain the jurisdiction and procedure. Proceedings are begun by making an application to a central office. The office refers all applications to the Arbitration and Conciliation Service (ACAS), which then puts a conciliation offer in touch with both parties to try to persuade them to agree to a negotiated settlement. Two-thirds of the cases begun are settled in this way. Those which are not are likely to result in a tribunal hearing. At proceedings before industrial tribunals legal representation is allowed, but legal aid is not available to pay for it. In practice it is quite common for the employer to be represented by a lawyer whilst the worker he dismissed is not; this may or may not account for the fact that only some 30 per cent of unfair dismissal claims which get as far as a tribunal hearing are successful. Unlike in the ordinary courts, however, the unsuccessful plaintiff is not normally liable to pay his successful opponent's costs; costs may be awarded only where the tribunal finds the proceedings were begun 'frivolously, vexatiously or otherwise unreasonably'.[1] Industrial tribunals hear cases in public; a glance at any local newspaper will show that they have become as happy a hunting-ground for reporters in search of a lurid story as the local magistrates' court. The volume of business is large. In 1985 there were 34,249 applications to industrial tribunals, 10,722 of which were decided after a hearing.

Appeals from industrial tribunals went to NIRC while it lasted; after NIRC had been abolished the Employment Protection Act 1975 set up a purpose-made Employment Appeal Tribunal.[2] This consists of judges nominated from time to time by the Lord Chancellor and by the Lord President for the judges in Scotland, and other members appointed by the Crown who 'shall be persons who appear to the Lord Chancellor and the Secretary of State to have special knowledge or experience of industrial relations, either as representatives of employers or as representatives of workers'. Appeal lies from industrial tribunals to the Appeal Tribunal on a question of law, and not on fact or mixed law and fact. The Appeal Tribunal is a superior court of record and its decisions are sometimes reported.[3]

If the parties consent, proceedings may be heard by a judge and one lay member but in default of such consent, proceedings must be before a judge and either two or four lay members so that in either case there are equal numbers of persons whose experience is as representatives of employers and of persons whose experience is as representatives of workers. There is a central office in London but hearings may be at any place in Great Britain. A party may be ordered to pay another party's costs, but only if the proceedings were unnecessary, improper or vexatious, or where there was unreasonable delay or other unreasonable behaviour in the course of conducting them. A party may be represented by anyone whom he desires to represent him. Legal aid, which is not

---

[1] Industrial Tribunals (Rules of Procedure) Regulations 1980 s.11.

[2] The provisions are now contained in the Employment Protection (Consolidation) Act 1978.

[3] Major decisions of the Employment Appeal Tribunal are reported in the *Industrial Cases Reports*, produced by the Incorporated Council of Law Reporting (see chapter 2), or in the *Industrial Relations Law Reports* which are a commercial production. So many were reported in its early days that in *Walls Meat Co.* v. *Khan* [1979] ICR 52, the Court of Appeal warned it to treat fewer matters as matters of law and hence susceptible to appeal. Lord Denning said 'If we are not careful, we shall find the Industrial Tribunals bent down under the weight of the law books or, what is worse, asleep under them.' The modern tendency is to move away from extensive reliance on decided cases in labour law.

available before an industrial tribunal, is available before the Appeal Tribunal. By its decision the Appeal Tribunal may exercise any of the powers of the body from whom the appeal was brought or remit the case to that body. From the Appeal Tribunal there is the possibility of a further appeal to the Court of Appeal and thence to the House of Lords. The Employment Appeal Tribunal disposed of 1,072 cases in 1986.

In addition to the matters already mentioned the jurisdiction of industrial tribunals has been increased by three important statutes. The Equal Pay Act 1970 was intended to eliminate discriminatory treatment as between men and women in pay and other conditions of employment; its provisions were grudgingly extended in 1984 after they had been condemned in 1982 by the European Court of Justice as failing to meet British obligations under EEC law; see chapter 36 below. The Sex Discrimination Act 1975 enacts a general prohibition in the employment field, in education, and in the provision of goods, facilities, services and housing. Claims or complaints under the Equal Pay Act and under the Sex Discrimination Act as regards employment go to industrial tribunals. Written contracts of employment typically fail to cover a number of issues that are likely to arise from work; by the Employment Protection (Contracts) Act 1978 a number of terms are automatically included to cover matters usually left unsaid, and if these are not observed complaint shall lie to industrial tribunals. These are rights of individual employees which only they can assert, though of course they commonly look to their trade unions for assistance.

The statutory provisions that have been mentioned amount to what is virtually a new branch of labour law. Parts of the old common law survive, so that an action for 'wrongful dismissal' may still be brought in the ordinary courts, where legal aid is available and damages are assessed in the usual way, but for relations between employers and employees it is now the industrial tribunals and the Appeal Tribunal which are the 'ordinary courts'. Obviously employed persons were at a disadvantage under the common law of 'master and servant'; provided the requisite notice was given the master could dismiss the servant without giving any reason; the servant could, after giving any requisite notice, terminate his service thus having equality before the law, which did not do him much good. Now the balance has been altered – and not only the balance, but the legal nature of the relationship. The master and servant relationship was purely contractual. Principles of contract are still vitally important in working out the details of the various statutory rights, but there is now a substantial element of an employed person having a 'property' in his employment. This is seen most clearly in *redundancy*. When a person starts being employed the employer must pay contributions to the Redundancy Fund (paid along with the weekly Social Security contributions) and if the employee has been continuously employed by the same employer for at least two years, compensation is payable if he is dismissed for redundancy, which in broad terms means that there is no longer any work for him. Smaller employers can recover part of the payment from the

Redundancy Fund. The purpose of redundancy payments was clearly described by the President of Industrial Tribunals in 1968:[1]

The stated purpose of the redundancy payments scheme is two-fold; it is to compensate for loss of security, and to encourage workers to accept redundancy without damaging industrial relations. A redundancy payment is compensation for loss of a right which a long-term employee has in his job . . . The purpose of redundancy pay is to compensate a worker for loss of a job, irrespective of whether that loss leads to unemployment. It is to compensate him for loss of security, possible loss of earnings and fringe benefits, and the uncertainty and anxiety of change of job.

We have now to regard an employee as a person whose contract of employment is to a large extent subject to statutory terms and who will acquire by long service in the same employment a quasi-property right which is more akin to the right of the holder of an office than to a contractual term. Henry Maine's *Ancient Law*, first published in 1884, contained the famous conclusion 'that the movement of the progressive societies has hitherto been a movement from *Status to Contract.*[2]' Maybe, but our present movement seems more just and forward-looking than when we thought only in terms of contract.

v Immigration appeals[3]

The Home Secretary has sweeping statutory powers to deport those who are not British citizens.[4] Under the Immigration Act 1971 the Home Secretary also has the widest statutory powers to prohibit the entry into Great Britain of those who are not British citizens. This Act requires him to make Immigration Rules; these Rules and any modifications to them are laid before Parliament and come into force unless Parliament disapproves them after 40 days. The Rules deal in considerable detail with who may and who may not be admitted, and for what purpose they are allowed in. The Rules are enforced by civil servants called immigration officers working at seaports and airports. The Home Secretary also has a wide power to deport, which is also contained in the Immigration Act 1971. Those who break the conditions under which they were permitted to enter the country are liable to be deported. Non-citizens may also be deported when on their conviction for a criminal offence the criminal court recommends them for deportation, or in any other case in which the Home Secretary considers their removal to be 'conducive to the public good'.

Originally there was no appeal either from an immigration officer's decision to

---

[1] *Wynes* v. *Southrepps Hall Broiler Farm Ltd.* [1968] ITR 407.
[2] Students are still recommended to read Maine, usually in editions with notes by Frederick Pollock. 'Status to Contract' comes at the end of Maine's chapter v.
[3] For further details see J. M. Evans, *Immigration law* (2nd ed. 1983), and Grant and Martin, *Immigration law and practice* (1982).
[4] Who is a British citizen and who is not is determined by the British Nationality Act 1981. It is an extremely complicated matter beyond the scope of this book. The details may be found in Evans, *Immigration law*, 72 *et seq.*, or in any standard work on constitutional law. Most Commonwealth citizens do not count as British citizens and are therefore liable to deportation.

refuse entry, nor was there any appeal from the Home Secretary's decision to deport.[1] This was most unsatisfactory. To turn a would-be immigrant away at the port of entry often involves great hardship to him and his family, and to deport someone who has made his home here is to inflict a drastic upheaval on him comparable to sending him to prison, and which carries almost as great a social stigma. Yet until comparatively recently successive governments of whatever political party strongly resisted the creation of any right of appeal. Eventually an official enquiry was set up, and, following its recommendations,[2] the present two-tier system of appeals was created by the Immigration Appeals Act 1969.

Most immigration appeals are heard in the first instance by an official called an *adjudication officer*. The Home Secretary determines how many of them there shall be, and the Lord Chancellor appoints them; in 1983 there were one Chief Adjudicator, 15 full-time adjudicators and a further 56 part-time adjudicators. The adjudicators sit in the major cities and at the usual ports of entry. Between them they disposed of 10,051 appeals in 1983. Above the adjudicators there is an Immigration Appeal Tribunal. Appeals normally go first to an adjudicator and then (provided leave to appeal is granted) to the Immigration Appeal Tribunal, but in certain types of case (including deportation orders made on the ground of 'conducive to the public good') the appeal bypasses the adjudicator and goes to the tribunal direct. The tribunal consists of a President, who must be a barrister or a solicitor of at least seven years' standing, and such other members (lay or legal) as the Lord Chancellor appoints. A tribunal of three is required for a hearing. Provided there is a legally qualified member to take the chair more than one panel may sit at once: in 1983 four panels were regularly sitting. The Lord Chancellor makes Rules which govern the procedure of the tribunal. The hearings are in public. It always sits in London. Applicants may be represented by a lawyer, a consular official or a representative of the United Kingdom Immigrants' Advisory Service; other persons may represent an applicant if the tribunal gives permission. No legal aid is available for representation before the tribunal, but applicants may get legal advice under the 'Green Form Scheme'. There is usually a hearing and it is usually public, but the tribunal has a discretion to hold it in private, and indeed to decide the case on the papers without a hearing. The tribunal handles a considerable volume of work. In 1985 it disposed of 729 cases, and considered 3,425 applications for leave to appeal. The decisions of the Immigration Appeal Tribunal, like those of the Social Security Commissioners, form an important body of specialist case-law. The most important ones are reported in the 'Immigration Appeals' which are published by HMSO.[3]

---

[1] When the power to deport aliens was first introduced by the Aliens Act 1905 there was a right of appeal to a local board, but this was abolished on the outbreak of the First World War and was not reinstated afterwards.

[2] The Report of the Committee on Immigration Appeals (Wilson Committee) (1967) Cmnd 3387.

[3] In 1980 it was proposed to discontinue the series to save money, but it was retained after protests from the Council on Tribunals.

From the Immigration Appeal Tribunal no further appeal lies to the ordinary courts, either on the merits or on point of law; but its decisions may (and often have been) attacked by way of judicial review.

Such rights of appeal as there are in immigration cases were grudgingly conceded by reluctant governments, and they are not comprehensive. One big practical limitation is that in many cases where an immigration officer refuses entry, the right of appeal may not be exercised while the applicant remains in the United Kingdom, which means that the applicant must go back home and pursue his appeal from there; this was contrary to what was proposed by the Committee which originally advised that an appeal system be set up, and seems to have been done largely to make it harder to appeal. In a number of other cases there is no right of appeal at all, notably where the Home Secretary when deporting someone because it is 'conducive to the public good' states that this is being done on grounds of national security; where this happens the usual practice is for the Home Secretary to set up an informal tribunal to hear what the deportee has to say, but since it is not the practice to give him the details of any allegations against him he is not usually able to make much of a defence.[1] Immigration appeals have certainly come in for plenty of criticism, but it is sometimes difficult to disentangle criticism of the adjudicators and the Immigration Appeal Tribunal from criticism of the current set of Immigration Rules, and opposition to all forms of immigration control.

vi Rent Tribunals and Rent Assessment Committees

The control of rents and tenancies of dwelling houses began in the 1914–18 war. The influx of workers to factory areas resulted in landlords charging inflated rents. Rent Restriction Acts controlled the rent at which lower-priced housing could be let unfurnished and gave the tenant security of tenure. Lettings to which these Acts applied were categorised as *controlled tenancies*. A controlled tenancy gave security of tenure lasting as long as the original tenant was in occupation, and continued by a kind of statutory succession to members of his family; this remains a feature of the present system of rent control. The rent for a controlled tenancy was fixed by reference to the rent in 1914 initially, and later by a formula applied to the annual rateable value. Disputes arising from controlled tenancies were handled by the county courts. The legislation was intended to be temporary, but rent restriction continued and still exists. Rent control is a politically contentious matter, and its scope has been expanded and contracted repeatedly as the party in power at Westminster has changed.

The present method of fixing maximum rents dates from 1965. The Rent Act 1965 expanded rent restriction, which at that time applied to only a small section of the very cheapest housing, to lettings of all unfurnished property up to a

[1] See *R.* v. *Secretary of State ex pte. Hosenball* [1977] 1 WLR 766.

rateable value of £1,500 in London and £750 elsewhere, and established a new official called a rent officer. Either landlord or tenant can apply to him; his duty is then to determine and register a fair rent. From the rent officer there may be an appeal to a Rent Assessment Committee. The Committees are independent bodies, some members being appointed by the Lord Chancellor (to provide legally qualified chairmen) and the others by the minister. Decisions are registered and the tenant need pay no more rent than that which is registered. Tenancies to which this arrangement applies are called *protected tenancies*. At first, controlled tenancies which existed under the earlier legislation continued to be governed by that legislation, but eventually[1] these were converted into protected tenancies, whereupon the rent officer and the Rent Assessment Committee became the only machinery for determining the rent of unfurnished housing subject to rent control.

Because rent control did not at first apply to furnished lettings, landlords took to furnishing their houses before they let them, and by 1945 it was clear that furnished lettings would also have to be controlled. At the time it was not thought practicable to bring them within the existing system, and the Furnished Houses (Rent Control) Act 1946 provided for the setting-up of tribunals to assess rents for dwellings that were let with furniture or with services, including attendance, heating, lighting or hot water supply, subject to limits of rateable value which are now £1,500 in London and £750 elsewhere. This created a dual system, one for furnished and one for unfurnished dwellings. Matters became still more complicated when Rent Assessment Committees were set up in 1965, because there were then two sets of tribunals as well. Eventually the two were amalgamated. The Rent Act 1974 turned most furnished lettings into protected tenancies, thereby expanding the jurisdiction of the rent officer and the Rent Assessment Committee and greatly reducing that of the Rent Tribunal. And the Rent Act 1977 abolished Rent Tribunals as separate bodies and transferred their remaining functions to the Rent Assessment Committees – a change which was more apparent than real, because by then the local Rent Assessment Committee and the local Rent Tribunal usually consisted of the same people. Lest the scheme be too easy for tenants to understand, however, the complication was added that when carrying out what would have been the work of a Rent Tribunal, the Rent Assessment Committee should still be called a Rent Tribunal!

The minister appoints members of panels for Rent Assessment Committees (*alias* Rent Tribunals) on a regional basis, with a regional president. The panels have lawyers, surveyors and laymen; a particular Committee could be made up of any three members but in practice there is normally a lawyer, a surveyor and a layman, the lawyer commonly being chairman. The usual practice is to inspect the properties in the morning and hear the case in the afternoon of the same day. They sit in public. The Rent Act 1977 lays down matters that are to be taken into account in deciding what is a fair rent for a protected tenancy; these follow usual

---

[1] By the Housing Act 1980 s.64; the period of overlap lasted 15 years.

practices in valuation except for the statutory requirement in section 70(2) that a 'reasonable rent' must be fixed ignoring any value attributable to scarcity. In 1985 Rent Assessment Committees disposed of 13,053 cases, and a further 3,067 in their capacity as Rent Tribunals.

When they were established after the Second World War the Rent Tribunals had a bad reputation. They were often adversely criticised by the High Court and few lawyers had a good word to say for them. There was some truth in some of the criticisms, especially that they were often too off-hand and informal, but it must be remembered that lawyers are unlikely to think well of any tribunal which was set up to interfere with rights of property, and in particular one which was set up in response to a report which said that a tribunal was preferable to the courts because tenants had 'a great dread of ever having to go to court to get a decision'.[1] One no longer hears the same sort of criticism of Rent Assessment Committees and Rent Tribunals. The Council on Tribunals made an examination of Rent Tribunals during 1961 and found that most of the complaints received from members of the public amounted to no more than a grievance about a particular decision. A general criticism which is heard, however, concerns the way in which jurisdiction over housing matters is now split between rent officers, tribunals and the ordinary courts. If a tenant thinks his rent is too high, he goes to a rent officer and Rent Assessment Committee (or maybe a Rent Assessment Committee masquerading as a Rent Tribunal); if he wishes to contest a notice to quit, or compel his landlord to carry out repairs, the case goes to the county court; and if the landlord gets tired of him and harasses him to make him leave there will be a prosecution in the criminal courts. This is undoubtedly confusing to many people, especially tenants, and it has even been suggested that there is need for one single 'housing court'.[2] But in 1987 the Lord Chancellor's Department Civil Justice Review, which had commissioned a survey, published a Consultation Paper in which it rejected the idea. (See chapter 8 above.) The types of issue that each of these bodies deals with are sufficiently distinct, it said, to justify separate courts dealing with them.

vii The Lands Tribunal

When in the later eighteenth century Parliament gave extensive powers for the compulsory acquisition of land, it was the practice to provide that the compensation to be paid should, in the absence of agreement, be determined by a jury. Later, and notably by the Lands Clauses Act 1945, the alternative of arbitrators was introduced. Each side appointed its own arbitrator, and the two arbitrators appointed an umpire who would decide if the arbitrators failed to agree. Then

---

[1] The Act was based on the recommendations in the Report of the Inter departmental Committee on Rent Control (Ridley Committee), (1945) Cmd 6621. There was no appeal on point of law until it was given by the Tribunals and Inquiries Act 1958.
[2] See A. Arden, 'A fair hearing? The case for a Housing Court', [1977] *Legal Action Group Bulletin* 27.

towards the end of the nineteenth century statutes began to provide for a single arbitrator appointed by a government department. The next step came from the provisions of the Finance Act 1910 for the taxation of land values; this required an independent arbitrator to determine values, and the method adopted was to make a Reference Committee of the Lord Chief Justice, the Master of the Rolls and the President of the Surveyors' Institution, who appointed persons to act as official arbitrators. This scheme was later applied for the settlement of disputed compensation on acquisitions by government departments or a public or local authority, and a number of other similar matters. The official arbitrators were a satisfactory tribunal on valuation but legal questions so often arise in these matters that it was decided to create a tribunal that would have professional skill in law as well as in valuation. The Lands Tribunal Act 1949 provided for the establishment of a tribunal consisting of: a president who must be either a person who has held judicial office (not necessarily in England) or be a barrister of at least seven years' standing, and other members (now eight in number) who must be barristers or solicitors of like standing or persons experienced in the valuation of land, appointed after consultation with the President of the Royal Institution of Chartered Surveyors. All appointments are made by the Lord Chancellor who has power to dismiss if, in his opinion, the person is unfit to continue in office or incapable of performing his duties. The jurisdiction of the tribunal may be exercised by any one or more of its members, so that the composition of the tribunal can be adjusted as between legal and valuation experts according to the nature of the case.

When the Lands Tribunal was set up it was intended that it should deal with all matters of the valuation of land and allied matters and that whenever some new occasion for assessing value or compensation should arise the jurisdiction would be given to it. As a result the jurisdiction is varied. The annual *Judicial Statistics* show that the tribunal disposed of 1,596 cases in 1985, though as with law courts a substantial proportion of cases are withdrawn or settled. The most numerous were rating appeals (920) with compulsory purchase cases (346) as the next largest figure. The tribunal is based in London but sittings are held in provincial towns as need be; this is connected with the practice of inspecting land and buildings in appropriate cases. In its hearings the tribunal normally follows the judicial practice of oral evidence on oath. It has a discretion as to costs. In compulsory purchase cases, it usually awards costs against a landowner who has rejected an offer by the public authority which is greater than the value which the tribunal eventually puts upon the land.

viii Tax Commissioners

In the past, the General Commissioners of Income Tax were appointed by the Land Tax Commissioners (a defunct body) from their own number and their activities were confined to their own district. Since 1958 vacancies are filled by persons appointed by the Lord Chancellor. General Commissioners are local unpaid people sitting from time to time, rather like justices of the peace, and they have their own clerk. The Special Commissioners (six in number) are civil servants, appointed by the Lord Chancellor from the practising Bar and from senior ranks of the Revenue; they sit, sometimes in pairs, sometimes singly, in London and in a number of provincial towns. There are also part-time Special Commissioners. Persons dissatisfied with assessments may appeal to the Commissioners. In some cases there is an option between appealing to the General Commissioners or to the Special Commissioners, though some appeals must be to the Special Commissioners. In 1985, 22,125 contentious appeals were set down for hearing before the General Commissioners, and 721 before the Special Commissioners. The tax-payer may present his case in person, or by a solicitor, barrister or accountant. The Crown is usually represented by an Inspector of Taxes or a representative of the Commissioners of Inland Revenue, counsel being briefed occasionally. From the decision of the Commissioners of Income Tax there is an appeal by case stated – but only on points of law – to the High Court. In some cases an appeal lies from the Special Commissioners to a special tribunal which is to rehear the case. An appeal then lies from the tribunal to the High Court on points of law. There are other tribunals and boards for special matters. From the High Court there is an appeal to the Court of Appeal, and thence, with leave, to the House of Lords: under the leapfrogging procedure it may be possible to go direct from the High Court to the House of Lords.

ix Professional and other organisations

There are a great number and a great variety of groups of persons formed for their mutual benefit; societies, clubs, associations, professions, trade unions and so on. It is of their nature that they should be largely self-governing, and this must involve some jurisdiction over their own members in such matters as imposing fines for breaches of rules and suspension or expulsion from the society. Lawyers usually call such procedures *domestic tribunals* – a name which is apt to mislead, because the word 'domestic' has now become so much associated with family matters. There are many instances, particularly with the professions,[1] in which Parliament has intervened and provided for a judicial organ. The powers of the Disciplinary Tribunal to fine, suspend or strike solicitors off the Roll (subject to an appeal to the High Court) and of the Inns of Court to control barristers are discussed in chapter 27. Since 1931 architects have been subject to the control of the Architects' Registration Council with a statutory disciplinary committee. Appeal lies to the High Court. For doctors there is a General Medical Council which, by the Medical Act 1978, has a statutory disciplinary committee with powers to remove a medical practitioner's name from the Medical Register;

---

[1] On the common law position, see D. Lloyd, 'The disciplinary powers of professional bodies', (1950) 13 Mod. LR 281.

appeal lies to the Judicial Committee of the Privy Council.[1] Before the present arrangements were introduced in 1950, a doctor could be struck off without any appeal to the courts. A similar statutory scheme for dentists, introduced in 1956, is now contained in the Dentists Act 1983; a scheme for opticians was introduced in 1958. Statutes also regulate the professional discipline of midwives, nurses, pharmacists and veterinary surgeons, giving a right of appeal to the High Court. The Professions Supplementary to Medicine Act 1960 provides machinery for registering chiropodists, dieticians, medical laboratory technicians, occupational therapists, physiotherapists, radiographers and remedial gymnasts and for their professional organisation and conduct. Disciplinary powers are vested in a Committee for each profession, with an appeal to the Privy Council.

Problems have arisen in the past over the powers of domestic tribunals to gather evidence, and in particular over whether they may compel unwilling witnesses to come and testify before them.[2] When a disciplinary tribunal is set up by Parliament the modern tendency is to give it the power to issue *subpoenas*. These are orders to witnesses to attend or else face proceedings for contempt of court, and are the method of compelling testimony in the civil proceedings in the ordinary courts. Where the tribunal does not have this power, the Queen's Bench Division of the High Court has a discretionary power to issue a subpoena on its behalf. It is also the accepted practice in recent legislation to provide for professional disciplinary tribunals to have the assistance of legal assessors.

In trades and professions that are not so regulated by statute, a member has a far more limited right to go to the law courts. All that he can do is to ask for judicial review, which in effect means that he can get the disciplinary proceedings set aside if there has been a failure in the basic requirements of a judicial process or other errors of a strictly limited kind. (See chapter 17 below.) It is only where a right of appeal is definitely given that the merits of a decision can be examined by the courts.[3]

---

[1] The Privy Council has long been associated with medical matters. Sir John Simon, who in 1848 was the first medical officer of health for the City of London and later Medical Officer of the Privy Council (and so not to be confused with a later Sir John Simon who became Lord Simon and Lord Chancellor), took a most active part in organising the medical profession as well as in shaping our law of public health. His book, *English sanitary institutions* (1890), is far more interesting than its title or appearance suggests.

[2] See the Report of the Committee on the Powers of Subpoena of Disciplinary Tribunals, (1960) Cmnd 1033.

[3] The distinction can be seen in *Hughes* v. *Architects' Registration Council* [1957] 2 QB 550, a precedent containing much wisdom on the rationale of the discipline of professional bodies. J. G. Miller, 'The Disciplinary Jurisdiction of Professional Tribunals', (1962) 25 Mod. LR 531, examines the grounds on which disciplinary action may be taken.

x The Restrictive Practices Court[1]

In most countries monopolies and restrictive trade practices have long been regarded as undesirable and against the public interest and there is some form of legal restraint.[2] The obvious method is to define the arrangements and practices that are regarded as undesirable and to prohibit them. The prohibited practice is put into much the same position as if it were a criminal offence; somebody has to ascertain the facts, bring the prosecution, prove that the alleged monopoly or restrictive practice comes within the definition laid down by law, and so get a verdict against those responsible. That method, which is accepted in the United States and Canada, has not been followed in this country. When it was decided after the war of 1939–45 that there should be machinery for dealing with monopolies and restrictive practices it was believed that it would be more efficacious to set up tribunals to hold a case-by-case inquiry, taking particular instances and deciding whether there was anything undesirable in the particular circumstances.

In 1948 the body which is now called the Monopolies and Mergers Commission was set up.[3] This is essentially a standing body for investigation and report. Its functions are limited to the investigation of matters referred to it by the minister or the Director of Fair Trading, and the publication of reports: it has no power of its own to force those whom it condemns for behaviour contrary to the public interest to amend their conduct. But its reports may lead to action by ministers or by Parliament – as when in 1973 the Secretary of State acted on a report of the Monopolies Commission to reduce the prices which manufacturers were permitted to charge for tranquillising drugs.[4]

Following a series of reports by the Monopolies Commission,[5] new machinery was set up to deal with the restrictive trade practices part of the Monopolies Commission jurisdiction by the Restrictive Trade Practices Act 1956. (The current statute is now the Restrictive Trade Practices Act 1976.) Unlike the Monopolies Commission, this machinery contains compulsory powers to make those responsible for restrictive practices desist. All restrictive practices as

---

[1] In March 1988 a government Green Paper, Review of Restrictive Trade Practices Policy (Cm 331), was published with a view to provoking public debate about possible changes in this area of the law.

[2] On the legal aspect, the most modern account is V. Korah, *Competition law of Britain and the Common Market* (3d ed. 1982). See also J. Lever, *The law of restrictive practices and resale price maintenance* (1964), Lord Wilberforce, A. Campbell and N. Ellis, *The law of restrictive trade practices and monopolies* (2nd ed. 1966, with supplement [1969]), and R. B. Stevens and B. S. Yamey, *The Restrictive Practices Court: A study in judicial process and economic policy* (1965).

[3] It was originally called the Monopolies and Restrictive Practices Commission. It lost its power to investigate restrictive trade practices in 1956, but acquired a power to investigate mergers in 1965, after which it was given its present title.

[4] See *Hoffman-LaRoche* v. *Secretary of State* [1975] AC 295.

[5] Especially its Report on Collective Discrimination (1955) Cmnd 9504.

defined in the Act must be registered with the Director of Fair Trading, who examines them and, if he considers them to be contrary to the public interest, may refer them to the Restrictive Practices Court. The court then decides if the practice falls within the scope of the Act and, if it does, it must condemn it as contrary to the public interest unless it is shown to fall within one of the eight 'gateways' which are opened for such practices by section 19 of the Act. The court has powers to enforce compliance.[1]

The constitution of the Restrictive Practices Court is laid down by the Restrictive Practices Court Act 1976. It consists of five judges, three from the High Court, one from the Court of Session in Scotland and one from the Supreme Court of Northern Ireland. The Lord Chancellor selects one of these judges to be President. In addition there are not more than ten other members appointed by the Crown on the recommendation of the Lord Chancellor from persons qualified by virtue of their knowledge of or experience in industry, commerce or public affairs. These members are appointed for a fixed period not less than three years and they may be paid. They are removable by the Lord Chancellor for inability or misbehaviour or on the ground of any employment or interest incompatible with the functions of a member of the court. The court may sit as a single court or in two or more divisions, and in private or in open court, the quorum being a presiding judge and two of the lay members. On a question of law the judge's opinion will prevail, whilst on other matters the decision of the court is by a majority vote. On questions of law there is appeal to the Court of Appeal or to the equivalent court for Scotland or Northern Ireland. Cases are heard much as they would be in the High Court, with counsel appearing for the Director of Fair Trading and for the parties to the agreement, with the calling of evidence, submissions, and a reasoned judgment. It is clear from the *Judicial Statistics* that the court has had a falling volume of work. Until 1971 it was handling between 50 and 100 references on restrictive agreements a year; in 1986 there were only 23 references of all types. That does not mean that the court and its jurisdiction is unimportant, however; it is probably the case that because of the jurisdiction, manufacturers and suppliers now avoid making restrictive agreements, rather than that the law is generally flouted.

The Restrictive Practices Court acquired an additional jurisdiction by the Fair Trading Act 1973. This Act, which is mainly concerned with consumer protection, established the office of Director of Fair Trading. Where it appears to

---

[1] Special provision is made for resale price maintenance agreements. At one time, suppliers used to force retailers to sell at their recommended minimum prices by blacklisting those who sold more cheaply. The Restrictive Practices Act 1956 forbade this practice, but made resale price maintenance agreements legally enforceable by the supplier, which previously they usually were not. A statute in 1964 invalidated them, but left it open to a supplier to apply to the Restrictive Practices Court, which was given power to declare a particular agreement valid if it found it to be in the public interest on various specified grounds; this legislation is now contained in the Resale Prices Act 1976. At present resale price maintenance agreements are lawful and enforceable in relation to books and medicines, but that is all. The difficulty of defending a price maintenance agreement is described in *Books are different*, ed. R. E. Barker and G. R. Davis (1966).

the Director that a person carrying on a business has persisted in a course of action which is detrimental to the interests of consumers in the United Kingdom and is to be regarded as unfair to consumers, the Director is required to seek a written assurance from that person that he will mend his ways. If that assurance is not forthcoming, or is made and broken, the Director may bring proceedings against him before the Restrictive Practices Court. Alternatively, the Director may take these proceedings in the county court.

The machinery described in this section is no longer the only legal weapon against unfair trade competition and restrictive trade practices, because since the United Kingdom joined the EEC in 1973 it has been possible to attack them as infringing EEC law. If such agreements are in breach of Articles 85 or 86 of the EEC Treaty and have repercussions on business in other EEC countries as well, a person affected by them may complain to the EEC Commission.[1] The Commission has powers to investigate the practice, and if it condemns it, those responsible will be required to stop it or face financial penalties which the Commission will recover by using the ordinary courts. The decisions of the Commission may be reviewed by the European Court of Justice; see chapter 36.

xi Royal Commissions and committees of inquiry

There are a few Royal Commissions that are permanent bodies for administration, and there are many Standing Committees in connection with government departments, but the ordinary Royal Commission or Departmental Committee is temporary, being appointed to inquire into a particular matter and ceasing to exist as soon as it has made its Report. The distinction between a Royal Commission and a Departmental Committee is largely one of dignity and standing.[2] A Royal Commission is appointed by the Crown, which means that the proposal for the inquiry comes before the government, and the names of the members are put forward by the Prime Minister. It is in constitutional position independent of any government department. A Departmental Committee is appointed by a minister, or by two ministers jointly. The purpose in either case is to have an inquiry that is official in the sense that it is paid for out of public funds and has the resources of the public service available to it, yet is independent of the government and of Parliament. The persons appointed may be expert, or they may be persons of experience in public affairs. To be a member of one of these bodies is a form of part-time voluntary work, similar to that of justices of the peace.

There are occasions when an official inquiry is set up to investigate allegations of public maladministration or of some supposed scandal, but that is not the usual situation. These inquiries are usually into some part of the public service or of social institutions where it appears that developments or a new departure may be

---

[1] For an example, see *Hassleblad (GB) Ltd.* v. *Orbinson* [1985] QB 745.
[2] See R. E. Wraith and G. B. Lamb, *Public inquiries as an instrument of government* (1971).

desirable. What is needed is a survey of the facts, assessments of relative opinion, specialist and general, and a set of recommendations that can form a basis for new legislation or new administrative practices. Such inquiries do not form any part of the machinery of justice: they are not concerned with the rights of individuals among themselves or as against the State, but with the policy that ought to be adopted for future action. There would be no need to mention these inquiries if it were not for one characteristic of their procedure, namely the taking of evidence.

The usual practice of Royal Commissions and of Departmental Committees is to receive evidence from organisations and individuals who may be expected to be able to contribute relevant information or opinions. A Royal Commission usually sits in public to hear such evidence, and publishes a verbatim transcript and the memoranda. A Departmental Committee generally does not do that, but some committees (notably the Ministers' Powers Committee and the Franks Committee)[1] have taken evidence in public and published their material. The procedure does, however, strongly suggest a judicial proceeding. Witnesses are examined on statements that have been made, and the questioning or cross-examination is obviously based on the practice in law courts. But the purpose is to inform the Commission or Committee about the general situation and of the opinion of the organisations and individuals who are called to give evidence, and however much the calling and questioning of witnesses resembles judicial procedure it is not in fact a judicial or quasi-judicial function.

There are, however, some occasions when an inquiry is needed into allegations of misconduct or into some supposed public scandal. Usually that kind of inquiry is needed because there are insufficient grounds for bringing legal proceedings or because the conduct that is alleged is not legally wrongful. The establishing of such an inquiry raises an important point of law. There is no doubt that the Crown, or a Minister of the Crown, can appoint persons to make an inquiry, for that is no more than asking for advice, but there is no power in the Crown to set up any new kind of jurisdiction. The Act of 1641 which abolished the Star Chamber specifically prohibited the Crown from setting up any new kind of court. In ordinary inquiries by Royal Commissions and Departmental Committees this problem does not arise because the organisations and people concerned are quite happy to give evidence voluntarily. If, however, an inquiry is to be made into allegations of malpractice or misconduct it may be desirable that the Commission or Committee should be armed with compulsory powers. The Tribunals of Inquiry (Evidence) Act 1921 was passed for that purpose: it provides that, if a resolution is passed by both Houses of Parliament for a tribunal be established for inquiring into a definite matter of urgent public importance, then the tribunal has the powers of the High Court as regards witnesses. Witnesses can then be summoned to attend, compelled to give evidence and produce documents, and they are entitled to the same immunities as they would

[1] See chapter 14.

be if they were witnesses before the High Court. There have only been 19 tribunals of inquiry under this Act, but the occasions have generally given rise to a great deal of public interest and discussion. Five were into police conduct, an area in which the Home Secretary now has powers to order an inquiry with compulsory powers under the Police Act 1964. The most recent examples of inquiries under the 1921 Act are the inquiry into the Aberfan disaster in 1966,[1] the inquiry into the 'Bloody Sunday' shootings in Londonderry in 1972[2] and the inquiry into the collapse of the Vehicle and General Insurance Company in the same year.[3]

This type of inquiry has been criticised on the ground that the procedure is unfair to persons who may be involved.[4] The ordinary rule in our civil and criminal courts is that witnesses are called by the parties, and the party calling a witness has the opportunity of eliciting his evidence. There are no 'parties' before a tribunal of inquiry. All the witnesses are called by the tribunal and examined by counsel for the tribunal. It is inevitable that some witnesses will say things that reflect upon other people, but it is not feasible to allow everyone who is mentioned to be regarded as a defendant and so be legally represented and allowed to cross-examine, for the proceedings would be endless. Following particular concern about certain aspects of the inquiry into the Profumo affair in 1963[5] a Royal Commission was appointed to examine these problems. In its report in 1966[6] it made a number of recommendations designed to see that witnesses are informed as to what is likely to be said about them and that they have adequate opportunity to put forward their own story, all of which have remained 'on the shelf' ever since.

Whatever procedure a tribunal of inquiry follows, the result can only be a report of the findings of the tribunal: that is to say, there cannot be a decision as to legal rights or as to criminal liability. It is therefore hardly right to regard these tribunals as being part of the machinery of justice for they do not make 'decisions' that are comparable in any way with those of the ordinary courts, of special tribunals or of ministers.

---

[1] Report of the Tribunal to Inquire into the Disaster at Aberfan. HC 553 (1967).
[2] Report of the Tribunal appointed to inquire into the events of Sunday 30 January 1972, which led to loss of life in connection with the procession in Londonderry on that day. (HL 101, HC 220.)
[3] Report of the Tribunal appointed to inquire into certain issues related to the circumstances leading up to the cessation of trading by the Vehicle and General Insurance Co. Ltd. (HL 80, HC 133.)
[4] G. W. Keeton, *Trial by tribunal* (1960), is a study of some of them.
[5] (1963) Cmnd 2152. Lord Denning (then a Law Lord and later Master of the Rolls) was asked to examine the circumstances leading to the resignation of Mr Profumo, formerly Secretary of State for War, who had apparently been sharing the embraces of a courtesan with the assistant Russian naval attaché. It is generally accepted that Lord Denning's Report was an excellent and fair account of what had occurred, but that is ascribed to Lord Denning's personal attributes: he heard the witnesses in private and conducted his inquiry as he saw fit, and excellent as the results were it can hardly be regarded as a good precedent.
[6] Cmnd 3121.

16

THE DISTINCTION BETWEEN MINISTERS' DECISIONS, TRIBUNALS AND LAW COURTS

The best way to grasp the distinction between administrative and judicial decisions is to look at both in action. In the judicial process we have the judge, who is a known person and not associated with any party to the proceedings. The evidence tendered to the court is available to all parties, and there are opportunities for testing and criticising evidence tendered by an opposing party; parties may be legally represented and put forward arguments on facts or on law. The judge is expected to base his decision on law and to explain what he has done by 'giving reasons'. The assumption is that some law must be applicable and that this law is ascertainable by a process of considering principles that can be found in books of authority. The judge often has to exercise a discretion, but he will generally find that there is some precedent and that he cannot do just whatever he thinks would be best. There are times when a judge does have such a wide choice that it is proper to say he can decide on the ground of what he thinks is the best policy, but that is regarded as the result of there being gaps in the law; he may have to make policy decisions, but that is not his real business.

The administrative process, as, for example, the exercise of powers conferred on a minister as the head of a government department, is for the most part not open to public inspection. In a matter of any importance there is a first stage of collecting information on everything that appears relevant. The core of it is the file of papers, and the file gets bigger with correspondence, memoranda and minutes. If it is a matter in which a statute prescribes the holding of an inquiry, then the inquiry is held and the report of the inquiry is added to the papers. Other departments may be consulted, and the opinions of experts, including legal advisers, may be obtained. The mass of paper, which may be considerable, is made manageable by the preparation of analyses and summaries. Then comes the question: 'Who actually decides?' Many people think that this is a most pertinent question and that if it were not for veils of secrecy they could get a clear answer. This idea comes from a lack of understanding of the structure and functions of the staff of a government department. It may be that in a particular ministry all matters of a certain kind go to a particular person or persons of a particular grade, and that this is where the decision is ordinarily made. But the

144

decision is in form and in law the decision of the minister. A most important part of a civil servant's job is to understand the limits of what he should do without reference to a higher official or to his minister. Much depends on the extent to which a case falls within clearly settled departmental practice or raises a new issue on which a policy decision is required. The minister also must understand what he can do on his own responsibility and when he ought to go to the Prime Minister or to the cabinet. Some matters must clearly go to the minister, as when replies must be made in Parliament, but the governing consideration is that the minister is responsible to Parliament for everything done in his name irrespective of whether he had in fact authorised it or had even heard of the matter.[1] Hence the minister is entitled to expect from the staff of his department a very high standard of care and an acute sense of the level at which a decision should be taken. It may thus happen that a matter which is not of itself of much importance but which may have political repercussions will go to the minister whilst something that is intrinsically of far greater importance can properly be settled by an official of moderate position. The decision, given in the name of the minister and not disclosing the identity of the person who actually made the decision, is an inevitable result of giving a power to a minister, for such a power cannot be exercised in any other way and remain consistent with ministerial responsibility.

Local government authorities have to decide many matters that affect the rights of citizens. Common instances are the control of development under the Town and Country Planning Acts and compulsory acquisition of land. These matters are thrashed out in committees, which either report to the council or make the actual decision under delegated powers; the committee members have the help of reports and advice from the council's officials and come to a conclusion on grounds of policy. The notion of responsibility attaches to these decisions: if attacked, they must be defended in a council meeting, and the ultimate arbiter is the electorate. There is, however, in virtually all these matters, either a right of appeal to a minister or a necessity for the council to secure the approval of a minister, so that an aggrieved person complains to the minister. The centre of interest thus shifts to the minister and to the process that he follows, and hence the decisions of local authorities need not be considered separately from decisions by ministers.

The administrative process is principally used for matters that are to be decided on policy, which means that the decision may be based upon any grounds or reasons that appear appropriate to the person who makes the decision, though ministers often have to decide issues by applying a known rule to facts established by evidence. The fact that the courts have more scope for policy than earlier

---

[1] Responsibility really depends on the attitude of the House of Commons. Questions are not allowed on the decisions of law courts. The House might accept a minister's contention that he should not answer for the exercise of a power that has obvious similarities with what is accepted as the business of law courts, but that does not extend to such matters as approval of slum clearance schemes or compulsory purchase orders even when in the circumstances the High Court would hold that the minister's behaviour was within the scope of judicial review.

145

writers recognised and that government departments often have a highly developed system of precedent tends to blur the line between law and policy, but it does not remove the distinction.[1]

The conception of law as being essentially fixed and binding runs through the judicial process. A judge is left virtually uncriticised and uncontrolled for the very good reason that he must work within well-understood limits; he must apply the law as he finds it, which includes doing his best to produce something intelligible and consistent when legal sources are confused or insufficient. The administrative process is free from those limits; a decision may be deliberately based on expediency, the state of the public finances, repercussions on other government policy, public opinion or any other of the numerous factors that determine the wisdom or practicality of the action in question. It may be that the judicial process and the administrative process might with advantage borrow a little from each other, but we confuse them at our peril, for the values of liberal democracy are not so tough that they can stand unlimited maltreatment.

If we consider all the agencies mentioned in the last section and look at the process which they follow, a sharp distinction appears between these deciding agencies and ministers. In all these agencies there is a tribunal of known composition that hears a case, applies a known rule to the case as established and so arrives at a conclusion. There are some instances where this analysis is less obviously applicable, as with Supplementary Benefit Appeal Tribunals before 1980, but these are anomalies rather than characteristics of special tribunals. There may be scope for policy, as there often is before law courts, but the typical instance is a tribunal applying Acts and subordinate legislation: a Social Security Appeal Tribunal, for instance, could no more refuse a claim because of the state of the public finances than a county court could refuse a tenant the protection of the Rent Acts because those acts have been an obstacle to a sensible housing policy.

It was once the practice to lump together ministers and special tribunals, as if they were merely different forms of the same kind of body. That had a number of unfortunate results. It is the exercise of powers by ministers that attracts much criticism and often creates strong feeling, for it is in the very nature of policy decisions that they should often turn on factors that are controversial. Policy often depends on conceptions of finance, priorities and allocations between competing claims, and whether 'the time is ripe', all of which are matters on which dispute is commoner than agreement. If special tribunals are thought of as belonging to the same category as ministerial decisions then people will suppose that decisions of tribunals may also depend on the minister's view. This false identification has been helped by the widespread use of the term 'administrative

[1] There was once a school of thought that regarded law and policy as being substantially the same thing: see Robson, *Justice and administrative law* (3rd ed. 1951), 432. But this view surely comes to little more than arguing that dividing lines are impossible to define, and therefore they do not exist, and therefore the two things are the same.

tribunal'.[1] When (as usual) the chief point in creating a tribunal is to provide an independent body to decide disputes, it is particularly important to avoid phrases that suggest that the tribunal is really the minister in disguise.

When proposals for new legislation are being prepared in a government department are there any principles for choosing between courts, tribunals and the minister? It is commonly believed that the Civil Service likes to keep as much as possible in their own hands and particularly wants to by-pass the law courts. That is not borne out by the evidence tendered to various enquiries. Departments have quite enough to do and do not want to have the trouble and the responsibility of numerous decisions in individual cases if it appears feasible to pass that work over to some other agency. The cardinal point is that the minister is going to become responsible for some service or process, and the minister must therefore keep in its own hands the making of all decisions that are vital to carrying out the minister's functions. If we take, for example, the compulsory acquisition of land, all the statutes vest the ultimate decision in a minister because if the power were vested in any independent body then that body could stultify the performance of the minister's functions. If it is decided as a matter of government policy that a new motorway is to be built between A and B, it is obvious that land will have to be acquired, and that someone must have ultimate responsibility for deciding the route that the motorway is to follow. If an independent court or body had the power to say whether any particular piece of land could be acquired or not, then that would be equivalent to deciding upon the route of the motorway, and whether there could be a motorway at all. No minister can be expected to agree to legislation that would remove from his control the carrying out of projects which rest upon policy decisions for which he has a responsibility to Parliament. When we look at the compensation to be paid we see that the government is concerned with the law that determines the basis for valuations, but that any particular valuation is left to the independent Lands Tribunal. In the same way the determination of whether a particular applicant is or is not entitled to benefit under the Social Security Acts, or how much benefit, is left to independent adjudication. There have been instances in which a ministry has kept control of a class of decisions that were not, as events went, at all necessary to safeguard the working of a scheme, but those have been miscalculations due to excess of caution and not to any general objection to some independent adjudication.

If decisions in certain matters are to be retained in the ministry, there is a further question as to whether the statute should lay down any procedure to be followed or not. There is a fairly standard procedure for the holding of inquiries before an inspector, and this is required by a number of statutes. This procedure was devised in the past as a substitute for private bill procedure, in order to save

[1] The high water mark of infelicitous phraseology is to be found in Professor Robson's book, *Justice and administrative law*, in which he uses the phrase 'trial by Whitehall' to include decisions of ministers and determinations by special tribunals.

both money and time, but it is now so well established that it is used in matters that would never have justified a private Act. Where the matter is one of a different kind, without any aura of private bill procedure, a statute may very well lay down no procedure to be followed but simply confer upon the minister the power and the duty to make decisions. The minister may then establish some procedure which may include a public inquiry or hearing, but any such procedure is an administrative arrangement and is not obligatory. Alternatively the method by which the decisions are made may not be divulged; all that is known to the outside world is that applications are received and that a decision comes from the ministry.

If the disputes that are likely to arise are not of a kind that would have a direct effect upon the work of the ministry, there is a definite advantage from the ministry's point of view in passing the work over to some independent body. Whether the work should be done by the law courts, or by a tribunal created for the purpose, rests upon a number of considerations. It is sometimes supposed that ministries set up special tribunals because they will carry out the ministry's policies, and some people even think that the minister, in selecting the members of such tribunals, deliberately looks for persons who will either be subservient to the ministry or can be relied upon to be sympathetic. There is no truth in that, and indeed it would defeat the whole object of establishing a tribunal, which is to provide an independent method of adjudication in matters in which the ministry does not mind whether the decision in any particular case goes one way or another. The choice between sending the disputes to the law courts and setting up a special tribunal is in practice made by considering their respective merits. Law courts have certain obvious advantages: they already exist, they have a known procedure, their behaviour is fairly predictable and they are eminently respectable. A minister who tells the Commons that disputes under his Bill are to go to the law courts does not have to argue that point; all lawyers and some other people will accept that as being obvious, whereas proposals for creating a special tribunal may have to be supported by arguments in favour of some special provision. Inevitably these advantages have to be considered in comparison with the characteristics of law courts.

(1) Special tribunals may make provision for deciding cases at very little cost to the parties. The cost of the officials and buildings used comes out of public funds. Where poor people are chiefly concerned, as in some matters under the Social Security Acts, the applicant merely has to attend; witnesses are not usually needed, but if the applicant has to call a witness (other than a full-time salaried trade union official) the cost is paid by the Treasury. An appeal from a tribunal costs the applicant nothing at all. In most tribunals there is far less need to employ lawyers than there is in the law courts, and parties are often unrepresented professionally. Of course part of the saving of cost to the parties is at the expense of the taxpayer, but taking this into account there is still an absolute saving in cost,

for the salaries are lower than in the judiciary, and the buildings and so forth are not specialised.

(2) There may be less delay before cases are heard. If there is an increase in the number of cases the minister may be able to expand the service to deal with it. This flexibility is also a characteristic of the magistrates' courts, where extra courts can be held to deal with a pressure of cases. An increase in the work of professional judges generally means delay in hearing cases, for an increase in the number of judges has not in the past been made until at least two years after the need for that increase had become acute. In some cases, however, special tribunals have been more dilatory than law courts.

(3) The procedure of law courts is very difficult for litigants in person. Special tribunals can adopt a more informal method, rendering it far easier for the inexperienced to present their case adequately. Even where solicitors are engaged there are great advantages, the saving of time and trouble being due to factors much like those mentioned for arbitrations.

(4) Special tribunals can avoid the rigidity of precedent that often hampers the law courts. There is sometimes a need for a break with past practice. It is not uncommon for judges in law courts to regret that they cannot make a new start interpreting a statute or a line of cases. A special tribunal is unlikely to achieve the futility of saying that a conclusion is 'ridiculous' and yet necessary because of precedent.[1] Much of the law depends upon standards of measuring rods: negligence is measured against a hypothetical 'reasonable man', whilst various words, such as 'in repair' for houses and 'sea-worthy' for ships, have come to denote an ascertainable standard. If the standard of public health works had been left to the judges to evolve, encumbered by the doctrine of precedent, we might still be living in fear of cholera epidemics. The more rapidly changes are occurring the more quickly must standards change or new standards be established. A special tribunal may escape the baleful influence of precedent upon precedent.

(5) Special tribunals are devised to meet particular needs. That is noticeable mainly in respect of their composition. A lawyer chairman is now usual, and the other members are likely to have expert knowledge or be well versed in the kind of matters that are to come before the tribunal.[2]

Examples that have been given earlier in this chapter include worker and employer members of national insurance tribunals, lawyers and surveyors for the

---

[1] For examples see Scrutton LJ in *Hill* v. *Aldershot Corporation* [1933] 1 KB 259; Cross J in *McVeigh* v. *Arthur Sanderson* [1969] 1 WLR 410; and Fox J in *Munby* v. *Furlong* [1976] 1 QB 259 (reversed by the Court of Appeal, [1977] Ch. D. 359).

[2] On the kind of people who are appointed to special tribunals, see S. McCorquodale, 'The composition of administrative tribunals', [1962] *Public Law* 298; W. E. Cavenagh and D. Newton, 'The membership of two administrative tribunals', (1970) 48 *Public Administration* 449 and 'Administrative tribunals: How people become members', (1971) 49 *Public Administration* 197.

Lands Tribunal and so on. There are also requirements for some tribunals of persons with general experience of public affairs and of the social services. There may also be provisions about the kind of evidence a tribunal may need and about the way in which it is to go about its business. The points can be illustrated by two examples:

(1) Suppose that we have to decide whether a field is foul with twitch. In a law court the judge would hear expert evidence on each side, which means one or more witnesses saying that the land is foul and other witnesses saying that it is clean. An Agricultural Land Tribunal would also hear such evidence, but then the members who include men of farming experience would inspect the land. The tribunal would almost certainly come to the right conclusion, whereas the law court, by clinging to its conception of a trial and evidence, may easily go wrong on the simplest of facts. A substantial amount of work goes to arbitration for similar reasons.

(2) The review of compulsory detention in mental hospitals would be grossly unsuitable for the ordinary courts. Patients are often very disturbed and it would not be sensible to convey them to the court-house, or for the proceedings to take place in open court. Also, much specialist knowledge is required to deal with the sort of issues which are likely to arise. These difficulties are met by Mental Health Review Tribunals, which invariably have a doctor as one of the members, which sit in private, and which go to see the patient instead of vice versa.

The strong points of tribunals cannot be ignored. This is not a claim that special tribunals are always better than law courts, either generally or in the particular points mentioned. It is impossible to discuss whether one tribunal is better than another unless we know the kind of work it has to do. The most important thing is personnel with adequate knowledge and experience and opportunity to use that knowledge. There is no good reason why law courts should be more expensive, dilatory and hidebound than special tribunals: but reform of these matters would not do away with the need for special tribunals. Law in its full range has become far too complex for any group of people with a similar training to handle all of it. The work has got to be spread over different institutions to secure efficiency.

A real problem with tribunals is that there is no unified system. This brings a risk of fragmentation and isolation. Virtually the only link between the different tribunals is the Council on Tribunals.

The Council on Tribunals in its earlier years was perhaps not as effective as it should have been. This was not the fault of the members. The Council was given a large field to supervise through having the two subjects of Tribunals and Inquiries, yet all its members are part-time volunteers and it has never been provided with adequate staff. Unpaid and part-time members cannot be expected to go through vast quantities of paper, draft Rules and so on, and record their findings and views within the time-limits set by departmental and parliamentary requirements. Visiting and seeing various tribunals and inquiries at work is most time-consuming for members and staff and yet getting down to the grass-roots is essential. It is, for example, by observing the actual process of ascertaining a party's case from his own account of the matter and from what his witnesses may have to say, that it becomes apparent whether insistence on applying the law of evidence would assist the course of justice or be a hindrance. The sound principle is to go to the grass-roots and watch and listen. The Council does what it can. In 1985–86 it managed about 150 assorted visits. This was a substantial work-load for the members, but not many visits considering the number of tribunals and inquiries there are.

The Council on Tribunals may well develop into a far more useful institution if it is given sufficient resources. On some matters there is a dearth of information and the Council would be a suitable body to gather it. The efficiency of some tribunals would probably be improved by training courses for members. Training courses for magistrates are considered valuable, both by those who practice in the magistrates' courts and by magistrates themselves. The preparation of training courses benefits from the feed-back from the participants, and so that is a self-improving exercise.

17

CONTROL BY THE LAW COURTS

Judicial control is exercised either on appeal or by review. An appeal is a complaint that a decision of the inferior tribunal was wrong through mistake as to the facts or the law or both. There is no general right to appeal from a lower to a higher court, or from a special tribunal to the ordinary courts. Hence, when dealing with any jurisdiction, it is necessary to look at the statutes to see if any right of appeal is given, and if so whether it is on fact or law or both. Within the hierarchy of ordinary courts, a system of appeals has been in existence for many years, whereas until comparatively recently it has been exceptional for appeals to lie from a special tribunal to the ordinary courts. There was a widespread feeling that there ought generally to be a right of appeal on a point of law and, following on recommendations of the Franks Committee, the Tribunals and Inquiries Act 1958 provided for such appeals in respect of a number of tribunals. Where an appeal to the ordinary courts does lie it is normally to the High Court; although as we have seen there are a number of important tribunals which have their own special appeal tribunal, from which appeal lies not to the High Court but to the Court of Appeal. Where there is a right of appeal to the ordinary courts this usually means that the High Court or the Court of Appeal has the power to give the decision which the tribunal should have given; but sometimes it is provided that the appeal shall be by a process called 'case stated'. On appeal by case stated, the court is asked to provide the tribunal trying the case with the answer to a specific question of law, which it then uses to reach its decision.

Judicial review is the process by which the law courts seek to ensure that those who have powers or duties of a public nature exercise them according to law. The principles which the courts apply form a body of rules known as administrative law. Special tribunals are within the range of administrative law, as are justices of the peace and coroners; but it reaches far beyond them to control many of the official actions of the ministers of the Crown and, at a lower level of government, the acts of local authorities. This form of judicial control was originally exercised by the Court of Queen's Bench, and its functions are now carried out by the Queen's Bench Division of the High Court. A series of remedies are at its disposal: writs of habeas corpus, the prerogative orders of mandamus, prohibition and certiorari, declarations, plus injunctions and the power to award damages if appropriate; these powers have already been described in chapter 6(ii).

Judicial review is similar to the ordinary process of appeal in that the purpose of both is to correct a decision by some official person or body which was wrong. The difference between them is that an appeal is positive, whereas judicial review is negative. On judicial review the Queen's Bench Division will point out the error and indicate the limits within which the body must operate, and may even quash the proceedings or command the tribunal or official to do what should be done, but it will never do itself what the tribunal, minister or official ought to have done. On an appeal, however, the appeal court usually has power not only to point out the lower court's error but also to make whatever judgment or order it should have made.

At one time administrative law was a subject both difficult and obscure. Basic principles were hidden by a mass of technical rules about which particular remedy was available in favour of what particular applicant against which particular type of respondent in what particular type of case. In addition, the courts were unwilling to recognise that when dealing with applications for judicial review against ministers and central or local government officials they were really controlling executive power, and preferred to pretend that the only bodies whose business they reviewed were courts or legal tribunals. Hence they invariably used to start off by asking themselves the question whether the person whose conduct they were asked to review had 'a duty to act judicially', instead of the simple question whether it was proper and sensible for this type of act by this sort of official to be reviewed on this sort of ground in a court of law. Over the last 30 years, however, a great simplification has taken place. As has already been described in chapter 6, the procedure for judicial review has been simplified and standardised in a way which enables the courts to concentrate upon principles rather than upon whether the applicant has asked for the correct remedy.[1] The courts are now willing to recognise reality when asked to review the acts of ministers and other officials, and no longer needlessly complicate matters by pretending that every official whose acts they are prepared to review is in some mysterious way a judge.[2] The result is that the principles of judicial review are at last becoming clear.[3]

The first principle is that judicial review is available against a tribunal or official

[1] Although not with total success, because a litigant may still fail against the merits if he asked for damages or a declaration where he should have sought judicial review: *O'Reilly* v. *Mackman* [1984] 2 AC 249. See Professor H. W. R. Wade, 'Procedure and prerogative in public law', (1985) 101 LQR 180.

[2] See *Ridge* v. *Baldwin* [1964] AC 40, especially the speech of Lord Reid.

[3] Standard works on the subject are S. A. de Smith, *Judicial review of administrative action* (5th ed. 1985); H. W. R. Wade, *Administrative law* (5th ed. 1982); Craig, *Administrative law* (1983); R. J. F. Gordon, *Judicial review: Law and procedure* (1985). See also the 450 page report by *Justice, Administrative Justice, Some Necessary Reforms* (1988). The exposition in this section owes much to Lord Diplock's judgment in *Council of Civil Service Unions* v. *Minister for the Civil Service* [1985] AC 374.

who has acted upon an error of law. This principle has only become established recently. Originally, judicial review lay only where the error of law had caused the tribunal or official to act beyond its jurisdiction: where it led an ecclesiastical court to attempt to try a man for a felony, for example, or where justices of the peace sent a man to prison in circumstances under which they had no power to do so. All courts, tribunals and public officers keep official records, and from an early date in legal history the Court of King's Bench would examine these records to see whether an excess of jurisdiction was disclosed. The court then expanded the scope of its interference by two routes. The first was through the concept of 'error on the face of the record'. It was held during the eighteenth century that proceedings could be quashed not only for jurisdictional errors that showed up in the official record, but for any error of law that was revealed there. In the second half of this century 'error on the face of the record' in this extended sense became an important means of correcting mistakes of law committed by special tribunals from whose decision there lay no right of appeal on point of law as such. Thus when a tribunal was set up to determine the compensation payable to those who lost their jobs in hospitals when the National Health Service took over the private hospitals, and an Act of Parliament decreed that the compensation should be calculated taking certain matters into account, the High Court was able to intervene when the tribunal announced that it had calculated an award leaving those matters out of account.[1]

At one time, the High Court would only quash for error on the face of the record when the error was contained in the formal documents which comprised the official record of the court or public official; but since the Second World War the idea of 'the record' has been progressively expanded so that it now includes any written reasons given by the tribunal or authority for its decision, and even includes reasons given orally.[2] The High Court was always ready to review a decision made in excess of jurisdiction even where this was not apparent from the official court record, and this became the second route by which judicial review for excess of jurisdiction eventually developed into judicial review for any error of law, because the courts gradually stretched the concept of what amounts to an 'excess of jurisdiction'. Originally it meant that the tribunal or official had tried to do something which it was the business of someone else to do; as long as the tribunal or official was basically engaged upon the work they were supposed to do, then they were not acting outside their jurisdiction merely because they made some mistake in the law which had to be applied. Then in 1969 there was a remarkable feat of judicial sleight of hand: the House of Lords propounded the doctrine that because special tribunals are only authorised to decide cases

---

[1] *R. v. Northumberland Compensation Appeal Tribunal ex pte. Shaw* [1951] 1 KB 711; [1952] 1 KB 338.
[2] *R. v. Knightsbridge Crown Court, ex pte. International Sporting Club (London) Ltd* [1982] QB 304. The courts have not yet ruled that it amounts to an error on the face of the record when no reasons are given for a decision, but from the spirit of a number of recent decisions this might be the next development.

according to law, they are acting outside the scope of their authority in deciding a case contrary to law, and any error of law by a tribunal therefore amounts to an excess of jurisdiction giving rise to the possibility of judicial review.[1]

A tribunal called the Foreign Compensation Commission had the task of distributing a compensation fund among British subjects and companies whose property had been damaged or confiscated in the fighting in Egypt in 1957. The tribunal refused to pay a British company whose property had been confiscated by the Egyptian authorities and handed over to an Egyptian company. It did so on the ground that by statute there could be no payment whether either the claimant or his 'successor in title' was foreign, and this claimant's successor in title was the Egyptian company, a foreigner. This was absurd, because confiscation of property was one of the cases for which compensation was intended. The provision about foreign successors in title was obviously meant to cover the case where the claimant had handed his property over to a foreign national, not where one had forcibly taken it from him. On the face of it there was nothing that the claimant could do, however, because so far from there being a right of appeal to the courts on point of law, the relevant statute even provided that decisions of the tribunal 'shall not be called into question in any court of law'. Nevertheless, the House of Lords said that the tribunal's error of law took it outside its jurisdiction, that the clause prohibiting interference by the law courts was ineffective to bar judicial review, and so it managed to quash the decision. The implications of this decision are profound and the courts are still trying to work them out. If the case is to be taken at face value then 'error on the face of the record' is redundant, because judicial review invariably lies where there is an error of law, whether or not it is contained in something which the court is prepared to call 'the record': indeed, some of the cases since *Anisminic* suggest that this is now the position.[2]

It also means that there is a big overlap between judicial review and the ordinary process of appeal in any case in which a statute gives the right of appeal from the tribunal to the law courts on point of law. This does not mean that one or other procedure must be unnecessary, however, because as we have seen the powers of the law courts are different according to whether they are hearing an appeal or an application for judicial review. Where appeal and judicial review overlap, the courts usually allow the person who is aggrieved by the decision to pursue whichever remedy suits him best,[3] or even both at once.[4]

The second ground upon which judicial review may be sought is *irrationality*: where a decision 'is so outrageous in its defiance of logic or of accepted moral standards that no sensible person who had applied his mind to the question to be decided could have arrived at it'.[5] Applications for judicial review under this

---

[1] *Anisminic Ltd.* v. *Foreign Compensation Commission* [1969] 2 AC 147.
[2] *In re Racal Communications Ltd.* [1981] AC 374; *R.* v. *Greater Manchester Coroner ex pte. Tal* [1985] QB 67.
[3] *R.* v. *Ipswich Crown Court ex pte. Baldwin* [1981] 1 All ER 596.
[4] As in *Hanson* v. *Church Commissioners* [1978] QB 823.
[5] Lord Diplock in *CCSU* v. *Minister for the Civil Service* [1985] AC at 410.

heading often concern the use of statutory powers for purposes other than those for which Parliament conferred them. A public authority is given power to take some specific action, which it takes, and this is attacked on the ground that the action could only be validly taken in pursuit of some broader purpose, which was not the purpose on this occasion. Thus the Home Secretary has the power to cancel television licences; this, said the courts, existed to enable him to punish those who broke the terms of the licence or failed to pay the fee, and they quashed his revocation of a licence when this was done in order to make the owner of a television buy a new licence at an increased fee.[1]

In another case a minister had the power to licence airlines to fly particular routes. His refusal to licence Laker Airways was struck down because the reason for the refusal was to protect the monopoly enjoyed by British Airways, whereas the enabling Act required him to use his licensing powers to prevent British Airways getting a monopoly.[2]

The reverse of this situation occurs where some official is given a wide statutory duty to promote some broad objective, and under colour of promoting it he does something which, in the view of the courts, no reasonable person could ever see as promoting it. Thus in a celebrated case in 1983 the courts struck down a plan by the Greater London Council to reduce bus and tube fares by 25%, and to make good lost revenue out of the rates, partly because this could not possibly be viewed as a proper means of carrying out a general statutory duty to run public transport in London on a basis of financial self-sufficiency.[3] But the courts are prepared to condemn a decision as unreasonable on more general grounds than these.

The court is entitled to investigate the action of the local authority with a view to seeing whether they have taken into account matters which they ought not to take into account, or, conversely, have refused to take into account or neglected to take into account matters which they ought to take into account. Once that question is answered in favour of the local authority, it may still be possible to say that, although the local authority have kept within the four corners of the matters which they ought to consider, they have nevertheless come to a conclusion so unreasonable that no reasonable authority could ever have come to it.[4]

Thus they quashed a decision of a city council to ban the local rugby club from playing on the city recreation ground as a punishment for refusing to utter a public condemnation of a proposed rugby tour of South Africa.[5]

[1] *Congreve* v. *Home Office* [1976] QB 629.
[2] *Laker Airways* v. *Department of Trade* [1977] 2 All ER 182.
[3] *Bromley LBC* v. *Greater London Council* [1983] 1 AC 768.
[4] Lord Greene MR in *Associated Provincial Picture Houses Ltd.* v. *Wednesbury Corporation* [1948] 1 KB 223 at 233. Because this is the leading case this type of behaviour is usually known as 'Wednesbury unreasonableness'; which is rather unfair to the inhabitants of Wednesbury because in that case the Court of Appeal found the corporation had behaved entirely reasonably.
[5] *Wheeler* v. *Leicester City Council* [1985] AC 1054. Lord Templeman said: 'the laws of this country are not like the laws of Nazi Germany. A private individual or a private organisation cannot be obliged to display zeal in the pursuit of an object sought by a public authority and cannot be obliged to publish views dictated by a public authority.'

Whilst the courts repeatedly say they have the power to quash a decision simply because it is unreasonable, in practice they rarely quash decisions on grounds of unreasonableness alone. Because they are conscious of the need to avoid getting into the position where they are regularly remaking decisions of competent authorities merely because they disagree with them, they have adopted a narrow definition of 'unreasonableness'. In this context 'unreasonable' does not mean that the court disagrees with what was done, or even that it thinks most reasonable people would disagree with it: it is unreasonable only if the court thinks that no reasonable person or body of persons could have done it – and public bodies and authorities rarely make decisions which are as bizarre as that.[1]

In the nature of things it is usually the decisions of public authorities, not special tribunals, which are judicially reviewed on grounds of irrationality. Irrationality is the obvious ground for attacking an abuse of discretion, and whereas public authorities have wide discretionary powers, tribunals generally do not. Tribunals sometimes act unreasonably, it is true, but because they have less room for manoeuvre their unreasonable behaviour will usually involve an error of law and the decision will be reviewed on that ground rather than because it is unreasonable. However, insofar as tribunals do have wide discretionary powers, their decisions, like the decisions of public officials, can be reviewed on grounds of unreasonableness alone. Magistrates, for example, have wide discretionary powers when it comes to sentencing, and on a number of occasions particularly weird sentences have been successfully attacked by way of judicial review.[2]

The third broad ground upon which judicial review may be sought is 'procedural impropriety', where the applicant complains not of the decision as such, but that the official or tribunal reached it disregarding the procedure which should have been followed. The most obvious case is where an Act of Parliament requires some step to be taken and it is omitted: where the minister is required to hold an enquiry before making a planning decision, for example, and he makes the decision without holding the enquiry; or when before introducing some scheme or proposal he is required by statute to give advance notice and hear objections, and he gives inadequate notice or gives no notice at all.[3]

Usually the procedural step will have been required by statute, but the courts sometimes intervene where the tribunal or official merely announced that he

---

[1] In this connection see *Secretary of State for Education* v. *Tameside Borough Council* [1977] AC 1014, where the courts condemned a minister who had power to overrule 'unreasonable' decisions for doing this too readily. An Act of Parliament empowered the minister to overrule a decision of a local education authority if he was satisfied that they were 'proposing to act unreasonably'. He tried to use this power to prevent a local authority preserving grammar schools, contrary to the government's current educational policies. The directive was struck down: disagreeing with their educational policy was not the same as having grounds to think they were behaving unreasonably.

[2] *R.* v. *St Albans Justices ex pte. Cinnamond* (1980) 2 Cr Ap R(S) 235. The cases are reviewed by M. Wasik in [1984] Crim LR 272.

[3] As in *Lee* v. *Department of Education and Science* (1967) 66 LGR 211, where the minister gave parents only four days to formulate objections to a plan to reorganise a school.

would follow a certain procedure, and then went back on his word.[1] 'Procedural impropriety' goes wider than this, however, and also covers cases where the proceedings failed to comply with certain minimum unwritten standards of fairness which are usually called 'the rules of natural justice'. These rules are two, and lawyers usually dignify and obscure them by putting them into Latin. The first is *audi alteram partem*: literally, 'hear both sides'. In the case of a tribunal which is entrusted with the task of settling a dispute between two citizens or between a citizen and some public official or department, this means exactly what it says: the tribunal must give both sides an opportunity to state their case before it decides between them. To take an obvious example, judicial review lies if a bench of magistrates dismisses an information against a defendant without hearing the prosecution case, or if (as occasionally happens) the magistrates hear the prosecution case and then absent-mindedly convict before hearing the case for the defence. The rule is said to apply not only to independent tribunals, but also to public officials who have to make decisions adversely affecting others. In these cases there are not two sides, however, and the rule has to be modified so that it is almost a different rule. In this sort of context *audi alterem partem* is taken to mean that before making a decision which will adversely affect another person, the official must normally listen to what that person has to say: the rule is not so much 'hear both sides' as 'do not condemn another person unheard'. Thus an authority which has power to demolish houses erected without its permission must invite the builder to explain himself before it sends a gang of men to knock it down;[2] a licensing authority which has power to revoke a trader's licence for misbehaviour must hear him before it closes his business down;[3] and an authority with power to remove a person from public office must give him a chance to answer the case against him.[4]

Of course, the courts do not invariably impose this rule of natural justice upon each and every minister and official. There are some powers which exist for the protection of the public which would fail in their intended purpose if the official had to invite the intended victim for an explanation in advance: if a magistrate had to ask a suspected criminal his views on the matter before issuing a search-warrant or a warrant for his arrest, for example, the clear-up rate for serious

[1] For example in *CCSU* v. *Minister for the Civil Service* [1985] AC 374, a trade union sought judicial review where there was a settled practice of consulting the union about major changes in the terms of staff employed at GCHQ, an intelligence agency, and the responsible minister suddenly introduced without prior consultation a ban on union membership. The application for judicial review succeeded at first instance, and failed in the House of Lords only because of overriding reasons of national security.

[2] As in *Cooper* v. *Wandsworth Board of Works* (1863) 14 CB (NS) 180.

[3] *R.* v. *Gaming Board ex pte. Benaim* [1970] 2 QB 417 (where the point at issue was refusal to grant a licence rather than the withdrawal of one already granted).

[4] *Ridge* v. *Baldwin* [1964] AC 40. There is a crucial legal distinction between an *office-holder* and an ordinary employee, even one employed by a public authority. Employees were never given the benefit of judicial review and it was necessary to give them a statutory right not to be unfairly dismissed: see above chapter 15(iv).

crimes would obviously be considerably lower than it is. The case-law on how far this rule of natural justice applies to public officials is therefore extensive and complicated and must be left to the books on administrative law.

The second rule of natural justice is *nemo iudex in sua causa*: literally, no one must be judged in his own case. Once again, the scope and application of this rule is clear in the case of magistrates, coroners, and other independent tribunals. Here it means that the tribunal which is charged with resolving a dispute between two sides must be independent of both. If it is not – or even if it looks as if it is not – then its decision is liable to be overset by judicial review. For example, the High Court overturned the decision of a Rent Assessment Committee when the landlord whose rent it had reduced complained that the tribunal chairman lived with his parents in another of their properties, and had been helping them and various of their other tenants to appeal against their rents.[1]

As with the previous rule, the application of this rule of natural justice to public officials is far less clear. Some public officials, such as certain licensing authorities, are charged with the task of hunting down shady operators and closing their businesses down. If their investigations reveal one, how can we expect them to be independent in deciding whether or not to shut his business down? Other public officials, like ministers, are expected to have a policy, and are given statutory powers by Parliament to put it into effect. Ministers have powers to reorganise schools, roads and railways, and we expect them to use them to carry out the educational or transport policies of the government of the day. How can we expect a minister to be completely independent when deciding whether or not to use the powers in a way which will necessarily tread upon a number of sensitive public toes? At one time, the courts took the view that this difficulty made it impossible to apply this part of the rules of natural justice to public officials altogether. More recently, however, a different view has emerged. Nowadays the courts usually say that an official in such a position need not be wholly independent, but nevertheless has a duty to listen patiently to objections from those who will be adversely affected while he still has an open mind.[2]

It is not clear precisely what the effect of this is. It is hard, of course, to prove the official listened with a closed mind, even if he did, unless he is unwise enough to announce a final decision before inviting objections; and sometimes this rule of natural justice may only mean that he must invite objections from those affected a decent interval before his decision is announced. But even so, the possibility of judicial review may serve some limited useful purpose in this type of case. The process of consultation may lead to an improvement in the details of a scheme, even if there was never the slightest chance that it would cause the whole scheme to be dropped.

[1] *Metropolitan Properties (FGC) Ltd.* v. *Lannon* [1969] 1 QB 577.
[2] As they have said in several planning cases where the local council, which was the planning authority, had a financial interest in the matter, or was concerned because it affected its overall planning policy for an area: *R* v. *Sevenoaks DC ex pte. Terry* [1985] 3 All ER 226; *R.* v. *St Edmundsbury BC ex pte. Investors in Industry* [1985] 1 WLR 1168.

The result of the Franks Committee, the ensuing legislation and the present attitude of the courts is to bring special tribunals and ministers' decisions nearer to lawyers' conceptions of the way that adjudication ought to be conducted. What is now happening is another great expansion of the common law. Is it going to resemble the time in the seventeenth century when common law took over the commercial jurisdiction of Admiralty and made a mess of it? In that expansion the common lawyers began by having no idea of what commercial people needed: lawyers could not or would not look at their common law principles afresh, and for a century the merchants suffered. Or is it going to be more like law and equity, where the long drawn-out attacks by the common lawyers on the Chancery court resulted in the end in a widened and revitalised common law? It depends on how much lawyers are rigid and set in their ways.

The strong point of lawyers is their notion of the *way* in which disputes should be decided. The ideas that lie at the back of a trial in our law courts represent a great contribution to civilisation. They are: (1) an adjudicator with an open mind, (2) a definite formulation of the issue that is to be decided, (3) that parties must have a full and equal opportunity to present their cases, (4) that the best available evidence must be produced, (5) that irrelevant material must be excluded, (6) that a body of accepted principles must be applied, and (7) that reasons for the decision must be given. It all sounds good and looks impeccable as a specification for producing satisfactory results. But we should be suspicious when lawyers preach these principles at tribunals and to public officials, because the goods which lawyers themselves deliver under this specification often fail to comply. When dealing with principle (3), a well-known writer on administrative law says this: 'Of course, the right to a hearing has always been sacred in courts of law, and any legal decision given without proper consideration of both sides would be set aside on appeal.'[1]

Yet consider the position of a prisoner not so long ago. He could be and often was interrogated. He could not see depositions against him or have copies of them until 1836. It is true that he could bring witnesses by 1702, but he could not have counsel in felony until 1836, and could not give evidence until 1898. There was no right of appeal until 1907. But of course these bits of common law only dealt with trivial things, like hanging a man by the neck until he is dead, and hardly affected important matters like real property.[2]

Now let us look at the admirable position that the best evidence should be produced: what does that mean? Anyone might think that the best evidence would usually include the evidence of the parties, yet the common law did not

[1] H. W. R. Wade in the first edition of *Administrative law* (1961), 142.
[2] Nor is the common law above reproach in these matters today. In 1985 there was an appeal from Jamaica in a case where the defendant had been deserted by his barrister at the trial and the judge had refused an adjournment to allow him to find a replacement. The Privy Council was unable to see anything fundamentally wrong with this, and affirmed his conviction for murder (which in Jamaica still carries the death sentence): *R. v. Robinson* [1985] AC 956.

allow the parties to give evidence until 1851 in civil actions and, as mentioned above, until 1898 in criminal charges. These restrictions have gone, but the lawyers' rules on what is evidence are still so fantastic that if a research worker were to follow them he would be rebuked for being silly and incompetent. For lawyers, we start with the proposition that what constitutes evidence is not based on reasoning or experiment but on authority; judges have laid down in decided cases what can and what cannot be evidence. It is open for a defendant to argue, for example, that photographs taken of him in the act of committing a criminal offence are not admissible because this is 'contrary to authority'.[1]

A court is allowed to take 'judicial notice' of many matters of common knowledge so that it is not necessary to produce evidence to establish that cats are kept for domestic purposes, that Christmas is celebrated on 25 December or who is Prime Minister. A court may also have 'visual evidence', as that a boy who was in court, actually aged 15, was under the age of 18.[2]

But apart from special rules that are not of common occurrence, evidence means oral statements of witnesses or documents, subject to admissibility. Again and again, tribunals are assailed by lawyers who try to force stupid and restrictive rules of procedure and evidence upon them. Fortunately, in modern times their attempts have generally failed, and it is increasingly one of the advantages of special tribunals that they need not follow archaic rules of pleading and evidence.[3]

The important question is whether this judicialising process is having a good effect. On the whole it is probably the case that special tribunals are all the better for some superintendence, in the same way that magistrates' courts and their workings need to be kept under review: sensible rules of procedure, adequate and well-qualified staff and suitable buildings have to be provided, and memoranda on new legislation and so on help the administration of justice. The independence of the judiciary is not diminished one scrap by the activities of the Home Office, and the Lord Chancellor advised by the Council on Tribunals may perform a similar function in respect of tribunals. But when we turn to inquiries relating to the acquisition of land or use of land, the result of recent changes is, from a national point of view, deplorable. As the processes have become more judicialised they have become slower, subject to delays and uncertainties, and far more expensive.

The basic trouble is that a procedure that is substantially judicial is not suitable for these matters. In some cases there has already been a government decision that, for example, road construction or improvement is to take place. For some

---

[1] *Dodson* [1985] 1 WLR 971. The argument failed. What is remarkable is that such a point can be seriously argued in a law court and even taken on appeal.
[2] Hence a conviction for selling liquor to a person under the age of 18 was sustained although there was no oral evidence of age: *Wallworth* v. *Balmer* [1966] 1 WLR 16.
[3] *R.* v. *Criminal Injuries Compensation Board ex pte. Moore* [1965] 1 QB 456. *R.* v. *General Medical Council ex pte. Gee* [1987] 1 WLR 564.

road work there is virtually no choice of site; if a cross-roads is to have a roundabout it must be at the cross-roads. For other works there may be a choice of site and if the new road is built someone is going to have to give up some land somewhere. For local authority proposals, the elected local council has approved some scheme and the question is now whether that should be confirmed by the central government. Or there may be a question of whether an area should be redeveloped, and if so what kind of redevelopment should take place. The minister has to make the decision, and the original purpose of the inquiry was to make quite sure that all the facts and views would be collected. The inquiry was not an occasion for justifying a proposal: the justification was to be made to the popularly elected local council or by the minister if challenged in Parliament. The problem, where there is one, is that democratic accountability through Parliament or local government has not been effective; and so we take the inquiry, the inspector's report and the minister's decision, and try to turn them into a kind of public trial of the merits of the project. The present inquiry system involves a vast amount of oral evidence, with the cumbersome habit of counsel repeating everything once or twice. To establish that, if shops are pulled down and new shops are built, the rent of the new shops is likely to be greater than the rents of the existing shops (or some similar proposition), can take an astonishing time, and pounds disappear as the clock ticks minutes. The substance of a project is often a choice between different sites, plans or operations and this, with the balancing of relative merits, is a very different business from adjudication in law courts. A lawyer naturally looks at things from his client's viewpoint: if the minister can be forced into producing a reasoned case there is just a chance that he may slip up or be deflected, and if his client does in the end lose his land (as he generally does) he has at least had a run for his money. The result is, however, that getting things done in England is becoming increasingly difficult. The Minister of Transport has said that it takes three years to get through the preliminaries for building a road; highway engineers say that the time is between three and seven years before the work can start. In the middle of the last century it was possible for promoters to go by private bill, get Parliamentary authority to acquire land, get the land, build a railway and be operating it in less time than it now takes to be allowed to start the construction of major works. The problem of giving the individual a reasonable deal, and at the same time not taking too long to get on with public works has not been solved. Private bill procedure became too expensive and clumsy, and provisional order was tried as a substitute and found to be little better; the ministerial inquiry system was much quicker and cheaper in its earlier days, and now if we are in need of roads, docks, power plants and so on, we must wait years and years, and sometimes so long that when the project can be begun it is no longer adequate. In 1956 an inquiry into a proposed nuclear power station at Bradwell in Essex lasted three days; the inquiry into the proposed Sizewell 'B' station lasted for 340 days spanning more than two years (and cost in the region of £15 million). All this raises problems which are beyond the scope of this book.[1] It is mentioned here merely to make the point that lawyers' ideas of administering justice are not always applicable to running the business of the country. The legal discipline was evolved for deciding defined and relatively simple issues according to a body of accepted principles: it cannot be applied unchanged to issues of policy and it cannot be a substitute for the control that Parliament should (but sometimes fails to) exercise. The idea of judicialising inquiries has led to increased opportunities for judicial review. Courts cannot control policy decisions (beyond securing that any requirements of procedure are satisfied) without a real danger that the judges may substitute their own ideas of policy for those of the ministers. It is quite as necessary to provide against being ruled by judges as it is to guard against being judged by ministers.

[1] See Gabrielle Ganz, *Administrative procedures* (1974); C. Harlow and R. Rawlings, *Law and administration* (1984), chapters 14 and 15.

18

THE PARLIAMENTARY COMMISSIONER FOR ADMINISTRATION

A theme that runs through all discussion of special tribunals and law courts is protection of the individual against the State. In the past the need was for protection against arbitrary arrest, imprisonment, taxation and other injustices that make up the story of constitutional struggles and the triumph of Parliament. For these matters there is no controversy over the form of protection: that is by judicial process. For instance, if a person is wrongly detained or wrongly refused bail there is a remedy, and the problems that arise involve the machinery, such as speedy access to legal aid and no delay in getting before a judge or court. But there is no agreement on the best form of protection against administrative injustice: there is debate on what that means and how much of it there is and on the merits of proposed remedies. Lawyers tend to think that there should be an extension of the powers of the courts so that a body of administrative law could be developed and applied. A very different idea reached England in the 1950s, that of the Ombudsman, an old institution in Sweden and which spread to Denmark and Norway and on to other countries. The idea of having someone with the power to look into any complaint against government departments, local councils, courts, hospitals, prisons, railways and anything else in the public sector is immensely attractive, and if that is taken further so that not only are complaints investigated but wrongs are put right, there we have the remedy for which we have all been waiting. Of course nobody with any sense of the realities could suppose that any Ombudsman could do all that; in countries which have an Ombudsman there is considerable variation in his powers,[1] and what may work in a small country would not necessarily suit a country of 55 million inhabitants. If there were to be an Ombudsman in this country, we certainly could not just adopt one of the existing patterns. What did happen was that ideas which began with an Ombudsman who would fit in with our particular conditions ended with a Parliamentary Commissioner for Administration, who is so different from other specimens that he seems a different species. The basic idea of the Ombudsman is that people with grievances take their complaints to him, yet the first rule about

---

[1] W. Gelhorn, *Ombudsmen and others* (1967) describes the position at that time in Denmark, Finland, New Zealand, Norway, Sweden, Yugoslavia, Poland, the Soviet Union and Japan.

the Parliamentary Commissioner is that he cannot investigate a complaint unless it comes to him from a Member of Parliament.

The argument for this was put in a White Paper in 1965.[1]

In Britain, Parliament is the place for ventilating the grievances of the citizen – by history, tradition and past and present practice. It is one of the functions of the elected Member of Parliament to try to secure that his constituents do not suffer injustice at the hand of the government. The procedures of Parliamentary Questions, Adjournment Debates and Debates on Supply have developed for this purpose under the British pattern of Parliamentary government. Members are continually taking up constituents' complaints in correspondence with ministers, and bringing citizens' grievances, great or small to Parliament, where ministers individually and Her Majesty's Government collectively are accountable. We do not want to create any new institution which would erode the functions of Members of Parliament in this respect nor to replace remedies which the British Constitution already provides. Our proposal is to develop those remedies still further. We shall give Members of Parliament a better instrument which they can use to protect the citizen, namely, the services of a Parliamentary Commissioner for Administration.

These proposals were carried out by the Parliamentary Commissioner Act 1967. The Parliamentary Commissioner is appointed by the Crown and holds office on terms similar to those applying to the superior judges except for a retiring age of 65. He is an *ex officio* member of the Council on Tribunals. The essential nature of the institution of the Parliamentary Commissioner is contained in the last sentence of the quotation from the White Paper: the viewpoint is that of a Member of Parliament who has what many members call a 'political surgery'. A member with good contacts and sufficient secretarial assistance can cope with the ordinary run of requests and complaints but there have always been some dead ends. If a member looks into a complaint and it seems to him that a government department is in some way at fault, he can write to the minister or ask a Question, or he may be able to get the matter before the Commons in some other way, but he cannot go behind the minister's statement. The Parliamentary Commissioner for Administration provides a means of doing so in certain cases. The problem with this arrangement from the citizen's point of view is that he may not know about it and may waste time trying to take his complaint to the Commissioner direct, or he may follow the proper procedure but come up against a Member of Parliament who is not sufficiently diligent to refer the matter on. To get around these problems, the Parliamentary Commissioner has been known to hand apparently genuine complaints sent directly to him to a Member of Parliament in order that the Member of Parliament may start proceedings in the proper form.[2]

[1] The Parliamentary Commissioner for Administration, Cmnd 2767.
[2] Sir Cecil Clothier, the Parliamentary Commissioner, admitted this in an address he gave in 1984, which is printed as 'Legal problems of an Ombudsman', (1984) 81 Law Soc. Gaz. 3108.

The 1967 Act allows a member to refer to the Commissioner a complaint received from an individual (whether one of his constituents or not) or from a company or other body (though not a complaint from a local or public authority). The Commissioner must then decide whether the matter is within the area in which he can investigate, as set out in the Act and consisting of a list of government departments but excluding a number of matters.[1]

In 1986 the Commissioner received 759 complaints; 611 were rejected because they obviously were, or proved after preliminary investigation to be, outside his jurisdiction. In 195 cases the investigation was completed and the result reported to the member. When an investigation is made, the object is not simply to find whether there was injustice but to find whether there was injustice caused by maladministration. 'Maladministration' is not defined, though as a guide 'bias, neglect, inattention, delay, incompetence, perversity, turpitude, arbitrariness and so on' have been cited. The Commissioner has the same powers as the High Court to examine witnesses on oath and to call for the production of documents, but the effective part of his powers is that he can require anyone in the department concerned, from the minister down through the staff, to furnish information, and he can and of course does look at the department's files (except for Cabinet proceedings and papers). These investigations are carried out in private by the Commissioner himself and a team of investigators. The government may prevent him from divulging information which it would be contrary to the public interest to divulge but he cannot be prevented from reporting his finding. The Commissioner has no power to order remedial action. Where the central government is concerned, this is of little consequence because remedial action is in fact taken if his findings show that such action is desirable; unfortunately the same is not always true as far as local authorities are concerned. (See page 167 below.) The Commissioner's prime function after investigating is to report. He gives the member the result of any inquiry, but as an officer of Parliament he reports, by annual report with additional special reports if he sees fit, and these reports come before a Select Committee of the House of Commons. Both the Commissioner's reports and the reports of the Select Committee are then published.

Inevitably, the institution of the Parliamentary Commissioner for Administration has disappointed people who expected an Ombudsman with extensive powers as well as people who looked forward to disclosures of juicy scandals. In reality it is much more like an audit, an impression perhaps helped by the fact that the first Commissioner previously held the office of Controller and Auditor General and reported to the Public Accounts Committee. The parallel with audit

---

[1] Further details may be found in 'The Parliamentary Commissioner for Administration', (1968) 10 *Journal SPTL*, by Sir Edward Compton (the then Commissioner); P. Jackson, 'The work of the Parliamentary Commissioner for Administration', [1971] *Public Law* 39. D. W. Williams, *Maladministration* (1976); the report by *Justice*, 'Our Fettered Ombudsman' (1977); and the address by Sir Cecil Clothier mentioned in the footnote above.

extends to the effect on departments: the object is not so much to catch people out as to ensure that proper methods are followed. It is only in a very wide sense that the Commissioner can be regarded as part of the machinery of justice – indeed, he is actually prohibited by Act of Parliament from investigating any case where the person aggrieved has a right of appeal to a special tribunal or a remedy by way of proceedings in a court of law[1] – but he is still referred to as the Ombudsman, with associated ideas about people appealing to him. The reality is that the Parliamentary Commissioner for Admininstration is a good and effective addition to public administration within a Parliamentary system.

The institution has been enough of a success to be copied. In 1973 an Act of Parliament provided for the appointment of two Health Service Commissioners, one for England and one for Wales; see chapter 15(ii). The Local Government Act 1974 provided for a Commission for Local Administration for England, which consists of three Local Commissioners and the Parliamentary Commissioner, and a similar Commission for Wales which consists of one Local Commissioner and the Parliamentary Commissioner. The principles are analogous to those applied to the Parliamentary Commissioner in that complaints should first be made to the Council department concerned and if that fails to satisfy, then a member of the authority should be asked to take the matter up. As with the Parliamentary Commissioner, the process is intended to reinforce the traditional role of a local elected member and there are very substantial limitations on the scope of investigations by Commissioners. They are concerned with maladministration, and apart from that they cannot go into the merits of decisions. As with the Parliamentary Commissioner, many of the complaints that people want to make, such as the level of rates or the conduct of police officers, are not within the sphere of these 'Ombudsmen'. Another problem is that some local authorities, unlike central government departments, stubbornly refuse to put matters right when maladministration is reported. This has led to pressure to give the Local Commission powers of enforcement.[2]

---

[1] By s.5(2) of the Parliamentary Commissioner Act 1967. The matter is discussed by Prof. A. W. Bradley in 'The role of the Ombudsman in relation to the protection of citizens' rights', [1980] 39 Camb. LJ 304.

[2] See *Local government: Enforcement of remedies* (1986) HC 448.

IV

CRIMINAL JURISDICTION

19

COURTS WITH ORIGINAL CRIMINAL JURISDICTION

Jurisdiction over serious crimes belongs to the Crown Court. This was created by the Courts Act 1971, and its constitutional document is now the Supreme Court Act 1981. This legal entity is usually spoken and written about as if it were a number of separate courts – 'Cambridge Crown Court', 'Snaresbrook Crown Court' and so forth. However, like the High Court, the Crown Court is really one single court with a number of branches operating in various places simultaneously. There are some 90 different Crown Court centres, one in every substantial town. The theory that the Crown Court is a single entity has an important legal consequence, namely that Crown Court jurisdiction is not territorial: a serious crime can be tried at the Crown Court in any part of the country, whether near or far from the place where it was committed. Trial in the Crown Court takes place before a legally qualified judge and, if there is a plea of 'not guilty', a jury. For the most serious offences the judge will be a High Court Judge, but most indictments are tried before a lower grade of full-time professional judge called a Circuit Judge, or a part-time legally-qualified judge called a Recorder or Assistant Recorder. The procedure is known as 'trial on indictment', because an indictment is the name for the formal document which states the offence for which the defendant is tried. The less serious criminal offences are tried in the magistrates' courts, of which there are at present around 630. Their constitutional document is the Magistrates' Courts Act 1980. Unlike the Crown Court, the jurisdiction of the magistrates' courts is broadly territorial, and the procedure which is followed in these courts is known as 'summary trial'. In a magistrates' court there is neither a judge nor a jury, and whether the defendant pleads guilty or not guilty, his case is heard and determined by a bench of magistrates, otherwise known as 'justices of the peace' or 'justices'. The bench usually consists of two or three lay justices, but exceptionally – and quite commonly in London – it will consist of a single stipendiary magistrate, who is full-time, paid and legally qualified. In either case the bench will be assisted – and in the case of lay magistrates, sometimes considerably more than assisted – by a legally qualified clerk.

Before the Crown Court was created in 1971 there were two overlapping but distinct systems of courts which tried offences on indictment: Assizes and Quarter Sessions. Both had ancient origins.

Jurisdiction over serious crime had become a matter for the judges by the fourteenth century. This jurisdiction was exercised primarily in the counties where the offences were committed, the court being that of the itinerant judge with a commission of *oyer and terminer* and gaol delivery. The civil work done by the itinerant justice was under the commission of assize, and the name of 'Assizes' became the common term for the court of the itinerant judge for both civil and criminal work. Lesser crime at first was dealt with in surviving local and franchise courts. The system was hardly satisfactory, since the jurisdiction of the inferior courts was limited, and too much of the time of the itinerant judge was taken up in hearing criminal cases of no great importance. The remedy was found in the office of justice of the peace. This office has late twelfth-century origins, but the important steps were taken in the fourteenth century. A statute provided that 'worthy' men were to be appointed to keep the peace and hear and determine felonies. Further statutes enacted that they were to hold their sessions four times a year; these gatherings became known as 'Quarter Sessions'. Before these statutes these worthy men were more conservators of the peace than justices; the duty of hearing and determining felonies made them 'justices of the peace', or more simply 'justices'. Justices of the peace were originally for counties only, but towns rose in importance and bargained with the King to get a charter giving them some measure of independence of their county, and these incorporated towns, called boroughs, commonly received the right to have their own justices of the peace. Hence there became two categories of justices; county justices with jurisdiction throughout the county, and borough justices with jurisdiction confined to their borough. For centuries we had a system where the most serious indictable offences were tried at Assizes, and the less serious ones at Quarter Sessions.

Assizes were a travelling court presided over by a High Court Judge. They visited the assize centres, which were generally the county towns, three or four times a year, originally only in the period when the High Court was on vacation. The assize system is described more fully elsewhere in this book.[1]

The constitution of Quarter Sessions varied as between Borough and County Sessions. Borough Quarter Sessions were originally composed in many and various ways, depending on the charter of the borough in question, but the Municipal Corporations Act 1835 laid down that when a borough had its own Quarter Sessions the court should consist of a legally qualified judge, called a Recorder,[2] who was appointed by the Crown, and paid for his services.

---

[1] See chapter 1. Those interested in their origins should consult J. S. Cockburn, *A history of English Assizes 1558–1714* (1972).

[2] The title Recorder has stood for three distinct offices: first, the judge at Borough Quarter Sessions; secondly, the full-time judges who formerly presided at the Crown Courts at Liverpool and Manchester; and thirdly, the part-time professional judge who does much of the work of the Crown Court today.

Recorders had to be barristers of at least five years' standing, and Recorderships of boroughs were attractive offices for barristers, because they could be combined with continued practice at the Bar, and were a usual stepping-stone to the High Court Bench. Hence they generally attracted people who were very suitable to preside over a jury trial. Until 1971 County Quarter Sessions, on the other hand, consisted of the justices of the peace for the county (or a number of them) assembled together. At one time it was not unusual to find that the bench consisted of twenty or more justices, and even when the maximum number was reduced by statute to nine in 1949 there could still be an inconveniently large body to preside over a jury trial. To make matters worse, they were free to elect their own chairman, who could be and at one time usually was a person with no legal training or qualifications. It was not until 1962 that County Quarter Sessions were required to have a legally qualified chairman, but long before then it had become usual to appoint one; and where there was a legally qualified chairman it inevitably happened that he became the centre of the proceedings, and the lay justices took a back seat.

The main problem in the post-war period was not the need to improve the quality of the various courts, however, but the need to cope with the increasing pressure of work. Two major social facts of our times are the soaring rate of divorce, and the ever-rising tide of crime. As the first inevitably led to big changes in the civil courts, so the second led to the complete rearrangement of the courts for trying serious criminal cases. The scale of the problem can be seen from figure 4. In fact matters were even more serious than the mere number of cases suggests, because whilst the number of defendants has increased, the speed at which the criminal courts get through their case-load has decreased; there are various reasons for this, but it mainly stems from the fact that legal aid now ensures that most defendants on serious charges have lawyers to defend them, and defence lawyers, unlike unrepresented defendants, usually put up a spirited and time-consuming fight. The result has been a continuing problem about the time which accused persons have to wait for trial. Pre-trial delays are an unmitigated evil for many reasons. They are needlessly stressful for the defendant, who has criminal proceedings endlessly hanging over his head, and are often quite as stressful for the witnesses. They make the criminal justice system inefficient, because during the delay vital witnesses may die, or go missing, or forget, with the result that the guilty get acquitted. Because many defendants have to be remanded in custody pending trial, delays also lead to hideous overcrowding and inhumane conditions in prisons, and to injustice to those who are held in custody; because although the time spent awaiting trial counts towards a defendant's sentence if he is convicted and sentenced to imprisonment, this is no consolation if he is fined or given a sentence shorter than the time he has already spent in prison; and even if such a defendant is eventually acquitted he has no right to compensation for his detention pending trial.

Before 1971 there were a number of attempts to contain the problem of delay

Courts with original criminal jurisdiction

Notifiable offences[a] recorded by the police per 100,000 population in England and Wales

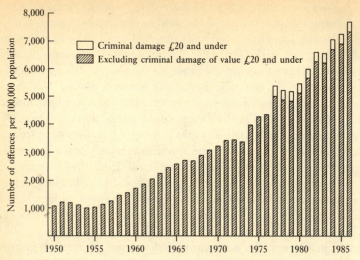

Criminal damage £20 and under

Excluding criminal damage of value £20 and under

[a] Indicates offences in 1978 and earlier years

Based on *Criminal Statistics*, HMSO

The caseload of the criminal courts 1965–85[b]

Year	Magistrates' courts	Assizes and Quarter Sessions to 1971, Crown Court 1972 onward		
	(1) Total persons proceeded against	(2) Total persons for trial or sentence	(3) Persons for trial	(4) Persons for sentence
1965	1,439,000	35,000	27,000	9,000
1970	1,777,000	58,000	44,000	14,000
1975	2,111,000	81,000	63,000	17,000
1980	2,378,000	88,000	74,000	14,000
1985	2,147,000	106,000	99,000	8,000

[b] Rounded to nearest 1,000

Based on *Criminal Statistics*, HMSO

Figure 4 The crime rate and the caseload of the criminal courts

within the existing system. There were rearrangements in the itineraries of the Assize Judges, and redistributions of work between Assizes and Quarter Sessions.[1] A lot of the less serious work was diverted downwards to the magistrates'

[1] Notably the Administration of Justice Act 1962, which carried out the recommendations of the Streatfield Committee, (1961) Cmnd 1289, and the Administration of Justice Act 1964, which reorganised Quarter Sessions in Greater London. For further details see the seventh edition of this book.

174

courts, and a lot of the more serious cases were diverted sideways into additional courts which were specially created. By far the oldest of these was in London, where since 1834 there had been a Central Criminal Court, commonly known as the Old Bailey, which acted as the Assize Court for the populous London area, and also as Quarter Sessions for the City of London. There were four sittings a year, but as each lasted for up to three months it was virtually a continuous court. As well as having a High Court Judge continually assigned to it, it had a number of full-time salaried judges of its own: namely the Recorder of the City of London, the Common Serjeant and various additional judges. Each sat separately, so there were several courts in session simultaneously. The other special courts were the Crown Court at Liverpool and the Crown Court at Manchester, which were established by statute in 1956. Each of these had a full-time judge called the Recorder, and the courts were in constant session.

In their day these measures prevented matters getting worse too quickly for a while, but there continued to be serious delays before trial. Furthermore, because Assizes dealt with civil work too, and because for obvious reasons the criminal work had to be given preference, delays in criminal cases had deplorable repercussions on civil litigation as well. Between 1967 and 1969 the Beeching Commission[1] concluded that the problems were inherent in the way in which the existing system of criminal courts was organised. The main cause of inadequacy was that everything was tied to the areas of local government, that is to counties, boroughs and London, and there was virtually no recognition of the principle of organising a service in the way which was most efficient and convenient to the public. In many instances, for example, two Quarter Sessions sat in the same town, one for the county and one for the borough. Other public services had long had a head office, regional offices and an operations level of offices sited so as to be convenient and accessible to people within an appropriate 'catchment area', but the system of criminal justice was rooted in history and insofar as it was ever intelligently planned it was devised for travel on horseback. A related problem was that the responsibility for the appointment and payment of staff, the provision of buildings and general organisation was inconveniently split between central and local government, with the result that no one was in overall control. And a final difficulty was that the whole system operated on the basis that the level of work would require courts to sit occasionally, when the rate of crime in many areas clearly required courts which were in continuous session. The Beeching Commission recommended that Assizes and Quarter Sessions should be abolished and replaced by a centrally organised system of criminal courts which could if need be sit continuously. Their recommendations were enacted by the Courts Act 1971, which gave us our present system.

---

[1] Royal Commission on Assizes and Quarter Sessions, (1969) Cmnd 4153.

175

i The Crown Court

The essence of the system which we now have for trying cases on indictment is that there is notionally only one higher court, namely the Crown Court, which is separate from the High Court, but is organised and run together with the High Court as part of an integrated system. Just as the High Court consists of a number of judges sitting for the most part singly in court-rooms in London or twenty-six places in the provinces, so the Crown Court consists of judges (with juries in cases that are defended) sitting singly or in some cases with justices of the peace in court-rooms at some 90 centres in London and elsewhere in England and Wales. The Crown Court thus sits at more centres than the High Court, and necessarily also uses a bigger pool of judges. High Court Judges sit in the Crown Court, and have jurisdiction to try any kind of case there, but are used only for the most serious cases. The bulk of the work is done by Circuit Judges, Recorders and Assistant Recorders. The qualities and qualifications of these different types of judges are discussed in chapter 31.

For the purpose of administering the higher courts, civil as well as criminal, England and Wales is divided into six circuits, each based on a major city: Midland and Oxford (Birmingham), North Eastern (Leeds), Northern (Manchester), South-Eastern (London), Wales and Chester (Cardiff) and Western (Bristol). Each has its own staff of administrators, and its own presiding judge. Within each circuit there are a number of court centres which are ranked in three levels of importance, and at all of them the Crown Court sits. The first-tier and second-tier centres are regularly visited by High Court Judges,[1] and there the full range of indictable offences can be tried. The third-tier centres are usually visited only by Circuit Judges and Recorders, and are for the trial of less weighty matters. The various centres are listed in an Appendix to this book, together with a map. The system is less rigid than the map suggests, however, and can be adjusted, temporarily or otherwise, to meet demand. Section 78 of the Supreme Court Act 1981 provides that any Crown Court business may be conducted at any time or place in England and Wales which the Lord Chancellor may direct. Thus High Court Judges are sometimes sent to third-tier centres, and the Crown Court occasionally sits at remote places – Penzance, for example – which are not regular centres at all.

Because High Court Judges are considered more suitable than Circuit Judges and Recorders for handling difficult and sensitive cases, rules are made to distribute cases to the type of judge who is best fitted to deal with it. By section 75 of the Supreme Court Act 1981 the Lord Chief Justice, with the concurrence of the Lord Chancellor, issues Practice Directions which grade indictable offences in various categories of seriousness and allocate them between the different types

[1] The difference between a first- and a second-tier centre is that High Court Judges sit at first-tier centres for the conduct of civil business: see chapter 6.

of Crown Court judge. Directions given in 1987[1] set up a four-fold classification. Class 1 consists of a small number of offences of the greatest difficulty and seriousness which must always be tried by a High Court Judge; it includes treason, murder, and offences under the Official Secrets Act 1911 s.1. A particular murder may, however, be released for trial by a Circuit Judge approved by the Lord Chief Justice. Class 2 comprises a small number of slightly less serious offences, which must be tried by a High Court Judge unless the presiding judge of the Circuit orders otherwise in a particular case: manslaughter, abortion and related offences, rape, sexual intercourse with girls under 13, sedition, mutiny and certain other offences. Rapes and serious sexual offences against children may only be released for trial before a Circuit Judge who has been approved by the Lord Chief Justice. Class 4, which is very large, consists of offences which, although triable by a High Court Judge, are normally to be tried by a Circuit Judge or a Recorder. It includes wounding, theft, fraud, robbery, burglary, and reckless driving. Class 3 is a residual category consisting of all offences not in any of the other classes. These may be tried by any judge competent to sit in the Crown Court and no legislative preference is expressed. Causing death by reckless driving, for example, comes into this category. Class 3 offences are normally listed for trial by a High Court Judge.

As a matter of law any Crown Court has jurisdiction to try any indictable offence from any part of the country. Where a case is sent for trial is in the first instance a matter for the magistrates at the committal proceedings. The magistrates are not completely free to send the case where they please, however, because defined catchment areas are fixed by the presiding judges of the circuits and the magistrates are expected to adhere to these. For offences in class 1, 2 or 3 they will commit to the most convenient first- or second-tier court. For a class 4 offence they commit to the Crown Court which has been administratively designated as the normal court to receive their committals; if this is a third-tier court they may nevertheless commit to a first- or second-tier court if they think there are circumstances which make trial before a High Court Judge desirable. The court officials who prepare the lists have power to overrule the decision of the magistrates and to send the case to a different court, a power which enables them to divert cases around legal traffic-jams in particular locations. The place where a case is to be tried may be hotly disputed, not only on grounds of convenience but also because of allegations of local racial or other influences, any of which may be thought to affect jurors. For this reason both the prosecutor and the defendant are given a right to object to a proposed venue, and such objections must be heard in open court before a High Court Judge.

The Crown Court system is almost entirely based on rational analysis and planning and there is only one marked survival of ancient privilege: nothing must

---

[1] Practice Direction (Crime: Crown Court Classification and allocation) [1987] 1 WLR 1671.

appear to be altered that affects the dignity of the City of London. The Crown Court sitting in the City of London accordingly continues to be known as the Central Criminal Court (Old Bailey) and the Lord Mayor of the City and the Aldermen of the City are entitled, as they were in the past, to sit as judges in the Old Bailey (which they have in fact done only in a ceremonial way). The working judges in the Old Bailey are the visiting Queen's Bench Division judges, the Recorder, the Common Serjeant, and a number of Circuit Judges. The Recorder continues to be appointed by the City (and then is appointed by the Crown to exercise judicial functions) and the Common Serjeant continues to be appointed by the Crown, but by statute both are now Circuit Judges. The City continues to own the court-house but must make it available for courts and must not alter it without consent of the Lord Chancellor.

Justices of the Peace were members of the court in the days of County Quarter Sessions, and when these were abolished in 1971 there was much discussion as to whether they should play any part in the Crown Court. The Beeching Commission recommended that justices should sit (but only as assessors) but by the Courts Act 1971 they were given a definite place as full members of the court for certain purposes. When the Crown Court is sitting as an appeal court from decisions in the magistrates' court, or dealing with cases committed by a magistrates' court to the Crown Court for sentence, it is required by statute to sit with a number of justices of the peace in addition to a judge (and there is no jury). For most purposes there must be not less than two and not more than four, but the number varies according to the type of business, and for licensing appeals and appeals from a juvenile court there are further requirements about their sex and experience. The details are to be found in the Crown Court Rules which are made by a statutory Committee.[1]

For trials on indictment the presence of justices is possible but not mandatory. The Practice Direction which classifies offences for trial before the various types of judge originally decreed that all Class 4 offences were suitable for Circuit Judges or Recorders sitting with justices, but in 1986 the Direction was revised so that magistrates are only to be used in proceedings for Class 4 offences where the defendant pleads guilty. This means that they may take part in sentencing offenders but no longer in trials where the defendant's guilt is contested. In all the instances when justices sit they are theoretically full members of the court, and it is provided by statute that in the event of disagreement the decision may be by a majority, subject to the judge's casting vote if the panel is evenly divided; but a Court of Appeal decision limits this to decisions on point of fact, and lays down that on any question of law the justices must accept the judge's ruling.[2]

In the Crown Court, unlike in the magistrates' courts, the prosecutor must be legally represented and if he is a lay person he is not permitted to conduct his own case.[3] The defendant is entitled to conduct his defence in person if he wishes, but

[1] The current set is the Crown Court Rules 1982, SI 1982 as amended in 1984.
[2] *R* v. *Orpin* [1975] QB 283.   [3] *R.* v. *George Maxwell (Developments) Ltd.* [1980] 2 All ER 99.

it has become very rare for him to do so. If the matter is sufficiently serious for the Crown Court he will usually be willing to pay for legal representation if he can afford it, and if he cannot afford to pay he will always get legal aid, because since the late 1960s it has been official policy to see that no defendant in the Crown Court is left unrepresented because he is too poor.[1]

Representation usually means a barrister, but there are some cases where a solicitor is permitted to appear. The rules on rights of audience are made by the Lord Chancellor acting under delegated statutory powers, and they are complicated. There is a running battle between the two sides of the legal profession over this, solicitors wishing to obtain the right of audience in the Crown Court and barristers seeking to keep it as their exclusive preserve, and the present rules embody a messy compromise, partly based on history. Before the Crown Court came into being barristers alone could appear at Assizes, but it was up to each court of Quarter Sessions to make its own rules on who could appear, and some – mainly ones remote from London – gave audience to solicitors. The present rules accordingly permit solicitors to appear in Class 4 cases tried at Caernarvon, Barnstaple, Bodmin, Doncaster, and (subject to further restrictions) at Lincoln. Elsewhere barristers enjoy the exclusive right of audience for Crown Court trials. When the Crown Court is hearing an appeal from a magistrates' court at any centre, a solicitor is permitted to appear, provided he or a member of his firm appeared in the proceedings appealed from. When the Crown Prosecution Service came into being it was widely expected that Crown Prosecutors would be permitted to conduct their own Crown Court cases, but the Bar fought hard to defend its monopoly, and succeeded, at least temporarily. The Crown Prosecution Service must for the present brief counsel to conduct its cases, but section 4 of the Prosecution of Offences Act 1985 empowers the Lord Chancellor to grant Crown Prosecutors rights of audience in future if he so decides.

The reforms which gave us the Crown Court system in 1971 were largely inspired by a desire to reduce the unacceptable delays which occurred because the existing system of courts was unable to cope with the rising pressure of work. Unfortunately the new system has not succeeded in eliminating delays, and as with the earlier attempts to streamline the system of Quarter Sessions and Assizes, the best that can be said is that the changes have slowed the pace at which matters have been getting steadily worse. The Crown Court, like its predecessors, has been struggling to keep up with the ever-rising volume of work, and the only consolation for reformers is the thought that without the Courts Act 1971 things would have been indescribable by now.

It is not easy to analyse the problem of delay intelligibly. Before 1972 figures on time spent awaiting trial were not regularly published and are only to be obtained from occasional studies,[2] and the annual figures since then have not always

---

[1] See chapter 40. In 1986, 118,463 persons were tried on indictment; all but 679 were legally represented, 1,669 privately and 116,115 on legal aid.

[2] Notably the Home Office Research Unit paper, *Time spent awaiting trial* (1960), the Streatfield

appeared in a form which made them comparable with what came before.[1] In addition there are differences in local conditions, so that there is often congestion in some courts and not in others. Nevertheless a picture emerges which is inescapably gloomy. A study in 1956[2] showed that the average time between committal by the magistrates and trial was around five weeks, with better figures in London where courts were in permanent session. The problem, insofar as there was one, was that in the provinces a defendant might have to wait nearly twice as long as this for trial at Assizes. In 1961 the Magistrates' Association told the Streatfield Committee that a norm of not more than four weeks' waiting time was feasible and the Beeching Commission said: 'We think it right that the aim should be to hold the waiting time as close as possible to four weeks, particularly when the accused is in custody.'[3]

In 1972, when the Crown Court first came into operation, the average period of delay between committal and trial across the country had risen to over 11 weeks, which varied locally from six to seven weeks in places where the courts were least crowded to almost 23 weeks in London. For a short time the Crown Court gained on the backlog of work and waiting times began to fall; but by 1979 the average delay had risen to over 17 weeks, with a local average of nine to ten weeks where things were going well and an average of over 30 weeks in London. There were horrifying instances where cases took more than a year to come to trial when defendants were remanded in custody, and over two years when they were free on bail. A determined attempt to tackle the problem followed in which many extra permanent judges were appointed and a large number of temporary Assistant Recorders were drafted in to help, and since then waiting lists have shortened; but in 1986 the national average waiting time was still 14 weeks from committal to trial, with nine weeks where the courts were least congested, and delays of over 23 weeks in London. It is hard to disagree when *The Times* began a leading article by saying 'The manner in which men and women are held prisoner while awaiting trial is a blot on English criminal justice.'[4]

One solution to these problems is to go on providing more resources: more judges, and more courtrooms for the trial of cases, as is already being done. The number of Circuit Judges rose from 307 in 1979 to 371 in 1985, and the number of Recorders from 412 to 445. In 1985 it was announced that an extra 40 courtrooms were being planned and should be available by 1988. Another method is to divert yet more cases from the Crown Court to the magistrates'

Committee (1961) Cmnd 1289 and the special statistical survey conducted for the Beeching Commission and published as a supplement to its Report (1969) Cmnd 4153.

[1] The information was given in *Statistics of Judicial Administration* for 1972–74, and since then has appeared in the annual *Judicial Statistics*.

[2] Published as *Time spent awaiting trial* in 1960.

[3] (1969) Cmnd 4153 para. 200.

[4] 1 November 1984. The Judicial Statistics for 1987, which appeared when this book was at the proof stage, show waiting times down to 12.3 weeks nationally and 19.6 weeks in London. This is encouraging, even if it does not mean the problem of delay is solved.

courts, where delays are generally less, and where delays matter less if they do occur because fewer of the cases involve defendants who will be held in custody pending trial. This was done wholesale when the Criminal Law Act 1977, enacting the proposals of the James Committee, provided that drink-driving offences and many others should be triable only in the magistrates' courts, and made another list of offences which were previously triable on indictment only into 'either-way offences', triable summarily with the consent of the accused. There may be further scope for this sort of change, but clearly there are limits to how much of the excess of Crown Court work can be dumped onto the magistrates' courts, because in some parts of the country these are already overworked and experiencing serious delays. Part of the problem of Crown Court delay could be simply that too few of the people in the story have any real perception that delay is a problem, and another approach to Crown Court delays is to try to instil a sense of urgency into court officials and lawyers acting on both sides. In Scotland there exists the '110-day rule' – a statutory rule, first enacted in 1701, which provides that if a person is not brought to trial within 110 days of committal the proceedings are automatically terminated. Similar rules exist in some jurisdictions in the United States. In the hope that a deadline might concentrate the minds of those involved, a section was included in the Prosecution of Offences Act 1985 giving the Secretary of State power to fix similar time-limits in England: 'custody time limits', setting a maximum length of time after which a person remanded in custody would have to be released on bail, and 'overall time limits', at the end of which a defendant if not tried, would be deemed acquitted. Following an experiment in certain areas, Regulations were made in 1987 making 'custody time limits' officially binding in the experimental areas.[1] (No overall time limits have yet been imposed in any areas). The 'custody time limits' are 70 days from first appearance to committal for trial, and 112 days from committal to the start of the Crown Court proceedings. The success of the scheme in these areas will determine whether the idea is more extensively applied. The court has a discretion to override the time limit, and where the real cause of the delay is simply an excess of work 'the main effect of custody time limits could be time-consuming discussions in court about whether or not the delay is attributable to the prosecution'.[2]

Another point to consider is the amount of time that trials take up. In our system, which provides for a very speedy disposal where the defendant pleads guilty and very protracted proceedings where he contests the case, Crown Court productivity is closely related to how many defendants plead guilty, and this in turn depends on a balance between the incentives which the system offers guilty people to induce them to plead guilty – quicker trial dates, lower costs and lower

[1] Prosecution of Offences (Custody Time Limits) Regulations 1987, SI 1987, 299.
[2] Corbett and Korn, 'Custody time limits in serious and complex cases: Will they work in practice?', [1987] Crim. LR 737; see also Julie Vennard in [1985] Crim. LR 73–83.

sentences – and the chance they think they have of a jury incorrectly acquitting them.[1]

The practices of lawyers are also important. A prosecuting counsel who has read and mastered his brief days before the trial will present a complicated case much more quickly than one who reads it for the first time in the train on the way to court. A defence counsel who advises his client to plead guilty when the case is about to start wastes court time, but saves it if his advice is given and accepted early enough for another contested case to be listed instead. Yet the way in which the work in barristers' chambers is organised ensures that barristers, who have a virtual monopoly of appearing in the Crown Court, quite often get their briefs too late to do adequate preparation. It may be that in order to tackle the problem of Crown Court delay effectively we need not merely more court-rooms and more judges, but a major review of criminal justice, embracing questions of Crown Court jurisdiction, the rules of criminal evidence and procedure, the question of who has the right of audience in the Crown Court, and also the way the work is organised at the criminal Bar.

Before leaving the higher criminal courts there are two historical points which are worth mentioning. The first is that at one time all peers, and the wife or widow (until remarriage) of a peer, charged with treason or felony,[2] had to be tried by peers. If Parliament was not sitting the trial could take place before the Lord High Steward with a panel of peers to act as a jury. The last case was in 1686. If Parliament was in session the trial was in the House of Lords. The court consisted of such of the lords of Parliament who cared to attend during the whole of the proceedings, and they were judges of both fact and law; although it was usual for a number of judges to attend to advise. The last occasion on which this amazing procedure was used was in 1935 when Lord de Clifford was tried for manslaughter in the driving of a motor-car and acquitted. The cost of this prosecution was £700 at a time when a trial at the Central Criminal Court would have cost the prosecution £75, and shortly afterwards the House passed a motion condemning the trial of peers by peers.[3] It was abolished without opposition in 1948.

The second historical point to mention is that the Queen's Bench Division of the High Court at one time had an important original criminal jurisdiction. This fell into disuse early in this century and was eventually abolished in 1971. It is briefly described in chapter 6.

---

[1] See I. R. Scott, 'Crown Court productivity', [1980] Crim. LR 293.
[2] Felonies were originally the more serious criminal offences, the less serious being called misdemeanours. At one time there were important differences in the criminal procedure applicable to each, one of which was that peers were tried before the House of Lords for felony whereas for misdemeanours they were tried before the ordinary courts. The distinctions between felonies and misdemeanours were removed one by one over the years, and the last ones disappeared when the Criminal Law Act 1967 abolished felonies as a separate category.
[3] The *Proceedings on the trial of Lord de Clifford* were published by HMSO in 1936. The debate is 99 HL Deb. 5 Cols.381–418.

ii Magistrates' courts

The Crown Court has a high level of public visibility because of the serious crimes which are tried there, but it carries only a small amount of the burden of criminal justice. Well over 90 per cent of all criminal cases are dealt with in magistrates' courts. Most of this work is fairly trivial, but much of it is not. As well as minor motoring offences, the magistrates try large numbers of thefts, frauds, woundings and assaults, and more than half the number of people who go to prison nowadays are sent there by the magistrates' courts. At present there are about 630 magistrates' courts, and they are served by some 24,000 justices, of whom almost all are laymen; only 50 or so are professional stipendiary magistrates. Justices are appointed by the Queen acting through the Lord Chancellor, by whom they may also be dismissed; their qualifications, training, appointment and dismissal are discussed in chapter 33. Magistrates' courts vary greatly in size and volume of business. In the depths of the country there may be a single court sitting less than one day a week, but in a big city there will be a big court-house with a number of courts sitting simultaneously on every working day. It is the second type which has come to predominate in recent years, and not simply because of the increasing amount of crime. At the Home Office, which is the government department with responsibility for magistrates' courts, the policy has long been in favour of fewer and larger courts, in order to achieve economies of scale. Whilst the total number of justices has increased very greatly – by 7,500 from 1975 to 1985 – the number of separate benches has been steadily reduced. The 630 benches of the present day have replaced more than 1,000 which existed forty years ago.

'Magistrates' courts' is the dignified title which these courts were given by the Justices of the Peace Act 1949. Before that they were officially known as Courts of Summary Jurisdiction (often shortened to Summary Courts), or, when sitting for certain purposes, Petty Sessions. They were given their present title because changes in the values of words had led to criticism: 'summary' suggests something hurried, whilst 'petty' has come to carry a derogatory meaning. In everyday speech they were formerly known as 'police courts', and sometimes they still are. This was once a proper legal title, but only for the court of the stipendiary magistrate in London, whose official title was then 'metropolitan police magistrate'.[1] Whether used properly or improperly it was a most unfortunate name, because it gave the impression that these courts were and were meant to be controlled by the police.

The chief work of the magistrates is the hearing and determining of lesser offences, but they have a puzzling array of other duties. They hold committal proceedings in serious cases in order to decide if there is a matter fit to be sent to the Crown Court; they licence public houses and betting shops, and compel

---

[1] Because the first stipendiary magistrates paid their own police and personally controlled them.

husbands and fathers to maintain their deserted wives and children; they issue witness-orders, search-warrants, and detention warrants empowering the police to hold suspects for questioning; and they order the destruction of dangerous dogs. This remarkable range of business stems from the history of the office of justice of the peace, which was touched upon in the previous section.[1]

In the fifteenth and sixteenth centuries a great deal of administrative work was given by Parliament to the justices and they became the local government of the counties as well as their courts of criminal justice – a state of affairs which lasted until elected county councils were set up in 1888. Their licensing functions are a remnant of their former administrative duties, and so in a sense is their matrimonial jurisdiction, which they acquired as an off-shoot of their duties in respect of the poor-law. Committal proceedings, and their powers to issue warrants, stem from the fact that at one time they also fulfilled most of the duties which are nowadays carried out by the police. At one time it was the magistrates who hunted down suspected criminals, had them arrested, and sent them for trial at Assizes or Quarter Sessions. A statute of 1555 required the justices to question the suspect and other witnesses and record their answers in writing; the dossier they prepared was then forwarded to the court of trial and used as the basis of the case against the accused. When police forces were created in the nineteenth century, policemen quietly took over from the magistrates the job of catching criminals and 'getting up' the case against them, and the magistrates' job changed into that of someone who assesses the strength of the case prepared by the police and makes sure that only cases where there is a chance of obtaining a conviction are sent to trial. The change of function was recognised by a statute of 1848 which required their preliminary investigation to be conducted with a measure of legal formality. For many years evidence at committal proceedings was heard orally, which was usually a great waste of time where the police had already obtained written statements from the prosecution witnesses, because the magistrates could just as easily decide if there was a case fit to send to trial by reading the statements. Thus in 1967 the magistrates were given the power to commit for trial on an examination of the papers, provided the defendant is legally represented and consents, and most committals now take this form. Committal proceedings are discussed in greater detail below; see chapter 22(iv).

Unlike the Crown Court, the magistrates' courts are still organised and administered locally. The principal area of organisation is the 'Commission area'. The name comes from the Commission of the Peace, which is the formal document, emanating from the Lord Chancellor, which sets out the functions and duties of the justices for a given area and authorises them to act. At one time it used also to list the justices by name, and when a justice was appointed he was said to be 'put on the Commission', but since 1973 each justice has been appointed by a separate instrument. There are 90 Commission areas. Each

---

[1] A useful account of the history of justices is Esther Moir, *The Justice of the Peace* (1969).

county is a Commission area, and London is divided into six areas. Each Commission area (except the Inner London area, which has a separate arrangement for historical reasons) is administered by a Magistrates' Courts Committee. The constitution of these Committees is laid down by statute[1] and they are almost entirely composed of magistrates from that area. The Magistrates' Courts Committee appoints the justices' clerks and the administrative staff, and is responsible for providing court-rooms and equipment. The Home Office provides 80 per cent of the necessary funds and is the department responsible for the running of the magistrates' courts. The remaining 20 per cent comes from the local authority.

Commission areas are subdivided into various 'petty sessional divisions'. For each of these there is a bench of magistrates assigned to hear cases in that division, with a court-house where they will conduct business on a regular basis, and a justices' clerk, who may belong exclusively to that bench or whose services they may share with one or more other benches. Benches vary greatly in size. The smallest consist of a dozen justices or less, and never sit as more than one court at a time, and the largest number 150 or more, who sit as battery of courts in almost permanent session. The organisation of petty sessional divisions within the Commission area is done by the Home Secretary. In this he acts on the recommendation of the Magistrates' Courts Committee, but in the last resort he can require them to make reorganisations if necessary. The jurisdiction of the local bench is not limited to offences committed within that particular petty sessional division, but the jurisdiction of magistrates is partly territorial in the sense that it is limited to offences committed within the Commission area. Section 2 of the Magistrates' Courts Act 1980 restricts justices to trying summary offences which occurred in the Commission area, but insofar as they may deal with indictable offences at all, they deal with them wherever they were committed.

Where the bench consists of lay justices, the Magistrates' Courts Act normally requires at least two magistrates to be present. The maximum number who may sit together is fixed by Rules laid down by the Lord Chancellor. The present maximum is seven.[2] This number is too large, because so big a bench is difficult to address, and renders rapid consultation between the chairman and the members almost impossible; but there are few problems in practice, because lay benches are rarely composed of more than two or three. Stipendiary magistrates may sit alone for most purposes, and for committal proceedings a lay bench may consist of one.

Each petty sessional division is required to elect a chairman and one or more deputy chairman to act in his absence. The chairman presides when the justices

[1] Justices of the Peace Act 1979 s.20; Magistrates' Courts Committee (Constitution) Rules 1973. These Committees were introduced in 1949 on the recommendation of the Committee on Justices' Clerks (1944) Cmd 6507.
[2] Justices of the Peace (Size and Chairmanship of Bench) Rules 1986, SI 86/923.

act as a body, as when they have meetings for business, and the chairman or one of his deputies presides in the courtroom when judicial business is being conducted. The chairmanship of justices has had a not-too-happy history. The choice of chairman is supposed to be a democratic one, but especially on the smaller benches the tendency has often been for the office to go to the most senior justice, who then considers he has a right to it for ever, and takes grave offence if his colleagues try to replace him with anyone else. The Lord Chancellor makes Rules governing the election of the chairman, the 1986 version of which provides that the chairman shall be elected annually, and that where the same person has held office for five years he must stand down for at least three years unless in postal ballot three-quarters of his colleagues vote to waive this requirement.[1]

A key position in the magistrates' court is occupied by the justices' clerk, who is both legal advisor and manager. In his capacity as manager he takes care of the business of the bench, listing the cases for hearing, collecting the fines and compensation orders, and generally handling the paper-work. He also carries out many of the routine processes of summary jurisdiction, such as the issue of process, the summoning of witnesses, adjournments, transfer of enforcement to another court in whose area the defendant resides; and he also has the power to grant legal aid. If he is clerk to a small bench he will do this in person, but the clerk to a big city bench will have a sizeable staff of subordinates and his job will be that of director and supervisor. In his capacity of legal advisor he sits as clerk of the court where he guides the lay justices on procedure and advises them on the law. The clerk to a small bench will regularly sit in court himself, but where several courts sit at once he obviously cannot be in two places at the same time and the task of clerking the court will fall to a deputy clerk, or one of a number of assistants usually known as 'court clerks'. The justices' clerk remains under a duty to advise the magistrates even where this is the arrangement, and he may be called upon for help if any of 'his' – or 'her', because nowadays a number of justices' clerks are women – justices get in difficulties.

Much criticism of lay justices has centred round the clerk and the way he performs his duties. The principal trouble has arisen from the clerk accompanying the justices when they retire to discuss a case. It has long been recognised that justices may consult their clerk in private, but this has to be reconciled with the principle that it is the justices who make the decision, not the clerk. If the clerk always retires with the justices, or apparently decides for himself whether he goes out with them, or if he stays with them until they come back, a defendant or an advocate may believe that the clerk takes part in their decisions, or even tells them what to decide and what sentence to impose. Suspicion may also arise even when justices having retired send for their clerk, and he returns into court before they

---

[1] A worse problem used to exist in boroughs, because by statute the mayor – who might never have been in court before – was not only a justice *ex officio* but also entitled to take the chair. Mayors lost the right to preside in 1949 and ceased to be justices *ex officio* in 1968.

do; a defending solicitor may assert that there was no point of law or anything in the case on which the justices could have needed their clerk and deduce from that that the clerk had gone in to tell the justices what to do. In 1952 the Divisional Court startled justices and their clerks by appearing to rule in *R. v. East Kerrier Justices*[1] that clerks could not join justices in their retiring room except when there was a point of law. This was a quite unworkable proposition. Questions of law and fact are often closely intertwined: for example, the justices may need advice on the law of evidence in order to decide a question of fact; or when sentencing the justices may need guidance on the options legally open to them, and it might be highly undesirable to hold a debate on the subject in the presence of the defendant. Thus the *East Kerrier* decision has been heavily glossed by statute, in a series of decided cases and by various Practice Directions.[2]

The present position is roughly as follows. First, it is the duty of the justices' clerk to advise on questions of law and questions of mixed fact and law, and where it is a question of law, and the law is clear, the magistrates are expected to follow his advice; but it is not his duty to advise them on questions of fact. Secondly, he need not always wait to be asked, but 'may, at any time when he thinks he should do so, bring to the attention of the justices or justice any point of law, practice or procedure that is or may be involved in any question so arising'.[3]

Thirdly, he should advise in open court as far as possible; and although he may advise the justices privately he should normally wait to be asked and should normally return to court as soon as his advice has been given. Fourthly, it is part of his job to keep notes of the evidence as it is given, and it is proper for the justices to refresh their memories from his notes if they wish to do so.

From the number of times which this matter has come before the Divisional Court in recent years, it is plain that the rules governing the role of the justices' clerk are neither clear nor easy to apply. Various proposals have been made over the years to alter and clarify the position, usually in such a way as to elevate the status of the clerk. In 1964 there was a proposal that the clerk should be in a position similar to that of a judge advocate in a court martial. He should sit with two lay justices and he would have sole responsibility for ruling on questions of law, practice and procedure but would leave all the issues of fact to the two lay justices.[4] His rulings on law or practice or procedure would be given in open court. It is usual in considering any proposal of this kind to refer to the clerk's 'summing up' but his functions would not be like that of a judge summing up to a jury: it would not review the evidence but be confined to matters of law, practice and procedure and so be relatively brief. In 1966 Lord Parker CJ thought the

---

[1] [1952] 2 QB 719.
[2] Justices of the Peace Act 1979 s.28(3); Practice Notes: [1953] 1 WLR 1416; [1954] 1 WLR 213; [1981] 1 WLR 1163. The case-law, which is too bulky to list here, will be found in *Stone's Justices' Manual* Vol. 1 paras. 1–5. The most recent additions are reviewed in (1986) 150 JPN 340, 357.
[3] Justices of the Peace Act 1979 s.28(3).
[4] K. C. Clarke, 'The justices' clerk' [1964] Crim. LR 620, 697.

answer was to make a full-time clerk to the justices one of the justices himself. But a major objection to this is that magistrates need a clerk both to make notes and to remind them of things because whilst concentrating on a case it is very easy to overlook something that is relevant; if the clerk were a magistrate then the court in which he was sitting would need a clerk, and the clerk, if sitting as a magistrate, would not be acting as a clerk.[1]

The real difficulty about any proposal to raise the status of the clerk and to give him judicial functions, however, is whether the people who hold these jobs are really up to playing a bigger role. If the justices' clerks proper were the only people who sat as clerks in magistrates' courts there would be little difficulty. The modern justices' clerk must be a barrister or solicitor of five or more years' standing, and nowadays he is almost always a full-time professional with much experience behind him. But the same is far from true of the court-clerks who in practice do the bulk of the actual advising, many of whom are virtually unqualified, raw and young. The qualifications of justices' clerks and court clerks are further discussed in chapter 33.

It has already been mentioned that the magistrates' courts, like the higher criminal courts before the Courts Act 1971, are still locally organised and administered. The main authority is the local Magistrates' Courts Committee, and the power of the central government to interfere with their autonomy is limited: both as a matter of law, and also as a matter of practice, because central government responsibility for magistrates' courts is split between the Home Office, which handles finance, and the Lord Chancellor's Department, which deals with the appointment, removal and training of justices. This state of affairs has a number of major drawbacks.

The first is that it leads to great differences in the way that summary justice is administered in different areas. Of course, there is nothing wrong with local diversity as such. Often it is harmlessly picturesque, as when in the days of Quarter Sessions it was the custom in Dorset for the chairman to sit wearing a top hat. But in certain fundamental matters it is very mischievous. It is very unfair, for example, if a man who steals or punches a policeman or drives recklessly stands to go to prison in county A whereas in counties B, C or D he would probably get off with a fine or a probation order. And yet this seems to be the case. In 1985 the Home Office released figures which showed the most startling diversities in sentencing, so that, for example, in Brighton the justices gaoled some 30 per cent of those whom they dealt with for indictable offences, whereas in Lewes they gaoled only 14 per cent.[2]

As identified by a recent Home Office study,[3] the cause of this problem is that

---

[1] This point is made by Sir Frank Milton, the chief metropolitan magistrate, in his book *The English magistracy* (1967).

[2] These figures were issued to the National Association of Probation Officers, and extracts were published in *The Times* 27 November 1985.

[3] Tarling, Moxon and Jones, *Sentencing of Adults and Juveniles in Magistrates' Courts*, in *Managing criminal justice*, (ed. David Moxon) Home Office Research and Planning Unit (1985).

each bench operates in isolation, and although benches usually behave with internal consistency, most know little of sentencing practice outside their own courtroom and practically nothing of what goes on beyond their local Commission area. For many years the Home Office and the Magistrates' Association have tried to counteract this problem by issuing general guidance on sentencing, but evidently general advice is not enough. Similarly, it seems that some benches are quite generous in granting poor defendants legal aid, whilst others are rather mean, and different benches vary greatly in their willingness to grant bail to defendants pending trial.

A second drawback to the local organisation of magistrates' courts is that it sometimes means a physical distribution of courts which is neither economically efficient nor convenient to the users. Until the local government reorganisation of 1972 there were separate Commission areas for counties and for boroughs, and the distribution of petty sessions often still reflected the long-vanished division of counties into hundreds.[1]

As a result, it sometimes happened that an area comprising a town and the surrounding country that formed an obvious unit for shopping and services was divided into two for summary jurisdiction, each of which was in a separate Commission area, a state of affairs which was inconvenient and wasteful. The problems of inconvenience were largely solved by the Local Government Act 1972 which redrew the counties to fit the way in which the population is now distributed, and combined the separate borough Commission areas with their surrounding counties – a move which was generally followed by a rationalisation of the petty sessional divisions. But in some parts of the country old traditions die hard, and in 1986 there were still over 80 benches with twelve justices or less, many of which sat less than 30 times a year. The separate existence of little benches like this is almost always a needless waste of resources.

The third problem which results from local rather than central organisation concerns the recruitment and training of suitable staff. By statute a justices' clerk must be a barrister or solicitor of at least five years' standing, but as will be explained in chapter 33 the statutory qualifications for court clerks are minimal. Although the Magistrates' Courts Committees in some Commission areas restrict these posts to those who hold proper legal qualifications and take care to train those whom they appoint, this costs money; and in some areas they appoint the cheapest and least qualified applicants and train them badly. Thus the level of competence of the staff varies much from place to place. A related difficulty is that because the magistrates' courts are administratively separate from the rest of the court system, the staff are not interchangeable, career prospects are limited, and it is therefore harder to attract good people to work in the magistrates' courts.

How then have the magistrates' courts escaped being taken over by the central government? The explanation is local pride and resistance in the provinces to

[1] The hundred was a Saxon administrative division, and probably once represented the area of land necessary to support 100 families.

central control. Some of this is irrational, but not all of it. If freedom from central control means freedom to be idiosyncratic about sentencing, legal aid and bail applications, which is bad, it also means freedom to experiment with more efficient ways of organising business, which is good. Many of the advances in summary justice in recent years have come from local initiative and not from the centre. For example pre-trial reviews in summary cases, which are now commended by the Home Office, were begun by go-ahead justices' clerks in Nottingham acting without any central directive or statutory authority. Central control often causes a stunting of initiative, a compulsive urge by everyone to refer to higher authority instead of making decisions, and an attitude of mind in which it becomes more important to apply a rule than to solve a problem. In 1971 the Home Office publicly raised the question whether magistrates' courts should become a central government responsibility as part of a unified court system. The Magistrates' Association and the Justices' Clerks' Society responded to the Home Office memorandum in favour, but the Local Authority Associations were opposed to any such change. The government thereupon decided to leave the present position alone – a news item which the *Daily Telegraph* rather misleadingly reported under the headline 'Magistrates Stay Under the Control of Town Halls' – and there for the present the matter rests.[1]

Trial on indictment is much older than summary trial, and summary trial started life as an exception to the normal type of proceedings. Although it has become the more usual mode of trial, it remains in legal theory an exception. Thus all offences are presumed to be indictable, and for an offence to be capable of summary trial some statutory authority must be found which gives the magistrates jurisdiction over it, either in addition to the Crown Court or exclusively. The first summary offences were extremely minor matters like profane swearing and robbing orchards, which were not thought serious enough to warrant trial on indictment in any circumstances. During the nineteenth century, however, summary trial began to be thought suitable for matters which were potentially more serious, and a number of new crimes were created which could be tried either summarily or on indictment at the option of the prosecutor. Meanwhile it became accepted that the full procedures of the criminal law should not be applied to children and that trial on indictment before a jury was too cumbersome for adults charged with trifling thefts. Thus a number of indictable offences were made triable summarily in certain circumstances, usually at the option of the defendant. This development was carried further in the twentieth century, mainly in order to relieve the higher courts of some of their excess business. At one time different offences had different procedures for deciding when they should be tried summarily and when they should be tried on

[1] Another reason why magistrates' courts remain in local control is said to be rivalry between the Home Office – which is at present in part-control of them – and the Lord Chancellor's Department, which would almost certainly acquire control of them completely in the event of rearrangement, since the Lord Chancellor's Department runs the rest of the court system.

indictment, and there was no uniformity. By the 1970s offences could be divided into six different categories: purely indictable offences, purely summary offences, and four intermediate classes of offence triable either way, each with a different set of rules. In addition, there was little overall planning, and many crimes triable only on indictment were less serious than similar matters which magistrates could try. This hideous tangle was referred to a committee headed by Lord Justice James,[1] and this produced some excellent proposals for rationalisation, almost all of which were enacted in the Criminal Law Act 1977. This divides offences into three categories. First, there are 'offences triable only on indictment' – often called 'purely indictable offences'. Into this category are placed those offences which are considered to be too weighty for summary trial even at their least serious: the main examples are homicide, rape, kidnapping, robbery, wounding with intent, conspiracy and spying. Magistrates may not try this type of offence at all, and their only duty is to check that the prosecution evidence discloses the elements of the offence charged, and if it does to commit the case to the Crown Court for trial. Secondly, there are 'offences triable only summarily', alias 'summary offences' or 'purely summary offences'. These are all those which are officially considered unsuitable for the Crown Court, even at their most serious. This category largely consists of an enormous list of fairly trivial regulatory offences like having a television without a licence and failing to inform the Minister of Agriculture of the castration of a breeding bull; but it also contains a number of more substantial offences, including assaulting the police, threatening or insulting behaviour likely to lead to a breach of the peace, indecent exposure, using motor-vehicles under the influence of alcohol, and criminal damage below a value which at the time of writing is £400, but which the Criminal Justice Bill proposes to raise to £2,000. These offences are exclusively triable in the magistrates' courts, and they only come before the Crown Court where the defendant appeals against conviction or sentence; see chapter 21 below.

The third category is 'offences triable either way', usually known as 'either-way offences'. This consists of offences which are often trivial, but are frequently serious enough to justify taking up the time of the Crown Court: the most common examples are theft, fraud, burglary, reckless driving, indecent assault, arson, criminal damage in excess of £400 (shortly to become £2,000), drug offences, and the less serious offences of wounding. Where it is an either-way offence the Director of Public Prosecutions (or a Crown Prosecutor acting for him) has the right to require the case to be tried in the Crown Court. Where, as is usual, this power is not exercised, it is up to the magistrates to decide whether the case is more suitable for summary trial or for trial on indictment, which they do at a preliminary investigation known as 'mode of trial proceedings'.

Mode of trial proceedings begin with the clerk of the court reading the charge to the defendant, after which first the prosecution and then the defence have the

[1] Report of the Committee on the Distribution of Criminal Business between the Crown Court and the Magistrates' Courts (James Committee), (1975) Cmnd 6323.

opportunity to express their views on whether the case should be tried summarily or should go to the Crown Court. The magistrates then form a view as to the appropriate method of trial. In doing so section 19 (3) of the Magistrates' Courts Act requires them to consider 'whether the circumstances make the offence one of serious character; whether the punishment which a magistrates' court would have power to inflict for it would be adequate; and any other circumstances which appear to the court to make it more suitable for the offence to be tried in one way rather than the other'. If they decide to send the case to the Crown Court their decision is final, the defendant has no right to argue with them: they simply tell him, and go on to the next stage, which will be a committal for trial (see chapter 22). If they decide it is a suitable case for summary trial then it can only be tried summarily provided the defendant consents to this, and the magistrates must therefore tell him what their view is and ask him if he consents to summary trial. If he consents they then proceed to try him – either then, or after an adjournment. If he does not consent he has to be tried on indictment, and the magistrates then hold committal proceedings. In fact the great majority of defendants do consent; the criminal statistics for 1985 reveal that approximately eight out of every ten either-way offences are tried summarily in the magistrates' courts.[1]

With two major exceptions the Criminal Law Act 1977 divides crimes between the Crown Court and the magistrates in a rational and fair manner. The first concerns assaulting the police. Prosecutions for this offence sometimes involve issues of civil liberties and allegations of excessive force by the police. In this respect they are like civil actions for malicious prosecution and false imprisonment which for civil libertarian reasons carry a right to jury trial. The offence is also seriously regarded and a conviction often lands the defendant in prison. It is therefore both odd and rather unfair that assaulting the police is a purely summary offence and the defendant has no right to jury trial. Before 1977 it was triable either summarily, when the maximum penalty was six months (nine on a second conviction), or on indictment, when it was two years; but the choice as to mode of trial lay with the prosecution. The James Committee thought this was indefensible and recommended that it should be an either-way offence, with a right to jury trial at the defendant's option, 'unless the maximum penalties are severely curtailed'. But the Home Office, which was responsible for drafting the Criminal Law Act 1977, wanted it to be a summary offence only – because, so cynics say, magistrates are readier to believe police evidence than are juries. The issue was fudged by reducing the maximum penalty from two years to six months; but as this was all that the magistrates could usually give for the offence anyway the maximum penalty was not in truth 'severely curtailed'. The other oddity concerns petty thefts, which are either-way offences, and in the form of

---

[1] But a recent Home Office study shows that the proportion of either-way offences committed to the Crown Court is increasing: Riley and Vennard, Triable-Either-Way Cases: Crown Court or Magistrates' Court?, Home Office Research Study 98, (1988).

shoplifting are said to take up some 14 per cent of the time of the Crown Court, at any rate in London. The punishment for minor shoplifting is hardly ever more than a fine, and the James Committee recommended that theft of property below £20 in value should be a summary offence only. However, as was mentioned earlier, this proposal in the Bill was defeated in Parliament after a lot of heated opposition, mainly on the ground that a conviction for theft, however petty, has a very serious effect on a person's reputation. Quite why a conviction for petty theft should be so much more damaging than one for the purely summary offences of minor vandalism, fare-dodging or indecent exposure nobody can ever explain; but some legal matters are so emotional that rational argument becomes impossible.

Something which is undoubtedly inconvenient in the present system is the fact that the Crown Court cannot deal with any related summary offences when it disposes of an indictable offence. If a man gets drunk, accidentally kills someone with his car and then drives off without stopping he has clearly committed two summary offences – failure to stop and drunken driving – and arguably has also committed the indictable offences of manslaughter and causing death by reckless driving. If he is tried for these at the Crown Court it is time-wasting and inconvenient if the case has to be in effect reheard in the magistrates' court before he can be dealt with for the drink-driving and the failure to stop: but if he is to be punished for these, that is what must happen. Over the years there were one or two piecemeal changes under which the Crown Court acquired jurisdiction to deal with specific summary offences committed in connection with specific indictable offences, and the Criminal Justice Bill which is before Parliament at the time of writing will solve the problem by giving the Crown Court wide general powers to deal with incidental summary offences.

Although the rules which have been mentioned permit almost all serious offences to go to the Crown Court they are not enough to ensure that this always happens, and occasionally very serious cases which should have gone to the Crown Court end up before the magistrates. This can happen because English criminal procedure gives the prosecutor a free choice in what offence he charges, and requires the court to try the offence which was charged, not the one which should have been. Thus it is open to the prosecutor if he wishes to undercharge, which he sometimes does, usually in order to make sure of getting a guilty plea. This not infrequently happens with motoring cases. Many or most fatal highway accidents are prima facie cases of causing death by reckless driving. This is a purely indictable offence with a maximum penalty of five years, but offending drivers are often prosecuted in the magistrates' courts for such purely summary offences as careless driving or excess blood alcohol, to which in such cases they are inclined to plead guilty. This saves a deal of valuable time for the Crown Court, the prosecutors and the police; at the cost, sometimes, of great feelings of outrage in the relatives of the deceased.

20

CORONERS' COURTS

The coroner's court may be mentioned in connection with criminal courts, for although it is not a criminal court it has some connection with criminal proceedings.[1] There are some 350 coronerships in England and Wales. It is a very old office, originally designed for protecting the fiscal rights of the Crown. Violent deaths were a concern of the coroner because in the past they sometimes brought revenue to the Crown through fines, deodands,[2] and forfeiture of the chattels of a convicted person. The coroner also had the custody of many records. In the course of time the holding of inquests on sudden deaths became the substantial part of the work of coroners. Nowadays the coroner is largely governed by statute, namely the Coroners Act 1988, which consolidates earlier legislation, and Rules made by the Lord Chancellor under delegated powers which this Act gives him. However, it is still the case that the office has more survivals of past ages than any other part of our system. Except where there are special rights, coroners for counties are appointed by the local government authority for the area in question, the appointments being made from barristers, solicitors or legally qualified medical practitioners. The amount of work, and the salary, varies considerably in different localities. Cases are brought to the notice of the coroner by the police, by various public authorities, and by members of the public. The coroner, with the assistance of his officer or the police generally, makes enough inquiries to decide whether an inquest is necessary. An inquest must be held when the dead body of a person is lying in the jurisdiction and there is reasonable cause to suspect that such person has died a violent or unnatural death, or a sudden death of which the cause is unknown, or has died in prison or in other places or circumstances mentioned by statute. In the case of a sudden death of which the cause is unknown, the coroner can order a post-mortem examination, and if the result shows death from natural causes the coroner may dispense with an inquest. Originally an inquest always involved a jury; but in 1926 the coroner

---

[1] The standard work is Knapman and Powers, *Thurston's Coronership* (3rd ed. 1985).
[2] An object that caused a death was forfeited. 'Horses, oxen, carts, boats, millwheels and cauldrons were the commonest of deodands' (Pollock and Maitland, *History of English Law* (2nd ed. 1898) II, 471–72). The object or its value was often devoted to pious uses. The rule of deodand represented a survival of very early ideas. Abolition came in 1846, hastened, it is said, by fears that whole railway trains might get forfeited.

was given the power to dispense with a jury in certain types of case, and this power was widened considerably by the Criminal Law Act 1977.

The coroner's court is a court of law, but it cannot be fitted into any classification of courts. Law courts are primarily concerned with *issues*, that is, the decision of points as between contesting parties. The coroner's court is a fact-finding body, incapable of trying any issue, civil or criminal. It is not part of the function of the court to attach blame to anyone for the death which has occurred, and if the verdict indirectly implies that someone is to blame, no civil or criminal court is later bound by that finding; although obviously the police and the dependants may find the inquest useful as a preliminary survey of the evidence. This was not always the case: at one time the decisions of coroners' courts were much concerned with the public attachment of blame for deaths, and when blame was so attached, unpleasant legal consequences would often follow automatically. At one time it was open for the inquest to return a verdict of murder, manslaughter or infanticide by a named person, and where such a verdict was returned the person accused was then automatically committed for trial. The opportunities for a coroner's court to commit for trial in this way were reduced in 1926, when it was provided by statute that where a coroner was officially notified that somebody had been charged before the justices with homicide he must adjourn his inquest until after the criminal proceedings. Where the police had not charged anyone, however, there was nothing to stop the inquest being held and resulting in a committal for trial. This was unsatisfactory, for the coroner's court does not have to observe any rules of evidence, and this placed suspected persons in a difficult position: some inquests contrived to look like badly conducted trials for murder. In 1977, following the recommendation of the Broderick Committee,[1] inquests were forbidden by statute to pronounce any person guilty of murder, manslaughter or infanticide, and the power to commit for trial was taken away altogether. It still remained possible, however, for a coroner's jury to act to cast the public blame for a death upon someone by returning a verdict with a 'rider' that so-and-so was to blame. But this is now prohibited by the Coroner's Rules 1984, s.42 of which provides that no verdict shall be framed in such a way as to appear to determine any question of civil or criminal liability.[2]

This change has not been fully understood by the public, nor is it altogether liked by those who do understand it. Most sudden deaths are not particularly

---

[1] Report of the Committee on Death Certification and Coroners (1971) Cmnd 4810. There were earlier committees on coroners, including one in 1936 (Cmd 5070).

[2] The change was originally made in 1980, very quickly after the relatives of one Blair Peach, who had died from a blow to the head in the course of a political demonstration in London, tried to use the inquest as a means of establishing that the fatal blow had been struck by the police: *R.* v. *Hammersmith Coroner ex pte. Peach* [1980] 2 WLR 496. For their further efforts, see *Peach* v. *Metropolitan Police Commissioner* [1986] QB 1064. In *R.* v. *Southwark Coroner ex pte. Hicks* [1987] 1 WLR 1624, it was held that a coroner's jury is nevertheless entitled to record a verdict of 'lack of care' when someone in prison is given insufficient medical treatment.

sinister and it is quite sufficient for an inquest to be held which is solely concerned with establishing the cause of death. But there are some which give rise to acute public anxiety, particularly those in which the police are thought to be involved, or are said to have been insufficiently enthusiastic in looking for the people who were; and here there is a widespread feeling that what is needed is a public inquiry which is able to establish responsibility for the disaster as well as the physical cause of death. However, the trouble with coroner's courts when it comes to these highly contentious cases is that they are simply not up to the job of dealing with them properly and it is not really safe to entrust them with the responsibility of publicly apportioning blame: which is partly why their powers to do this have been largely taken away. The local coroner may be a doctor rather than a lawyer, perhaps with little idea of the legal requirements of procedural fairness. Coroners, furthermore, are appointed by local authorities, not central government, and there is little or no quality control. The responsibility for summoning a jury rests with an official called the 'coroner's officer', who is usually a policeman, which does not boost public confidence in a case where it looks as if the police may be to blame for the death.[1] And if something does go badly wrong at an inquest there is no regular appeal system, only the possibility of an application for judicial review (see chapter 17). The Broderick Committee made a great many useful proposals in relation to these matters, including that coroners should need a legal qualification for appointment, and that the Lord Chancellor should be responsible for appointing and dismissing them. What really seems to be needed, however, is some kind of superior coroner's court to handle the difficult and contentious cases. A report by *Justice* in 1986[2] suggested that coroners' courts should be arranged in groups under the supervision of a senior coroner, who would be more experienced and to whom the more difficult cases could be referred.

[1] Before the Coroner's Juries Act 1983 regulated who is eligible for service on coroner's jury, there was room for considerable abuse: see the previous edition of this book.
[2] *Coroners' Courts in England and Wales.*

21

COURTS WITH APPELLATE CRIMINAL JURISDICTION

The remaining part of the system of courts for criminal matters is concerned with criminal appeals. Before describing the courts which deal with these it is worth considering what the purpose of criminal appeal is supposed to be, and what functions we would expect courts of criminal appeal to perform in an ideal legal world. Broadly speaking, the main function of criminal appeal must surely be to see that the trial in the court of first instance reached the correct result, and to put the matter right if it did not. From the defendant's point of view, this means quashing the conviction and substituting an acquittal where he was innocent, and where he was guilty, reducing the sentence if it was unreasonably severe. From the prosecution's point of view it means the converse – substituting convictions for undeserved acquittals, and increasing sentences which are unreasonably light. But there is also a secondary purpose in a system of criminal appeals, and that is to safeguard the integrity of the system of criminal justice by making sure that criminal cases are tried according to due process of law. For example, every defendant, however manifestly guilty and no matter how vile, surely has a legitimate complaint if he was convicted on the basis of a confession extracted from him by torture, or by a jury consisting of a panel of his victims, presided over by a judge who was the brother of the policeman who investigated the case. Similarly, the prosecution is entitled to complain if the court, without justification, dismisses the case against the defendant unheard. In this sort of situation the party who appeals is complaining about the way in which the court of trial conducted its business; he may or may not be objecting to the result itself. And when in such a case the appeal succeeds, it will often be the procedure rather than the result it produced which the appeal court condemns, and the appeal court may have no view – and probably not even the material upon which to form a view – as to whether the defendant should have been acquitted or convicted. Here it makes little sense for the appeal court to substitute an acquittal for a conviction, or vice versa, and the only sensible thing it can do is to quash the original proceedings on account of what went wrong, and order a new trial to take place in accordance with due process of law.

When we look at the system of criminal appeals which we have in England today there are a number of obvious respects in which it falls short of this ideal. In the first place, the system is very lop-sided, because whilst the defendant can generally appeal the prosecution generally cannot. To some extent this is quite right and proper, because in our society the rule against double jeopardy is widely accepted as a useful principle, and according to this it is not fair to put a defendant in peril of conviction twice. It follows that once a defendant has been acquitted by a criminal court on the merits, that must be the end of the matter and there can be no further proceedings merely because the prosecution is disappointed at the result. It by no means follows, however, that the prosecution should be unable to appeal if the trial court acquitted the defendant not on the merits, but because it wrongly refused to give the prosecution a hearing according to due process of law; or that the prosecution should be unable to complain if on conviction the court imposed a derisory sentence. Secondly, the present system of criminal appeals sometimes fails to recognise the vital distinction between allowing a defence appeal on the merits – quashing a conviction because the defendant is seen to be innocent – and quashing a conviction because of some failure to apply due process of law. Thus there are many situations in which convictions are quashed and acquittals entered when it would be much more sensible to send the case back for a retrial. These points will be developed later.

A defendant who is disgruntled with his conviction in the magistrates' court, or considers that his sentence was too severe, has a right of appeal to the Crown Court, which for this purpose consists of a Circuit Judge or Recorder sitting together with magistrates; the judge is usually an experienced one, and the number of magistrates is between two and four. The appeal can be on the ground that the justices came to a wrong conclusion as to the facts, or as to the law applicable, or both. An appeal on fact is a true rehearing of the case: the witnesses are heard again, new witnesses can be called, and the appeal is like a new trial before a different tribunal. The powers of the Crown Court on an appeal are very wide. They can confirm, reverse or vary the sentence; they can send the case back to the magistrates' court for further hearing; they can do anything that the magistrates' court could have done. Their power to vary the sentence includes the power to increase it; however, as the prosecution cannot appeal to the Crown Court it is only in a position to vary those sentences against which the defendant appeals.

The defendant who wishes to appeal against the decision of a magistrates' court on some point of law has an alternative route open to him, and that is to appeal to the High Court. The Crown Court has power to hear appeals on point of law, and frequently does so; but an appeal to the Crown Court on law alone is little use if an authoritative ruling is required, for the views of a Circuit Judge or Recorder do not carry much weight in other jurisdictions. In such a case the defendant is likely to seek a High Court ruling on the matter. Furthermore, although the prosecution has no right of appeal to the Crown Court, it does have the same right to appeal to the High Court on point of law as the defence. Hence a prosecution appeal against the decision of a magistrates' court will necessarily be an appeal to the High Court.

For this purpose the High Court consists of a panel of two or three judges sitting together, and it is known as the Divisional Court. It typically consists of one Lord Justice of Appeal sitting with one High Court Judge, but in an important case it may well consist of three judges, with the Lord Chief Justice presiding. An appeal to the High Court may take one of two forms: it may be either a procedure called 'case stated', or an application for judicial review. In the first of these, the aggrieved party asks the magistrates' court to state a case, which means that an account of the case, giving the findings of fact and the decision made by the magistrates' court is drawn up, and on the basis of this document the legal point that arises is argued before the High Court. If the magistrates' court neglects or refuses to state a case when required, it can be compelled to do so. On hearing a case stated the powers of the Divisional Court are wide: by statute it may 'reverse, affirm, or amend the determination in respect of which the case has been stated, or remit the matter to justices, with the opinion of the court thereon, or make such other order in relation to the matter, and may make such orders as to costs as to the court may seem fit'.[1]

Thus on a successful prosecution appeal, one of the things which the court may do is to send the case back with directions to the magistrates to convict. (Surprisingly, however, the court is not considered to have the power to send the case back for a retrial.) The case stated procedure is primarily designed for the situation where the magistrates follow the correct procedures but make an error of substantive criminal law; where, for example, they convict a defendant of theft of a bicycle which they are satisfied he intended to return after using it without permission, because they wrongly imagine that theft of a bicycle is an offence which can be committed even where there was no intention permanently to deprive. Where the objection is that the magistrates failed to comply with the rules of criminal procedure – for example by hearing a case which they had no jurisdiction to hear, or refusing to hear a case which they were legally obliged to hear, or by refusing to allow one of the parties to call relevant evidence – the appropriate procedure is not to ask the magistrates to state a case but to apply for their decision to be judicially reviewed. (The process of judicial review was outlined in the section of this book on tribunals.)

Judicial review is not automatically available, and the applicant must first obtain leave from a single judge before the case can proceed. If leave is obtained, then where the application is to review the decision of a magistrates' court it is heard before the Divisional Court in much the same way as a case stated. If the complaint is made out, the court may make one of three orders: *mandamus*, which requires the magistrates to hear the case, or take some other action which they are wrongfully refusing to take; *prohibition*, which requires them not to hear a case

---

[1] Summary Jurisdiction Act 1857 s.6.

which they have no legal power to hear; or *certiorari*, which is an order quashing a decision reached in disregard of the proper procedures. When quashing a decision by *certiorari*, the Divisional Court also has the additional powers to remit the case to the magistrates to reconsider it and reach a decision in accordance with the Divisional Court's findings, and to replace an unlawful sentence with a lawful one which it considers fit. If a conviction is quashed the proceedings before the magistrates are rendered void, but by contrast with the position when the Court of Appeal (Criminal Division) quashes a conviction on appeal from trial on indictment in the Crown Court, this does not mean that the defendant is acquitted; technically, at least, it then is open to the prosecution to prosecute him again. Similarly, if an acquittal is quashed the defendant is not thereby convicted, and further proceedings would have to be taken to bring this about. This situation arises rarely, however, because the situations in which an acquittal may be judicially reviewed are restricted.[1] Where the defendant first appealed to the Crown Court rather than to the Divisional Court, either defence or prosecution can then appeal to the Divisional Court against the decision of the Crown Court in the same way as they could have appealed from the magistrates' court. But, as will be explained below, there is no right of appeal to the Divisional Court against a decision of the Crown Court other than one made when it was hearing an appeal from a magistrates' court.

If a bench of magistrates have made some obvious and indisputable error which is recognised as such by everyone including the magistrates themselves, it would be very cumbersome and expensive if the only way of correcting it was by an inevitably successful appeal to the Crown Court or Divisional Court. Hence in 1972 magistrates' courts were given an extremely useful power to review their own mistakes and correct them. By what is now section 142 of the Magistrates Courts Act 1980, the magistrates who tried and convicted a defendant who pleaded not guilty have 28 days within which they may declare the trial invalid and order a retrial before different justices. Where they have sentenced an offender they have 28 days within which they may vary or rescind the sentence.

As far as appeals from magistrates' courts are concerned, the rules of criminal appeal, although rather complicated, form a fairly satisfactory structure. The defendant who complains of a miscarriage of justice in that he was convicted of an offence which he did not commit, is entitled as of right to have the whole of the evidence against him re-examined by a new tribunal which hears it again first-hand. And if either the prosecution or the defence claims that it did not get due process of law, the complaint is examined by a court which has power to see that due process is then done, either by correcting the error itself, or by making the justices do what they ought to have done; and it is possible for there to be another trial.

When it comes to appeals from the Crown Court trying cases on indictment as

---

[1] See *R. v. Dorking Justices ex pte. Harrington* [1984] AC 473.

a court of first instance, the position is less satisfactory. It is an astonishing fact that until 1907 there was no system of appeals from trial on indictment at all. Two courts – the Queen's Bench Division of the High Court and a special court called the Court for Crown Cases Reserved – had a limited jurisdiction to entertain appeals on certain technical points of law; but there was no tribunal that was competent to deal with the straightforward complaint that the court of trial had succeeded in convicting a person who was innocent.[1] The man who was simply not guilty, and could prove it, had to ask the Crown (meaning the Home Office) for a pardon; and if this was not forthcoming he was left to console himself with the thought that if England had the best legal system in the world he was lucky indeed not to be a foreigner. The appalling miscarriage of justice which resulted in Adolf Beck serving years of a sentence for an offence that he could not have committed, led in 1907 to the creation of the Court of Criminal Appeal to hear appeals from trial on indictment. This court was separate from the Court of Appeal which heard appeals in civil cases – a situation which occasionally caused confusion when as a result the two courts sometimes reached conflicting decisions on the same point of law. There was also the feeling that the Court of Criminal Appeal was rather inferior in quality as a tribunal for taking appeals, because apart from the Lord Chief Justice, who was its head, the judges who staffed it were all puisne judges, of the same level as many of those whose decisions were being appealed from. In 1966 these considerations led to the abolition of the Court of Criminal Appeal and its replacement with the Court of Appeal (Criminal Division), which is an integral part of a single Court of Appeal.[2]

Some of the flavour of the earlier court remains, however, because by section 9 of the Supreme Court Act 1981, the Lord Chief Justice has power to require puisne judges to sit in the Court of Appeal (Criminal Division), and in practice the panel nearly always consists of a Lord Justice of Appeal (or the Lord Chief Justice himself) presiding, flanked by two puisne judges of the Queen's Bench Division. The Criminal Division, like the Civil Division, sits in the Law Courts in London. It normally sits in three divisions which are running simultaneously, but at particularly busy periods there are four. It is usually exceedingly busy. The job of preparing the papers and generally keeping the court running occupies a staff of 80.

However hard its members work, it is obvious that a court based in London and consisting of nine or twelve judges sitting in three or four divisions cannot possibly hear all the appeals from all the defendants who are disgruntled by the outcome of a trial on indictment in the same sort of way in which the Crown Court with some 700 professional judges and 25,000 magistrates sitting at some

---

[1] The best account of the position before 1907 is contained in M. L. Friedland, *Double jeopardy* (1969) pp. 238–63.

[2] As a result of the Report of the Interdepartmental Committee on the Court of Criminal Appeal (Donovan Committee) (1965) Cmnd 2755. Lawyers' views were given in a *Justice* report, *Criminal appeals* (1964).

90 different places around the country is able to hear all the appeals from those defendants who feel they have suffered a miscarriage of justice in the course of summary trial. It follows that drastic restrictions have to be imposed on those who may appeal to the Court of Appeal (Criminal Division), and the process of hearing appeals has to be greatly speeded up. The restriction takes the form of requiring most would-be appellants to obtain leave to appeal. Except where the appeal is based on a pure point of law – that is to say, in any case where a defendant is asserting that he was convicted for something which he did not do, and in any appeal against sentence – the paperwork with which the defendant begins his appeal is read by one of a number of teams of judges who are detailed to do this task in what would otherwise be their leisure hours, and the appeal goes no further unless the judge thinks the papers disclose an arguable case. If the single judge refuses leave, the defendant has the right to renew his application to the whole court – which when it happens usually means that a panel of judges sitting in a division of the Court of Appeal (Criminal Division) then study the papers. Additionally, the Home Secretary has the power to override a refusal of leave and to require the appeal to be heard. But in fact most would-be appeals never get beyond the stage of an unsuccessful application for leave. In 1986, for example, there were some 6,300 applications for leave to appeal, of which only some 1,500 were granted.

If leave to appeal is granted, the appeal does not consist of a rehearing as it does on appeal from the magistrates' court to the Crown Court, with the tribunal approaching the whole evidence in the case afresh. The appellant must establish one of a number of specified 'grounds of appeal' as listed in the Criminal Appeal Act 1968, which in basic terms means that he must state what he claims was wrong with his trial. A transcript is made of the short-hand note (or audio-recording) of those parts of the original proceedings of which the defendant complains. These are read in advance by the panel of judges assigned to hear it, and counsel address argument to them based upon it. The outcome is that the appeal generally fails. Table 6 shows how much lower the success rate is on appeal to the Court of Appeal (Criminal Division) than it is on appeal from the magistrates' courts. In the Crown Court, some 25 to 30 per cent of appeals against conviction succeed, and nearly 50 per cent of appeals against sentence, but of appellants in the Court of Appeal (Criminal Division) only some 10 per cent succeed in appeals against conviction and 20 per cent succeed in appeals against sentence. It is hard to believe that so many more appeals from magistrates' courts succeed simply because magistrates are so much the more prone to make a hash of a trial and produce a miscarriage of justice.

The sad truth is that the defendant who seeks to appeal on the ground that the Crown Court convicted him when he was innocent gets a poor deal compared with the defendant who makes the same complaint about what happened at summary trial. This much is abundantly clear from a series of famous cases in which defendants who were clearly not guilty failed to get their cases re-opened by the normal appeal process and had their convictions quashed only after political pressure had been brought to bear, and the Home Secretary had used his statutory power to require to the Court of Appeal (Criminal Division) to take another look at the case. The most famous one in recent years was the case of the unfortunate Luke Dougherty, who was convicted of shoplifting at a time when he was, to the knowledge of some 54 other passengers, on a coach trip miles away.[1]

If it takes the intervention of the Home Secretary before a miscarriage of justice as clear as this gets a proper airing, one cannot but fear there are many other unhappy cases which never get looked at at all. Clearly there is something wrong here, and we must ask what it is. It is not the attitude of the judges and officials in the Court of Appeal (Criminal Division), who are mainly a body of fair-minded and extremely hard-working people, which is responsible for this. Part of the problem is that the court was set up by statute and can only exercise such powers as statute gives it, and the rest of the problem is that the court is seriously overworked. The Criminal Appeal Act 1968 does not entitle the defendant to a rehearing, but instead requires him to show that one of three specified grounds for appeal are present:

(a) that the conviction should be set aside on the ground that under all the circumstances of the case it is unsafe or unsatisfactory; or
(b) that the judgment of the court of trial should be set aside on the ground of a wrong decision of any question of law; or
(c) that there was a material irregularity in the course of the trial.

Of these, two – that there was a 'material irregularity in the course of the trial', and that there was 'a wrong decision on any question of law' – are not applicable to the case where the trial was conducted according to due process of law, but where due process resulted in the conviction of an innocent man. If this is what the appellant is trying to say, then he can appeal only if he makes out ground (a) – 'that the conviction should be set aside on the ground that under all the circumstances of the case it is unsafe or unsatisfactory'. But he is usually in a weak position to do this, first because the burden rests on him to show it, and secondly because he has to rely on a transcript of the evidence rather than a re-hearing of the evidence, and from a mere written transcript of the evidence the true unsatisfactory nature of the conviction based upon it may not appear. The court does have a power to call the trial witnesses and hear them again, but the defendant cannot insist on this being done, and the court is extremely reluctant to do it. Given the way in which the court is arranged, its reluctance is quite understandable. The wholesale re-hearing of witnesses from every corner of the country in London would be a great burden for the witnesses, and as listening to the witnesses would take much longer than reading the transcript of their original

[1] See the Report of the Departmental Committee on Evidence of Identification in Criminal Cases (Devlin Report) HC 338 (1976). See also Sir Henry Fisher's Report into the Confait Case: HC 90 (1977). *Criminal trials: The search for truth*, a Fabian Society pamphlet by Tom Sargant and Peter Hill published in 1986, deserves careful study.

Table 6. Appeals against conviction and/or sentence disposed of by the Crown Court and the Court of Appeal (Criminal Division)

Appeals against conviction[a] disposed of, by court and result
England and Wales

Number of appellants

	The Crown Court				The Court of Appeal			
	Total number of appellants	Result			Total number of appellants	Result		
		Conviction confirmed or appeal abandoned	Conviction quashed[b]			Conviction confirmed or appeal abandoned	Conviction quashed[c]	
Year			Number	Percentage of number of appellants			Number	Percentage of number of appellants
1976	5,220	3,668	1,552	30	1,528	1,378	150	10
1977	5,553	4,024	1,529	28	1,521	1,391	130	9
1978	5,902	4,228	1,674	28	1,360	1,235	125	9
1979	5,726	4,200	1,526	27	1,420	1,310	110	8
1980	6,357	4,669	1,688	27	1,389	1,272	117	8
1981	6,202	4,514	1,688	27	1,418	1,282	136	10
1982	6,083	4,393	1,690	27	1,352	1,239	113	8
1983	6,420	4,532	1,888	29	1,421	1,287	134	9
1984	6,769	5,013	1,756	26	1,735	1,549	186	11
1985	7,383	5,560	1,823	25	1,397	1,228	169	12
1986	6,473	4,737	1,736	27	1,892	1,730	162	9

[a] Including appeals against both conviction and sentence.
[b] Including cases remitted to magistrates' courts.
[c] Including cases in which a retrial was ordered, but excluding cases in which the conviction was quashed on some counts but confirmed on others or the conviction for a lesser offence was substituted.

Appeals against sentence[a] disposed of, by court and result
England and Wales

Year	The Crown Court					The Court of Appeal				
	Total number of defendants sentenced at magistrates' courts[b,c] (thousands)	Appellants against sentence[d]		Appellants whose conviction was quashed or sentence varied		Total number of defendants sentenced at the Crown Court[e] (thousands)	Appellants against sentence[d]		Appellants whose conviction was quashed or sentence varied	
		Number	Percentage of number of defendants sentenced	Number	Percentage of appellants		Number	Percentage of number of defendants sentenced	Number	Percentage of appellants
1976	1,905	10,007	0.5	4,929	49	67	5,373	8	605	11
1977	1,834	10,386	0.6	5,209	50	68	5,030	7	733	15
1978	1,769	11,275	0.6	5,401	48	69	5,253	8	731	14
1979	1,749	10,889	0.6	5,317	49	60	4,596	8	789	17
1980	2,041	11,440	0.6	5,801	51	68	4,758	7	807	17
1981	1,924	10,735	0.6	5,454	51	72	4,757	7	972	20
1982	1,844	10,815	0.6	5,575	52	75	5,557	7	1,233	22
1983	2,013	11,965	0.6	6,029	50	83	5,456	6	1,120	21
1984	1,881	12,860	0.7	6,295	49	82	7,177	9	1,670	23
1985	1,822	15,193	0.8	6,915	46	90	6,274	7	1,189	19
1986	1,809	13,431	0.7	6,245	46	86	8,168	10	1,328	16

[a]Including appeals against both conviction and sentence.
[b]The totals for 1976–78 include an element of double counting of persons sentenced at one court appearance for indictable and for non-indictable offences.
[c]The figures for 1976–82 exclude defendants given probation orders or conditional discharge orders.
[d]Including defendants appealing against both conviction and sentence but excluding those appealing against sentence after breach of an order.
[e]Excluding those sentenced for murder and, for figures prior to 1983, those given probation orders.

From *Criminal Statistics* 1986

evidence, it would prevent the Court of Appeal (Criminal Division) keeping abreast of the work. Perhaps the burden on witnesses of coming to London to repeat their testimony could be solved if the original trial was recorded on videotape, which could then be played to the Court of Appeal. But only a massive increase in judicial manpower could get around the problem of finding time to listen to the evidence, either on tape or in the flesh.

By contrast, the defendant who complains of some failure of due process at the trial is in a strong position. A failure to give him due process will almost invariably amount to either an 'error of law' or a 'material irregularity in the course of the trial', or both; and, most important, it will usually involve some event which can be proved to have taken place, frequently because it is preserved for all to see in the written transcript of the trial. But the position here is not altogether satisfactory either, because if the defendant who has suffered a genuine miscarriage of justice is in too weak a position, the defendant who complains of a failure of due process is in one which is too strong. The trouble now is that where a ground of appeal is established, the powers of the Court of Appeal (Criminal Division) to dispose of the case are very limited: in fact so limited as sometimes to prevent it doing what common sense requires. Usually the only thing that the court is able to do when the appellant can show some failure of due process at the trial is to quash the conviction and let the appellant go free. It has virtually no power to order a retrial and, because a section of the Criminal Appeal Act provides that when the Court of Appeal has quashed a conviction this counts as if a jury had acquitted him of the offence (and it is a basic principle of criminal procedure that a man cannot be retried once a jury has acquitted him) the prosecutor is unable to bring further proceedings. In consequence it is all too easy for someone who is clearly guilty of a crime to get off on appeal because of a technical irregularity.

Where a ground of appeal is made out, the wording of the Criminal Appeal Act 1968 requires the Court of Appeal (Criminal Division) to quash the conviction unless it feels able to apply the following proviso:

Provided that the Court may, notwithstanding that they are of opinion that the point raised in the appeal might be decided in favour of the appellant, dismiss the appeal if they consider that no miscarriage of justice has actually occurred.

At first sight this suggests that the court can uphold the conviction wherever it thinks the appellant was really guilty, and this may be what Parliament originally intended it to mean. However, the courts have always refused to interpret it this way, because this would involve forming a judgment on the appellant's guilt or innocence on the transcript of the evidence at the trial and without actually seeing the witnesses, something the judges are understandably reluctant to do. So they interpret it to mean that where there has been an 'error of law' or a 'material irregularity' they can only affirm the conviction where they are certain that no reasonable jury, properly directed, could have failed to convict: a test which necessarily excludes many cases in which the judges themselves may feel that he is probably guilty. A case may reek of guilt, but the Court of Appeal may be unable to say that a jury would infallibly have convicted, and may therefore feel bound to quash the conviction. Furthermore, it is not logical to expect the Court of Appeal to apply the proviso to uphold the defendant's conviction for offence A in the fairly common situation when his complaint is that he was convicted of the wrong offence, because his crime amounted to offence B. Here too the court must usually quash the conviction, because although it does have a power to substitute a conviction of one offence for another, it is narrowly defined and is often not available.[1]

The obvious thing to do in many of these cases would be to order the case to be retried: but as the law stands the circumstances in which a retrial can be ordered are very limited. This is clearly unsatisfactory, particularly when it is contrasted with the position in Scotland, Northern Ireland and most of the British Commonwealth, where the courts of criminal appeal have a wide power to order retrials. At the time of writing the Criminal Justice Bill which is now before Parliament contains a clause which will give the Court of Appeal a general power to order a retrial. If enacted, this will be a great improvement.[2]

The Criminal Appeal Act also gives the defendant a right to appeal against sentence. As with an appeal against conviction, he may only appeal against sentence with leave. The procedure for hearing appeals against sentence is in principle much the same as for hearing appeals against conviction, only the hearing is usually much shorter because the prosecution is generally not represented and usually the only argument which the court hears comes from the appellant. The explanation for this is said to be the tradition that the prosecution take no part in the sentencing process – a matter which is further discussed in chapter 24. It is not a very satisfactory state of affairs, however, because as the process of sentencing has become increasingly governed by rules of law, judicial precedents and 'guidelines' issued by the Court of Appeal, so the court often needs to hear both sides of the argument before it makes up its mind. The present Lord Chief Justice, Lord Lane, has publicly stated that the prosecution ought to be represented on sentencing appeals, and it is likely that this will eventually come about. Sentencing appeals form a large part of the work of the Court of Appeal (Criminal Division), notwithstanding the requirement of leave to appeal. Until 1966 there was a powerful deterrent in that the court had power to increase the sentence as well as to decrease it. The power, or at any rate its exercise in certain cases, was a matter of controversy and in 1966, following a recommendation of the Donovan Committee[3] it was abolished. The result, as figure 5 shows,

---

[1] Illogical as it is, the proviso has occasionally been used to uphold a conviction in this sort of situation – notably in *Ayres* [1984] AC 447.

[2] Unfortunately the drafting leaves some significant and unnecessary gaps. The editor tried to draw attention to them in an article in (1988) 138 NLJ 315, but was unable to persuade the Home Office to do anything about them.

[3] Report of the Interdepartmental Committee on the Court of Criminal Appeal (Donovan Committee) (1965) Cmnd 2755.

Year	1963	1964	1965	1966	1967	1968	1969	1970	1971	1972	1973	1974	1975	1976	1977	1978	1979	1980	1981	1982	1983	1984	1985	1986
Applications for leave to appeal	2,497	2,699	2,852	4,403	5,798	7,898	8,613	8,280	6,309	6,261	6,171	4,840	5,545	6,302	6,056	6,198	5,456	5,610	6,214	6,572	6,482	7,987	7,921	7,696

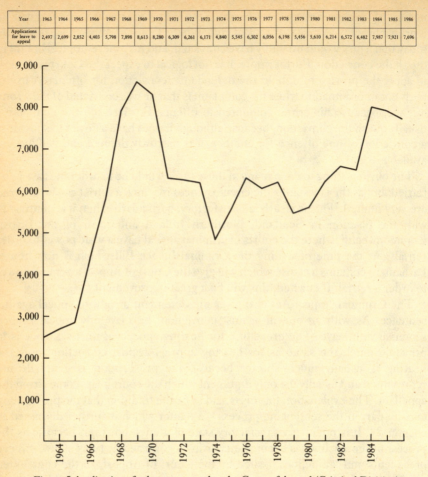

Figure 5 Applications for leave to appeal to the Court of Appeal (Criminal Division)

was an enormous increase in the number of appeals against sentence. Many of these were from appellants who really had no cause to complain about their sentence but who felt that they had nothing to lose. Leave to appeal was likely to be refused in these cases, but they still had considerable nuisance value, because as has already been explained, a really persistent appellant who is refused leave to appeal can renew his application to the full court. To deal with this situation, the court took to ordering that the time the appellant spent in custody awaiting the final determination of his appeal should not count as part of his sentence served. This too was controversial, and in 1987 it was unsuccessfully challenged in the European Court of Human Rights.[1]

Until recently the prosecution had no right of appeal from what took place at

[1] *Monnell and Morris* v. *U.K.*, (1988) 10 EHRR 205.

208

the Crown Court, whether its cause of disgruntlement was an unjustified acquittal or an over-lenient sentence following conviction.

No one in England has seriously complained about the prosecution's inability to appeal when the jury has acquitted on the merits as it saw them, because as was explained at the beginning of this section it is considered to be an important principle of justice in this country that the prosecution should be able to inflict upon a defendant a trial according to due process of law only once. It is by no means so obvious, however, why the prosecution should have no right of appeal if the court of trial refuses to give them due process of law even once: as for example in one leading case where the judge quite improperly directed the jury to acquit without allowing the prosecution to present its case.[1]

If the magistrates did this at summary trial the prosecution could certainly appeal, yet the prosecution has no right to appeal from the Crown Court to the Court of Appeal (Criminal Division) against an acquittal even in such circumstances as this, and the right to apply to the Divisional Court for judicial review does not apply here either, because the Supreme Court Act 1981 expressly provides that there shall be no judicial review of proceedings in the Crown Court which are part of a trial on indictment (as against part of an appeal from a decision of the magistrates' court). This problem is still with us and there is no legislative proposal before Parliament to correct it. A further problem used to be that if the acquittal was the result of a dubious ruling on a point of law from a High Court Judge, it might be reported in the law reports and thus become a precedent to mislead other judges. To deal with this problem, the Criminal Justice Act of 1972 created a device called an 'Attorney-General's Reference', under which the Court of Appeal (Criminal Division) has the chance to anathematise the error without upsetting the conviction. The procedure is that if the Attorney-General desires the opinion of the Court of Appeal on a point of law that arose in a case where there was an acquittal on indictment, he can refer the point to the Court of Appeal (which can in turn further refer the point to the House of Lords). At the hearing of the reference the acquitted person can, if he likes, be represented by counsel and gets his costs paid out of public funds, but he need not pay any attention to such proceedings: the law even provides for him to be anonymous. The hearing of a reference by the Attorney-General is in no way an appeal or retrial: it is aimed at getting an opinion on a legal question and the 'judgment' ends with the words 'Opinion accordingly'. To make the position absolutely clear, section 36(7) of the 1972 Act says 'A reference under this section shall not affect the trial in relation to which the reference is made or any acquittal in that trial.' The question of prosecution appeal against an over-lenient sentence is discussed in chapter 24.

From the Divisional Court and from the Court of Appeal (Criminal Division), a final appeal lies to the House of Lords. In either case leave to appeal is needed

---

[1] *R. v. Middlesex Justices ex pte. DPP* [1952] 2 All ER 312.

and appeal lies only on a point of law. At one time the right of appeal was narrower: there was no appeal from the Divisional Court, and for appeals from the Court of Criminal Appeal (as it then was) it was necessary to obtain a certificate from the Attorney-General that the appeal raised a point of law of exceptional public importance. It was thought to be wrong that a decision as to further appeal should lie with a person who is a politician and a member of the government, and in 1960 when a right to appeal to the House of Lords from the Divisional Court was created, the requirement of the Attorney-General's *fiat* was abolished at the same time. The present position about obtaining leave to appeal is that there are two requirements: *first*, the court below must certify that a point of law of general public importance is involved; *second*, it must appear to the court below or to the House of Lords that the point is one which ought to be considered by that House. So if the court below says 'No' to the first requirement, nothing further can be done; but if they say 'Yes' to the first question and 'No' to the second, one can go to the House of Lords and ask them to say 'Yes' to the second, and if they will do so, the appeal can proceed. Although the prosecution has no right of appeal from the Crown Court to the Criminal Division of the Court of Appeal, it does – surprisingly – have a right to appeal from either the Court of Appeal or the Divisional Court to the House of Lords. Thus, as happened in one celebrated case,[1] the Court of Appeal can quash a murder conviction on point of law, whereupon the prosecution appeals to the House of Lords which restores it. In principle appeal lies to the House of Lords from any decision of the Divisional Court or the Court of Appeal (Criminal Division), including the decision as to sentence. But because there must be a point of law involved, and controversial sentencing decisions do not usually raise points of law, it is very rare for a case on sentencing to reach the House of Lords.

Unfortunately it cannot be said that the House of Lords have made a satisfactory contribution to the development of the criminal law. There have been a number of instances where leave to appeal was given in the hope that they would sort out some point of confusion, and their pronouncements only added to the state of confusion.[2] There have been other cases where they have produced retrogressive interpretations of the law which have been unpopular with the courts below and have been the subject of bitter attacks in the legal press. In 1961 the House of Lords made such a mess of the law of murder that it provoked a storm of criticism throughout the common law countries and had to be corrected by statute.[3] In 1962 they decided on slender authority that there existed a crime called conspiracy to corrupt public morals, and in the process expressed views about the judges having a residual power to create new criminal offences in the

---

[1] *DPP* v. *Smith* [1961] AC 290.

[2] As for example on when a person can be guilty of attempt if the crime he sets out to commit is impossible: where the House of Lords decision in *Haughton* v. *Smith* [1975] AC 476 had to be reversed by the Criminal Attempts Act 1981; and on the meaning of 'appropriation' in the crime of theft, which the decision in *Morris* [1984] AC 320 leaves completely obscure.

[3] *DPP* v. *Smith* [1961] AC 290, corrected by the Criminal Justice Act 1967 s.8.

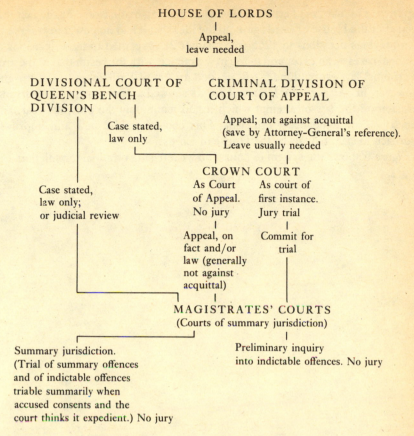

Figure 6 System of courts exercising criminal jurisdiction

area of public morals which were so reactionary that if they had been applied there would have been a call for legislation.[1] In 1982 they redefined the word 'recklessness', which forms part of the definition of many serious criminal offences, greatly widening its meaning and thereby widening the definition of a whole range of criminal offences.[2] The subsequent efforts of the lower courts to distinguish it have added many complications to the criminal law. Why does this sort of thing keep happening?

The root of the trouble is probably that the total number of Law Lords is small, and there have been considerable periods of time when it was difficult to compose a panel which contained judges who had either theoretical interests or recent

[1] *Shaw* v. *DPP* [1962] AC 220. Seaborne Davies, 'The House of Lords and the criminal law' (1961) 6 *Journal SPTL* is an article that should be read by everyone who cares for the traditions of liberal jurisprudence.
[2] *Caldwell* [1982] AC 341.

experience in matters of criminal law. Matters were made worse by the fact that even after the House of Lords gave up the idea that it had no power to reverse its own previous decisions in 1966 (see chapter 2), it seemed to treat decisions in criminal cases as an exception to the new practice, with the result that in the area of criminal law every blunder still needed an Act of Parliament to put it right. However, in *Shivpuri*[1] the House of Lords showed a new spirit, and reversed a decision on the law of attempt which it had made only the previous year, and which had attracted heavy criticism. This could herald a new and improved approach to criminal law by the House of Lords.

Figure 6 shows the system of courts now exercising criminal jurisdiction.

[1] [1987] AC 1.

22

THE PROCESS OF PROSECUTION

As far as the courts are concerned, a prosecution is begun when someone 'lays an information' – that is to say, when someone makes a formal complaint to the magistrates. But this is obviously only part of the story. Going backwards in time, before an information is laid, someone has to make the decision to do this, and before making the decision someone will have carried out an investigation. Moving forwards in time, laying an information is only a very early stage in a prosecution, and many other steps must be taken before the prosecutor and the defendant get their 'day in court' at which the defendant pleads guilty or not guilty, and on conviction is then sentenced. Some of these earlier steps are carried out by the police, and others by the Crown Prosecution Service. The way in which responsibility is now divided up between these two bodies is something which has only recently come about, and it is necessary to give some account of the recent historical background.

In most countries the police investigate and a public prosecutor who is separate from the police then carries out the prosecution if there is to be one. In England, on the other hand, the position was until recently far more complicated. The police, and a number of different public agencies like the Inland Revenue, the Customs and Excise and the Trading Standards Departments of local authorities, had (and have) the job of investigating crime; but there was no public prosecutor, and each of these various agencies would then make the decision to prosecute, and carry on the proceedings once they were begun. Where, as is usual, the investigation was carried out by the police, it would be the police who prosecuted. If the case was heard in the magistrates' court it would at one time be a policeman who presented and argued the case for the prosecution, and if it was tried on indictment the police would instruct solicitors who briefed counsel to appear for them. More recently most police forces had acquired the services of prosecuting solicitors employed by the local authority to present the cases in the magistrates' courts and to make the necessary preparations for the trials in the Crown Court, but even where this was the arrangement it was the police who were in charge, because the legal position was that the prosecuting solicitors were subordinated to the police whose instructions they were bound to carry out. Other investigating agencies also handled their own prosecutions. When the police or some other public agency prosecuted, the theory – which dated back to the days before such agencies existed – was that the prosecution was not carried on by an official agency, but was being done by an individual who happened to work for such an agency. As Professor Jackson wrote in earlier editions of this book:

When 'the police' prosecute, the legal analysis is that an individual has instituted proceedings, and the fact that this individual is a police officer does not alter the nature of the prosecution. If William Styles is the name of a prosecutor, the law is not concerned with his occupation: he may be a grocer, or a police excise officer, but he remains William Styles the prosecutor.

Because this was the theory, it was generally the case that William Styles the grocer had just as much right to start and carry on a prosecution as William Styles the policeman. When it was William Styles the grocer who was prosecuting we called this a 'private prosecution'.[1] Until recently there were a substantial number of these. Most of these took place because certain police forces as a matter of policy and resources declined to undertake certain types of prosecution – as in London, where the Metropolitan Police declined to prosecute shoplifters and left this to the proprietors. A few, however, were the work of private vigilantes, as when Mrs Mary Whitehouse successfully prosecuted the newspaper *Gay News* for blasphemy for attributing homosexuality to Jesus Christ.[2]

Standing in a corner of this maze of overlapping powers and responsibilities was a figure who until recently had a very misleading title: the Director of Public Prosecutions. As with so many of our institutions, the form his office used to have has to be explained by reference to its development. In the middle of the nineteenth century very serious or difficult criminal matters were often reported to the Home Office. The Home Office might give advice, or it might decide to give active assistance by handing the case over to the Treasury Solicitor.[3] Counsel would then be briefed. In serious cases the prosecution would be taken by either the Attorney-General or the Solicitor General, whose job it was, then as now, to represent the government in legal proceedings. If neither of these took the brief it would go to one of a small group of counsel who became known as Treasury Counsel. At various times in the nineteenth century the idea was put forward of putting a public official in overall command of the prosecution process. Eventually the office of Director of Public Prosecutions was created in 1879, but it was then purely advisory, and from 1884 to 1908 his office was

---

[1] The right to bring one remains: see chapter 22(ii).

[2] *Lemon* [1979] AC 406.

[3] The Home Office and other Departments have 'legal advisors' on their own staff, but these do not practise; if there is conveyancing to be done, or proceedings to be brought or defended, it must go to the department's solicitor, and the Treasury Solicitor was appointed solicitor to the Home Office in 1842. The Treasury Solicitor acts for several government departments, and some have their own solicitor. The Treasury Solicitor is not to be confused with the Official Solicitor, whose office and duties are described in (1966) 63 Law Soc. Gaz. 270, 335.

merged with that of Treasury Solicitor. Then the offices were separated, and the Director of Public Prosecutions was given a job which would more accurately have been described as advisor and co-ordinator. His functions were laid down in rules made by the Attorney-General with the approval of the Lord Chancellor and the Home Secretary. A large part of his function was to give advice on prosecutions when the police and other public agencies asked for it. His consent was needed before a prosecution for certain types of offence was instituted, and he alone could prosecute for one or two of the most serious crimes. Certain categories of offence had to be reported to his department, and he had the right to take any prosecution over, either to carry it through, or with a view to suppressing it.

This scheme – or absence of any scheme – was inelegant and confusing. But it was not the untidiness of it which began to cause disquiet. It was widely felt that it worked less than fairly, mainly because in many situations it put the investigation and the conduct of the prosecution in the same set of public hands: those of the police. To prosecute someone is to do something which can cause him grave damage, even if the prosecution fails, and is therefore a decision which needs to be taken with a degree of detachment. 'A police officer who carries out an investigation, inevitably and properly, forms a view as to the guilt of the suspect. Having done so, without any kind of improper motive, he may be inclined to shut his mind to other evidence telling against the guilt of the suspect or to overestimate the strength of the evidence he has assembled.'[1] Likewise, those who carry on prosecutions with the authority and power of the state behind them need to act in a way which is detached and scrupulously fair. It is important that they do not obstruct the defence in its search for evidence, and if they themselves discover evidence which tends to show the accused is innocent they should not suppress it. Unfortunately in police prosecutions this sort of thing did happen from time to time.[2]

There was also the opposite problem: a risk that the police would not press charges with sufficient vigour, and would too readily compromise serious cases with pleas of guilty to minor offences in order to save time and trouble for policemen who would avoid having to attend court in the event of a guilty plea. Another major criticism was that the responsibility for prosecuting offences was divided among so many different agencies that no one was politically accountable over policy matters. Nobody wants the prosecution process to be politically accountable in the sense that the Prime Minister, or any other minister accountable to Parliament issues directions as to who shall be prosecuted for what, and when; but we do expect there to be political accountability in the sense that there should be some person or persons who can be required to give a

[1] Report of the Royal Commission on Criminal Procedure Cmnd 8092 para. 6–24.
[2] See for example *Derbyshire* v. *Lancs. C.C.* (1983) 133 NLJ 65, where the police took a statement from a witness; he then gave a more favourable statement to the defence solicitor, which he showed to the police – and they confiscated it from him!

215

reasoned explanation of what is happening, and who can be made to listen to advice and recommendation in general terms. There was little accountability in this sense in the system as it was. Prosecution policy was a matter for each individual police force, and each police force was accountable only to its police authority. Police authorities were little inclined to ask questions about prosecution policies, and, as they consist of magistrates as well as representatives of the local authorities, are several stages removed from democratic control. The Director of Public Prosecutions was under the control of the Attorney-General, who is a minister responsible to Parliament; but as has been explained, the Director's job was itself mainly advisory, and he had little actual control. In some ways the system was inefficient as well. Policemen are trained to carry out investigations and to catch criminals, not to operate the machinery of the courts. As this falls outside the scope of their expertise it is something they are likely to do badly. If they prosecute badly, this is a waste of the time which they ought to be spending on doing what they are able to do well; and a badly conducted prosecution is liable to fail, so wasting other people's time and money.

If police control of the prosecution process caused disquiet, there was greater disquiet over the powers of the police to investigate crime. The problem with police and the prosecution process was that the law gave them powers to do something which should have been somebody else's job; but the problem with police investigations of crime was that they lacked adequate powers to do what was their proper job beyond any possible dispute. To solve crimes, especially serious crimes, the police need to be able to exercise various coercive powers against other citizens. They need to be able to search property for clues and suspects, to seize clues, and to arrest suspects and hold them for questioning. But in each of these areas the powers which the police had were chaotic, vague and frequently insufficient. For example, to search property for clues the police generally needed (and still need) a warrant from a magistrate, which can only be issued under a statutory power to do so; and although magistrates had a statutory power to issue search-warrants to look for stolen goods, no power existed to issue one to look for evidence of a murder. When it came to interrogating suspects, the powers of the police were regulated in a haphazard way by various circulars issued by the Home Office, and a set of guidelines issued by the judges and known as the 'Judges Rules'.[1]

These were singularly deficient, because they were all written against the background of a legal rule which said that the police officially had no powers of interrogation at all, because their power to arrest suspects was in legal theory only a power to bring suspects before the courts as the first stage in starting a prosecution, not a power to question them to see if there was enough evidence to justify the prosecution taking place. This was highly unsatisfactory. It goes without saying, of course, that if the police had always stayed strictly within their

---

[1] For details of their origins and what they contained see the 7th edition of this book, pp. 232–35.

216

legal powers they would have solved few crimes. What happened was that the police regularly exceeded their narrow powers, and everybody systematically condoned the illegality. By and large the courts were prepared to admit the evidence which they had gathered, although it had been gathered illegally. Those responsible for dealing with complaints of police misbehaviour did not take it seriously if the police had exceeded their powers when behaving in a manner which was reasonable in all the circumstances. Thus the only means that existed to make the police keep within the law was the occasional civil action which someone brought when what the police had done amounted to a wrong like trespass to land or false imprisonment, for which damages can be claimed, and obviously there were not many of these where the person who had been unlawfully treated had been convicted and sent to prison. On balance it was no doubt better that the police overstepped their powers to solve crimes than that crimes remained unsolved, but it was a bad state of affairs, because if everything the police were doing was technically illegal, then neither the courts nor anyone else could make detailed rules to say how they must do it. If in strict law the police may not hold a suspect for interrogation at all, there can be no legal rules determining how long he may be held for interrogation, or on how he is to be treated whilst he is so held, and everything takes place in a kind of legal no-man's land.

In 1978 these matters were causing sufficient disquiet that a Royal Commission on Criminal Procedure was set up to examine the powers of the police, and the prosecution process, and to make recommendations. The chairman was Sir Cyril Philips, who had been Vice-Chancellor of the University of London. Over the next three years twelve research studies were commissioned and in 1981 the Commission produced a radical and well-argued report.[1]

In outline, its proposals were that the powers of the police to investigate offences should be rationalised, extended and codified; that in order to make sure the police kept within their new range of powers the procedure for dealing with complaints against the police should be strengthened; and that the conduct of prosecutions should be taken away from the police and given to an independent prosecution authority. Over the next few years the Philips Committee's proposals were enacted, although with some changes of detail, in two major pieces of legislation: the Police and Criminal Evidence Act 1984 (usually known as 'PACE'), and the Prosecution of Offences Act 1985.

i Investigation and interrogation: the police

The Police and Criminal Evidence Act 1984 (PACE) is now the source of the law on the powers of the police to stop and search people in the street, to enter and search property, to search for clues and seize them, to arrest suspects, to search

---

[1] Report of the Royal Commission on Criminal Procedure, Cmnd 8092.

their bodies, take their fingerprints and obtain bodily samples from them, and to detain them for questioning. It is a big Act containing 122 sections and seven schedules. Nor is this all, because sections 66 and 67 provide for the Home Secretary to issue Codes of Practice giving the police further and more detailed guidance on how their powers in the Act are to be used. The following discussion will be limited to the powers of the police to arrest suspects and question them. PACE and its subsidiary Codes have already given rise to a number of detailed works on the subject of police powers,[1] and these should be consulted for further information.

The police have power to arrest anyone if a magistrate has issued a warrant for his arrest. In addition, they have wide powers to arrest without warrant in certain cases. As under the previous law, they may do this wherever they have reasonable grounds for suspecting that someone has committed an 'arrestable offence', which broadly speaking means one which is punishable with five or more years' imprisonment. This covers theft, burglary, fraud, criminal damage, wounding and most sexual offences. Under PACE they have also acquired a power to arrest without warrant for an offence which does not come within this definition where any of a number of 'general arrest conditions' are satisfied, the most important of which concern people who refuse to give their name and address, or give ones which are manifestly false. On arrest, the suspect must be taken as soon as practicable to a 'designated police station', which will be one where there will be a sergeant or officer of higher rank who is designated 'custody officer'. When the suspect is brought in, the custody officer must decide whether there is sufficient evidence to charge him: that is to say, to make a formal accusation against him, a copy of which will eventually find its way to the magistrates' court where it will set the court machinery in operation against him. If there is insufficient evidence for this the suspect must be released, 'unless the custody officer has reasonable grounds for believing that his detention without being charged is necessary to secure or preserve evidence relating to an offence for which he is under arrest *or to obtain such evidence by questioning him*'. Thus there is no power to arrest simply for the purpose of questioning; but if someone has been validly arrested under the general powers to arrest he may be kept in custody for this purpose. The initial decision to hold the suspect for questioning enables him to be kept at the police station for up to 24 hours, during which time another officer of at least inspector's rank is required to review the detention at stated intervals. At the end of the 24 hours the suspect must ordinarily be charged or released. However, if the offence he is suspected of committing is a 'serious arrestable offence' – a term exhaustively defined in section 116 of the Act – an officer of the rank of superintendent or above may order his detention for further questioning provided certain conditions are fulfilled. By this procedure his time in the police

---

[1] Notably M. Zander, *The police and Criminal Evidence Act 1984* (1985); Robilliard and McEwan, *Police powers and the individual* (1986). Copies of the various Codes of Practice can be bought in bookshops.

station may be extended from 24 to 36 hours. If the police wish to hold the suspect longer than this without charge, then they must go to the magistrates' court and seek what is called a 'warrant of further detention', which the magistrates are empowered to grant in the case of a serious arrestable offence, provided they consider the investigation is being conducted diligently and expeditiously, and his continued detention is necessary 'to secure or preserve evidence relating to an offence for which he is under arrest or to obtain such evidence by questioning him'. A warrant of further detention enables him to be held for a further 36 hours, and is renewable; but the interrogation must come to an end after 96 hours in custody, beyond which the suspect may not be further detained without charge. At this point the police must either release the suspect, or charge him. If they charge him, they are not permitted to go on questioning him thereafter.

It is always said that the English criminal justice system is accusatorial, not inquisitorial, and one of the ways in which it is usually said to show that it is not inquisitorial is that it does not provide for any kind of official interrogation of the accused. In this way our system is usually said to be radically different from most legal systems on the Continent, where the accused can be formally interrogated by an examining magistrate. Many years ago our system was not so different from those of our continental neighbours, because as was mentioned earlier our magistrates formerly had a statutory duty to interrogate suspects (see chapter 19(ii) above). In more recent times, interrogation used to take place, but the police did it, not the examining magistrate, and it was unofficial, lacking any legal basis. Thanks to PACE, interrogation is now both present and supported by a legal basis.

It has also traditionally been said that no one in this country is compelled to answer police questions. Although the police now have the power to detain for questioning, this is still true in the sense that no one is obliged to answer their questions in the sense that he commits a criminal offence by refusing to answer their questions.[1] Indeed Code 'C', which governs the treatment of persons detained for questioning, requires the police to caution a suspect before questioning, and to remind him of his right to remain silent, just as the Judges' Rules required in the days before PACE. What is new, in theory if not in practice, is that the police can now legally compel the suspect to stay in the police station and listen to their questions. This is not to say that they can question him as severely as they choose, because Code 'C' lays down strict rules as to the length of periods of questioning, and the provision of refreshment and rest. But it is obviously not easy to remain silent during questioning which may extend over a period of 96 hours, even if it is conducted in a civilised manner. The psychologi-

[1] There are some important exceptions to this. The Road Traffic Act 1972 gives the police various powers to require information from drivers and owners of cars, making it a criminal offence to refuse to give such information, and the Prevention of Terrorism Act 1984 makes it an offence not to give the police information about acts of terrorism.

cal pressure to say at least something in answer to police questioning is great, and in practice only a small proportion of suspects persist in a refusal to talk. A research study carried out for the Royal Commission on Criminal Procedure revealed that only some 6.5 per cent of suspects in London and 3.8 per cent of suspects in Birmingham refused to say anything.[1]

The suspect undoubtedly has right of silence in the sense that he usually commits no crime by refusing to talk: but does the law go further and require the court which eventually tries him to disregard his refusal to explain himself to the police, however suspicious, when considering whether the prosecution have proved the case against him? In other words, is his failure to talk not merely no crime in itself, but not even admissible evidence of his having committed the crime which is under investigation? Broadly speaking this is indeed the position, at any rate at the time of writing. If the case is tried by magistrates they are meant to disregard the defendant's suspicious silence in the police station, and if there is a jury the judge must tell them to disregard it. Where an innocent suspect would undoubtedly have given the police an explanation it goes against common sense to tell the jury that they must not count the silence of the accused against him, and everyone suspects that many juries would be affected by it whatever the judge chose to tell them; but the legal profession sees this as an important principle. Despite the fact that lawyers writing to the newspapers commonly treat it as an ancient and immutable principle of the common law, dating back to Magna Carta if not to Noah's Flood, in truth the principle is comparatively modern, becoming settled only during the present century.[2] But it has such a powerful hold over the public imagination that when the Criminal Law Revision Committee in its Eleventh Report on criminal evidence recommended that the court should be officially entitled to draw adverse inferences from the silence of the accused in the face of police questioning,[3] there was such an outcry that it killed the whole of of the report, and the Committee's six years' work was cast aside. Since then, however, there has been a slight but significant move in the direction which the Criminal Law Revision Committee recommended. A decision of the Court of Appeal (Criminal Division) held that silence in the police station could count against a suspect when he had his solicitor with him. The usual rule, they said, depended on the fact that a suspect was not on equal terms with the police, but this was not the case when he had his solicitor with him:[4] this was an unimportant decision at the time, because suspects rarely had solicitors with them at the police station, but it becomes very important now that the presence of a solicitor is becoming more common, as is explained below. And where a suspect refuses not to talk, but to give what is called an 'intimate sample' – a sample of blood, semen

[1] Baldwin and McConville, *Confessions in Crown Court trials*, Royal Commission Research Study No. 5 (1980).
[2] As late as 1919 the Court of Criminal Appeal was prepared to say that suspicious silence to the police could amount to corroboration: see *Feiginbaum* [1919] 1 KB 431.
[3] Eleventh Report – Evidence (General) (1972) Cmnd 4991.
[4] *Chandler* [1976] 1 WLR 585.

and so forth – section 62 of PACE provides that a court trying him for an offence 'may draw such inferences from the refusal as appear proper; and the refusal may, on the basis of such inferences, be treated as, or capable of amounting to, corroboration of any evidence against the person in relation to which the refusal is material'. At the time of writing the police are getting increasingly restive about the fact that an accused person's suspicious silence is not evidence against him. Eventually the rule may be reversed by legislation, although the government resisted pressure to include a provision in the current Criminal Justice Bill to alter it.

An important change wrought by PACE concerns the right of a suspect to have legal advice when he is being held in the police station. Before 1984 there was no statutory basis for any such right, and although the Judges' Rules said that every person under investigation should be able to consult and communicate with a solicitor, it was not the usual practice for persons detained for questioning to have the help of solicitors. The Philips Committee wished to promote the availability of legal advice to suspects in police stations as a counterbalance to the general extension of police powers. As a result, Section 58 of PACE now provides that 'A person arrested and held in custody in a police station or other premises shall be entitled, if he so requests, to consult a solicitor privately at any time', and in Code 'C' it is laid down that the police must inform the suspect of this right. The police are permitted to delay complying with a request to send for a solicitor only where the suspect is held for a serious arrestable offence, and where a police officer or superintendent authorises it, which he is allowed to do only where he has reasonable grounds for believing that sending for a solicitor immediately would lead to interference with the evidence, injury to other persons, a warning to other suspects, or hindrance in the recovery of the proceeds of the crime.

It is all very well for an Act of Parliament to say that a suspect has a right to have a solicitor present in the police station, but how as a practical matter can it be possible to provide a probably penniless man with a solicitor in a police station at short notice at three o'clock in the morning? This vital question was not confronted until the Police and Criminal Evidence Bill was already before Parliament, at which point the government eventually conceded an amendment which created the possibility of legal aid being available for advice given to suspects in the police station. Then, very late in the day, the Lord Chancellor's Department tried to negotiate with the Law Society as the body which administers legal aid, to set up a rota of solicitors to provide 24-hour a day cover for the purpose. The government became alarmed at the likely cost, and fixed a level of remuneration so low that an insufficient number of solicitors were willing to join the scheme. When PACE was brought into force it was reported that there was only some 60% coverage under the '24-hour scheme'. At the time of writing the Lord Chancellor's Department is conducting research into the working of the scheme and there is a possibility that it may be improved in future; see further chapter 40(iv).

It is a terrible thing for a person's family when he simply disappears, and the fact that he knows his family will be worrying about him adds greatly to the anxiety of a person who is held for questioning. Thus, in addition to giving him the right to see a solicitor, PACE also gives the suspect the right to have a friend or relative told where he is. The word to the friend or relative may be delayed by the police to the same extent as the telephone-call to the solicitor.

Before PACE the duties of the police to keep written records about those whom they held in custody were rather vague, and practice varied from place to place. PACE and the Codes of Practice now require the police to open a 'custody record' for each person who is arrested, and lay down in considerable detail the information that the police must record in it. Of this the detainee or his lawyer is entitled to have a copy.

If a suspect's silence in the face of police questioning does not count as evidence against him, there is no doubt at all that what a talkative suspect says to the police may be used as evidence against him. In general, the 'hearsay rule' prevents witness A telling the court what non-witness B said happened in order to prove that the event occurred, but there has always been a massive exception to this in the case of extra-judicial admissions and confessions by the accused. Such evidence has its dangers. A person may have confessed falsely because of improper pressure, and feeble-minded people have been known to confess under pressure which was not in any way improper. For this reason many legal systems, including that of Scotland, refuse to permit a person to be convicted on evidence of his extra-judicial confession unless there is supporting evidence. In England, by contrast, a confession is theoretically sufficient evidence to support a conviction even if it stands on its own, provided the court believes that it was true; but there are certain safeguards, which are now codified in sections 76 to 78 of PACE. If the defence asserts that a confession was obtained by oppression, or in consequence of anything that was likely to make it unreliable, the court is bound to reject it as evidence unless the prosecution disproves this. In addition, the court has a discretion to reject a confession (or any other piece of evidence) if it considers it would render the trial unfair – which means that it can reject confessions obtained where the police had been exceeding their statutory powers – and the court is also required to exercise caution over the confessions of those who are mentally handicapped. On trial on indictment, where there is a judge and jury, this means that the judge will scrutinise the confession and if he rejects it the jury will never hear of it. On summary trial, however, it will be the magistrates who decide to reject the confession, and the magistrates who must then go on to try the case, pretending that they have not heard about the confession: something which seriously blunts the effect of these rules when it comes to summary trial.

In practice it is much more usual for a defendant to claim that the police are lying when they say that he confessed than for him to say that he was induced to make a false confession, and in the past much courtroom time has been taken up with disputes as to whether this was so. Once tape-recorders were invented the obvious answer was for the police to record their interrogations, so putting the questions of what the defendant said beyond the area of dispute. Surprisingly, the police stoutly resisted this obvious move for 25 years, and the Home Office backed them up in their refusal. Many obscure reasons were given, but everyone suspected the truth to be that the police were afraid that their methods of interrogation would not stand up to public scrutiny. Eventually some forces were persuaded to experiment, and the police found to their pleasure that for every case where the tape revealed something embarrassing to them there were several cases where the tape prevented a defendant from falsely denying the confession that he had made,[1] and they were rapidly converted to the idea. PACE now contains a provision requiring the Home Secretary to issue a Code of Practice governing the tape recording of interviews with suspects, and to make the use of tape recordings compulsory by issuing orders. At the time of writing the Code is in preparation, and tape recording of interviews with suspects is being introduced nation-wide as fast as the equipment can be bought and the policemen trained to use it.

Where the police exceed their powers in the course of investigating an offence, the person who was on the receiving end can sue them for damages if what they did amounts to a tort – as it will do where they arrest him without power to do so, for example, or beat him up, or illegally search his property. At one time he could only sue the individual officer responsible, but this difficulty is eased by the Police Act 1964 which makes the chief constable liable for a civil wrong committed by any member of his force. When the chief constable is held liable the local police authority is legally obliged to indemnify him. The fact that evidence was obtained illegally may induce the court to reject it. If evidence was illegally gathered this does not automatically make it inadmissible, but where a defendant is prosecuted on the basis of such evidence, section 78 of PACE gives the court a discretion to reject it if the judge or magistrate thinks that admitting it would render the trial unfair.

In addition to these indirect controls, it is also an offence against the police code of discipline if an officer fails to observe the limits on his powers laid down in PACE or the Codes of Practice, and it is possible for a citizen who is aggrieved to make an official complaint against the policeman responsible. At one time there was no formal procedure for making complaints against the police. The Police Act 1964 established one, but it did not satisfy the public because it operated by obliging the police to investigate the complaint against themselves, something it was widely thought that they were reluctant to do. The Police Act 1976 was intended to improve matters by adding an independent element in the process called the Police Complaints Board; but the procedure under this Act was unsatisfactory, first because the Board had to be informed of every complaint no matter how trivial, and secondly because there was not much the Board could do about the complaint if it was serious. The Royal Commission on Criminal Procedure made it plain that a more efficient police complaints procedure was needed if the police were to be given the increased powers they recommended,

[1] The story is told by Baldwin, [1985] Crim. LR 695.

and Part IX of PACE seeks to provide one. Under these provisions the responsibility for dealing with complaints against the police is divided between the chief constable of the force concerned, and a new body called the Police Complaints Authority. This has twelve members appointed by the Home Secretary, a chairman appointed by the Queen, and 56 supporting staff. The members must not include anyone who is or has been in the police. In the first instance a complaint against the police goes to the chief constable. On receiving it he must decide whether he should deal with it on his own, or bring in the Police Complaints Authority; he is bound to refer the case to the Authority if the complaint is that the police killed or seriously injured someone, and certain other grave matters; in other cases he may refer the case to the Authority; and the Authority has the power to call a case in even where the chief constable does not propose to refer it to them. One of three things may happen next, depending on whether the chief constable is handling the matter or the Police Complaints Authority has become involved. (1) If the chief constable is handling it he may try for an 'informal resolution' of the complaint, probably by means of an explanation and apology. This is obviously suitable for many complaints of a fairly trivial nature: bad language, slowness in answering a 999 call, and so forth. (2) Alternatively, he may decide to have a formal investigation, which will be conducted either by a senior officer of his own force or by one from another force. (3) Where the Police Complaints Authority is involved there will be a formal investigation carried out by the police, but it will be done under the Authority's direction and supervision. In cases (2) or (3) the investigation will eventually produce a report, which will go to the chief constable. On this he will take one of three following courses of action, depending on what it reveals. (1) If the report says there is no substance in the complaint he may let the matter drop; but the Police Complaints Authority must be informed and may require him to take action. (2) If the report suggests a crime has been committed he must, save in exceptional circumstances, hand the matter to the Director of Public Prosecutions for criminal charges. (3) If the report reveals a breach of the police code of discipline falling short of a criminal offence, he will institute disciplinary proceedings against the officer. In a minor case these will take place before the chief constable or his deputy, but if the breach of discipline is serious it will be heard by a police disciplinary tribunal.

The main reason for introducing this new procedure was that the old procedure was thought to be ineffective. As far as complaints against the Metropolitan Police were concerned, one writer says

In 1984, 8 per cent of all complaints actually investigated were held to be substantiated. *Not one* complaint involving harassment, racial discrimination, false evidence or perjury was found substantiated; the same was true in 1983. Only 20 of 1410 complaints of assault – 1.5 per cent. – were substantiated. Either those who do bother to complain are all liars, or there is something wrong with the system.[1]

[1] Lustgarten, *The governance of police* (1986) p. 154.

The root of the problem, unfortunately, seems to be that the nature of police work builds up very strong feelings of solidarity between policemen, making them unwilling to reveal anything that will get their comrades into trouble and ready to lie where necessary to get them out of it. However many lay representatives we add to the Police Complaints Authority, or extra paper powers we give it, this will not get around that problem. Even the replacement of the present system by a full-time body of professional investigators to carry out the investigation in place of the police – a course some people have recommended – is hardly likely to break through the 'wall of silence'. The sort of difficulties that can be encountered are vividly illustrated by the 'Holloway Road Incident'. In August 1983 a gang of Metropolitan policemen leapt out of a transit van and beat up a gang of innocent youths, for no apparent reason. A series of police investigations into the matter got nowhere; the Police Complaints Authority replaced the Police Complaints Board, and in February 1986 this reported that a conspiracy of silence was protecting the guilty men. Eventually, following a fierce campaign in the newspapers and an official offer of immunity to any accomplice who informed, a further investigation produced evidence which landed five policemen in prison in July 1987; a mere four years after the incident.[1]

PACE was a very controversial piece of legislation, and we should not leave it without considering some of the arguments raised against it when it was being enacted. It was bitterly resisted by the political left, who were opposed to extending the powers of the police on ideological grounds. At least for a while after it was passed, it was official Labour Party policy to work for its repeal. It seems extraordinarily naive in a major political party to think that the police can do their job properly with the uncertain and limited powers which they had before. If PACE was repealed and the police were given back their previous inadequate and uncertain powers, a state of affairs would return in which they routinely exceeded them and this was officially condoned. If those who want to see PACE repealed accept that, then they have a dangerous attitude to the rule of law. Were the critics right to the extent that PACE gives the police too many powers? Since the Act came into force the biggest complainers have been the police themselves, who are always talking about it as if it cut their powers down, and so made their job more difficult to do. The truth of the matter seems to be that PACE extended the powers of the police in theory, but curtailed them in practice, because now the limits on their powers have to be noticed, whereas previously they could often be ignored. If the powers of the police turn out to be too wide in certain respects they can be narrowed, and if the new rules prove too narrow they can be extended. And meanwhile rules are rules, and not just pious aspirations.

Before leaving this subject it is convenient to say a little about how the police are organised in England. Unlike in most other countries we have no national

---

[1] See Robert East, 'Police brutality: lessons of the Holloway Road', and Brian Hilliard, 'Holloway Road: Unfinished business' (1987) 137 NLJ, 1010 and 1035.

police force, but a series of locally-based forces which in theory are not subject to central government control. The old pattern of provincial police was that each county had its own force, local control being vested in a Standing Joint Committee which consisted of persons appointed by the County Council and by the magistrates in Quarter Sessions, and borough forces were placed under a Watch Committee appointed by the Borough Council. The Metropolitan Police Force was anomalous in that it covered the Greater London area and that it was under the direct control of the Home Office. The police for the technical City of London are a separate force under a commissioner appointed by the City. The pattern of provincial police was established in the nineteenth century. During the first half of this century it became clear that small police forces cannot provide that kind of organisation or specialisation that are required for modern conditions. There was some demand for a national police force, but a Royal Commission on the Police[1] considered the whole basis of policing and took the view that there should continue to be local forces but that by a process of amalgamation we should have fewer but larger forces. This has been carried out, and nowadays there are forty-three police forces: the Metropolitan Police and the City Police in London, and forty-one provincial forces.

To the question 'Who is responsible for the police in England and Wales?' no clear answer can be given.[2] The Metropolitan Police is under the direct control of the Home Secretary, but for provincial forces the responsibility is divided three ways between the chief constable, the police authority, and the Home Office. The Police Act 1964, section 5(1) says 'The police force . . . shall be under the direction and control of the chief constable', and this means that the real control over what a particular police force does resides in the chief constable. Each force has a 'police authority' composed of two-thirds members of the local authorities and one-third of magistrates. The main statutory duty of this body is concerned with administration, including buildings, equipment and finance. It appoints the chief constable, subject to Home Office approval. Once he is appointed the police authority has no power to tell him how to do his job, and they have no power to remove him except for corruption or misconduct. Some police authorities have tried to control their chief constable by limiting the resources they give him, but as the Home Office has power to give him what has been refused, this is not particularly effective.[3] The Home Office has no direct control, but in practice it exercises a strong influence. It operates a system of grants, and also issues circulars to police forces giving detailed directions as to how certain parts of their work should be carried out. In theory every chief constable is free to put the latest circular in the waste-paper basket if he wishes to, but in practice

[1] Report of the Royal Commission on the Police (1962) Cmnd 1728, ch. V.
[2] See Lustgarten, *The governance of police* (1986).
[3] Thus the Court of Appeal recently held that the Home Office could equip a police force with CS gas and plastic bullets even when the local Police Authority objected: *R.* v. *Home Secretary ex pte. Northumbria Police Authority*, [1988] 2 WLR 590.

none would ever dream of doing so. The fact that except for the Metropolitan Police all the police in this country are free from direct political control, whether at local or central government level, is usually said to be one of the corner-stones of our liberty. The other side of the coin, however, is that the police are not in any real sense politically accountable either. If neither local nor national politicians can tell the police who they may or may not investigate, it is equally true that there is little that the community – particularly the local community – can do to make the police take notice of their views on how they should go about their job of policing them. The local police authority is virtually powerless, and although the chief constable would probably take great notice of what the Home Office said to him, if any citizens approached the central government about the policing in their area they would doubtless be told it was not the central government's business. In the 1980s this led to various bitter and inconclusive arguments between chief constables and those who spoke or claimed to speak for the local community, and in 1982 the Home Secretary issued a circular to chief constables advising them to set up local committees to advise them on relations with the community. Section 106 of PACE now requires this to be done.

ii The Crown Prosecution Service

The Crown Prosecution Service was created by the Prosecution of Offences Act 1985 as an independent body to take over the process of prosecution from the police. It 'went live' in certain parts of the country on 1 April 1986, and elsewhere on 1 October 1986. The titular head of the service is the Attorney-General – a function he combines uneasily with his other functions as the government's chief legal representative, and the head of the Bar, a body which views the new service with dark suspicion lest it should eventually undermine the monopoly of barristers as advocates in the Crown Court. The real head of the new Service is the Director of Public Prosecutions. He presides in London over a headquarters based in Queen Anne's Gate. From there the Director and his headquarters staff run an empire which is divided into four regions, within which are 31 areas. Each of these is the area of one or more police forces – except in London, where the area for which the Metropolitan Police are responsible is divided into two areas as far as the Crown Prosecution Service is concerned. For each area there is a Chief Crown Prosecutor. Below him there are Branch Prosecutors, who run offices in the larger towns. These are manned by a number of Crown Prosecutors, who do the prosecuting, and their office staff. By law any Crown Prosecutor, of whatever level, has the power to take in the name of the Director of Public Prosecutions any step in connection with a prosecution which the Director has legal authority to take; but the Service's internal rules require the more sensitive decisions to be referred up the chain of command. Crown Prosecutors are barristers or solicitors: many were formerly prosecuting solicitors employed by local authorities under the system which the Crown Prosecution Service has replaced. When up to strength, the Service was originally intended to have some 1,500 lawyers working for it, and in April 1987 this figure was raised to 1,700. The total number of posts, including secretarial posts, which the Crown Prosecution Service is allocated is around 4,500. At the time of writing, however, it is still seriously under strength.

The Crown Prosecution Service is national, centralised, and forms part of the Civil Service. In this respect it is not what was envisaged by the Philips Commission.[1] A national service, the Commission said, would be too bureaucratic, out of touch with local feeling, and unsatisfying to work for because those who had to do the job of prosecuting would feel remote from the positions of power. Hence it recommended a locally-based service with a certain amount of central co-ordination; and it also proposed that in each area it should have some kind of local supervisory authority. None of this cut any ice with the government when it came to designing the new service, however, and it opted for a heavily centralised service with no vestige of local control. This was surprising in a Conservative government which has generally been against expanding the Civil Service, and strongly in favour of trying to make public services more accountable to the public. The choice of a heavily centralised service may have been unwise, because many of the complaints that have been made about the new service since it was created have been of the sort of things which the Philips Commission said would be caused by a centrally directed service.

The main function of the Crown Prosecution Service is 'to take over the conduct of all criminal proceedings, other than specified proceedings, instituted on behalf of a police force (whether by a member of that force or by any other person)'.[2] This sounds like a very big change from the position as it used to be. Although it is a major change, however, it is not quite so great as it first appears. First, the duty of the Crown Prosecution Service is not to start prosecutions, but only to 'take over' the ones that the police have decided to begin: the decision to institute a prosecution remains in the hands of the police. Secondly, the only prosecutions the Service is obliged to take over are those begun by the police.

To take the second of these points first, there are many agencies involved in investigating crime apart from the police. These include local authorities, the Customs and Excise, the Inland Revenue, and the Department of Health and Social Security. It is reckoned that some fifth of all prosecutions are started by these bodies rather than by the police, and the Crown Prosecution Service has no duty to take over these. It is strange that when the Crown Prosecution Service was created it was not given the job of conducting their prosecutions as well, because the argument in favour of having a prosecution conducted by an organisation which is detached from the process of investigation is exactly the same in the case

[1] Royal Commission on Criminal Procedure, (1981) Cmnd 8092, para 7.21 *et seq.*
[2] Prosecution of Offences Act 1985 s.3(1)(a). This section actually states this to be the function of the Director of Public Prosecutions, but the Act presupposes that his duties are to be carried out by the Crown Prosecution Service on his behalf.

of these agencies as it is with the police. Indeed, it is stronger, because these bodies may have a financial interest in the outcome of the prosecution which the police will never have. Yet the Philips Commission saw no need for the Crown Prosecution Service to handle these cases, and the Prosecution of Offences Act follows where Philips led. What the Philips Commission did recommend, however, was that the right of a private individual to start a prosecution should be greatly curtailed, and here the Conservative government – keen as ever to promote private enterprise – disagreed. Consequently in the Prosecution of Offences Act the right to bring a private prosecution is retained intact. The argument against private prosecutions is that no prosecution should be brought unless there is a good chance of success, and private prosecutions are often half-baked at best, and more commonly the hopeless efforts of people who are vindictive, or are cranks; as in the case a few years ago where one Roger Gleaves, a man with multiple convictions for buggery and wounding, started a whole series of private prosecutions for criminal libel against those who had exposed his latest enterprise, which consisted of setting up a chain of hostels for young boys who had run away from home.[1]

On the other hand, the possibility of someone bringing a private prosecution is something of a check upon official lethargy, incompetence and corruption: as in the case in 1974 where Police Constable Joy reported someone for a motoring offence, his superiors wanted to drop the case when the motorist turned out to be an MP, and Joy was able to see justice done by bringing a private prosecution.[2]

In our system of criminal justice, the victim of the offence is in a very weak position, and the threat of bringing a private prosecution is virtually the only card he has to play if in his case the police or the Crown Prosecution Service refuse to do their job. It is therefore as well that the Prosecution of Offences Act did not take it away from him. Where any prosecution is brought by someone other than the police the Crown Prosecution Service has the right to take it over. If it was rightly brought but the person who started the proceedings lacks the funds to carry on with the case this power enables the Crown Prosecution Service to see the case through, and where it is a hopeless case which should never have been started, the Crown Prosecution Service can take it over and stop it. So at least in theory there is a restriction on the damage that a private prosecutor can do if he is cranky or vindictive.

---

[1] Because of various peculiarities in the law of criminal libel, which were later corrected by s.74 of PACE, the journalists whom he prosecuted were unable to prove his criminal record by proving the fact that he had been convicted, but were forced to prove that the offences of which he had been convicted had actually been committed by calling the prosecution witnesses at those trials to give evidence on their behalf: all of which necessitated the journalists undergoing a trial at the Old Bailey which lasted for several weeks before they were eventually acquitted. The judge ordered their costs to be paid out of public funds, and said that he would have ordered the private prosecutor to pay if he had had any money. See *The Guardian* 20 February 1980. The Law Commission recommended major changes in the law of criminal libel in a Report in 1985 (LC 149 Cmnd 9618), but this, like many of its best reports, seems destined for the shelf.

[2] See the article by A. F. Wilcox, *The Times* 18 September 1977.

It is a little surprising to find that it is the police who still make the decision as to whether or not to start a prosecution, because a large part of the thinking behind setting up the Crown Prosecution Service was that there needed to be stricter control over the process of starting prosecutions to make sure that inherently weak cases did not come before the courts at all. A prosecution is started by laying an information before the magistrates, which means taking one of two formal steps: arresting the suspect, formally charging him, and sending a copy of the charge-sheet to the magistrates' court office, or requesting the magistrates to issue a summons requiring him to appear before them – the course usually taken where the offence is not serious enough to justify an arrest. Under the Prosecution of Offences Act, it is not the Crown Prosecution Service but the police who take these initial steps – or decide not to take them. The Crown Prosecution Service can exercise control, but only inasmuch as it has the power by statute to stop any case in which the police have instituted a prosecution. By section 23 of the Prosecution of Offences Act, the Crown Prosecutor can stop any case simply by informing the court that he is stopping it, provided that things have not yet reached the point where the prosecution witnesses have begun to testify in the case of a summary trial, and provided the magistrates have not yet committed for trial where the case was destined for the Crown Court. But psychologically it is harder for a Crown Prosecutor to tell the police that the prosecution they have started is to be stopped than it is for the Crown Prosecutor to tell them in advance that no prosecution should be begun. The first course involves an implied rebuke and a judgment the police have behaved ineptly, the second course does not. At the time of writing a number of commentators are gloomily saying that because of this, the aim of the Prosecution of Offences Act to reduce the number of weak cases that are brought before the courts is unlikely to be achieved – but it is still early days and the commentators may be proved wrong. A further and more intractable difficulty with the arrangement under which it is the police who make the decision to start a prosecution is that the Crown Prosecution Service cannot make sure that strong cases are not dropped at the end of the investigation where charges really should be brought. In this situation the Crown Prosecutor may never get to hear of the matter, because the police must charge or summons the man or the file will never reach his desk.[1]

Nor does the Crown Prosecutor have any power to require the police to continue their investigations if it looks as if there ought to be a strong case against a defendant whom they have charged, but the police have failed to uncover it. All this puts the English Crown Prosecutor in a much weaker position than his counterpart in other countries, Scotland included. On paper these problems look serious limitations on the usefulness of the new Service, and it is therefore surprising to find that they all date back to the scheme designed by the Philips

---

[1] However s.8(2) of the Prosecution of Offences Act does empower the Attorney-General to make Regulations requiring chief constables to give him information. Under such Regulations he could routinely demand information about alleged crimes when the police have not started prosecutions.

Commission. and are not the consequence of a reluctant government watering down the Philips scheme. Whether these theoretical problems turn out to be problems in practice will depend on the kind of relationship that develops between the Crown Prosecution Service and the police. If good relations develop in future, it may become standard practice for the police to seek advice from the Crown Prosecution Service before they charge or apply for a summons in a tricky case, and the police may be receptive to requests for further investigations even if further investigations cannot be required. If this does not happen it may eventually be necessary to give the Crown Prosecution Service more extensive powers.

Where, as is usual, the prosecution goes ahead, it is the responsibility of the Crown Prosecution Service to arrange for a qualified person to present the case to the court. For proceedings in magistrates' courts this is simple, because whether the Crown Prosecutor is a barrister or a solicitor he will be eligible to take the case. In the magistrates' courts it is Crown Prosecutors who are now doing the work which was previously done by local prosecuting solicitors on behalf of the police, and which in seven police authorities – including the Metropolitan Police Area – was still largely done by policemen acting as advocates. (Or rather this is what is meant to be happening; in a number of places there are still such staff shortages in the Crown Prosecution Service that many magistrates' court cases have to be presented by solicitors in private practice engaged as agents for the Service.) In the Crown Court the matter is more difficult. Before the Crown Prosecution Service was created, the police, or the local prosecuting solicitors' department acting for the police, would have to brief counsel to appear. The local prosecuting solicitor, being a solicitor, could only take a Crown Court case himself if it was one of the limited class of proceedings for which solicitors have the right of audience in all Crown Courts, or if the Crown Court was one of those where solicitors have the right of audience in all proceedings (see chapter 19(i) above). For the purpose of creating an efficient and economical public service it would have been sensible to enable the new Crown Prosecutors to take their own cases in the Crown Court as well as in the magistrates' courts. The classic arguments for requiring prosecutors to use counsel to present their cases to the Crown Court are two: first that the case should be handled by someone who is independent of the process of investigation and hence able to take a detached view of the matter, and secondly that the consequence of a conviction in the Crown Court is likely to be a very serious matter for the defendant, making it unfair to expose him to the risk of this being brought about by the dubious tactics of a prosecutor who does not know the rules or the ethics of the professional lawyer. Neither of these arguments apply against the Crown Prosecutor as advocate, since he is both independent of the investigation and legally qualified. Even if the Crown Prosecutor could take the case himself it would often make good economic sense for him to brief counsel, particularly in London and other places where barristers abound. But it makes no economic sense at all to require a Crown Prosecutor who operates in a town miles away from the nearest Bar and who is able and willing to take the case in the local Crown Court to brief counsel who must come from many miles away. And it makes even less sense if, as all too often happens because of the way that the criminal Bar manages its business, the counsel who was originally briefed is unable to take the case and the man who eventually appears is a replacement found at the last minute whose sole preparation consists of a hasty attempt to read the papers on the train.[1]

Accordingly the Philips Commission recommended that Crown Prosecutors should be given a wider right of audience in the Crown Court than was accorded to prosecuting solicitors. A majority of members thought that they should be given the right of audience in a specified range of matters, others that they should be permitted to take any type of case. However, as is explained elsewhere in this book[2] this was not done, mainly in response to effective lobbying from the Bar, which was afraid of losing business. The Prosecution of Offences Act enables the Lord Chancellor to give Crown Prosecutors extended rights of audience, but the Lord Chancellor of the day, Lord Hailsham, anxiously assured the Bar that this provision would not be brought into force, and the Attorney-General – taking off his wig marked 'head of the Crown Prosecution Service' and putting on his wig marked 'head of the Bar' – wrote a letter to *The Times* to similar effect which concluded: 'I am sure that I do not need to emphasize that I personally remain wholly committed to the principle of a strong and independent Bar'.[3]

The result, broadly speaking, is that Crown Prosecutors have no right of audience in the Crown Court, and all prosecution work must still be done there through counsel. If the Crown Prosecutor is a solicitor, he can appear to the limited extent that a solicitor has rights of audience; if he is a barrister his right of audience will be no greater, because by the rules of conduct for the Bar, a barrister who is an employee rather than in private practice has only very limited rights to represent his employer in court. His office as Crown Prosecutor gives him no extra rights of audience. Up to now, the Crown Prosecution Service seems to have been so short of staff at all levels that the inability of Crown Prosecutors to appear in the Crown Court has been the least of its worries, but once the Service gets over its teething troubles this is likely to be a sore point for the future. As the classic arguments for requiring counsel to conduct Crown Court prosecutions do not apply where Crown Prosecutors are involved, the only remaining arguments for retaining the barristers' monopoly over Crown Court prosecution work are distinctly weak. One is that it is vital that those who

[1] The Bar is reluctant to admit this happens, but one only has to watch a Crown Court in operation to see that it does. A year or two ago the editor watched the start of a fraud trial which was expected to be complicated and for which two weeks had been allowed. After floundering badly in his opening speech, prosecuting counsel turned to the judge and said 'I do beg your pardon, your honour – on the train this morning I realised this case was going to be difficult to open.'

[2] See chapter 30.

[3] *The Times* 6 August 1984.

prosecute in court should do defence work from time to time as well; but this has never been the position in the magistrates' courts, and no one suggests that prosecutions are conducted in an overbearing fashion there. The other is that it is essential to preserve the Bar's monopoly of the Crown Court because the Bar needs it as a training-ground and as source of work for newly-fledged barristers, the loss of which would be bad for recruitment to the Bar. But it is the lure of advocacy that attracts some of the more able people to the Crown Prosecution Service, and the smaller the amount of advocacy Crown Prosecutors can do, the fewer really able people the service is likely to attract. A healthy Crown Prosecution Service is just as important to the country as a healthy and prosperous Bar.

As practically all prosecutions in the Crown Court must still be conducted by counsel, the question arises as to who is in charge of a Crown Court prosecution once counsel has been briefed. A number of difficult decisions may have to be taken, particularly in relation to dropping charges in return for guilty pleas. If the defendant is about to stand trial on a charge of raping a girl of 14, for example, he may offer to plead guilty to the lesser offence of intercourse with a girl under the age of 16 if the prosecution will accept his plea of not guilty to the more serious charge. Whether or not to accept his offer may be a delicate question, because it will involve balancing the unpleasantness for the girl in having to give evidence if the rape charge is persisted in against the risk of the defendant's receiving an inadequate sentence for what he has done if the rape charge is dropped. Who has to make this and similar decisions: the Crown Prosecutor or the barrister? Before the Prosecution of Offences Act 1985 no one knew the answer to this question, and the point is not covered anywhere in the Act. So the Bar set up a committee under Mr Justice Farquharson to consider the matter. This laid down the rule that the Crown Prosecutor had the final word on such matters in the period leading up to the trial, but that when the trial is about to start, or is actually in progress, and it is no longer practicable for the Crown Prosecutor to withdraw his instructions and brief a different barrister, the barrister is in charge and has the final word in the case of disagreement.[1]

This was the only sensible answer that could be given, and not surprisingly the Crown Prosecution Service welcomed it. But it is an interesting comment on relative status of the Bar and the Crown Prosecution Service that everyone assumed that it was quite right and proper for the Bar to tell the Crown Prosecution Service how far it was willing to obey the instructions of its client, and it never occurred to anybody that he who pays the piper normally calls the tune.

At the time of writing the Crown Prosecution Service is less than two years old, but it must already qualify as the most unpopular development in the administration of justice that has taken place in recent years. It has generated a mass of comment in the general and the legal press, nearly all of which has been bitterly

[1] The report is printed in (1986) 83 Law Soc. Gaz. 3599–3603.

critical. From this it seems that the police dislike it, and that those who administer the courts dislike it. The general impression is that the new service has added nothing to the machinery of criminal justice except a new layer of bureaucracy and delay. Yet it seemed a good idea when the Philips Commission recommended it, and the Conservative government, despite its general aversion to bureaucracy and increased public spending, accepted it. What are the problems? Why have they come about?

The main criticism is that the Crown Prosecution Service is slow. Files on cases which formerly stayed in the hands of the police throughout now have to be passed from the police to the Crown Prosecution Service, and 'the administrative staff for the new Service, or the police, or both, seem unable to prepare files for court within the generous periods of time allowed. More and more cases are being adjourned and the effect is cumulative, causing court lists to become clogged with a great mass of cases which are not yet ready for trial or committal.'[1] The delays so caused are making the prisons even more seriously overcrowded with prisoners on remand awaiting trial. The second and related criticism is that cases often seem to be handled by people who do not know their job. To take one example out of many, a lawyer writes:

I appeared for the defence before the Crown Courts in the Midlands in three cases last week. In no case was the CPS prepared for the hearing. In the first case I was to make a bail application in chambers for an alleged ringleader in an affray. The court clerk from the CPS attended without counsel and no case papers, grabbed a passing barrister and instructed him to ask for an adjournment . . . In the second case, the CPS simply forgot to brief counsel to attend in an allegation alleging assault, the judge refused an adjournment, a passing counsel was again grabbed, given 30 minutes to prepare the case and the defendant was bound over to keep the peace . . . The third case was the most worrying. The defendant, a man who was severely mentally ill, had assaulted a nurse at an open hospital for the mentally ill. He was a danger to himself and others and was properly remanded in custody by the justices. Five weeks passed and his condition deteriorated. The defence solicitors then effectively took over the administration of the case. In one day they had the defendant produced before the justices, committed to the Crown Court and arraigned before it . . . I can only speak from my own experience, but it appears that papers are lost, counsel is not briefed in time, administration procedures are not followed and important cases are not expedited. For an individual defendant this is most unjust.[2]

That there is truth in these complaints is admitted by the outgoing Director of Public Prosecutions, Sir Thomas Hetherington, in the first Annual Report on the service.[3] Whilst condemning much of the criticism as unjustified, he says 'On a

---

[1] Editorial, (1987) 151 JPN, 689.

[2] *The Times* 20 November 1987.

[3] HMSO 23 July 1987. The document is magnificently presented in a style that resembles a directors' report from the most expensive sort of public company, with some three-and-a-half of its 49 pages devoted to photographs of its staff, one of which is a full-page glossy portrait of the Director of Public Prosecutions, reminiscent of the opening page of *Country Life*. The cost is £8.30, and since

number of occasions, particularly in the beginning, we did fail to provide an acceptable level of service.'

To a large extent these problems seem to have been the result of the Service being set up without either the time or the money to do it properly. Everyone simply overlooked the practical problems involved in recruiting a force of 1,500 competent and dedicated lawyers. The levels of pay offered were not high enough to tempt enough lawyers of sufficiently high quality to join the service. This was particularly the case in London, where the problem of recruitment was made all the worse by the high cost of living and the fact that there was practically nothing in the way of an existing local service to build on, so that a very large number of lawyers had to be recruited all at once. Consequently the Service went into business in London with nearly 50 per cent of its posts unfilled, and many of the staff it had managed to recruit being raw, inexperienced and young. Because of the shortage of Crown Prosecutors it was decided that much of the actual prosecuting would be farmed out to local solicitors as agents, and the Crown Prosecutors would be kept in the office doing the administration – to the disappointment of those who enjoyed or had hoped to enjoy the thrill of advocacy. The general sense of disorganisation and the persistent public criticism of the new service caused bad morale – which spread to other parts of the country when members of the Service found themselves under pressure to go and work in London. Morale was made needlessly worse by a senseless Civil Service rule which ensured that a number of experienced prosecutors recruited from the superseded local prosecuting solicitors' departments were paid less for doing the same job than inexperienced people recruited from elsewhere. Having started badly, labour relations within the Service seem to have stayed bad. At the time of writing the management of the Service is being sued by the union that represents Crown Prosecutors because it has decided on grounds of staff shortages to use its unqualified staff to 'vet' some of the cases it receives to see whether the prosecution is fit to go ahead: something which on the face of it seems contrary to many of the arguments for creating the Service.[1] To be fair, not all the problems are the fault of the Service. The Crown Prosecution Service went into operation at the same time as a new scheme under which the prosecution are obliged to disclose their case to the defence in advance of summary trial, and the inevitable delays that this has caused have often been unfairly laid at the Crown Prosecution Service's door. And matters may appear worse than they really are. The fact that all the initial problems were at their worst in London, where they are most visible to the national press, has made sure that the worst possible impression was created. In his annual report in 1987, the Director of Public Prosecution bravely described these difficulties as transitional problems, and expressed hope 'that

the Lord Chancellor's Department can produce the Civil Justice Review General Issues Document consisting of 112 information-packed pages for £2 one feels that here if nowhere else the Crown Prosecution Service has not given value for money.
[1] The union has won the first round: *R* v. *DPP ex pte First Division Assn* 1988 138 NLJ 158.

next year will be a less difficult year for staff and will produce a more favourable industrial relations climate than has prevailed thus far in the new Service. In a more settled environment and with greater experience of new systems the Service should be able to improve its public image significantly in the coming year.' Other commentators, notably the editor of the *New Law Journal*,[1] think the difficulties may be more serious. 'One cannot help but think that CPS management has been hiding serious structural and operational difficulties under the ubiquitous "teething problems".' But even if the problems are really only teething problems, they have given the Crown Prosecution Service a bad start. It may be some years before they cease to have an effect on the calibre of staff it is able to recruit.

As far as public relations are concerned, the Crown Prosecution Service faces the extra problem that even if it does achieve what it was meant to achieve, the benefits are not the sort of thing for which the public is likely to give it any thanks. A stipendary magistrate has described the possible benefits of the Service as three: 'firstly, to release the police for other duties; secondly, to greatly speed up the administration of justice in magistrates' courts; and thirdly, to reduce the lists by enabling the prosecution to exercise a far greater discretion in deciding whether or not to proceed with a prosecution which may have doubtful prospects of success'.[2] The first two benefits, if they materialise, are likely to be masked by the rising level of crime and hence the generally increasing work-load of the police and the criminal courts. The third gain, that weak cases are dropped at an early stage, is not likely to make the Service popular with the general public either. The people who will benefit from this will be defendants, some of whom will be innocent and others guilty. The innocent will accept the benefit ungratefully as nothing less than their due, the guilty will keep quiet. The people who will write letters to the newspapers and to their MPs will probably be the victims of the crimes, and they are likely to be even more annoyed because their cases have been suppressed by what they see as a faceless bureaucracy than they would have been if the defendant had been tried in open court and acquitted. Up to now, the Crown Prosecution Service has adopted the practice of having nothing whatever to do with victims or their families, taking the view that this is not part of their job. It will get no credit and only blame for doing its necessary job of weeding out weak prosecution cases unless it is prepared to explain to the victim why this has been done.

The Roskill Committee on Fraud Trials[3] reported that serious commercial frauds were beyond the abilities of the police to investigate efficiently, and recommended the creation of a Serious Fraud Office to investigate and prepare such cases for trial. These recommendations were carried out by the Criminal Justice Act 1987, which was brought into force almost as soon as it was passed.

[1] Editorial, vol. 137 30 October 1987, p. 1003.
[2] Ronald Bartle, 'The Crown Prosecution Service: a view from the bench', (1987) 137 NLJ 33.
[3] HMSO (1986).

The Serious Fraud Office has a staff of about 90, including 26 lawyers and 17 accountants. Like the Crown Prosecution Service, it is responsible to the Attorney-General. Unlike the Crown Prosecution Service it has the power to investigate as well as to prosecute, and unlike the police it also has the power to require its suspects to co-operate with its investigations under pain of prosecution if they refuse.

iii The decision to prosecute

It is commonly believed that the police and the Crown Prosecution Service have a duty to prosecute a criminal offence if they have sufficient evidence against an alleged offender. This is the formal position in some legal systems: in West Germany, for example. But it is not and has never been the position in England. Prosecution is always a matter of discretion; a potential prosecutor must consider each case and decide whether he thinks criminal proceedings are justified. Until recently the discretion was a matter for the police, but since the Crown Prosecution Service came into being the discretion is now to be exercised twice over: the police must decide whether or not they will institute proceedings, and the Crown Prosecutor must decide whether he will carry on or drop the case.

Before the Crown Prosecution Service came into being the decision to prosecute was generally in the hands of the police, and as police forces are local they were free to adopt their own policies. Consequently, the question whether a given breach of the criminal law resulted in a prosecution if it was detected could easily depend on where in the country it took place. This was obviously unsatisfactory, and one of the reasons why the Royal Commission on Criminal Procedure recommended setting up the Crown Prosecution Service was that it would ensure the discretion to prosecute was uniformly exercised.[1]

Even before the Crown Prosecution Service was set up, some moves were made to encourage a standard approach. In 1982 the Attorney-General produced some guidelines for prosecutors, notably the '51 per cent rule': the notion that no prosecution should be instituted except where the prosecutor thought there was a better than evens chance that the court would convict on the evidence he could put before it.[2] And in 1985 the Home Office, having first set up an official working party to consider the matter, issued a circular to all police forces, setting out official guidance on when they should let offenders go with a formal caution instead of prosecuting them.[3]

As far as the Crown Prosecution Service is concerned, the position is now formalised by section 10 of the Prosecution of Offences Act 1985, which requires the Director of Public Prosecutions to issue a Code of Practice to Crown

[1] (1981) Cmnd 8092 para. 6.40 *et seq.*
[2] These guidelines were published by the Home Office in February 1983. They are reproduced in (1983) 147 JPN 228.
[3] Circular 14/1985. It was printed in the JPN in two instalments, 16 March and 23 March 1985, 173 and 190.

Prosecutors covering, among other things, when it is proper to start proceedings and when proceedings begun by the police should be stopped. This Code is published each year as an appendix to the Director's Annual Report.[1] Although it is officially directed to the Crown Prosecution Service there is no doubt that in practice it will influence the police as well. (There is nothing to require private prosecutors to take any notice of it, however, and it is open to any person who is disgruntled by a decision not to prosecute made in compliance with the Code to start his own prosecution if he has the time and money.)

The relevant part of the Code for Crown Prosecutors is six pages long, but it is possible to summarise it briefly. In deciding whether to start a prosecution or to carry on with one, the prosecutor must first be satisfied that there is sufficient evidence. 'A prosecution should not be started or continued unless the Crown Prosecutor is satisfied that there is admissible, substantial and reliable evidence that a criminal offence known to the law has been committed by an identifiable person.' At one time it was generally said that a prosecution is justified if the prosecutor believes in the guilt of the suspect and thinks the evidence against him would justify a conviction if the court believed it: in which circumstances lawyers would say there was a 'prima facie case'. But the Code, like the Attorney-General's guidelines in 1982, adopts the stricter test of whether it is more likely than not that the court of trial will believe this evidence: this is known as the '51 per cent rule'. 'The Crown Prosecution Service does not support the proposition that a bare prima facie case is enough, but rather will apply the test of whether there is a realistic prospect of conviction.' As a practical matter it is no doubt sensible that the courts should not be troubled with prosecutions which are likely to fail when they need all the time available to them to cope with the ones that are likely to succeed. But the '51 per cent rule' can cause great outrage to the victims and their families. Parents who believe their child has been indecently assaulted are likely to be grievously affronted to be told that there will be no prosecution because there is a less than evens chance that as a child she will be believed, and will probably think that the question of whether she is telling lies should be a matter for a court which has heard her rather than for an official sitting in an office who has merely read the file; there have been cases where official refusals to prosecute have been followed by private prosecutions.[2]

If he is satisfied about the evidence, the prosecutor must then consider whether the public interest would be served by bringing a prosecution. Under the heading 'public interest' he must weigh up a number of different factors.[3] The

[1] For its own use the Crown Prosecution Service has amplified the Code with a *Crown Prosecution policy manual*. It is impossible to say more about this, important as it doubtless is, because it is classified as a 'restricted document', no doubt in deference to the view of the Royal Commission on Legal Services that the prosecution process should be 'open and accountable'. ((1981) Cmnd 8092 p. 141.)

[2] For further discussion of the merits of this test see Glanville Williams 'Letting off the guilty and prosecuting the innocent' [1985] Crim LR 115, and Peter Worboys, 'Convicting the right person on the right evidence' [1985] Crim LR 764.

[3] A. J. Ashworth, 'The "Public Interest" Element in Prosecutions' (1987) Crim. LR 595.

first is the gravity of the offence. If someone appears to have committed a murder or a rape, for example, it is almost inconceivable that there should not be a prosecution provided the evidence is likely to stand up. If the offence is less serious – like a fairly minor theft, for example – a number of matters may tip the balance against bringing proceedings. These include the fact that the court would probably impose no more than a nominal penalty; the fact that the allegation is stale, particularly if it is three or more years old; that the offender is young, making it undesirable to give him a criminal record at an early stage in his life, or that he is old and infirm, or physically or mentally ill; and the fact that the original complainant does not now want the offender to be prosecuted.

The question whether or not to prosecute is closely linked with the question of whether the case is a suitable one for the police to give a caution.[1] This is recognised in the Code for Prosecutors, which makes a number of references to the Home Office guidelines on cautioning.[2] These guidelines advise the police to caution in the same sort of cases as the Code for Prosecutors advises against a prosecution. In the case of adult offenders, the Home Office guidelines assume that a caution will be the exception rather than the rule, but as far as juveniles are concerned they suggest that cautioning ought to be the rule and a prosecution the exception. Again, one of the factors pointing towards a caution rather than a charge is the fact that the complainant does not want the offender to be prosecuted; in some areas this has been made the basis for various schemes under which the offender makes reparation to the victim as part of a deal with the police under which no charge is brought. The guidelines on cautioning stress that no caution should be given unless the police have evidence enough to justify a prosecution, which means evidence to satisfy the '51 per cent rule'. If the evidence is not strong enough to justify a prosecution the police must drop the case, and they must not use cautions in order to appear to do something about crimes they have not really solved. Furthermore, cautions must be given only where the offender clearly admits the offence, and where the offender (or his parents if he is a juvenile) agree to this being done. This is important, because cautions are recorded in police records, and the defendant's history of cautions will be cited together with his convictions if a later court has to decide how to sentence him.

The Home Office circulars on cautioning were introduced in the attempt to produce a more uniform practice in cautioning, but despite the fact that the police normally obey such circulars, the *Criminal Statistics* for 1986 show that big differences still exist between different police forces. If and when the Crown Prosecution Service is operating efficiently, these differences may begin to disappear.

What remedy is available to the citizen who feels that the discretion to prosecute has been exercised unreasonably? In theory an exercise of the

[1] On the history of cautioning see chapter 25 below.
[2] Circular 14/1985; printed in (1985) 149 JP 173, 190.

discretion can be challenged in the High Court by way of judicial review,[1] but there has yet to be a case where the challenge succeeded. In order to succeed, the applicant would have to show that the decision was so unreasonable that no reasonable policeman or Crown Prosecutor could ever have made it, which is something he is hardly likely to be in a position to do. If the person who is dissatisfied is the victim of the offence, or anyone else who is outraged at a failure to prosecute, it is usually open to him to start a private prosecution. But he cannot do this for certain types of offence where there is a statutory requirement that the consent of some official – usually the Attorney-General or the Director of Public Prosecutions – must be obtained before there can be a prosecution, and where no such consent is needed the Crown Prosecution Service may still thwart him by taking the prosecution over and suppressing it.[2]

If the person aggrieved is the defendant he may sometimes have a remedy in the doctrine of *abuse of process*. In recent years the courts have been developing the theory that a criminal court must refuse to entertain a prosecution if it is brought under various circumstances that render the whole proceedings unfair. So far this theory is very nebulous, and this book is not the place for a detailed discussion of it.[3] Suffice it here to say that there have been cases where the Divisional Court has quashed proceedings in magistrates' courts where prosecutors started criminal proceedings for fairly minor offences, let them go to sleep, and then tried to press ahead with them when the defendant no longer had access to the evidence he needed to defend the charge. It is likely the doctrine of abuse of process would be invoked in other situations: for example, where someone had been induced to give evidence against an accomplice by a promise of immunity from prosecution which was later broken.[4] It must also be remembered that in the Crown Court the jury has an unfettered discretion to acquit a defendant, even where the evidence points plainly to his guilt, and if someone was prosecuted where to do so was plainly very harsh, the outcome might be a technically perverse but morally defensible acquittal.

iv The position of the defendant

In his memoirs Sir Henry Hawkins, later Baron Brampton, describes a trial at the Old Bailey as they were commonly conducted about the time that he was called to

---

[1] See chapter 17 above.

[2] In several cases where this happened the would-be prosecutor then tried, always unsuccessfully, to have the take-over decision judicially reviewed: see *Raymond* v. *AG* [1982] QB 839.

[3] The cases are reviewed by Rosemary Pattenden, 'The power of the courts to stay a criminal prosecution', [1985] Crim. LR 175.

[4] There is no doubt that the doctrine of abuse of process applies in the Crown Court as well as in the magistrates' courts; but as no judicial review lies from a trial on indictment in the Crown Court, and the defendant is limited to the grounds of appeal that are listed in the Criminal Appeal Act 1968, it is not clear what redress the defendant would have if in the Crown Court the judge wrongly refuses to suppress a prosecution which amounts to an abuse of process.

the Bar in 1843. The prisoner Jones, accused of picking pockets, pleaded 'not guilty'.

The accused having 'held up his hand', and the jury having solemnly sworn to hearken to the evidence, and 'to well and truly try, and due deliverance make', etc., the witness for the prosecution climbs into the box, which was like a pulpit, and before he has time to look round and see where the voice comes from, he is examined as follows by the prosecuting counsel:

'I think you were walking up Ludgate Hill on Thursday, 25th, about half past two in the afternoon, and suddenly felt a tug at your pocket and missed your handkerchief, which the constable now produces. Is that it?'

'Yes, sir.'

'I suppose you have nothing to ask him?' says the judge. 'Next witness.'

Constable stands up.

'Were you following the prosecutor on this occasion when he was robbed on Ludgate Hill and did you see the prisoner put his hand into the prosecutor's pocket and take this handkerchief out of it?'

'Yes, sir.'

Judge to prisoner: 'Nothing to say, I suppose?' Then to the jury: 'Gentlemen, I suppose you have no doubt? I have none.'

Jury: 'Guilty, my lord', as if to oblige his lordship.

Judge to prisoner: 'Jones, we have met before – we shall not meet again for some time – seven years' transportation. Next case.'

Time: two minutes, fifty-three seconds.

Perhaps this case was a high example of expedition, because it was not always that learned counsel could put his questions so neatly; but it may be taken that these after-dinner trials did not occupy on the average more than *four minutes* each.

A sentence of seven years could not be given today in such a casual way, but it is as well to keep the not-too-distant past in mind, for continuity of institutions may lead us to take for granted some practices that should be questioned.

In order to have a fair chance of defending himself, a person who is being prosecuted for a crime needs two things. First, he must have access to legal help and advice. Secondly, he must know in advance the nature of the case against him, so that he has the opportunity to call evidence to rebut it. Thirdly, his chance of preparing his defence efficiently is much improved if he is a free man, and it is important that where possible he should be allowed his freedom pending trial.

Legal advice and representation

The troubles of an accused person begin whilst he is in the hands of the police, before he is ever brought to court. The right of the accused to consult a lawyer at this stage, and the arrangements for ensuring that as a practical matter he is able to exercise it were described earlier in an earlier section of this chapter.

When it comes to legal representation at trial, it is surprising to learn that until

241

not so very long ago the accused did not merely have practical difficulties in obtaining it: it was actually forbidden. He was allowed to have counsel to represent him if the offence charged was legally classified as a misdemeanour, but if it was treason or a felony he was obliged to conduct his defence in person. As misdemeanours were, generally speaking, the less serious types of offence, and treason and felonies usually involved the risk of being sentenced to death, the position which the law took on the matter involved a hideous paradox: the worse the trouble the defendant was in, the less were the safeguards against a wrongful conviction. In treason trials counsel were allowed by a statute in 1696 – one passed, it is said, because of public disquiet about the series of wrongful treason convictions which had been brought about by the perjuries of Titus Oates. The accused finally acquired the right to have counsel to represent him in all cases by a statute of 1837.

If the accused is to be represented, he must be represented by a lawyer who has the right of audience in the court concerned. In a magistrates' court this means that he may be represented by a barrister or a solicitor; but as solicitors have only limited rights of audience in the Crown Court, his legal representative in the Crown Court must usually be a barrister. The right of the accused to be legally represented at his trial also implies a right in the opposite direction: the accused can conduct his own defence if he prefers. A defendant who wishes to do this is entitled to have a person of his choice beside him to prompt and help him – a figure usually called a 'McKenzie man' after the leading case in which this right was officially upheld.[1] McKenzie men are likely to be unqualified, but there is nothing to stop a defendant using a solicitor in this capacity if he is able to find one willing to oblige.

The defendant's theoretical right to be represented by a lawyer is useless to him unless he can afford to pay the fee. For many decades after the right to have legal representation was established, this practical difficulty ensured that many or most defendants were unrepresented. Since the Second World War the growth of legal aid in criminal cases has made the right to legal representation a reality. Nowadays almost every defendant in the Crown Court is represented by a lawyer, and his services will usually be paid for from the public purse. If the defendant needed a lawyer and one was unreasonably refused his conviction would probably be overturned on appeal.[2]

In the magistrates' courts, the extent to which the defendants are legally represented varies considerably from place to place, depending on the attitude of the local bench to legal aid; but it is rare in any magistrates' court to find a

[1] *McKenzie* v. *McKenzie* [1971] P 33. This was a civil case; the case which holds that the same applies in the criminal courts in *Kirk* (1983) 76 Cr. Ap. R. 194. At one time justices had a discretion to permit an unqualified person of the accused's choice to go further and actually to put his case for him, but this power is probably now obsolete: see *O'Toole* v. *Scott* [1965] AC 939.
[2] See *Kirk* (1982) 76 Cr. Ap. R., 194; but consider the amazing Privy Council decision in *Robinson* [1985] AC 956.

defendant who is unrepresented if he is facing any really serious charge. Legal aid in criminal cases is more fully discussed in chapter 40 below.

At present, legal representation for the defence means buying the services of lawyers in private practice, usually out of public funds. Until recently everyone has assumed that this is the best and indeed the only way to go about it. But nowadays different approaches to the matter are found in other countries. In some places the public prosecutor has an opposite number in the shape of a state official called a 'public defender', whose job is to conduct the defence of those persons who wish him to do so. This scheme exists in three States of Australia, and in a number of jurisdictions of the USA; there is also an experimental scheme in existence in British Columbia. A Scottish Royal Commission in 1980 recommended the Scots to experiment with the idea – a suggestion that has not yet been taken up.[1] In 1987 a committee of *Justice* published a report entitled *A Public Defender* which puts the case for such an institution in England.

One argument for this is that under the present system the accused does not always get an efficient and competent defence. Many solicitors – including many of the most competent ones – view criminal work, especially criminal work on legal aid, as sordid, ill-paid and unpleasant, and refuse to touch it. Thus whilst the defendant has a choice of solicitor in theory, in practice he often has to put up with what he can get. Whilst many or most solicitors engaged in this kind of work are highly conscientious, 'some solicitors run what can fairly be described as a legal conveyor belt. Their offices are conveniently situated opposite police stations or magistrates' courts. They employ clerks to take statements and sit in at trials. They fail to trace potential witnesses, and their briefs to counsel often consist solely of the depositions and the proofs they have taken from the accused and his witnesses.'[2]

In the Crown Court, where solicitors generally have no right of audience, the person who eventually appears for the defence must be a barrister. From the defendant's point of view this often means that he has the disquieting experience of finding that on the day of the trial his case is handled not by the person to whom he explained it earlier but by a stranger whom he has never seen in his life before, and, if the solicitor briefed him badly or too late, by a stranger who knows little or nothing about the case. Even if the case was well prepared, and counsel had had a conference with the defendant well before the trial, the inscrutable workings of the Bar may still ensure that someone else turns up on the day. The following passage from a judgment of the Court of Appeal is revealing:

We sympathise with the appellant to this extent: to be told on the Friday that counsel instructed to conduct his defence to a serious charge, in whom he had confidence and with whom he had had a long conference, would not be available on the following Monday, when the trial had been fixed to start on that day for that counsel's convenience, must have

---

[1] Royal Commission on Legal Services in Scotland (Hughes Commission), (1980) Cmnd 7846.
[2] Sargant and Hill, *Criminal trials – The search for truth*, Fabian Research Series No. 349, (1986) p. 10.

been very worrying. Let it be said at once that there is nothing in our papers to suggest any fault whatever on the part of the counsel or, indeed, of his clerk. Nevertheless from our combined experience we agree entirely with the comment of the learned judge below that 'this is the sort of situation that very frequently arises'. . . . We appreciate that . . . the Code of Conduct for the Bar provides that 'briefs are in general accepted on the understanding that the barrister concerned may be unavoidably prevented by a conflicting professional engagement from attending the case'. Nevertheless, particularly in criminal cases, both in contested matters and in pleas of guilty, we feel that there is a danger that all concerned may forget the very real feelings of frustration and deep anxiety that a defendant left in the lurch in this way may experience, even though it may be that nothing anyone could have done could have avoided the situation.[1]

Whilst expressing sympathy with the defendant, the Court of Appeal refused to accept that any of this gave him a valid ground of appeal: which is not surprising, because the Court of Appeal generally takes the hard-nosed view that defendants have to accept responsibility for the shortcomings of their legal advisors and representatives, even if it means they must stay wrongfully in gaol. In recent years the rates of pay for doing defence work on legal aid have been the subject of public spending cuts. The result is that lawyers who continue to do defence work on legal aid find it increasingly difficult to make it pay, and must either subsidise it from other parts of their practice, or else skimp on the work. The more the work is skimped, the more commonly the case is ill-prepared. Lawyers in private practice would say the answer is to provide more public money for criminal legal aid so that it is more profitable, the abler practitioners are attracted to it, and all are able to give the work sufficient time. But if the public is to spend more money, perhaps a public defender would give better value in return. In theory it might provide a better and more uniform standard of service, with more effective quality control.

Recent experience with the Crown Prosecution Service will raise many doubts as to whether a state agency in the shape of a public defender would really be more efficient at performing the tasks at present done by defence lawyers in private practice. But there is no doubt at all that a public defender could do some necessary jobs for defendants which a network of private practitioners is barely able to do at all. Laboratories for forensic science and centralised banks of information held by computers are routinely available to the police when they are getting up a case. But these are the sort of facilities which no firm of solicitors, however well-heeled, could possibly afford. At present, broadly speaking, the position is that if the defence wish to make use of such facilities they must beg a favour of the Home Office or of the police. A national public defender would be able to afford some of these back-up services of its own, and it would stand on an equal footing with the police and the Crown Prosecution Service in the matter of access to the services that it would be uneconomical for the state to provide in duplicate.

[1] *Breslin* (1985) 80 Cr. Ap. R. 226. 228.

Knowing the case that must be met

At one time the accused would know virtually nothing of the case he had to meet beyond what was disclosed in the indictment, and this was a source of little information for most defendants – not least because it used to be written in Latin.

As far as trials on indictment are concerned the practice of telling the defendant the nature of the case against him has been firmly established since the nineteenth century, when there was a change in the function of examining magistrates and the modern system of committal proceedings was established. Formerly, the duty of the magistrates was essentially to get up the case. They had a statutory duty to interrogate the accused and the witnesses on oath, to record what they said in writing, and to forward these *depositions* to the court to which he was then *committed for trial*. Whether the magistrates examined the witnesses in the presence of the accused, or told him what the witnesses had said if they examined them privately, was a matter for their discretion. When the police took over the job of getting up the case the magistrates' preliminary inquiry was retained, but its form and function changed. Its main purpose thereafter was to act as a filter to remove those cases from the system in which the police had collected too little evidence to justify a trial,[1] and its subsidiary purpose was to act as a mechanism by which the defendant was informed of the evidence against him. With this in mind, the accused was given a statutory right to be present during the examination of the witnesses by a statute of 1848; and the courts completed the picture by later ruling that if the prosecution wished to use evidence that had not been put forward at the committal proceedings, they were obliged to tell him what it was before the trial.[2]

Some mechanism is needed to achieve the purposes for which committal proceedings exist, but they are a complicated and rather troublesome way of achieving them.

In the first place, committal proceedings involve a judicial hearing which is normally held in public. Thus, not only is the defendant informed of the evidence which the prosecution propose to use against him; the information is shared with the world at large. If the case is sufficiently newsworthy, the newspapers will have their reporters there, and at one time they could then print the whole of the evidence at the committal and make it front-page news. This could be very unfair, because the magistrates might allow in evidence highly prejudicial matters which, if later held inadmissible at the trial, would probably be known to the jury from the newspaper account.[3]

In 1967 this problem was tackled by a Criminal Justice Act which drastically

[1] A function previously performed by the Grand Jury, which was then left without any useful function – although it was not abolished until 1933. An account of the last days of the Grand Jury in England is given by Devlin, *The criminal prosecution in England* (1960). In the USA the Grand Jury still operates.
[2] The story is told by Lord Devlin in *The criminal prosecution in England*, chapter 4.
[3] Various lurid cases in which this took place are described in earlier editions of this book.

curtailed the right of the press to report committal proceedings. The ordinary rule is that reporting is now limited to matters of formal record, such as the court, names of those concerned, the charges and the committal or other result. Full reporting is allowable if the defendant asks for reporting restrictions to be lifted; if there are two or more defendants only one of whom wants the restriction lifted the court has a discretion in the matter.[1] Full reporting is also allowed if the justices do not commit for trial, or after a trial is concluded.

Another trouble is that committal proceedings can be needlessly time-consuming. Until 1967 all the prosecution witnesses had to attend in person to give their evidence orally, while the court clerk wrote it down in long-hand at dictation speed. This wasted enormous amounts of the time of the magistrates, court-staff and police, and it was intolerable for the non-police witnesses, who had to give an account to the police, then to give evidence at the committal proceedings and then, if the case was fought, to go through the whole performance yet again at the trial. Two important changes were made by the Criminal Justice Act 1967 in an attempt to improve matters. First, the prosecution is now allowed to tender the written statements of its witnesses at committal proceedings provided the defence does not object. Secondly, and more radically, the magistrates are now permitted to commit for trial 'without consideration of the evidence' if certain conditions are met: namely, where the prosecution case consists of written statements copies of which have been given to the defence, the accused is legally represented and his lawyer does not object. Because this procedure is now contained in section 6(2) of the Magistrates' Court Act 1980, it is usually called a 'section 6(2) committal'; alternatively it is called a 'short form' or 'paper' committal. If the accused's lawyer objects to the procedure, the justices must then hold committal proceedings in which they consider the evidence: nowadays these are usually referred to as 'old-style committals'. The great majority of committals are now 'paper committals', but 'old-style committals' take place in a significant minority of cases. Where defence lawyers insist on an 'old-style committal' it may be because they hope that the magistrates can be persuaded not to commit the case for trial; but the usual reason will be that they provide an opportunity for a closer look at the prosecution witnesses, and having seen and heard them it is easier to advise on whether the best course at the trial is to fight or to plead guilty.

The main criticism that is made of committal proceedings today is that they are redundant as a filter for weak cases, and that as a method for informing the defendant of the case against him they are needlessly complicated. One of the major arguments for creating the Crown Prosecution Service was that it would act as a filter for weak cases. If the Crown Prosecution Service does this, why do

[1] The original provision was for restrictions to be lifted if any one of the defendants asked for it. This was changed in 1981 in response to the trial of Mr Jeremy Thorpe in 1979, in which one of co-defendants had caused the restriction to be lifted allegedly because a newspaper had paid him to do so.

246

we need a further filter in the shape of committal proceedings? When the Royal Commission on Criminal Procedure proposed the Crown Prosecution Service it also proposed the abolition of committal proceedings; instead of there being a scrutiny by magistrates in every case, the file would bypass the magistrates and go straight to the Crown Court except where the defendant specifically asked for a review of the evidence.[1] When the Crown Prosecution Service gets into its stride, a reform along these lines will probably be carried out. As for informing the defendant of the case against him, this could surely be done quite adequately by requiring the prosecution to serve on him a copy of the statements that their witnesses have made to the police – as they already do when preparing for a 'paper committal'.

In summary trials the defendant until recently had no right to any information about the prosecution case in advance. The police or the prosecuting solicitors would usually give the defence a copy of any statement that the defendant had made to the police, and they would sometimes tell the defence what the prosecution witnesses were expected to say; but if they were feeling awkward they could refuse all information, and the defendant might then arrive at court knowing nothing more than what was revealed in the three or four lines of typescript outlining the offence in the summons or charge. In this situation the prosecution evidence might take him completely by surprise. 'Trial by ambush' is how such proceedings were often described.

This was a sore point among defence lawyers for many years. Then in 1975 the James Committee[2] identified this problem as a reason why some defendants who had the option of summary trial or trial on indictment would choose trial on indictment although summary trial was otherwise more suitable, and recommended that the law be changed to require advance disclosure of the prosecution case. This led to section 48 of the Criminal Law Act 1977, which empowered the Lord Chancellor to make rules requiring disclosure: but successive Lord Chancellors failed to make any rules. Nevertheless a number of go-ahead justices' clerks began to experiment with voluntary schemes for advance disclosure, and from these experiments it seemed that where defendants and their lawyers knew the strength of the prosecution case in advance the usual result was a plea of guilty instead of a fought case.[3]

Soothed by this message, the Lord Chancellor eventually made the Magistrates' Courts (Advance Disclosure) Rules 1985. Unfortunately these embrace the principle of advance disclosure rather half-heartedly. They only apply to either-way offences, and thus do not apply to summary offences – although this category includes such potentially serious matters as assaulting or obstructing the police and threatening or insulting behaviour in public places.

---

[1] (1981) Cmnd 8092 para. 8.24 *et seq.*
[2] Report of the Committee on the Distribution of Criminal Business between the Crown Court and Magistrates' Courts, (1975) Cmnd 6323.
[3] The various schemes are reviewed in J. Baldwin, *Pre-trial justice* (1985).

They do not require the prosecution to give the defence a copy of the statements made by their witnesses, but permit them to offer a summary – which is necessarily less informative, and may be coloured by the prosecution views about the case.[1] And instead of requiring the prosecutor to give the information, the Rules merely require him to tell the defence of their right to request it. The idea of this was to make sure that the police and the Crown Prosecution Service do not waste their time preparing copies or summaries of statements that no one really wants; but by enabling unmeritorious defendants to ask for advance disclosure at the last minute when everyone is getting ready for a trial, the effect has been to provide a useful delaying tactic for putting off the evil day. What with the time taken up by writing summaries, and with cases being adjourned following belated tactical requests by defendants for advance disclosure, the most obvious result of the 1985 Rules has been to slow down the speed of summary trial.

The necessity for the defendant to have advance notice of the evidence that will be used against him is an aspect of the principle that a court must hear both sides of the argument and must not condemn a man unheard. If one party to litigation is to have a chance to answer his opponent's case, he must know what his opponent is saying, and if the opportunity is to be a fair one he must know this long enough in advance to consider the evidence and collect the evidence he needs to counter it. If this cannot be done the risk of a miscarriage of justice is created. On this argument there is an equally strong case for saying that the defence ought also to be required to disclose its case before the trial. To take an extreme example, if a man accused of an offence saves his alibi until the day of the trial and springs it on the prosecution as a surprise, it is then too late for the police to make any enquiries necessary to see if it is false. In recent years some minimal steps have been taken towards requiring advance disclosure from the defence. Since 1967 defendants in the Crown Courts have been required to give advance notice of an alibi, and since 1987 they must give advance notice of expert evidence as well.[2] But these provisions do not apply to summary trials, and even in the Crown Court the basic rule is still that the defence can hoard its evidence until the last minute, and spring it on the prosecution as a surprise. Only when the requirement of disclosure is made general will we really be able to say that the rules of English criminal procedure and evidence are designed to discover the truth rather than to obscure it.

Bail

A defendant may be held in custody pending trial, or he may be released on bail. The question of bail may arise at different stages in the proceedings. When a person has been arrested and taken to a police station the police may either let

---

[1] See J. Baldwin and A. Mulvaney, 'Advance disclosure in the Magistrates' Courts: How useful are the prosecution summaries?' [1987] Crim. LR 805.
[2] Crown Court (Advance Notice of Expert Evidence) Rules 1987, made under powers contained in PACE 1984 s.81.

him go unconditionally, or grant him what is called 'police bail' – which means that they may release him on condition that he later returns to the police station, or later attends at the magistrates' court. If the police keep him under arrest after they have charged him, section 46 of PACE requires them to take him before a magistrates' court 'as soon as is practicable and in any event not later than the first sitting after he is charged with the offence', and says they must take him to a place where a court will be sitting if the local court is not due to sit on the day of the charge or the day following. If the case is simple and the court is not a busy one the magistrates may be able to dispose of the case then and there; but usually they will have to adjourn the proceedings. Where the case is not serious the magistrates may simply order the defendant to be released during the adjournment period, but if the case is serious they may (and sometimes must) go further and *remand* him. A remand is either a remand in custody, which means that he stays in prison, or else a remand on bail, which means that he is free but placed under an obligation to appear for the adjourned proceedings breach of which is a criminal offence. When at last he is tried and convicted, the question of bail may arise again if he lodges an appeal. Here we are concerned with the question of bail between the defendant's first appearance in the magistrates' court and his eventual trial.

It is a serious matter to deprive a person of his liberty pending trial. A remand in custody will usually be an appalling disruption of the life of the defendant and his family. In a number of obvious ways it makes it difficult for him to prepare his defence if he is in prison. It also imposes a strain on public resources in conveying accused persons to and from prison and in keeping them in prisons where overcrowding is endemic and costs to the State are always increasing: in recent years, up to 20 per cent of the prison population has consisted of people on remand awaiting trial. It follows that a defendant should be granted bail wherever this can be safely done. The law on the subject is contained in the Bail Act 1976. This was based on the Report of a Home Office Working Party entitled *Bail procedures in magistrates' courts* published in 1974.[1] The Act was intended to encourage a more uniform approach and a more liberal attitude.

The Bail Act works by creating what is generally called a 'right to bail' in the case of someone who is awaiting trial. However the right is not an unqualified one, because Schedule I of the Act sets out a number of broadly-defined circumstances in which bail may be refused.

In the first place, bail may be refused if there are substantial grounds for believing that the defendant would do any of the following: (a) fail to surrender to custody (b) commit an offence while on bail, or (c) interfere with witnesses or otherwise obstruct the course of justice. The case for refusing bail in cases (a) or (c) is obvious, but case (b) sticks in some people's throats. At the stage of a bail application it has not yet been formally proved that the defendant committed an

---

[1] (HMSO, but not a command paper.) Further details about the earlier law and the background to the Report are given in the previous edition of this book.

offence once, and the criminal justice system supposedly presumes a person innocent until he is proved to be guilty. How can we fairly refuse a man bail for fear that he will repeat the offence when we are meant to assume that he is innocent? The explanation is a pragmatic one. If the defendant is a professional criminal – a burglar, for example – he may expect to go to prison following his eventual trial, and if released on bail he will probably be tempted to put in a vigorous spell of overtime awaiting trial in order to make sure his wife and family are provided for whilst he is inside.

A further ground upon which bail may be refused is where it is necessary to keep the defendant in custody for his own protection. This might be the case where the crime has aroused fierce local feeling against him – if he is accused of offences against young children, for example – or where the police fear he is likely to be assassinated by a violent co-defendant who is anxious to shut his mouth. Bail is sometimes refused on this ground where the defendant has been threatening to kill himself. Bail may also be refused where the defendant is already serving a prison sentence – obviously there is no point granting bail to a person who must in any case go back to gaol – and bail may be refused if he was granted bail earlier and was arrested for failing to come back to court or for breaking the conditions on which the bail was granted.

Finally, bail may be refused where the court has insufficient information upon which to make a decision. This will often be the case when the defendant makes his first appearance in the magistrates' court following the arrest and charge, and in these circumstances, of course, bail may be granted on a later application. But even then there may be a lack of information, particularly where he is unrepresented. In this case all the information the court is likely to have will come from the police, and this may give less than a balanced view. This problem is partly met by legal aid for bail applications, fortified by the duty solicitor scheme (see chapter 40, section iv); but legal representation does not wholly solve the problem because assertion is no substitute for information – even in bail proceedings, where the formal rules of evidence do not apply. Here we probably have something to learn from various schemes in the United States; some information about them is given in the report of the Home Office Working Party which preceded the Bail Act. The main feature of these schemes is that a standard form is completed about a defendant before he appears in court so that the court has information about his home background, residence, employment record and so forth. In this country there have been a number of pilot schemes of this type, and they have recently been reviewed by the VERA Institute.[1] In this way it is possible to put information before the Crown Prosecution Service and before the magistrates to complement, and sometimes to neutralise the information they receive from the police. Such schemes clearly have the potential for making bail procedures work more fairly, but they obviously depend on enough people being available to carry out the necessary work involved.

[1] *Probation service work on bail with the Crown Prosecution Service* (1987).

In deciding whether to grant or refuse bail on one of the prescribed grounds the Bail Act requires the court to consider a number of matters. These include the seriousness of the offence and the likely sentence on conviction; the reasoning here is that defendants are more likely to run away from the prospect of a long prison sentence than a short one. Another factor is 'the character, antecedents, associations and community ties of the defendant'. What this means among other things is that if the defendant is homeless he is likely to be refused bail. This is understandable, but it is also harsh, because homelessness is a misfortune and to refuse bail because of it is to pile one misfortune on another. A partial solution to this problem has been the creation of a number of 'bail hostels'. If a place in one of these is available, a homeless person may be granted bail on condition he goes to live in the hostel, which will probably be preferable to imprisoning him pending trial. In 1987 the Home Secretary announced that the number of bail hostels was to be increased from 16 to 25. The other factors which the magistrates are obliged to take into account are how the defendant has previously behaved when granted bail, and the strength or otherwise of the evidence against him: the weaker the prosecution case, the greater the likelihood of eventual acquittal, and the more unjust a period of detention pending trial. This list of factors is not exclusive, and the magistrates are also bound to consider 'any others which appear to be relevant': the fact that the defendant or a member of his family is seriously ill, for example, or the fact that he is able to provide sureties (see below).

All of this applies only where the defendant is charged with an offence which is punishable with imprisonment. If the offence is not punishable with imprisonment, the grounds for refusing bail are confined to persons who have previously been granted bail and failed to appear in accordance with the terms of that bail.

Bail, if granted, may be unconditional. If it is, then the defendant is free to go, subject only to his obligation to surrender to his bail at the next stage of the proceedings. If he absconds – something more commonly referred to 'jumping bail' or 'going over the side' – he thereby commits a criminal offence for which he may be arrested and for which he will be punished if and when he is caught. Very often, however, the court does not grant bail unconditionally but makes it subject to conditions. Provided they are reasonable, the court may impose any conditions that seem necessary to make sure that the defendant does not abscond, does not interfere with witnesses, and does not commit further offences whilst on bail. If they think the defendant might be tempted to flee abroad, a condition might be the surrender of his passport. During the miners' strike some magistrates imposed a condition on pickets arrested for picket-line violence: namely, that they did not do further picketing whilst on bail, and their decision was upheld by the Divisional Court.[1]

A very usual condition of bail is that the applicant provides a *surety*. This is some person other than the defendant himself who is willing, in effect, to make a

[1] *R. v. Mansfield Justices ex pte. Sharkey* [1985] QB 613.

bet with the court that the defendant will turn up as he has promised; this bet is called a *recognisance*. If the person on bail absconds the surety is obliged to pay. No money has to be handed over at the time of entering into the recognisance, but the prosecution may object to a surety on various grounds, including that he is unlikely to be able to pay if the necessity arises. In principle the court decides on the suitability of sureties by questioning them, but this is difficult if they are not there and cannot be brought to court quickly. Section 8 of the Bail Act 1976 meets this difficulty by enabling the magistrates to grant bail provided sureties for certain sums are forthcoming, leaving it up to the police (and certain other officials) to see if the defendant's sureties looks good for the sum involved and to take the recognisances if they do. A person who is rejected as a surety in these circumstances has a right of appeal to the court.[1]

If the magistrates decide to remand a defendant in custody pending trial, that is not the end of the matter, because there are four separate and independent routes by which their refusal of bail may be challenged. First, it is often possible for him to ask the magistrates to change their mind. When they commit a person for trial, the magistrates deal with the question of bail pending trial once and for all; but where they remand pending summary trial, mode of trial proceedings or committal proceedings, they are not permitted to remand in custody for longer than eight days at a time, and at each remand there is the possibility of a further application for bail. The opportunities offered by this were severely curtailed by a decision of the Divisional Court which ruled that a fresh application may not be made unless new facts have emerged; where his case for bail remains the same, the defendant must not be permitted to pester the original bench of magistrates to change their minds, or try to persuade a differently constituted bench to act as a court of appeal on their colleagues.[2]

However, where the defendant is remanded in custody at his first appearance because the magistrates have insufficient information upon which to grant him bail, there will usually be sufficient new information at his second appearance to justify a fresh application, and further applications remain a possibility where the situation has changed – as will often be the case where, following a lengthy remand in custody, the magistrates eventually hold committal proceedings and commit him for trial.

Where the magistrates refuse bail, the second method by which the defendant may seek to challenge their decision by making a bail application to a High Court judge in chambers. At one time this was the only way in which the defendant could challenge a repeated bail refusal on its merits, and for various reasons it was not a good one. Legal aid was not (and is not) available for such an application, and those who could not afford to pay for their own lawyer had to use a cut-price procedure under which the Official Solicitor acted for them. Furthermore,

---

[1] There is a useful article on sureties by James Morton, 'Sureties', (1985) 135 NLJ 981.
[2] *R.* v. *Nottingham Justices ex pte. Davies* [1981] QB 38.

involving a High Court Judge in what were often fairly routine cases was something of a sledgehammer to crack a nut. Thus in 1982 the Criminal Justice Act provided a third method: an application to the Crown Court – where it will normally be heard by a Circuit Judge or Recorder. An application to the Crown Court is something which most defendants can make locally, unlike an application to the High Court, and legal aid may be obtained for making the application. Surprisingly, although it makes the procedure of applying to a High Court Judge largely redundant, that procedure has not been abolished, and the defendant is free to try first one and then the other, or even both at the same time – as well as, or as an alternative to trying to make fresh bail applications to the magistrates. The fourth possible method of challenging a refusal of bail is to apply for the decision of the magistrates to be judicially reviewed (see chapter 17 above). This is of little or no use when what is at issue is the merits of the decision, but it is appropriate where the defendant claims their decision was not open to them as a matter of law, or broke some essential rule of procedure.

Two criticisms of the use of bail are persistently made: that bail is granted too infrequently, and that it is too often granted where it should be refused. At first sight these criticisms seem to cancel one another out, but it is possible that there could be truth in both.

It is obviously a matter of serious concern if people are being remanded in custody where there is no pressing reason. But is this happening? A number of studies over the years have pointed out that a substantial proportion of those who are remanded in custody are acquitted or are convicted and not given a custodial sentence: recent figures suggest that those acquitted number some 3 per cent, and those who are convicted but receive no custodial sentence are somewhere between a third and a half. The inference usually drawn is that the result of such cases shows that bail should have been given and that a remand in custody was unjustifiable. But this does not necessarily follow. The court may, for example, give a non-custodial sentence precisely because the defendant has already spent some time in prison. The courts must make each decision in the light of the information available to them at the time they make it, so *ex post facto* assessments of bail decisions are really not conclusive.[1]

What is more disquieting, however, is a Home Office study which shows there are enormous variations in the extent to which bail is granted by magistrates in different parts of the country.[2] Against a national average of some 16 per cent of defendants remanded in custody, it is difficult to see what can sensibly explain the fact that Dorset magistrates remand 31 per cent in custody and North Yorkshire magistrates 37 per cent. It is difficult to believe that these areas have more villainous villains than the rest of the country, or a population in greater need of protection from them. It does look as if a change of policy by the magistrates

[1] See paras. 78–81 of the *Report of the Working Party on Bail* (1974) (page 249 above).
[2] Peter Jones, 'Remand decisions at Magistrates' Courts', in *Managing criminal justice*, ed. David Moxon, Home Office Research and Planning Unit (1985).

in certain commission areas could make a useful impression on prison overcrowding.

The criticism that bail is granted too readily is usually made in response to a particular incident where a defendant who was remanded on bail has used the opportunity to commit some very serious offence. There have been a number of such cases over the years. The most striking concerned Winston Silcott, who murdered a policeman during the Broadwater Farm riot in 1985. On his conviction for murder in 1987 it was revealed that he committed the murder when he was on bail awaiting trial for another murder – bail that had been granted notwithstanding his serious criminal record which included other offences of violence in the past. This case provoked a public outcry against the Bail Act. But isolated incidents of this sort, however horrible, do not show that the courts are generally granting bail in cases where they should not. Much less do they show that the principles in the Bail Act are wrong, because in all of these cases, including Silcott's, there existed ample grounds for remanding the offender in custody if the courts had had their wits about them. What they really show is that in any system there are bound to be some mistakes. What is unsatisfactory, however, is that whereas the defendant has four different ways available to him for challenging an allegedly unreasonable refusal of bail, the prosecution has no means at all of challenging a grant of bail, however grossly unreasonable, except perhaps by judicial review. There is surely a strong case for allowing the prosecution the right to appeal to the Crown Court against a grant of bail.[1]

[1] At the time of writing, a clause in the Criminal Justice Bill at present before Parliament would impose a duty on a court to give reasons if it grants bail to a person who is accused of murder, rape, or certain other serious offences.

23

CRIMINAL PROCEDURE

Practically all criminal cases come before justices of the peace, either to be tried summarily or for committal proceedings. Most of the summary cases and a few that are more serious are begun by the prosecutor 'laying an information' which comes before a justice or a justices' clerk, who authorises the issue of a summons which will be served on the defendant. A summons states the alleged offence and gives the date and place where the defendant is to appear. In the case of a person who would probably disregard a summons, the prosecutor may ask for a warrant of arrest as the initial step; this application must be made upon a sworn statement. The granting of summonses and warrants need not be done in open court; in the case of warrants for arrest it would often be unwise to advertise the steps that are being taken. In many cases there is neither summons nor warrant, for the accused has been arrested and charged at the police station and he appears before the magistrates' court on police bail or in custody. Where the police proceed by this method a copy of the charge-sheet is sent to the magistrates' court, and this constitutes 'laying the information'.

A defendant must as a general rule be present in court during committal proceedings and at a trial on indictment;[1] there are exceptions to this, however, notably where the accused behaves in a disorderly manner and disrupts the proceedings.[2] Personal attendance by the defendant is not always necessary for summary trials. First, the defendant in a magistrates' court has a right 'to appear' by solicitor or counsel. Secondly, where the defendant fails to appear, a magistrates' court may, on proof of service of a summons, either require the defendant to appear (and may issue a warrant for his arrest) or may hear the case in his absence (although it may not impose a custodial sentence on an absent defendant, nor may it usually disqualify him from driving). Thirdly, since 1957 there has been a procedure under which a person who is accused of a minor offence may plead guilty by post. This applies to any summary offence for which

---

[1] The leading case is *Lee Kun* (1916) 11 Cr. Ap. R 293.

[2] This has always been the case at trials on indictment, but formerly it did not apply at committal proceedings, and if a defendant seriously disturbed the proceedings, as happened with Kray (who was at the time serving a life sentence for murder and had nothing to lose), the only course was to ask a judge to authorise the preferment of a voluntary bill of indictment. A provision in the Criminal Justice Act 1972 enabled committal proceedings to take place in the absence of a disruptive defendant.

the maximum penalty does not exceed three months' imprisonment. The defendant gets, together with the summons, a brief statement of the police evidence, and a form on which he can if he wishes plead guilty, say that he does not intend to appear, and set out any mitigating circumstances. He need not reply, and if he wants to defend the case he must appear. Most defendants who can use this procedure do plead guilty by post, and their statements are read out in court without any witnesses attending, which saves a great deal of time and trouble. The bulk of minor motoring offences have long been dealt with in this way. A development which goes still further in this direction is the fixed penalty scheme, first introduced for parking offences in 1960, and extended to speeding and a number of other motoring offences in 1986. Here the police give the motorist the option of paying a penalty fixed by statute if he does not wish the case to go to court. Where he opts to pay the fixed penalty, as he almost always does, the magistrates' court is by-passed altogether, unless the penalty is left unpaid.

In a summary case with the defendant present, the substance of the charge is read out and he is asked whether he pleads guilty or not guilty. If he admits it, that is, 'pleads guilty', the court may wish to hear the more important evidence, but more often it is thought sufficient for the Crown Prosecutor to give a short account of the facts. The defendant may also address the justices, or evidence may be given by himself or by others in the hope of inducing the bench to impose a light or nominal sentence.

If the defendant pleads not guilty, the trial proceeds. In describing this procedure it will be convenient to assume that the defendant is represented by a solicitor. This used not to be common, the usual pattern being a defendant in person appearing against a prosecutor in the shape of a policeman. In the last 20 years there has been a major change, with first prosecuting solicitors and then Crown Prosecutors replacing the police as prosecutors, and the majority of defendants accused of 'either-way' offences now being represented on legal aid. There are still a good many summary trials in which the defendant is unrepresented, however, and where this is so the procedure that is about to be described is not invariably followed. But by describing what happens when legal advisers are present, we can get a sketch of what is supposed to happen in all cases.

After the plea of 'not guilty' the solicitor for the prosecution will 'open the case', that is, he will describe the prosecution's allegations and indicate the way in which this story is going to be substantiated. This 'opening' is not evidence, and the advocate must be careful not to make statements that cannot be supported by the evidence he is going to call. The witnesses for the prosecution are then called. Each witness is first questioned by the prosecution, this process being the 'examination in chief'; then he is 'cross-examined' by the defence, and then sometimes 're-examined' by the prosecution. A large mass of rules of evidence restrict the questions that may be asked: these rules are highly technical and difficult to understand. On the whole they are meant to protect the defendant (but occasionally they have the opposite effect). After the prosecution has called all the evidence that is to be given, the defence may submit that there is no case to answer. That means that he contends that if all the evidence for the prosecution is believed that would not establish the commission of the alleged offence. The justices must then consider this submission, and if they decide that there is a case to be answered the defence must be put forward. The defendant's advocate may 'open the defence', and call witnesses, including the defendant himself: these witnesses will give their evidence in the same way as the witnesses for the prosecution, except that the examination in chief is now conducted by the defence and the cross-examination by the prosecution. It is possible, in some circumstances, for the prosecution to call witnesses to rebut the evidence given for the defence. If the only evidence for the defence is that of the defendant himself, then instead of 'opening' the case the defendant's advocate must call the defendant and address the court afterwards. When there are other witnesses besides the defendant the justices may allow an address to the court after the evidence for the defence instead of the 'opening'. Further speeches are not allowed unless there is a point of law to be argued. The justices must then decide whether to convict or acquit: for this purpose they frequently retire to their own room so that they can discuss the case freely. If they decide to convict, the prosecutor will usually be asked to state what he knows about the defendant. During the hearing of the case the prosecution is generally speaking not allowed to give evidence to the effect that the defendant is of bad reputation or has been previously convicted of some offence, but after conviction it is considered relevant to assist the court in determining the sentence that should be imposed.

If the offence in question is triable only on indictment, the justices do not try the case but hold a preliminary enquiry, now more usually known as committal proceedings. A general account of these was given in chapter 22(iv) above. If the offence is an 'either-way offence' – that is, it is triable either summarily or on indictment – the justices hold what are called 'mode of trial proceedings' to determine whether they should try it summarily or whether it should be tried on indictment in the Crown Court. These proceedings were described in chapter 19(ii). Where summary trial is not the outcome of the mode of trial proceedings, committal proceedings will then follow. The great majority of committals are now 'paper committals'; but where there is an 'old-style committal' it follows roughly the same form as a summary trial, except that the court clerk takes the evidence down in writing and reads it over to each witness, who then signs it. These written statements of evidence are called 'depositions'. If the justices think that there is a *prima facie* case against the defendant, he is given the opportunity to give evidence and to call witnesses in defence, and the defence evidence is also recorded. The depositions, and a copy of any statement that the defendant may have made, are transmitted to the clerk of the trial court. Where it is a 'paper committal' what is sent is the statements which the prosecution witnesses made to the police, these being the basis upon which the justices then commit for trial. By law these are then deemed to be depositions. On the basis of the depositions the indictment is drawn up – usually by members of the administrative staff at the court of trial, but by counsel if the case looks difficult. The case will then be tried as soon as the workload of the Crown Court permits.

If the magistrates refuse to commit for trial when they ought to do so, or commit in a case where they ought not to do so, it is possible to attack their decision by means of an application for judicial review (see chapter 17 above). However, any judge of the High Court is empowered by statute to commit a person for trial, and as a practical matter an easier solution for the dissatisfied prosecutor is to apply to a judge for the exercise of this power. When a judge commits a person for trial he is said to *prefer a voluntary bill of indictment*.[1]

Until the later part of the eighteenth century trials on indictment, like summary trials 20 years ago, were commonly conducted with neither the prosecution nor the defence represented by lawyers.[2] For many years the prosecution has invariably been represented by counsel, and nowadays the defence are almost always represented by counsel as well, usually paid for by legal aid. In general outline a trial on indictment follows the lines given for a summary trial. The defendant is *arraigned*, that is called upon to plead, on each count of the indictment separately, so that he may plead not guilty to some counts and guilty on others.[3]

The arraignment takes place before he is given in charge to the jury and the jury does not hear about any pleas of guilty because that might prejudice them against him; the jury is to try the count or counts on which he has pleaded not guilty. The evidence and the speeches follow a similar order to that adopted in summary trial, with the defence having the last word. The judge's summing up is essentially in the form 'if you find such and such allegations to be true, your verdict must be so and so', although to enable the jury to come to their conclusion the judge may review any of the evidence and comment upon it. If the jury return a verdict of 'not guilty' that is final; no appeal lies against an acquittal, as has already been explained (chapter 21), and the defendant cannot be tried again for

[1] The power to prefer a voluntary bill formerly belonged to the Grand Jury, something which enabled it to take action against persons other than those whom magistrates had committed for trial. The power was transferred to High Court Judges when the Grand Jury was abolished in 1933.
[2] See two important studies by Professor John H. Langbein, 'The criminal trial before the lawyers', (1985) 45 *U of Chicago Law Review* 263–316, and 'Shaping the eighteenth-century criminal trial: A view from the Ryder Sources', (1983) 50 *U of Chicago LR* 1–136.
[3] There are other possible pleas, but these are rare and some of them are obsolete. There can be a plea that the defendant has already been tried and convicted (*autrefois convict*) or acquitted (*autrefois acquit*), or a plea to the jurisdiction (that the court has no jurisdiction), or that the defendant has received a Royal pardon, or that he demurs (that the facts alleged by the prosecution do not disclose a criminal offence). The defence can normally raise any of these matters on a plea of not guilty and that is the usual course. There is a special procedure for deciding whether a defendant is 'fit to plead', usually because of his mental condition. Where the defendant refuses to make any plea at all this used to present a serious difficulty, and until 1772 there was a savage practice called *peine forte et dure* under which he was ceremonially pressed beneath heavy weights until he either changed his mind or died. Nowadays a plea of not guilty is entered on his behalf.

the same offence. There may be special verdict that the accused is not guilty by reason of insanity.[1]

In the past the most notable characteristic of jury trial in England was the requirement of unanimity in the verdict; that was not a result of rational argument but of historical development. Trial by jury came into our law to take the place of ordeals, that is, or *judicium dei* which was a single voice. Even the number of a jury is sometimes said to have been fixed at twelve because there were twelve Apostles. The requirement of a unanimous verdict was generally justified in modern times on two grounds. First, since criminal process used to be disadvantageous to the accused, the balance was redressed in his favour by the jury having to be unanimous. Secondly, it is very difficult to feel quite sure that an accused really is guilty because so often there are lingering doubts about witnesses and their evidence, but if every juror is satisfied there cannot be much room for wrongful conviction. But it was not a convenient rule because of the effect that a single obstinate juror might have. A juror who simply refused to agree could wear down the others and eventually get them to agree so that the whole tiring business could be finished. But far more sinister was the possibility of a juror being got at or 'nobbled' on behalf of the accused. It was following a number of allegations of this happening that the Criminal Justice Act 1967 made it possible for a jury to return a majority verdict. These are now allowable where there are not less than eleven jurors and ten of them agree on the verdict, or where there are ten and nine of them agree on the verdict. Despite majority verdicts, allegations of jury-nobbling are still made, and it is possible that there may be an attempt at some time in the future to reduce the size of the majority still further. The position in England is still considerably more generous to the accused than it is in Scotland, where the jury of fifteen has always been able to convict if eight of its members vote for a conviction. The majority of jurors laid down by statute are needed to acquit the defendant as well as to convict him. If they are unable to reach the necessary majority for a conviction or an acquittal the jury is said to be 'hung', and the consequence is that the defendant is put up for trial a second time. In theory there is nothing to stop this happening repeatedly if successive juries disagree, but by convention the proceedings are usually dropped if the second jury disagrees.

The major question about trial on indictment is whether judge and jury constitute a satisfactory tribunal. The problem of judges in criminal trials is the same as in civil cases, being, in the words of Lord Davey, that: 'All English judges are impartial, but not all have the power of divesting themselves of prejudice'. This personal factor is inevitable, since tribunals must be composed of men and

---

[1] The verdict used to be 'guilty of the act (or omission), but so insane as not to be responsible, according to the law, for his action at the time when the act was done (or the omission made)'. This curious verdict, devised by Queen Victoria, was treated as one of acquittal, with the result that no appeal could be made. The Criminal Procedure (Insanity) Act 1964 altered the form of the verdict and gave a right of appeal. On mental disorder and criminal proceedings see chapter 24.

not machines. One judge, who was a great authority upon ecclesiastical law, will be remembered for his severity in all bigamy cases: as a pillar of the church he considered that all infringements of morality were necessarily serious offences. Whether a trial was held before this judge, or before one of his colleagues who was an agnostic, might make a difference to the sentence. The extent to which a body of people, judges or others, is prejudiced is always a matter of dispute; the ecclesiastical lawyer and the agnostic doubtless considered each other to be hopelessly prejudiced. Trial by a single judge is perhaps not the best method; if ten out of a dozen judges can appear unprejudiced, the other two judges may well discredit the whole system. In most countries it is the practice to have three or more judges together, with or without some system of jury. The traditional English method in criminal cases has been the single judge with jury, and the use of three judges would presumably be regarded as too expensive if there was any chance of its being politically acceptable. The main question about jury trial is whether it has merits that should ensure its retention in our legal system. This question cannot however be dissociated from problems of machinery, such as the qualification of jurors and the methods of summoning a panel and selecting a jury. These matters are discussed in Part V, where the method of appointment of judges is also discussed.

There is much that is good in the way in which trials in this country are conducted. Cases are disposed of without adjournments (other than from day to day) except in a very few cases and yet the proceedings are not hurried. The defendant usually has ample opportunity to challenge the evidence against him and he is not usually harried or brow-beaten either by the prosecutor or by the judge. However there are a number of matters which cause disquiet.

i Guilty pleas – plea bargaining

It is a feature of criminal trials in the common law that two radically different forms of procedure are followed, depending on whether there is a plea of guilty or not guilty. On a plea of not guilty, the prosecution must prove the case according to strict rules of evidence, which normally require them to produce their witnesses in court for oral examination and cross-examination. This takes up a large amount of time and money. If the case is tried on indictment there will also be a jury, which slows things down still further because everything must be explained to them in simple terms. In the magistrates' court a simple fought case will take up most of a morning, and in the Crown Court it will take a day or a couple of days. On a plea of guilty, most of the time-consuming elements are dispensed with. Witnesses are not usually called to testify about the details of what happened, and the court usually proceeds on the basis of the facts as recounted by the prosecutor. In the Crown Court there is no jury and everything is done by the judge. A case of homicide, which if contested would take several days at least, can be dealt with in 40 minutes.[1] In the magistrates' courts a guilty plea would probably take less than half that time – very much less if the defendant pleads guilty by letter. The police like guilty pleas, because they can be getting on with what they see as more important duties if they are not hanging around the courts waiting to give evidence. Judges, magistrates, court administrators and Home Office officials like them too, because they enable the criminal courts to get through their caseload, and so keep down pre-trial delays. Indeed, if between a half and a third of Crown Court defendants and the vast majority of defendants in the magistrates' courts did not plead guilty the criminal justice system would immediately seize up. Consequently the system has developed a number of incentives to encourage guilty pleas.

One of these is the possibility of an earlier disposal of the case: guilty pleas can usually be dealt with much sooner than contested cases. The second incentive is to do with costs. Fighting the case will obviously cost the defendant more by way of his own lawyer's fees, and the courts also regard the fact that he has fought the case as a proper reason for making him pay more of the prosecution costs if he loses.[2] But the main incentive is that the courts give the person who pleads guilty a discount on his sentence, which is customarily around two-thirds of what it would have been if he had contested the case. There is no secret about this, and it is done quite openly. In one case Lord Justice Lawton said the following:

The appellant, no doubt, was advised by his counsel, and rightly advised, that if he pleaded guilty he was likely to be more leniently dealt with than if he pleaded not guilty. This is the practice of the Courts and in the judgment of this Court a very wise practice indeed. It can be justified (despite what some academic writers have said about it) on the ground that a man who admits his guilt is in a more penitent mood than one who denies it and persists in telling lies in support of his denial. Morality and common sense both envisage that the penitent thief should be dealt with more leniently than the impenitent one. The sooner it is appreciated by those charged with criminal offences that they will be more leniently dealt with if, being guilty, they plead guilty, the better it will be for them and the better it will be for the public.[3]

As no attempt is ever made to discover whether a particular guilty plea stems from penitence or a cynical calculation that it will enable the defendant to resume his criminal career more quickly, and as the discount may be withheld where the case against the defendant was a clear one (although he may then be just as penitent as where it would have taken time and trouble to prove the case against him), this justification for the discount is of course a piece of humbug. The real justification for the discount is that by pleading guilty the defendant has saved the

[1] See the case of Deborah Philpott, *The Independent* 24 July 1987.
[2] For costs, see chapter 38.
[3] *Coffey* (1982) 74 Cr. Ap. R 168, 169.

criminal justice system time and trouble, and has possibly saved the victim of the offence a nasty experience in having to give evidence; and for this it is necessary to reward him in public, to encourage his criminal friends to do the same.

Since guilty pleas involve both benefits and disadvantages to prosecution and defence they are often preceded by negotiations in which each side tries to get the best deal that it can. This process is usually called 'plea bargaining'. In the USA it is a highly-developed part of the criminal justice process, and involves not only the prosecution and defence but the judge as well. In England things have not gone quite so far, and plea-bargaining is usually confined to prosecution and defence, with the judge staying firmly out of it. If plea-bargaining occurs in the early stages it will take place between the defendant and the police. During interrogation the suspect may offer to 'cough' certain offences if the police drop their interest in others. If an informal deal is struck, nothing about these other offences will ever reach the charge-sheet, let alone the court. Plea-bargaining at later stages will involve the defendant (or his lawyers), and the Crown Prosecution Service; or the defence lawyers and prosecuting counsel if the case has reached the Crown Court when the bargaining takes place. Once again there will be a proposal from one side or other that in return for a plea of guilty to charge X, charge Y will be withdrawn; if you will drop the murder charge, say, we will plead guilty to manslaughter, or to causing death by reckless driving. The legal basis for such a deal is the ability of the prosecution to drop a charge. In the very early stages, the Crown Prosecutor has an unfettered power to drop a case, or part of one, simply by announcing that he is dropping it (see chapter 22(ii) above). Dropping a charge in the later stages of a case usually requires more formality: the defendant is put up to plead 'not guilty', the prosecution offers no evidence, and the court enters a formal acquittal. For this the consent of the court is needed, at least in theory, and judges have been known to refuse.[1] The most celebrated case was that of Sutcliffe, the 'Yorkshire Ripper', in 1981, where the Attorney-General wanted to drop the murder charges in return for a plea of guilty to manslaughter and the judge would not allow it. In general, however, the judge or magistrates are as anxious to save time as everyone else and are very happy to agree to the arrangement.

Negotiations between the prosecution and the defence can limit the offences for which a person is convicted, but they cannot control the sentence he gets except insofar as the maximum sentence the court can impose is controlled by the offence for which the defendant stands convicted. What sentence is imposed within that limit is a matter for the magistrates or the judge, and the prosecution is not even permitted to make a recommendation. As it does not enable the defendant to know exactly where he stands if he pleads guilty, this limited kind of

[1] In *Jenkins* (1986) 83 Cr. Ap. R 152, the Court of Appeal recently cast doubt on this and said that the judge had no power to insist on the prosecution calling evidence, but the decision is suspect because the court failed to deal with a line of earlier cases which held the opposite. They are set out in *Archbold's criminal pleading and practice* (42nd ed. 1985) para. 4–122.

plea-bargaining has limited attractions for defendants. This has led to attempts to involve the judge in the process, getting him to say in advance what sentence he would give in the event of a guilty plea, and what it would be if the case was fought to a finish. In the United States this practice is now widespread. Some years ago there were signs of it beginning in England, but then it was resoundingly condemned by the Court of Appeal in a case called *Turner* in 1970.[1]

Whilst it is in order for prosecution and defence to discuss the matter of pleas, and whilst it may be proper for them to discuss a possible arrangement with the judge in advance of the hearing to see if he will agree to it, the Court of Appeal said it is quite improper for him to tell them that he will impose such-and-such a sentence if the defendant pleads guilty, but so-and-so if he is convicted after a contested trial. If he does this it will be construed as judicial pressure to plead guilty, and if the defendant is induced to plead guilty by overt pressure from the judge this makes the plea a nullity and the conviction will be set aside. Notwithstanding this decision one still hears from practitioners sometimes of judges joining in the plea-bargaining process, and incidents where it has happened sometimes come to light on appeal, but it now seems to be exceptional.

The dangers of plea-bargaining, even in its attenuated English form, are obvious. The first is that defendants get too readily pushed into pleading guilty for fear of what their lawyers tell them may happen to them if they do not; if this happened many would get the feeling that a fair trial has been denied them, and some, perhaps, plead guilty where they are really innocent. In 1977 two researchers, John Baldwin and Michael McConville, published a book called *Negotiated justice* which was based on interviews with 150 defendants who had entered guilty pleas. Many of those whom they had interviewed claimed to have had experiences of this sort. This book produced an outburst of anger from the legal profession, which was furious at the suggestion that lawyers were putting improper pressure on their clients to plead guilty. The high point of the attack on their methods and their conclusions was when a High Court Judge when speaking at a dinner of academic lawyers likened legal research that consists of interviewing defendants to medical research that canvasses the opinions of flies that buzz round wounds. Clearly the legal system exists for lawyers, and no one else is fit to express any views about its workings, particularly if his only contact with it has been to get a prison sentence out of it rather than a livelihood.

The second problem is that it leads to some defendants getting less than their just deserts because the prosecution in its anxiety to save time and trouble settles for pleas of guilty to an offence substantially less serious than the facts of the case really warrant. It is a basic rule of sentencing that the judge must sentence for the offence of which the defendant stands convicted, not for the one he thinks he really committed, so an under-charge usually results in a substantial under-sentence. There are two versions of the crime of arson, for example, one where

[1] [1970] 2 QB 321.

263

the offender intended to endanger life or was reckless as to whether he did so, and a less serious one where he did not; and where a man had petrol-bombed an occupied building, and the prosecutor had unwisely settled for a plea of guilty to the lesser form of arson, the Court of Appeal felt obliged to reduce the sentence to the one that should have been imposed on a defendant who was unaware of any risk to human life.[1]

The third problem with plea-bargaining is that it leads to cases being ineptly dealt with because the court has insufficient information. Whilst the trial that follows a plea of not guilty is elaborate and thorough, what comes after a guilty plea is a very cut-price affair. Generally no evidence is called about the circumstances of the crime, and for this the court relies on the prosecutor's assertions. Some years ago the courts realised that this could be unfair to the defendant where, for example, he is prosecuted for wounding, the prosecutor says he made an unprovoked attack upon the victim, but in truth the victim really did provoke him. So they decided that in such a case the defendant must be permitted to make counter-assertions, and the judge must sentence on the basis of these unless he is prepared to resolve the conflict by calling evidence (see chapter 24 below). But where, as often happens, the judge does not trouble to call evidence this procedure can result in an inappropriate sentence for the opposite reason: because the court accepts a version of facts which is false, but this time false in his favour.

The root of the problem is that we have two different types of procedure – one for where the defendant pleads not guilty which is over-elaborate and too time consuming, and another following a guilty plea which is almost as slap-dash and cursory as the type of trial which Hawkins described; see pages 240–241 above. Because our courts have too much business, and insufficient resources to give all defendants the elaborate form of trial, we allow only the bravest and most persistent defendants to use it, and pressure the rest into accepting the sub-standard version; then, if we are lawyers, we probably write letters to the newspapers saying the English criminal trial is the Envy of the World. Perhaps this is true in that we still do better than the United States, where contested trials are even more complicated and time-consuming, and plea-bargaining has become far more pervasive as a result. But we do substantially worse than many other legal systems – that of Germany, for example – where they have only one version of a trial, less complicated than our contested trial but more elaborate than our guilty hearing, and no pressure has to be applied to make defendants choose one rather than the other. It is interesting to note that the widespread use of guilty pleas, and the accompanying plea-bargaining, is quite a modern development in the common law. In the days when criminal trials were quick and brutal it seems that almost everyone pleaded 'not guilty', and those who tried to plead 'guilty' were actually pressed by the judges to change their plea. Rough as it

---

[1] *Booker* [1982] Crim. LR 378.

was, at least the system meant that each case was disposed of on the basis of first-hand evidence. Quick as it was, it was not so much quicker than the way in which we deal with guilty pleas today.[1]

ii The rules of criminal evidence

In criminal cases there are a number of strict and complicated rules about what does and does not constitute evidence, and how witnesses may and may not be examined in court. Whilst there is a grain of sense at the bottom of most of them there is no doubt that many of them have long parted company with the reasons for their existence. Together they amount to a cumbersome structure which makes contested criminal trials take longer than they need, and in some cases quite needlessly reduces the prosecution's chance of securing a conviction. Such problems undoubtedly encourage prosecutors to make unsatisfactory plea-bargains. Worse, they sometimes prevent the parties being able to put information before the court which is unquestionably relevant to the guilt or innocence of the accused. When a witness is prevented from imparting relevant information this makes a mockery of his oath that he will tell 'the truth, the whole truth and nothing but the truth', and it inhibits the court from doing its proper job, which must be to discover the truth in order to do justice based upon it.

This book is not the place for a full account of all the exclusionary rules of criminal evidence, but it is worth saying a little about the best-known one, which is the hearsay rule. Under this a witness is not permitted to repeat what another person told him happened if the purpose of his repeating what was said is to show the court that it did happen: to establish that it happened it is necessary to call the man who saw it with his own eyes, and get him to repeat the tale. Where that person is available to give evidence it is obviously sensible to get the tale from him direct, instead of relying on a second-hand tale which may have been changed in the telling. But the hearsay rule goes further, and says that if that person is not available to tell it the tale must not be told at all, which is ridiculously restrictive. If a person, now dead, said that it was the defendant who attacked him, this fact must ordinarily be kept from the court;[2] and if a child of three or four is indecently assaulted, or witnesses the murder of his mother, no one may recount what he told them of the incident; in theory the child must be brought to court to give his evidence like an adult – and as this is usually impracticable, the court must do without his evidence altogether. When strictly enforced, the hearsay rule

---

[1] For all these points the editor is heavily indebted to the writings of Professor John H. Langbein. See 'The criminal trial before the lawyers', (1978) 45 *U of Chicago LR* 263–316; 'Torture and plea bargaining', (1978) 46 *U of Chicago LR* 3–22; 'Land without plea-bargaining: How the Germans do it', (1979) 78 *U of Michigan LR* 204–25; 'Shaping the eighteenth-century criminal trial: A view from the Ryder Sources', (1983) 50 *U of Chicago LR* 1–136.

[2] There are some exceptions, notably where the deceased person's statement amounts to a 'dying declaration'. The House of Lords recently created a further exception in *Andrews* [1987] AC 281, covering the case where the statement was made immediately after the attack.

also needlessly inhibits witnesses. A man is giving evidence as to why he remembered the time when he started to drive home. He says: 'I had to be home by ten, and it was getting very foggy, so at nine I rang Muriel, and I says, "Muriel, what's the fog like your end?" and she says . . .' At this point he is stopped. What Muriel says is hearsay, and not admissible. The poor man is confused and bewildered, for his natural way of speaking is apparently taboo: the proper course is to go in for circumlocution whereby he makes it clear that in consequence of information received he decided to leave earlier than he otherwise would have done. The hearsay rule is supposed to protect the defendant, but in practice it can have the opposite result. In one leading case it prevented a white man from calling evidence to show that the three-year-old child he was accused of assaulting had described her attacker as black[1] and it has also prevented a defendant calling evidence to show that someone else has confessed to the crime, or has been talking in a way that suggests a suspicious amount of inside knowledge.[2]

The main rule about examining witnesses is that a witness must appear either for the prosecution or for the defence. They must appear as a supporter of one or other of the parties, in other words, and they are not called by the court to tell their story from a position of impartiality. This makes both sides unwilling to call witnesses where it is unclear whose side they are on, and if a witness looks too impartial the result may be that he is not called at all. It also affects how witnesses can be questioned. The party calling a witness is not normally allowed to ask him 'leading questions' – a privilege which is reserved for his opponent when he cross-examines him. A 'leading question' is one which suggests the answer the questioner wants to hear. 'Was the car he was driving green?' instead of 'What colour was the car he was driving?' This creates a difficulty with a witness who probably knows something useful and important, but is either forgetful or reluctant to talk. If the side that thinks he may be useful to them calls him they may be able to get nothing out of him without using leading questions, which they cannot use unless the judge is prepared to rule that he is 'hostile' – meaning that he is being deliberately obstructive. If they call him, and fail to get anything out of him, their opponents can then put leading questions to him in cross-examination, and so may get him to tell the wrong tale. So they probably decide not to take the risk of calling him. Their opponents probably take the same decision, and the result is that the court has to decide the case without the benefit of evidence which might have shed a useful light on the case. The sensible solution would be for the judge to call such a witness, question him, and then tender him for cross-examination by both sides. This is what is routinely done in most continental legal systems. It could be done here, for judges in a criminal case do have a discretionary power to call witnesses, and at one time they used to exercise it. But in recent years the practice has been very much discouraged, and it is rarely done.

In the nature of things, the account a witness gives of an incident immediately

[1] *Sparkes* [1964] AC 964.
[2] *Blastland* [1986] AC 41.

after it occurs is likely to be fuller and more reliable than what he attempts to remember about it in court months or even years afterwards. So it would be helpful in discovering the truth if the party calling a witness could put in evidence his previous statements to supplement the testimony he gives in court. This, needless to say, he is not allowed to do. Nor is the witness allowed to use his previous statement to prompt himself when he is in the witness-box; to use a note to refresh one's memory the note must be contemporaneous or nearly con-temporaneous – which in practice means that a policeman may prompt himself from his notebook but nobody else may use a prompt at all. This is very silly, particularly as a witness, although not permitted to have his statement with him in the witness-box, is permitted and encouraged to read the statement outside the door of the court just before he goes in to give his evidence. This turns the process of giving evidence into a memory-game, such as is played at children's parties. The law, it seems, turns the most elementary rules of psychology on their head. By insisting that only courtroom testimony is acceptable it assumes, first that memory is improved with time, and secondly, that stress improves the process of recall.

A final point concerns cross-examination. It is considered a matter of the greatest importance that each side should be able to test the evidence against him by cross-examining his opponent's witnesses. Cross-examination is supposed to be the great instrument for sifting, probing and testing evidence. The best way to check whether this is so is to listen to a jury trial where there is medical evidence. When the doctor called by the prosecution has given his evidence he may be cross-examined as to the tests he applied and asked in respect of each of them whether such a test is conclusive and the doctor is likely to answer that it is not. Counsel will later suggest to the jury that as the doctor did not make any conclusive test his evidence is not proof. The judge may, or may not, explain to the jury that clinical diagnosis commonly depends on the coexistence of different symptoms which considered individually are not conclusive, but once a view has been formed it is not so easy to dislodge it. Counsel's questions are not designed to sift and test the evidence, for the evidence is usually an honest professional medical report: a particular line of questioning is adopted because experience shows that it is likely to confuse and mislead the jury. An eminent psychiatrist has observed that: 'The judicial process does not seem to be designed primarily for the ascertainment of fact: and if it is not so designed, it is hardly surprising that it is not very successful.'[1]

Children as witnesses can get frightened and upset, and in this state they are easily pressed to retract their earlier evidence. To see a young child demolished

---

[1] 'The judicial process and the ascertainment of fact', by Dr Eliot Slater, (1961) 24 Mod. LR 721. Dr Slater does not like the fancy dress used in court. It is commonly said that wigs and robes and some pageantry make the higher courts more impressive, though who is impressed and to what effect is unexplained: obviously criminals are not 'impressed' unless that means they come back to court again because they liked it so much on an earlier occasion.

by cross-examination from an eminent QC is something that is physically sickening to watch. With ordinary adult witnesses cross-examination is often less than an instrument of truth. Let us suppose that a witness was driving his car along a street towards traffic lights some distance away, when he was overtaken by a motor-cyclist who appeared to ignore the traffic lights and to crash into a van that was coming out with the lights in its favour. The car driver will be cross-examined on how fast he and the motor-cyclist were going, how far each was from the road markings when the lights went amber, the other traffic that was about, the time of day, the weather and maybe other things. These questions may all be relevant, but on most of these points the witness cannot give a precise answer: people do not notice everything that happens, particularly when it does not appear at the time to be unusual or in any way to matter to their own affairs. But the cross-examination is conducted as if the witness does know the answers and is concealing them: counsel must drag out the truth. If a witness says he does not know, and keeps on repeating that, counsel can get no further, but most people cannot bear the strain of persistent questioning and clutch at any suggestion of certainty. The witness ends up by giving detailed evidence which he is now certain is the truth. If a similar cross-examination can lead another witness into details that cannot be reconciled with that of the car driver, then counsel has established that there is a conflict of evidence. Counsel do this, and often do it so well, in good faith. It is a traditional method of truth-finding, which has in its day uncovered witchcraft, and that which is ancient in the common law is not to be doubted.

A number of sensible proposals to change some of the more absurd rules of criminal evidence were made by the Criminal Law Revision Committee in its Eleventh Report in 1972.[1] Unfortunately it began this report by recommending an encroachment on the right of silence (see chapter 22(i) above). This proved such an emotive matter, and created such a public outcry, that no government then or thereafter has wanted to have anything to do with implementing the Report even shorn of these proposals. A few of the less controversial parts of the Report have been quietly implemented in unobtrusive parts of other legislation. But we are a long way off the radical overhaul of the law of criminal evidence that is badly needed.

iii The place of the victim

Most serious criminal offences have an identifiable human victim. In the early days of the criminal law it was he, or his surviving relatives, who had the job of setting the law in motion against the offender, and the possibility of a private prosecution still survives as a relic of those days. Where the State does the job of prosecuting, as it usually has done in modern times, no one has taken much official notice of the victim. He may be used as a prosecution witness if there is a

[1] (1972) Cmnd 4991.

plea of 'not guilty', but he has no special position in the prosecution process, which is free to carry on without considering his interests – and often does.

In recent years there has been a growth of public interest in the victim. A 'victim movement' has begun in the USA, and the ideas which it has generated have spread to this country. This has had a political impact. When the House of Commons Home Affairs Committee was formed it took victims of crime as the subject for its first report. This brought a response from the government in which it announced increased consideration for victims as an item of government policy.[1] Various proposals which are meant to improve the position of the victim are contained in the Criminal Justice Bill which is before Parliament at the time of writing.

One manifestation of increased interest in victims of crime has been the growth of voluntary groups concerned with their welfare. Someone who is the victim of a crime is usually shocked and frightened, and often more bewildered by the legal system than the person who has been arrested for the offence. In the past he might get some sympathy and advice from the police, but that would be his lot. In 1974 the first 'victim support scheme' began in Bristol: a group of volunteers made themselves available to visit the victims of crime to offer help, advice and moral support. The scheme was rapidly copied elsewhere and we are now on the way to having a national network of such schemes. The National Association of Victim Support Schemes (NAVSS) now co-ordinates their efforts (and also publishes an annual report). More aggressive in their approach are various self-help groups, such as the Campaign Against Drunken Driving (CADD), the membership of which consists of those whose relatives have been killed in alcohol-related traffic accidents. As well as offering comfort and moral support, this group runs publicity campaigns against drunk-driving, and puts pressure on prosecutors not to bargain guilty pleas in return for dropping the serious charges against drunken drivers who have killed.

By definition the victim of a crime will suffer loss. Where he loses property he may be able to claim on his insurance, but otherwise he is likely to be out of pocket. The criminal is theoretically liable to compensate him, but until modern times the victim could only enforce his rights against the criminal by suing him in the civil courts, and as a class criminals are not usually worth the cost and trouble of suing in the civil courts. Most systems of justice have long allowed the criminal courts to award compensation against the offender, so relieving the victim of the bother of bringing a civil action, but ours did not. This was corrected in 1972 when they were given the power to make compensation orders, the details of which are discussed later (chapter 24 below). A study in 1985 showed that the courts often failed to make compensation orders in cases where they could do so.[2] The trouble, it seems, is that it is nobody's job to ask for one. The victim has no

---

[1] The Committee Report is HC 43 (1984–85). The Government response was a White Paper, (1985) Cmnd 9457.
[2] Shapland, Willmore and Duff, *Victims in the criminal justice system*.

official standing in the process, and is not entitled to ask for a compensation order, so they are made only if the prosecution asks for it, or the court happens to think of it unasked.

Most criminals are too poor to pay large compensation orders, and many are too poor to pay anything at all. Thus if the victims of crime are to be compensated effectively, there has to be provision for compensation from the State. In England this began in 1964 when the Criminal Injuries Compensation Board was set up. In theory this was a hole-and-corner exercise; the Board had no statutory basis and was established simply by the government's executive act, which meant that all its payments were strictly speaking *ex gratia* and no one could sue if his claim was refused. In practice this did not matter, however, because the Board always behaved as if it were legally obliged to pay those whose cases fell within the limits of the scheme the government had devised, and it allowed its refusals to be challenged in the courts. The scheme pays only those who are the victims of crimes of violence, and only the more seriously injured among these: if the claim is not worth a sum which is at present £550, the claimant gets nothing at all and is left to his rights against the attacker, such as they are. As part of its proclaimed policy of helping victims, the present government has included a proposal in the current Criminal Justice Bill to put the Criminal Injuries Scheme on a statutory footing, so giving claimants the legal right to sue. As they can sue in practice anyway this is a largely cosmetic change. At the same time the government proposed to make a real change to the detriment of victims by raising the threshold to £1,000 in order to save money, but this penny-pinching idea was dropped in the face of public opposition.

Despite these various improvements in his position, the victim of a crime in England is still poorly off compared with his counterpart in many other legal systems. The root of the trouble is that he still has no kind of official standing in the process, and neither the prosecution nor the court is obliged to take any notice of his interests or even to tell him what is going on. Thus he is often not informed, let alone consulted about what charges are brought against the offender; and if serious charges are brought which the prosecution then decide to drop in exchange for trivial ones, or to abandon altogether, it need not tell him, let alone ask his permission. If a man is prosecuted for rape of a girl aged 15 – a charge that implies she did not consent to intercourse with him – the prosecution can accept his guilty plea to unlawful sexual intercourse – a charge that implies she did consent – without considering her feelings or asking her what she thinks about it. The victim has no right to be told how the case is progressing, or when the case is to be heard, and if he is not needed as a witness because the defendant decides to plead guilty, the first the victim may hear of the matter is when he reads about the outcome in the local paper. If the victim is needed as a witness, probably no one will look after him when he comes to court, or explain what is going to happen, and he may find himself waiting for hours outside in the company of the defendant's friends and relations. If there is a guilty plea the defence are free to say in mitigation that it was really the victim's fault – that he provoked the fight by getting drunk and using bad language, or if a woman, that she invited the rape by her immoral life-style or her unchaste behaviour – and the victim has no right to put her side of the story before the court if neither the prosecutor nor the court feel they wish to call her; the local paper, of course, will only report what it has heard in court, and may print the defence's version of the story without the victim having any chance to put the record straight.[1]

None of these matters will be effectively cured until in England, as in France and many other countries, the victim has a right to be made a party to the prosecution. None of the recent legal changes in England really alter the victim's status as an official non-person. Indeed one of them makes his position worse, and that is the creation of the Crown Prosecution Service. Decisions about how the prosecution is to be conducted were formerly in the hands of the police, who were also the people with whom the victim had dealings face-to-face. The victim was therefore able to bring his views on the matter to the attention of those who were making the decisions. But the decision-making is now in the hands of the Crown Prosecution Service, and it is not considered to be part of their job to bother about anyone so insignificant as the victim. The Home Office guide to the Prosecution of Offences Act says: 'It is not envisaged that the new service will have direct or personal contact with witnesses and it will be under no duty to make contact with victims, witnesses or others after disposal of the case.'

[1] On all this, see Shapland, Willmore and Duff, *Victims in the criminal justice system*. A paper by Shapland and Cohen, 'Facilities for victims: the role of the police and of the courts', [1987] Crim. LR 28 shows that in some ways the police have attempted to respond to the criticisms made earlier.

24

THE PROCESS OF SENTENCING

The process of sentencing an offender must be sharply distinguished from the process of a trial.[1] In the case of a trial on indictment, the verdict is that of a jury whilst the sentence is given by the judge. The distinction does not, of course, hold good for magistrates' courts; but whether the trial is on indictment or summary, there are certain principles that must be observed: there are strict rules of evidence, the burden of proof must be satisfied, and the issue to be decided must be clearly formulated. If the result of the trial is a conviction, or if the offender pleads guilty, the court must then decide whether a penalty is to be imposed, and if so, what it is to be. For every offence the law prescribes the penalties that may be imposed. Murder, and a few other offences, are exceptional in that there is only one penalty, so that the judge has no option and there can be no question of the amount of punishment. In most cases the law prescribes a maximum punishment, the court being free to impose a less amount. The court thus has a free hand within the limits laid down for the offence in question. In exercising the available choice the court is thus in a very different position than it is during the trial: for the process of sentencing, the court is left to exercise its discretion. Of course, this is not to say that the court is free to be as arbitrary and capricious as it likes. Sentencers are guided by various official publications and by exhortations from the higher courts, and sentences which are unduly heavy – but not, at least at the time of writing, those which are unreasonably lenient – are liable to be overturned on appeal. There is a further restriction on the exercise of sentencing discretion by magistrates, because by statute they may imprison no one for longer than six months (or twelve months for two either-way offences) nor impose a fine above a level which is fixed from time to time (£2,000 at the time of writing). Where the magistrates convict of an either-way offence, however, they may commit the offender to the Crown Court for sentence if they think their limited powers of punishment do not enable justice to be done.

Before discussing the process of sentencing it is desirable to mention the various measures available to the court.

[1] See Cross, *The English sentencing system* (3rd ed. 1981); Nigel Walker, *Sentencing: Theory, law and practice* (1985); D. A. Thomas, *Principles of sentencing* (2nd ed. 1982); A. J. Ashworth, *Sentencing and penal policy* (1983).

1 Death

Death by hanging was the punishment for murder; it was temporarily suspended in 1965 and the suspension was made permanent in 1970. It remains a possible penalty for treason and for certain forms of piracy.

2 Imprisonment

Imprisonment, as such, is generally limited to offenders over the age of 21. (Persons under 21 may be sentenced to youth custody, or a period at a detention centre or an attendance centre, sentences which are discussed later.) Nowadays it is generally recognised that the effects of imprisonment on offenders are usually bad. Compared with other penal measures it is very expensive to keep a person in prison. Furthermore, in recent years prisons have been permanently over-crowded. In 1987, there were roughly speaking 50,000 people crammed into prisons designed to hold no more than 40,000. Overcrowding means

very considerable cell sharing: thus in May 1981 about 4,900 prisoners were living three and 11,000 were living two to cells certified as suitable for one man. The cells which these prisoners share are by and large not pleasant, warm, well lit and ventilated rooms, but spartan, gloomy and stagnant. Although they are reasonably large for one man, by the time two or three beds are installed there is little room for other furniture and the cells are extremely cramped . . . in some locals [i.e. local prisons], prisoners are locked up for 22 hours or more each day. There is, of course, no integral sanitation in the great majority of local prisons. Therefore, an inmate wishing to urinate or defecate at a time when the cell is locked must use a chamber pot within six or eight feet of his companions, and either retain the contents until 'slopping out' is possible, which may be many hours later, or, an alternative sometimes resorted to, throw them out of the window.[1]

Imprisonment is also very expensive: it has been estimated that it costs some £13,000 to keep someone in prison for a year, whereas a year's probation costs only £730.[2]

  For all these reasons imprisonment is now officially recognised as a course of last resort, and the courts are encouraged to use imprisonment as sparingly as possible. Section 20(1) of the Powers of Criminal Courts Act forbids a court to impose a prison sentence on a person who has not been in prison before, except where it believes no other course is appropriate. In a case in 1980[3] the Court of Appeal added that even where an immediate custodial sentence is necessary, it should be 'as short as possible, consistent only with the duty to protect the interests of the public and to punish and deter the criminal'.

[1] *Report of Her Majesty's Chief Inspector of Prisons for England and Wales 1981* (Home Office 1981), quoted in D. E. Smith, *Research on prison overcrowding*, Home Office Research and Planning Unit, Research Bulletin 15 (1983).
[2] *The cost of penal measures*, NACRO (National Association for the Care and Resettlement of Offenders) 1987.
[3] *Bibi* [1980] 1 WLR 1193.

There are various types of prison, ranging in spectrum from open prisons on the one hand to maximum security prisons on the other. At one time it was the court which determined the type of imprisonment that the offender had to undergo. Since the Criminal Justice Act 1948, however, the classification, disposal and treatment of the prisoner has been determined by the civil service department responsible for running prisons: the Prison Commission until 1963, and thereafter the Prison Department of the Home Office. The length of sentence, however, remains (at least in theory) a matter for the court and, subject to the statutory maximum for the offence in question, the court may have a choice of imprisonment for life, imprisonment for a fixed term, a sentence of suspended imprisonment, and a partly suspended sentence. In the case of a persistent offender, section 28 of the Powers of Criminal Courts Act 1973 sometimes gives the court the option of imposing an *extended sentence*, which may exceed the statutory maximum penalty for the offence which he has committed.

Where a person receives a life sentence, he rarely spends the rest of his life in prison, because the Home Secretary has the power to release such a prisoner on licence, and in most cases he does so eventually. The Home Secretary used to have an unfettered discretion in the matter, but since 1967 he may only order release on the recommendation of the Parole Board (see below), and after consultation with the Lord Chief Justice and with the trial judge if available.[1] The average period served on a life sentence is around nine years, but there are great variations, and it is certainly not the case that everyone is released from a life sentence after this period: for example Kenneth Barlow, who was imprisoned for murdering his wife, served 26 years before he was released in 1984,[2] and the recidivist child-murderer John Straffen was sent to prison in 1953 and remains there to this day. Furthermore, a person released on licence from a life sentence may be recalled to prison, not only where he commits a further offence, but if his behaviour gives cause for suspicion.[3] Figures issued by the Home Office in 1985 show that some 15 per cent of those released on licence are recalled within five years. When a mandatory life sentence for murder was introduced to replace death by hanging, the sentencing judge was given a power to recommend that a minimum term be served before the murderer's release. Some judges regularly make a recommendation, others do not; but, curiously, even where such recommendation is made neither the Home Secretary nor the Parole Board are bound by it. (In truth, this provision was really a piece of window-dressing to make the abolition of the death penalty more acceptable to the public.)

---

[1] The Home Secretary's practice of routinely waiting three or four years before beginning to consider cases was condemned by the Divisional Court in *R. v. Home Secretary ex pte. Handscomb*, *The Times* 4 March 1987.

[2] *The Times* 4 January 1984.

[3] In *Weeks* v. *U.K.*, *The Times* 5 March 1987, the European Court of Human Rights held that the existing recall procedure was defective because he was not given sufficient opportunity to challenge the information upon which the recall was based.

Fixed terms of imprisonment rarely exceed 15 years, but (subject to the statutory maximum for the offence, of course) they may be of any length.[1] Where someone is sentenced for several offences at once, the terms imposed may be consecutive or concurrent. If the offences are unrelated to one another, consecutive sentences may be imposed, but if they were all part of the same transaction it is usual for them to be concurrent, which means that it it only the heaviest of the various sentences imposed which in reality must be served. As an aid to prison discipline, it has long been the case that every fixed-term prisoner is automatically granted remission of one-third of his sentence for good conduct, unless it is forfeited as a punishment for misbehaviour. Since 1967 there has also existed the possibility of *parole*. This is discretionary release on licence at an earlier stage in the course of a fixed sentence – subject, as with those released whilst serving life-sentences, to the possibility of recall. The Home Secretary appoints a national Parole Board[2] and a Local Review Committee for every prison. Recommendations go to the Home Office and the Home Office refers these and other cases to the Parole Board; the Parole Board recommends release on licence in certain cases; and, in theory, the Home Secretary uses his discretion to accept or reject the recommendation. In practice the Home Secretary is personally involved in only a very few notorious cases, his discretion being exercised by Home Office officials, and a favourable recommendation from the Parole Board almost always means that parole is granted.[3] When parole was first introduced in 1967 it was only available to a prisoner who had served one-third of his sentence or twelve months, whichever was the longer; in 1984 the twelve months was reduced to six months, so making parole a possibility for a wider range of offenders.

Is parole satisfactory? The answer must be that it is not entirely so. The initial sentencing decision is made in public after the convicted criminal has had ample opportunity to make his representations, and if it is unreasonable he has an opportunity to appeal. When parole is granted or withheld, the prisoner is in effect being resentenced; but the decision to grant or withhold parole is an administrative one, made in secret; the prisoner is not given reasons for refusal; he may be left to wonder why he was refused parole when another prisoner whose case is apparently similar was granted it, and if he thinks the outcome is unreasonable he has no opportunity to appeal. To some extent parole also undermines the authority of the courts, because it means they no longer decide how long a convicted criminal shall serve, but only fix the maximum he may be required to serve. A judge may solemnly sentence an offender to 18 months imprisonment, only to find that six months later he is back in town on parole; or a

[1] For some years, the record for a fixed term was the 42 years imposed on Blake for spying in 1961, but in 1986 it was surpassed by the 45-year sentence on the terrorist Hindawi for attempting to blow up an aeroplane containing 380 passengers.

[2] Sarah McCabe, 'The Powers and Purposes of the Parole Board' (1985) Crim. LR 489.

[3] But in 1983 the Home Secretary did announce that would no longer grant parole to drug-traffickers or to certain types of violent offender. His decision was unsuccessfully attacked in the courts: *re Findlay* [1985] AC 319.

judge may sentence a group of offenders according to their culpability as he sees it, giving sentences carefully graded from six months' imprisonment to two years – only to find that the whole gang is back on the streets again after serving six months. Yet, satisfactory or not, we have now become heavily dependent upon parole. In round figures, in 1987 there were around 50,000 people in prisons which were designed to hold around 40,000. Meanwhile, there are regularly around 6,000 prisoners out on parole. With our prisons so overcrowded despite the widespread use of parole, it is almost inconceivable that parole could be abolished. In some Commonwealth countries which have a system of parole, the judge fixes the proportion of a sentence which must be served before parole may be considered, and a reform on these lines is the most which it is practicable to expect in England.

Suspended sentences were introduced in 1967. A court which passes a sentence of imprisonment of not more than two years may order that the sentence shall not take effect unless during a period specified in the order (known as the 'operational period') of not less than one year or more than two years the offender commits another offence punishable with imprisonment. If the offender gets through the operational period without being convicted of a second offence nothing further happens, but if he is convicted of a second offence committed during the period then he will be sentenced in the ordinary way for the second offence and the suspended sentence for the first offence may be 'activated'. A suspended sentence is thus a threat that hangs over the offender; he knows that if he gets caught committing an offence during the operational period he is liable to be punished for the first offence. However, a suspended sentence is not invariably activated. By statute, the court (which usually means the court dealing with him for the further offence) is obliged to order that the suspended sentence shall take effect with the original length unaltered unless it 'is of opinion that it would be unjust to do so in view of all the circumstances which have arisen since the suspended sentence was passed, including the facts of the subsequent offence'. If the court does think it would be unjust, it may substitute a lesser length, or vary the original order so that it continues for a longer time, or even make no order. Since 1982, it has been possible for the court to suspend part of a sentence; this power applies where the sentence is between three months and two years; at least 28 days must be served immediately, and at least a quarter of the sentence must be suspended. It is not open to the court to combine a suspended sentence with probation, but it is possible for a Crown Court to make a suspended sentence supervision order. This puts the offender under the supervision of a probation officer for a period not exceeding the operational period of the sentence.

276

3 Youth custody and detention centres

For offenders under the age of 21, who may not be sent to prison, there are *detention centres* and *youth custody centres*. These, like prisons for adults, are regarded as sentences of last resort, and the courts are discouraged from using them if there is a realistic alternative.

Detention centres are custodial institutions for offenders between the ages of 14 and 21 who are thought to be in need of disciplinary treatment: the regime is intended to provide a 'short, sharp shock'. The shock consists of a heavy emphasis on discipline, physical training and fitness; shortness is guaranteed by a provision in the Criminal Justice Act 1982 that a detention centre order may not be for longer than four months (or for shorter than 21 days). There are around 20 detention centres, and they are all for men; detention centres orders may only be made against male offenders. *Youth custody centres* are, in the main, what used to be known as Borstal institutions: special prisons for young offenders, where the emphasis is on training and rehabilitation rather than on mere custody. Until 1982, the courts were given a curious choice when dealing with offenders aged between 17 and 21 who were in trouble too deep for a detention centre. The court could sentence them to 'Borstal training', which meant that they were detained in a Borstal institution for an indeterminate period of between six months and two years, according to the discretion of the prison authorities; or they could send them to prison, but only for any period not exceeding six months, or for any period in excess of three years. The idea behind this curious restriction was that the right thing to do with a young offender who merited a sentence of between six months and three years was to send him for Borstal training, but judges generally disagreed with this thinking, and disliked the rule because it fettered their discretion to impose a prison sentence of a length which they regarded as appropriate. Hence by the Criminal Justice Act 1982 the position was changed. The court may now sentence an offender aged between 15 and 21 to a period of 'youth custody'. The sentence is determinate, subject to parole and remission. In the case of an offender under the age of 17, it must not exceed one year; for a female over 17 it may be any term up to the maximum penalty for the offence she has committed, and for a male over 17, who unlike his sister may be sent to a detention centre for up to four months, the sentence may be any term between four months and the statutory maximum for the offence. The sentence will normally, but not invariably, be served in a 'youth custody centre'. (The Criminal Justice Bill at present before Parliament is likely to make various changes, the most important of which is the amalgamation of youth custody orders and detention centre orders into one single form of penalty.) Where a person aged between 17 and 21 commits murder, which carries a mandatory sentence of life imprisonment, he receives a sentence of custody for life. There are special provisions for the detention of persons under 17 years of age who commit murder or other offences punishable with life imprisonment in the case of an adult.

A milder penal measure for offenders under 21 is the *attendance centre*. These are places usually run by volunteers on Saturday afternoons where young offenders are kept under firm discipline and are occupied in activities like physical training and handicrafts. The idea is not only to punish the offender by taking away his leisure, but also to teach him how to make less anti-social use of it in future. An order usually requires 12 hours' attendance, which will usually involve two Saturday sessions. Unlike youth custody and detention centres, which are only open to offenders over the age of 15, attendance centres may be used for offenders aged from 10 to 21.

4 Hospital orders

If an offender is mentally disturbed, the court may sometimes compulsorily commit him to a mental hospital as an alternative to imposing a punishment. The power to do this is contained in the Mental Health Act 1983 section 37. This provides that before a hospital order can be made, the court must be satisfied on the evidence of two doctors (one of whom must be a specialist in mental health) that the offender is suffering from 'mental illness, psychopathic disorder, severe mental impairment or mental impairment'; that the nature of the illness makes it appropriate for him to be detained in a hospital for treatment; and, in the case of psychopathic disorder or mental impairment, that treatment will either make him better or at least prevent him becoming worse. If these conditions are fulfilled the court may make a hospital order; but it is not obliged to do so, because the section also requires the court to be satisfied that a hospital order is the best course to take 'having regard to all the circumstances including the nature of the offence and the character and antecedents of the offender, and to the other available methods of dealing with him'. Thus, for example, the court can still send a dangerous psychopath to prison for life if it thinks the chances of his improvement in mental hospital are slender and that prison is the safest place for him to be.

The effect of a hospital order is that the person is compulsorily admitted to a mental hospital for treatment, and he is thereafter in much the same position as someone who has been civilly committed or 'sectioned'; see chapter 15(iii) above. Whether or not he is released is then a medical decision for the hospital authorities. To meet cases where a court feels that detention should not be ended without full consideration of the interests of the public, section 41 of the Mental Health Act allows a court 'having regard to the nature of the offence, the antecedents of the offender and the risk of his committing further offences if set at large' to make a hospital order together with an order restricting discharge, either without limit of time or for a specified period. Only the Crown Court may do this, but a magistrates' court may commit a person to the Crown Court with a view to such an order being made. The effect of such an order is to prevent discharge taking place except on the authority of the Home Secretary. The rights of patients compulsorily detained under hospital orders are protected by Mental Health Review Tribunals, to which they may appeal, and which may authorise their release, even in the case of restricted patients. This was discussed in chapter 15(iii).

The Mental Health Act 1983 lays down that a hospital order must specify a particular hospital, and that before such an order is made there must be a place in that hospital available. The choice of hospital usually lies between one of the secure hospitals under the immediate control of the Secretary of State (Broadmoor, Rampton and Moss Side) and an ordinary National Health Service mental hospital. In the ordinary mental hospitals, a change in the attitude to mental disorder has resulted in their having far fewer locked wards or none at all, and hence they have become progressively less well equipped to cope with possibly dangerous patients sent to them by the criminal courts. This has led to resistance from the staff: there have even been cases where the nurses threatened to strike at the prospect of having to accept a particular offender.[1]

The result has been severe overcrowding in the special hospitals, which have had to take cases unsuitable for their type of regime, and a number of scandalous cases where the courts have been obliged to send offenders who needed mental treatment to prison because there was nowhere else for them to go. In 1974 the Butler Committee on Mentally Abnormal Offenders urgently recommended the creation of a new set of 'regional secure units'[2] to take the cases for which ordinary mental hospitals are no longer suitable; but it took ten years and a great deal of pressure before any were built, and in 1985 the Court of Appeal, when hearing the appeal of yet another mentally disturbed offender who had been sent to prison because no place could be found for her in a mental hospital, expressed the view that 'nothing had been done'.[3]

There are two other measures which a court may adopt in the case of a mentally disturbed offender. First, as an alternative to a hospital order, the court may make a guardianship order. This places the offender under the guardianship of the local social services authority or of a person of whom they approve. The guardian may require the offender to live at a particular address, or obtain medical treatment. Secondly, the court may make a psychiatric probation order. Under the Powers of Criminal Courts Act 1973 a court may put a mentally disturbed offender who is not bad enough for a hospital order on probation, subject to a condition that he receives treatment as a resident patient, an outpatient, or from a psychiatrist outside a hospital.

[1] See *The Times* 29 and 31 October 1975.
[2] Cmnd 5698.
[3] *R* v. *Porter, The Times* 22 January 1985.

5 Community Service Orders

Where a person aged 16 or over is convicted of an offence punishable with imprisonment, the court may make a community service order requiring him to perform unpaid work for not less than 40 or more than 240 hours (120 hours if he is under 17). Before an order can be made the court must be satisfied from a report by a probation officer or social worker that the offender is a suitable person to perform work under such an order: it must be possible to make arrangements for him in the area where he lives; and the offender must consent. The arrangements for work must avoid conflict with the offender's religious beliefs or interference with the time at which he normally works or goes to school. The kind of work envisaged is the sort commonly done by volunteers, such as digging old people's gardens, helping with adventure playgrounds, clearing water courses and improving public amenities. In doing the work the offender is in a position similar to that of voluntary workers, and is often working together with them; but in his case, failure to do the work can result in a fine, or even revocation of the order and some more unpleasant form of punishment in its place.

6 Fines

Unlike community service orders, which were only introduced in 1972, fines are a very ancient form of penalty. In the early days of the common law the defendant was ordered to be imprisoned, whereupon he bargained for his release on payment and made an end (*finem facere*) of the matter. Later fines became a penal measure in their own right, and nowadays they are by far the most common penalty, as table 7 shows (pages 288–89 below).

Where a person is convicted on indictment there is no limit to the fine which the Crown Court may impose,[1] except perhaps the vague provision of the Bill of Rights 1688 that fines must not be unreasonable. The magistrates' courts, when trying either-way offences, are forbidden by statute to fine above a limit which is raised from time to time and which at present stands at £2,000 for any one offence. When trying a summary offence, a magistrates' court is limited to a maximum fine which is stated in the statute which creates the offence. Formerly the maximum penalty was always expressed as a sum of money, which was inconvenient, because inflation continually eroded the real value of penalties and frequently made them derisory. So the Criminal Justice Act 1982 provides that fines for summary offences shall be determined by reference to a five-point scale, the cash value of which the Home Secretary sets from time to time. At present the scale is as follows: level 1 – £50; level 2 – £100; level 3 – £400; level 5 – £2,000.

When a fine has been imposed it is necessary to extract the money from the

---

[1] The Criminal Law Act 1977 s.32(1) sweeps away all existing statutory maxima as far as the Crown Court is concerned and gives it complete freedom.

offender, and fines, unlike civil debts, can be enforced if necessary by imprisoning the defaulter.

When deciding on the size of a fine the courts think mainly in terms of a tariff related to what he has done. When dealing with an offender who is poor they are ready to fine below the usual level, according to his actual ability to pay; but the courts resolutely refuse to fine a man more heavily merely because he is rich. In consequence fines bear much less heavily upon defendants who are well-off. In some countries this problem is solved by the sensible device of calculating fines, not in cash, but as a proportion of the offender's income. Various writers have pressed the idea in England, but it has so far completely failed to attract official support.[1]

7 Compensation orders

There is a widespread feeling that criminals ought to be forced to make good the losses they cause. The most obvious ground is that the victim has a moral and a legal right to be compensated by the wrongdoer, but it is also argued that having to make reparation is a valuable element in the treatment of offenders. Yet until recently the criminal courts in this country had hardly any powers to order compensation, and made little use of such as they had. In 1972 this was changed when criminal courts were given a general power to make compensation orders in favour of the victim of the offence.[2]

As with fines, there is no upper limit to the sum which the Crown Court may award, but magistrates' courts are limited to a maximum of £2,000. In general, however, fairly small sums are awarded even for serious loss or damage, because by statute the courts must have regard to what the offender can afford to pay. If the victim wishes to make the offender compensate him more fully he may still sue him in the civil courts, if he thinks it worth the cost and trouble, but in awarding damages the civil court must take account of the compensation order. Compensation orders are intended for straightforward cases where the extent of the loss is clear, but subject to this they are available for any kind of loss or damage caused by any type of crime. There is one curious exception, however, which is that no compensation order can be made 'in respect of injury, loss or damage due to an accident arising out of the presence of a motor vehicle on a road'. The official reasons for this restriction are that such losses are usually covered by the offending driver's insurance, and that assessing the losses resulting from traffic accidents is often a complicated exercise which a criminal court is ill-equipped to perform. Neither is convincing. The fact that the offender

[1] Ashworth, *Sentencing and penal policy* (1983) p. 288. At the time of writing attempts are being made to amend the Criminal Justice Bill to take care of the problem; they may or may not succeed.

[2] As a result of the report by the Advisory Council on the Penal System, *Reparation by the offender* HMSO (1970). The relevant statute is now the Powers of Criminal Courts Act 1973 ss.35–38 (as amended).

is insured guarantees the victim a solvent defendant to sue, but he still has the trouble and expense of suing him; and the difficulty of calculating awards in difficult cases is no reason for refusing to allow the courts to make awards in cases which are straightforward. (There is something strange, too, about a situation in which a compensation order can be made against a cyclist who negligently cycles into a car and scratches it, but not against a driver who negligently wrecks a cycle, or its rider, or both.) The real reason is probably that traffic cases form a large part of the business of the magistrates' courts, and it is feared that if compensation orders were regularly sought in these cases, this would slow them down.[1]

A study published in 1985 revealed that the courts were frequently not making compensation orders in cases where they could usefully do so.[2] In the light of this the government has put a clause in the present Criminal Justice Bill which if enacted will require a court which fails to make such an order when dealing with an offender to give the reason why it did not make one. This would go some way to encourage a greater use of compensation orders; but a large part of the problem here is that the court needs information from the victim before it knows how much to award, and this information is often lacking because the victim at present has no official standing in the proceedings and may be completely unaware of the trial until it is over.

The usual reason why a court does not make a compensation order, of course, is that it would be pointless because the offender has neither money nor the prospect of getting any. Thus a prudent person insures against loss or damage to his property. The risk of personal injury by criminal acts is not ordinarily covered by insurance, but since 1964 there has been the Criminal Injuries Compensation Scheme which makes payments out of public funds for personal injury directly attributable to a crime of violence (which once again excludes ordinary traffic offences).

8 Confiscation

If it is widely felt that a criminal should be made to compensate his victim, it is equally widely felt that he should not be allowed to profit from his crime; yet until recently there was no certain means of preventing this happening. Fines are calculated on the basis of the harm done, not the profit which accrued from it; compensation orders presuppose an identifiable victim who has been hurt by the crime, and there may not be one; and sending an offender to prison does not prevent him enjoying the fruits of his crime on his release. The problem was dramatically demonstrated in a case in 1980[3] where the House of Lords felt

---

[1] A clause in the Criminal Justice Bill which is before Parliament at the time of writing would empower the courts to make a compensation order where the driver was not insured and there was no possibility of a claim against the Motor Insurers' Bureau.

[2] Shapland, Willmore and Duff, *Victims in the criminal justice system* (1985).

[3] *Cuthbertson and others* (1981) AC 470. The problems were thoroughly analysed by a committee chaired by Sir Derek Hodgson whose findings were printed as *The profits of crime and their recovery* (1984).

bound to quash various orders which had the effect of forfeiting assets worth some £750,000 which the defendants had amassed in the course of extensively trafficking in drugs. In an attempt to plug this particular gap, a number of complicated confiscation provisions were included in the Drug Trafficking Offences Act 1986, and general powers to make orders confiscating the profits of all types of crimes are proposed in the current Criminal Justice Bill.

9 Prohibitions and disqualifications

Sometimes the criminal courts have, in addition to their other powers, a power to ban the offender from carrying on the activity in the course of which the crime was committed. The most obvious example is the power to disqualify an offender from driving, which a court is generally obliged to do when convicting of a blood-alcohol offence, and which it has a discretionary power to do for many other motoring offences, and wherever an offence punishable with two or more years' imprisonment has been committed with the help of a car. There are many others. Thus, the courts may disqualify persons from acting as company directors who have committed offences in the course of running companies, prohibit those found guilty of public health offences from running restaurants, prohibit those convicted of cruelty to animals from keeping animals, and, under the Public Order Act 1986, ban convicted soccer hooligans from attending football matches.

10 Discharge and binding over

These are the most lenient ways of dealing with an offender, except for probation which is considered in a later section. A 'discharge' is where the court, notwithstanding the conviction, formally resolves to impose no penalty at all for the offence. Discharges are governed by section 7 of the Powers of Criminal Courts Act 1973, which lays down three conditions. First, the offence must not be one where the penalty is fixed by law; as treason and murder are the only ones that fall into this category this is not a significant restriction. Secondly, the court must feel that no punishment is called for, and thirdly, it must feel that the case is unsuitable for a probation order as is likely to be the case where, for example, the offender is an old person of previously good character and it would be pointless to add him to the probation officer's caseload. A discharge may be absolute or conditional. Where a court grants an absolute discharge the offender is quit of all punishment. Where – more usually – the court grants a conditional discharge, he goes free provided he does not reoffend during a period fixed by the court, which must not exceed three years. If he reoffends during this time he may be punished for the original offence as well as the subsequent one. Where an offender is 'bound over' he must usually enter into a form of written undertaking called a *recognisance*, by which he promises to pay a specified sum of money to the crown if he misbehaves himself during a certain length of time. Unlike the power to grant a discharge, which is regulated by a clear statutory provision in a modern Act of Parliament, the law governing binding over is ancient, complex and obscure, and is in some need of clarification and reform.[1]

11 Probation

The process of placing an offender on probation grew out of the practice of binding over.[2] It was realised during the last century that many persons bound over for offences would be more likely to conduct themselves properly and be less likely to commit further offences if during the period for which they were bound over they could be placed under the supervision of some person. Probation emerged from a combination of binding over an offender with provision for his supervision, but although the value of this course was realised there was a serious difficulty in that the courts had no system of officers or other facilities for undertaking the supervision of offenders.[3]

In the last quarter of the nineteenth century some religious bodies began to appoint 'police court missionaries', a movement that grew rapidly and provided many courts with a useful and trustworthy handyman. Many magistrates' courts used to inform offenders that they would be under the supervision of a police court missionary, thus in effect introducing probation. Thus by the beginning of this century the practise of placing on probation was common, but it was informal, and its use was necessarily confined to those courts where there were police court missionaries. The Probation of Offenders Act 1907 gave statutory effect to probation, and empowered the courts to appoint paid probation officers. The Criminal Justice Act of 1925 made the appointment of probation officers compulsory in all magistrates' courts. Although some courts responded by appointing part-time officers who worked for little pay from a sense of missionary zeal, this Act brought about a change. Gradually probation officers ceased to be zealous amateurs and became a body of full-time, paid professionals.

The structure of the probation service as it now is was created by the Criminal Justice Act 1948. Its constitution is now contained in the Powers of the Criminal Courts Act 1973, the Criminal Law Act 1977 and the Criminal Justice Act 1982 and Probation Rules made under delegated powers. Probation officers are, as they always have been, officers of the court; however, they are appointed not by the court, but by area Probation Committees. There are 56 probation areas, each

---

[1] In 1987 the Law Commission produced a working paper – *Binding over: The issues*.
[2] The standard book is Jarvis, *Probation Officer's manual* (3rd ed. 1980). There is a comprehensive survey in the *Report of the Departmental Committee on the Probation Service* (1962) Cmnd 1650, which is the main Report, and the Second Report, (1962) Cmnd 1800 on the probation hostel system. Further material developments are in the Home Office *Reports on the Work of the Probation and After-care Department 1962–1965* (1966) Cmnd 1307 and *1966–1968* (1969) Cmnd 4233, and the Home Office's *Statement of National Objectives and Priorities of the Probation Service of England and Wales* (1980), which is printed in Nigel Walker, *Sentencing theory, law and practice* (1985) appendix H.
[3] A fuller account of the history of the service will be found in the last edition of this book pp. 353–54.

more or less corresponding with a local government area, each with its own committee. Committees consist of magistrates, judges nominated by the Lord Chancellor, and certain co-opted members. The service is under the general control and direction of the Home Office, which provides an inspectorate, and in the name of the Secretary of State makes the Probation Rules which govern the qualification, appointment and duties of probation officers. The costs of the service are shared by central and local government.[1]

Probation is secured by an order made by the court requiring the person to be under the supervision of a probation officer, and containing such other terms, called 'requirements' as may be specially appropriate. The court must explain in ordinary language the meaning of a probation order and its requirements, and the offender must express his willingness to comply with the requirements. The supervision is to be by a probation officer assigned to the petty sessional division in which the offender resides or will reside. Thus, there may be two courts involved: the court that made the order (Crown Court or magistrates' court) and the supervising court. The court that made the order can discharge it, whilst the supervising court (which is always a magistrates' court) can amend it. Probation is not available for persons under 17: for them, its place is taken by a Supervision Order (for which, unlike probation, the consent of the offender is not necessary).

A distinction has to be made between breach of the requirements of a probation order and conviction for a fresh offence during the period of probation. A fresh conviction may itself be a breach of requirement, but it must be dealt with as being a fresh conviction.

(1) For breach of requirement the probationer is brought before either the magistrates' court that made the order or the supervising court (whether the order was made by a magistrates' court or by a higher court). If the magistrates are satisfied that there has been a breach of requirement, they can

(a)   fine up to £400, or
(b)   order him to attend at an attendance centre (Criminal Justice Act 1982 s.17)
(c)   if the probation order was made by a magistrates' court, deal with the offender for the original offence in any way that they could have done if he had just been convicted; if the probation order was made by the Crown Court, commit him to the Crown Court which court can then deal with him as if he had just been convicted.

Courses (a) and (b) leave the probation order still in force, whereas course (c) ends the probation order.

---

[1] The Probation Rules lay down minimum professional qualifications for probation officers, and to obtain the necessary qualification the would-be probation officer must undergo training. At one time the probation service managed its own training, but nowadays probation officers train side-by-side with those who intend to go into other types of social work. In 1971 a Central Council for Education and Training in Social Work came into existence, which has the responsibility for providing training in social work for local authority personal social services, the hospital and educational services, the probation and after-care service and for similar services provided by voluntary organisations. The Council is an independent statutory body, and there is one basic professional qualification in social work.

(2) Where a new offence is committed, the new offence is tried before an appropriate court and the offender is sentenced for that offence. This fresh conviction also makes the offender liable to be sentenced for the offence for which he was put on probation, and any complication is merely as to the court that should deal with it. If the same court made the probation or conditional discharge order and subsequently convicts of a further offence there is no difficulty. Where different courts are involved the principles are:

(a)   if the order was made by a magistrates' court and the new conviction by the Crown Court, the Crown Court can sentence for the original offence after they have sentenced for the fresh offence;

(b)   if the order was made by magistrates' court X and the new conviction is in magistrates' court Y, then court Y after sentencing for the new offence can sentence for the original offence if court X agree to that course;

(c)   if the order was made by the Crown Court and the new conviction is by a magistrates' court, the magistrates' court sentences for the new offence and either commits the offender (in custody or bail) to the Crown Court to be dealt with there for the original offence, or causes the new offence to be reported to the Crown Court;

(d)   if the order was made by the Crown Court and the new conviction is by the Crown Court, there is machinery for securing the production of the offender before the court that made the order.

If it seems that probation would be a suitable course the court must consider whether there should be any special requirements. The probation officer will 'advise assist and befriend' the probationer, but if it is desired to enforce some specific rule, such as that the probationer shall abstain from alcoholic liquor, or not associate with some named person, that must be made a requirement. The range of possible requirements is thus immense, which on the whole is a good thing, although it does allow unsuitable requirements to be made on occasion. There are limitations upon a requirement relating to residence, including a rule that residence in an institution may not extend beyond 12 months. An important power is that on suitable medical evidence a probation order may contain requirements for the treatment of mental conditions, and this may include residence in an institution. The agreement of the hospital or of the doctor concerned must be obtained before such a condition is made.

The greater part of the work of probation officers has been the supervision of offenders, but there has been a steady widening of their duties. Since 1957 they have acted as welfare officers in divorce proceedings. In matrimonial jurisdiction the recognition of conciliation (in the sense of making an official attempt to negotiate an end to the dispute) added to the duties of probation officers, who may act as conciliators and report to the justices. The amount to be inserted in a maintenance order may be determined after an investigation by probation officers. The same process may be used for the amount of fines: a fine supervision order may be made to help an offender who is feckless and who needs help in putting aside money to meet his obligations. The Criminal Justice Act 1948 required probation officers to undertake after-care of persons discharged from custody if they are required to do so, thus giving statutory authority to that which was already happening in practice. Some years later it was realised that the problems of release begin when a man enters prison, so that some welfare service is needed during his sentence. Voluntary agencies formerly provided a measure of such services but in the 1960s the probation service took them over. (After 1964 the service was officially entitled 'The Probation and After-Care Service'; it reverted to its former title in 1982, whilst retaining its responsibility for after-care.) After-care also arises on discharges from youth custody and detention centres. Since 1966 the prison welfare officers have been probation officers. The Criminal Justice Act 1967 added to the work of the Probation Service by introducing parole. Probation officers are responsible for supervision and principal and senior officers are members of local review committees and of the National Parole Board. When community service orders were introduced in 1972, the task of supervising them also fell on the shoulders of the probation service.

In recent years the crime rate has been steadily rising, prisons have become ever more crowded, and there has been a widespread recognition that prison, whilst a deterrent for others, is entirely bad for the person who is sent there. The result has been an anxious search for alternative ways of dealing with offenders. This has put the probation service very much in the front line in the fight against crime. Probation statistics[1] reveal an increasing use of probation particularly for offenders with previous criminal records, who in earlier days might have expected to be sent to prison. In a time of cuts in public services the Probation Service has moderately expanded. In 1979 some 5,400 probation officers were supervising some 139,000 persons, by 1985 there were 6,200, and 151,000 under supervision.

In order to sentence intelligently, the judge or bench of magistrates needs to know considerably more than what the maximum penalty for the offence in question is. In addition, they also need to know (1) what the various punishments and other courses actually involve and what they may or may not be expected to achieve, (2) the details of what the offender actually did, and what were the mitigating circumstances, if any, (3) the offender's character, and previous criminal record, if any, and (4) what is the current sentencing practice in this type of case. When the first edition of this book appeared in 1939 sentencers were often disgracefully ill-informed about all these matters except the second, and the author wrote the following. 'An English criminal trial, properly conducted, is one of the best products of our law, provided you walk out of court before the sentence is given: if you stay to the end, you may find that it takes far less time and enquiry to settle a man's prospects in life than it has taken to find out whether he

---

[1] *Probation Statistics* are published annually by the Home Office.

Table 7. *Offenders sentenced by type of court, type of sentence or order and type of offence*

England and Wales

Number of offenders (thousands) and percentages

Type of sentence or order	1985	1986 Number of offenders				1986 Percentage of total offenders sentenced		
	Total	Total	Indictable offences	Summary offences — Offences (excluding motoring offences)	Summary offences — Motoring offences	Indictable offences	Summary offences — Offences (excluding motoring offences)	Summary offences — Motoring offences
Magistrates' courts								
Absolute discharge	18.1	17.7	2.1	5.8	9.8	1	1	1[b]
Conditional discharge	74.9	68.3	46.6	18.6	3.1	16	4	—[b]
Probation order	35.1	32.9	27.6	3.7	1.6	9	1	—[b]
Supervision order	12.1	9.4	8.6	0.7	0.1	3	—[b]	—[b]
Fine	1,572.5	1,591.0	143.2	401.2	1,046.6	48	90	98
Community service order	29.2	26.6	22.0	2.8	1.8	7	1	—[b]
Attendance centre order	14.0	10.4	9.3	1.1	—[a]	3	—[b]	—[b]
Care order	1.4	0.9	0.9	—[a]	—[a]	—[b]	—[b]	—[b]
Detention centre order	9.3	6.8	6.1	0.6	0.1	2	—[b]	—[b]
Youth custody	7.9	6.1	5.6	0.4	0.1	2	—[b]	—[b]
Imprisonment								
Fully suspended	18.8	15.5	12.6	1.6	1.4	4	—[b]	—[b]
Partly suspended	0.3	0.2	0.2	—[a]	—[a]	—[b]	—[b]	—[b]
Unsuspended	18.2	14.9	11.8	1.7	1.3	4	—[b]	—[b]
Otherwise dealt with	9.8	8.5	3.1	5.2	0.2	1	1	—[b]
Total	1,821.6	1,809.0	299.5	443.5	1,066.1	100	100	100

The Crown Court								
Absolute discharge	0.2	0.1	0.2	—[a]	—[a]	—[b]	1	3
Conditional discharge	4.0	3.9	3.9	—[a]	—[a]	5	7	3
Probation order	7.2	7.2	7.2	—[a]	—[a]	8	9	11
Supervision order	0.3	0.3	0.3	—[a]	—[a]	—[b]	—	—
Fine	7.5	7.2	7.1	—[a]	—[a]	8	11	20
Community service order	9.1	8.6	8.5	—[a]	—[a]	10	12	13
Attendance centre order	0.2	0.2	0.2	—	—	—[b]	—	1
Care order	0.1	0.1	0.1	—	—	—[b]	—	—
Detention centre order	2.3	2.0	2.0	—[a]	—[a]	2	2	—
Youth custody	13.2	12.1	12.1	—[a]	—[a]	14	13	2
Imprisonment								
Fully suspended	12.1	12.1	12.2	—[a]	—[a]	14	8	5
Partly suspended	3.5	2.9	2.9	—[a]	—[a]	—	2	—
Unsuspended	28.6	28.0	27.8	0.1	0.1	33	33	39
Otherwise dealt with	1.5	1.3	1.3	—[a]	—[a]	1	4	3
Total	89.7	85.9	85.6	0.2	0.2	100	100	100
All courts								
Absolute discharge	18.3	17.8	2.2	5.8	9.8	1	1	1
Conditional discharge	78.9	72.2	50.5	18.6	3.1	13	4	—[b]
Probation order	42.4	40.1	34.8	3.7	1.6	9	1	—[b]
Supervision order	12.4	9.6	8.8	0.7	0.1	2	—[b]	—[b]
Fine	1,580.0	1,598.1	150.3	401.2	1,046.7	39	90	98
Community service order	38.3	35.1	30.5	2.8	1.8	8	1	—[b]
Attendance centre order	14.2	10.6	9.4	1.1	—[a]	2	—[b]	—[b]
Care order	1.5	1.0	1.0	—[a]	—[a]	—[b]	—[b]	—[b]
Detention centre order	11.6	8.8	8.0	0.6	0.1	2	—[b]	—[b]
Youth custody	21.1	18.2	17.6	0.5	0.1	5	—[b]	—[b]
Imprisonment								
Fully suspended	30.9	27.7	24.7	1.6	1.4	6	—[b]	—[b]
Partly suspended	3.9	3.1	3.1	—[a]	—	1	—[b]	—[b]
Unsuspended	46.7	42.8	39.7	1.8	1.4	10	—[b]	—[b]
Otherwise dealt with	11.3	9.8	4.3	5.2	0.2	1	1	—[b]
Total	1,911.3	1,895.0	385.0	443.7	1,066.3	100	100	100

[a] Less than 50.
[b] Less than 0.5 per cent.
Source: From *Criminal Statistics* 1986.

took a suitcase out of a parked car' – a state of affairs which led him to suggest that the process of sentencing should be removed from the hands of the court and given to an independent sentencing authority. Matters have much improved since, and nobody seriously advocates this course today. But the sentencing process still has its imperfections, as the following discussion will show.

1 What the various punishments involve and what they may be expected to achieve

Judges and magistrates can learn certain things on the job in court including, if necessary, what their formal powers of sentencing are and what are current levels of sentencing in practice. Such things are regularly discussed in court, and they can be guided on such matters by court officials and by the lawyers in the case. But nobody in court describes what the inside of a prison is like; nobody reports back to the court how a given offender is behaving as a result of the sentence they gave him; and no one tells a judge or magistrate in court what the usual effects of particular types of sentence are known by criminologists to be. Thus for broader questions, such as what a particular punishment actually involves and what it can reasonably be expected to achieve, sentencers must rely on special training. So we must ask two questions: what training do sentencers receive, and how much does it contain about these matters?

When the first edition of this book appeared, the answer was 'none at all'. Neither magistrates nor judges were given any kind of instruction in their formal powers and duties, let alone broader criminological matters. It was quite possible for a barrister to acquire a substantial practice and be appointed a stipendiary magistrate, a Recorder, or even a High Court Judge and be no better informed in criminological matters than any ordinary citizen. A barrister who is appointed a judge would at least usually know what his formal powers are, but a layman appointed as a magistrate would be unlikely to know even this. Since the Second World War, however, things have greatly changed. In 1948 the Royal Commission on Justices of the Peace recommended instruction for magistrates, and said 'It is essential that every justice should understand the meaning of the various sentences that can be given and orders that can be made'.[1] As is explained elsewhere in this book, there is now a two-stage course training for new magistrates, which has been compulsory since 1964; see chapter 33(ii). This includes not only lectures, but visits to prisons, youth custody centres and so forth. Further training days are arranged for experienced magistrates who are keen enough to volunteer for them, and sentencing exercises frequently form part of these. Training for judges took longer to establish.

There was a strong feeling at the Bar and among the older judges that the only requirement a judge needs for sentencing is a feel for the 'going rate', and a curious idea that the very notion of judicial training was a threat to the idea of

[1] (1948) Cmnd 7463 para. 90.

judicial independence, or was in some way insulting both to bench and Bar. In 1963, however, the Lord Chief Justice called a series of meetings of practising lawyers to discuss problems of sentencing, and this was followed by a series of sentencing conferences, and by the holding of various voluntary courses for newly-appointed judges – courses which included visits to penal institutions. In 1975 a working party was set up jointly with the Home Secretary, the Lord Chancellor and the Lord Chief Justice under the Chairmanship of Lord Justice Bridge (now Lord Bridge).[1]

As a concession to those who were hostile to the idea of judges needing to be trained in sentencing, the Bridge Committee rejected the term 'judicial training' in favour of 'judicial studies', but under cover of this euphemism recommended a system of judicial training. Training, including training in sentencing matters, now regularly takes place. There is a Judicial Studies Board, with a salaried director, which holds regular training courses, and newly-appointed judges are required to attend a course there. The Bridge Committee thought such courses should last for two weeks; attendance for three or four days is all that is required at present – not much, but certainly a step in the right direction. Refresher courses for more experienced judges are also available; nowadays, when a person is appointed a Recorder or a Circuit Judge, it is made plain to him that he is expected to go to a number of refresher courses. Much of the time at these courses is necessarily taken up with other matters, but there are some lectures on sentencing and penology. There are also some visits to prisons and similar places, and there are plans to increase their number.

The training judges receive in general penological matters, though better than nothing, is neither very thorough nor very systematic. Unfortunately, however, there is a real difficulty giving them any more systematic training in these matters than we manage to do at present. In this country, judges are not trained for the career from an early age, as in most countries, but are recruited from the ranks of practising lawyers already middle-aged. If they have any ability at all – and it is highly desirable that they should have – they will be extremely busy people, with little time for prolonged training courses. Once they are judges they will still be very busy people with comparatively little spare time. Things are unlikely to be much improved except by changing the upbringing of lawyers. In order to get legal qualifications, it is necessary to make some study of criminal law and criminal evidence and procedure, but a study of the treatment of offenders is not compulsory. Every law student is expected to know how the system of law courts was altered during the nineteenth century, but he may be accounted legally educated without ever having heard of the Report of the Gladstone Committee of 1895, of the steps taken to carry out its recommendations, and the later developments. Is it too much to hope that the legal profession may come to regard the subject of sentencing as being as important as, say, the rules of evidence and procedure?

[1] *Report of the Working Party on Judicial Studies and Information* (1978).

All this raises two important questions: what body of scientific knowledge exists on penological matters, and how useful is any of it for a sentencer to know? Over the last 40 years a large volume of criminological research has been done. The work is shared between the universities, with the Home Office sponsoring and assisting, and the Home Office Research Unit. In 1958 the Home Secretary announced his desire to see a National Institute of Criminology in Cambridge, and the Institute was established in 1959; at Oxford what is now called the Centre for Criminological Research has existed since 1970. Criminology has become accepted as an optional subject in law courses in many universities. A large part of the research that is done is more of interest to those concerned with policy than it is to the courts: for decisions whether to increase facilities, alter age limits, maintain or revise the prison regime and so forth. Thirty years ago was a time of great optimism when it was widely believed that criminological research would also be of much immediate use in the sentencing process: that with a little more time and money spent on it, we would reach a state where we knew scientifically what the right 'treatment' for each type of offender and offence was, and courts would be able to sentence to cure offenders of their wrongdoing in much the same way as doctors can prescribe effective treatment for an illness once they have properly diagnosed it. This optimism is now a thing of the past, because if criminological research has shown anything at all it seems to be that there is no type of sentence which is notably more successful than any other in reforming offenders. In this area, many hopes have been raised, only to be rudely dashed. In theories of sentencing, as in criminology generally, there has been

something of a tendency to stagger from one policy prescription to another – in this country, the treatment of offenders, then situational crime prevention, then social crime prevention; in the United States, the treatment of offenders, then deterrence, selective incapacitation, and so on – often with a strong tendency to what two Canadian criminologists have called 'panaceaphilia' (this will solve everything) when a new policy is proposed, to 'negativitis' (this has been absolutely useless) when one moves on from one policy to the next.[1]

Nowadays criminologists would be the first to admit that they are in no position to give sentencers all the answers. They cannot even explain the continual rise in crime which is such a dark feature of our times, and certainly cannot tell us how to end it by appropriate 'treatment' of offenders in the courts. However, it does not follow from this that all knowledge of penology for sentencers is useless. Information can be of negative as well as positive value. If criminology does not enable the court to choose the sentence which will infallibly cure the offender of his anti-social tendencies, it is still useful for the court to know that statistically a prison sentence is not more likely to deter him from future misbehaviour than any

[1] Professor Anthony Bottoms, 'Reflections on the criminological enterprise', [1987] Camb. LJ 240, 253; referring to Gendreau and Ross, 'Correctional potency: Treatment and deterrence on trial', in Roesch and Corrado (eds.), *Evaluation and criminal justice policy* (1981) p. 30.

other course, that imprisoning people is nearly always bad for them, and that the value of a prison sentence to society in general lies only in its effect on the victim's morale, the certainty that the offender cannot reoffend whilst he is inside, the possible deterrent effect on others, and a public recognition that some offences are so grave that imprisonment is the only appropriate course. At a more practical level, it is still important for a sentencer to know what in real terms he is letting the offender in for when he subjects him to imprisonment or youth custody, puts him on probation, or inflicts any other penalty upon him.

2 The details of the offence

Where the defendant pleads not guilty the case will be proved against him by witnesses who give evidence to the court, and the sentencer obviously has full details of what happened. Where the defendant pleads guilty, however, as he does in the majority of cases, usually no witnesses are called. Generally, all that happens is that the prosecution lawyer outlines the offence to the court as he understands it, after which the defendant or his lawyer makes a speech in mitigation, in which he usually tries to put the best complexion on the matter that he can. Quite often the result is that the court is presented with conflicting versions of what happened which are so far apart that the sentence should be quite different, according to which version is believed. For example, where the defendant pleads guilty to assault or wounding, the prosecution may say that the defendant launched an unprovoked attack on a victim who was peacefully minding his own business, and in mitigation the defendant may claim that the victim insulted him and hit him first. At one time, when this sort of situation arose, the sentencer was expected to decide by hunch or instinct which version he preferred, and sentence accordingly; which was potentially very unfair to the defendant, who might be sent to prison on the basis of false allegations which there had not even been an attempt to support by evidence. In recent years, the Court of Appeal has ruled that where, following a guilty plea, prosecution and defence accounts of the incident conflict, the sentencer has a choice. Either he must hear witnesses and decide on the basis of evidence what really did happen, or he must accept the defence version and use that as the basis for his sentence.[1]

This ruling avoids a risk of over-severity to the defendant, but it is not wholly satisfactory, because it means that if the court does not bother to hear evidence the defendant may be seriously under-sentenced. Furthermore, it can be exceedingly offensive for the victim if the defence make untrue allegations against him in mitigation, and without checking the court then sentences upon the basis that they are true. Nor is it always sufficient to ensure that no injustice is

---

[1] *Newton* (1982) 77 Cr. Ap. R. 13. Most of the credit for this development must go to Dr D. A. Thomas, who identified the problem in his writings, particularly 'Establishing the factual basis for sentencing' [1970] Crim. LR 80. Later cases qualify *Newton* by saying that the judge may reject the defence version without calling witnesses if it is obviously incredible.

done to the defendant. More recent decisions say that none of this applies where a defendant puts forward in mitigation something which does not actually conflict with the prosecution's version of events. Thus, for example, the defendant in one case pleaded guilty to possessing drugs with intent to supply. In mitigation he asserted through counsel that he had been acting under threats. This story did not conflict with anything the prosecution had said, which was simply that he was found with a quantity of drugs in his car of a size suggesting that he meant to supply it to others. The Court of Appeal said that here there was no duty on the judge to hear evidence before rejecting the story about threats.[1] In most other European legal systems, the USSR included, there is no special procedure for guilty pleas, and in any remotely serious case the court will hear evidence before it decides what sort of penal measure to impose. In this respect, if in no other, it is hard to accept that our criminal justice system is the best and fairest in the world.

It goes without saying that the court must sentence the offender for the offence of which he stands convicted, and not for other crimes which the court suspects he may have done. There is a partial exception to this, however, and this is the procedure known as *taking offences into consideration*. If at the time that he is sentenced the defendant is prepared to admit he has committed other offences, the court may sentence him taking these other offences into account. At first sight this looks an extraordinary thing for an offender to do, but in fact it is in everyone's interests that he should do this, including his own. It makes it possible for the police to clear up a large number of unsolved crimes. It saves the prosecuting authorities the time, cost and trouble of further prosecutions. And the offender, for his part, usually receives a sentence which amounts to less than he would have received if he had been separately prosecuted for the extra offences, and comes out of prison with a clear start ahead of him and no chance of further proceedings; because although there is no formal bar to a future prosecution for these offences, it is the invariable practice not to prosecute for them.[2] The common offences to be taken into consideration are theft, obtaining by deception and burglary, which in the Crown Court carry maximum penalties high enough to cover both the offence for which there is a conviction and the offences taken into consideration. Where the maximum available is regarded as insufficient, then the court should refuse to take other offences into consideration. Hence magistrates' courts can rarely follow this practice.

3 The character and background of the offender

Here the court gets its information from four different sources. The first is the police, who in any remotely serious case prepare an 'antecedents statement' on the offender. This is prepared in writing, but a police officer comes to court and

[1] *Ogunti* [1987] Crim. LR 836; in fact the judge had heard evidence before he rejected the story.
[2] If the conviction on which he has been sentenced should be quashed on appeal, then there could be a prosecution for any of the offences taken into consideration.

speaks to the report, usually by answering questions about it put to him by prosecuting counsel. At one time the police were inclined to give their views about the general way of life of the defendant unsupported by any evidence, and using phrases that made good headlines in evening papers. In a leading case in 1943 they were castigated for this[1] and since then the practice has usually been to confine these statements to particulars of the offender's age, education and employment, the date of arrest, whether the prisoner had been on bail, and a statement summarising any previous convictions.[2] A copy of the statement is available to the defence in advance if they want it, and the defence has the opportunity of challenging the information it contains if it wishes to do so, and they may require proof by evidence of the parts which they do not accept.

The second source of information is likely to be the social enquiry report which is prepared by the probation service. This gives the court information about the offender's character, personality, education, present employment (if any) and employment prospects. It also usually contains information about the offender's attitude to the offence. In preparing the report, the officer is officially encouraged to give an opinion as to the kind of sentence which is suitable for the offender, and most probation officers do venture an opinion,[3] and although judges occasionally make harsh remarks about these recommendations in a majority of cases they seem to follow them. These reports are generally prepared before the trial, provided the probation service has time enough to do so, in order to enable the court to sentence the offender immediately after conviction where possible. This is felt to be important 'to demonstrate that persons who commit serious offences are punished; and the public impact of the sentence is much reduced if it is made known at a later date than the finding of guilt'.[4]

There are disadvantages in pre-trial reports, however. In the preparation of a pre-trial report it always has to be borne in mind that the defendant may be acquitted, and some enquiries cannot be made without his consent. The terms of the report may be affected because the probation officer interviewing the defendant before trial should not proceed as if he has committed the offence unless he admits it, whereas in interviewing him after conviction there can be a much franker discussion and a franker report about the reasons for his behaviour. Thus probation officers are generally reluctant to prepare social enquiry reports if the defendant intends to plead not guilty. If pre-trial reports have not been made, the court can call for them after conviction, when it can also call for more

---

[1] *Van Peltz* [1943] 1 KB 157. After she was convicted of larceny the police statement said: 'for many years past this woman has led a loose and immoral life, and she has associated constantly with convicted thieves in the West End of London . . . This woman is undoubtedly an adventuress. She is regarded as a very dangerous woman indeed. She is completely unscrupulous and for many years past she has lived entirely on her wits.'

[2] Their content and so forth is now regulated by a Practice Direction, [1966] 1 WLR 1184.

[3] The form and content is governed by Home Office circulars: see HO circ. (1983) no. 17. The Home Office Research Study 48, *Social enquiry reports: A survey* contains a great deal of other information.

[4] *The Committee on the Business of the Criminal Courts (Streatfield Committee)* (1961) Cmnd 1289 para. 310.

information if a social enquiry report which has been prepared pre-trial is not sufficiently informative; but this will necessarily mean an adjournment between conviction and sentence.

Social enquiry reports were introduced in 1934 for juvenile offenders, and their use since has extended to cases involving adult offenders. In certain situations the court is now obliged by statute to obtain one before passing sentence. Thus one must normally be obtained before sentencing a juvenile, before imposing a first custodial sentence on an offender under the age of 21, and before making a community service order. Since 1967 the Home Secretary has had the power to make regulations requiring the court to obtain one before passing any type of sentence on any class of offender, but no such regulations have been made. Instead, the Home Office has preferred to exhort their wider use by issuing circulars, and the Court of Appeal has added its encouragement by comments in various judgments. As a result, social enquiry reports are now obtained on practically all offenders sentenced by the Crown Court, and on many of those sentenced by magistrates' courts as well. Social enquiry reports, like the antecedents statements which the police prepare, are available to the defence in advance, and the defendant may challenge unfavourable statements contained in them and may require the probation officer responsible to come and give evidence.

A third source of information about the offender could be other specialist reports obtained at the request of the court. These may be medical or psychiatric reports, a court normally has a discretion to ask for, and which it is obliged to obtain before making a hospital order or a psychiatric probation order. Other reports may be obtained where juvenile offenders are concerned, in particular, reports from the school they attend and reports from any social worker who has been involved with their family.

The final source of information is the offender himself, from what is said on his behalf in mitigation of sentence. Where a defendant has an odds-on chance of being sent to prison, there are various stories which the court is likely to be told: that he has just been offered a job which he will be unable to take up if he gets a custodial sentence; that he has recently formed a stable relationship with a steady young woman who has been a moderating influence on his life, whom he will marry if he stays out of prison; and that he can afford to pay a sizeable fine or compensation order should the court decide on a non-custodial sentence. Sometimes stories of this sort are backed up by witnesses who can vouch for them, when they are likely to be true. Sometimes they are supported by letters, when they are probably true but may be false. 'There seems to be an Irish agency in North London', James Morton recently wrote, 'which provides open letters of reference and offers of employment to defendants. In the last few weeks I had one which began "Dear Sir/Madam, With reference to your interview last Friday we have pleasure in offering you a job as a driver . . .".'[1]

[1] *Handling criminal cases: A guide to preparation and defence* (1986) para. 7.08.

Quite often these and similar stories come out as mere assertions which the defence lawyer makes in his speech in mitigation, and then they are quite likely to be false. As a matter of professional behaviour, the position of the defence lawyer is that he is bound to put forward such information in mitigation as his client tells him to put forward, and, although he must not repeat what he knows to be false he is under no duty to check that it is true. If defence lawyers do not check the information is true the prosecution certainly will not, because although the defence have a right to know in advance what will be contained in the antecedents statement and the social enquiry report, there is no obligation on the defence to tell the prosecution what facts they propose to assert in mitigation; and even if they were able to check it in advance a prosecution attempt to point out its inaccuracies might probably be viewed as the cardinal sin of 'seeking to influence the court in regard to sentence' (see page 300). The result is that sometimes the sentencer can be misled, with serious results.[1]

A recurrent problem has been where the court has been misled about the offender's finances and, usually as an alternative to sending him to prison, has imposed a substantial fine or compensation order which he has then been unable to pay. This has recently induced the Court of Appeal to rule that contrary to what is generally the case, defence counsel does have a duty to the court to check the facts about his client's finances before mitigating on the basis that he is in a good position to pay.[2]

It is surely a bad thing that the defence are ever permitted to put forward any matter in mitigation by way of mere assertions, with no evidence to back it up. When we read in the newspapers that counsel has made a speech in mitigation on behalf of a gang of youths on the basis of their deep remorse, and that after sentence was passed they laughed, jeered and swore at the judge as they left the dock, it makes one feel that there is something seriously wrong with the sentencing system.[3]

4 Current sentencing practice

In most ages there has been a widely held feeling that a criminal deserves and ought to receive a measure of punishment appropriate to the crime. For many centuries that view was reflected in the fact that many or most offences carried penalties which were mandatory. Nowadays very few offences have mandatory penalties, but the same view, justified by some people on the ground that

[1] As in the celebrated case of Guardsman Holdsworth in 1977. He was originally sentenced to three years' imprisonment for grievous bodily harm to a young woman which he inflicted in an attempt to rape. There was a public outcry when the Court of Appeal substituted a six-month suspended sentence on being told that this would enable him to resume his promising career in the Coldstream Guards – and a worse one when the Army then proceeded to throw him out: *The Times* 18–23 June 1977.
[2] *Bond* [1986] Crim. LR 413.
[3] *The Independent* 7 October 1987.

punishment should be expiatory or retributive, has moulded the attitude of our courts in exercising their sentencing discretion. The conception has been that every crime has a measure of punishment; the customary sentence may be mitigated or even increased for special circumstances, but in an ordinary case such and such an offence 'warrants' a sentence of such-and-such a type and size. The traditional method of sentencing has some merits. It is in accordance with the usual reaction of ordinary people and it appears to uphold the obligatory nature of the law. Uniformity is associated with justice; when persons guilty of apparently similar offences are given dissimilar sentences there is apt to be a feeling that it is unfair. It is felt that judges ought to do the customary thing, for then people know what to expect. The customary thing must of course alter as time goes by, but it should not alter too fast. A more modern view is that the object of the criminal law is the protection of the community. As regards people who have already committed offences, that purpose can be served in three main ways. First, if an offender can be reformed or rehabilitated he will no longer be a menace. Secondly, he may be prevented from further harmful acts by being kept in custody. And thirdly, the thought of having to endure punishment may deter the person who has offended and deter other people from committing offences. The question of which sentence to impose is then largely one of trying to forecast what would be the effect of each type of sentence that the court could impose. It is not until we look at the probabilities attendant upon each course of action that we can make the best choice. The treatment is made to fit the offender rather than to fit the offence. It is sometimes thought that this process of individualisation means that offenders all get off more lightly; many do, but some get heavier sentences. Broadly speaking, the courts are at present in the process of trying to consider the individual offender without completely abandoning their notion of each type of offence having a proper quantum of punishment. The traditional view is apt to be taken most firmly at the top and bottom of the scale; it is felt that a really serious offence should be visited with imprisonment appropriate to its gravity, whilst for a relatively minor offence it would be disproportionate and wrong to go beyond a light sentence. It is only when there is room to manoeuvre, either because the offence does not clearly fall into the category of grave or minor, or because there are some exceptional characteristics, that a court feels free to look at the future needs of the offender.

In the light of this it is clear that uniformity in sentences is neither possible nor desirable. What is highly desirable, and also possible, is that the courts should adopt a uniform approach to the process of sentencing. Sentencers should be in agreement as to the types of offence which must be handled according to a 'tariff' approach, and the types where individualised sentences are acceptable. Where the tariff approach prevails, the tariff should be uniform and should not vary from judge to judge and court to court. Where offences permit sentences to be individualised, sentencers should follow a broadly similar approach as to those factors which point to an individualised sentence in a particular case, and make similar assumptions about what type of sentence is meant to achieve what type of result. If there is great disparity between the sentences of different courts which cannot be explained by reference to a body of principles which are known and accepted by the criminal courts generally, it means that the sentencing is arbitrary, which is wrong, because it is a basic legal notion that like cases must be treated alike. It is equally wrong if principles of sentencing exist, but some sentencers depart from them. If an offender receives a sentence heavier than accepted principles allow for – if a first offender with an excellent record is given a sentence of immediate imprisonment for a minor shoplifting, for example – the injustice is very dubious. The injustice is no less real if the sentence is unreasonably lenient – a sentence of only six months imprisonment for manslaughter on a man who killed a cyclist by deliberately running him over, for example, or a non-custodial sentence for a rape.[1]

Here the offender has nothing to complain about, but such a sentence makes a grievance for similar offenders who correctly received heavier sentences, outrages the victim (or his surviving relatives), discourages the police who feel their efforts were in vain, and undermines the deterrent effect of the law, which is made to look like a lottery, unworthy of public respect. Worse still, an over-lenient sentence could lead to the premature release of an offender who was dangerous and likely to do further harm unless restrained.

For the more serious offences, the current principles of sentencing are laid down by the Court of Appeal from time to time in the course of deciding appeals against sentence imposed in the Crown Court. To take two examples, important judgments in recent years have stated the principles to be applied in rape[2] and causing death by reckless driving.[3] The cases which contain these pronouncements are published in the various series of law reports (of which there is now one entirely devoted to sentencing),[4] and they are digested in various books and journals available to judges and lawyers (and ordinary members of the public too, if they wish to read them). Of particular note is Dr D. A. Thomas's *Principles of sentencing*, and the Home Office booklet called *The sentence of the court*.[5]

Magistrates get less guidance from the Court of Appeal than do judges in the Crown Court, because cases of the sort which they have to try rarely come before it. However, for some years in motoring cases they have extensively used a set of guidelines prepared by the Magistrates' Association and approved by the Lord Chancellor and the Lord Chief Justice. In 1987, it was announced that those guidelines would shortly be extended to cover other common offences too. The

---

[1] Both of these are real examples, unfortunately. For the manslaughter, see 'Motor vehicles as weapons of offence' [1985] Crim. LR 29. The rape case occurred in 1982 and caused a big public outcry. There is an account of it by Sheila Jeffreys and Jill Radford in *Causes for concern* ed. Scraton and Gordon (1984).

[2] *Roberts* [1982] 1 WLR 133; *Billam* [1986] 1 WLR 349.

[3] *Boswell* [1984] 1 WLR 1047.

[4] *Criminal Appeal Reports (Sentencing)*, published by Sweet and Maxwell.

[5] HMSO. First published in 1964, and regularly revised since.

journal *The Justice of the Peace* carries a weekly digest which includes a regular selection of recent sentences, including sentences imposed by magistrates' courts – culled in the main from the pages of local newspapers. Sentencing also forms part of the training which magistrates receive (see chapter 33(ii)).

To ensure that they know and understand the currently accepted principles of sentencing, judges and magistrates at present depend entirely on their own experience and training, and they cannot rely on getting help from the counsel appearing before them. This contrasts sharply with the position when it comes to their knowing the substance of the criminal law and the rules of criminal evidence and procedure, where it is considered to be part of the duty of the advocate to bring to the attention of the court any legal rule which is relevant to the case. Obviously, counsel is entitled to emphasise the ones which suit his client's case the best; but it is considered to be a breach of professional etiquette for an advocate deliberately not to mention cases or statutes which invalidate the argument he puts, hoping that neither his opponent nor the judge has heard of them. Thus as far as rules of criminal law and evidence are concerned, the more competent and informed the advocates are, the less chance there is of the judge making a mistake by overlooking something vital. This largely goes by the board, however, when it comes to the principles of sentencing. Rule 163 of the Code of Conduct for the Bar says 'Prosecuting counsel should not attempt by advocacy to influence the court in regard to sentence', and this is interpreted to mean that he must do nothing more than outline the facts which are relevant to sentence if these have not already appeared from the evidence heard during the trial. Defence counsel, on the other hand, is placed under no such restraint. He is quite at liberty to suggest, either directly or obliquely, what the appropriate sentence is, and in doing so his duty to his client is 'to see that he gets rather less than he probably deserves'.[1]

A respectable defence lawyer would not of course deliberately mislead by saying that something was an approved principle of sentencing which he knew was not. But it seems that there are quite often cases in which defending lawyers, through ignorance or otherwise, advance arguments in mitigation which are contrary to accepted principles.[2] If this happens the prosecuting lawyer may not correct him, and if the judge or magistrates swallow the argument and let the offender off lightly when they should not, that is just his good luck. Conservative-minded lawyers usually defend this extraordinary state of affairs by saying it is an ancient and basic tradition of English justice that the prosecutor plays no part in sentencing; but this is misleading, because the tradition is neither basic nor ancient. In the first place, the prosecutor is in truth deeply involved in sentencing, albeit at one remove, because he both selects the charge which the defendant must face and helps to select the court which will try it, his decision on both of these matters often being heavily influenced by what penalty he thinks the

[1] James Morton, *Handling criminal cases: A guide to preparation and defence* (1986) para. 7.10.
[2] See Ashworth, *Sentencing and penal policy* (1983) p. 426.

defendant ought to get. And secondly, in earlier days he used to be free to suggest a penalty to the court, and did. Furthermore, the tradition, such as it is, conflicts with another and much more important tradition of justice: *audi alteram partem* – the rule that a court must hear both sides of the argument before it makes up its mind. As one writer puts it, 'Judicial decision-making in the common law is based on the adversary system, but that system is uniquely abandoned when it comes to sentencing.'[1] The history of the matter is that at one time it was the accepted custom for prosecuting counsel to be coarse, heavy-handed and overbearing, and part of their stock-in-trade was to make an emotional appeal for a heavy sentence.[2]

In the nineteenth century the Bar, to its credit, consciously adopted a more civilised approach to prosecuting, and the rule that prosecuting counsel must not make any suggestions about sentence dates from then. This restraint may have made sense in the days when most defendants were unrepresented, and when judges generally needed no encouragement to be severe. It makes no sense at all now that any defendant who is in serious trouble is almost certain to have a lawyer who will be trying to persuade the court to take a merciful course. Nowadays the rule is probably largely responsible for those occasional ridiculously lenient sentences which get wide press coverage, provoke a public outcry, and give a wholly false impression that our courts are going soft on crime.

As the law stands, the defendant may appeal against a sentence but not the prosecution. This means that a mechanism of control exists to make sure that judges do not depart from accepted principles of sentencing in one direction, but nothing except their good sense and training exists to prevent them departing from them in the other. If a judge or magistrate imposes a sentence which is too severe the decision can be reversed, but a sentence which is unreasonably lenient must stand, and the most that can happen is for the person responsible to get a confidential rebuke from the Lord Chancellor. This is very different from the position in most other countries. Even in common law jurisdictions like Canada, Australia and New Zealand it has been felt necessary to give the prosecution some sort of appeal against an unreasonably lenient sentence, in order, as an Australian judge put it, 'to enable the courts to establish and maintain adequate standards of punishment for crime, to enable idiosyncratic views of individual judges as to particular crimes or types of crime to be corrected, and occasionally to correct a sentence which is so disproportionate to the seriousness of the crime as to shock the public conscience'.[3] The usual pattern is for an appeal to lie only with the consent of the Attorney-General.

In England any suggestion of giving the prosecution a right of appeal against over-lenient sentence has traditionally provoked great hostility from lawyers,

[1] Graham Zellick, 'The Role of Prosecuting Counsel in Sentencing', [1979] Crim. LR 493, 494.
[2] For two striking examples see *Horne Tooke* (1777) 20 *State Trials* 657, 781, and *Hales* (1729) 17 *State Trials* 267, 295.
[3] King CJ in *Osenkowski* (1982) 5 *Australian Criminal Reports* 394.

largely on the ground that it would go against the theory that the prosecution plays no part in sentencing. In recent years, however, public pressure has been building up for a change in the law, and some leading lawyers have altered their views. When the Police and Criminal Evidence Bill first appeared, the government proposed to extend the Attorney-General's Reference procedure (see page 209) to sentencing. This would have given the Court of Appeal the power to anathematise aberrant sentences without actually being able to increase them. When this idea was proposed in 1984 it had to be dropped in the face of strong legal opposition to any kind of prosecution appeal on sentence. But when it was resurrected in the Criminal Justice Bill in 1986, it provoked the wrath of the Lord Chief Justice and several Law Lords on the ground that it was a flaccid half-measure: what was needed, they said, was a prosecution of right of appeal coupled with a power to increase sentence. The government was converted to this view, and it seems certain that the Criminal Justice Act that eventually arises from the present Criminal Justice Bill will create a limited prosecution right of appeal which is capable of leading to the sentence being increased.[1]

Various criticisms have been made of the sentencing system in the previous pages. The most serious were the absence of reliable means for making sure that the facts of cases are properly investigated before sentence is passed, and the dishonesty of a system under which the judge, for public consumption, says the sentence is X, and the executive, for administrative reasons, then privately makes the sentence Y. Other serious criticisms are sometimes made, and we must briefly consider them as well.

It is sometimes said that our sentencing system is a failure inasmuch as it is not reducing crime: the crime rate continues to rise, despite what the courts are doing, therefore our sentencing system is wrong. The problem, however, is that crime rates are rising similarly throughout Western Europe, and that they seem to go on rising no matter what penal measures are adopted. The rising crime rate seems to be something that is endemic in our kind of society, and the most any sentencing system can do is to react to the problem. No one who has seriously examined the phenomenon of rising crime thinks it can be solved by a different method of sentencing offenders.

It is frequently said that in England our sentencing is far too severe, in proof of which it is usually said that we imprison more persons per head of the population than most other Western European countries: 81 per 100,000 in 1981, as compared with 72 in France and 23 in the Netherlands. Our sentencing may or may not be too severe, but if it is, such figures do not prove it. Needless severity is one possible explanation for them, but they can equally well be explained by a higher population of criminals, or more efficient police. A study by the Home Office Research and Planning Unit concluded that 'as indicators of judicial attitudes to imprisonment, the figures take no account of differences in crime

---

[1] I tried to put forward the case for an appeal in an article in [1987] Crim. LR 724. (Editor).

rates, detection rates, the proportions of suspects proceeded against, and the relative seriousness of offending'.[1]

Two criticisms in which there is undoubtedly some truth are that the English sentencing system has become needlessly complicated, and is increasingly confused in its objectives. Rising crime causes two opposite concerns, which provoke newspaper headlines alternately: one is that sentencing is insufficiently deterrent, and the other is that our prisons are overcrowded. One consequence of this has already been mentioned: our two-faced combination of a judicial sentence which is severe, and a parole system which often mitigates the severity by two-thirds. Another is the reaction of Parliament in giving more and more increasingly detailed directions to the judges in how they must go about the business of sentencing, much of which is confusing and self-contradictory. Before a judge passes sentence nowadays, he must pick his way through a maze of statutory directions which gets more complicated every year. Dr David Thomas, the well-known writer on sentencing, gives as an example the rigmarole that must precede the imposition of a partly suspended sentence. Because of a combination of various statutory provisions,

The approved approach requires the sentencer first to consider all other alternatives to custody, conclude that a sentence of imprisonment is necessary, fix the length of that sentence, consider whether the sentence can be suspended in full, decide against that, consider whether the sentence can be suspended in part, and if it can, decide what portion of the sentence should be served in the first instance. This approach involves the judge in taking decisions for which it is impossible to give sensible reasons: once he has reached the stage of deciding that a sentence of imprisonment is necessary and fixed the length of the sentence, he has exhausted all relevant considerations, and must begin to use some of them again.[2]

Part of the trouble is that in recent years we have invented a number of new kinds of sentence without really thinking out what they are supposed to do and where they fit into the scale with other penal measures. At one time the judge had a primary decision to make: is this a case for punishment, or for some non-punitive measure designed to rehabilitate the individual? Once that decision was made there were imprisonment and fines, which were clearly punitive, and probation, binding-over and discharging, which were individual and rehabilitative. Now we have, among other things, suspended sentences, partly suspended sentences, community service orders, compensation orders, confiscation orders, and various kinds of disqualification, and nobody knows quite where they go in the list. Judge A may think a suspended sentence is meant to be punitive, but when he gives a drunken driver a suspended sentence for killing a cyclist or pedestrian the

[1] P. Softley, *The use of custody: Some European comparisons* Home Office Research and Planning Unit, Research Bulletin 16 (1983).

[2] D. A. Thomas, 'Sentencing and some current questions', in *The psychology of sentencing: approaches to consistency and disparity* (1988), ed. Pennington and Lloyd-Bostock.

local press will probably scream he has let the driver off. If Judge A thinks community service orders are punitive and Judge B thinks they are rehabilitative there will obviously be a disparity of sentencing between the courts over which they preside.

At present it falls to our over-worked Court of Appeal to attempt to make sense of all these nonsenses by issuing occasional guideline judgments as and when the appropriate case comes before them. In some countries, notably various jurisdictions in the USA, the legislature tries to resolve the questions of principle by making detailed sentencing guidelines by statute. This has the disadvantage of being inherently too rigid. One solution that has been proposed is to set up a Sentencing Council, presided over by the Lord Chief Justice. This could discuss these general sentencing dilemmas hypothetically without waiting for a case upon which to hang the decision, and their rulings could then be issued in the form of Practice Directions.[1]

[1] See Ashworth, *Sentencing and penal policy* (1983) chapter 11. There was at one time an Advisory Council on the penal system. This was abolished in 1979.

25

JUVENILE COURTS[1]

Traditionally the minimum age for criminal responsibility in England was 7. It was raised by statute to 8 in 1933, and in 1963 it was further raised to 10, where it remains today.[2] A child over the age of 10 can incur criminal liability, but only where he can be shown to have 'mischievous discretion' – that is to say, where he knew not only what he was doing but also that it was morally wrong. A person who has become 14 and is under the age of 17 is defined by statute as a 'young person'. A young person is not protected by the requirement of 'mischievous discretion', but like a child, he must usually be tried before a special court called the *juvenile court*. In the juvenile court virtually all offences are treated as summary offences. There is no right for the child to elect trial on indictment. The only cases which must be sent for trial are homicide, certain grave offences for which there can be detention under direction of the Home Secretary, and cases where a child is charged together with an adult.

Until the middle of the last century there was no special provision for the trial of children; if the offence charged was indictable the trial would be before a jury at Assizes or Quarter Sessions, whilst a petty offence would be tried summarily before justices in the usual way. An Act of 1847 allowed offenders under 14 to be tried summarily for stealing. This policy was widely extended by the Summary Jurisdiction Act 1879 with the result that offenders under 16 could be tried summarily for nearly all the indictable offences. These changes merely simplified proceedings against young offenders, who were still tried in the same courts and subjected to the same conditions as adults. The Children Act of 1908 represented the success of a long agitation, and established the principle that young offenders must be treated differently from adults. Offenders under 16 had to be tried in a juvenile court, which was a court of summary jurisdiction sitting in a different place or at a different time from the ordinary sittings of the court, thus avoiding bringing the juvenile offender into contact with older professional criminals and undesirable persons. Prison for children was abolished, except in

---

[1] The standard practitioners' book is Clarke Hall and Morrison, *The law relating to children and young persons* (10th ed. 1985). An interesting account of their development and present state is Alison Morris and Henri Giller, *Understanding juvenile justice* (1987).
[2] The Children and Young Persons Act 1969 contained a section raising the age to 14, but it was never brought into force.

exceptional circumstances for those between 14 and 16, in favour of methods aiming at reformation of the offender rather than punishment. The courts that tried young offenders were still the ordinary benches of justices. The practice of selecting certain justices for this work began in the London area under an Act of 1920, whereby a juvenile court consisted of a metropolitan stipendiary magistrate and two lay justices (of whom one had to be a woman); the Home Secretary nominated the justices, taking account of their suitability for the work.

In 1927 a Committee on the Treatment of Young Offenders issued a report[1] which led to statutory changes which were consolidated in the Children and Young Persons Act 1933. This is still the main Act which governs the composition of the courts and general matters of procedure, but there are also Rules made by the Lord Chancellor under powers contained in various statutes. The justices in each area make up a panel among themselves of those justices who are thought to be most suitable for work in juvenile courts; ordinarily there is one panel for each petty sessional division, but divisions may be combined so that there is a single panel for all the courts in a combined area. Every three years the panel must be reconsidered, existing members still being eligible. Rules provide that no justice shall be a member of a juvenile court panel after he has attained the age of 65, with an exception for stipendiary magistrates and any justices specially exempted by the Lord Chancellor. Before he may adjudicate in a juvenile court, a panel member is required to undergo extra training (see chapter 33(ii)). The Lord Chancellor, in considering the appointment of new justices, may give special attention to the needs of the juvenile court panel. The panel appoints a chairman. A juvenile court consists of not more than three justices drawn from this panel, and must include one man and one woman. Juvenile courts are still magistrates' courts, but they must hold separate sessions, preferably in a different room from the ordinary court-room; if an ordinary court-room is used, the juvenile court must not be held within an hour before or after its use for another court. Throughout the proceedings care is taken to see that the juvenile does not come into contact with adult offenders. This is necessary both before and after the case is tried. A juvenile who is remanded, or who is committed for trial without bail, is remanded to the care of a local authority; but if he is too unruly to be safely committed to the care of the local authority he may be sent to a remand centre for 17- to 21-year-olds provided by the Home Office, or if one is not available he will be sent to wait in prison.

Although proceedings in the juvenile court are in outline the same as proceedings in an ordinary magistrates' court, in a number of respects they are less formal. In many courts an ordinary room is used, so that the justices sit at a table and there are no special court furnishings. Policemen may be instructed to attend in plain clothes. Legal representatives may appear, and since 1982 are legally required to do so in some serious cases; but if they do not, a parent or

---

[1] (1927) Cmd 2831 (Maloney Committee).

guardian (or in their absence any relative or other suitable person) may conduct the defence. Instead of the charge being read to him, as in an adult court, the charge is explained in simple language so that the juvenile can understand it. Instead of being asked whether he pleads guilty or not guilty, he is usually asked whether he 'admits' the charge or 'denies' it. Another modification is the form of the oath. On the ground that children are taught that swearing is a bad thing, the oath instead of begining 'I swear' begins 'I promise'. There is a very sensible provision that if a child or young person 'instead of asking questions by way of cross-examination, makes assertions, the court shall then put to the witness such questions as it thinks necessary'; but unfortunately this does not apply to parents or other lay advocates who must apparently know how to cross-examine. If the case is proved, the juvenile court does not convict, but 'makes a finding of guilt', and instead of sentencing it 'makes an order'. The conduct of the court is largely in the hands of the chairman whose role is much greater than in an adult court. It requires much skill and experience together with the knack of being able to talk with children without losing their respect. For these reasons the rules require the chairman or deputy chairman always to be present in order to preside. The courts are not open to the public; press reporters may be present, but all other persons must be connected with the case or authorised by the court to be present. Newspaper reports of the case must not give the names or anything that will reveal the identity of the child or young person who appears before these courts, whether he appears as a defendant or as a witness. The court has a discretion to release the name of a child if it seems in the interests of justice to do so.

The Children and Young Persons Act 1933 produced a very important principle that is still fundamental. Section 44(1) of that Act, as amended in 1969, is as follows:

Every court in dealing with a child or young person who is brought before it, either as an offender or otherwise, shall have regard to the welfare of the child or young person and shall in a proper case take steps for removing him from undesirable surroundings and for securing that proper provision is made for his education and training.

There seems nothing very revolutionary about these words today, but at the time they represented something of a breakthrough in the face of legal tradition. The ordinary practice in the criminal courts was to measure the punishment against the gravity of the offence and the welfare of the offender was not considered save in exceptional cases. To apply the principle of the welfare of the child, the court had to consider what would be the effect on the child of any of the possible orders that the court could make, and for this the magistrates had to know what these orders actually meant in practice and they also needed reliable information about the child himself. In those days, in the adult courts we saw judges, who knew practically nothing about the inside of a prison, imprisoning offenders of whose circumstances they were equally ignorant. Our more civilised practices in these matters today originated in the juvenile courts.

Quite apart from the question of prosecuting juveniles for criminal offences, the State has a number of compulsory civil law powers to intervene where children are being ill-treated or neglected, or are beyond their parents' control. In cases of urgency, a child can be taken away from its parents for up to 28 days by what is called a 'place of safety order'[1]. Children can be permanently removed from their parents by means of a 'care order', and there are other less drastic procedures. Although these are civil law matters, they are operated by the magistrates' courts, and with the exception of place of safety orders which can be issued by any magistrate at any place, the business is conducted in the juvenile court. It may seem odd that the jurisdiction should have fallen to juvenile courts for they are specialised magistrates' courts and commonly regarded as criminal courts. This type of work found its way into the magistrates' court as an off-shoot of their power to punish offenders. In the nineteenth century various offences of cruelty to children were created for which parents could be punished, and in 1889 the magistrates' court was given the power to remove the child as well as to penalise the parents. This power was later extended to other situations where the parents were not guilty of any offence.[2]

It has long been recognised that the issues of juvenile crime and children in need of care and protection merge into one another. At each end of the spectrum the difference is clear. If a child has committed something like a rape or a murder the public need to be protected from him, and a child who is accused of a very serious crime should be entitled to a judicial proceeding and adjudication before the question of dealing with him is considered. At the opposite end, a child who is left unprovided with a home and normal care (whether through natural catastrophe such as being orphaned or by defect of parents or other failure of arrangements for his care) needs to be looked after, not punished, and does not need an adjudication any more than the victim of a physical accident needs a judicial proceeding before he can be admitted to hospital. Between these extremes there is an area in which cases may be dealt with through courts or by administrative procedures. Children who are not being properly looked after, who are disobedient, truanting, staying out late at night and so on, may be seen as in need of better care; and if nothing is done about them, such children commonly get involved in burglary, vandalism, and other matters which in the case of adults are treated as criminal offences. There is no logical dividing line and the use made of either method has depended on the facilities available. In the earlier days of juvenile courts the social services were inadequate and hence the jurisdiction of the court was expanded. Then, after the 1939–45 war there came a great increase and strengthening of social services, and a strong body of public

[1] A period of 28 days is generally said to be far too long, and the Government White Paper, *The Law on Child Care and Family Services* (1987) Cm 62 recommends a maximum of no more than 8 days. In July 1988 this recommendation was endorsed in the *Report of the Inquiry into Child Abuse in Cleveland 1987*, Cm 412.
[2] See J. S. Heywood, *Children in care* (3rd ed. 1978).

opinion was in favour of removing as many of these cases as possible from the ambit of the courts and handing them over to the social services. However there were, and still are, serious differences of opinion on these matters, and it is necessary to examine the different opinions in order to understand the legal changes which have taken place over the last 20 years.

There is one point of view which is usually associated with the political left. At the risk of over-simplification, this view is that juvenile misbehaviour is the direct result of deprivation and bad social conditions. When a child or a young person steals, burgles or vandalises he is not to be blamed or punished for this: the appropriate response is to remove him from bad influences and improve his conditions. As the courts, particularly the criminal courts, are primarily concerned with matters of guilt and blame, they should not usually be involved in these cases. In the most serious cases, perhaps, the public must be protected by measures of restraint which it is desirable that only a court of law should impose. Otherwise, however, the courts should be involved only to the extent necessary to remove the child or young person from the control of his parents or other bad influences upon him, and to give the local social services department the powers they need to do for him what his best interests require. This point of view gained strength in the 1960s from the fact that the rate of juvenile crime had been steadily rising for some years, a fact which made people doubt whether the current practice of prosecuting juveniles as offenders before the juvenile courts had any practical value in the prevention of crime. It also gained strength from the prevailing optimism among criminologists that their researches were likely before long to produce cures for crime in the form of effective 'treatment' for offenders.

This point of view had its greatest impact in Scotland. There, the Kilbrandon Committee reported in 1964.[1] Their diagnosis was

In terms of the treatment measures to be applied, the children appearing before the courts, whatever the precise circumstances in which they do so, show a basic similarity of underlying situation. The distinguishing factor is their common need for special measures of education and training, the normal upbringing processes for whatever reason having failed or fallen short.

That being so, the need as they saw it was for a specialised treatment agency or panel, and that should be a lay body with knowledge and experience, independent and neither a court of law nor a local authority committee. If there were a dispute on the facts, the case would go to a law court and if the allegation was upheld, the case would be remitted to the panel for consideration of treatment measures. These recommendations were substantially carried out by the Social Work (Scotland) Act 1968.[2] The Scottish system of 'children's hearings' has now been

---

[1] *Report on Children and Young Persons: Scotland* (1964) Cmnd 2306.

[2] Proposals for some form of child welfare committee have often been inspired by Scandinavian practice, but the Kilbrandon version seems to be original. A comparative study of the Swedish Child

in existence for nearly 20 years and is often held up in England as a successful model which we ought to copy. Among those who have studied it carefully it has its critics, however;[1] but despite some people's misgivings about certain aspects of the scheme it is fair to say that the Scots seem generally content with it.[2]

In England this philosophy did not so thoroughly prevail. There was a lot of public discussion, an official inquiry and a series of public proposals, some of which included the idea of replacing the juvenile court with some kind of less formal body.[3] However, in 1968 the Labour government, which was then in power, produced a scheme in a White Paper entitled *Children in trouble*[4] which retained the present system of juvenile courts, whilst shifting the emphasis of their work away from criminal proceedings against juveniles and towards civil care proceedings. Criminal proceedings for children under 14 were to be abolished, leaving civil 'care proceedings' as the only possibility for this age-group; juvenile courts were to lose their powers to impose any kind of custody upon young persons between the ages of 14 and 16, for whom the possibility of criminal proceedings was to remain; and the main method for dealing with children and young persons in trouble, whether they came before the court by way of care proceedings or on a criminal prosecution, was to be the 'care order' which gave the local authority social services department a wide discretion as to what to do with them. These proposals were enacted in the Children and Young Persons Act 1969. However, there was a change of government in 1970 before the Act was implemented, and the Conservative government promptly said that it would not bring some of the Act into force. In the end much of the 1969 Act was never brought into effect, and in the Criminal Justice Act 1982 a later Conservative government undid some of the parts of the 1969 scheme which were in force.

The problem with implementing the 1969 scheme in England was that an influential body of opinion did not accept the basic idea behind it. Many people, usually on the political right, are firmly committed to the idea that people are morally responsible for their acts even if they are young, and refuse to accept that deprivation and bad social conditions can properly excuse them from blame and punishment. Thus the Conservative Bow Group wrote:

It is easy to find excuses for children who have shown signs of anti-social behaviour, but we do feel that a child over the age of 10 is old enough to be responsible for his actions, or at least to appreciate the difference between right and wrong, and if not he should be corrected.[5]

Welfare Board and the Californian Juvenile Court System is made by O. Nyquist, *Juvenile justice* (1969), vol. XII in *Cambridge Studies in Criminology*.
[1] See Morris and Giller, *Understanding juvenile justice* (1987), pp. 244–45.
[2] A short account of the system in action is given by A. H. Manchester, 'Impressions of the Scottish system of juvenile justice', (1985) 149 JPN 552–55.
[3] See Committee on Children and Young Persons (Ingleby Committee) (1960) Cmnd 1191; *Crime: A challenge to us all* (1964), published by the Labour Party; a government White Paper, *The child, the family and the young offender* (1965) Cmnd 2742; and a further White Paper, *Children in trouble* (1968) Cmnd 3601.　　　　　　　　　　　　　　　　[4] (1968) Cmnd 3601.
[5] *Crime and the Labour Party* (1964). Quoted in Morris and Giller, p. 89.

For them, largely removing the powers of the juvenile court to punish was quite unacceptable. Furthermore, after the Act the rate of juvenile crime did not, as some of its sponsors had hoped, decline; indeed, it continued to rise. There were plenty of people who directly attributed the continued rise to the Act. There was also a widespread feeling among magistrates and the police that the 1969 Act seriously undermined the protection of the public. Before the 1969 Act, the powers of the juvenile court included sending a young offender to an 'approved school' or to a remand home. After the Act, however, the most serious measure which the juvenile court could now apply to many young offenders was to make a care order putting them under the control of the local authority. In some places the local authority was said to be willing then to allow the young offenders upon whom care orders had been made to go home. Thus where the juvenile court decided that A was the ringleader and B and C had merely followed his lead, they might fine B and C, and make a care order on A – only to find that A had been allowed home and had apparently suffered a less serious penalty than his less blameworthy followers. In 1975 the Chairman of a Metropolitan Juvenile Court wrote

Out of all this emerges a frighteningly large number of children able to cock a snook at authority and totally untrained to accept the discipline essential for the survival of a democracy. By all means let us continue to examine and reexamine our methods of dealing with this very complex problem as well as at the same time trying to eradicate some of the social ends that are the root cause. But, in the meantime, all involved have a duty to the community and to the children to perform, and we are being forced to do it very badly indeed.[1]

About this time another trend of thought also began to emerge, shared by a number of people on both sides of politics: concern about what is sometimes called 'welfare totalitarianism'. It is undesirable, so it is said, to give welfare officials broad discretionary powers to organize people's lives for them whether they like it or not. Certain things should only be done, so it is said, when certain facts have been proved against the child by means of a judicial process. Thus a further criticism of the 1969 Act was that it increased the powers of officials to interfere with the life of the child, and undermined such judicial safeguards as it formerly had. It is a combination of these trends of thought which underlie the refusal to implement much of the 1969 Act, and the amendments to it which were enacted in 1982. The general trend of the 1982 changes was to increase the powers of the court and correspondingly to reduce the discretionary powers of the local authority, probation service and prison authorities in dealing with the child or young person once the court had handed him over to them. Borstal training (which was to have been abolished for offenders below the age of 17 under the scheme in the 1969 Act) was replaced by 'youth custody', a sentence

---

[1] Letter in *The Times* from Mrs Renee Soskin, Chairman of the Camden Juvenile Court, 10 December 1975.

which remains available to the juvenile court for offenders over the age of 15; and, whereas Borstal training ended when the prison authorities chose to end it, youth custody is for a term fixed by the court. Care orders – the most severe measure available to the court for offenders under 14 – were modified so that it became possible for the court to impose a condition preventing the local authority promptly letting the child or young person go home. Supervision orders, which are the juvenile court equivalent of probation orders, were modified to enable the court to impose certain conditions. And in various situations the court was required to see that the child was legally represented before an order is made against him.

As a result of the Children and Young Persons Act 1969 and its amendments, the following are the measures that a juvenile court may now order upon a finding of guilt in criminal proceedings:

(1) *Youth custody* (see page 277) This is available where the offender is 15 and provided the offence is punishable with imprisonment if committed by an adult.

(2) *Detention centre* (see page 277) This is available where the offender is a male over the age of 14 and provided the offence is punishable with imprisonment if committed by an adult.

Youth custody and detention centres are the most severe penalties available to the juvenile court. As explained, they may only be used against juvenile offenders who are in the upper age-bracket and who have committed what amount in law to serious offences. The Criminal Justice Act 1982 section 1 also imposes a further restriction: neither may be imposed unless the court

is of the opinion that no other method of dealing with him is appropriate because it appears to the court that he is unable or unwilling to respond to non-custodial penalties or because a custodial sentence is necessary for the protection of the public or because the offence was so serious that a non-custodial sentence cannot be justified.

(3) *Attendance centre* (see page 278) These are available for juvenile offenders of 10 and upwards. The offence must be one which carries imprisonment in the case of an adult.

(4) *Community service order* (see page 280) This is available where the offence carries imprisonment in the case of an adult. Originally these were only available for adult offenders, but the Criminal Justice Act 1982 permits their use in the juvenile court if the offender is aged 16.

(5) *Care order* Care orders were introduced in 1969[1] and are available for juvenile offenders of any age. In 1969 the idea was that these orders should be widely used, and the Children and Young Persons Act 1969 laid down no restrictions on their use in criminal proceedings against a juvenile except that he must be found guilty of an offence which carries imprisonment in the case of an adult. The Criminal Justice Act 1982, however, restricts their use by imposing

[1] They are largely derived from an earlier power to make what was called a 'fit person order' (the fit person usually being a local authority). For further details see the previous edition of this book.

two further requirements: that a care order is appropriate because of the seriousness of the offence, and that the child or young person is in need of care or control which he is unlikely to receive unless the court makes a care order. It also requires the child or young person to be legally represented (on legal aid if necessary) before a care order can lawfully be made.

The effect of a care order is to remove existing parental rights over the child or young person and to vest them in the local authority. Under the 1969 Act as originally enacted the magistrates simply made the care order, after which the local authority decided what to do with the child or young person. The local authority had (and still has) the power to restrict his liberty by sending him to a community home, but it was also open to them to allow him to stay with his parents, and it was entirely a matter for them to choose what to do. This led to some problems, as has already been mentioned, and the Criminal Justice Act 1982 gives the juvenile court a power – narrowly defined and available only where the offender was already subject to a care order – to forbid the local authority to allow him home. A care order is indeterminate and lasts until the juvenile reaches the age of 18 (or 19 if he was 16 or over when it was made). However, on application by the local authority, the juvenile or his parent, the juvenile court may discharge the order, or substitute a supervision order (see below).

(6) *Supervision order* This is the juvenile equivalent of a probation order (see page 285). The main differences between supervision orders and probation orders are two. First, an adult may not be made the subject of a probation order unless he consents, whereas a juvenile does not have to consent before a supervision order is made upon him. Secondly, whereas probation orders are supervised by the probation service, the person who supervises a supervision order need not be a probation officer. By statute the court makes an order placing the juvenile 'under the supervision of a local authority designated by the order or of a probation officer'. In practice, younger offenders are usually placed under the supervision of the local authority – which means in practice a local authority social worker – and older ones are placed under the supervision of a probation officer. It is the duty of the supervisor 'to advise, assist and befriend the supervised person'. Under the 1969 Act it was possible for a supervision order to carry with it a requirement that the juvenile should live with a named individual, or should undergo mental treatment. In addition it was (and still is) possible for the court to impose a condition that the supervised person should comply with directions given by the supervisor about living at a specified address for a specified period and taking part in various activities which the supervisor thinks would be good for him. These orders are known as *intermediate treatment*: so called because under the earlier law the choice lay between leaving the child at home permanently and taking him away from home permanently, and what was created then was a procedure for removing him from home for certain periods, something which was intermediate between the previous choices. The 1969 Act expressly left it up to the supervisor to decide whether and to what extent he

313

exercised the power the court gave him. However, as we have seen, it was the policy of the Criminal Justice Act 1982 to extend the authority of the court and to reduce the discretionary powers of the welfare agencies, and hence the 1982 Act gave the juvenile court an additional power to make directions in such matters which bind both the juvenile and his supervisor. Directions which may be attached to a supervision order in this way include a *night restriction order* imposing a curfew on the juvenile for up to 30 nights, and directions prohibiting him from taking part in certain activities – for example, attending certain football matches.

(7) *Fines* A juvenile may be fined for an offence, subject to a maximum of £50 for a child and £200 for a young person. For many years a limited power has existed to make the parent pay the fine. The Criminal Justice Act 1982 now requires the court to make the parents pay the fine unless certain conditions are met. If the court makes a compensation order in favour of the victim of the offence, the parent can be made to pay for this as well.

(8) *Bind over* A juvenile offender can be bound over, but only with his consent. The juvenile court also has power to order his parent or guardian to enter into a recognizance to take proper care and exercise proper control over him.

In addition to these powers, compensation orders and forfeiture orders can be made against juvenile offenders in the same sort of way as they are made against adult offenders, and it is also open to the juvenile court to grant a conditional or an absolute discharge.

If a child starts behaving in a delinquent way and the police find that he has broken the law and he is over 10, criminal proceedings do not necessarily follow, for a decision to prosecute is not automatic but a matter for discretion; (see chapter 22(iii)). It is an old police practice to give informal cautions, to young and old, about the possible consequences of continuing in wrongful ways. For juveniles a more formal system began in the 1950s and has become general. There is no statutory basis; it derives from the office of constable and his duty to prevent crime. The usual course is that the child and his parents are asked to attend at a police station, and there a uniformed superintendent or senior inspector warns the child of the likely consequences should he offend again. This in effect supposes that the offence is admitted, that it is not grave, and that neither the parents nor any party objects to this course. Although cautioning is largely associated with younger offenders, it is applied to offenders of all age groups in respect of all manner of offences. In recent years it has been official government policy to encourage this form of 'diversion' for juveniles. Following criticism by the Royal Commission on Criminal Procedure about the wide variety of practices which operated in different police areas,[1] a working party was set up consisting of a number of Chief Police Officers and a group of Home Office officials, which in 1985 resulted in a Home Office circular being issued to all police forces urging

---

[1] (1981) Cmnd 8029; for the Royal Commission see chapter 22 above.

Table 8. *Juvenile offenders cautioned for indictable offences as a percentage of those either cautioned or found guilty of indictable offences by age and sex (1983–86)*

| | Age, group and sex | | | | | |
| | 10 and under 14 | | | 14 and under 17 | | |
Year	Male	Female	Both	Male	Female	Both
1983	74	90	82	42	68	55
1984	75	91	83	45	71	58
1985	79	93	86	51	78	64
1986	81	94	87	55	80	67

Source: Criminal Statistics, 1986.

the wider use of cautions, and setting out various basic principles which must be followed.[1] In particular it was suggested that cautioning should only be used where the evidence is strong enough to support a prosecution; the juvenile must admit the offence and accept his guilt; and his parents must consent to the caution being issued. The *Criminal Statistics* in recent years show a proportionately greater use of cautioning for juveniles, and a corresponding reduction in the proportion who are prosecuted in the juvenile court. (See table 8.)

Civil care proceedings can be started in the juvenile court by the local authority, the police, and (subject to some restrictions) by an officer of the National Society for the Prevention of Cruelty to Children. The court has to be satisfied that one of six conditions relating to the child or young person are fulfilled before it may make an order: (1) present ill-treatment or neglect, (2) probability of future ill-treatment or neglect, in the light of what has happened to another child of the family, (3) exposure to moral danger, (4) that he is beyond parental control, (5) that he is not attending school, or (6) that he is guilty of a criminal offence. In addition, the court must also be satisfied that he is in need of care or control which he is unlikely to get unless a court order is made. It must be noted that a finding of (6) – that the child or young person has committed a criminal offence – is not a conviction: it merely establishes what the Act calls an 'offence condition', so enabling an order to be made. If the conditions are made out and the court decides to make an order, it may order the parent or guardian to enter into a recognisance to take proper care of the child and exercise proper control over him, or it may make a care order or a supervision order. The care orders and supervision orders which are made in civil care proceedings are basically the same as those that are made in criminal proceedings, which have been described above. An important difference is that when making these orders in civil care proceedings, the juvenile court does not have the power to impose conditions on a reluctant local authority which the Criminal Justice Act 1982

[1] Circular 14/1985; printed in (1985) 149 JP 173, 190.

gives it when making care or supervision orders in criminal proceedings. The fact that care proceedings are civil rather than criminal has some important consequences: the court can act if satisfied on the balance of probabilities, and need not be convinced beyond reasonable doubt, and the juvenile and his parents are compellable witnesses. In general, civil care proceedings are more inquisitorial and less adversarial in nature than criminal proceedings. Nevertheless, care proceedings can sometimes degenerate into a bitter adversarial battle between the parents and the local authority in the course of which the real interests of the child or young person are lost sight of. In such a situation the court usually has a duty to appoint a suitable person to act as *guardian ad litem* to represent the interests of the juvenile.[1]

The juvenile court is a jurisdictional oddity because the same group of magistrates, sitting in the same court, have to attempt to deal with both civil and criminal proceedings. This leads to a frequent criticism that juvenile courts tend to do neither particularly well: in criminal cases they forget they are trying a crime and occasionally fail to give the child or young person the safeguards which are traditionally granted to an accused person in a criminal court, whereas in civil cases they can too easily think they are trying a crime, and start insisting, for example, that the local authority prove beyond all reasonable doubt that a child is being neglected or ill-treated before they will make a care order. The original logic behind the composite jurisdiction of the juvenile court was that both parts involved children: but nowadays not everyone accepts the logic of this, and there are those who think it is a mistake to have one tribunal which handles both juvenile crime and care proceedings. The view is sometimes expressed that the juvenile court should be abolished and its work distributed elsewhere. With an increased use of cautioning only the most serious examples of juvenile crime need be prosecuted, it is said, and these could as well or better go before the ordinary criminal courts, if their procedures and powers were suitably modified when dealing with juveniles. The proper place for care orders, it is said, is the Domestic Court, where related questions of custody and access are handled (see chapter 26), or the Family Court if we ever get one.[2]

---

[1] In recent years criticism has been made of much of the law relating to care orders. A Government White Paper, *The Law on Child Care and Family Services* (1987) Cm 62 argues for wholesale revision of the grounds upon which care orders can be made. These recommendations were endorsed by the *Report of the Inquiry into Child Abuse in Cleveland 1987*, (1988) Cm 412. It is thought likely that there will be legislation in the near future.

[2] See Morris and Giller, *Understanding juvenile justice* chapter 8.

26

THE MATRIMONIAL JURISDICTION OF MAGISTRATES – THE DOMESTIC COURT

As was mentioned earlier (chapter 6(iii)), magistrates' courts have jurisdiction over a range of family law matters. This is obviously something which falls outside the general scope of a chapter on the criminal courts, but until day dawns for a unified Family Court (see chapter 6(iii)) it is necessary to deal with this in the general context of the magistrates' courts.

For those who are looking at the English legal system for the first time, it must seem distinctly odd that the magistrates' courts have any jurisdiction in family law matters. Magistrates' courts are primarily criminal courts, family law is primarily civil law and we would therefore expect family law to be a matter for the High Court and the county court, not for the magistrates' courts. The explanation for this jurisdiction is partly historical. As was mentioned earlier (chapter 19(ii)) the magistrates at one time had a large number of administrative functions, and these included the administration of the poor law. As part of this they had power to punish those who failed to maintain their dependants and who ended up a charge on the poor-rate as a result. A section of the poor were illegitimate children, and here the magistrates tried to identify the men responsible for their appearance in the world and make them pay for their upkeep. Hence the magistrates' jurisdiction to make what were originally called bastardy orders, and were later euphemistically renamed affiliation orders. (As a distinct type of order these have now been abolished, but magistrates can still order a parent to maintain an illegitimate child as part of their general jurisdiction to order maintenance for children.) The rest of the jurisdiction of magistrates in family law matters is of more recent growth. As part of their ordinary criminal jurisdiction, magistrates have always been able to punish those who use violence to others, including their wives and families, and in the light of this it seemed natural enough in 1878 to empower magistrates to make orders of non-cohabitation, maintenance and custody of children, where a husband has been convicted of an aggravated assault upon his wife.[1] Subsequent statutes extended the grounds upon which such

---

[1] It is interesting to note that originally the power was limited to the case of an *aggravated* assault: a relic of the belief that the common law permitted a husband to beat his wife as long as it was no more than 'reasonable chastisement'. (According to some authorities, chastisement was reasonable provided the stick was no thicker than a man's thumb!)

orders could be made, abolished non-cohabitation orders, and created new forms of order, including orders that the spouse shall not use violence against the other spouse, and orders evicting a violent spouse from the matrimonial home. When Parliament made it possible for children who were being neglected or abused to be removed from their parents and placed in the care of the local authority, it provided that this too should be done by orders made in the magistrates' courts. (See the previous chapter.)

In recent years the domestic jurisdiction of magistrates has suffered much criticism. Part of the trouble was the basis upon which much of the jurisdiction had to be exercised. As was explained earlier (chapter 6(iii)), the law relating to divorce and judicial separation, which are operated by the High Court and the county courts, was radically refashioned in 1969 to remove as far as possible the notion of the 'matrimonial offence'. Henceforth, divorce and judicial separation were available not because one party to the marriage was able to prove some piece of misbehaviour by the other, but rather because it was shown that the marriage had irretrievably broken down. Similar principles thereafter governed the way in which the High Court and the county court exercised their ancillary jurisdiction to order maintenance and rearrange the matrimonial property. Yet the powers of the magistrates' courts to order maintenance between separated spouses continued to be exercisable only where the applicant proved that the respondent had committed one of a specified series of sordid acts: desertion, cruelty, adultery, that he had caught a venereal disease, that he had taken to drink and so forth. As it was generally the less well-off who took their matrimonial disputes to the magistrates' courts, whereas the better-off would go to the civil courts, it looked very much as if there was one law for the rich and another for the poor. This led the Finer Committee on One Parent Families[1] to criticize the domestic jurisdiction of magistrates as a 'secondary system' designed 'for what were considered to be the wider requirements of the poor'. In 1976 the Law Commission produced an important Report [2] which recommended that the powers of the magistrates over custody and financial provision should be completely recast so as to follow the same general lines as the law in the High Court and county courts. This was carried out by the Domestic Proceedings and Magistrates' Courts Act 1978 (DPMCA 1978), which, with the Guardianship of Minors Act 1971 (as amended by the Family Law Reform Act 1987), is now the legal basis for the powers of the magistrates' courts in this area. A deeper source of trouble is the widespread feeling that the magistrates' courts are a fundamentally unsuitable forum for handling family law matters. Their main business is crime: the public trial of wrongdoers by an accusatorial and adversarial method, followed by their punishment. This, it has often been said, makes them unfitted to investigate family disputes where each side may be equally to blame and the aim should not

---

[1] 1974 Cmnd 5629; vol. 2 app. 5 para. 6.
[2] *Report on Matrimonial Jurisdiction in Magistrates' Courts*, (1976) Law Com. 77.

be to find if an accusation is true and to blame and punish if it is, but to get to the bottom of a difficult and complex problem and impose a sensible solution. Serious attempts have been made to make the magistrates' court when engaged on family matters behave differently from when it is trying criminals, and much progress has been made; but despite this, there are still those who say – reasonably or otherwise – that it is demeaning for otherwise law-abiding citizens to have their matrimonial difficulties investigated by a tribunal which is associated in the public mind with the trial of breathalysed drivers, shoplifters, 'flashers' and drunks.

The first step in the progress towards de-criminalising the family law jurisdiction of magistrates was a statute in 1936 which required them to sit in private when engaged on family matters. It was also then provided that the court must sit with at least one magistrate of each sex. The second big step was in 1978, when the Domestic Proceedings and Magistrates' Courts Act (DPMCA 1978) required every bench to form a separate 'domestic panel' of justices. To join a domestic panel, a justice must undergo special training, and only a member of the domestic panel may adjudicate in family cases. The amount of training they receive was increased in 1986, and they must now undergo 12 or more hours of further training every three years. Where the local bench is too small to create its own domestic panel, it must pool resources with another bench or benches to make a combined domestic panel. The DPMCA 1978 also tried to separate the family jurisdiction of the magistrates from their criminal jurisdiction by a change of name. Section 67(1) of the Magistrates' Courts Act 1980 (as it now is) provides: 'Magistrates' Courts constituted in accordance with the provisions of this section and sitting for the purpose of hearing domestic proceedings shall be known as domestic courts'. However, it is one thing to say that a court has a new name, and another to persuade the public to use it or think of the old court in new terms. Most people still talk about 'the magistrates' court' rather than the 'domestic court', and the complaint about ventilating family matters in a criminal court is still heard. It is unlikely to be stilled unless and until there is a family court which is separate and distinct from the magistrates' court system – with or without the participation of people who happen to be magistrates as members (see chapter 6(iii)).

The main business of the domestic court is as follows.

1 Orders for financial provision

Under section 1 of the DPMCA 1978, either party to a marriage may apply to the domestic court for financial provision where the other

(a)   has failed to provide reasonable maintenance for the applicant, or
(b)   has failed to provide or make a proper contribution towards reasonable maintenance for any child of the family, or

(c) has behaved in such a way that the applicant cannot reasonably be expected to live with the respondent, or

(d) has deserted the applicant.

In such a case the court may make an order for periodical payments – usually referred to as 'maintenance orders' – and in addition or alternatively it may order a lump sum payment of up to £500. In addition, section 11B of the Guardianship of Minors Act 1971 (as amended) gives the domestic court power to order one parent to make orders for periodical or lump sum payments for the support of a child on the application of the other parent. This power partly overlaps with the court's powers under the DPMCA 1978, but it is wider, because whereas one has to be married to the respondent in order to apply under the DPMCA 1978, under the Guardianship of Minors Act anyone who is a 'parent' may seek an order to make the other 'parent' pay, and by an amendment to the Guardianship of Minors Act which was made in 1987 the word 'parent' now includes the natural father and mother, whether or not they are married. This is an important change, because although the father of an illegitimate child has always had a duty to support it, until 1987 this could only be enforced by a special procedure called *affiliation*, which was generally less favourable to the child, and had a number of criminal overtones. The assumptions behind affiliation proceedings were two: first, that illegitimate children were usually the result of a casual sexual encounter between a woman living at home or on her own and a man who thereafter denied that he had ever set eyes on her, and secondly, that 'loose' women frequently made false allegations of paternity against respectable men. The centre-piece of affiliation proceedings was thus the woman's adduction of strict proof that the respondent was the 'putative father'. These assumptions no longer held good by the 1980s, when some 19 per cent of births are illegitimate, and of these probably half are the product of stable unions outside marriage, where the partners have just 'not done the paper-work'. It was to meet this changed social reality as well as to be fairer to the illegitimate child that affiliation proceedings were abolished, and in their place the civil procedure by which a father can be compelled to support his legitimate children was extended to cover his illegitimate children as well. Obviously, genuine disputes about paternity will sometimes arise under the new law as under the old, and when they do it will sometimes be necessary for the court to order scientific tests in the hope of resolving the issue. The courts have had certain powers to order blood-tests since 1969, and the Family Law Reform Act 1987 widens them in various ways, introducing the possibility of tests on human tissues other than blood as well. This is important, because tissue-tests are now able to tell us much more than blood-tests formerly could. Until recently, a blood test was never more than conclusive in the negative sense of showing that someone could not possibly be the child's father, but now a process called 'DNA fingerprinting' makes it possible to say that one person is definitely another person's father by comparing samples of body tissue.[1]

---

[1] For an explanation, see Kelly, Rankin and Wink, 'Method of application of DNA fingerprinting: a guide for the non-scientist', [1987] Crim. LR 105.

Someone who is without financial support is entitled to social security payments from the DHSS, and many of those who end up on social security are in this position because their husband or father is failing to carry out his legal obligation to maintain them. Where this is the case, the DHSS has the right to recover what it has paid out by taking proceedings in its own name in the domestic court. Where the spouse or child has obtained their own order, anything paid under it will be deducted from the social security payments. If the maintenance payments are less than the social security, or are paid irregularly, it is possible to arrange for the payments to be made to the DHSS, which then keeps the maintenance money and pays in full.

2 Protection from violence

Under sections 16–18 of the DPMCA 1978, the domestic court may make two types of order. The first, generally called a personal protection order, orders the respondent not to use, or threaten to use violence against the applicant, or against a child of the family. The second, called an exclusion order, requires the respondent to leave the matrimonial home, or forbids him to enter it, or both; and it may also require him to allow an applicant whom he has thrown out of the matrimonial home to return to it. These powers of the domestic court considerably overlap with similar powers exercisable by the county courts (see chapter 6(iii)), but in various ways they are less effective. Broadly speaking, it requires worse behaviour by the respondent before the domestic court can act, and when it can act it is sometimes less able to do so speedily in emergencies than can the superior courts. The domestic court can sometimes make expedited orders, lasting for 28 days, without notice to the respondent, but to get such an order in emergency it is necessary as a practical matter to get a hearing. In the superior courts, unlike the domestic court, administrative arrangements are made to see that a judge is always available to hear emergency applications. For applicants who live near a county court this is obviously an advantage.

3 The custody of children and related matters

Here the domestic court has an array of powers most of which are also available in the High Court and the county courts. On the application of either parent, it may make a *custody order*. This gives the successful applicant the right to possess the child, and to control his life generally. A parent with custody can therefore decide what persons the child shall and shall not see, and unless qualified a custody order would make it possible for one parent to prevent the child seeing the other parent. For this reason a custody order frequently contains a term granting the other parent reasonable access to the child. Custody orders can only be made in favour of someone who is the parent of the child, and in the past this left foster-parents in an unprotected position, because they had no control over the removal of a child from their household, even where he had lived with them for a long time, and now regarded them as his real parents. To meet this problem the Children Act 1975 (which was not brought into force until 1985) created the *custodianship order.* A custodianship order can be made in favour of any person, other than a parent, with whom the child has been living for three years (or 12 months if a person with custody of the child consents). The order suspends the right of the natural parents and vests legal custody in the applicant. As with custody orders, there may be a provision as to access by the natural parents, and the order may be revoked. Neither custody orders nor custodianship orders give the adult power to deal with the child's property, in the unlikely event of his having any, but this can be done by someone who obtains a *guardianship order.* Unlike custody and custodianship orders, guardianship orders may only be made (broadly speaking) where the child has no parent – as where both have died in a road crash, for example.[1] *Adoption orders* are altogether more drastic. They have the effect of obliterating the legal rights and duties between the child and his natural parents, and transferring them to the adopters once and for all. This step normally requires the consent of the natural parents, but in certain circumstances the court may dispense with their consent. After an adoption, the natural parents have no legal right to obtain access to the child, who may be brought up in complete ignorance of who they were. (But in such a case the child now has a statutory right to discover their identity when he reaches the age of 18.) Another function of the domestic court is to give consent to young people to marry where they are over 16, but below the age of majority, and their parents, who must consent, refuse to do so. This was an important function when 21 was the age of majority, but now that it has been reduced to 18 the situation arises rarely.

When a local authority wishes to exercise its powers to remove a child into care, this requires an order from the magistrates' court. Surprisingly this business is conducted in the juvenile court, and is not a matter for the domestic court. As the main business of the juvenile court is the punishment of juvenile offenders, and considerable efforts have been made to de-criminalise the jurisdiction of the magistrates in family matters, it is distinctly odd that this should still be so. (The juvenile court is described in chapter 25.)

Most of the orders which the domestic court can make it can later vary or revoke, and a sizeable part of the court's business is hearing and determining applications by those who are affected by custody or maintenance orders to alter them because circumstances have changed since they were made. Where orders are disobeyed, proceedings must usually be taken to enforce them. Personal protection orders and eviction orders will be enforced by arrest. The domestic court may attach a power of arrest when making the order, and where this has been done the person who broke the order can be arrested straight away. If no

---

[1] There is obviously a degree of overlap between these various orders, and the Law Commission recently issued Working Paper 96 which discussed the possibility of restructuring them (October 1986).

power of arrest was attached, the victim of the breach of the order must ask the domestic court to issue a warrant for his arrest. In either case the upshot will be an arrest, following which the respondent will be brought before the court and fined, or committed to prison for up to two months. Financial provision orders are often enforced by attachment of earnings, a procedure described elsewhere in this book (chapter 9).[1] Unlike other civil debts, they may also be enforced by committing the defaulter to prison if he refuses to pay. This may be a deterrent against future default, but as he earns nothing in prison it is of little practical help in getting him to pay his arrears. Yet justices are convinced that imprisonment has to stay unless something more effective than attachment of earnings can be devised. Attachment of earnings presupposes a pay-packet, and an employer who can be required to take something out of it. The trouble with attachment of earnings is that defendants who fail to pay maintenance orders are often self-employed, or are shiftless men with no jobs, or with jobs they change faster than the machinery of justice can keep up with. The Magistrates' Association once put forward the idea that a man's liabilities for maintenance should form part of his PAYE deductions, when they would be automatically deducted from his pay however often he changed his employment, but the suggestion was very unen-thusiastically received by the Inland Revenue. Thus a promising line for avoiding committals to prison got nowhere.

Appeal against a decision of the domestic court making or refusing to make an order, or revoking or varying an order, lies to the Family Division of the High Court. In some cases the appeal can be heard by a single judge, and then it can be heard by a High Court Judge sitting out of London. The appeal may be on law or on fact or on both. It is conducted on the notes made by the justices' clerk at the original hearing. There is some difference of opinion as to whether this is better than the usual method of appeal from the magistrates' court, which is by a complete rehearing in the Crown Court, supplemented by an appeal to the Divisional Court on points of law (see chapter 21). By going to the Family Division, the law in this area is kept more consistent and magistrates get authoritative rulings. But the individual who wants his case reconsidered on the merits might do better by a rehearing in the Crown Court. From the juvenile court there is no appeal to the Family Division, but it is possible to appeal to the Crown Court (plus appeal to the Divisional Court on point of law) in the usual way. The fact that local authority care proceedings take place in the juvenile court rather than the domestic court does at least mean the possibility of an appeal by way of rehearing in these cases. There is one situation where there is no appeal from the domestic court, and that is against grant or refusal of permission for a minor to marry.

Table 9 gives an indication of the volume of business in the domestic court.

---

[1] As well as its own orders, the domestic court also has the job of enforcing in this way the orders of other courts which are registered with it for this purpose, and this amounts to quite a lot of its business: see table 9.

Table 9. *Applications for orders in domestic proceedings at magistrates' courts by type of application*[a]

	1983	1984	1985	1986
Maintenance (including affiliation orders)[b]	37,340	36,670	33,270	32,630
Custody, access and guardianship[b]	22,420	23,320	21,420	21,760
Permission to marry	70	70	70	40
Applications to vary orders	61,980	59,910	58,410	54,530
Applications to enforce orders (including application to register orders from other courts)	113,250	108,210	167,080	157,770

[a]Includes estimates for a few courts in each year for which there was no data returned.
[b]Includes application made jointly for affiliation and guardianship orders. The figures given are the number of proceedings.
Source: 'Statistics of domestic proceedings in magistrates' courts in England and Wales 1986', *Home Office Statistical Bulletin* 17 (1987).

V

THE PERSONNEL OF
THE LAW

27

SOLICITORS

The most striking thing about the legal profession in England is the division into solicitors and barristers.[1] As the solicitors far outnumber the barristers,[2] and the layman has more contact with solicitors than with barristers, what is technically the junior part of the profession may be described first. The profession of solicitor took its present form relatively recently. In earlier times the barristers practically constituted the whole profession, the men who eventually evolved into solicitors being then far more lowly members of society. The old courts of King's Bench and Common Pleas had attached to them a number of attorneys who were appointed and controlled by the judges. These attorneys represented their clients and so could take many of the formal steps required for litigation. Some measure of legal ability or knowledge of procedure was required before a judge would admit a man as an attorney, but on the whole the attorneys were not sufficiently learned for the more important work of framing and then presenting a case; the more skilled work fell to the barristers. The rise of the Court of Chancery led to the need for a class of men corresponding to the common law attorneys; the counterpart of the attorneys were the solicitors of the Chancery Court, whose chief work was perhaps to 'solicit' (worry or bribe) the officials so that the customary delays of Chancery proceedings were reduced as far as possible. The ecclesiastical and admiralty courts had a similar class of men called proctors. In the fifteenth century the attorneys had often been housed in the Inns of Court where the barristers were organised, but in the later sixteenth century the barristers ejected the attorneys. The barrister was a gentleman and he could not be expected to mix with mere attorneys. The humbler branch prospered, and in 1739 the Society of Gentlemen Practisers in the Courts of Law and Equity was founded as a body to which attorneys, solicitors and proctors could belong. The London attorneys generally became solicitors as well; the decline in the courts having proctors led to a virtual disappearance of proctors as a separate body, so that there emerged a combined profession that adopted the name of 'solicitor' instead of the more dignified name of attorney. In 1831 the Society of Gentlemen

---

[1] The practitioners' book is Cordery, *The law relating to solicitors* (7th ed. 1981). See also Shurman, *The practical skills of the solicitor* (2nd ed. 1985).
[2] In 1986 there were some 47,000 practising solicitors, of whom some 43,000 were involved in private practice. In the same year the practising Bar numbered less than 6,000.

Practisers and other smaller societies were merged into the chartered body called the Incorporated Law Society, renamed the Law Society in 1903. It has always been a voluntary organisation, and this principle is still maintained, solicitors joining the Law Society or not, according to their inclination.[1]

The Society provides some club facilities for its members, but its activities in looking after the interests of solicitors are of course of benefit to all members of the profession whether they belong to the Society or not. Most solicitors do belong to the Law Society: in 1986 there were 47,830 practising solicitors of whom only 10,205 were not members. A special point about the Society is that it is more than an ordinary professional organisation: the Society has been entrusted with statutory duties affecting members of the public as well as regulating and controlling solicitors.

Since the earlier eighteenth century, admission as a solicitor has depended upon a combination of the idea of apprenticeship with that of examination. In 1877 the control of examinations was given to the Law Society, although the formal admission of solicitors remained with the Master of the Rolls. The pattern was for a period, ranging from five years for a non-graduate to three years for a graduate, to be served under written articles with a solicitor and the passing of an Intermediate and a Final Examination. In 1922 law graduates were exempted from the Intermediate Examination. Also in 1922 it was provided that all articled clerks other than law graduates must spend an 'academic year'. The later changes are discussed in the chapter of this book on legal education (chapter 29).

In the past there were heavy stamp duties upon becoming a solicitor. After admission the young solicitor commonly obtains a position as a salaried assistant. Before the war the newly admitted man could not expect a salary much in excess of £200 a year, and that salary was not likely to be greatly increased for two or three years; a substantial or profitable partnership was generally postponed until the solicitor was in his late twenties. There was a shortage of solicitors at the end of the war, and much higher salaries were paid. In 1958 the Law Society said the range for newly qualified solicitors was £600 to £700; by 1970 a figure of £2,000 was nearer the mark for London and the big cities; in 1986, newly qualified solicitors were earning an average of £12,840 in central London, and after three and a half years of practice they were earning over £22,000. Pay out of London tends to be lower, especially in the less prosperous parts of the country. By no means all solicitors are in private practice. The chief executives of many local authorities are solicitors, and there are other solicitors on their staffs. Those wishing to enter the local government service often serve articles with the authority, but some appointments are made from solicitors who have served

[1] The Solicitors Act 1941 provided that membership of the Law Society could be made compulsory for all practising solicitors by Order of the Lord Chancellor if he were satisfied on a poll of all practising solicitors that at least two-thirds of those voting were in favour of that course. After that Act, the Society increased its membership and steps for making membership compulsory were not taken. The provision was not included in the consolidating Solicitors Act 1974 and it is no longer law.

articles in private practice. Quite a number of solicitors are employed as justices' clerks or their assistants, and the Crown Prosecution Service employs others. The central government departments, nationalised industries, the larger trading and industrial concerns and various public bodies all have legal departments. Barristers may be preferred where the writing of legal opinions forms a large part of the work, as in some government departments, but there are many more solicitors in these salaried positions than there are barristers. With so many openings there is little chance that the admitted solicitor will fail to make a living. A few solicitors make large incomes; if clients will bring their work to a solicitor, his firm can expand into a firm with a number of partners and a team of salaried solicitors and legal executives and a large office staff. Taking the average across the whole of the country, however, large firms with many staff are rare, the average number of partners in a firm being between three and four. In London and the south-east, firms tend to be larger and some of the major London commercial firms are enormous: in 1987 one of them, for example, had 95 partners, over 290 assistant solicitors and 79 articled clerks. There is a tendency, however, for firms to get bigger, and in the provinces those firms that wish to compete for commercial work with the big London firms are amalgamating in order to be able to offer the same collection of specialist skills.

Solicitors may act as advocates in magistrates' courts, in county courts, and tribunals, but (apart from some Crown Courts – see chapter 19) the advocacy in all other courts is confined to barristers. Advocacy does not account for a large amount of the work of solicitors, and many or most solicitors do none whatever. In contrast to the barrister, the solicitor is more of a businessman, having an office to run and a substantial correspondence to deal with. An important part of the work of solicitors has traditionally been concerned with the conveyance of land, which includes negotiations preceding sales and leases, with the drawing up of appropriate documents; that part of their work involves the law of landlord and tenant and of town and country planning and compulsory purchase. An ordinary mixed practice is also likely to have some matrimonial cases, wills, probate and intestacies, and matters arising from employment and the conduct of business affairs. In central London and big cities there are solicitors with practices that are mainly concerned with commercial, financial and allied matters. But this does not mean that a solicitor in a less specialised firm cannot cope with difficult cases: a solicitor who is consulted in, say, a difficult matter of company organisation and finance, can go to a barrister for an opinion or for drafting documents, or seek the help of an accountant or tax expert who may have no legal qualifications. As the law becomes more complicated, however, it is becoming increasingly difficult for small firms to compete with the large firms which can offer advice on such matters without making the client wait while they go outside for it. At the time of writing, major changes are taking place in the economics of solicitors' practices. For a great many years some 50 to 60 per cent of the income of solicitors as a profession was derived from conveyancing, and this source of income was guaranteed by two legal rules. The first was that solicitors had by statute a monopoly on conveyancing, and the second was that their charges were 'scale fees' fixed by delegated legislation as a proportion of the value of the property. The scale fee was often generous for the amount of work involved, and conveyancing was in consequence highly profitable; indeed, it usually carried much of the rest of a solicitor's business, especially criminal court advocacy and small claims, out of which it was (and is) extremely difficult to make much of a return. The social justice of this was not apparent to those who had to buy or sell houses, however, and after a lot of public discussion, and following a report of the Prices and Incomes Board, scale fees were abolished in 1973. This left solicitors to fix their own conveyancing charges. The result was that they began to undercut one another and the price – and hence the profitability – of conveyancing began to fall.[1]

More recently it is the solicitors' conveyancing monopoly which has been under vigorous attack. The first attack came from various unqualified 'cut-price conveyancers', who set up in illegal competition. Following a brief period when the Law Society tried vainly to suppress them by bringing prosecutions, the government came to the aid of the cut-price conveyancers with the Administration of Justice Act 1985. This broke the solicitors' monopoly to the extent of permitting such people to do conveyancing for gain, provided they register as 'licensed conveyancers' and submit themselves to a regulatory scheme.[2]

This alone was not too serious for solicitors, because licensed conveyancers operating in small firms are unlikely to become common enough to make a large dent in the work of solicitors. A much bigger threat to the solicitors' conveyancing monopoly is posed by the banks and building societies, which would dearly love to be able to employ in-house lawyers or licensed conveyancers, and with them to offer the conveyancing as a service incidental to providing the finance to buy the house. This prospect is attractive to house-buyers, not least because banks and building societies, unlike solicitors, would not insist on the fees being paid in a lump sum, but would offer to spread them over the repayment period of the mortgage. The objection to conveyancing done by banks and building societies is that the customer gets a less good service: there could be conflicts of interest between the house-buyer and the bank or building society, and the in-house conveyancer might not give the buyer disinterested advice. This argument long prevented the law being changed so as to allow conveyancing to be done by a bank or building society when it is arranging a mortgage. The answer to this objection, however, is that the law should allow the customer a choice: as long as he knows what he is getting, why should he not be free to choose an inferior service if it is cheaper? In 1986 Parliament enacted the Building Societies Act, a section of

---

[1] Since 1984 the Law Society has published an annual statistical report which gives details on all matters of practice.

[2] As a result of a report in 1984, The First Report of the Conveyancing Committee (Farrand Committee), set up by the Lord Chancellor's Department.

which enables the Lord Chancellor to make Rules permitting building societies to offer conveyancing services subject to various conditions. At the time of writing this section has not been activated. When it comes into force it will present solicitors with the prospect of a very great reduction in their income from conveyancing, and the profession is anxious to stave off the evil day as long as possible. But many solicitors accept that the profession will lose and are developing plans to deal with the change when it comes. Some, especially the larger firms, are trying to move into other work, particularly commercial work concerned with companies, taxation and so forth. Solicitors would be better able to attract and hold this kind of commercial work if they could offer a 'package deal' to clients which included the services of people like accountants, surveyors, and so on; this is something which they cannot easily do at the moment, because the professional rules of solicitors' practice forbid them to make partnerships with other types of professional. Consequently, strong pressure is now building up within the solicitors' profession to change the rules of practice to permit 'mixed partnerships'. At the time of writing a debate is going on in the profession about it: the Law Society issued a discussion paper on Multi-Disciplinary Partnerships and Allied Topics in April 1987, and a decision is likely to be made on the question during 1988. Given the enormous size of some firms, it is also being questioned whether or not it is sensible for solicitors to be required to work in partnerships; there is a certain amount of pressure for them to be permitted to form corporate bodies, which would offer some organisational advantages[1]. Other firms of solicitors, generally the smaller ones, are moving the other way and trying to get into the business of estate agency as well as conveyancing. The first 'solicitor's property centre', providing what is described as 'a one-stop house sale package', opened in Crawley, Sussex, in 1985, and it has had many imitators. This would have been unthinkable only a few years ago, and shows a big change in professional attitudes. To run any kind of estate agency business it is essential to advertise, and solicitors' rules of etiquette most strictly forbade resort to this vulgar and undignified practice, which was seen as something fit for tradesmen but not for professional gentlemen. However, in 1979 the Benson Committee recommended that solicitors be permitted to advertise, and since 1984 the rules of conduct of the profession have permitted it, subject to limits.[2]

The organisation and running of solicitors' offices used to depend to no small extent on a class of unadmitted managing clerks. Many of these men were highly skilled in the more routine processes, so that the commonly expressed view was that the firm just could not get on without them. Many of these men worked all

---

[1] By June 1988 the Council of the Law Society had made new rules permitting solicitors to practise as corporations as an alternative to partnerships, but the issue of multi-disciplinary partnerships was still unresolved.

[2] Lawyers have long been permitted to advertise in the USA, and probably the brash forms of advertising existing there put the English profession off the idea until recently. One American attorney allegedly 'has a topless beauty on book matches bearing his name, with the words "When you are busted he'll appeal" '. [1984] 81 Law Soc. Gaz. 3230.

their lives in the same office; they had security rather than substantial salaries. Economic and social changes have made it easier for clerks in an office to become solicitors, but there are still a number of unadmitted men. There was an Association, with an examination scheme, which gave some measure of status, and this was replaced in 1963 by an Institute of Legal Executives. The senior grades are associate membership and fellowships, both obtainable by way of examinations. The Institute's members have grown from 3,000 in 1963 to 16,075 in 1987. It is a good development, though the choice of title is unfortunate for 'executive' is coming to mean the man at the top.

Solicitors are subject to much legal control. As officers of the court they are amenable to direct discipline by the judges[1] but whilst instances still occur of judges rebuking solicitors and making them personally liable for particular costs, the systematic regulation of the profession is divided between the Law Society and the Solicitors' Disciplinary Tribunal.

A person is not qualified to act as a solicitor unless three conditions are met. (1) He must be admitted as a solicitor. This requires a satisfactory compliance with the requirements for education and training (discussed above) and the Law Society must be satisfied as to his character and suitability to be a solicitor. The Law Society, with the concurrence of the Lord Chancellor, the Lord Chief Justice and the Master of the Rolls, makes regulations for the education and training of persons seeking to be admitted or to practice as solicitors. Admission as a solicitor normally follows automatically on a certificate of compliance with the education and training and of character and suitability. (2) His name must be entered on 'the roll'. The Master of the Rolls used to be the custodian of court records but by the metamorphosis of time he became a judge, and his custody of rolls is now only nominal. The roll is in fact kept by the Law Society; it used to be a long parchment roll with the names inscribed, but it is now kept in a computer. The importance of the roll is that entry of a name on, or removal from, or restoration to the roll is the formal record of whether a person is or is not a solicitor: a person 'struck off the roll' is no longer a solicitor. (3) He must hold a 'practising certificate' issued by the Law Society. A salaried solicitor who is an assistant in a firm of solicitors or in an office of central or local government or in a business or an industrial concern may not need a practising certificate, but if he is going to do conveyancing, issue process or do various kinds of legal work for reward, or appear as an advocate, he must have a practising certificate. Hence the issue of practising certificates is a key point in the position of the Law Society. In the first place, when a solicitor applies for a practising certificate, the Law Society

---

[1] This is statutory, being laid down by s.50 of the Solicitors Act 1974. To understand the law may need some research, for the provision is that the superior courts or a judge of those courts 'may exercise the same jurisdiction in respect of solicitors as any of the superior courts of law or equity from which the Supreme Court was constituted might have exercised immediately before the passing of the Supreme Court of Judicature Act 1973 in respect of any solicitor, attorney or proctor admitted to practise there'. For a summary of these powers, see *Udall* v. *Capri Lighting Ltd.* [1987] 3 WLR 465, 472.

can check as to whether he is 'in the clear' as regards the indemnity rules (i.e. has insurance cover against possible claims against him) and that he is not subject to any professional suspension, disqualification or outstanding inquiry. In the second place the Law Society charges a fee of an amount fixed by the Master of the Rolls with the concurrence of the Lord Chancellor and the Lord Chief Justice. These fees, together with the subscription of members, provide the money for the Society to perform its general duties. In 1987 a practising certificate cost £280, all of which went to the Law Society; in addition the solicitor was obliged to pay between £30 and £60 to the compensation fund (see below).

There is a general power for the Council of the Law Society to make rules with the concurrence of the Master of the Rolls for regulating the professional practice, conduct and discipline of solicitors. Major matters on which there are rules include the keeping of accounts, the handling of clients' money, auditing of accounts and sending an accountant's report to the Law Society; the powers of the Law Society to intervene when for any reason a solicitor becomes unable to continue handling his clients' affairs; the obligation of all solicitors to pay an annual levy to the 'Compensation Fund' which is maintained by the Law Society to relieve clients who have suffered loss through the dishonesty of a solicitor or his employee; and the obligation of a solicitor to be insured against claims arising from his practice. (As to this, since 1976 the Law Society negotiated a master insurance policy, and all solicitors in private practice must take cover under this scheme.)

Complaints against solicitors or members of their staff are handled by two agencies. The Law Society investigates complaints, and has power to impose minor sanctions. There is also a statutory body called the Solicitors Disciplinary Tribunal, with power to fine solicitors, suspend them from practice, or strike them off the roll, to which the Law Society refers those cases which its investigations reveal to be serious and apparently well-founded.

For many years the Law Society investigated complaints against solicitors through a Professional Purposes Committee. During the 1970s and early 1980s there was increasing public discontent about the way in which this body operated. Part of the problem was that it would not investigate an allegation of professional negligence. For negligence rather than misconduct a disgruntled client had no option but to sue the solicitor in the courts. The Law Society was not to blame for this; the difficulty was that the Law Society's powers are laid down by statute, and the investigation of negligence by solicitors was not one of them. But this reason usually failed to impress disgruntled clients, many of whom found the distinction between negligence and misconduct rather over-subtle for them. The other problem was that there was a widespread feeling that a system consisting of lawyers investigating the misdeeds of lawyers was far too cozy, and the Law Society was too ready to take the solicitor's side even where the complaint was well founded. Particularly irritating was its habit of answering complaints it considered unfounded with letters warning the complainant he had libelled the solicitor by making the complaint.[1]

The Solicitors' Act 1974 tried to correct the feeling that there was insufficient external scrutiny by creating the office of 'lay observer', who monitors the Law Society's investigations and issues an annual published report. In 1979 the Benson Commission on Legal Services[2] also recommended that the Law Society be given power to investigate professional negligence, and that its investigating machinery be made still more independent by the addition of lay members to the Law Society Committee in charge of investigations. Nothing was done at the time. Then matters came to a head in 1983 with a scandalous incident in which the Law Society failed to investigate a well-founded complaint that a solicitor who was a former member of the Council of the Law Society had over-charged his client by £131,000. This led to the client bringing a law-suit against the Law Society for negligence – which the Law Society eventually compromised – and a large amount of unpleasant and damaging publicity. The Law Society then conducted its own internal inquiry into the affair which led to further bad publicity.[3]

The outcome brought two substantial changes. First, in 1986 the Law Society reformed its complaints procedure. Instead of complaints being handled by the staff of the Law Society under the direction of the Professional Purposes Committee, the Law Society has now set up something called the 'Solicitors' Complaints Bureau'. This consists of two committees: the Investigation Committee, which has seven lay members and four members who are solicitors, and an Adjudication Committee, with nine members who are solicitors on the Council of the Law Society and six lay members. The first of these Committees reviews the results of the investigations carried out by the Law Society's staff, and decides whether to forward them to the Adjudication Committee, which can impose certain sanctions, or prosecute before the Solicitors' Disciplinary Tribunal. Secondly, the Administration of Justice Act 1985 enlarged the Law Society's powers to enable it to investigate negligence as well as misconduct. In the same year the Law Society launched an arbitration scheme by which it is hoped that some complaints by dissatisfied clients can be informally resolved. It remains to be seen how these changes work out. The Law Society is very anxious that they should work well, because if the public is still dissatisfied with the way in which the Law Society investigates complaints against solicitors, the result would probably be the creation of some independent statutory body to investigate, and the matter would be taken out of their hands.

The Solicitors' Disciplinary Tribunal was created by the Solicitors' Act 1974.

---

[1] For an example, see Ole Hansen, 'Cooper and Lybrand's exposure: draft report on the society's regulatory functions – a reply' (1985) 82 Law Soc. Gaz. 2728.

[2] Royal Commission on Legal Services, (1979) Cmnd 7648.

[3] The incident is known as the 'Glanville Davies affair'. The report of the inquiry was published as a supplement to (1984) 81 Law Soc. Gaz.

Its functions are governed by that Act and by Rules made by the Lord Chancellor under powers contained in it. The members are chosen by the Master of the Rolls. Some are chosen from solicitors with at least ten years' standing and others are laymen. It normally sits as a panel of three (which is the quorum), and it is provided by statute that the solicitor members must always outnumber the laymen. The Solicitors' Disciplinary Tribunal was created to replace a body called the Solicitors' Disciplinary Committee. The earlier committee had the same functions as the Solicitors' Disciplinary Tribunal, but its members were all solicitors, and its name was unfortunate because it wrongly suggested that it was merely a committee of the Law Society, when in fact it was independent.[1]

This tribunal has power to fine a solicitor a sum of money which 'shall be forfeit to Her Majesty', to suspend him from practice, or to strike him off the roll; where this has been done, it also has power to reinstate him to the roll on his later application. The tribunal normally sits in private, but since 1985 it has had the power to sit in public. Its decisions are publicly announced, and are printed for all to read in the pages of the *Law Society's Gazette*. Appeal lies on some lesser matters to the Master of the Rolls and otherwise to the High Court.

It is only to be expected that the Law Society, like all major controlling bodies for professional activities, does not satisfy all members of the profession. In particular it is often said that the Law Society is dominated by the large City firms: a charge which hardly seems to be justified in the light of the constitution of the Society and the membership of the Council. In 1964 discontent with the Law Society led to the formation of the British Legal Association (BLA). This is a voluntary association of solicitors in England and Wales which was set up because a number of solicitors felt that their increasing practical and economic difficulties were not being adequately handled by the Law Society: the Law Society has its statutory duties and ties and the BLA intended to press the claims of solicitors without being inhibited by 'old habits, inherited attitudes and institutional arrangements'. It has a membership of around 1,800 and publishes a journal called the *Independent Solicitor*.

The position of solicitors also needs to be considered in relation to barristers, costs and legal aid and advice, all of which are discussed later.

[1] For further details see the previous edition of this book.

28

BARRISTERS

Barristers, known collectively as 'the Bar' and also collectively and individually as 'counsel', have a long history as a profession.[1] The distinction between attorneys and those who pleaded in court can be seen under Edward I, but the settlement of the Bar as a definite organisation probably took place later. Fortescue, writing in the fifteenth century, described the Inns of Court as well-established institutions. Lincoln's Inn, The Middle Temple, The Inner Temple, and Gray's Inn, together with lesser Inns that have disappeared, existed as bodies with an organisation much like Oxford and Cambridge colleges. The governing body was the Benchers, who were senior members who themselves filled any vacancies that occurred. One of the functions of the Inns was legal education, conducted by lectures and arguments. In rank below the Benchers came the Readers, who delivered lectures which were followed by arguments in which the next rank, the Utter-barristers, disputed with the Readers. The lowest rank of learners were the Inner-barristers. In the more formal arguments, called moots, the Benchers acted as judges and the cases were argued by two Utter-barristers and two Inner-barristers. It was a tense training which tended to keep the narrow requirements of procedure well to the fore. The other function of the Inn was the 'call to the Bar'. The exclusive right of the Bar to act as advocates in the superior courts rests on nothing but the attitude of the judges. A judge can allow a solicitor, or presumably anyone else, to conduct a case, but by convention this is not done. The judges have been content to accept the verdict of the Inns, so that a person becomes a barrister by the act of the Inn to which he belongs, subject to a rarely used supervisory power residing in the judges. The more successful barristers might rise to the rank of serjeants-at-law, an order that appears to have been established by the end of the fourteenth century. The Chief Justice of the Common Pleas, with the consent of the other judges, could present names to the Lord Chancellor of barristers of eminence who had been sixteen years in the law. If the Lord Chancellor called upon a barrister to become a serjeant, he had to do so, for it was a public office. It was, however, far more advantageous than burdensome to be a serjeant, for according to Fortescue: 'Neither is there any

[1] W. W. Boulton, *Conduct and etiquette at the Bar* (6th ed. 1975) is an excellent brief guide. Megarry, *Lawyer and litigant in England* (1962) gives an excellent account of barristers in action. *The Bar on trial* (1978), edited by Robert Hazell, gives a critical account of some of its practices.

man of laws throughout the universal world which by reason of his office gaineth so much as one of these serjeants.' Becoming a serjeant was a necessary prelude to becoming a judge. The serjeant ceased to be a member of his original Inn and joined Serjeants' Inn. The judges and the serjeants were therefore in close contact, forming an order quite apart from the rest of the barristers. The most momentous occasion in the career of a successful lawyer was becoming a serjeant. Thereafter he had the virtual certainty of becoming a judge, which was a trifling change compared to the gulf between ordinary barristers and serjeants. In the most important of the medieval courts, the Common Pleas, the serjeants had an exclusive right of audience. The relation between serjeants and judges was symbolised by the terms of address, for they were 'brother' to each other; in this capacity a serjeant could intervene in a case and, as *amicus curiae*, assist his brothers of the Bench by contributing his observations. This early history has profoundly affected our legal system, giving it the peculiarity of judicial office being more of an activity of the legal profession than an aspect of the public service: however, this antithesis does not imply any necessary antagonism between the two ideas.

During the eighteenth century lethargy overtook the Inns: legal education ceased and the emoluments of the Inns merely fattened the privileged few. By the earlier nineteenth century call to the Bar depended upon a student paying the fees and keeping twelve terms, of which there are four in each year, by eating the prescribed number of dinners each term. There were no examinations. The only instruction given was that students should 'read in chambers' with a barrister, and a student had to produce a certificate as evidence that he had pursued this type of study. This state of affairs was severely criticised in the era of reform that followed the Reform Bill of 1832. Change came in 1852, when the four Inns set up the Council of Legal Education. Instruction for students was re-introduced, and in 1872 a system of exminations replaced the certificate given by a barrister. Call to the Bar then depended upon keeping terms according to the practice of the eighteenth century, together with passing examinations and paying the fees. The changes of the last few years are considered in chapter 29 on legal education.

At present, it is still the case that barristers may not work in partnerships. Several barristers group together to form chambers, which means that they have rooms or share rooms adjoining each other, and employ a clerk (and subordinate office staff) in common. Each barrister pays his proportion of the rent and guarantees to the clerk a specified sum. The clerk, who receives commission upon the fees earned by each barrister, is a business manager rather than a clerk. Except in a few matters it is contrary to established usage for a barrister to be instructed by a lay client: the lay client must go to a solicitor, and the solicitor instructs the barrister. Hence barristers are dependent upon solicitors for almost all their work. In some cases the lay client tells the solicitor that he would like a particular barrister to be briefed, but in most cases the lay client leaves the solicitor to select a barrister. Whether the barrister is asked to advise, to draft some document, or to appear in court, he is sent a written brief, with the fee marked on it.[1]

The size of fee is settled between the solicitor and the barrister's clerk, it being against etiquette for the barrister himself to discuss his remuneration. Specialisation at the Bar means that solicitors never keep to one barrister or chambers for all their work; a firm of solicitors with a general practice will usually keep to a small circle of barristers for briefing in ordinary cases, sending their special cases to those with a specialised practice or of greater reputation. Until a barrister acquires a considerable reputation he is dependent upon his 'connection' with certain solicitors, yet a large part of Bar etiquette is concerned with maintaining the superior status of the Bar. Last century some barristers still lived in Lincoln's Inn Fields, and when this book first appeared in 1940 there were those who remembered a plate on the side door of one of these houses reading 'Tradesmen and Attorneys'. This spirit is not quite dead. Solicitors are still expected to go to the barrister's chambers: a busy solicitor with a large practice must wait upon a junior barrister. In the lower courts, where both barristers and solicitors may act as advocates, barristers sometimes refer to their barrister opponents as 'my learned friend', and to their solicitor opponents as 'my friend'. Of course the rules are not always observed, and the old class distinctions between the two branches of the profession have very much broken down. Many persons who would once have become barristers now become solicitors. The social distinction cannot survive a state of affairs in which many of the entrants into both sides of the profession have the same type of background, education and money.

The position of the Bar is due partly to its close association with politics, the judiciary and high positions, and partly to the large cash rewards that come to those who are very successful. Upwards of £100,000 a year is reached by a few barristers. Most barristers earn nowhere near this: a survey carried out by Messrs Coopers and Lybrand in 1986 revealed that average earnings for barristers aged between 32 and 37 and specialising in criminal work ranged between £6,140 and £11,880. Nevertheless, the great financial success that comes to a few has a dazzling effect upon both the profession and the public. The conditions of a barrister's work make it necessary for him to do the bulk of it personally; juniors can 'devil' for him, and by judicious management he can sometimes appear in two cases that are heard more or less at the same time, but naturally clients do not like a barrister to leave part of their case to a junior. If a practice increases there comes a time when the barrister has more work coming in than he can deal with. He will then consider becoming a Queen's Counsel,[2] commonly known as 'talking silk', because he may then wear a gown of silk instead of a stuff gown. Originally

---

[1] On briefs from the Crown the fee is fixed afterwards. For practice in legal aid cases see chapter 40 below.

[2] A Queen's Counsel (QC) automatically becomes a King's Counsel (KC) when the Sovereign is a King.

Queen's Counsel were appointed for the work of the Crown, but by the end of the eighteenth century it became a regular practice for successful men to apply for the appointment. The appointment is made by the Lord Chancellor; there are no official qualifications, but it is understood that at least ten years' standing is required, together with an indefinable degree of success as a junior. Before the appointment is made, the Lord Chancellor arranges for consultations to take place, first with the leaders of the various sections of the Bar concerned, and then with the judges. The purpose of becoming a QC has for long had nothing to do with Crown work. Nowadays there are just a number of conventions which give Queen's Counsel the position of a superior grade of barrister. To some extent they replace the order of serjeants, which decayed and died out during the last century, but unlike the serjeants the Queen's Counsel remain members of their old Inns. Queen's Counsel are generally known as 'leaders', because of a rule, abolished in 1977, that they must not appear in court unless an ordinary barrister called a 'junior' appears with them. These trappings apart, the real reason why a barrister aspires to be a Queen's Counsel is to do with the development of his practice. If Mr A is a successful junior with an increasing practice he may become overworked. A rule of conduct at the Bar is that 'Counsel is bound to accept any brief in the courts in which he professes to practice at a proper professional fee dependent on the length and difficulty of the case, but special circumstances may justify his refusal, at his discretion, to accept a particular brief': a doctrine generally known as the 'cab-rank principle'. So Mr A cannot avoid overwork by taking only those briefs that he would like to have. By taking silk he puts himself on a higher professional level and makes it plain to one and all that he now commands a higher range of fees. Until 1977 there was a rule, and there is still a convention, that a QC will only appear in a case if he is briefed together with a junior (see chapter 39 below). This puts the QC still further up-market, because anyone who wishes to have his services must generally expect to hire an assistant too. If he has chosen wisely, his better-paying clients will still wish to brief him, and he will get higher fees and avoid doing the lesser and ill-paid work that overburdened him as a junior. If he has made a mistake, he is in trouble, because he cannot go back to being a junior; he must either wait and hope, or accept any offer of a minor judicial appointment.

A strange rule is that barristers cannot sue for their fees. The idea behind this was originally the notion that a barrister was a gentleman, and a gentleman (unlike a tradesman) does not need to earn his living: although he may occasionally accept an *honorarium* as a thank-you present from a grateful client. At the back of a barrister's gown there is still a pocket called a 'fee bag', which is said to have been there originally so that clients could slip counsel his fee without embarrassing him. The rule does not mean that barristers often go unpaid; the instructing solicitor is responsible for paying counsel and it is professional misconduct if he fails to pay counsel's fee, whether or not he ever gets the money out of his client. Unfortunately, however, it does mean that if unscrupulous solicitors pay late, or fail to pay at all, the barrister has no recourse to law; all he can do is to report them to the Law Society. In the past this is a step which barristers have been reluctant to take because of fears that news would rapidly spread through the solicitors' profession and result in solicitors taking their trade to different counsel. To counter this problem, the Bar has now taken collective action. In 1987 it introduced a 'blacklist' and required all barristers to refuse to accept briefs from blacklisted solicitors except on payment in advance. The other side of a barrister's inability to sue for fees used to be his immunity from lawsuits by disgruntled clients if his performance failed to satisfy them. It used to be thought that this stemmed from the fact that there was no contract between them. In recent years, however, the law of negligence has greatly developed and it has become possible in many situations for A to sue B for causing him damage through his negligence even where there was no contract between them. As part of this development, the House of Lords decided in a series of cases that a barrister may now be liable to his client for negligence in certain situations, and his immunity is limited to what he actually says and does when conducting a case in court, and in the final stages of preparation just before the case comes up for trial.[1] Thus he may be liable if, for example, he negligently advises his client to start proceedings against someone who is clearly not liable, or to drop them against someone who clearly is; but he is not liable for an allegedly negligent decision to call or not to call a particular witness, or for a negligent failure to ask him the right questions when examining him in court. This immunity is based on considerations of public policy. First, it is generally thought right that everyone should be as free as possible from the constraints of possible civil liability in deciding what to say and do in court. Neither witnesses nor judges can be civilly liable for what they do there, and it is thought right that counsel should be in the same position. Secondly, a barrister has a duty to the court which in certain cases transcends his duty to his client; it is thought that he should be free to do his duty to the court without fear of repercussions from his client. And thirdly, if barristers could be sued for what they did in court, it is probable that most actions brought against them would be by litigants disgruntled at the outcome of their case; and disgruntlement with the outcome of one's case is adequately catered for – at least in theory – in the system of appeals. For what they do in the conduct of litigation, solicitors are immune to the same extent as barristers.

When it comes to managing its affairs, the Bar is theoretically in an extraordinarily privileged position. The head of the profession is the Attorney-General, and behind him in order of precedence is the Solicitor-General (who is always a barrister). These persons are important ministers to whom the government looks for disinterested legal advice: yet the Bar expects to be able to look to them as their leaders for support, sometimes even in struggles which the Bar is having with the government of the day. Sometimes the Bar is disappointed in its

---

[1] *Rondel* v. *Worsley* [1969] AC 191; *Saif Ali* v. *Mitchell* [1980] AC 198.

leaders, but on other occasions this built-in conflict of interest has given the Bar a very powerful voice in affairs of State. The Bar has also escaped regulation by Act of Parliament. Solicitors, and all other professions, are heavily regulated by statute. Parliament has passed Acts which lay down the constitution of their professional organisations, and regulates in considerable detail what they may and may not do and sometimes how much they may charge for doing it as well. Yet the Bar is governed by no Act of Parliament. It is free to make and unmake its own professional constitution, and to decide for itself what its rules of practice shall be.

Until recently, at least, the affairs of the Bar have often suffered as well as prospered as a result of the absence of any regulation imposed from outside. Much of the trouble has been the failure of the Bar to produce any single professional organisation with overall control of what goes on. In the past, everything was in the hands of the four independent Inns of Court, each of which had the right to call to the Bar and discipline and control its members. The Inns were (and are) controlled by their Benchers, who tended to be the judges and the most senior section of the profession. The first body which was set up to act for the Bar as a whole was the Council of Legal Education, created in 1852 to introduce uniform requirements for entry to the profession and to be responsible for teaching and examining. In 1883 there was set up the Bar Committee, renamed the Bar Council in 1894. This was intended to be a body through which the Bar spoke to and dealt with the outside world. This concerned itself with professional etiquette, the conduct of relations with solicitors, and suchlike matters; as it had little executive authority and less money, it was hardly in a position to concern itself with anything else. In 1966 another body was established, the Senate of the Four Inns of Court. This was intended to act collectively for the Inns in a large number of matters of common interest; but as executive authority still largely resided in the Inns, this body was not able to do much either, and the main result was a proliferation of committees to no great purpose. About this time the Bar began to face serious problems. The main one was the rapid increase in the number of barristers in practice in London, who had nowhere to do their work. It became clear that these were matters which only a strong central authority would be able to solve. In 1972 the Senate set up a committee under Lord Pearce, a Law Lord, which recommended 'one effective central governing body for the Bar'.[1] A rearrangement followed in 1974, but it fell considerably short of this ideal. The Senate was expanded to represent interests other than the four Inns of Court, but the Bar Council remained as an autonomous body not subject to the Senate's direction, and the new scheme failed to provide a workable professional association. Authority remained divided, and there was still a widespread feeling that the arrangements gave too much power to the senior end of the profession and too little to the junior end,

---

[1] First Interim Report of the Pearce Committee to the Senate of the Four Inns of Court (1972); second Interim Report (1973).

341

and too little say to barristers practising outside London, of whom there was an increasing number. Meanwhile accommodation problems in London continued and, from the general election of 1979 onwards, the Bar found itself in recurrent conflict with a government which was both unsympathetic to the restrictive practices of the professions, and determined to save public money spent on legal aid. Moved by a general sense of desperation, a committee under Lord Rawlinson recommended a new centralised constitution for the Bar in 1986. This was overwhelmingly accepted at an extraordinary meeting of the Bar in London and then in a subsequent poll. The new arrangements came into force on 1 January 1987.

The new professional organisation is called the General Council of the Bar, or 'Bar Council' for short.[1]

Its first three functions are listed as follows:

(a)   To be the governing body of the Bar.
(b)   To consider, lay down and implement general policy with regard to all matters affecting the Bar.
(c)   To maintain the standards, honour and independence of the Bar, to promote, preserve and improve the services and functions of the Bar, and to represent and act for the Bar generally as well as in its relations with others and also in matters affecting the administration of justice.[2]

The four Inns of Court have bound themselves to accept and implement the general policies which the Bar Council lays down (whilst reserving for themselves the right to opt out on twelve months' notice). The new Bar Council consists of 93 members. Eleven are members *ex officio*, including the Attorney-General and Solicitor-General, the leaders of each of the six circuits, and the chairmen of the various professional interest groups such as the Criminal Bar Association. Twelve members are appointed by the Benchers of the four Inns of Court, and a further twelve are elected by their circuits. Five are elected by the various professional interest groups. Thirty-nine barristers are elected on a vote of all practising barristers, of whom thirty must be juniors, and twelve juniors of under seven years' call. Twelve are elected to represent those barristers who do not practice at the Bar, but work as paid employees. There is also room for four other members co-opted by the rest. There is an Inns Council, which deals with matters particularly affecting the Inns of Court, and the decisions of which are binding on the Inns.

Complaints against barristers are first investigated by a Professional Conduct Committee of the Bar Council. At one time, action was only taken in cases of 'professional misconduct' – in other words, serious misbehaviour; in 1985 'breach of proper professional standards' were also made a disciplinary matter. If

[1] A consequence of its not being a statutory body is that a copy of the constitution is not something which is readily found in a law library. The editor obtained his copy by telephoning the office of the General Council of the Bar, which was kind enough to supply one free of charge.
[2] Constitution of the General Council of the Bar, s.1.

the Professional Conduct Committee thinks there is a case to answer it is heard before a Disciplinary Tribunal of five persons nominated by the President of the Inns Council, and consisting of a judge as chairman, three barristers, and a layman from a panel appointed by the Lord Chancellor. The hearing is normally in private. If the case is proved the tribunal has a choice of sentences ranging from removing the offending barrister's professional qualification (when he is 'disbarred'), through suspension from practice, ordering him to repay or forego fees, or admonishing him. From a decision of the Disciplinary Tribunal appeal lies to the judges who in this capacity act as a domestic appeal court and are known as Visitors. In 1986 there were around 200 complaints against barristers; three were disbarred and one was reprimanded. At the time of writing the Bar Council is also considering a scheme, like the one which now exists for solicitors, whereby the clients of a barrister who are dissatisfied with his services can go to independent arbitration.

As a body the Bar has many excellent qualities, including a very high standard of professional probity. A bad characteristic, however, is its extreme unwillingness to accept change. This is understandable when, like the monopoly of audience in the superior courts, the habit which the Bar is asked to give up is profitable. But the reluctance to change is equally strong in lesser matters, such as the insistence on wearing period costume for court appearances, and the inability to sue for fees. Big changes have happened to the Bar in recent years: although the most noticeable ones have been the sort which occur rather than are willed. The most obvious is the fact that the Bar has doubled in size and relocated much of itself outside London, as Table 10 shows. Nowadays there are signs of greater willingness to make changes. One attitude which seems to be changing involves the rule that each barrister must work on his own and that there be no partnerships. This is usually justified by an argument based on consumer choice: because barristers in a set of chambers are not in partnership the plaintiff can brief Mr X of those chambers whilst at the same time the defendant briefs Mr Y of those chambers – something which would be impossible if they were partners. From the barrister's point of view, the traditional arrangement also has the advantage that if he is successful all his profits come to him. However, it is

Table 10. *The size of the practising Bar*

| | Barristers in practice | Number of sets of chambers | | |
		In London	In provinces	Total
1970	2,584	169	74	243
1975	3,646	181	93	274
1980	4,589	202	109	311
1985	5,367	226	112	338

Note: The average was 10.6 barristers to a set of chambers in 1970, and 15.8 in 1985. A barrister who practises in London and also at a local Bar may be a member of more than one set of chambers.

very inconvenient in other ways. If Mr X or Mr Y fall ill it means their income immediately ceases, and if Mr Z wishes to join the chambers he has to do without inconvenient in other ways. If Mr X or Mr Y fall ill it means their income immediately ceases, and if Mr Z wishes to join the chambers he has to do without any income at all until his name is known. A few years ago an enterprising set of chambers introduced a 'fee pooling' scheme under which all its members pooled their fees and paid themselves regular salaries. In 1986, after talk of disciplining them for breach of the rules of professional conduct, the Bar Council was considering adjusting the rules of practice to permit fee-sharing schemes as long as they fell short of actual partnerships. At the time of writing a new Code of Conduct is being considered by the Bar. This would permit 'fee-pooling', and also certain restrained forms of advertising. It would also permit barristers to appear in the Crown Court without instructing solicitors being present (see chapter 30 below).

29

LEGAL EDUCATION[1]

Law is taught in this country at different academic levels ranging from university degree standards to the GCSE in schools. First-degree courses in law (or law in conjunction with other subjects) are offered by some thirty universities; the number of university law schools is well over thirty, because four of the colleges within London University have their separate law schools. There are also around two dozen polytechnics which offer CNAA courses that can lead to a degree. Polytechnics and Colleges of Further Education do a vast amount of non-degree law teaching as well, for there are over thirty bodies, including those concerned with accountancy, banking, business and various kinds of administration, which have law papers as part of their examinations, and law courses are needed for these. The Inns of Court Law School, which is controlled by the Council of Legal Education, is concerned solely with teaching for Bar examinations, and the College of Law (controlled by the Law Society) prepares students for the Law Society examinations. Neither of these organisations teach law for other purposes (but polytechnics also teach for some of the legal professional examinations of the Bar and of the Law Society).

In other countries an essential part of the education and training of lawyers has always been taking a degree in law. This has never been the case in England. Indeed, there is a noticeable tradition of anti-intellectualism in both branches of the legal profession in England, and particularly at the Bar. This has diminished in recent years; as more and more aspects of life have become regulated by laws, so the volume and range of legal knowledge that everyone needs for practice has grown, and it has now reached such a size that hardly anyone can seriously claim that it is possible to master it without long and systematic study. Yet old ideas die hard. In 1985 a Queen's Counsel prominent at the criminal Bar told the editor of this book that studying law at university was 'a complete waste of time', because any bright young man 'can pick up all he needs to know in six months of evening classes, and the rest as he goes along'.

[1] See the Report of the Committee on Legal Education (Ormrod Committee), (1971) Cmnd 4595. See also 'A survey of legal education in the United Kingdom' by Prof. J. F. Wilson for the Institute of Advanced Legal Studies (1966) 9 *Journal SPTL* 1 and 'A second survey of legal education in the United Kingdom' by Prof. J. F. Wilson and Dr S. B. Marsh (1975) 13 *Journal SPTL* 241. Both surveys were also separately published. Supplements to these surveys were published in 1978 and 1981.

Oxford and Cambridge were the only universities in England until the early nineteenth century, and the teaching of law in Oxford and Cambridge then meant the civil law, that is Roman law. In the later eighteenth century attempts were made to establish the teaching of common law, notably by Blackstone's lectures at Oxford in 1753 and the later foundation of the Vinerian chair, and the foundation of the Downing chair at Cambridge in 1800, but the studies languished. Effective university teaching of English law began in University College, London, in 1826, shortly followed by King's College, but development of university law schools was a slow process. When a Select Committee on Legal Education was set up by the House of Commons in 1846 there was virtually no institutional law teaching in England except for one professor in London. The Select Committee saw the need for both academic and professional training: for the academic part, the university law faculties needed to be revived, whilst for the professional training a 'special institution' was required. In response to the Select Committee and to other pressures, Oxford and Cambridge established law degrees in 1852 and 1855, and law faculties in 1872 and 1873. As new universities were founded there was an increase in university law teaching and by 1908 there were eight law faculties altogether. Provision for a 'special institution' for Bar students and a 'cognate institution' for solicitors made slow progress. The Council of Legal Education was formed by the Bar in 1852, but there was prolonged controversy over proposals to form a separate institution and the dream of a great school of law centred on the Inns of Court slowly died away. The Law Society had to work within the statutory scheme laid down by Act of Parliament in 1877, namely articled clerks who had to pass an Intermediate and a Final Examination. As articled clerks were dispersed all over the country, and nominally obliged to attend full-time the offices of their principals, the Law Society could do no more than organise lectures for them in London and in the main provincial centres. Articled clerks were allowed some time off for preparing for examinations and they mostly went to Gibson and Weldon, a firm of private law coaches. In an attempt to improve the position, the Law Society set up its own school of law in 1903 – which in 1962 was merged with Gibson and Weldon to form the College of Law.

A Committee on Legal Education (the Ormrod Committee) was appointed in 1967 and its Report was published in 1971.[1] This made a number of major recommendations, and some significant changes followed. It is convenient to examine the professional training of lawyers by taking stock of the situation up to the time of the Ormrod Report, to look at the Ormrod recommendations, and finally to examine the position today.

To go to the Bar it was (and still is) necessary to join one of the four Inns of Court, and there to 'keep terms' for three years. Before the Second World War no attempt was made to see that students studied law or learned anything of

[1] Cmnd 4595.

practice during the years in which terms were kept by eating dinners. The Council of Legal Education, which prescribed the examinations, provided lectures but attendance at these was voluntary. A graduate or undergraduate at a university had to keep terms but eat three dinners instead of the six required for others, and a law graduate might gain exemption from Part I of the Bar examination. Having passed the Bar Final examinations a student could be called, and he was then qualified to practice. The education and training required were far less onerous than those required for any other profession. In reality it usually mattered little for the practising Bar, because a man could not attract any work at once and he would therefore fill in time by fitting himself to practice by becoming a pupil to an established barrister, usually at a fee of 100 guineas for a year. It was hard to get a start at the Bar because solicitors would not send briefs to a beginner until they heard on the legal grape-vine that he could be expected to do the work competently. Further, since most of those who wanted to practise were graduates, the practising Bar had a high educational level. But the result was deplorable for overseas students and some others who did not go on to practice. The educational level for admittance to an Inn was lower than for universities and anyone who got through the examinations (which were regarded as relatively easy) could return to his own country as a barrister-at-law, apparently fully fledged, yet without any academic education or practical training or experience of courts and the administration of justice.

After the war the pattern of home students going to the Bar was affected by changing social patterns. The expansion of universities meant that there was a higher proportion of graduates, most of whom had been in receipt of grants whilst at university. Some of these were unable or reluctant to submit to a voluntary pupillage before they started earning at the Bar. Hence in 1959 a rule was made making a twelve month period of pupillage compulsory (although the pupil was not barred from practice during pupillage). In the 1950s there was a slump in practice at the Bar, but in the 1960s the slump turned into a boom. The situation then arose in which newcomers to the Bar could make an immediate living, and the rise in the amount of work resulted in some newly-called barristers taking so many cases that they were not benefiting from the pupillage required by the 1959 rules. Thus in 1965 the rules were changed again so that no barrister is permitted to practise until he has completed six of his twelve months' pupillage. At this time, the Bar examinations were not particularly difficult, and included neither practical training exercises nor compulsory attendance at any tutorials or lectures. In 1970 this was changed when a new examination scheme was introduced. The educational standard for entering an Inn was raised, and preparation for practice at the Bar now involved two stages. The *educational stage* was satisfied by obtaining a degree in law provided that it covered the necessary studies, or by passing a new pattern Part I. The *training stage* led to a new-style Part II examination, in which the questions were directed to testing the candidate's knowledge of the professional approach to legal problems of the kind which he was likely to encounter in the early years of practice at the English Bar, and his skill in the professional techniques of writing opinions and drafting pleadings and other documents required in civil and criminal litigation. It became compulsory to be instructed in advocacy and paper work, although there was no examination on those points. These changes did ensure some practical training, but even so they still left the requirements for the Bar at a lower level than those for solicitors, doctors and other professionals.

Training requirements to become a solicitor have always been stricter. Since the eighteenth century it has been necessary both to serve a period of apprenticeship called 'articles' and to pass an examination. Before the Second World War the period of articles was five or four years according to educational standards, and three years for a graduate. The value of articles varied: some principals saw that their articled clerks did learn their job, but there were other offices where they were regarded as a nuisance that had to be tolerated. In those days, articles were an expensive business, and had the effect of limiting admission to the profession to the children of the relatively well-off. In addition to the stamp duties which were then levied on articles of clerkship, it was generally necessary for an articled clerk to pay a premium to his principal, £250 or £300 often being required, and during his articles the clerk was paid nothing and had to be supported financially. Things began to change with changing social conditions after the war. The stamp duty was abolished, the practice of asking for premiums gradually ceased, and it became usual for the solicitor to pay a small salary to his articled clerk. It was (and still is) the case that two examinations had to be passed. Before the Second World War these were called the Intermediate and the Final. A law graduate received exemption from the legal part of the Intermediate. Unless he was a law graduate, the would-be solicitor was also required to take an 'academic year': a year's study, either at the Law Society's own school or at a provincial university. In 1962 there was a big rearrangement. The Law Society's school was amalgamated with the law-coaching firm of Gibson and Weldon and became the College of Law, with premises at London and Guildford (and later at Chester as well). The 'academic year' was abolished and a new scheme came into operation which rearranged the elements of articles, law school and Part I and Part II examinations. A non-graduate was required to attend a recognised law course, pass Part I, and then enter into articles, serve four years and pass Part II at the end of his articles. A graduate in a subject other than law had to pass Part I before articles, then serve two and a half years and pass Part II. A law graduate would normally get exemption from Part I, and he would then take Part II before articles and serve two years, or serve two and a half years and take Part II at the end.

The Ormrod Committee produced a number of recommendations. It thought that the law should become a graduate profession and that, subject to certain exceptions for mature students, the way in should be via a university degree. It said that there should be two stages in a lawyer's education, each part of which should be integrated into a coherent whole. The first should be the academic study of law. By that it did not mean that an attempt should be made to give a student a comprehensive coverage of all the law he may require in practice but that the student should study basic 'core' subjects in such a way that he would understand legal principles and acquire the equipment to ascertain the law as and when he wants it. This, they felt, should normally be achieved by reading for a law degree; for graduates in subjects other than law, or mature students, there should be a 'common professional examination', to be taken by those who intended to become either barristers or solicitors. The second stage should be the professional or vocational stage in which the student acquires the special skills needed for practice. This should consist of two elements: a new, compulsory vocational course lasting for one academic year, which should include practical exercises, additional law subjects, and non-law subjects of special concern to legal practitioners, and then a period of in-training such as pupillage, articles, or some other sort of restricted and supervised practice.

A compulsory vocational course for all entrants to the legal profession was a new element in legal training. The Inns of Court Law School (ICLS) provided lectures for the Bar Final, and the College of Law provided a residential course leading to the Law Society Part II examination, but attendance at neither was compulsory, and many would-be lawyers chose to do without them. So the question that faced the Ormrod Committee was who should provide these new courses. On this the Committee was not unanimous. A majority thought that the vocational courses should be provided by universities, the role of the professions being limited to seeing that the training was of adequate standard. Some people were optimistic enough to think that if vocational courses were brought within the normal pattern of higher education the cost of them might be provided by public funds through the University Grants Committee. There was never any chance of that: it has always been government policy that the cost of professional training other than that of doctors is not to be borne by public funds, and this has been reinforced by increasing financial pressure in the years following the Ormrod Report. A minority of the Committee thought it should be done by the existing professional schools. In the end, such vocational courses as we have were provided by a combination of the ICLS, the College of Law and a number of polytechnics, and the universities have played no part in the scheme.

The Ormrod recommendations were well received at the time, but enthusiasm began to wane when it became a question of putting them into effect.

The Law Society initially favoured the idea of a graduate-only profession, but in the end did not accept it. Under the current Qualifying Regulations it remains possible for a person to enter the profession straight from school: a school-leaver qualifies by serving five years' articles, attending a course and taking a special Solicitors' First Examination before going on to study for and take the Final Examination. In practice very few people became solicitors by this route, however, and the derogation from the Ormrod idea is largely a theoretical one. Most entrants to the profession nowadays hold university degrees, usually in law.

Provided the 'core' subjects have been covered,[1] for them the university law course counts as completion of the academic stage. For graduates in subjects other than law and for mature students, the Law Society tried to provide for the academic stage by setting up a 'common professional examination' to be operated jointly with the Bar. At the last moment negotiations broke down, however, and the Bar created its own separate Diploma examination; this was not before the Law Society had named its new examination the 'Common Professional Examination' – CPE for short – and it is still called this, despite the fact that it is not in fact common.[2] Before he is allowed to sit the CPE, the candidate is usually required by the Law Society to take one of the study courses which various polytechnics provide, but the requirement can be waived in special cases. For the first part of the 'vocational stage', the Law Society abolished its old Part II examination and replaced it with a new Final Examination, which is preceded by a compulsory twelve-month course. The teaching for the vocational course is provided by two sources: the College of Law, operating from centres in London, Guildford, Chester and York, and eight polytechnics in various parts of the country. These courses have to be paid for, which is a problem for some students, because they do not attract a mandatory grant from the local authority. Students whose local authorities are generous sometimes get a discretionary grant; the others have to find the money themselves or else abandon their ideas of entering the legal profession. Viewing a future solicitor as a good financial prospect, banks are usually ready to advance the student a loan, and some of the more prosperous firms of solicitors will lend or give the money where (as is usually the case) the student has already fixed up articles which are due to start once he has completed the Final. Prompted by a suggestion from the Law Society, the Ormrod Committee recommended the abolition of articles and their replacement with a period of 'restricted practice' under supervision. But this did not prove acceptable to solicitors in general, and service of two years in articles has been retained as the second part of the vocational stage; however, the Law Society now exercises a measure of control over the training an articled clerk receives, and lays down recommended minimum salaries for them.

The first thing that an aspirant barrister must do is to join an Inn of Court and 'keep terms'. This means that he must eat dinner in the hall of his Inn on three occasions during eight 'law terms', of which there are four in the year. This is a relic of the ancient days, when there was no formal training for a barrister and students literally 'ate their way to the Bar'. Imposing this on Bar students today is officially justified as something that helps them to identify with their Inn, to get to know their fellow members who are in practice, and pick up some of the corporate spirit of the profession. Unfortunately the truth is that the only people

---

[1] At present these are tort, contract, criminal law, land law, constitutional and administrative law, and the law of trusts; the Law Society reserves the right to add others.

[2] In 1988 there are new moves to make the Common Professional Examination common to both branches of the profession.

the student is likely to meet are other students in the same position as himself. Patterns of family life have changed in the last century, and the modern barrister, like the modern Oxford or Cambridge don, usually eats at home in the evenings with his wife and family instead of dining at his Inn. Lunch at an Inn of Court is, by contrast, a friendly, bustling, professional occasion when many barristers are present – but the student is required to dine, not lunch. The Ormrod Commitee said that dining 'should be adapted to present day conditions and so arranged that the hardship on students who live far from London is minimised'. This has not been done, and most students find dining burdensome and useless.

The Bar, unlike the Law Society, did accept the idea of graduate-only entry (with exceptions for mature students). Like the Law Society, the Bar counts a law degree as covering the academic stage of training – but, since 1981, it has insisted on a degree with first or second class honours. For graduates in other subjects and mature students the Bar has its own Diploma Examination, for which teaching is provided by the City University and the Polytechnic of Central London. The vocational stage consists of a year's course leading to an examination, and a period of pupillage. Before the Ormrod Report was published the Bar had already introduced a new final examination – which is now called the Bar examination – together with a year-long course of teaching at the ICLS and various practical exercises. With minor modifications this is still the scheme which is in force. Whether or not a candidate for the Bar examination is obliged to enrol for the ICLS course and take part in the practical exercises depends on whether or not he actually intends to practice at the Bar in England and Wales: many overseas students, a number of academic lawyers and others merely wish to acquire the professional qualifications so that they can put the words 'barrister at law' after their names. Those who do intend to practice must enrol for a year's course of lectures at the ICLS, and must also take part in a course of 'practical exercises'. These include court visits, practice in drafting legal documents, and training in advocacy. Some of this consists of filming the learner's performance and playing it back to him, a procedure which learners usually find very revealing. The ICLS course was originally open to anyone who had joined an Inn and passed the academic stage, and in the 1970s the efforts of the Council of Legal Education to make it into a serious-minded exercise nearly collapsed under the pressure of numbers. In 1981 the intake was limited to 1,000 students per annum, with priority given to those who do intend to practice at the Bar.

Pupillage continues much as it did before Ormrod. It still lasts twelve months (as against two years' articles for a solicitor), during the second six months of which the pupil is permitted to take his own cases if anyone will brief him. Pupilmasters no longer exact premiums, but it is still the case that a Bar pupil must expect virtually no pay during his twelve months' pupillage, and during that time must usually support himself. Nor is this the only difficulty that faces the would-be Bar pupil compared with the intending articled clerk. Whereas law-students are usually able to arrange articles with a firm of solicitors whilst they are still at university, and before they have spent time and money on vocational training, pupillage must usually be arranged after joining an Inn (at a fee) and embarking on the vocational course. Thus the would-be Bar pupil risks his time and money before he knows whether or not he will be able to take the next step in his professional career. Solicitors usually only offer articles to people they hope and expect to employ when they have qualified; but in London – where most barristers are still based – a pupillage is no guarantee whatever of an eventual place in chambers, and barristers routinely take on far more pupils than they will eventually be able to find room for as tenants. At the end of pupillage, surplus pupils must look for a tenancy elsewhere, and if they cannot find one, give up the Bar. The Bar usually justifies this by saying that it enables them to select the barristers of the future according to merit fairly tested, and gives every aspirant a fair and equal chance. Sceptics say that the real attraction of the system is that it enables barristers to have their future colleagues on twelve months' free trial without obligation, so relieving them of the need to waste time and energy on kinder selection procedures, and meanwhile gives them research assistance without the discomfort of having to pay for it. In the early 1980s the Bar, which had previously been able to attract almost all of the most able law students, found to its chagrin that many of the best people were now tending to become solicitors instead. In response to this pressure the London Bar has begun to provide an increasing number of grants and awards to ensure some financial support for worthy students during pupillage. At the provincial Bar it is already the case that pupillages are mainly offered only where there is a prospect of a tenancy, and it may be that in time the need to ensure a supply of good recruits makes the London Bar adopt the same approach.

It is a feature of the present age that the law is continually changing. Thus for lawyers who have trained and qualified, there is the continual problem of keeping their knowledge up-to-date. Some manage to find time to do so, at least within their particular areas of expertise, whilst others lamentably do not. This raises the question whether it is enough to require a lawyer to be trained at the outset of his career. In 1979 the Benson Commission[1] said that 'persons practising a profession need to keep abreast of changes and it is the function of the governing body of a profession to ensure that every member is properly equipped with up-to-date and comprehensive knowledge, both in his own interests and in those of his clients and of the profession'.

The Law Society encourages its local branches to put on courses of lectures which are voluntary, and in a small way it has now started to make further training compulsory. Since 1985, new recruits to the profession are required to attend a specified number of further training sessions in the first three years of practice – but this does not, of course, apply to the old ones whose knowledge is most likely to be out of date. At the moment there is no sign of any requirements of continuing education at the Bar.

[1] Royal Commission on Legal Services, (1979) Cmnd 7648 paras. 39, 89.

30

SHOULD THE PROFESSION
CONTINUE TO BE DIVIDED
INTO BARRISTERS AND
SOLICITORS?

The distinction between the Bar and solicitors is, on the face of it, somewhat odd.[1] There is nothing peculiar in having specialists within a profession, but it is unusual to find that the citizen is obliged to employ two men to do the work that he would willingly entrust to one of them. Fortunately for the citizen, for most types of the legal business this situation does not arise. 'The business of the legal professions is as to about nine-tenths concerned with matters affecting the daily life of the community outside the courts, and the remaining one-tenth which attracts great public attention, is litigation and criminal business.'[2] For litigation in the civil or criminal courts, however, the citizen frequently has to employ both a solicitor and a barrister, whether he wants to do so or not. The Bar has a virtual monopoly in the conduct of cases in the higher civil and criminal courts (together with a virtual monopoly over all but the lowest judicial appointments). And although barristers conduct cases in the higher courts, the preparation of these cases has to be done by solicitors, not barristers, and it is a rule that no barrister may deal directly with a client, as clients have access to barristers only through solicitors. Broadly speaking, this division suits the Bar very well and it is anxious to maintain it. This is partly for obvious reasons: the monopoly over litigation in the High Court and in the Crown Court suits them because litigation is their bread and butter and no one else is allowed to share it, and the monopoly over judicial appointments provides a small profession of self-employed men with a relatively large source of pensionable jobs to move into when they are getting old. But there is a less obvious reason why the Bar likes to keep the present division of labour. It is because it feels that if the present demarcation rules broke down, the result would quickly be an amalgamation between the two branches of the

[1] See Peter Reeves, *Are two legal professions necessary?* (1986).
[2] Sir Thomas Lund, formerly Secretary-General of the Law Society, 'The future pattern of the profession', (1966) 63 Law Soc. Gaz. 127.

353

profession, in which the Bar, being only some 6,000 strong, would disappear without trace into a sea of 47,000 solicitors. Solicitors have always been less content with the situation, particularly the Bar's monopoly of judicial appointments. Until recently, however, their own conveyancing monopoly ensured solicitors sufficient profitable work to keep them fairly happy, and whilst they would grumble about the Bar's monopolies occasionally, they were not cross enough to campaign very actively to have them removed. Since the solicitors' conveyancing monopoly came under attack, however, their attitude to the Bar has changed. In 1986 the Law Society began a public agitation for solicitors to be given greater rights of audience in the higher courts, and the Bar retaliated by demanding the right to have direct access to its clients. After a bitter war of words, both professions referred their differences to a working party chaired by Lady Marre, a prominent social worker who was a former chairman of the central appeals advisory committee for the BBC and IBA and a sometime member of the Lord Chancellor's Advisory Committee on Legal Aid. The Marre Committee is expected to report in 1988. Meanwhile, it is an uncomfortable fact of life for both branches of the profession that there is a government in power which is strongly opposed to all sorts of monopolies, even professional ones; whatever the Marre Committee recommends, it looks as if the present forced division of work is unlikely to remain for long.

In the late 1960s the Beeching Commission[1] had to consider the effect of rationalising the superior courts on the qualification for appointment as Circuit Judges. No question then arose over High Court Judges who were then and still are appointed exclusively from the Bar. But there was a difference of opinion over Circuit Judges because they took over the criminal work of Quarter Sessions, and a person was qualified to be a chairman of Quarter Sessions if he was a solicitor as well as if he was a barrister. The Beeching Commission came down by a majority on the side of qualification for Circuit Judges being either barristers or solicitors. Predictably the resulting Bill ignored solicitors, for it was a Lord Chancellor's Bill and he and all the higher civil servants in his department are barristers. The debate in the House of Lords on this part of the Bill and the ensuing correspondence in *The Times* 'showed the power of emotion as well as logic that can be brought to bear on both sides of this question'.[2] The principal argument was that to get satisfactory judges, appointments must be made from those with advocacy experience, from which it was deduced that, since advocacy in the higher criminal courts is almost entirely confined to barristers, appointments of Circuit Judges should be made solely from the Bar. However, in county courts solicitors do much of the advocacy and on that argument solicitors should be eligible for the county court Bench. The reality is that appointments to the Bench are often made with little regard to whether the practice of the person appointed has lain in the matters that will come before him as a judge: barristers practising

[1] Royal Commission on Assizes and Quarter Sessions, (1969) Cmnd 4153.
[2] *The Times*, leading article, 7 December 1970.

in commercial work regularly become judges who take criminal cases, and there are many other circumstances in which newly-appointed judges have to do unaccustomed work. The dividing line between county court and High Court jurisdiction is the financial amount of the claim, and magistrates' courts try a great many indictable offences; thus advocates (who may be solicitors) have to deal with matters which, if the claim were larger or the defendant opted for jury trial, would have to be presented by barristers.

The other main argument put forward by the Lord Chancellor (Lord Hailsham) in the House of Lords was that appointing solicitors would 'lead to fusion'.[1] Obviously if the professions were fused there would no longer be room for questions about who does what, but fusion does not arise if certain appointments may be held by persons with different qualifications: at present among stipendiary magistrates some are barristers, and others are solicitors, and among coroners there are barristers, solicitors and medical practitioners.

As a result of these debates the Lord Chancellor had discussions with the Bar Council and the Law Society and produced the present compromise position which was enacted in the Courts Act 1971. Recorders may be appointed from solicitors as well as from barristers of ten years' standing. The qualification for Circuit Judges became a barrister of ten years' standing or a Recorder who has held that office for three years, so that a solicitor can only become qualified for appointment as a Circuit Judge after three years' service as a Recorder. By this route some solicitors reach the Circuit Bench, but the numbers are small: of fifty Circuit Judges appointed in 1986, only nine were solicitors. A Circuit Judge who is a barrister may be promoted to the High Court Bench, but this is not possible if he is a solicitor. When the Supreme Court Act 1981 was a Bill before Parliament, the Law Society fought an unsuccessful campaign to have this restriction removed, and in the course of the public dispute which led to the Marre Committee, the Law Society tried again to re-open the question of solicitors as High Court Judges. Surprisingly, perhaps, they found a supporter in Lord Donaldson, Master of the Rolls, who said

There have been most distinguished judges who started their professional lives as solicitors and then transferred to the Bar. Who could think that they would have been any less successful if they had first acquired the necessary experience at the Bar and then become solicitors? ... I should like to see this ineligibility removed, on the strict understanding that appointments would be purely on merit and that there would be no question of reverse discrimination.[2]

A second matter is the right of audience allowed to solicitors. As has already been mentioned, barristers have the virtual monopoly of conducting the more important civil cases in the High Court and the more important criminal cases in

---

[1] Fear of fusion seems to be an occupational disorder that is endemic on the Woolsack, for the previous Lord Chancellor, Lord Gardiner, suffered from the same neurosis: see his address to the Bentham Club in 1970, *Two lawyers or one?*

[2] In an interview printed in (1986) 1 *Counsel* at p. 20.

the Crown Court. Recently, both monopolies have been under attack. Following a much-publicised test case which proved inconclusive, a Practice Direction was issued in 1986 giving solicitors the right to make formal and unopposed applications in the High Court. Thus, for example, a solicitor instead of a barrister may now appear to read out in court a statement on behalf of his client when a libel action has been settled in the final stages.[1]

As far as right of audience in the Crown Court was concerned, an uneasy compromise was reached when the Crown Court was set up in 1971. One of the courts which the Crown Court replaced was Quarter Sessions, and in some Quarter Sessions solicitors as well as barristers were permitted to appear. Under the Courts Act 1971, the Lord Chancellor can make rules governing the right of solicitors to appear in the Crown Court, and the rules so made give solicitors the right of audience in those places and for the conduct of those matters where they had the right of audience in Quarter Sessions before the Crown Court came into being (see chapter 19, section i above). There matters rested peacefully until the advent of the Crown Prosecution Service (see page 232 above).[2]

The question then arose whether a Crown Prosecutor, who might be either a barrister or a solicitor, should be permitted to conduct his own cases in the Crown Court. The Bar was strongly opposed to this: not only did it stand to lose a lot of prosecution work, but a state of affairs in which prosecutions could be conducted by solicitors would almost certainly lead to a general right for solicitors to defend as well. In the end the issue was fudged. The Prosecution of Offences Act empowers the Lord Chancellor to permit Crown Prosecutors (whether barristers or solicitors) to appear in the Crown Court, but the Lord Chancellor (Lord Hailsham) and the Attorney-General (Sir Michael Havers) assured the Bar that only over their dead bodies would this be done.[3] It has already been argued that wider rights of audience for solicitors in the Crown Court would probably result in a more efficient use of public money, and it therefore seems unlikely that the Bar's present near-monopoly of Crown Court work will long survive the rigours of the present political climate, despite the efforts of sympathetic Attorney-Generals and Lord Chancellors to shelter it from the Thatcherite blast.

A third matter is the rule that forbids a client to brief a barrister directly, and

[1] Practice Direction [1986] 1 WLR 545. The test-case was *Abse* v. *Smith* [1986] QB 536.
[2] On this, as on much else, the Royal Commission on Legal Services (Benson Commission) (1979) Cmnd 7648 proposed no change; seven members wanted wider rights of audience, but seven was a minority.
[3] In the House of Lords, Lord Hailsham reminded everyone that he was a barrister, the father of two barristers, and devoted to his own branch of the profession. Sir Michael Havers attended a meeting of the Bar Committee considering the Bar's response to the proposal, and wrote to *The Times* saying 'I am sure that I do not need to emphasize that I personally remain wholly committed to the principle of a strong and independent Bar.' A remarkable double performance, considering both were Ministers of the Crown and so presumably were expected to offer the government impartial advice. Furthermore, the Attorney-General is also head of the Crown Prosecution Service and therefore not wholly without responsibility for its finance and morale.

requires him to do so through a solicitor. At one time barristers were free to accept briefs direct: the present rule was laid down by the Bar Committee (the predecessor of the Bar Council) in 1888. Since the rule was invented it has been a serious breach of professional etiquette for barristers to deal directly with clients, for which it has been known for barristers to be disbarred. The rule has some slight advantages for the Bar. It preserves the peace of the Temple against importunate visits or telephone-calls from the great unwashed and, given the quaint custom that barristers cannot sue for their fees, it usually ensures that they eventually get paid. The real winners from this restrictive practice, however, are solicitors. If somebody wants expert legal advice which only a barrister can give him, he has to obtain it via a solicitor, who naturally extracts a toll on the way. In the days when solicitors were mainly general practitioners and rarely had specialist knowledge, this enriched solicitors without doing any harm to the Bar. But now that solicitors do specialise, particularly in London, and are free to advertise the fact, the rule creates a risk that clients who need specialist advice will take their trade to a specialist solicitor rather than a specialist barrister in order to avoid paying twice. The rule has already been abandoned by the Bar as far as overseas clients are concerned: these may now approach a barrister directly. In recent years, the Bar has used the threat to abandon the rule altogether as a bargaining counter when the Law Society has showed signs of upsetting other aspects of the overall work-sharing scheme, and it is likely that any big alteration in the rights of audience in the higher courts or the eligibility for judicial appointments would be coupled with direct access by clients to the Bar.

Both the Bar and the Law Society claim that the higher public interest is served by the existence of two separate professions, as well as by as many of the restrictive rules as they are currently anxious to defend. At the AGM of the Bar in 1976 Sir Peter Rawlinson (now Lord Rawlinson) even claimed that the liberty of subject actually depended upon the continued existence of a divided profession.[1] We may well ask, however, whether the whole business is anything more than a demarcation dispute similar to the celebrated issue in the shipyards of whether carpenters or metal workers should have the right to drill holes through panels consisting of both wood and metal.

If we look at all this without the froth of polemics there seem to be four main arguments in favour of the present arrangements. The first is that when it comes to a law-suit there is an advantage in the case being presented by a person who can take a fresh view of the evidence. In working up a case a solicitor may lose objectivity in outlook; when you know your client and are quite certain that he is telling the truth it may become difficult to realise that a court may see the matter in a different light. In litigation the most important faculty, from the viewpoint of the client's interest, is ability to forecast what a court will do. In fact, the law itself

---

[1] He is quoted in Hazell, *The Bar on trial* (1979) p. 170. The plausibility of the claim is reduced in that the Bar has made the same claim for jury trial, the right of silence, and most other things in the legal system that are old and apparently irrational.

can be described as the basis of predictions of what judges will say and do. The best estimate of the probable course of a case can be made by a person who looks at it in an impersonal way. But if the greater efficiency of separate persons to prepare and present a case is admitted, this does not settle the question, for we must consider the cost, and whether the litigant should be forced to pay for a first-class service when he would prefer to pay less for one which is only second class. Looking at matters from the solicitor's angle there seem to be three types of case.

(1) There are the ordinary cases in magistrates' courts and county courts in which solicitors are accustomed to appear. Advocacy must of course be done by a solicitor in person and not by an unadmitted member of his staff and that brings in the question of cost. Where, as in London and some other places, there are junior counsel not yet established in practice who are glad to take briefs at low fees, it may be cheaper for the client if counsel is briefed; the solicitor does not himself have to waste hours in waiting about but can send a clerk to 'hold the brief', and in some simple cases the barrister is permitted to do it all on his own without anyone in attendance. It is allowable for a solicitor to whom a legal aid case is assigned to take in a counsel provided that the total cost is not more than it would have been if the solicitor had taken the case himself.

(2) There are cases that a solicitor knows he could handle perfectly well but which he is not allowed to take. Undefended divorce used to be in this category before divorce became a county court matter. There are still criminal matters which could well be handled by solicitors. When a solicitor has appeared in a magistrates' court and his client appeals to the Crown Court after a conviction or is committed to the Crown Court for sentence, the solicitor is allowed to take the case in the Crown Court; presumably he can do it quite as well before the Circuit Judge sitting with magistrates in the Crown Court as he did before other magistrates at the original hearing. Yet he is not permitted to take the case if the Crown Court hears it at first instance rather than on appeal or after committal for sentence. It may be said that solicitors do not at present have any experience of advocacy before juries following pleas of not guilty, but of course if you are not allowed to do something you cannot possibly have experience of doing it. There is little doubt that if solicitors were allowed to appear in a wider range of criminal proceedings there would be some saving of cost, mainly to the advantage of the legal aid fund.

(3) There are the more difficult cases. Of course it sometimes happens that a solicitor who has spent a long time over an involved case is in a better position to present it, and then he may have the mortification of seeing counsel floundering badly. In such a case the solicitor will nearly always be in court whilst the case is heard, and he must in practice spend nearly as much time over the case as he would do if he were able to conduct it altogether. Here the use of counsel does put up the cost, but probably it is generally worth it on the basis that counsel is a specialist in presenting cases.

The second argument for the present arrangements is said to be that the integrity and quality of our judges is largely a consequence of having a separate Bar. It is not suggested that barristers are more honourable than solicitors for there are not grounds for such a supposition.[1] The issues are far more subtle than integrity as meaning legally permissible as opposed to legally wrongful actions. The conduct by advocates in cases before the courts calls for the observance of standards and frankness. Thus, in dealing with legal points an advocate should cite relevant precedents whether their bearing is for or against his case. On issues of fact there is a well-understood distinction between concealing evidence and not asking questions of a witness that might result in unwelcome answers. Proceedings in the higher courts are conducted on the basis that barristers understand these things and observe the proprieties. 'Integrity' thus denotes reliability in pursuing and adhering to a particular pattern of behaviour in the highly conventional setting of a particular system of judges and law courts. Obviously 'integrity' in this sense is more easily ensured by having a small number of persons engaged in these activities, by their close association with each other and with the judges through their Inns and Bar messes and by the general conditions under which they work as independent professional men who are isolated from the lay clients. A small and closely-knit Bar is also an advantage when persons have to be considered for appointment as judges; indeed Henry Cecil regarded this as being of major importance for what he calls 'sieving' candidates.[2] What these views really amount to is a belief in the essential goodness of the present system of Bench and Bar; there is much to be said in favour of this but it is too cosy a view. The size of the judiciary has increased very greatly in recent years (see chapter 31), and so has that of the Bar (see chapter 28). An expanding system cannot be expected to work on a basis of 'We at the top know everyone in our field and can settle promotions and appointments by having a word with each other.'

Another reason for maintaining a separate Bar is connected with the 'cab rank principle' (see page 339). Where there is only one profession, a firm of lawyers (such as solicitors in England) is free to decline to act for a particular person; someone who is unpopular for social, political, racial or other grounds, or who wants to attack some trade or industrial interests, may find that the legal firms of great reputation all regret that they cannot help him because of the interests of their other clients. In our system such a person can always have the service of counsel, and even eminent counsel if he can afford it; the 'cab rank principle' means that counsel who appear on one side might just as well have been on the other side if their brief had got in first. In criminal courts a small number of counsel may be found sharing the work, sometimes prosecuting and sometimes

[1] Henry Cecil (H. C. Leon, a former county court judge), *The English judge* (1970) p. 14, considered the incidence of disciplinary action against barristers and solicitors and found no significant difference.
[2] *The English judge* p. 14ff. He thought no judicial appointment should go to solicitors.

defending. This is undoubtedly a merit, although that does not imply that every restrictive practice within the existing state of affairs must be maintained.

The main argument in favour of the present arrangements is usually said to be the need for specialisation. The legal profession, like every other learned profession, needs its specialists, and they must be available to all who need them. A divided profession is said to ensure this, and the job-sharing and the restrictive practices are said to be necessary to keep in existence two separate professions. To some extent the top end of the Bar meets the need for specialists, but to say that having a separate Bar is the best and only way in which specialist skills can be made available is absurd. The process of specialisation occurs among solicitors as well as at the Bar; the practice of some firms is virtually confined to a few matters, whilst in others one partner is a specialist. For consultative work there is no reason why the specialist should be a barrister, or even have any legal qualifications at all. A layman who wants legal advice may have to go to a solicitor in some cases, whilst in others he can consult other people such as tax experts and accountants. Nor can the Bar be described as a remotely efficient machine for the production of well-qualified experts. Medical, engineering and other specialists are people who first acquired general practitioner qualifications, and then specialised. A young barrister starts off taking briefs as soon as he is allowed to do so, that is after a course containing a few practical exercises and a mere six months in chambers: a quarter of the time that a solicitor must spend in articles. Beginners in advocacy, whether barristers or solicitors, are often unbelievably bad: courts try to be kind to them, for a young practitioner cannot learn the work except by doing it. In time he will either drop out or become competent. It is absurd to keep up the pretence that all barristers are specialists when a large proportion of them are less experienced and less competent than the solicitor who briefs them. For all barristers to have a credible standing as specialists, the legal profession needs restructuring to provide a body of general practitioners and specialists who would be drawn from those practitioners. In terms of our existing system it would mean that all lawyers would have to start as solicitors and that at an appropriate stage in their experience they would cease to be GPs and become barristers. A system of that kind would be compatible with the Bar being a separate body, centred on the Inns of Court and Bar messes, and with professional rules and usages much as at present; nor would it then seem ridiculous if some kinds of legal work and some appointments were reserved for barristers. In 1986 this was one of the ideas which the Law Society put forward in a discussion document which was widely circulated.[1]

In a very hostile response the Bar castigated all their proposals.[2] 'They are not in the public interest. They are self-contradictory, contain new and unjustifiable

[1] *Lawyers and the courts: Time for some changes: A discussion paper issued by the Law Society's Contentious Business Committee* (January 1986).
[2] *Lawyers and the courts: The response of the Bar to a discussion paper issued by the Law Society's Contentious Business Committee* (June 1986).

restrictive practices and are ill thought out and unspecific in respects which are fundamental to any sensible discussion of them.' But the best of the specific arguments which the Bar could find to hurl against this particular proposal were that solicitors' firms would be reluctant to take as articled clerks people they thought likely to decamp to a specialist Bar, and that a person's self-removal to the Bar would come at a time when he had acquired family commitments which would make him reluctant to uproot himself. This is not very convincing, particularly when set against the inconvenience which the present system causes a person who has just graduated from university, who must often choose between two professions before he is sure of his suitability for one rather than the other, and who may often be forced to take an expensive leap in the dark.

If the Bar and the solicitors were fused, it is probable that there would be a slight reduction in cost, but perhaps the saving would not be as drastic as some people think.[1] Specialisation would still be needed. Either firms would become much larger, so that the more common forms of specialised work would be done by a particular partner, or else the specialist in one firm would be 'briefed' by another firm. If the total number of lawyers is to remain about the same, and their standard of living is to remain about the same, the cost to litigants will hardly change. There may be a certain saving in overhead costs when a particular type of legal work is done on a larger scale; at present most solicitors regard litigation as rather a nuisance if litigious matters only come to their office occasionally. Large firms in a combined profession might effect some further economy, but this would not solve the problem of the cost of litigation; in any case the payments to witnesses and other heavy out-of-pocket expenses would not be affected by such a reorganisation of the legal profession.

When the Royal Commission on Legal Services was set up in 1976, it was widely expected that big changes in the structure of the profession would be recommended. They were not. Indeed, 'For those favouring radical reform of our creaking and increasingly costly legal system, the Benson Commission was an expensive waste of time.'[2] Since then, the fact that the Royal Commission recommended no major changes has been repeatedly used by the Bar as an argument in favour of no changes at all. Time will tell whether the Marre Committee takes a similarly conservative line.

[1] M. Zander, *Lawyers and the public interest* (1968) chapter 13, thinks there would be a saving in cost as well as other advantages.
[2] *The Times*, leading article, 17 July 1985.

31

JUDGES

By long usage, the expression 'the superior judges' or simply 'the judges' usually means the judges of the High Court, Court of Appeal and the Law Lords.[1] It is these judges who are the centre of interest when we think of 'the courts', the development of the law and the administration of justice. For many years there have been other judges. Before 1971 there were county court judges, the Chancellors of the Chancery Courts of Lancaster and Durham, the Recorder and Common Serjeant of the City of London, Recorders of boroughs and a number of legal chairmen of Quarter Sessions, together with deputy recorders and deputy chairmen, but they were not regarded as forming a corps of lower-tier judges.[2] There was a system of county courts, but other courts below the level of the High Court were fragmented and largely governed by piece-meal legislation. The Courts Act 1971 not only restructured the courts but also rationalised the lower judiciary (see chapter 19(i) above). There is now a single rank of full-time lesser judges, namely Circuit Judges, taking civil and criminal work, supplemented by new-style Recorders who are part-time professional judges. The qualifications for appointment were discussed in the last section.

In the years before the Second World War a serious problem was insufficient judicial strength. It was the practice for statute to lay down the maximum number of judges that could be appointed. Thus the Supreme Court of Judicature (Consolidation) Act 1925 provided that the Chancery Division should have six puisne judges, the King's Bench seventeen, and the Probate Divorce and Admiralty Division two puisne judges; the Court of Appeal was to have five ordinary judges. In the 1930s the courts were working badly with delays and general inefficiency, but the official inquiries of the time make curious reading.[3] Although many observers thought the root of the problem was that there were not

---

[1] An excellent full length study is *Judges on trial*, by Simon Shetreet (1976). Very readable discourses are Sir Brian McKenna, 'The Judge and the common man', (1969) 32 Mod. LR 603, Henry Cecil (H. C. Leon, a former county court judge), *The English judge*, (1970) and D. Pannick, *Judges* (1987). B. Abel-Smith and R. Stevens, *In search of justice* (1968) deals with some of the issues in a trenchant way at pp. 166–96. A Report, *The judiciary* (1972), by a sub-committee of *Justice* is also interesting.

[2] For details of how these various judges were appointed see the 7th edition of this book, pp. 456–57.

[3] Reports of the Business of the Courts Committee, (1933) Cmd 4265, (1934) Cmd 4471, (1936) Cmd 5066 and the Report of the Royal Commission on the Despatch of Business at Common Law, Cmd 5065.

enough judges, no one at an official level seemed to be prepared to accept that obvious fact, and the assumption was that the quality of the judges would be reduced if the number was increased.[1]

The favoured remedy for speeding the course of justice was reform of the rules of procedure – which needed reform anyway, but was not enough to solve the problem. Eventually the need for more judges was recognised. Beginning in 1944, there was statute after statute which raised the maximum number of High Court Judges, so that by 1965 it had risen to 63. The number of county court judges was also raised, so that the maximum of 60 before the war had become 80 by 1955.[2] With a rising volume of work, it became obvious that an adequate judicial strength should not depend on revision by statute, which meant that an increase would not be put forward until several years after the need had become acute, and in 1968 a new scheme was introduced under which the statute laid down a maximum number of judges, but the government was given power to raise the maximum by Order in Council. This power was exercised on a number of occasions, and then as far as the High Court and the Court of Appeal were concerned the Supreme Court Act 1981 began the process again with a new statutory maximum, which the government once again has power to override. In 1986 the number of Law Lords stood at 9 (with a possible maximum of 11), the number of Lords Justices of Appeal was 22 (with a possible maximum of 23) and the number of High Court Judges stood at its maximum of 79. In November 1987 one of the first acts of the new Lord Chancellor, Lord Mackay, was to announce that the maximum number of judges in the Court of Appeal would be raised to 28 and the number of High Court Judges to 85. As far as appointments to the lower judiciary are concerned, the maximum numbers are simply determined by the executive. The Courts Act 1971 provides that the maximum number of Circuit Judges shall be such as may be determined from time to time by the Lord Chancellor with the concurrence of the Minister for the Civil Service. In 1976 there were 268, and ten years later the number had risen to 391. Recorders are paid fees on a piecework basis and there is no procedure for fixing the maximum number of Recorders who may be appointed. In 1976 there were 328; ten years later there were 540. The Courts Act 1971 and the Supreme Court Act 1981 also contain provisions for temporary appointments to help out the regular judges when there is pressure of work. Retired High Court and Appeal Court Judges, if willing, can be called back to sit in the High Court and the Court of Appeal. Barristers of standing to be appointed as High Court Judges may be temporarily appointed as Deputy High Court Judges. Retired Circuit Judges, High Court Judges and Appeal Court Judges, if willing, can be called back to sit in the Crown Court or the county court – for which purpose they then go by the title of 'Deputy Circuit Judge'. And barristers or solicitors qualified for appointment as

---

[1] The most instructive discussion is in chapter 10 of the Report of the Royal Commission on the Despatch of Business at Common Law, (1936) Cmd 5065.
[2] Further details of the gradual increase will be found in earlier editions of this book.

Recorders may be employed as Assistant Recorders – a temporary post which is nowadays used by the Lord Chancellor's Department to try out people to see if they are suitable for a permanent appointment.

All the superior judges (that is the judges of the House of Lords, the Court of Appeal and the High Court), Circuit Judges and Recorders are appointed by the Crown[1] on the recommendation of the Lord Chancellor. The Prime Minister nominates the Lords Justices of Appeal, the Lord Chief Justice, the Master of the Rolls and the President of the Family Division (although it is commonly assumed that the Prime Minister is guided by the Lord Chancellor). In the old days when judicial posts were few in number and the Lord Chancellor could personally assess the field for every post himself, he acted largely on the basis of what he himself had heard. With increasing numbers of appointments, people began to wonder how he managed, and there were dark rumours about secret files, blacklists, and so forth. To dispel the sense of mystery, in 1986 the Lord Chancellor's Department published a booklet entitled *Judicial Appointment* which is available for all to read. From this we learn that within the Lord Chancellor's Department there is a body of officials called the Judicial Appointments Group. Potential appointees come to their notice either because they write in and say they are interested in a judicial appointment, or because their names are mentioned by judges and 'senior members of the profession' with whom the senior officials in the Judicial Appointments Group regularly consult. Files are opened on these candidates – and remain open when they have obtained a position. Into this file will go factual information about the candidate, and opinions which have been expressed about him. At some point, a person under consideration for appointment is likely to be interviewed, and this will put more information about him on file. The part of the information which is purely factual is open for the candidate to see, but the opinions which have been expressed about him are usually given in strict confidence, and these he is never shown. However, the Lord Chancellor or the senior members of the Judicial Appointments Group are usually willing to give judges and would-be judges general advice about their prospects, and this is likely to show an applicant in what standing he is held.

For centuries it was the case that there was no regular system of promotion. The Court of Appeal and the House of Lords were filled by promotions from below, but there was little movement from the lower judiciary to the High Court, and an appointment to the County Court bench – and more recently to a Circuit Judgeship – was regarded as the end of the road.[2] In the last ten years this has

---

[1] The Recorder of the City of London has always been appointed to his office by the City, but he is appointed by the Crown to exercise judicial functions, thus reconciling the privileges of the City with the general principle of Crown appointments. The Common Serjeant is a Crown appointment. The Courts Act 1971 makes the holders of these offices Circuit Judges.

[2] Only one county court judge was elevated to the High Court bench from the creation of county courts in 1846 until after the Second World War. Professor Jackson disapproved of judicial promotion and in earlier editions of this book he defended the former state of affairs.

greatly changed. The Lord Chancellor's Department has made it plain that it expects the people who are appointed Recorders to have proved themselves as Assistant Recorders, and Circuit Judges to have proved their worth as Recorders or Assistant Recorders. Whilst the majority of appointments to the High Court Bench are still made from persons eminent in practice at the Bar, most of them have been new-style Recorders, and there are a number of High Court Judges in office who have been promoted from the Circuit Bench. There are signs that the judiciary is developing a career structure with a promotional ladder, like other areas of public service; although no one puts his foot on the first rung until he has reached his middle age.

The Lord Chancellor, who is nominated by the Prime Minister, occupies an anomalous position. For some purposes he is the head of the judiciary and his powers are extensive. Not only is he in charge of judicial appointments, but he sits as a Law Lord in the House of Lords to hear cases and determine cases in so far as his other official duties permit. Yet he is invariably a member of the cabinet. As a cabinet minister, the Lord Chancellor holds office upon the usual political terms, which means that ordinarily he will vacate office if the government changes. Hence when there is a change of government, the new Prime Minister will have to fill the office of Lord Chancellor just as he has to fill the office of Chancellor of the Exchequer, Home Secretary and so on. The office of Lord Chancellor was originally that of secretary to the King and legal qualifications are still not required by law, but it is nowadays unthinkable that we should have a non-lawyer in this office. The choice of a Lord Chancellor must in practice be made from among those barristers who have adequate standing, but within this range the choice is governed by political considerations; the Prime Minister wants someone who will perform the judicial functions adequately and who will also be a welcome addition to the cabinet. A barrister who has rendered service to a political party may find his reward in being made Lord Chancellor when his party gets into office.[1]

On various occasions, however, the Prime Minister of the day has chosen to appoint as Lord Chancellor a judge who has not been particularly active in politics: Lord Sankey, appointed in 1929, was then a Lord Justice of Appeal, and Lord Maugham (appointed in 1938), Lord Simonds (appointed in 1951) and Lord Mackay (appointed in 1987) were Law Lords at the time of their appointment.[2] An ordinary judgeship is a permanent appointment, whereas he who achieves the Lord Chancellorship may rejoice in his peerage, his salary of £79,400, and his great dignity, only to find that his political party is turned out of

---

[1] Various authors have written *Lives of the Lord Chancellors*: Lord Campbell (1848) wrote one covering the period from the earliest periods down to George IV. Atlay's *Victorian Chancellors* (1906) takes up the record, and Professor R. F. V. Heuston continues it with his two volumes of *Lives of the Lord Chancellors* (1964) and (1987) – both mines of information on the exercise of the Lord Chancellor's powers, notably on the appointment of judges. All contain as much political as legal history.

[2] Lord Mackay, uniquely, was a Scots lawyer who had been a Scottish judge, and had been promoted to the House of Lords from the Scottish bench.

office and that he is a virtual nobody. As an ex-Lord Chancellor, who has held the key to judicial appointments, it is unthinkable for him to go back to practice at the Bar. To compensate for these inconveniences, ex-Lord Chancellors are entitled to a substantial pension, and by convention they are expected to do something towards earning it by sitting from time to time in the Judicial Committee of the Privy Council and in the House of Lords in its judicial capacity. Not all do this. When Lord Kilmuir ceased to be Lord Chancellor in 1962 he later accepted a commercial appointment, choosing not to draw his pension. Lord Dilhorne, who ceased to be Lord Chancellor in 1964, continued to sit and was later appointed a Lord of Appeal in Ordinary (a Law Lord).

The statutory qualifications are that a Circuit Judge must be a barrister of at least ten years' standing or a Recorder who has held that office for at least five years; a Recorder must be a barrister or solicitor of at least ten years' standing; a puisne judge of the High Court must be a barrister of at least ten years' standing. A barrister of at least fifteen years' standing, or an existing High Court Judge, qualifies for appointment as a Lord Justice of Appeal (i.e. a judge of the Court of Appeal). The qualifications for appointment as a Lord Justice of Appeal also qualify for appointment as Lord Chief Justice, Master of the Rolls, or President of the Family Division. The Lords of Appeal in Ordinary (the Law Lords) must be appointed from barristers or advocates of fifteen years' standing or from persons who have held high judicial office in England, Scotland or Northern Ireland for two years. Since most barristers begin to practice when they are still young, and judges are never appointed from those under forty and quite often from those over fifty, the requisite standing at the Bar is usually attained many years before there is any chance of judicial appointment.

The House of Commons Disqualification Act 1957 contains a list of judicial offices which disqualify for membership of the House of Commons, and the Courts Act 1971 adds Circuit Judges to that list. There is no disqualification for Recorders, but their court sittings are arranged so that no Recorder who is an MP sits judicially in his own constituency.[1] All the superior judges receive a formal summons to attend the House of Lords 'to advise'; but this is a survival from ancient times and nowadays they would not attend unless their advice was sought on some specific matter, and this is something which is not likely to happen.[2] The Law Lords are life peers, and the Lord Chancellor is always a peer. Other judges may receive peerages, it being the usual practice to give a peerage to the Lord Chief Justice and the Master of the Rolls. In the old days the peerages so

---

[1] Before 1971 the term Recorder meant the person who was chairman of Quarter Sessions for a borough. Old-style Recorders could be MPs provided they did not sit for the borough in which they sat as Recorder.

[2] The judges used regularly to attend the House of Lords to advise when it was hearing appeals, in the days before the present judicial House of Lords came into being, when the legislative House of Lords also acted as the court of final appeal, and the practice continued from time to time until the early years of this century. The judges used also to attend at the trial of peers; the last case was in 1936, and peers lost their right to be tried before the House of Lords in 1948.

given were hereditary, but since the Life Peerages Act 1958 it has been the practice for life peerages to be given.

These legal rules about disqualification from membership of the House of Commons are supplemented by conventions about the public conduct and activities of judges. Much of the conventional pattern is illustrated by the position of the Lords of Appeal, the Lord Chief Justice and other judges who are peers; as peers they have in law the right to attend the House of Lords in its legislative (that is, non-judicial) capacity and there to do anything that any other peers can do. By convention they may take part in debates provided that they avoid 'political' matters. Generally speaking law reform, whether of the substantive law or of procedure and evidence, is regarded as 'non-political', and so is the use or disuse of particular punishments, despite the way in which in the past so many of the judges and so many Conservative ladies appeared to have similar views about the desirability of floggings and hangings. In 1966 Lord Parker, then Lord Chief Justice, introduced a bill in the Lords to require the registration of buildings used for entertainments, dancing and playing games and to confer powers of control on the local authorities: something which was noted with comment in *The Times*.[1]

By convention, judges who are not peers also avoid making public pronounce-ments on matters of public controversy. This convention is fortified by what are usually referred to as the 'Kilmuir Rules'.[2] These are a directive which the then Lord Chancellor, Lord Kilmuir, issued to the judges in 1955, in which he warned them of the need to avoid such pronouncements, and instructed them that if they wished to make any extra-judicial utterances they should seek his approval first. Most judges are content to abide by this: few have chosen to break the convention, and it is said that whenever the Lord Chancellor has asked the judiciary whether they wish the rules to be changed the overwhelming response has been to say no. The convention exists to make sure that the judiciary is seen to be non-partisan and independent. As Mr Bernard Levin vividly put it,

a visibly impartial and independent system of law is crucial to a free society. But this includes an essential element of remoteness, even of inhumanity, in the judges and their work. The only excuse for a judge with opinions is that he refrains from expressing them; the moment he steps into controversy, or even indicates that he has views, all respect for the law itself will collapse, as the public abruptly realises that the august figure, wigged and robed, who embodies the rule of law and its truly vital function as the foundation of our liberties, is only a daft old geezer with funny clothes who thinks that pubs should be made illegal and that all homosexuals should have their whatsits cut off.[3]

In 1986 a strident challenge to the convention was issued by Judge Pickles, a Circuit Judge whose conduct of trials has attracted the attention of the Court of

[1] 25 May 1966.
[2] The text of the Rules is set out in [1986] *Public Law* 383.
[3] Commenting on the affair of Judge Pickles in *The Times* 28 February 1986.

Appeal on more than one occasion.[1] In a series of newspaper articles and broadcasts and then in a book, he gave the world his views on a large number of topics – including his views on Lord Hailsham, the Lord Chancellor, whom he described as a 'quixotic dictator'. Lord Hailsham ignored the attacks; indeed he could hardly do anything else unless he was prepared to remove Judge Pickles from office, which he could hardly do for something as comparatively trivial as a breach of the Kilmuir Rules. This provokes the thought that there is no sense in having rules if there is nothing that can be done to enforce them; nor is there much need for them if in practice almost everyone who is to be subjected to them is going to behave in conformity with them even if no rule is laid down. One of the first things that Lord Mackay did when he became Lord Chancellor in 1987 was to announce that the Kilmuir Rules were to be relaxed.

There is a substantial difference in the terms upon which the superior judges hold office and the terms applicable to Circuit Judges and Recorders. All the superior judges other than the Lord Chancellor hold office 'during good behaviour subject to a power of removal by Her Majesty on an address presented to Her Majesty by both Houses of Parliament', this being the provision of the Supreme Court Act 1981 which ultimately derives from the Act of Settlement 1701. There may be a petition to either House, or the matter may originate with a member, there being some authority for saying that it must be in the Commons. The charge against the judge must be formulated and he must be given an opportunity to answer the charges. As only one judge (and he an Irish one)[2] has been removed since the Act of Settlement there is little authority for stating the procedure, and the interpretation of the statute is by no means certain.[3]

On any interpretation, however, the provisions do what they were intended to do when they were first formulated in the Act of Settlement: that is, they secure the independence of the superior judges from the executive. The judges are not protected in any way from change made by statute; Parliament can alter the terms upon which they hold office, alter their salaries, or make any other change. The cabinet system of government has for many years meant that the distinction between executive and legislature is thoroughly blurred. The cabinet, considered as a group of ministers of the Crown, cannot interfere with the judges; the cabinet considered as the leaders of a political party with a sufficient majority could

---

[1] In 1977 he was criticised for plea-bargaining (*R*. v. *Atkinson*, 67 Cr Ap. R 200), and in 1986 the Court of Appeal described his overbearing behaviour towards a defence counsel as 'deplorable' (*The Times* 27 June 1986).

[2] Sir Jonah Barrington, judge of the Irish Admiralty Court, who with immense difficulty was removed in 1830 for helping himself to money which suitors had paid into court.

[3] The statute is obscure and could be read in any one of three senses: (a) the Queen can dismiss a judge *either* for misbehaviour, *or* where Parliament has presented an address for his removal (for misbehaviour or anything else); (b) the Queen can only dismiss a judge when he is *both* guilty of misbehaviour *and* the subject of an address for his removal; (c) the Queen can only remove a judge who is the subject of an address from Parliament; and if an address is presented, it matters not whether he has really misbehaved, because a judge who is the subject of an address is deemed to be guilty of misbehaviour.

interfere with the judges by causing the passing of appropriate legislation. By convention a judge may not be criticised in Parliament unless there is a substantive motion;[1] apart from such a motion a decision of the courts may be criticised, but only upon the supposition that the complaint is about the law and not about the conduct of the judge. Circuit Judges and Recorders have no such security of tenure. The Courts Act 1971 provides that 'The Lord Chancellor may, if he thinks fit, remove a Circuit Judge from office on the ground of incapacity or misbehaviour', and a Recorder is removable on those grounds and also for failure to comply with the requirements of his appointment as to when he would be available to sit in court. The distinction is obvious when we consider what can happen if either type of judge is convicted of a serious criminal offence. In the case of a Circuit Judge or Recorder, the Lord Chancellor will formally ask him for an explanation, and if no adequate explanation is forthcoming he will give him the sack forthwith: as he did in 1983 when, incredibly, a Circuit Judge was convicted of smuggling 125 litres of whisky and 9,000 cigarettes in company with a stall-holder from the East End of London.[2] If a superior judge should commit an offence there is no disciplinary power that the Lord Chancellor or the Lord Chief Justice can exercise. There may be consultation at a high level to decide whether he should be asked to resign, but his statutory security against being dismissed except on an address from both Houses of Parliament effectively prevents him being removed for reasons which are good as well as for reasons which are bad.

The present rules governing the dismissal of judges undoubtedly ensure the independence of the judiciary inasmuch as they prevent judges being sacked by the government of the day for politically inconvenient decisions. This is obviously most desirable. But it is arguable that they go too far, and also prevent effective discipline being exercised over judges who are guilty of what is recognisable as plain misconduct by anyone of any political persuasion. Where judicial misbehaviour involves deciding a case the wrong way, the appeal system generally enables the right decision to be reached in the end;[3] but not enough can be done to correct the bad effect that misbehaviour by a judge has on members of the public who are not involved in the particular case in which it occurred. Misbehaviour by a judge, whether it takes place on the bench or off the bench, undermines public confidence in the administration of justice, and also damages

---

[1] In 1965 there was a motion deploring the action of Mr Justice Stamp who had committed a man to prison for contempt in the course of a wardship case heard in chambers. Mr Justice Stamp was following established practice but there was much public criticism and the Rules were altered to ensure that there must be an announcement in open court.

[2] *The Times* 6 December 1983. The judge in question was a former Conservative MP who as a legislator had the habit of calling for severity for wrongdoers: see page 87 above. In practice a Circuit Judge or Recorder who is prosecuted for a serious offence is more likely to resign well in advance of his conviction – as in the case of the Recorder who in November 1984 was convicted of fraud and theft: *The Times* 23 November 1984.

[3] But not always; for example, there is no prosecution appeal if a trial judge quite improperly directs a jury to acquit a criminal (see chapter 21).

public respect for the law of the land; if nothing is seen to be done about it, the damage goes unrepaired. This must be so when the judge commits a serious criminal offence and remains in office. If those who enforce the law are seen to break it when they get the chance, why should anyone else be expected to keep it if he thinks he can get away with it? The case of judges who are convicted of blood-alcohol offences illustrates the point. In 1969 Lord Justice Russell (as he then was)[1] was convicted of driving a motor-vehicle when he had drunk so much that witnesses described him as 'staggering'. Like most defendants on a breathalyser charge he was only fined and disqualified; but the offence is serious enough to carry the possibility of imprisonment for a first offence, and some drivers have been sent to prison in similar circumstances. Despite some adverse public comment he did not resign; as he was a superior judge there was no practical possibility of dismissing him. His example made it morally impossible for the Lord Chancellor thereafter to dismiss any Circuit Judges who similarly offended, of whom there have since been a number,[2] and it also seems to have led him to abandon his previous policy of dismissing magistrates who were convicted of drink-driving offences. Of course it was partly because of ambivalent public attitudes to drunken driving that all this was possible. But there can be little doubt that the example of a procession of judges being convicted of the offence and staying in office to judge others reinforced the public attitudes which Parliament was actively trying to change. It would surely not undermine the independence of the judiciary in the least if, on conviction of any criminal offence punishable with imprisonment, a judge was automatically disqualified from office. Scarcely less damaging than when a judge gets convicted of a crime is the situation that arises when a judge behaves so badly when trying a case, or makes some public remark which is so outrageously biased, that the public or a section of it thereafter doubts his balance and impartiality; as when a High Court Judge threatened to lock a jury up all night if they did not reach a verdict in time to enable him to catch a train which would get him to a dinner engagement,[3] or when another judge described the law which legalised homosexual behaviour in private as 'a buggers' charter which enabled perverts and homosexuals to pursue their perversions in private',[4] or when another judge interrupted defence counsel's closing speech by saying 'Oh God!', putting his head on his hands, and groaning aloud until he had finished.[5]

[1] Lord Russell of Killowen as he later became; despite this incident he was promoted to be a Law Lord, and in that capacity sat on various criminal appeals, including at least one in a blood-alcohol case.
[2] One Circuit Judge was convicted in 1973 and a High Court Judge was convicted in 1975. In answer to a Parliamentary question on 18 December 1986, the Attorney-General said that three Circuit Judges had been convicted since 1984.
[3] See *R.* v. *McKenna* [1960] 1 QB 411.
[4] Mr Justice Melford Stevenson; who for this outburst was publicly reprimanded by the Lord Chancellor (*The Daily Telegraph* 5 July 1978). This judge also had the possibly unique distinction of being reversed three times by the Court of Appeal in one week, in the course of which his behaviour in court was severely criticised by that court twice in the same day: *The Times* 20 February 1976.
[5] *R.* v. *Hircock* [1970] 1 QB 67.

At present the most that ever happens in this sort of case is that the judge receives a public rebuke from the Lord Chancellor, and is quietly moved into less sensitive work for a while. More usually nothing visible happens at all. If this sort of behaviour is repeated, the offending judge ought surely to be removed from office, whatever his judicial rank, and it is impossible to see how removing him could be said to undermine the independence of the judiciary. The matter must be kept in proportion. The standards of judicial behaviour, both on and off the bench, are normally extremely high. But it is because standards are usually so high that these lamentable lapses are so newsworthy. And being newsworthy, they create a bad public impression far in excess of the size of the problem in statistical terms.

People generally think of judges as ancient men. This is hardly surprising, because there was no retiring age for superior judges until 1959. County court judges had long been subject to a retiring age of 72 with possible extensions to 75, and this was adopted for Circuit Judges under the Courts Act 1971. Justices of the peace were subjected to a retiring age in 1949 (see chapter 33(iii)). A superior judge could be removed on an address if he became incapacitated by senility, but apart from this there was nothing to stop him sitting in extreme old age – and some did. For many years a retiring age for superior judges was staunchly resisted. In his evidence before the Royal Commission on the Despatch of Business at Common Law[1] Lord Hewart, the Lord Chief Justice, opposed it on the grounds that a retiring age would deprive the bench of such men as Mr Justice Avory – who continued to sit on the bench until a few days before his death at the age of 83 with his faculties unimpaired. One of the greatest judges there has ever been in the common law countries was Oliver Wendell Holmes of the American Supreme Court, who was nearly 90 when he retired from the bench in 1932.[2]

Unfortunately a retiring age is bound to exclude some men who have years of work before them; but the sound argument for a retiring age is that judges must inspire confidence, and that on the whole people do not care to be judged by those who belong to a generation that is generally inactive. Under the Judicial Pensions Act 1959, superior judges were at last subjected to a retiring age of 75.[3] Their pensions are on a graduated scale, starting with one-quarter of the last annual salary in the case of a judge who retires after five years' service or less, and rising by annual increments of one-fortieth to a maximum of one-half of the last annual salary after fifteen years. A judge may elect to retire when he becomes 70, and he will then receive the graduated pension to which his length of service entitles him. Despite the introduction of a retiring age for superior judges, however, it is still true to say that as a body the judiciary is rather old. The retiring

[1] (1936) Cmd 5065.
[2] In England, Lord Halsbury is thought to hold the record when he sat at the age of 93 – by which time he was suffering from deafness: Heuston, *Lives of the Lord Chancellors* (1964) p. 77.
[3] The provision about the retiring age for High Court Judges and Lord Justices of Appeal is now contained in the Supreme Court Act 1981. The law relating to judicial pensions is consolidated in the Judicial Pensions Act 1981.

ages for both Circuit Judges and superior judges are between ten and fifteen years older than those found in most other careers, and partly as a result of this the average age of the full-time judiciary is about 60 and until recently, nearer 70 in the House of Lords.[1]

In modern times the impression of agedness was accentuated by the fact that the retiring age for superior judges did not apply to those who had been appointed before 1959, some of whom went on to sit long after it would have been sensible for them to retire. Lord Diplock, for example, continued to sit in the House of Lords until his death in 1985 at the age of 77, and for the last part of his time he was so ill he could barely speak. Lord Denning – that paragon of judges – persisted as Master of the Rolls into extreme old age until at 83 he had to resign in unfortunate circumstances.[2] Furthermore, there is no retiring age for Lord Chancellors: this permitted Lord Hailsham to continue until he was nearly 80 and physically infirm; and there is no age beyond which retired judges may not be brought back into temporary service as helpers-out in the Court of Appeal or courts below: this has enabled a number of notionally retired judges to keep on sitting until an advanced age.

A retiring age, and particularly a high one, is no guarantee against the problem of the judge whose faculties become dimmed at an earlier age. Over the years there have been a number of cases, the most famous being that of Mr Justice Stephen, a much-respected late Victorian judge, who suffered a stroke at the age of 56, progressively lost his mental grasp, and eventually had to resign in the face of mounting public criticism of his performance on the bench. When this sort of case arises, one of his seniors is usually able to have a quiet word with the judge and he is persuaded to resign. But this cannot always happen. For some considerable time before Lord Chief Justice Widgery resigned in 1980 he was visibly and distressingly half-senile, and as the office of Lord Chief Justice is vitally important, the whole administration of justice suffered as a result. Bearing in mind the fatefulness of the decisions that lie in a judge's hands, there is something to be said for requiring them to undergo periodic medical examinations.[3] Since 1973 the Lord Chancellor has had the power by statute to remove from office any superior judge who is so incapacitated by illness that he is unable to resign.

It is not usual for a judge to resign before the retiring age except where circumstances force him to do so. In 1970 Mr Justice Fisher resigned, having been a judge for only two-and-a-half years, in order to take up an appointment with a merchant bank at a substantially higher salary than he was receiving as a

---

[1] See J. A. G. Griffith, *The politics of the judiciary* (3rd ed. 1985) pp. 27–28.
[2] He took to writing popular books, in one of which he succeeded in libelling a group of jurors who proceeded to sue him. Unlike some of the judges who have stuck to the bench despite criminal convictions, he had the sense to realise that it was impossible for him to stay in office when he was the defendant in a civil action to which he had no defence. He tells the story movingly in *The closing chapter* (1983).
[3] See Dr Eliot Slater, 'The judicial process and the ascertainment of fact' (1961) 24 Mod. LR 723.

judge. Some lawyers, including Lord Dilhorne (an ex-Lord Chancellor) thought it was 'unprecedented and inexcusable' that a judge should relinquish his appointment in favour of one more attractive. A judge receives a knighthood and has much prestige, and these endure when he gives up his office. Further, if there should be grounds for thinking that anyone on the bench is negotiating with commercial interests for his future employment, that would seriously damage the reputation of the judiciary. On the other hand, if a man does accept a judgeship and finds that he has made a mistake, it seems quite unreasonable that he should be expected to stick it out until he can retire without comment. Leaving all questions of kindness to the judge aside, and thinking solely of the public, a judge who loathes his work is likely to do it badly. But emotions were aroused: since Bracton in the thirteenth century there has been something sacerdotal about the judiciary; it is not right to leave one's order unless there are compelling reasons.

The salaries of judges were at one time directly fixed by statute. The puisne judges were given £5,000 a year in 1832 and that remained unchanged until 1954. There was no income tax in 1832 but when that tax was introduced in 1842 there was no exemption for judges and they have always had to pay tax at the same rate as other people. The need for better pay for judges was apparent in the post-war years and in 1954 all salaries were raised, and further increases were given by the Judges Remuneration Act 1965. This Act provided for the pay of the superior judges to be increased in future by an Order in Council, subject to the approval of both Houses of Parliament. When the Courts Act 1971 created the rank of Circuit Judge, their pay was made 'such salary as may be determined by the Lord Chancellor with the consent of the Minister for the Civil Service', and in 1973 the system of the government determining the judges' pay without the intervention of Parliament was extended to the superior judges as well. Instead of a salary, Recorders are paid fees for the days they sit; these are also laid down by the Lord Chancellor with the approval of the Minister for the Civil Service. In setting judicial pay, the government is advised by an independent review body. In 1987, judicial salaries were as follows: Lord Chancellor £79,400; Lord Chief Justice £81,000; Law Lords and Master of the Rolls £74,750; Lords Justices, Vice-Chancellor, and the President of the Family Division £71,750; High Court Judges £65,000; Circuit Judges £43,000. The judges' salaries are charged upon the Consolidated Fund, the older constitutional law books explaining that this secures the payment of the judges even if Parliament does not meet. The point today is that the legislation providing for these payments remains in force until it is repealed, so that the payments to judges, unlike the payment of the civil service, do not have to be discussed each year and be authorised by annual votes.

To many people judicial salaries sound like wealth untold. But are they high enough to secure enough judges of sufficient quality? As all the superior judges and nearly all the Circuit Judges are appointed from the ranks of successful barristers, this depends on how judicial salaries compare at any given time with the money that can be earned by senior practitioners at the Bar. Judicial office, unlike a Bar practice, carries a pension at the end, for the promise of which a successful barrister would usually be ready to accept a slight drop in pay when he becomes a judge; but he would be unlikely to accept judicial office if it meant a very large drop in income. At the time of writing there seems to be no difficulty in filling the small number of higher posts which fall vacant, but it is not easy to find enough suitable persons to be Circuit Judges. In April 1986 the Lord Chancellor told Parliament that for the last two years he had been trying to increase the number of Circuit Judges by 10 per cent and two years later only an extra 7 per cent had been recruited. It is sometimes thought that the substantial salaries paid to our judges were designed to lessen the chance of corruption by putting a judge into a position where he is not likely to be tempted. There is no evidence that the far lower salaries which have traditionally been paid to French judges lead to corruption. The French judge, by entering the judicial profession when he is under 30, belongs to a State judicial service and his salary is fixed in accordance with the salaries paid in other forms of public service. In England we have to tempt men to leave private practice of a lucrative nature, and this is the reason for the salary; corruption is eliminated by professional tradition, which is perhaps the only effective method under any system.

Those looking for a justification for our expensive system of appointing judges from the ranks of middle-aged barristers who are enjoying success at the Bar will point out that it does ensure we have judges of sufficient age, maturity and confidence to take effective command in their courts and to exercise proper control over the advocates who appear before them. This is certainly true. They are also likely to say that it ensures us judges with good legal knowledge and experience, and so saves us the trouble of having to train them. Unfortunately this is only partly true. A large part of the function of most judges, including High Court Judges, is to try serious criminal cases. Contrary to popular imagination, barristers generally dislike criminal work because they find it sordid and comparatively ill-paid, and the able ones tend to get out of it and to specialise in civil matters. As judges are chosen from the abler section of the Bar, this means that judges are regularly appointed who are unfamiliar with a large part of the work which they must do after they are appointed. Being able, they can quickly pick it up – but left to themselves they are likely to make blunders in the process. This difficulty was eventually recognised when the Judicial Studies Board was set up in response to the report of the Bridge Committee in 1978.[1] The work of this body was discussed in the section of this book on sentencing (chapter 24).

An important question is whether politics enter into the appointment of judges, not in the sense of appointing a person simply because of his politics, but in terms of whether the choice between possible candidates has been influenced by party considerations. There is no doubt that in the past much attention was paid to the claims of party. Out of 139 appointments made between 1832 and

---

[1] Report of the Working Party on Judicial Studies and Information (Bridge Committee) 1978.

1906, 80 of these appointed were Members of Parliament at the time of their appointment, and of these 63 were appointed whilst their party was in office, leaving a mere 17 appointments made from those in political opposition.[1] Obituary notices in *The Times* used to point out whether the judicial appointment was due to professional standing or political services: we used to find 'The Bar, however, did not regard him as a likely candidate for judicial honours till his astonishing Parliamentary success at the General Election', or that 'On its merits the appointment was welcomed by the Bar . . . moreover he had some political claim on the party in power.'[2]

The most obvious use of judgeships as political rewards arose with the Law Officers. Each government appoints an Attorney-General and a Solicitor-General, who are practising barristers normally with Parliamentary seats. The functions of the Law Officers are to advise the government in legal matters and to conduct important litigation. The job of an Attorney-General is to support his party in power; he is avowedly a partisan who is expected to fight for the government with all the zeal he can show. Yet until recently an absurd convention gave the Attorney-General a first claim on the highly coveted office of Lord Chief Justice if it fell vacant. The fierce opponent of a minority in the course of a week might shed his counsel's wig and gown and appear in scarlet robes to hold the scales of justice between those he had so recently denounced and those he had so recently supported. In 1922 this system landed the country with Lord Hewart as Lord Chief Justice, who proved to be a judge so biased and incompetent that he seems to have caused a reaction against it.[3]

Hewart's successor, Lord Caldecote, had been Attorney-General once, but a decent interval before, and all the subsequent Lord Chief Justices from Lord Goddard in 1946 to Lord Lane in 1980 have been Law Lords or Lords Justices of Appeal, none of whom had ever played a prominent part in politics. The last occasion on which a government Law Officer was rewarded with any high judicial office in England was when the Solicitor-General, Sir Jocelyn Simon, was made President of the Probate, Divorce and Admiralty Division in 1962 – an appointment for which his attainments as a lawyer would in any case have suited him. When Lord Donaldson became Master of the Rolls in 1982 there were

---

[1] These figures were given by H. J. Laski in an essay on 'The technique of judicial appointment', published in *Studies in Law and Politics* (1932), 163. There is much information about politics and judicial appointments in Heuston, *Lives of the Lord Chancellors 1885–1940*. On p. 522 there is an excellent statement of principles by Lord Hailsham (Lord Chancellor 1928–29 and 1935–38, and father of the Lord Hailsham who was Lord Chancellor until 1987) which incidentally shows that being a Member of Parliament can be a hindrance to a judicial appointment if the government wants to avoid a by-election.

[2] *The Times* 21 August 1934 and 26 July 1938.

[3] When the Lord Chief Justiceship fell vacant in 1921, Gordon Hewart was Attorney-General, but the state of Lloyd George's government was such that he did not care to lose his efficient Attorney-General and risk losing a by-election. Hence a High Court Judge aged 78 (Lord Trevethin) was appointed to keep the place warm. In 1922 Lord Trevethin was astonished to be told that he had resigned, and Hewart was promptly appointed in his place.

those who said it was a political appointment; but he had never been in Parliament. The 'political' label was attached to him because when already a judge of five years' standing he had become President of the politically contentious National Industrial Relations Court (see chapter 15(iv)). It must not be supposed that there ought to be any ban upon the appointment of barristers who have been in the House of Commons or otherwise active in politics; it is even the other way round, for our bench gains from having some judges who have been much concerned with political life.[1]

There are really two propositions. The first is that politics should be disregarded in making appointments, and the second is that a man should not be taken from the office of Attorney-General or other ministerial office to go straight upon the bench. There is no evidence that disregard of these principles will lead to biased decisions. It is implicit in the notion of political debts that accounts can be settled. A judgeship means the end of a career at the Bar or in politics; there is no recent instance of a judge resigning and going back to practice or to politics, although it can hardly be said that he may not do so. There has been no apparent connection in the last hundred years between the political antecedents and the decisions of judges. The point is primarily one of public confidence, that people may feel sure that those on the bench have been appointed for legal eminence and suitability and not for political reward or by way of disposing of an embarrassing colleague.

English conditions tend to produce a certain measure of uniformity in the outlook of the judges. Judges are of different political faiths, different religions or agnostic, and have varying degrees of intelligence and cultural attainments. Yet there is something that enables us to talk about the judges almost as we do about the cabinet, tacitly postulating a body of people whose varying inclinations will appear homogeneous. This is not strange when we remember that judges have had careers that are similar in outline. Generally there has been a period of university, followed by call to the Bar, perhaps some politics, becoming a Queen's Counsel, and then the bench. Invariably there has been success at the Bar. Now the Bar is one of the few openings left in which someone with a small amount of money may rise by his own personal exertions to a position of great eminence. The vigorous individualism by which men in a small way could become great manufacturers largely belongs to a past economic order. The classic Victorian precepts for success in life survive at the Bar. Other professions tend to produce individualists, but the conditions are less propitious (except for film stars and pop singers). Successful barristers, and hence the judges, are not likely to be very critical of the legal order. The existing system has brought them large incomes and position and has produced a disposition to resist change. The appointment of judges fairly late in life, and their continuance on the bench as elderly men,

---

[1] Lord Haldane thought experience in the House of Commons helped 'in checking the danger of abstractness in mental outlook'. See his *Autobiography* (1931) p. 69.

strengthens this tendency. Individual judges have been active in the cause of law reform, but as a body their attitude has been less than lukewarm towards it.

As well as general scepticism towards the need for legal change, the judiciary as a body also shares certain views of what is and is not in the public interest that seem to be derived from their background and training. Professor J. A. G. Griffith identifies these as: sensitivity towards the interests of the State, particularly in the preservation of public order; the protection of property rights; and sympathy towards certain political and economic ideas which are generally associated with the right rather than with the left – distrust of organised labour, and dislike of collective schemes which trench upon the freedom of the individual to make and spend his money as he likes.[1]

Some years ago, if less today, a number of serious clashes occurred between the ideas of judges and modern social tendencies. For many years now Parliament has been passing legislation that is often called 'social'. The common law is on the whole highly individualistic, upholding the liberty of individuals to enter into such contracts as they see fit and allowing property owners to do what they like with their property (subject of course to limitations). Modern legislation often cuts across these ideas: statutes regulating conditions of employment and statutes aimed at slum clearance and a better standard of housing obviously conflict with the policy of the common law. In fact, it is generally taken for granted that social legislation is meant to interfere or control, yet when one of these statutes came before the courts the process was this: 'The common law upholds freedom of contract and rights of property; we presume that Parliament means to legislate in accordance with existing law; therefore we will start by assuming that Parliament did not intend to alter freedom of contract or rights of property.' It is not surprising that with such an assumption the courts often succeeded in wrecking a statute.[2]

This was one of the results of a too-rigid theory of precedent: the courts have applied canons of construction originally derived from a philosophy of individualism and of *laissez faire* in a society which has abandoned that philosophy for over half a century. Fortunately, this particular trouble seems to have subsided. Presumably the judges, like nearly all sections of people, have come to accept some views about public action that would have seemed dangerously revolutionary not so many years so. Another factor is that there has been less room for administration to come before the courts, for one reaction to certain types of decision has been to take various types of matter away from the judges and to give them to special tribunals.

The notion of a judge being 'impartial' needs more thought than it is commonly given. Strong views may obviously affect decisions, but general

---

[1] *The politics of the judiciary* (3rd ed. 1985).
[2] See Llewlyn Davies, 'The interpretation of statutes in the light of their policy by the English Courts', (1935) 35 *Columbia Law Review* 519; Jennings, 'Courts and administrative law', (1936) 49 *Harvard Law Review* 426.

outlook and mental habits can have just as much influence without being so noticeable. Whatever the conscious effort to be impartial, and here our judges have a high standard, there is always the 'prejudice' or 'bias' or as Holmes called it the 'inarticulate major premiss' of the judge.[1] The more thoughtful judges recognise the difficulty. Sixty-five years ago Lord Justice Scrutton, in discussing the need for impartiality, said:

This is rather difficult to attain in any system. I am not speaking of conscious impartiality; but the habits you are trained in, the people with whom you mix, lead to your having a certain class of ideas of such a nature that, when you have to deal with other ideas, you do not give as sound and accurate judgments as you would wish. This is one of the great difficulties at present with Labour. Labour says: 'Where are your impartial judges? They all move in the same circle as the employers, and they are educated and nursed in the same ideas as the employers. How can a Labour man or a trade unionist get impartial justice?' It is very difficult sometimes to be sure that you have put yourself into a thoroughly impartial position between two disputants, one of your own class and one not of your class. Even in matters outside trade-unionist cases (to some extent in workmen's compensation cases) it is sometimes difficult to be sure, hard as you have tried, that you have put yourself in a perfectly impartial position between the two litigants.[2]

It is sometimes argued that the whole matter is one of social class, for there are few barristers and hence few judges of working-class origin. Our judges do on the whole come from homes that are not working-class;[3] it would be harder for a working-class man to become a judge than for him to become a high official in a government department. The class factor cannot be ignored.[4]

But in its simple form, social class is not a complete explanation. If we seek for a body of men coming from much the same social class and having had much the same education and nurture as the judges, we may find it in the administrative group of the home civil service, but it is difficult to find in the administrative class as a whole the habits of mind discernible in the judges. Similar as they may have been at first, at the age of 50 he who has been at the Bar and he who has become an administrator will have developed a different cast of mind. The judge sees a compensation claim as an issue between two persons, and from this angle the bias is against making A pay money to B unless A is at fault. The administrative mind realises that if an injured workman is not compensated by his employer the cost will fall on public funds; whether it is better to make the employer pay (as under the old Workmen's Compensation Acts) or to pay out of a fund partly contributed

---

[1] Oliver Wendell Holmes, 'The path of the law', (1897) 10 *Harvard Law Review* 455, 465–66.
[2] (1921) Camb. LJ 8.
[3] After examining various studies, Prof. J. A. G. Griffith concludes that 'in broad terms, four out of five full-time professional judges are products of public [i.e. private and fee-paying] schools, and of Oxford or Cambridge'. *The politics of the judiciary* (3rd ed. 1985) p. 28.
[4] How else can we explain a judge saying when he sentences a man for kicking his wife, 'If you had been a miner in South Wales, I might have overlooked it. But you are a cultured gentleman living in a respected part of the community'? See the obituary of Sir Neville Faulks, *The Times* 17 October 1985.

through weekly stamping of cards and partly from State funds (as under the National Insurance system now in force) is a matter of policy and that is not to be determined by ideas of 'fault'. Social legislation can rarely be comprehended by seeing its effects solely as an issue between two individuals, but the isolated issue is the centre of traditional common law technique. If we turn to the legal battles over trade-union activity, the bias generally seems to have been against organised labour. In issues where employees are in conflict with employers, it is doubtful whether a judiciary trained and selected on the English pattern can be entirely satisfactory. It is not easy for anyone who has not been intimately involved in industrial relations to appreciate the issues that arise; the nuances can be so easily missed, and points of enormous importance in the eyes of a party may seem small or even ridiculous. If the training of lawyers were to be broadened, and if the selection of judges were widened, we should probably still get this trouble. Probably the best answer, when we find something that the judiciary does not do very well, is to look for some other way of doing it. Industrial tribunals, with experienced laymen and a lawyer chairman, undoubtedly provide a better way of handling questions of unfair dismissal and related matters than do the ordinary courts presided over by judges alone.

Some years ago Professor Jaffe of Harvard put forward the view that the English judge no longer has the role of oracle and law-maker that belonged to his predecessors.[1] 'There have been great judges in England, Coke, Bacon, Holt, Mansfield, Blackburn, Willes. Is the "great" English judge a relic of the past? Are these gods dead today, the victims of their irrelevance? Or have they moved to America where a new Parthenon is flourishing?' In previous editions of this book Professor Jackson broadly agreed with this. The great judges of the past, he said, were those who were able to take a fragmented collection of cases which seemed to have no common principle in them, and draw out of them some new and brilliant principle that gave a foundation for future development. But this, he said, can only be done where Parliament has left room for it to be done. From the time of the Great Reform Bill onwards, Parliament has been continually active in reforming and reshaping the law, and this simply leaves no room for the great judge of the past to operate. This view is difficult to accept. Whilst it is true that Parliament has stolen much of the show, there are still large areas where the judges of today have been able to exercise their skills in developing the law, and in modern times they have sometimes done this every bit as brilliantly as their predecessors. In 1932, the House of Lords decided *Donoghue* v. *Stevenson*,[2] in which Lords Atkin and Macmillan took a disorganised collection of previously unconnected decisions and derived from them the general principle that a person is liable to pay damages if he hurts someone else by acting negligently. This principle has been of enormous importance. Scarcely less impressive is the way in

---

[1] L. L. Jaffe, *English and American judges as lawmakers* (1969), based on lectures he gave in Oxford in 1967.
[2] [1932] AC 562.

which Lord Diplock and his colleagues more recently stated the principles of judicial review in such a way as to make them intelligible; see chapter 17 above.

These reorganisations of the law, however, are of fairly narrow compass. We do not expect to find English judges producing major decisions which cause important social changes affecting the lives of large numbers of people, as the judges of the Supreme Court of the United States did when they forbade the segregation of blacks from whites in schools, for example, or ruled that States must supply free lawyers to all poor persons facing serious criminal trials.[1]

This does not reflect any difference in intelligence between American judges and ours, nor has it much to do with any difference in political views or social backgrounds, nor is it solely because Parliament is so active that it leaves nothing in these areas for the judges to do. The real explanation is the difference between the constitutions of the two countries, and the powers of the courts in relation to the powers of the legislature. The United States has a written constitution, the provisions of which override statute law. This puts the American Supreme Court Judges, who interpret the constitution, in a doubly powerful position compared with their British colleagues. In the first place it means that, unlike our judges, they can declare a statute void if it stands in their way. Confronted with a British statute which provided for segregated schools, or required the poor to pay for legal representation, an English judge would either have to apply it, or resign. Secondly, the constitution of the USA contains in its Bill of Rights a collection of general statements upon which the judges can base the concrete rulings with which they decide the revolutionary case. A provision such as Article XIV:

All persons born or naturalized in the United States, . . . are citizens of the United States and of the State wherein they reside. No State shall make or enforce any law which shall abridge the privileges or immunities of citizens of the United States; nor shall any State deprive any person of life, liberty, or property, without due process of law; nor deny to any person within its jurisdiction the equal protection of the laws

can be made the basis of almost any expansive decision in the general area of human rights. English judges, on the other hand, have to derive their basic principles from other sources, usually previous judicial decisions. In the absence of these, they must invent the principles. This they are understandably reluctant to do, because those who oppose what they are trying to achieve will say with some justice that the judges invented the principle as a pretext for the decision and the resulting social upheaval. Recently, some of our more adventurous judges have begun to look for a source of basic principles for action in the European Convention on Human Rights; but there are limits to what they can do with this, because it does not as such form part of English law, and certainly does not prevail against a statute. The arguments for incorporating the European Convention into our law are considered in chapter 35.

[1] *Gideon* v. *Wainwright* (1963) 372 US 335.

These considerations bring us to the question of whether the office of a judge now occupies such an important position as it did years ago. The answer must be that in some ways it does not. Not only is there the point that the activities of judges as law-makers are nowadays dwarfed by the activities of Parliament: there is also the question of numbers. Last century before the Judicature Acts 1873–5, 'the judges' numbered about 25. A hundred years later the number of superior judges was nearly 200. The social position and prestige of an office depends on factors which include the size of the elite and the number of other high positions. These days there were not only far more judges but also far more top civil servants, chairmen of boards and other persons in high positions in public affairs, and so the importance of a judge – even a High Court Judge – has declined. Before the Second World War the appointment of a High Court Judge was something of an event, and *The Times* would announce it and give an account of the new judge's career. Now *The Times* does not ordinarily report such an appointment and lawyers have to pick up these happenings from brief references in a legal journal. By contrast, the headship of a Division of the High Court and appointments to the Court of Appeal and the House of Lords are still newsworthy. To hold judicial office at this level is still to hold an office of major public importance.

32

JURIES

Nothing in the whole of the English legal system generates so much heated and emotional argument as the merits and demerits of the jury.[1] No debate on the subject is complete without a few eulogistic remarks on the value of juries quoted from lawyers of the past. These are apt to mislead us unless we bear in mind two vital facts which are usually forgotten. The first is that the composition of juries has changed dramatically over the years, and in particular since the Criminal Justice Act 1972 abolished the property qualification and made eligible for jury service almost everyone who is entitled to vote in elections. The second is that their place and function within the legal system has also dramatically changed.

To take the second point first, jury trial used to be almost universal as a method of deciding cases, both civil and criminal, whereas now it is applicable to only a small fraction of either. The position in the eighteenth century was that a trial by jury was the method of determining any civil action for debt or damages brought in one of the courts of common law,[2] which is to say that they were used for the overwhelming majority of civil cases. Up to the same period, it was also the method by which almost every criminal case was tried: the number of offences which could be tried summarily was tiny, making trial on indictment the usual method, and as in those days almost everyone pleaded 'not guilty' nearly every indictment resulted in a trial by jury actually taking place; see pages 264–65 above.

In civil cases, as explained earlier (chapter 7) a series of legislative changes between 1854 and 1933 first made jury trial optional rather than compulsory, and then virtually abolished it altogether. It now survives in trials for fraud, libel, slander, malicious prosecution and false imprisonment – cases of a type which usually attract a lot of attention, but which are only a minute proportion of the caseload of the civil courts. In criminal cases, a stream of legislation through the nineteenth and twentieth centuries gradually increased the number of offences triable summarily by magistrates, making jury trial an option in some of the cases where it was previously compulsory, and not even optional in others. Thus in

---

[1] W. R. Cornish, *The jury*, (1968) contains a great deal of information. A well-known commentator is Lord Devlin, *Trial by jury* (1956), (revised version 1971). Glanville Williams, *The proof of guilt* (3rd ed. 1963) has a chapter on jury trial, generally adverse.
[2] The Court of Common Pleas, the Court of King's Bench, and the Exchequer. Juries were not used in the Admiralty Court, the Ecclesiastical Courts or in Chancery.

1985 some two million cases were dealt with summarily, and the number of cases which went on indictment was less than 100,000. Furthermore, pressure of work in the criminal courts has led to an official policy of encouraging defendants to plead guilty, something which between half and two-thirds of defendants facing trial on indictment in the Crown Court now do. Where the defendant pleads guilty there is no jury and the case is disposed of by judge alone, so even in those criminal cases which do get as far as the Crown Court, a jury is used in considerably less than half – although these of course tend to be the more newsworthy ones. Thus by a process much of which has hardly been noticed, and most of which has generated little public controversy, the role of the jury in England has been enormously reduced.

The qualifications for jury service are now contained in the Juries Act 1974, which codifies a number of previous statutes on the subject, principally the Criminal Justice Act 1972. Before 1972 a juror had to be over 21 and under 60 years of age and be (1) a £10 freeholder, or (2) a £20 long leaseholder, or (3) a householder in the valuation list of £30 in London or Middlesex or £20 elsewhere, or (4) occupy a house with not less than fifteen windows: qualifications (2), (3) and (4) were due to the Juries Act 1825. The only qualification that mattered in practice was being the occupier of a house having the required rateable value; that was known to the local authority for rating purposes, and other information was obtained on forms sent to each household. The effective qualification for jury service changed with the fall in the value of money and reassessments for rating. It used to mean that jury service was largely confined to the middle and upper classes. A few years before the war, a ward in Cambridge which consisted partly of working-class houses and partly of middle-class houses contained just under 5,000 parliamentary electors, and the list showed 187 jurors: roughly one juror to every 26 electors. The views and prejudices of jurors were more apt to be those of the middle classes than those of the poorer classes.[1]

Revaluation of dwelling-houses for rating, and particularly the new lists in 1963, resulted in nearly all occupiers suddenly becoming jurors. Liability for jury service was thus extended not by deliberation but by a sidewind of local government finance. In earlier years the property qualifications did give some selection that was defensible in a community in which education and responsibility tended to go with wealth expressed in housing: but once the rules let in any head of a household who was not so poor as to be homeless, there was little sense in keeping out his wife, lodger, or grown-up child. Such a system could not be reconciled with ideas of sexual equality or of giving young people full legal

[1] This tendency was all the more marked in the case of 'special jurors'. A special juror was (1) an esquire or of higher rank, or (2) a merchant or banker, or (3) someone who occupied a dwelling-house in the valuation list at not less than £100 in larger towns or £50 elsewhere, or (4) someone who occupied premises of the annual value of at least £100, or £300 if it was a farm, and a jury limited to such persons could be ordered in certain types of case. Special juries were abolished without opposition in 1949. Further details will be found in earlier editions of this book, especially the first.

capacity. A Committee on Jury Service which reported in 1965[1] recommended that the basic qualification for jury service should be citizenship as evidenced by inclusion in the electoral register as a parliamentary elector. This change was enacted in 1972, and is now contained in section 1 of the Juries Act 1974. The basic qualification is being on the electoral register. In addition he (or she) must be between the ages of 18 and 65.[2] In addition, he must have been ordinarily resident in the United Kingdom, the Channel Islands or the Isle of Man for any period of at least five years since attaining the age of thirteen. A person who falls within this definition may however be ineligible, disqualified or excused. Those who are *ineligible* include the judiciary and a long list of others who are or have been concerned with the administration of justice during the last ten years, and also clergy and persons who are mentally ill. Persons who are *disqualified* are those with criminal records. At first only those with serious records were excluded, but following a number of scandals about criminals serving on juries the rules were tightened up by the Juries (Disqualification) Act 1984 so that a person is ineligible to serve if he has ever received a prison sentence of five years or more, or any custodial sentence within the last ten years, or a probation order within the last five. Persons are *excusable* where they are eligible to serve but have the right to refuse. In this list are members of the House of Commons, officers of either House, serving members of the armed forces, and practising doctors or members of allied professions. Persons are also excusable from jury service if they have attended for jury service during the past two years, or, as sometimes happens, if the judge before whom they have previously done jury service has excused them from future jury service for a longer period (which may be for the rest of their lives). In principle, jury service still has its medieval characteristic of being compulsory: a person who is duly summoned and who fails to attend, or who attends and is unfit for service by reason of drink and drugs, is liable to a fine. However, the court officials have a discretion to let someone off jury service if there is a good reason, which usually ensures that such people as the mothers of young children and students with examinations to sit are not required to serve, and in addition the judge has a general discretion to excuse a person from attending. In case of doubt the practice is usually to excuse, which is sensible because a reluctant juror is unlikely to do his job well. For centuries jurors were unpaid, and there were many instances of jurors suffering considerable loss through having to attend for a case that lasted several days or even weeks. Since 1949 all persons who are summoned and attend, whether they actually serve or not, are entitled to draw travelling and subsistence allowances, and to receive compensation for financial loss within carefully defined limits.

At one time the summoning of jurors was the responsibility of the sheriff

[1] Report of the Departmental Committee on Jury Service, Chairman Lord Morris of Borth-y-Gest, (1965) Cmnd 2627.
[2] At the time of writing there is a proposal in the Criminal Justice Bill before Parliament to raise the age to 70.

(which in practice meant the under-sheriff or deputy) and he did it from a list of eligible persons called the Jurors Book. The Courts Act 1971 transferred responsibility for jurors to the Lord Chancellor and the job is done by the officials of the Crown Court. There is now no Jurors Book. The process of getting jurors begins with the compilation of electoral registers. Forms are distributed to occupiers of houses requiring a return of the names of persons who live there and whether they are over 18 years or over 65. The electoral registration officer makes up a copy of the register to show which persons on it are between the ages of 18 and 65 and sends it to the designated officers of the courts. That gives a list of persons for each area who appear to be qualified as jurors, but takes no account of ineligibility or disqualification: to do so would involve asking questions of well over 30 million voters whereas the total number of jurors needed is only a tiny fraction of this. From this list, a batch of possible jurors called a *panel* is summoned by the court officials. In the past a panel was summoned for each session of a court, but now that courts are continuous a court officer has to provide a panel to cover a convenient period and fresh panels as may be required. If his estimate is that a panel of say 100 is needed, he makes a random list of maybe 150 or more names from his list;[1] he may exclude some names which he recognises as ineligible, such as a judge or a celebrated local criminal, but he does not make enquiries about the persons named. The officer then sends out a summons to each person to attend for jury service; the summons is accompanied by a notice about qualifications, grounds for ineligibility and excusal, and it explains what the person concerned should do to have the summons cancelled. But since people do not always read or understand notices sent to them, the Juries Act contains a provision which permits the court officer to question a person who attends to establish whether he is qualified. There is a further provision that if a person attends but strikes the court official as unable to act effectively as a juror through disability or want of English, the official may ask the judge to decide whether or not to discharge him; or the judge may excuse such a person from his own observation. It is an offence for any person summoned for jury service to make false statements or knowingly to act as a juror when he knows he is ineligible or disqualified.

The court officials select from the panel the groups of twelve jurors who are to try each case by *ballot*: that is to say they are chosen by drawing lots.[2] However, the composition of the jury may be affected by either side exercising their right of

---

[1] If there is a miscalculation and the result is an insufficient number the judge has a statutory power to press-gang 'any persons who are in, or are in the vicinity of the court' for service. This is exceedingly rare, but a case occurred in Cambridge Crown Court on 24 April 1985, when two persons were requisitioned from the City Council offices adjoining. The ancient term for this procedure is 'praying a tales'.

[2] At one time the jury was sometimes selected by 'striking': the sheriff selected a panel of 48 names, each party took it in turns to strike out names until there were only 24 left, and then lots were drawn to select the final 12. An account of how this worked, and how it could be manipulated in political cases, is contained in earlier editions of this book.

challenge as well as by the operation of the ballot. As a safeguard against the court officials summoning a prejudiced panel, a party to any proceedings (or his representative) has the right to know the names and addresses of the whole panel, and a party aggrieved may 'challenge the array' if he can show grounds for thinking it was not fairly chosen. Such challenges are extremely rare. Alternatively, individual jurors may be challenged after their name has been drawn by ballot and before they are sworn. This is called a 'challenge to the polls'. In any case, criminal or civil, either side may challenge any juror if he can give a reason why he is unsuitable to serve: this is called making a 'challenge for cause'. In a criminal case both prosecution and defence also have the right to challenge jurors without giving reasons. At the time of writing each defendant can make three such 'peremptory challenges'.[1]

The Crown technically has no right of peremptory challenge as such, but may require any juror whose name is balloted to go back into the panel to serve only as a last resort when there is no one else left. In practice this gives the prosecution what usually amounts to an unlimited right of peremptory challenge. Sometimes the judge takes a hand in the selection. In recent years there have been cases in which black defendants persuaded the judges to influence the composition of the jury so as to make sure that it contains blacks, usually by asking white jurors who are balloted to stand by; but not all judges are willing to do this, and there is some doubt as to whether it is strictly legal.[2]

The rules on eligibility, disqualification and challenge was intended to ensure that juries do not contain people whose personal qualities make them unfit to serve as jurors or who have reasons to be biased. They seem quite inadequate to keep unsuitable people off juries; worse, whilst they do not enable a party to identify and remove jurors who have reason to be biased against him, they do sometimes enable him to pack a jury so that it is biased against the other side. One only has to read the newspapers and the law reports to find cases in which it has been discovered, usually too late, that some of the jurors were grossly unsuitable, or had reasons to be biased, and those are only the cases in which the matter came to light. Thus one Old Bailey trial costing thousands of pounds was abandoned when it was found that one of the jurors, an Asian woman, could not understand English.[3] A fraud trial had to be abandoned when two young female jurors got drunk during the lunch adjournment and one started to make sexual advances to a male colleague during defence counsel's closing speech.[4]

During the miners' strike, when there was intense ill-feeling between those miners who were on strike and the 'scabs' who were not, a striking miner accused

---

[1] The number was fixed at seven in 1948 and reduced to three in 1977. At the time of writing there is a proposal in the Criminal Justice Bill 1987 to abolish it altogether: see below.
[2] The cases are *Broderick* [1970] Crim. LR 155; *Binns* [1982] Crim. LR 522; *Bansal* [1985] Crim. LR 151; *McCalla* [1986] Crim. LR 335. The issues are discussed by Alan Dashwood. 'Juries in a multi-racial society', [1972] Crim. LR 85.   [3] *The Times* 6 February 1986.
[4] *The Sun* 1 October 1981. They were fined £100 and it was estimated that abandoning the trial wasted £10,000 of public money.

of damaging a 'scab' miner's car discovered after his conviction that one of the jurors was another 'scab'.[1]

In a case where some mental hospital nurses were on trial for assaulting their patients, it emerged that one of the jurors was prejudiced against the defendants by what he had heard about the affair from his wife, herself a mental nurse, and that he had preached his prejudices to three other jurors as he drove them to and from court over the previous ten days.[2]

In another case, a jury was said to have convicted because the foreman of the jury happened to know the defendant had a criminal record, and revealed it to the others at a crucial moment in their deliberations.[3] When matters of this sort come out at the trial, the trial is usually abandoned, and when it comes to light afterwards an appeal is occasionally allowed; but by then the damage has been done. This sort of thing should be prevented. The problem with the rules on disqualification and unfitness is that no systematic check is made to see if the persons summoned are disqualified, and they depend entirely on self-reporting. The onus is put on the juror to point the matter out – which he is unlikely to do if he is dishonest. He is even less likely to do so if he has no English and therefore cannot read the paragraph in the notice the Lord Chancellor's Department sends to jurors telling them they may be excused if they have no English. And the rules about challenge are ineffective to exclude unfit and biased jurors because the parties have virtually no information to go on. All they are given, if they choose to ask for it, is the names and addresses of the whole panel which has been summoned for jury service; they do not even have their occupations, as they did before 1971. Unless a party has the facilities for large-scale detective work he can only exercise his right to challenge a juror on hunch, or in the rare case where he happens to recognise him.

The people who do have the capacity for large-scale detective work are the police. In 1978 it was revealed in the course of the trial of Aubrey, Berry and Campbell for offences under the Official Secrets Act (the 'ABC Trial')[4] that for some years it had been the practice for the prosecution to ask the police to 'vet' the jury panel for them in major cases to provide information with which to exercise their right to challenge for cause, or more usually, to 'stand jurors by' without having to give a reason. The practice had grown up at trials at the Old Bailey, and had first come to the government's notice in 1974, when the Attorney-General had issued guidelines restricting its use. Amid rising public

---

[1] *Pennington* (1985) 81 Cr. Ap. R 217. The clerk to one of the magistrates' courts in the area told the editor that every magistrate who was connected with the coal industry in any way was treated as disqualified when trying miners during the dispute.

[2] *Spencer* [1987] AC 128. In this case the conviction was eventually quashed by the House of Lords.

[3] *Thomson* 36 (1962) 46 Cr. Ap. R 72. The Court of Criminal Appeal refused to quash the conviction and complained about the fact that the secrecy of the jury-room had been violated by bringing the matter to its attention.

[4] See A. G. L. Nicol, 'Official secrets and jury vetting', [1979] Crim. LR 284. See also Peter Duff, 'Jury vetting – the jury under attack', (1983) 3 *Legal Studies* 159.

outcry, the Attorney-General made a public statement about the practice and published his guidelines (which were revised slightly in 1980).[1] In outline, these guidelines are as follows:

(1) Random selection, within the range of persons properly qualified for jury service, is the dominant principle to be followed.

(2) In any type of case it is proper for the police, either on the command of the DPP or of a chief constable, to check whether members of the jury panel have criminal records which disqualify them from jury service.

(3) In addition, there are 'certain exceptional types of case of public importance' where 'it is in the interests both of justice and the public' that there should be 'further safeguards against the possibility of bias' which include seeking information about jurors going beyond whether or not they are formally disqualified because of criminal records.

(4) 'The classes of case may be defined broadly as:
(a) cases in which national security is involved and part of the evidence is likely to be heard *in camera*;
(b) terrorist cases.'

(5) Extra information is needed in these cases because of the risk that jurors may later make improper use of evidence given in camera, or 'that a juror's political beliefs are so biased as to go beyond normally reflecting the broad spectrum of views and interests in the community ... to a degree which might interfere with his fair assessment of the facts of the case or lead him to exert improper pressure on his fellow jurors'.

(6) In such cases it is proper to look further than the criminal records office, and to enquire what information is held on the jurors by the police 'special branches'.

(7) Such checks must only be made with the personal authority of the Attorney-General or the DPP (who must notify the Attorney-General).

(8), (9) and (10) The DPP will decide how much to pass on to prosecuting counsel, who must not use it unless there is a strong reason for thinking the juror really is a security risk or is actually likely to be biased; but if he does use it to 'stand a juror by' he need not make the reason public.

(11) Prosecuting counsel should tell defence counsel if any of the information he so receives makes him think a juror may be biased against the accused (but he need not give away the reason).

(12) The DPP is to keep a record of when jury vetting takes place, and what use is made of the information it reveals.

Shortly afterwards, the legality of 'jury vetting' was twice challenged in the Court of Appeal. In a case where two police officers were charged with assault, and the judge had ordered the prosecution to disclose to the defence whether any of the jurors had criminal records, and the prosecution sought to have his order quashed, the Court of Appeal (Civil Division) publicly doubted whether jury-vetting could ever be legal.[2] But shortly afterwards the Court of Appeal (Criminal

[1] The Attorney-General's official statement on the history of the practice is printed in (1980) 71 Cr. Ap. R 30, and the full text of the current version of the *Guidelines* is in (1981) 72 Cr. Ap. R 14.
[2] *R. v. Sheffield Crown Court ex pte. Brownlow* [1980] QB 530. In fact the Court of Appeal refused to intervene because it had no statutory power to entertain the appeal.

Division) disapproved of this view and upheld a conviction in a case where jury-vetting had taken place apparently quite outside the Attorney-General's guidelines, and a juror had been 'stood by' although he was not disqualified from serving.[1]

For the moment, the practice seems to be accepted as legal. There is much about it, however, which seems highly undesirable. There is every reason why the police should check that none of the jury panel are actually disqualified to serve,[2] and perhaps there is a case for further checks if the jurors are to hear information which it would endanger the country if they leaked to the KGB. But there are clear dangers in giving the prosecution what almost amounts to a power in national security cases to purge the jury of those whom they think are likely to be unsympathetic to the prosecution. There is also the problem of 'inequality of arms': although both sides have access to the names on the jury panel, usually it will only be the prosecution which is actually in a position to make this sort of check, and the defence must rely on the judgment of the prosecution as to what information it will release as likely to assist the defence. It raises issues of civil liberty for the members of the jury panel as well. It is bad enough for them that they are compelled to serve against their will, and when this is also made the excuse for Big Brother to snoop into their private lives it is intolerable.

If jury vetting and the right to 'stand by' creates a risk of the prosecution manipulating the composition of a jury to make it biased against the accused, the defendant's right of peremptory challenge at present creates a much greater risk of the defence shaping a jury with an anti-prosecution bias. Before eligibility for jury service was extended in the 1960s and 1970s, defendants rarely bothered to exercise their right of challenge. One juror looked much like another, and there was nothing much to be gained by replacing one respectable middle-class male with another. When all sorts and conditions of men (and women) became eligible for jury service this abruptly changed. It became a common practice for the defendant in a weak case to challenge off the jury anyone who looked respectable, in the hope that his replacement would look disreputable, on the assumption that disreputable-looking people are sympathetic to defendants. It was for this reason that the number of peremptory challenges was reduced in 1977 from seven to three: but since each defendant has three challenges this trick can still be played where there are several defendants and they pool their resources. The art of challenge reached its height in fraud cases, where there are typically a number of defendants, and there is also the possibility of challenging anyone who looks intelligent, on the added assumption that even a jury of respectable citizens will be reluctant to convict if it cannot make head or tale of the prosecution case. In 1986 the Roskill Committee on Fraud Trials examined the practice and

---

[1] *Mason* (1980) 71 Cr. Ap. R 157.

[2] In September 1987, following some public allegations of 'jury nobbling' the Home Secretary announced the introduction of random police checks to deter those with criminal records from attending for jury service. Amazingly, this move was attacked by the Law Society, which evidently thinks it is right that the law should prohibit something which is permitted in practice to happen.

concluded that 'the current situation bids fair to bring the whole system of jury trial into public disrepute'[1] and recommended that in fraud trials the right of peremptory challenge should be abolished. To treat both sides equally, it recommended the abolition of the prosecution right to 'stand by' as well. The government, true to its 'law and order' image, initially responded to this with a clause in the present Criminal Justice Bill to abolish the defendant's peremptory challenge whilst retaining the prosecution right to 'stand by'. Parliamentary pressure did not succeed in getting the prosecution right to 'stand by' abolished too, but it did persuade the government to announce that the Attorney-General will shortly issue an official direction restricting its use.

The present system, under which the provision of a jury which is qualified, fit and unbiased depends partly on self-reporting by the jurors themselves and partly on the machinations of the parties, seems inherently unsatisfactory. The only possible reform is to make this vital task the responsibility of the court. There should be automatic checks on whether the jurors are disqualified by criminal records, and the court officials should have the routine task of examining the persons summoned to see if they can see, hear, read, write, and understand spoken English. The question of bias is a little harder. In some other common law jurisdictions, notably in North America, when prospective jurors have been chosen they are questioned as to their fitness to sit in the case, a process known as *voire dire*[2]. It often takes up a great deal of time, and is widely thought to be a source of greater abuses than those which we have here. But there the questioning is done by the lawyers representing the parties, who necessarily try to get jurors who will be sympathetic to their case rather than jurors who will be genuinely unbiased. It would surely be a different matter if it were the judge who put a few simple questions in open court to each juror: such as whether he had any connection with the defendant or with any of the witnesses. There is nothing in law to prevent the judge doing this at the moment if he wishes to, and there is no reason why it should not be made the general practice.[3]

In this country we are used to the idea of jury trial and so we take it for granted. But on the face of it, it is an extraordinary notion. Magistrates are carefully chosen and trained, and judges are chosen only from those who have great experience in the trial of cases: but a jury is a bunch of completely untrained amateurs selected at random. As Professor Hogan says:

Of course trial by jury is one of our sacred cows. But, you know, if we'd long had trial by judge in criminal cases and I were now to suggest that his reasoned and professional judgment as to facts and inferences should be replaced by the blanket verdict of pretty well

---

[1] Fraud Trials Committee Report HMSO (1986) para. 7.37. This report is not published as a command paper.

[2] In England a *voire dire* is when a judge hears evidence in the absence of the jury, e.g. where there is a disputed confession.

[3] In the ABC trial all the jurors were asked if they had served in any government service or in the Armed Forces where they had handled material classified as secret: see A. G. L. Nicol, 'Official secrets and jury-vetting', [1979] Crim. LR 284 at 286, who also gives other examples.

any twelve men and women placed in a cramped box and holed up there for days or even weeks at a time you would rightly think that I had taken leave of my senses.[1]

Why do we so value the jury system? A large part of the reason is that jury trial has long been regarded as a bulwark against oppression; it is part of our tradition and still surrounded by sentiment and emotion. In the late eighteenth century we get many professions of enthusiasm for trial by jury. Lord Camden said:

Trial by jury is indeed the foundation of our free constitution; take that away, and the whole fabric will soon moulder into dust. These are the sentiments of my youth – inculcated by precept, improved by experience, and warranted by example.[2]

When Erskine was made Lord Chancellor in 1806 he took 'Trial by Jury' as his motto, although it was said that 'By Bill in Equity' would have been more suitable for the Woolsack.[3] Erskine was so enthusiastic about juries that Lord Byron, after sitting next to Erskine at dinner and hearing about little else, felt that juries ought to be abolished.[4] Lord Loughborough, before his appointment as Lord Chancellor, declared that: 'Judges may err, judges may be corrupt. Their minds may be warped by interest, passion, and prejudice. But a jury is not liable to the same misleading influences.'[5] Even Lord Eldon, when he was Solicitor-General and found that for political reasons he could not oppose Fox's Libel Bill, began his speech 'by professing a most religious regard for the institution of juries, which he considered the greatest blessing which the British Constitution had secured to the subject'.[6] The older constitutional law books are in the same tradition.[7]

The same kind of views are still sometimes expressed today. Lord Devlin writes:

The first object of any tyrant in Whitehall would be to make Parliament utterly subservient to his will; and the next to overthrow or diminish trial by jury, for no tyrant could afford to leave a subject's freedom in the hands of twelve of his countrymen. So that trial by jury is more than an instrument of justice and more than one wheel of the constitution; it is the lamp that shows that freedom lives.[8]

Jury trial acquired this reputation in the eighteenth century when governments used to try to stamp out public criticism by prosecuting their critics for the crime of sedition – a notoriously vague offence – and juries sometimes rebelled against the practice by acquitting in the teeth of the judge's direction to convict.

[1] Letter to *The Times* 3 May 1982.
[2] Campbell, *Lives of the Lord Chancellors* 5th ed. VII, 35.
[3] Campbell VIII, 376.   [4] Campbell IX, 94.
[5] Campbell VII, 400.   [6] Campbell IX, 189.
[7] 'When questions evolved by political agitation are raised between the subject and the crown . . . it is conceived that, by the wit of man, no system could be devised more fitter' than jury trial (Broom, *Constitutional law* (1885) pp. 156–57).
[8] *Trial by jury* (1956) p. 164. Compare Lord Denning's remarks in *Ward* v. *James* [1966] 1 QB 273, 295: 'Let it not be supposed that this court is in any way opposed to trial by jury. It has been the bulwark of our liberties too long for any of us to seek to alter it.' F. G. Hails, 'Complete freedom', (1966) 116 *New Law Journal* 1245, writes: 'Restriction on the right to trial by jury even for a single class of criminal is the first step on the ladder to the police state. *Facilis sit in avernus descendere.*'

Professor Jackson's view on these cases, as expressed in previous editions of this book, was that they failed to justify the view that the jury was a protector of civil liberties.

I have examined many of the late eighteenth-century trials for seditious libel, and failed to find any justification for this view. In reading these cases I found it quite impossible to predict what the jury was going to do; for every acquittal there was a conviction to balance it. In 1792 Paine was convicted for publishing *The rights of man*,[1] whilst in 1793 his publisher Eaton was virtually acquitted.[2] The jury found Eaton 'guilty of publishing'; the judge pressed the jury to alter their verdict, but all the jury would agree to do was to alter it from 'Guilty of publishing' to 'Guilty of publishing that book'. As Fox's Libel Act had been passed, the effect was an acquittal . . . The list could be continued. The only cure for admiration of these juries is to read the *State Trials*, and ponder over the possibility that if the printer put 'guilty' when he meant 'not guilty' and vice versa you would not have noticed anything odd.

But this view surely takes insufficient account of the fact that in those days the Crown had all sorts of means of packing the jury with its supporters, and it regularly used them:[3] if the government had resort to these means, and juries still sometimes acquitted, juries surely did quite a lot to protect civil liberties. Without juries, one suspects the government would have won every time.

If juries were effective in protecting civil liberties two hundred years ago, that of course does not mean that they are effective now. Indeed, with jury trial no longer the method of determining most cases that come to court, their opportunity to do so now is limited. If we take the cases that are cited on the citizen and the State in standard books on constitutional law it will be found that juries played an insignificant part. A typical case concerning civil liberties is likely to arise from some action by police, immigration officers or other public officials purporting to act under statutory powers, and legal proceedings come before a magistrates' court. The case may be taken to the Divisional Court by way of judicial review or on case stated for a ruling on law, or go on appeal to the Crown Court. A jury does not come into any of those proceedings. A civil case may raise an issue of civil liberties – but juries are now rarely available in civil actions. In criminal cases tried on indictment, there must be a jury if there if a plea of not guilty and here the jury may possibly protect a person against some unjustifiable inroad upon his civil liberties. But even here a jury will nowadays be told, several times over, by counsel on each side and by the judge, that they the jury are to decide matters of fact but that they must take the law from the judge. Here the lawyers speak with two voices: they go on repeating that jury trial is a safeguard for civil liberties, which necessarily accepts the right of a jury on occasions to disregard what the trial judge says, whilst in court they hammer into juries an absolute obligation to accept what they are told. Despite this, however, there are still isolated occasions

---

[1] 22 *Howell's State Trials* 357.
[2] 22 *Howell's State Trials* 754, 786.
[3] See Bentham's pamphlet 'Elements of the art of packing as applied to special juries' (1821).

on which a jury rebels. In 1985 Mr Clive Ponting, a civil servant, was prosecuted for an offence under section 2 of the Official Secrets Act for leaking official documents relating to the sinking of the Argentine cruiser 'General Belgrano' during the Falklands war. Defendants in such cases have usually sold or given away information, the loss of which is damaging to national security, to the agent of some hostile power, but Ponting had leaked the information to a Labour MP for use in Parliamentary debates, and as the war was now over it could not be said that national security was endangered: the real objection to what he had done was that the disclosure was in breach of his obligation to the government, his employer, and embarrassing to them. To many people the prosecution looked distinctly heavy handed. But the wording of the Official Secrets Act covers leaks by civil servants, whether or not they endanger national security, and the judge accordingly gave the jury what amounted to a direction to convict – which they ignored and proceeded to acquit him.[1]

This verdict is said to have put the present government off trying to prosecute 'leaking' civil servants under the Official Secrets Act, and in its battle against Peter Wright's book *Spycatcher* and various associated campaigns, it has resorted to civil actions for breach of confidence, which are tried by judges without juries.[2] The conclusion must be that juries still have some part to play in protecting civil liberties, although it is undoubtedly a smaller part than is generally supposed.

If the part that juries play in the protection of civil liberties is small, then the real case for having them must depend on their utility in ordinary cases: that is, on how they perform in comparison with other possible methods when it comes to trying criminal cases on indictment, and in civil actions for fraud, defamation, malicious prosecution and false imprisonment. The abilities of judges and juries may be compared in several points.

The first is the problem of deciding whether a witness is to be believed or not. Skill in estimating the characters of others depends to a considerable extent upon experience, provided that 'experience' means that conclusions are in some way tested. Most doctors ultimately *know* whether their patients have been telling the truth. Schoolteachers and college tutors also have to take responsibility for their estimates of character. Businessmen are largely concerned with the same problem. When these people make mistakes, they sooner or later know that they have made a wrong estimate. Now a judge, by the very nature of his office, is not accustomed to testing his conclusions. He can live in the firm conviction that he is a shrewd judge of character. To some extent as counsel, and almost certainly as judge, he will very rarely find out when he has been wrong. A man who never knows of his mistakes is apt to think that he is generally right. A judge does not

[1] *The Times* 12 February 1985, reported the case with a cartoon of a jury saying 'We find the defendant not guilty – SO THERE.' A cartoon in *Private Eye* had a similar theme but with the jury reinforcing the message in sign-language.
[2] For the latest instalment at the time of writing, see *The Times* 22 December 1987.

always 'gain experience' on the problems of fact; he increases his self-assurance and his self-confidence. A learned judge once said that: 'The average English jury can understand most things which are put to them in plain language'. What this really means is that when a judge explains to a jury some subtle legal distinction, and the jury find a verdict in accordance with the judge's views, the judge deduces that the jury understood his plain language. No law teacher would make that assumption, because he tries to find out whether the plain language of lectures, textbooks and learned judges has been understood. There is little reason for supposing that in the matter of assessing credibility jurors are any better or any worse than judges: and a jury has the advantage that twelve heads are better than one. There is also the point that in our system judges are almost always middle-aged to elderly, and male. It must be an advantage for a jury, when it comes to assessing the credibility of women and young children, that some of its members will be women, and others may be parents with young children still at home.

The second is the question of applying the common public opinion of sensible men. The problem is really one of evidence. An old example can be taken from an action for libel. An epithet is defamatory because people regard it as such. Can we assume that judges and juries know this, or must evidence be produced to show what ordinary people think? When chocolate manufacturers (Messrs Fry) published a caricature of a well-known amateur golfer (Mr Tolley) without his leave in order to advertise their goods, Mr Tolley brought a libel action. It is clearly not defamatory to assert that a golfer eats chocolate; the only possible libel was that the public would believe that Mr Tolley had been paid to allow himself to be caricatured, and hence he was not a bona fide amateur at all. Naturally, there was no evidence that 'amateurs' receive money for the use of their names or portraits in advertisements. The jury found in favour of Mr Tolley. The Court of Appeal had to consider whether the jury were entitled to come to that finding, that is, the extent to which the jury could add their common knowledge to the evidence that had been given. Scrutton LJ said that 'A jury is certainly allowed to know something not in the evidence', but Greer LJ and Slesser LJ, who found that there was no evidence on which the jury could have acted, implied that advertising habits are outside a jury's knowledge.[1] The House of Lords thought otherwise.[2] Viscount Hailsham said: 'It is always difficult to determine with precision the amount of judicial knowledge which it is permissible to a judge or jury.' There is indeed no more difficult task than the devising of a method for ascertaining what is common knowledge. A jury may not be the perfect method, but a random selection from the public at large is surely better than relying upon such a select group as judges.

In such civil cases as are still tried by jury, the jury not only decides the issue of liability but also has to assess the damages. The amount of damages is not a

[1] [1930] 1 KB 467.   [2] [1931] AC 333.

matter upon which a jury is likely to show any special ability; it does not depend upon estimate of character, nor to any large extent upon general knowledge. Here, juries have a dismal record by comparison with judges, and it is for this reason among others that the judges have forced them out of personal injury claims, and actions for damages in general. Since 1933 the formal position has been that a jury has to be ordered on a charge of fraud, or in a claim for libel, slander, malicious prosecution or false imprisonment, unless the judge thinks the trial requires any extensive examination of documents or other investigations which cannot conveniently be made with a jury; and in other cases there is a discretion to order trial with a jury (see chapter 7). Most personal injury actions came before judges sitting alone, and the judges took considerable pains to be consistent with one another in their award of damages. Since 1951 counsel have been permitted to refer the judge to the amounts awarded in other cases. Since then, law publishers have regularly provided the profession with accounts of damages awards, and previous awards now amount to a kind of quasi-precedent, in which judges develop an expertise which juries cannot be expected to match.[1]

For a time there used to be a number of applications for juries and hence the case-law became confused. In 1937 the Court of Appeal ruled that the judge has a discretion whether to order a jury or not to do so, and that when his discretion has been exercised the Court of Appeal would not interfere.[2] Then in 1965 the Court of Appeal reconsidered the matter.[3] It said that judges should exercise their discretion to grant jury trial in personal injury cases sparingly, that the Court of Appeal would entertain appeals against the exercise of the discretion in future, and that it would also be more willing than previously to overturn awards of damages which juries had made. The result of this case was virtually to remove juries from personal injury actions.

Juries are still routinely used in defamation actions, and here they still get into the same sort of difficulty over the assessment of damages as they used to get into in personal injury cases. Their awards vary wildly, and nobody can begin to estimate in advance what the defendant is likely to be held liable to pay as data for the basis of a settlement. In a personal injury case there may be doubt as to whether the judge would award £4,000 or £5,000. In a libel action no one can predict whether the jury will award £500, £5,000, or £50,000. If on average the general run of awards is quite modest, from time to time juries award sums for libels which are astronomical compared with what a plaintiff might expect to get for a serious personal injury. And here, unlike in personal injury claims, the Court of Appeal usually refuses to interfere with the jury award. Jury awards are not reported so there is no accepted tariff by which to say that the award is

---

[1] The book is *Kemp and Kemp on the quantum of damages in personal injury and fatal accident claims*: a gloomy but intriguing book which is arranged in anatomical order: so much for skulls, so much for legs, so much for arms, etc. It is supplemented each month by a section in similar style in *Current Law*.

[2] *Hope* v. *Great Western Railway* [1937] 2 KB 130.

[3] [1966] 1 QB 273.

demonstrably wrong; the rules of defamation permit the plaintiff to recover 'substantial' damages whether or not he is financially any the worse off, and irrespective of whether anyone actually believed the libel. So it is difficult for them ever to say with any assurance that the sum awarded is so big that no reasonable jury would have given it.[1]

For these reasons the Faulks Committee, which was set up in 1971 to consider reforms to the law of defamation, recommended that the function of calculating damages in defamation cases should be taken away from the jury and given to the judge.[2] No serious objections have been made to this proposal, yet twelve years after the Committee reported there is no sign of its being enacted. The Committee also recommended a change in the law that normally requires the use of a jury in a defamation case. The present rule is that the court must order jury trial in a defamation case if either party wants it, and has a discretion to order trial by judge alone against the wish of one of the parties only where there are complicated documents to examine and so forth. In its place, the Committee proposed that the court should have a discretion to dispense with a jury if either party wished to do so. This recommendation, like most of the rest of the report, has borne no fruit.

The reason why juries are so bad at calculating damages is not entirely the fault of jurors. The main problem is that it is still the convention that no sums of money must be mentioned to them, and they have to be directed in non-monetary terms. Questions of money can only be settled by talking about figures. To send a jury away with the idea that if they find for the plaintiff they are to give 'substantial' damages means very little. Some jurymen feel that £100 is substantial, whilst others plunge for £100,000. The only reason why one may not talk money to a jury seems to be that no one has ever been allowed to. It is fitting to give the last word on the subject to the foreman of a jury which awarded the then huge sum of £34,000 to the TV star Telly Savalas in 1976, so attracting public criticism which moved him to write a letter to *The Times*:

I would comment that in circumstances where a jury has to decide, as men and women of the world, 'how much', the degree of uncertainty is so great that a random answer, consistent only with a total lack of any sort of yardstick, can be expected. Their Lordships would do as well to use an electronic random number indicating machine.

It is no betrayal of the secrets of the jury room to confess that, with the other jurors, I entered the Royal Courts of Justice on June 14 with not the remotest idea of what compensation is paid for anything except perhaps a dented boot and wing; haloes are outside our normal terms of reference. Apparently that is why we were asked. If that is so, the court had the outcome it deserved from the appointed procedure. I am thankful that I was not required to give judgment on something which really mattered.[3]

A jury may be as good or better than a judge in deciding a simple issue such as

[1] See *Blackshaw* v. *Lord* [1984] QB 1.
[2] *Report of the Committee on Defamation* (Faulks Committee) (1975) Cmnd 5909 para. 516.
[3] *The Times* 22 June 1976.

whether A is telling the truth when he says that B knifed him, or B when he says that he did not. But there can be little doubt that a jury of twelve is much inferior to a judge for complicated cases arising from commercial and financial dealings. The fundamental problem is that these cases are necessarily difficult and the facts necessarily take a long time to unravel. Years ago a special jury of the City of London (merchants, bankers and the like) could cope admirably with these cases,[1] but it is asking a lot from a modern jury: if the jurors have the intellectual capacity to master a complicated series of transactions and to keep their attention fixed for days and days on matters that do not concern their personal affairs, there is still the serious difficulty of obtaining a sound assessment from jurors who may have very little knowledge and understanding of the relevant business and financial practices. This was recognised in the civil jurisdiction long ago. In civil actions for fraud, defamation and certain other wrongs there still must be a jury if either party wants one, as we have seen: but under the Supreme Court Act 1981 section 69[2] the judge in such cases has power to dispense with a jury even against the wish of one of the parties where the trial requires any prolonged examination of documents or accounts or any scientific or legal investigation which cannot conveniently be made with a jury. Difficulty arises over criminal cases because a big fraud will almost invariably be serious enough for the Crown Court, and here there is no alternative to jury trial. In 1983, following increasing public disquiet about commercial fraud, an official Committee was set up under the chairmanship of Lord Roskill, a Law Lord, to consider the law and procedure in criminal trials for fraud. In its report in 1986[3] it said:

We think that, in general, the public believes that juries provide a satisfactory method of trial and this view is held by many of our witnesses. We do not know whether the public appreciates the complexity of some fraud trials or the extent to which confidence would be impaired if . . . it were generally realised that (a) trial by jury selected at random is sometimes a major contributory cause in preventing fraud cases from being brought to trial, (b) the difficulty of presenting a complex case often results in a decision to opt for less serious charges than the facts warrant.[4]

Accordingly it recommended, with one dissentient, that complicated commercial frauds should be tried not by a jury but before a special tribunal consisting of a judge and two lay members of appropriate experience in commercial matters, selected from a panel prepared by the Lord Chancellor. This sensible proposal attracted considerable public support, including some from prominent members of the Bar; but in the face of the usual outcry that it was a fundamental threat to civil liberties and would rapidly turn the country into a police state, the government did not take up this recommendation when it incorporated most of

---

[1] For special juries see note 1 on page 383 above.
[2] Originally enacted in the Administration of Justice Act 1933.
[3] *Fraud Trials Committee Report* HMSO 1986; not a command paper.
[4] *Fraud Trials Committee Report* para. 8.13.

the rest of the Roskill Committee's proposals in the Bill which became the Criminal Justice Act 1987.

A comment that is often heard is that juries in criminal cases are too soft-hearted and often acquit guilty men against the evidence. There is little doubt that the acquittal-rate before juries in contested cases is much higher than in contested cases in the magistrates' courts: a Home Office study in 1985 suggested it might be as much as twice as high.[1]

However, these figures do not necessarily mean that juries are too ready to acquit. There is the problem of whether we are comparing like with like: it could be that defendants who are in a position to choose between trial by magistrates and trial by jury tend to go for jury trial in those cases where their case is stronger anyway. And if juries really do acquit more readily than magistrates, it does not follow that it is the juries that are wrong. The argument can be stood upon its head: magistrates are too tough, because they often convict people whom juries would quite properly acquit. The difficulty in making any kind of study of the rightness or wrongness of acquittals is that it is usually impossible to say conclusively whether an acquitted defendant did or did not do it, and hence impossible in most cases to say whether he was rightly or wrongly acquitted. Two researchers, John Baldwin and Michael McConville, attempted a large-scale study which made the best of this difficulty.[2] They studied 370 jury trials which took place in Birmingham and 358 in London, and asked the judge, the police, the prosecution and the defence solicitors whether they thought the jury verdict was correct in the light of the evidence. (They were unable to ask the barristers, because the Senate predictably forbade their members to cooperate.)[3] Taking an acquittal as 'questionable' where the judge and at least one other respondent thought it was wrong, they found that some 25% of acquittals were 'questionable': a surprisingly large number. They also came up with a piece of data which was more alarming. Before this study everyone had tended to assume that if juries do sometimes irrationally acquit, they never irrationally convict. But Baldwin and McConville also found in adopting a similar test that at least 5 per cent of convictions looked doubtful – which is very worrying, bearing in mind how difficult it is for a person to appeal against a conviction if his only criticism is that the jury convicted him against the weight of the evidence (see chapter 21). This clearly suggests that juries are not always rational in their verdicts; but it does not tell us, of course, that trial by judge alone or trial by magistrates would necessarily be any better.

A further practical difficulty in assessing the performance of juries is that the

[1] See Julie Vennard, 'The outcome of contested trials' in *Managing criminal justice* (a collection of papers by the Home Office Research and Planning Unit) ed. Moxon (1985).
[2] *Jury trials* (1979).
[3] *Jury trials* p. 24. Among the reasons given for the refusal was that if barristers spoke their minds to researchers, in future 'the jury might be less likely to give credence to the arguments of counsel if they knew that counsel might privately hold a different view of the case'!

one set of people no researcher is permitted to question about how juries go about their business is the jurors themselves. The jury verdict is nothing more than a conclusion: 'guilty' or 'not guilty'.[1] No reasons are given, and verdicts are a mystery that is officially inscrutable. For certain very limited purposes the judge may sometimes put questions to the jury about their verdict, mainly to gather further information to use in sentencing,[2] but otherwise no one is permitted to know how the verdict was reached. In the past it was always said to be unlawful for anyone to question a jury about the reasons for their verdict, or for a juror to disclose them, but it was not clear exactly what criminal offence would be committed. Following the sensational trial and acquittal of Mr Jeremy Thorpe, former leader of the Liberal Party, on charges of incitement and conspiracy to murder, one of the jurors leaked an account of their debates to the press. Legal proceedings were brought against the newspaper and failed.[3]

In response to this, section 8 of the Contempt of Court Act 1981 was enacted, which makes it the offence of contempt of court to disclose or publish what went on in the jury room – even in connection with a piece of genuine and serious research. Even where something bad is said to have happened which impugns the correctness of a conviction, the Court of Appeal usually refuses to listen: that the jurors did not really agree on the verdict, for example,[4] or that the majority wanted to acquit the accused until one juror produced a list of the accused's previous convictions.[5] In this last case the court dismissed the appeal with an approving quotation from an earlier case[6] where it was argued that if the secrets of the jury room were penetrated, 'differences of individual opinion might be made manifest which, at the least, could not fail to diminish the confidence that the public rightly has in the general propriety of criminal verdicts'. The public believes the jury system works well, and it must not be disabused by anything so vulgar as facts which suggest that it does not, even if they show that someone was wrongfully convicted. This is all very odd, because it is normally axiomatic that a court is expected to give reasons for its judgment, and a repeated criticism that lawyers have made of special tribunals is that they sometimes fail to do so (see chapter 14 above).

---

[1] In theory the judge has the alternative of putting a series of questions to the jury, the answers to which he then analyses to decide whether they add up to guilty or not guilty. This is called asking for a 'special verdict'. But in criminal cases it is officially discouraged, and nowadays is never done.

[2] This is officially permitted in manslaughter cases, where the range of facts which could support a conviction for the offence is extremely wide and it is sometimes vital for the judge to know if the defendant was convicted on the basis that he killed by gross negligence, or intentionally when suffering from diminished responsibility as a result of a disease of the mind which makes him very dangerous; otherwise it is strongly discouraged – *Solomon and Triumph* [1984] Crim. LR 433, *Wilcox* [1984] Crim. LR 690.

[3] *Attorney-General* v. *New Statesman* [1981] QB 1.

[4] *Ellis* v. *Deheer* [1922] 2 KB 113; *Boston* v. *W. S. Bagshaw* [1966] 1 WLR 1135.

[5] *Thomson* (1962) 46 Cr. Ap. R 72.

[6] *Armstrong* (1922) 16 Cr. Ap. R 149.

If we want first hand evidence of how the jury system works, we must either try to set up experiments using shadow or simulated juries,[1] or rely on the odd snippets which jurors happen to tell us – since 1981, in breach of the criminal law. It seems fair and proper to give a juror the last word on the whole subject.[2]

I wonder whether the profession would be interested in a juryman's view of the legal system. These are some impressions received during a recent three-week stint at the London Crown Courts.

(1) Triviality: Almost without exception the cases were of the utmost triviality. After two days spent in deciding whether someone had taken 65p from a gas meter or three days deciding whether someone had broken a window in a pub, jurymen whose daily lives and livelihoods were suffering while they did their duty as citizens tended to become resentful. They were also very conscious of the cost to public funds.

(2) Delay: With 12 months or more delay in cases coming to court, witnesses were forced to swear to matters of detail which they could not possibly have remembered, then stick to them under cross-examination for fear of perjury or having their whole evidence discredited. This induced a general atmosphere of disbelief and unreality.

(3) Pencils and Wigs: To someone from the outside world the conduct of trials at the speed at which a judge can operate a pencil is far from engagingly quaint. There is a shorthand writer too. Yet in the outside world the electronic age has been with us for some years. Without having given the matter any previous thought I became an anti-wig man too. The effect of retaining this obsolete article of dress is to intimidate the non-lawyers present. This may be justifiable in the case of a judge, but surely not with counsel. These aspects of justice give laymen a sense of participation in some antiquated ritual and suggest that the law is centuries out of date.

(4) Evidence: Jurymen swear to try a case on the evidence put in front of them. In practice they may well reach a decision on the basis of the evidence which is not put in front of them, either reading between the lines or drawing deductions from, for instance, the accused not going into the witness box. This is because neither side is concerned to tell the jury the truth, only its 'case'. In this connection I was surprised at some of the summings up. Judges tended to read their longhand notes almost verbatim and with no indication of what might be considered salient or crucial points.

(5) Conviction: I received the impression that there must be large numbers of guilty people being found not guilty. This is particularly the case at the beginning of a session when juries are green and appear to believe that there is a reasonable doubt if no one has actually seen the accused's hand in the till. The typical jury at Newington Causeway seemed to contain one Irishman and one coloured man both of whom were liable, as a matter of principle, not to believe a single word of the police evidence. Another regular member was the tender-hearted fellow who disliked sitting in judgment on a fellow creature and could not face the responsibility of convicting anyone of anything. The remaining nine had to be very sure of themselves and include one or two strong-minded members to overcome this built-in not-guilty faction. The system appeared to me to be

---

[1] S. McCabe and R. Purves, *The shadow jury at work* (1974); LSE Jury Project, 'Juries and the rules of evidence', [1973] Crim. LR 208; A. P. Sealy and W. R. Cornish, 'Jurors and their verdicts', (1973) 36 Mod. LR 496. A useful short account of this and other material is *The British jury system* (1975), a report of a conference held in 1974 at the Institute of Criminology in Cambridge.
[2] Letter published in (1973) 123 NLJ 952.

saved from total wreck only by the innate sharp-wittedness of the average Londoner. Your electrician's mate from Shepherd's Bush knew exactly what was what and could judge as well as anyone who was and wasn't telling the truth.

(6) Sentences: I think it is fair to say that juries were often astonished, sometimes appalled, at the leniency of sentences – an interesting reversal of 18th and 19th century days. This leniency was sometimes used as an argument for acquittal: 'Why bother to find him guilty if . . .'

(7) Women: [The writer complained that there were so few women; this has changed sharply since the qualifications for jury service were extended to include those who were not householders.]

(8) Police: The treatment of police witnesses by counsel and occasionally by a judge left me wondering why anyone goes on being a policeman. When the only defence is to convince the jury that the police are a bunch of hardened liars I suppose this is inevitable, but there were occasions when it seemed as though the police were in the dock rather than the accused. One judge ordered a police witness to be reported to his superiors for giving what could be construed as false evidence after a clever counsel had tied him up in verbal knots and even the jury were lost in a maze of double negatives.

(9) Administration: Jurymen appeared to get less consideration than anyone else involved in the courts. Most of our time was spent in a hideous cafeteria which we were forbidden to leave because fresh jurors were always being required as cases ended. Throughout the session we were short of elementary conveniences such as pegs on which to hang our coats, paper in the lavatories and soap in the basins. We all felt it a pity that lawyers were debarred from jury service.

The least worst legal system in the world?

33

LAY JUSTICES AND STIPENDIARY MAGISTRATES

The task of trying cases and sentencing offenders in the magistrates' courts of this country is almost entirely done by a force of amateur justices.[1] Of these there were 27,000 in 1987, of whom nearly 24,000 were active. Their number has been increased steadily in an attempt to keep pace with the rise in crime. Only some 55 magistrates are paid, full-time professionals – 'stipendiary magistrates'. There is at first something odd in the office of justice of the peace continuing in an age that has been steadily turning away from the amateur in favour of the professional. One might have expected that in the years since 1945 the unpaid justice would have been replaced by paid magistrates, yet the system of lay justices not only continues but is more firmly established today than it was before the war.

In the 1920s and 1930s there was a growing body of criticism of justices. Some people thought that there had been a deterioration in the standards of magistrates' courts, but a more likely explanation is that a more vocal type of defendant had been appearing there. An important factor was the rise in the number of cases under the Road Traffic Acts: in 1910–14 road traffic cases were under 10 per cent of the total, but by 1938 they had reached 60 per cent. The justices of an earlier age had dealt mainly with the poor, but motor cars brought the middle and upper classes into contact with institutions that they had not previously known, and they did not like what they found.[2]

For most people 'the law' means the police, magistrates' courts and county courts. Respect for law and confidence in the judicial system depend very much upon the conduct of cases in inferior courts. One might have expected that the government would have shown some response to the criticism,[3] but until the

---

[1] See Sir Thomas Skyrme, *The changing image of the magistracy* (1979). Sir Thomas writes with unrivalled personal experience, because from 1947 to 1977 he was an official in the Lord Chancellor's Department with responsibility for the appointment of magistrates. See also Elisabeth Burney, *Magistrates, the court and the community* (1979).

[2] It is no new thing for indignation to arise when a wealthier class comes into contact with institutions previously confined to poorer classes. Prison reform has always been stimulated by the protests of political prisoners. A number of ladies, sent to prison for their violence in the suffragette movement, refused the regulation prison bath, pointing out that the baths were too dirty; unbathed but triumphant, these ladies secured some improvement in prison conditions.

[3] See for example *English justice* (1932) by 'Solicitor' (the late C. L. Hodgkinson, a practising solicitor); Charles Muir, *Justice in a depressed area* (1936) and the first edition of this book (1940).

Second World War there seemed to be no awareness of the damage that was being done by the increasing loss of confidence in the administration of summary justice. But here, as elsewhere, the war wrought a major change. The mobilisation for war of the population of this country and its resources was carried out through a code of Defence Regulations, with orders, rules and by-laws, most of which were enforced through the magistrates' courts. For 1939–45, Assizes and Quarter Sessions found 1,754 persons guilty, whereas in magistrates' courts 1,275,889 persons were found guilty. Blackout offences accounted for 928,397 of these convictions, and doubtless there were many other offences which were not particularly serious, but the load of serious cases was substantial. The effect of magistrates' courts having an important place in the war effort was two-fold. It stimulated many justices into taking their duties more seriously, and it led to the government finding time for some reforms even during the war.

The prevalent view at the end of the war was that magistrates' courts had done their work reasonably well, but at the same time there was greater awareness of the need for reform. A Royal Commission on Justices of the Peace was appointed in 1946, with wide terms of reference, covering in particular the selection and removal of justices, matters of qualification and disqualification, chairmen of benches, juvenile court panels, expenses of justices, and stipendiary magistrates, and it produced a major report in 1948.[1] A striking thing was that all the associations and virtually all the individuals who tendered evidence were agreed that the system of lay justices should continue, although there was a general acceptance of the view that there might well be an increase in the number of stipendiary magistrates. It was left for a member of the Commission, Lord Merthyr, to say in his Minority Report that it is merely a question of time before lay justices disappear, and that it would be better if we came gradually to have a system of stipendiaries. All the other members accepted the desirability of the continuance of lay justices, with the result that the main Report was concerned with improving the present system. Both this Report and the parallel Report of the Justices' Clerks Committee were well received, and all the principal recommendations requiring legislation were carried out by the Justices of the Peace Act 1949. This remained the main source of law on the powers and responsibilities of magistrates until it was replaced by the Justices of the Peace Act 1979, which codified the 1949 Act together with later Acts which had amended it. The matters concerning justices and their courts fall under a number of headings:

J. W. Robertson Scott, then editor of *The Countryman*, made great efforts to persuade his fellow-justices and the public that reform was necessary: a letter to *The Times* of 23 October 1935 was a notable contribution.

[1] Cmnd 7463. The Report and Minutes, together with the Report of the Justices' Clerks Committee, (alias the Roche Committee), (1944) Cmnd 6507, gives an authoritative account of the system of justices over the preceding generation, and is of permanent value to students of the development of our institutions.

i The appointment of justices

As was mentioned on page 184, justices are appointed for a specified 'Commission area', which usually corresponds with a county. Lay justices are appointed by the Lord Chancellor[1] on behalf of and in the name of the Crown; stipendiaries are appointed by the Crown. Anciently there was a property qualification of land to the value of £20 a year, raised to £100 in 1732, but all property qualifications were abolished in 1906. Since 1919 women have been eligible. Originally justices were paid four shillings a day during their sessions, that being about sixteen times the wages of a day labourer, but the decline in the value of money led to the office becoming unpaid; by the end of the seventeenth century the remuneration merely provided a free dinner for the bench, and today their services are entirely gratuitous (although they are paid expenses).

Appointments have long been influenced by political considerations, and this has generated much controversy. It became the practice during the eighteenth century for the Lord-Lieutenant of a county to make recommendations to the Lord Chancellor for the appointment of justices (although Lord Chancellors have always considered that they could act on any information from any source). Those who read Surtees will find in *Hillingdon Hall* that Mr Jorrocks became a justice because he was a Whig and the Lord-Lieutenant thought that there were too many Tories on the bench. In the late years of the nineteenth century and the early years of the twentieth there was great dissatisfaction with the political aspect of the magistracy. A Royal Commission on the Selection of Justices of the Peace, which reported in 1910[2] found that county benches were largely Conservatives, due to the politics of the Lords Lieutenant. The Commission recommended that the Lord Chancellor should set up advisory committees in counties and in the various commission areas, and that these should advise the Lord Chancellor on appointments. These committees were set up, and appointments came to be made through their advice – as they still are today. The composition of these committees was in the hands of the Lord Chancellor and the membership was supposed to be secret, but it was common knowledge that political parties dominated. In some areas things worked well, but at the worst the practice was for the committee to decide upon the quota of new appointments that should go to each party, so that each party produced its names on the basis of 'If you agree to our names we will agree to yours'. Under that system there was little serious

---

[1] Within the Duchy of Lancaster, the Chancellor of the Duchy performs the functions that are elsewhere performed by the Lord Chancellor. The Duchy now means, in modern local government terms, Greater Manchester, Merseyside and Lancashire. The Chancellor of the Duchy is a political minister in the government; since his duties in respect of the Duchy take up little time he is available for other government duties. See Skyrme, *The changing image of the magistracy* (1979) pp. 215–16.

[2] (1910) Cd 5250. The way in which the justices might be alien to the ways of thought of the ordinary people is seen in the figures for Wales; Appendix VI to the Minutes of Evidence, (1910) Cd 5358. Despite the enormous preponderance of Nonconformists in Wales, the justices comprised 478 Nonconformists and 1,006 members of the Church of England.

inquiry into the suitability of persons to be appointed, and the office was sometimes used as a reward for faithful political service. The Royal Commission of 1946 accepted that too much attention had been paid to political opinions in the appointment of justices in the past, but was divided as to whether it was wrong for politics to play any part in the appointment of justices at all. The minority thought that politics should be entirely ignored, both in selecting persons to serve on advisory committees and in considering names of applicants. The majority, however, took the view that this is not practicable: so long as the political parties show a keen interest in appointments being given to their own supporters, it remains necessary to guard against a 'spoils system' or calculated exclusion of adherents of any particular party. The majority recommendation was that advisory committees should be less political in composition and that members should understand that they are not present to push party claims. It was also recommended that the name of the secretary to the committee should be made public and that it should be generally known that individuals or organisations can submit suggested names for consideration as justices. At the time these words largely fell on deaf ears, but when Lord Gardiner became Lord Chancellor in 1964 he made a determined effort to put these recommendations into practice. In November 1966 he sent a note to all advisory committees stressing that justices should represent all shades of opinion, and that their political views should be taken into account in order to get a balance on the bench, not in order to exclude as far as possible one's political opponents. The note also urged advisory committees to try to appoint more justices from persons who are independent of any political party.[1]

In an attempt to widen the section of the community from whom justices of the peace are recruited, some publicity was then given to the way in which justices are appointed. In 1967 a booklet, *The appointment and duties of Justices of the Peace in England and Wales*, was prepared and widely circulated. Some advisory committees went so far as to publish a statement in a local newspaper that the committee was going to consider making recommendations and inviting the public to send them names. At first the step had mixed results: in one area over 80 names were submitted for 7 appointments and sponsoring bodies wanted to know why 'their' candidates were rejected. Nevertheless public advertisement has now become a widespread practice. At the same time a step was taken away from the secrecy which had traditionally surrounded these matters. Previously, the members of advisory committees had been expected to guard the fact of their membership like a state secret, but in 1967 the Lord Chancellor announced that he would not object if a member of an advisory committee wished to emerge into the limelight. At the time of writing, the Lord Chancellor's Department is planning to go much further and to make the membership of advisory committees public.

In public discussion there has been so much said about politics that it has

---

[1] *The Times* 3 December 1966. The text is printed in full in the previous edition of this book.

probably not been generally appreciated that the main difficulty that advisory committees have is finding enough suitable men and women to become justices. Such persons must be suitable in character and temperament, they must come from various sections of the community, and their distribution geographically is important, particularly in rural areas. In areas where much of the population is black or Asian it is important to find magistrates who come from the same groups. It is also desirable to obtain a balance of age and sex. In recent years the Lord Chancellor's Department has tried quite hard to make the composition of the magistracy reflect a good social mix, but without complete success. By 1977 the proportion of women had greatly risen, from 1:3.5 in 1947 to 1:1.7, but it has not been so easy to increase the number of workers in relation to the number of professional people. In 1977 only 8.2 per cent of justices were manual workers, as compared with 10 per cent who were doctors or dentists, and 12.5 per cent who were teachers. Part of the trouble is that being a magistrate requires giving up a large amount of time. Normally a magistrate is expected to sit at least 26 times a year, and is also expected to attend training sessions. Those who work for wages rather than salaries do not find it easy to get time off work. In times of unemployment, workers are reluctant to risk their jobs by even asking: in 1984 the Lord Chancellor's Department was said to be very concerned about the number of magistrates who were resigning for this reason.[1] Also, it seems that workers who could make time to be magistrates are often reluctant to take office because they fear what their workmates will have to say about it.[2] By contrast, the Lord Chancellor's Department has recently been more successful in recruiting black magistrates. In 1987 it announced that the proportion of blacks among the recent appointments was much the same as the proportion of blacks in the population as a whole.

When a list of possible candidates has been assembled, the advisory committee must then decide who to recommend. In the past, the way things worked would ensure that many or most of the nominees were known to some or all of the committee, but the attempt to widen the field of recruitment in recent years means that this is no longer the case. The practice therefore grew up for advisory committees to interview candidates, and since 1970 this has been universally adopted. In some places, the interview is even 'structured', with the candidate being given written problems to read, upon which he then must make his comments.

When the advisory committee has eventually settled the list the names and particulars are sent to the Lord Chancellor. If the Lord Chancellor approves the

[1] *The Times* 1 May 1984. The Royal Commission of 1946 considered whether magistrates' courts might sit in the evenings to get around this problem, but rejected it. The idea seems less feasible now, with changes for the worse in public transport and greater difficulty in persuading the support staff to work 'unsocial hours'.
[2] See Skyrme, *The changing image of the magistracy*, from whom the figures mentioned earlier are also quoted.

list, the persons are formally offered appointment, but appointment is not made until the person has been told about the commitments that must be met if he or she is appointed. There are two undertakings which must be given. One is to do a fair share of the work, and the other is to do the required training. He is then sent a note from the Lord Chancellor's office explaining that he will be expected to undergo training in two stages during the twelve months following his appointment. If the person is able and willing to give the undertakings, the formal appointment is then made. The new justice takes the oath of allegiance and the judicial oath: 'I swear by Almighty God that I will well and truly serve our Sovereign Lady Queen Elizabeth the Second in the office of Justice of the Peace, and I will do right to all manner of people after the laws and usages of the realm without fear or favour, affection or ill-will.' But he may not adjudicate until he has completed the requirements of training, which are considered in the next section.

By statute, justices are entitled to a travelling allowance for attending court or courses of instruction, a general subsistence allowance, and an allowance for loss of earnings or necessary expenditure in getting someone to look after a one-man business or a household during absence on official duty. The rates are prescribed by regulations. These allowances cannot be claimed unless there has been a loss; there is nothing corresponding to the 'attendance allowance' for members of local government councils, which amount to payment simply for attending.

Until the Justices of the Peace Act 1968 there were 2,248 persons who were justices by virtue of some office that they held. They included 1,497 mayors and chairmen of local government councils, 424 lawyers nearly all of whom held some judicial office, 315 Privy Councillors and a mixed bag of dignitaries, mostly ecclesiastical. Before 1949 the list was even longer, ex-mayors also being *ex officio* justices for the year after they held office, a situation which led to some cosy little borough courts consisting of the mayor (who had never been on a bench until his year of office) and the ex-mayor whose experience was just a year more.[1] Nearly all *ex officio* justices were abolished in 1968, and the few that remained went five years later.[2]

The virtual abolition of *ex officio* justices was not based on any poor performance, however, but upon the rule introduced in 1964 that the training of justices should be compulsory. It had to be recognised that if newly appointed ordinary justices were to be obliged to attend training courses, and other justices encouraged to attend further courses, there is no room for other persons, however experienced in public affairs or learned in the law. The only exception allowed to remain concerns the City of London, where under ancient charters the Lord Mayor and Aldermen were *ex officio* justices and sat singly in their two justice rooms. The City always has a powerful lobby when any attempt is made to

[1] More details about *ex officio* justices will be found in earlier editions of this book.
[2] The Commissioner and Assistant Commissioner of Metropolitan Police were initially retained to enable them to perform some administrative functions that depended on their being justices. The Administration of Justice Act 1973 removed this anomaly.

reduce its privileges and in this case it must be said that aldermanic dispensation of justice has a good record. The result was a compromise. A commission of the peace now issues for the City, the justices named on the commission being appointed in the usual way, but the Lord Mayor and Aldermen continue to be justices and benches are made up from the combined strength. However, the traditional element is specially recognised in the Lord Mayor being the chairman and the eight aldermen who have last been Lord Mayor being deputy-chairmen. To guard against a case where the Lord Mayor or one of the aldermen does something scandalous, the Lord Chancellor has power to exclude any of them from sitting. A rationalist has some difficulty in stomaching the way the City gets away with retaining its undemocratic and peculiar institutions, but these things are peculiarities, not abuses, and in practice it works quite well.

ii The training of justices

Justices usually know very little about the duties they are to perform when they are appointed, and it is therefore necessary to give them some elementary instruction. It is obviously not practicable to give amateur justices a comprehensive legal education, and the objects of the training, as they are set out in the *Handbook for newly appointed justices* which they are given, is to enable them:

(a)   to understand the nature of their duties so that they shall acquire the judicial mind and accordingly act judicially whilst sitting on the bench;

(b)   to acquire an elementary knowledge of the law to follow with understanding any normal case they may be called on to hear;

(c)   to acquire a working knowledge of the rules of evidence particularly in relation to what is admissible and what inadmissible;

(d)   to learn the various courses which may be taken in dealing with offenders so that they understand the nature and purpose of the sentences which they impose, and other methods of treatment which they may use and the orders they may make and their effect;

(e)   to understand the relationship which should exist between members of the bench, the clerk to the justices, the probation officers and the staff of the courts, and the duties in court of the police and of advocates.

Like much else, the training of magistrates began with a recommendation of the Royal Commission of 1946.[1] This recommended that on appointment a justice should be required to give an undertaking that he would follow a prescribed scheme of instruction. The Justices of the Peace Act 1949 made it a duty of Magistrates' Court Committees (see chapter 19(ii)) to make and administer schemes for courses of instruction for justices of their area, but did not make such courses obligatory. The response was predictably uneven, and in 1964 the Lord Chancellor eventually announced that training for new

[1] Cmnd 7463.

magistrates would be compulsory, and he appointed a Training Officer and a National Advisory Council to advise him on the steps to be taken; the Advisory Council was replaced by a smaller Advisory Committee in 1974, and its work has now been taken over by the Judicial Studies Board (see page 291).

A two-part scheme of basic training was produced.[1] The *first stage* has to be completed before a new justice sits to adjudicate. It consists of attendance at courts as an observer and elementary instruction on the duties of magistrates. The *second stage* begins when the new justice has sat and adjudicated a few times, and it must be completed within twelve months of his being appointed to the commission. It consists of not less than eight sessions of instruction or practical exercises, each of one-and-a-half hours to two hours in length, visits to the local prison, a senior detention centre and a youth custody centre, and attendance as an observer at a magistrates' court other than the one where the new magistrate normally sits. There are further courses of basic training for magistrates who are appointed to the juvenile panel or the domestic panel, which must be completed within a year of being appointed to the panel. Enforcement of these requirements rests on an undertaking given before the person is appointed. There are no tests or examinations, but a certificate of attendance at courses and visits has to be signed and sent to the Lord Chancellor's office. At first there was no further training requirement (although attendance at voluntary courses was encouraged), but all magistrates appointed after 1 January 1980 are required to complete certain minimum refresher training, known as 'obligatory refresher training', alias 'ORT'. The minimum dose is twelve hours every three years until the age of 65, when the obligation ends.

The responsibility for administering the training is on the Magistrates' Courts Committee, who are issued with periodic notes of guidance by the Lord Chancellor. The usual step has been the appointment of a special sub-committee and a local training officer (commonly a justices' clerk) who keeps in touch with the Training Officer in the Lord Chancellor's office. The scheme of training introduced in 1966 worked fairly well in the following years, but a few Magistrates' Courts Committees failed to appoint training officers and were doing the minimum to satisfy the requirements for training. Thus the Administration of Justice Act 1973 gave the Lord Chancellor power to provide courses of instruction for justices, and also provided that if a Magistrates' Courts Committee failed to provide instruction the Lord Chancellor may do so, recovering the cost from the Magistrates' Courts Committee. This is a standard form of default power, intended not so much to be used as to act as a threat to ensure that those who have a duty carry it out. The power of the Lord Chancellor to provide training is intended to supplement that of the Magistrates' Courts Committees, not to effect a take-over.

Another source of training for justices is the Magistrates' Association which

[1] See *The training of justices of the peace in England and Wales* (1965) Cmnd 2856.

has branches covering the whole country. These branches arrange meetings open to all justices within a wide area. The Association holds national training conferences and training days. Some university extra-mural departments organise residential courses. The pattern of such meetings and courses varies: sometimes there are lectures followed by a discussion, sometimes intensive training 'workshops' built around practical problems. Judges, experienced justices, justices' clerks and others involved in the criminal justice system such as police, probation officers and prison governors all have a role to play here. The organising of such functions allows justices from all parts of the country to meet each other and exchange ideas. As for funding, some of these courses are approved for training purposes by the Lord Chancellor's Department and rank for full grant, whilst others are approved for such purposes by individual Magistrates' Courts Committees and course fees and expenses incurred by justices are met by the Committee.

In this section the emphasis has been on compulsory training. In practice, however, most magistrates need little compulsion, and tend to ask for more rather than less training.[1]

iii The retirement and removal of justices

The position has for long been that justices are appointed for life but have no security of tenure, being liable to be removed from the commission if the Lord Chancellor sees fit. By convention the Lord Chancellor must exercise this power in a judicial manner and justices are not removed except for good cause.

Historically, the main problem was not the retention of justices guilty of misconduct or scandalous behaviour but the retention of justices who were ineffective, particularly through old age. The first edition of this book described how one justice celebrated his 100th birthday by sitting in court. Perhaps he managed well, but the magistracy was full of people twenty and thirty years his junior who were deaf, doddering and senile. In 1938 the Lord Chancellor sent out a circular suggesting that justices who were incapacitated by old age or infirmity should have their names placed on a Supplemental List; they would then no longer be summoned to attend courts, but they would remain justices and could 'sign papers' for people and do similar work. In some districts there was a good response, but in other areas justices who had not sat for years, and who were perhaps wise not to have sat, feared removal if they remained inactive, and returned to active service; in those parts the circular was known as the 'Resurrection Circular'. Eventually, as a result of the recommendations of the Royal Commission in 1946, a statutory retiring age was introduced. The age was fixed at 75 in 1949, and in 1968 it was reduced to 70, which is the present retiring age. On reaching the age of 70 a justice does not cease to be a justice: retirement

[1] On this see the survey conducted by J. Baldwin, 'The Compulsory Training of Magistrates', [1975] Crim. LR 634.

is carried out by the gentler expedient of compulsorily putting the justice on the Supplemental List. The Lord Chancellor can also direct that a name be put on the list if he is satisfied 'either (a) by reason of that person's age or infirmity or other like cause it is expedient he should cease to exercise judicial functions as a justice for the area; or (b) that the justice declines or neglects to take a proper part in the exercise of those functions'.[1] Justices' clerks make returns of attendance to advisory committees, and it is the responsibility of those committees to keep the Lord Chancellor informed.

Serious misbehaviour by justices of the peace happens rarely, and when it does arise it has considerable news value.[2]

Considering how many justices of the peace there are, it is much to their credit as a body that misbehaviour is so rare. Out of some 27,000 magistrates, only about a dozen a year are removed from office. This may be done for some piece of scandalous misbehaviour, or for any less serious conduct which the Lord Chancellor considers likely to undermine public confidence if the person concerned continues to sit on the bench. At one time those who had been cited as co-respondents in divorces invariably had to go; more recently it was the practice to remove homosexuals, even after homosexual behaviour in private had ceased to be automatically illegal in 1967.[3] People are also removed sometimes for taking part in political demonstrations which are thought to be a threat to law and order; in 1985, not without some controversy, a woman magistrate was removed for taking part in a demonstration outside her court-house in favour of a CND supporter who refused to pay a fine, and for refusing to give the Lord Chancellor an undertaking not to do the same again.[4]

The usual reason for removal, however, is the commission of some criminal offence. For a minor traffic offence a magistrate can expect no more than a reprimand, but if it is more serious he will be removed if he does not resign. Difficulty has arisen over convictions for excess blood-alcohol. For many years any magistrate who incurred a conviction for drink-drive offences was automatically removed, but the practice was relaxed after the incident in which a Lord Justice of Appeal – who was practically irremovable by virtue of his office – did not resign after being so convicted, so making it morally impossible to remove Circuit Judges and Recorders who found themselves in this position (see chapter 31). Practice thereafter has been for a magistrate convicted of a drink-drive offence to be suspended from office for the period of his disqualification from driving, after which the Lord Chancellor may or may not remove him. It might have been thought that the cases of judges and magistrates were materially

[1] Justices of the Peace Act 1979 s. 8 (4).
[2] When a justice of the peace was convicted of a murder in 1985, the fact that he was a justice of the peace was given great prominence in the newspapers: see *The Times* 26 March 1985.
[3] See Skyrme, *The changing image of the magistracy* chapter 11. The editor does not know whether this is still the practice.
[4] The facts are fully stated by an official of the Lord Chancellor's Department in a letter in (1985) 135 NLJ 1029.

different. To sack a judge is to deprive him of his living, but to sack a magistrate is not; a judge, furthermore, can easily be removed from criminal to civil work, something which cannot usually be done with a magistrate. The spectacle of either judges or magistrates continuing in office after drink-drive convictions must surely do little to convince the public that drinking and driving is a serious matter, or that it is no light thing to be convicted of an offence which carries the possibility of a prison sentence.

When removing a justice of the peace from office the Lord Chancellor is not required to hold a formal hearing. It is a very painful step to take, however, and it is not taken lightly.[1] Unless the facts are very clear, therefore, it is the practice to write and ask the errant justice for an explanation before removing him. In some cases he may even be interviewed before this is done.

iv Stipendiary magistrates

In addition to lay justices there are a few professional, full-time stipendiary magistrates. At the time of writing there are about 55 of them, some 40 in London and 15 in various other busy centres.

The system of paid magistrates began in London. It had its origin in two great defects of the administration of justice in the metropolis in the eighteenth century, namely the poor quality of the justices and the absence of any adequate police force. An Act of 1792 set up seven public offices with paid magistrates, in addition to an existing office at Bow Street. Several Acts amending and extending the system followed. These paid magistrates were in charge of a few constables, and when the Metropolitan Police were established in 1829 they were placed under two magistrates. In 1839 the police were placed under a Commissioner and separated from the metropolitan magistrates.[2] The 1839 Act required these magistrates to be appointed from barristers, solicitors becoming eligible in 1949. In the central area of London, now called the Inner Area of Greater London, the more important part of summary jurisdiction has traditionally been exercised by professional stipendiary magistrates. The system of lay justices exists there too; at one time their work was restricted to minor matters and to juvenile courts, but the Administration of Justice Act of 1964 fully integrated the work of stipendiaries and lay justices. Where the case goes before a stipendiary, however, he continues to sit alone. The administrative system of Magistrates' Courts Committees (see chapter 19(ii)) is substantially varied to suit the particular circumstances of Inner London.

[1] Sir Thomas Skyrme, *The changing image of the magistracy* p. 145, describes how he had to write to a woman whose behaviour was showing signs of mental disturbance, temporarily suspending her from sitting, and 'the following morning the clerk to her court telephoned to tell me that she had been found dead with her head in a gas oven and my letter in her hand'!

[2] Remnants of the old system survived in the magistrates being styled Metropolitan Police Magistrates until the 1949 Act renamed them Metropolitan Stipendiary Magistrates, and the Commissioner of Police continued to be a justice of the peace (though he did not sit in court) until the Administration of Justice Act 1973.

The use of stipendiary magistrates outside London began with an Act of 1813 which allowed the appointment of a stipendiary for the Manchester area. A general power was given by the Municipal Corporations Act 1835 which was substantially re-enacted in 1882. The essence was that a borough could ask for a stipendiary and if that request was granted, as it normally was, the Crown made the appointment on the advice of the Home Secretary. When a vacancy occurred it could only be filled if the borough made a further request, and sometimes they did not: hence the number varied from time to time.[1]

If a stipendiary was needed for an area not covered by the Municipal Corporations Act it was necessary to have a special Act of Parliament; such Acts were passed from time to time. The Justices of the Peace Act 1949 simplified matters by giving the Crown a general power to appoint a stipendiary outside London, but it was only exercisable when the locality requested one, and as it was the locality which had to pay for him, not many requests were made.

Since the Administration of Justice Act 1973 the position has been different. The Crown, on the advice of the Lord Chancellor, may appoint a stipendiary, or more than one stipendiary, for any commission area outside the Inner London area (which is already served by metropolitan stipendiaries appointed under separate legislation) and the City of London. No request from the locality is needed; if the Lord Chancellor thinks an area needs a stipendiary he may appoint one, though doubtless there would be consultation. The salary is determined, like other judicial stipends, by the Lord Chancellor with consent of the Minister for the Civil Service, and like other judicial stipends it is charged on and paid out of the consolidated fund. To be eligible for appointment a candidate must be a barrister or solicitor of at least seven years' standing. By statute the maximum number of metropolitan stipendiaries is fixed at 60 and the number for outer London and the provinces at 40. There is power to raise this maximum number by Order in Council, but it has not been necessary to do so, because up to now only a little over half this number have been appointed. In addition, if the Lord Chancellor thinks it desirable to appoint a person as a stipendiary for a short period (not exceeding three months at one time) in order to avoid delays in the administration of justice in an area, he may do so and the temporary stipendiary will be paid for out of public funds. In recent years this power has proved useful in times of public disorder: during the miners' strike of 1984 the increase of work caused by 'flying pickets' was partly handled by a team of 'flying stipes'.[2]

As the limit on the number of stipendiary magistrates can be removed by Order in Council, the legal framework theoretically exists for the complete replacement of lay justices by stipendiary magistrates. There are no signs at the moment of this happening, but it is nevertheless interesting to consider the arguments for and against the idea.

[1] For further details of the position before 1949 see R. M. Jackson, 'Stipendiary magistrates and lay justices', (1946) 9 Mod. LR 1, and earlier editions of this book.
[2] See Rutherford and Gibson, 'Special hearings', [1987] Crim. LR 440.

In the past it has always been said that this would be quite impracticable to replace lay justices with stipendiaries because of the cost. Stipendiary magistrates need stipends, but lay justices do the job for expenses only. However, there is more to it than this, because the real question is which of the two groups are the more cost-effective. The cost of running a court is more than the cost of stipends or expenses to its judges. The court-room has to be paid for, repaired, heated and lit, and while it is open there are the salaries of the clerks and the rest of the assistant staff. Stipendiaries are generally recognised as able to get through the business much quicker than lay justices: some people say as much as three times quicker. If so, it is possible that stipendiary magistrates in place of lay justices might actually save the court system their stipends in other costs. Such research evidence as exists on the subject falls short of proving the point, but it certainly calls into question the traditional assumption that lay justices are cheaper.[1]

Relative speed is not all, of course. We must also take into account the quality of justice which each system delivers. In earlier editions of this book Professor Jackson forcibly put the point that stipendiary magistrates often succumb to the sheer boredom of dealing with petty crime day after day and become tetchy and irritable. This, he said, was all the more serious because they sit in court alone and thus have no one to restrain them; indeed, stipendiary magistrates are the only people who regularly administer criminal justice without any diffusion of responsibility. Eccentric stipendiaries there have been – including the formidable lady who in 1945 gave a station porter six weeks' imprisonment for stealing three tablets of soap[2] – but the general quality of justice which stipendiaries deliver seems to be high, and is often said to be higher than lay justices provide. A solicitor recently wrote that

The most immediate apparent difference is the speed and efficiency with which matters are dealt ... it is partly because they have the confidence to cut short long-winded advocates, to exclude irrelevant evidence and to indicate intended sentences at an earlier stage during mitigation. They also generally deal more robustly with applications for adjournments. The other obvious difference is the greater legal knowledge of stipendiaries ... From my inquiries of local solicitors, I have the strong impression that defence advocates feel they obtain, if anything, a fairer trial from stipendiaries. As far as penalties are concerned the general feeling is that stipendiaries are more consistent.[23]

This solicitor was a prosecuting solicitor, but his words are consistent with what this editor has often heard from lawyers who frequently defend. Defence lawyers sometimes also say that stipendiary magistrates are more inclined to stand up to the police on bail applications than are lay magistrates.

A further point in favour of stipendiaries is that they are better able than lay

---

[1] A useful review is 'Stipendiary and lay justices' by Paul Softley, (1985) 149 JPN 710.
[2] An incident in 1945 recounted by Softley, 'Stipendiary and lay justices'.
[3] Quoted by Alan Fraser, (1986) 150 JPN 312, 314.

justices to handle the occasional lengthy case which comes the way of the magistrates' court. Lay justices usually have a rota for sitting so that they have a day on the bench every week or two weeks, which often means that if they cannot deal with a case within the space of one or two days it has to be adjourned for a week or so. Doing judicial work by instalments is troublesome to everyone concerned, and the trouble can be avoided by a stipendiary who can sit day after day until the case is finished.

Despite the existence of a number of strong arguments in favour of stipendiaries, there is at present no public demand for them in the place of lay magistrates. This fact may reflect one of the standard arguments in favour of juries: that in a world where everything is increasingly taken out of our hands and run by experts, it is good for the lay voice to be heard.

v Justices' clerks and court clerks

A justices' clerk was originally the personal clerk to an individual justice.[1] Justices were entitled to take fees for some of their acts, and whilst some justices did their own clerical work and kept the fees, when a justice had a clerk it was customary for the clerk to take the fees due to his master. During the eighteenth century and first half of the nineteenth there was a tendency for the justices of a district to share the same clerk, and an Act of 1851 made it permissible to pay the clerk a salary; he became the clerk to the bench. The Justices Clerks Act 1877 required that clerks should be either lawyers or men who had worked as assistants to a justices' clerk. Each bench was left to appoint its own clerk. The clerk was paid an inclusive salary, which meant that he engaged his own assistants and paid them and all other expenses out of his salary; thus the more he paid out in wages, office expenses, stamps and stationery the less there was left for his personal remuneration. Some slight central control was introduced, and there were provisions for the Home Office to settle any disputes between the local authority and the justices about the appointment of a clerk or the amount of his salary.

A Committee which reported in 1934 on imprisonment in default of payment of fines[2] found it necessary to discuss the position of justices' clerks, since the recovery of fines and other payments (and imprisonment in default) depend so much on proper office work. It was shown that the obsolete method of paying clerks could result in needless imprisonment. In 1938 this led to the Home Secretary setting up a Committee on Justices' Clerks, which eventually reported in 1944.[3] The Committee found that the provision of a satisfactory system of clerks is bound up with the whole organisation, administration and finance of magistrates' courts; hence the Report covered a much wider field than might be

[1] The definitive study is Penny Darbyshire, *The magistrates' clerk* (1983).
[2] (1934) Cmd 4649.
[3] Cmd 6507.

expected from its title. One of its main recommendations was the creation of Magistrates' Courts Committees to look after the administrative side of magistrates' courts (see chapter 19, section ii). This and most of its other recommendations were carried out in the Justices of the Peace Act 1949; the relevant provisions are now mainly to be found in the Justices of the Peace Act 1979.

The subsequent history of justices' clerks has had three main themes. The first is the shift from part-time clerks to clerks who do the job full-time as their only employment. The second is the substitution of legally qualified clerks for people who had no legal qualifications. And the third is the general shift in the content of the job from giving legal advice to running an administrative empire.

Traditionally most clerks did the job part-time, many of them being local solicitors.[1] However, it has long been thought better to have full-time clerks if possible. A part-time clerk is likely from time to time to find that the duties of his clerkship and the calls of private practice conflict. The work of justices has increased in quantity and still more in complexity, so that a fair amount of reading and study is needed to keep up to date, and naturally a part-time clerk (who has the common difficulty of keeping up with matters affecting the general practice of a solicitor) is hardly going to find enough time for study in connection with a part-time appointment. The reason why most clerks were originally part-time is that if benches of magistrates were small, it was customary for each bench to have its own clerk, and a small bench did not generate enough work to justify a full-time employee. To some extent the general increase in the work-load of magistrates' courts has altered this, but the main alteration has resulted from the gradual amalgamation of petty sessional divisions to produce a smaller number of larger benches: something which it was originally very difficult to achieve, but which since 1949 has been possible by a simple administrative process.[2] Where it has not been thought suitable to amalgamate several divisions, the alternative method is to have one full-time clerk who acts for a clutch of neighbouring benches, and this too has been widely done. The result has been the virtual disappearance of the part-time clerk, and also a great reduction in the number of clerkships. In 1938 there were 822 justices' clerks, of whom 732 were part-time. In 1985 the number had shrunk to 323, of whom only 19 were part-time; for 1986 the figures were 315 and 14.

At one time many justices' clerks were not legally qualified. Paradoxically, it was mainly those who did the job full-time who were unqualified: the part-time clerks were usually solicitors. The Committee on Justices' Clerks felt that the time had come when long service with a clerk should not be a qualification for

[1] Probably the most famous one of these was the celebrated poisoner, Armstrong!
[2] At one time divisions had to be altered by a clumsy procedure involving Quarter Sessions, but this was replaced by a review by the Magistrates' Courts Committee and an Order by the Home Secretary. In the case of Domestic Panels, the Secretary of State can compel an amalgamation if the local Magistrates' Courts Committee drags its heels.

appointment, and that after a transition period only barristers or solicitors should be eligible. The provisions of the 1949 Act, now largely reproduced in the 1979 Act, are framed on that principle. Appointments are confined to barristers or solicitors of not less than five years' standing, (or less than five years' standing if they have had the specified amount of experience on the job), but preserving existing interests by making long service a qualification if a person had ten years' experience as an assistant before 1960, and making it easier for some experienced assistants to become solicitors. The result has been that the great majority of justices' clerks are now either barristers or solicitors, and the justices' clerk without legal qualifications is becoming a thing of the past. In 1975 the membership of the Justices' Clerks Society (to which all but 23 justices' clerks then belonged) showed that of 378 members, 254 were solicitors, 53 were barristers, and 71 were qualified by long service; in 1985, out of a membership of 312, 152 were solicitors, 120 barristers and only 21 were qualified by experience.

The third striking thing about justices' clerks is the way in which the nature of the job has changed. Originally the clerk would usually be the only functionary who worked for the bench, and much of his work would consist of advising the justices in court. The amalgamation of small benches, and the practice of having one full-time clerk to service several benches, means that nowadays the typical justices' clerk is primarily the head of a sizeable office. He advises the magistrates on the law in a general way, because it is usually he who is responsible for arranging their training, but the day-to-day work of sitting in court and offering immediate advice to lay magistrates as and when real problems arise is now generally done by one or more of a team of assistants: a deputy-clerk, or a deputy-clerk and a number of people still further down the ladder who are usually known as 'court clerks'.

Here there is a paradox. It was felt to be important for justices' clerks to be legally qualified so that lay magistrates should be advised in court by someone with a sound knowledge of the law, to avoid the situation where the blind lead the blind. It was with this in mind that the requirements about legal qualifications for justices' clerks were introduced. But these requirements apply only to the justices' clerk himself, and do not restrict those who may be appointed to the assistant posts. When it came to filling these posts it was up to each Magistrates' Courts Committee in each area to decide what qualifications they required, and some committees did not require any. As the pressure of business gradually tended to remove the justices' clerk himself from the courtroom, so his place was often taken by an assistant with no qualifications – and sometimes with little experience either. By this the policy of the 1949 Act in requiring justices' clerks to be properly qualified was considerably undermined, and in some places the quality of summary justice suffered as a result. It took a long time for Parliament or the Home Office to take action on this problem. In 1968 the Justices of the Peace Act was amended: not however to impose a statutory requirement, as with justices' clerks, but only to give the Secretary of State power to make rules about qualifications for assistant clerks by means of delegated legislation. It took the Home Office another six years to produce draft rules, and it was not until 1979 that the Justices' Clerks (Qualifications of Assistants) Rules were finally made.[1]

These rules are anything but stringent, because an assistant clerk counts as qualified to sit in court not only if he is a barrister or a solicitor, but also if he has passed the first but not the second part of the examination necessary to become one, or if he has 'successfully completed a relevant course'. What is meant by 'a relevant course' is the special part-time course for assistant clerks which is run by the Home Office – a much less serious course of training than qualifying as a barrister or a solicitor would be. The root of the problem, of course, is money. People with professional qualifications cost more than people without them; it suits some Magistrates' Courts Committees to save money by hiring unqualified assistant clerks, and it emphatically suits the Treasury which has to find some 80 per cent of the money for the Magistrates' Courts Committees to spend. The position is anything but satisfactory[2] and public pressure has been exerted to change it, including by the Justices' Clerks Society.[3] Nevertheless in 1987 the Home Secretary announced that there would be no change in the rules 'in the foreseeable future'.[4]

As has already been mentioned, justices' clerks and assistant staff are now appointed not by the bench for which they will work but by the local Magistrates' Courts Committee. The appointment of a justices' clerk (who is an office holder and who holds his office at the pleasure of the Magistrates' Courts Committee) requires the approval of the Home Office, and the Committee can be required to submit particulars of any other candidate for the appointment so that the Home Office may see what choice was before the Committee. Full-time clerks and staff are subject to a retiring age and are superannuable on the lines of staffs of local authorities. An important development since 1949 has been the growth of national joint negotiating machinery. Scales of salaries for clerks and their assistants and other conditions of service are now settled by two bodies of Whitley type. The management side is made up of representatives of Magistrates' Courts Committees, and of the paying authorities, with the Justices' Clerks Society or the Association of Magisterial Officers representing the officers' side. Clerks, whether full-time or part-time, are paid in accordance with scales varying with the size of the population of the division or divisions which they serve, whilst assistants are graded according to the responsibilities of each post.

The Justices' Clerks Society was established in 1839 to bring justices' clerks together. The Society is of course actively concerned about its members' salaries and conditions of service, but the Society is also concerned with the whole range of magisterial affairs and improvements of the law and administration. Represen-

---

[1] SI 1979 No. 570.
[2] For details, see Penny Darbyshire, *The magistrates' clerk* (1983).
[3] See their document 'Magistrates' court staff training' (1983).
[4] Reported in (1987) 151 JPN 1.

tative justices' clerks attend the meetings of the Council of the Magistrates' Association and are co-opted to the Committees. The Justices' Clerks Society is a voluntary body primarily dependent on the subscriptions of its members for its funds. There is no remuneration for all the work that is done in helping the Lord Chancellor, the Home Office or the Magistrates' Association. The Society consists of justices' clerks only, and as there are now only just over 300 of these, all this work is spread over a fairly small number of shoulders.

At one time the office of justices' clerk, like many others in the English justice system, existed in isolation, in as much as it represented no point on any kind of promotional ladder. There was no recognised way up to the position, or any clear upward route out of it. This is no longer the case. Those who are appointed as justices' clerks are almost invariably assistant or deputy clerks of ability and ambition, and some of the more promising justices' clerks have gone on to posts as stipendiary magistrates. Stipendiary magistrates are sometimes elevated to become Circuit Judges, and there are some former justices' clerks among the stipendiaries who have reached the Circuit Bench.

vi The Magistrates' Association

The Magistrates' Association was founded by some leading magistrates meeting in the Guildhall in 1920. In its earlier years it had a somewhat mixed reputation because it tended to press for reforms that seemed unnecessary to many conservatively-minded magistrates and chairmen of quarter sessions. Nevertheless, it grew in membership and strength and by the time of the Royal Commission in 1946 it had become an institution of some importance. Since then its membership has steadily increased and nowadays it has over 26,000 members. As the total number of lay magistrates is 27,000, there are few who do not belong to it. It is organised into 56 branches which cover the whole of the country, and there is a central office with a small staff in London. It issues a monthly journal, *The Magistrate*, that is sent to every member. It has always been a voluntary body, financed for the most part by the subscriptions of its members; but in recent years it has received a grant from the Lord Chancellor on account of the work that the Association does in support of his responsibility for training. From its beginning the Association's major activity has been the training of justices. A small book, *Notes for new magistrates*, was produced and a copy sent to each new magistrate; later the Lord Chancellor took over the distribution. Before the days when the State provided training for magistrates, the Association ran a postal training course. As already mentioned (chapter 33, section ii), it is still heavily involved in continuing education. Sentencing exercises and other activities are also organised by branches. In 1967, in response to public disquiet about the different levels of sentencing for motoring offences which prevailed in different areas, the Association issued its first list of 'Suggestions for traffic offence penalties'. These are regularly published, and have the approval of the

Lord Chancellor. So helpful have magistrates' courts found these that at the time of writing the scheme is about to be extended to other offences which they frequently have to try.

The branches elect representatives to the Council of the Association which meets in London three times a year. The Council elects Committees for the principal matters with which magistrates are concerned. There is frequent consultation between the Association and the Home Office and with the Lord Chancellor's Department. When a memorandum of evidence has to be prepared for an official body, the Association is in a very good position to collect views and material because inquiry can be made through the branches. It is often most important in the formulation of policy to be able to say 'This is how the legal or administrative machinery is working in the courts' or 'in such and such places or regions'. The Association has a good record of providing Royal Commissions, Departmental Committees, the Law Commission and other bodies with evidence based on observation and experience.

There can be little doubt that the quality of lay justices and their courts is very much better than when the first edition of this book appeared. The process of improvement owes most to a sound legislative basis, but it also owes much to the will among magistrates themselves to improve things, which has largely manifested itself through the efforts of the Magistrates' Association.

34

THE ADMINISTRATION OF THE COURTS

Perhaps the most astonishing chapter in the history of our law courts is that dealing with the official staff.[1] Medieval law had a poorly developed notion of contract and a highly developed law of property. Offices, such as clerkships in the courts, came to be regarded as property; the official had a freehold for life in the office, just as he might have such a freehold in land. As the work of the courts increased the staff was not increased accordingly, for that would have interfered with property: the process was for the office holder to continue to receive the fees, but for him to employ men to do the work. In the early nineteenth century the chief clerk of the King's Bench received on an average £6,280 a year, and paid his deputy £200 a year. The patronage to these highly paid or sinecure offices was partly in the government and partly in the judges: 'The fact that many highly placed people both in the fashionable and the judicial world had an interest in these offices, made the system extraordinarily difficult to eliminate.'[2]

Royal Commissions investigated, and a series of statutes ending with the Courts of Justice Salaries and Funds Act 1869 converted court officials into salaried officials with pension rights assimilated to the civil service. The Treasury was given some control over salaries and the establishment, but the methods of appointment remained substantially unchanged. Later legislation as a result of further Commissions and Committees brought the legal departments more under the control of the Lord Chancellor and the Treasury. The whole situation was reviewed by the Royal Commission on the Civil Service in their sixth Report in 1915.[3] They found that 'the present method of appointment in all the Legal Departments is nomination, subject, in the case of some of the higher officials, to certain qualifications imposed by statute, and in the case of the clerical staff generally, to a qualifying examination of an elementary character'. In general the head of each division nominated the appropriate officers, so that the appointments were made by the Lord Chancellor, the Lord Chief Justice, the Master of the Rolls, and the President of the Probate Division. 'After making full allowance

---

[1] Holdsworth, *History of English law* (1903) I, 246f., with appendices taken from Parliamentary Papers, is the most accessible account. *The black book of abuses*, (1819 and later editions) is a virulent contemporary exposure.
[2] Holdsworth, *History of English law* p. 250.
[3] (1915) Cd 7832. What is said in this book is taken from this Report except where other authority is cited.

for heredity in legal talent and for the tendency among members of certain distinguished families to adopt a legal career in successive generations, we believe that "influence", as it is commonly called, has had a considerable share in determining the appointments.' Of the seven King's Bench masters and two assistant masters, four were sons of judges and two or three were relations of judges. Of four Chancery masters, two were sons of dead judges and one was a nephew of the Lord Chancellor at the time of his appointment.[1] Of eight clerks of Assize, five were sons of judges. In evidence the following passage took place: 'The Clerk of Assizes Act was passed after the appointment of a Mr Bovill, who had been a cavalry officer. He really did not know much about it at first.' 'Was he the son of a judge?' 'He was the son of a Lord Chief Justice, and that raised rather a scandal, because his military methods did not quite accord with practice.'[2]

The Report notes that the Lord Chancellor had shown less tendency to appoint for family reasons; we might hazard the conjecture that he had more political debts to pay and put his party higher than his family. The higher official posts in the courts carried salaries up to £3,800 a year and the qualifications of barrister or solicitor were necessary. The ordinary clerkships were paid at rates similar to those in the civil service. The Commission's conclusion is not surprising: 'In the appointment of clerks the part played by "influence" appears to be less than in the case of the higher appointments, perhaps, because, in Lord Loreburn's words, these posts are "not an object of very great ambition".' The Commission recommended that the power of appointment (except for the Pay Office and the judges' clerks and secretaries) should be vested in the Lord Chancellor with an advisory committee from his own department, the civil service commission and a solicitor. That would have taken away the rights of the Lord Chief Justice and the President of the Probate Division and it was not accepted.

Under the Supreme Court of Judicature (Consolidation) Act 1925 the financial officers in the Supreme Court Pay Office were appointed by the Treasury and the clerks of that office through the civil service. The Masters in the King's Bench Division and Chancery Division were appointed by the heads of the Divisions; that is, by the Lord Chief Justice, the Lord Chancellor and the President respectively. The district registrars of the High Court were appointed by the Lord Chancellor and the district probate registrars by the President of the Probate Division. Two somewhat odd examples of judicial patronage continued. Clerks of Assize were appointed by the judge who was last on the Circuit when the vacancy occurred. In 1946 Parliament provided that Clerks of Assize should be appointed by the Lord Chief Justice and should be officers of the Supreme Court. Other duties previously performed by special circuit officers became the duties of the general body of Supreme Court officers. When a barrister was made a judge he took with him his clerk who thus became an official paid out of public

[1] Minutes of Evidence, (1915) Cd 8130 Question 50,660.
[2] Cd 81230 Questions 51,452, 51,453.

funds. Since 1954 judges' clerks have been appointed by the Lord Chancellor.

The position in county courts was investigated by the Royal Commission on the Civil Service and by the County Court Staff Committee in 1920.[1] These investigations showed a thoroughly unsatisfactory state of affairs. Registrars of county courts were appointed by the county court judge, subject to the approval of the Lord Chancellor. Remuneration depended upon the number of plaints. Since it is often possible for a plaintiff to choose in which county court he will commence proceedings, persons with a large volume of debt collecting could transfer their 'custom' to another court if a registrar was not sufficiently obliging: a registrar who wanted to keep his income at a satisfactory level had a strong temptation to lean in favour of creditors.[2]

The clerks in county courts were employees of the registrar. They were paid either from an allowance made by the Treasury for clerk-hire, or by the registrars personally. Their conditions of work, pay and security of employment depended upon the registrar. In some cases decrepit and senile clerks were still employed, since no pension was available and kindly registrars did not care to dismiss men who would have to resort to poor relief. Other registrars were not so kind-hearted. Some reforms were made by statute, consolidated in the County Courts Act 1934. The fact that some county courts have a small volume of business made it difficult to adopt a uniform system. All registrars were to be appointed by the Lord Chancellor, who (with the concurrence of the Treasury) directed the salary to be paid and whether the registrar was to be full-time or not.

The position in respect of Assizes and Quarter Sessions was far from uniform. Court-houses and their maintenance had to be provided by County and Borough Councils, and the council provided some of the services needed. The sheriff was responsible for summoning juries. The appointment of Clerks of Assize has already been described. Clerks of the peace and supporting staff for Quarter Sessions were paid by the county or borough.

It was obvious that the reorganisation of the courts by the Courts Act 1971 had to provide a new system. The relevant provisions of that Act are:

27. The Lord Chancellor may, with the concurrence of the Minister for the Civil Service as to numbers and salaries, appoint such officers and other staff for the Supreme Court[3] (including the district probate registries) and county courts as appear to him necessary –

(a) for setting up a unified administrative court service, and
(b) for discharging any functions in those courts conferred by or under this or any other Act on officers so appointed, and
(c) generally for carrying out the administrative work of those courts.

28. (1) The Secretary of State for the Environment may with the approval of the Treasury, provide, equip, maintain and manage such courts, offices, buildings, judges'

[1] (1920) Cmd 1049.
[2] Minutes of Evidence, (1915) Cd 7832 Question 51,908; (1920) Cmd 1049 p. 5.
[3] The Supreme Court now means the Court of Appeal, the High Court and the Crown Court.

lodgings and other accommodation as may be necessary or desirable for carrying on the business of the Supreme Court and county courts.

'Administration' of courts covers a wide range of services. There are few problems of the 'housekeeping' aspects, other than securing enough money to pay for sufficient court rooms, offices and so forth. The troublesome part of court administration is regulating the flow of cases. The administrators must programme the work of the courts but they cannot follow classical models of administration because they do not control the central operation of the institution, that is the trial and disposition of cases; in particular there must be nothing to suggest that the administration controls the judiciary. The Beeching Commission said this:

The administrative officers . . . shall exercise firm managerial control over all matters affecting the smooth running of the courts other than those which have a direct bearing upon the discharge of judicial functions. This being so, we consider it very necessary, on constitutional grounds, to provide a visible and effective safeguarding of the position of the judges serving the Circuits by assigning to each Circuit a senior member of the judiciary who will have a general responsibility for that Circuit and a particular responsibility for all matters affecting the judiciary there. (Para. 256)

The administrative structure is not laid down in the Courts Act 1971: it rests on directions given by the Lord Chancellor under statutory powers as to the location and sittings of the High Court and on directions by the Lord Chief Justice and the Lord Chancellor under statutory powers for the Crown Court under section 4. The arrangement is that the Lord Chief Justice nominates two Queen's Bench Division judges to each Circuit as Presiding Judges, the number of two ensuring that ordinarily there would be one of them in the area of the Circuit. There are also advisory committees covering all the circuits and liaison judges (Circuit Judges or Recorders) who are nominated to maintain contact with justices of the peace in the various Commission Areas.

Court administrators are not required to have legal qualifications but of the first appointments in 1970, four were solicitors and two more were barristers with administrative experience. In each Circuit the court administrator has a relatively small staff at the Circuit headquarters. Below the Circuit administrator there are courts administrators who have overall responsibility for the running of all locations of the High Court, Crown Courts and county courts. Day to day organisation is in the hands of chief clerks at the various centres. Under the new system, the staff of the Supreme Court – that is, the Court of Appeal, the High Court and the Crown Court – and county courts are part of the civil service, and have rank, pay and allowances accordingly. There were some difficulties in the transition, principally because some staff of courts regarded themselves as belonging to a special category and resented becoming 'mere' civil servants. Whilst the Lord Chancellor has general responsibility, matters of recruitment, pay and management come under the Civil Service Department.

The position of justices' clerks has been explained in chapter 33, section v above. It is a pity that inter-departmental jealousies and unwillingness to upset the *amour-propre* of local authorities prevented the staff of magistrates' courts being brought within a comprehensive system of staffing law courts, but we have to bow to this decision of politicians – for the time being.

VI

THE EUROPEAN DIMENSION

35

THE EUROPEAN CONVENTION ON HUMAN RIGHTS[1]

In 1949 the United Kingdom was one of a group of Western European countries which agreed to set up the Council of Europe. This organisation was responsible for the European Convention on Human Rights, an international treaty which binds the ratifying states to observe certain standards of behaviour towards individuals, and sets up at Strasbourg an administrative agency called the European Commission on Human Rights and a legal tribunal called the European Court of Human Rights to deal with complaints against member states whose laws allegedly infringe the terms of the Convention. Member states were free to choose whether or not to submit to jurisdiction over complaints lodged by individuals as well as by other member states. The United Kingdom at first refused to accept the right of individual petition, but in 1966 accepted it. Since then, a procession of persons disgruntled with United Kingdom laws, or with the decisions of United Kingdom courts, or with both, has taken its complaints to the European Commission on Human Rights at Strasbourg. At present, around 100 applications are being lodged against the United Kingdom every year.

The machinery for enforcing the Convention consists of a Committee of Foreign Ministers of member states, a body of Commissioners elected by the Committee, and a court composed of judges nominated by the member states. To set the machinery in motion, an individual makes a written application to the Commission, setting out his complaint. This is examined by a single Commissioner, called the *rapporteur*, and on the strength of his *rapport* the Commission decides whether or not to investigate further. Most applications are ruled inadmissible as falling outside the scope of the Convention altogether, either on the basis of the preliminary *rapport*, or, where the *rapporteur* suggests there is a *prima facie* case, as soon as arguments against admissibility have been submitted by the state against which the complaint has been made. If after this the Commission still finds the complaint to be admissible, it holds an investigation of

---

[1] Standard works are Sieghart, *The international law of human rights* (1983), Fawcett, *The application of the European Convention on Human Rights* (2nd ed. 1987), and Beddard, *Human rights and Europe* (2nd ed. 1980). An annual summary of what has been happening is published in the *Yearbook of the European Convention on Human Rights*. The Judgments and Decisions of the European Court of Human Rights are published as a serial.

the facts *in camera*, with the aim of procuring a friendly settlement to the dispute. If no friendly settlement is reached, the Commission then reports on the case to the Committee of Ministers, stating whether or not it considers the facts found disclose a breach of the Convention. In addition, the Commission may refer the matter to the court – as may the state complained about (although not the individual complainant). The number of cases which thus eventually get heard by the court is small, rarely exceeding half-a-dozen each year.

The European Court of Human Rights is composed of twenty-one judges, one for each member state. Occasionally all judges sit on a case, but usually cases are heard by a panel of no more than seven. The hearings are oral, and the court has funds available to provide legal aid for individual complainants to be legally represented. In due course the court pronounces in public on whether or not it finds the Convention has been violated.

If the European Court of Human Rights finds against the United Kingdom, that by itself does not have any instant effect as far as English law and the English courts are concerned. The law condemned remains in force, and the court decision called in question still stands. However, the United Kingdom has been pronounced in breach of its international obligations, and this is usually enough to cause the government to set the matter right by getting Parliament to change the offending law, and by compensating the person who suffered by it. As a result, proceedings before the European Court of Human Rights, where available, can prove highly effective in the long if not in the short run. For example, in 1971 a judgment for a prisoner against the United Kingdom led to the rapid alteration of the prison regulations so that they no longer denied prisoners the right to consult a lawyer unless the prison authorities consented; a decision in 1981 caused Parliament to remove the Home Secretary's power to veto the release of a person detained in a mental hospital subject to a restriction order imposed by the court (see page 125); a judgment for *The Sunday Times* against the United Kingdom led to the Contempt of Court Act 1981, which enlarged the right of the press to comment on pending litigation; a judgment in favour of a man whose telephone conversations were bugged by the police led to statutory controls on telephone tapping in the Interception of Communications Act 1985; and other decisions led to the statutory abolition of corporal punishment in state schools in 1986.

The great majority of applications do not get as far as the European Court of Human Rights. Where cases brought against the United Kingdom have gone as far as the Court, however, the United Kingdom has generally lost. Up to September 1985 the United Kingdom had been a party to fourteen cases that reached judgment and had lost in twelve. This is very embarrassing to Englishmen, and particularly to those who talk about Magna Carta and say that because of this we have the most highly developed protection of human rights in the world. It is particularly embarrassing to the successive British governments, which have had the unenviable job of defending these cases unsuccessfully, and which have enjoyed the experience of being condemned by a foreign authority as little as did Henry VIII.[1] They have been little consoled by the fact that the British judge almost invariably dissented. This has provoked two opposite reactions. One is agitation that the United Kingdom should either denounce the European Convention on Human Rights altogether, or at least not renew the right of individual petition when the time next comes to do so. After some hesitation the British Government did renew the right of individual petition in 1985, although this offended a number of Conservative MPs,[2] and this course does not look a political possibility at the moment. The opposite reaction is to campaign for the European Convention to be directly incorporated into British law by Act of Parliament, so that all of it would have immediate effect. This, it is said, would mean that the European Convention would be applied by our courts at home. There would then be little need for anyone to take their complaints to Strasbourg, and the embarrassing spectacle of Great Britain being repeatedly condemned in a foreign tribunal for failure to respect human rights would be avoided. In 1987 a Bill was introduced in Parliament to this effect, which attracted much attention, but predictably got nowhere without government support.

The arguments for and against doing this are worth examining. Besides the argument that incorporating the European Convention into British law would save us international embarrassment, the main reason advanced for doing this is that the human rights which it guarantees are immensely valuable and would be better protected here if the Convention was incorporated into British law than is the case at present. This would give us fairer laws and a legal system which worked more fairly, and everyone would be happier and better. This sort of argument does not usually appeal to those in government, who see and resent the prospect of a greater amount of judicial review, which means more interference from the lawyers and judges in the day-to-day doings of government servants and in the implementation of the government's favourite plans. But there are more respectable arguments against the scheme than the mere reluctance of those who have power to submit to legal controls. The first is that it would necessarily give the judges wider powers, and this would politicise them. This means more than that the judges would find themselves making decisions which pleased one political party and offended another – which they sometimes have to do already. It means that the judges would start making decisions that are 'political' in the broad sense that they are big decisions about how society is to be run, and thus the sort of decisions which we are accustomed to have made by Parliament as part of the democratic process. The rights which the European Convention contains are vague, and in various ways they conflict with one another; and where there is a

[1] See p. 9 above.
[2] Mr Teddy Taylor, MP, said 'I am against having laws made for Britain by elderly judges sitting in Strasbourg . . . The Strasbourg court keeps forcing the British Government to bring in laws that it does not want.' (*The Times* 25 October 1985.) For those who favour it, this is of course its main advantage.

conflict it is largely a matter of personal choice how the conflict is to be resolved. For example, the Convention protects both freedom of speech and freedom of religion: so we must resolve the question of where, by what means and how loudly one person is to be permitted to speak freely against another person's religion. One might think the obvious answer would be 'as loudly as he likes, as long as this does not interfere with another person actually practising his religion', but it is possible to hold other views on where the line should be drawn. In an English court case on the ambit of the crime of blasphemy, Lord Scarman – who is one of the public supporters of legislation to incorporate the European Convention into British law – referred in his judgment to the European Convention in terms which suggest he thought that if it were in force in Britain, it would justify a ban on publishing in a newspaper intended for homosexuals a poem which offended Christians who happened to read it because it rather crudely ascribed homosexuality to Christ.[1]

In that case, the House of Lords was dealing with the existing crime of blasphemy, which they decided made this publication potentially illegal. As things stand they could not have so decided if there had been no crime of blasphemy to hang this decision upon. But if the European Convention had been directly incorporated into British law, the courts could presumably have decided in favour of some sort of ban on this publication simply on the basis of the Convention even if there had been no existing criminal offence, had they agreed with Lord Scarman's interpretation of it. Indeed, Lord Scarman has publicly stated that if the Convention is incorporated by statute 'it will fill the gaps in our law. Our courts, for example, will be in a position to develop a modern and effective law of privacy. They will be able to protect victimised members of minority groups.'[2]

Whether books are banned because they offend a group of religious believers is surely a matter to be decided by Parliament, not by the courts, and so too are such matters as discrimination against minority groups and how far newspapers should be restrained from publishing matters which invade other people's privacy.

The second objection to making the Convention part of British law is that it would unsettle all sorts of rules which the process of litigation has satisfactorily settled. For example, over the years the powers of the police to make demonstrators move on have been worked out as the courts have construed the criminal offences of obstructing the highway, and assaulting and obstructing the police in the execution of their duty. The result does not please everyone, of course, but it is a reasonably satisfactory compromise, and it is unlikely that the courts would wish to alter the present rules. If the European Convention was brought directly into force then probably all the rules which have been developed would be re-litigated by hopeful defendants to see if the courts would strike them down as

[1] *Lemon* [1979] AC 617.   [2] Writing in *The Independent* 30 January 1987.

inconsistent with the 'right to freedom of peaceful assembly', which the Convention expressly protects. It is unlikely that the end result would be any different from the present law, and the only people who would gain would be the lawyers who would have a field-day with it first. Despite these objections, the idea of incorporating the European Convention into British law has attracted quite a lot of support from influential lawyers, and there was considerable press support when the Bill which attempted to do this came before Parliament in 1987. It is therefore quite possible that at some future date it may be done.

36

THE EUROPEAN
ECONOMIC
COMMUNITY

The second big change is the consequence of Great Britain's joining the EEC on 1 January 1973.[1] This was formally accomplished by Parliament enacting the European Communities Act 1972. This incorporates into the law of the United Kingdom as much of the EEC Treaty as is required by that Treaty to be given direct effect in the law of the nation states. One of the articles which was given immediate effect in this way was Article 177, which provides that matters of EEC law arising in the course of litigation in the United Kingdom always may be, and sometimes must be referred to the European Court[2] at Brussels for a ruling. All existing United Kingdom law contrary to the provisions of the Treaty are repealed by the Act, which also delegates to the legislative organs of the EEC the power to make, within the scope of the Treaty, laws which may then have force in Britain. Thus it is possible for laws to be made in Brussels regulating in Great Britain agriculture, the movement of goods, free trade, unfair trade competition, social security, the movement of workers and a number of other matters, even to the extent of repealing existing British statute and common law.[3]

The EEC Council and Commission can make laws for the United Kingdom in two different ways, one direct and the other indirect. It can issue *Regulations*. These are laws made under powers delegated to the EEC by the European Communities Act, and usually have immediate effect. Alternatively – and more commonly – it can issue *Directives*. These are formal commands to the member states, requiring them to change their laws if this is necessary to make them comply with some prescribed pattern. Whether in a given situation there can be a Regulation, or a Directive, or both, is laid down by the terms of the EEC Treaty.

---

[1] On this see Lawrence Collins, *European Community law in the United Kingdom* (1984). English textbooks on EEC law include Lipstein, *The law of the EEC* (1974), Lasok and Bridge, *Introduction to the law and institutions of the European Communities* (4th ed. 1987), and Wyatt and Dashwood, *Substantive law of the EEC* (1980).

[2] The full title of this body is the Court of Justice of the European Communities, but the 'European Court' is the name it has in the European Communities Act 1972.

[3] Whilst there is no doubt that EEC legislation can overrule existing British legislation that conflicts with it, no one really knows what the position would be if EEC legislation were passed to say 'x', and Parliament were then to pass conflicting legislation which said 'x is abolished: the answer is y'. As a matter of United Kingdom constitutional law, the position is probably that the British Act of Parliament would prevail: see Collins, *European Community law in the United Kingdom* pp. 23–33.

Directives, unlike Regulations, do not usually have any effect on the law of the United Kingdom until laws have been made here to comply with them, but they may exceptionally have direct effect. If a member state fails to comply with a Directive by amending its domestic laws within the time allowed for this, that state is considered to be in the wrong, and to prevent it profiting from its own wrong the Directive will be given immediate effect in any litigation to which that state is a party. Thus in one case an EEC Directive prohibited discrimination between men and women in employment matters, and did so in more general terms than the current British sex discrimination legislation, which permitted discrimination in the matter of retirement ages. Relying on English domestic law, an Area Health Authority compulsorily retired a female dietician earlier than it would have compulsorily retired a male dietician. It was held that because the United Kingdom was at fault in not complying with the Directive and because the Area Health Authority was an organ of the state, for the purpose of deciding the dietician's claim against the Area Health Authority the Directive must be treated as if it was already part of English law.[1] How far EEC Regulations and Directives have immediate effect in the United Kingdom is a complicated question, however, and for further information readers are advised to go to the standard works on EEC law, referred to at the beginning of this chapter.

The first and most obvious way in which EEC law has an impact on the machinery of justice in England is by giving rise to rights and duties which can be enforced in the English courts. For example, the English law of tort recognises a head of liability called *breach of statutory duty*, under which certain kinds of breach of certain kinds of statute can render the statute-breaker liable to compensate those who suffer loss or damage as a result. As the EEC Treaty has been incorporated into the law of this country by Parliament enacting it as a British statute, the English courts have sometimes held that where one person performs an act which contravenes a section of the Treaty, *alias* statute, he may be liable for breach of statutory duty. Thus Article 86 forbids the abuse of a dominant trading position, where this is done in some way which affects business between the member states of the EEC. In a case in 1984 the House of Lords held that where one trading organisation contravened this Article to the detriment of another, he could be sued for breach of statutory duty.[2]

Secondly, the European Communities Act may require a case which involves a point of EEC law to be heard by the Court of Justice of the European Communities, usually called the European Court. The EEC Treaty does not impose the European Court as a new all-purpose court of final appeal from the House of Lords; but the European Court may become involved in litigation originating in England in two important ways.

---

[1] *Marshall* v. *Southampton and South West Hampshire AHA*, [1986] QB 401.
[2] *Garden Cottage Foods Ltd* v. *Milk Marketing Board* [1984] AC 130. But the English courts have not consistently held that every breach of the EEC Treaty grounds such an action. There is an account of the various domestic remedies by Josephine Steiner, 'How to make the action suit the case', (1987) 12 *European Law Review* 102.

First, by Articles 169 and 170 of the EEC Treaty, a member state or the EEC Commission may seek a declaration from the European Court that another member state is in breach of its EEC Treaty obligations. Here, the European Court may be invited to say to the defendant state: 'you are in breach of your obligations to the EEC because one of your laws runs contrary to such and such a Treaty provision, Regulation or Directive'. An example was the celebrated tachograph case in 1979.[1] In the interests of road safety, an EEC Regulation made it compulsory to fit lorries with tachographs, which automatically record driving periods, speeds and distances covered. British lorry-drivers were vocally opposed to 'the spy in the cab', as they called it, and the Labour government, preferring trouble in Brussels to trouble with trade unions at home, refused to implement it. After three years of wrangling, the EEC Commission took proceedings against the government of the United Kingdom in the European Court of Justice, where the failure to implement the Regulation was condemned; after which the government brought in a Statutory Instrument making it compulsory to fit tachographs. It is usually the EEC Commission which takes proceedings under these sections, but proceedings are occasionally brought by member states. One such case involved a French fisherman who was prosecuted before the magistrates in Pembroke for fishing in British waters with a net smaller than the terms of a British statute allowed.[2] After the Frenchman had been convicted and fined and had returned to France, the French government sued the British government in the European Court, and obtained a declaration that the British statute was in conflict with an article of the EEC Treaty. This declaration did not have the automatic effect of invalidating the British statute or reversing the Frenchman's conviction, at least as far as English constitutional law is concerned. But, as when condemned by the European Court of Human Rights, Britain was publicly shown up as in breach of its obligations, and put under strong moral pressure to amend the offending law.

Secondly, where a point of EEC law arises in the course of a law-suit in the courts of a member state, a lower court or tribunal may, and a court or tribunal of final appeal must refer the matter to the European Court for a ruling. This is laid down in Article 177 of the EEC Treaty in order to ensure as far as possible that the courts of the various member states develop a single version of EEC law. According to Article 177, the power or duty to refer to the European Court for a preliminary ruling arises when a question is raised in any litigation on the interpretation of the EEC Treaty, or on the validity or interpretation of any EEC legislation, and the English court 'considers that a decision on the question is necessary to enable it to give judgment'. It is a precondition, therefore, that the English court thinks that the outcome of the case in hand depends on the point of EEC law which one of the parties has raised; if it considers EEC law irrelevant to the case before it, no reference can be made. If it finds EEC law relevant to the

---

[1] *Commission* v. *United Kingdom* [1979] ECR 419.
[2] *France* v. *U.K.* [1979] ECR 2923.

outcome, then, if it is the House of Lords,[1] the court is bound to refer it to the European Court. Article 177 says: 'Where any such question is raised in a case pending before a court or tribunal of a member state against whose decisions there is no judicial remedy under national law, that court or tribunal *shall* bring the matter before the Court of Justice.' On the face of it, it looks as if the House of Lords has no choice but to refer the question, however obvious the answer may be, and however bogus the dispute may really be. Thus in one criminal case[2] involving two men who had been convicted of importing a truck-load of pornographic books, pictures and films from Denmark, the House of Lords felt obliged to refer to the European Court the question whether or not the British statute prohibiting the importation of obscene matter conflicted with provisions in the EEC Treaty about the free movement of goods – in which case it would have been rendered inapplicable by it. It must have been obvious to all concerned, not least the defendant, that the answer was bound to be 'no', but the English criminal justice system had to wait for the European Court to say so.[3]

This sort of difficulty induced the French courts to invent the doctrine of the *acte clair*, which is that no court is bound to refer a point of EEC law to the European Court if the answer is obvious all along. This doctrine has now been given some measure of approval by the European Court itself.[4] The duty of the court of final appeal to make a reference has also been qualified by rulings that it does not arise when the European Court of Justice has already decided the point at issue, or when the appeal is only on an interlocutory matter;[5] but the court is free in these cases to make a reference if it so wishes. The lower courts and tribunals whose decisions can be appealed against have a choice under Article 177 between referring points of EEC law to the European Court and deciding them themselves. In a leading case in 1974[6] the Court of Appeal, presided over

---

[1] It is as yet unclear whether it is only the House of Lords which can be obliged to refer, or whether the same also goes for a court which effectively gives the final ruling in the instant case – as where the Court of Appeal refuses leave to appeal, or in a criminal case refuses to certify that a point of public importance is involved.

[2] *R. v. Henn and Darby* [1981] AC 850.

[3] Although in the light of *Conegate Ltd* v. *HM Customs and Excise* [1986] 1 CMLR 739, perhaps the answer was not quite so obvious. A company imported from West Germany a quantity of inflatable dolls, complete with female genitalia, for sale to masturbation enthusiasts in its chain of sex-shops. When they were confiscated as indecent articles by customs officers acting under powers given by a British statute, the European Court of Justice ruled that the seizure did contravene the EEC Treaty provisions concerning the free movement of goods. These dolls, disgusting objects as they were, were not *publications*, and by a quirk of the English law against pornography their manufacture and sale in England was legal; thus the European Court of Justice held that a ban on their importation into Britain could not be justified by an Article of the EEC Treaty permitting imports to be banned on grounds of public morality.

[4] *CILFIT Srl* v. *Ministry of Health* [1982] ECR 3415.

[5] See Collins, *European Community law in the United Kingdom* pp. 115 *et seq.* An interlocutory appeal is an appeal on a point of procedure which falls to be determined before the case is finally decided on the merits. The classic example would be an appeal against a decision of the lower court to grant an injunction pending trial.

[6] *Bulmer* v. *Bollinger* [1974] Ch. 401.

by Lord Denning, laid down some guidelines as to how this discretion should be exercised. It said that as references to the European Court take time and cost money, they should be made sparingly and only in cases of real difficulty and importance, and that the lower courts should be reluctant to make a reference against the wishes of one of the parties. When these pronouncements were made, some writers on EEC law criticised them as being too restrictive,[1] and English judges in more recent cases have expressed slightly greater enthusiasm for the idea of making references. However, the Court of Appeal decision appears to have set the tone of what has followed, because it remains true that only a small number of references are made by the English courts. Whereas the court systems of France and West Germany annually refer several dozen cases each to the European Court of Justice, the number of references annually from all the British courts has never reached double figures.[2]

Where an English court requests a preliminary ruling it notifies the Registry of the European Court, which then invites the parties to the case, other member states and the organs of the EEC to submit written arguments on the matter. There is a period of two months for this. At some time after this there is an oral hearing, which the interested parties may but need not attend, and later the European Court pronounces judgment. At one time, the whole process took about six months; but as a result of the creeping paralysis which seems eventually to affect all courts in every system, it is now taking nearer twelve. The ruling, when it appears, will say what the disputed rule of EEC law is; it will then be left for the English court to apply the ruling to the facts (as it finds them), and to decide if there is a conflict with domestic law. Frequently, however, the European Court ruling is so specific that it disposes of the issue for all intents and purposes.

The European Court is a large and expanding operation, which is already bursting out of the modern five-storey building in Luxembourg which was built for it in 1973. Indeed, at the time of writing there are serious proposals to create an additional, subsidiary court to handle staff and competition cases, and thus to relieve the main court of part of its work. At present the European Court has 13 judges, all full-time appointees – one for each of the 12 member states, plus an extra to ensure that there is never an equal division of votes. They may sit all together, but usually operate in 'chambers' of three. The judges are backed up by a large administrative staff of over 400, some 80 of whom are translators and interpreters. As might be expected, the court works on the Continental pattern, which involves a number of features which look distinctly odd to lawyers trained in the common law. There is great emphasis on written submissions, and oral argument plays a small part – a part made all the smaller by reason of the advocates having to speak to the bench via a microphone, headphones, and a

---

[1] See Freeman, 'References to the Court of Justice under Article 177', (1975) 28 *Current Legal Problems* 176.

[2] An annual Synopsis of the work of the Court of Justice of the EEC is published by the Office for the Official Publications of the EEC.

battery of translators. 'There is none of the drama, the cut and thrust and impromptu repartee of an English trial. The advocates deliver their set speeches: the rhetoric is subdued and often misunderstood, and humour intervenes rarely, and then lightly.'[1]

Another strange feature to common law eyes is the *Advocate General*. In a number of Continental countries a public official, known in France as the *ministère public*, can (and frequently does) intervene in civil litigation in order to put before the court aspects of the case which affect the state and the general public, which may be very different from the concerns of the parties themselves. This character is faithfully reproduced in the European Court in the form of a team of six Advocates General, who invariably address the court at the close of the oral hearing. A further continental feature is the style of the eventual judgment, which is single and usually brief. If they disagree on the outcome, the judges vote in private, the minority accepts the majority view, and a judgment is issued in the name of them all. There are no dissenting judgments, and the single judgment which appears is usually abstract and brief, with none of the discursive length of a judgment in a court of common law. The nearest European equivalent to this is the Advocate General's opinion, which is always published together with the judgment of the court, whether or not it accepted his views.

[1] Brown and Jacobs, *The Court of Justice of the European Communities* (2nd ed. 1984) p. 29.

37

THE IMPACT OF EUROPE ON THE ENGLISH LEGAL SYSTEM

The EEC has already had some impact on the substance of English law. Some EEC legislation has direct effect here, and much more has come into effect by being incorporated into English legislation. The European Convention on Human Rights has necessarily had a less marked effect. However, a series of small but significant changes have come about as Parliament has changed the law following rulings of the European Court of Human Rights. More important, perhaps, is the fact that English judges are now beginning to get 'Convention-minded'. They are becoming aware of the Convention, and are prepared to try to construe English law so as to avoid conflict with it where possible. In one case, for example, the House of Lords refused to give a criminal statute retrospective effect, partly because the European Convention says that no one shall be convicted of criminal offence for doing what was not a crime at the time he did it.[1]

It is less clear that the attitudes and practices of English courts and English lawyers have been altered by contact with Europe in its various manifestations. The EEC has exposed common lawyers to a different tradition of civil trial, a different philosophy to the interpretation of statutes, and a legal profession which is differently organised. There have been no major changes so far. However, in response to Europe, the Bar has already bent all its most hallowed rules of conduct. For practice overseas, members of the English Bar are now permitted to receive instructions directly from a lay client, to accept an annual fee, and to enter partnerships with foreign lawyers. It is likely that as a new generation of common lawyers grows up, many or most of whom have learnt about European ways during their days as law-students, the European influence will be much more widely felt.

[1] *Waddington* v. *Miak* [1974] 1 WLR 683.

VII

THE COST OF THE LAW

38

THE FINANCES OF THE LAW COURTS

In the past the growth of royal justice was partly due to the profits that accrued from exercising jurisdiction. The early itinerant justices were more concerned with safeguarding the King's fiscal rights than with the trial of ordinary actions. A law court was expected to show a profit for the King. It is some time since justice has been a substantial source of income, but the old idea survives in the idea that civil courts ought not to be run at a loss.

There is a substantial difference between the finances of civil courts and those of criminal courts. A civil court is a facility provided by the State and those who make use of the courts must pay the equivalent of an entrance fee and further fees for the various stages of the proceedings. Criminal courts are part of the machinery of the State for enforcing law and order and virtually the whole of the cost falls on public funds. The cost of running criminal courts and the cost of prosecutions may usefully be considered together.

The principle was originally that crime was a local matter to be dealt with locally at local cost. Counties had to provide court-houses, lodgings for Assize Judges and the salaries and outgoings required for Assize Courts and County Quarter Sessions. Boroughs that had their own Quarter Sessions had to meet the cost of court-houses, the salary of the Recorder and other expenses. The Assize Court Judges were paid (in their capacity of High Court Judges) out of the Consolidated Fund, but that is all that was paid for out of central funds: the rest had to be paid for by the local authorities out of the county or borough rates. Under the Courts Act 1971 all the criminal work that used to go to Assizes and Quarter Sessions goes to the Crown Court, and the cost of the court-houses, office accommodation, judges' lodgings, salaries of judges and staff, and all other expenses fall on central government funds. Magistrates' courts continue to be subject to the principle of local responsibility for the costs of crime, though by a complicated financial process (which takes into account fines received by the Exchequer) local authorities receive a grant of about 80 per cent of the cost.

Formerly the cost of prosecuting criminals used also to fall on local authority funds: so, for example, when the mail train robbers stopped the train in Buckinghamshire this meant that Buckinghamshire had to bear the heavy cost of prosecuting them. After the Courts Act 1971, prosecutions continued to be handled locally, but the Act gave the court of trial the power to order the costs of the prosecution to be paid out of central funds provided by the government, which enabled the burden to be spread more evenly. The Crown Prosecution Service which came into being in 1986, as a result of the Prosecution of Offences Act 1985, is paid for directly by the central government, and the cost of prosecuting offenders is borne as part of its total cost. Thus normally there is no question of the court ordering prosecution costs to be paid from central funds. However, the power to a limited extent remains. A court may no longer order central funds to pay the costs if a prosecution is brought by a local authority, but the court may still order prosecution costs to be paid from central funds if there is a private prosecution.

Where the defendant is convicted, the courts have long had power to order him to pay some or all of the prosecution costs, and this power is widely exercised. But it is a principle the courts must follow when making such an order that the order must bear some relation to the defendant's means: ordering him to pay money that he has not got and has no realistic prospect of ever getting would give the administrators who collect the payments a lot of trouble for nothing, and put the defendant for ever on the wrong side of the law. Thus it is quite impracticable to think of transferring the total cost of prosecuting criminals onto the shoulders of those who have caused the need to spend the money. However, the total amount that convicted criminals are made to contribute by way of costs comes to more than a token sum. In its first six months of full operation, the total expenditure of the Crown Prosecution Service was £58 million, of which £37 million were overheads and £21 million directly attributable to the costs of particular prosecutions; against this it was able to offset not quite £5 million in costs recovered from defendants. When the Crown Prosecution Service was created there was a feeling in some quarters that being prosecuted should henceforth be free, like hospital treatment or education. It is hard to understand this. No one is to be blamed for falling ill or for having children who must learn to read and write. But those who commit crimes are in the wrong, and can surely be expected to help repay society for the cost of prosecuting them just as they can be expected to compensate the victims for the harm they have done to them.

Traditionally there has been great reluctance to give the acquitted defendant the costs of his defence. The official attitude seems to be that as he was probably guilty he was lucky to be acquitted, and hence should not have the impertinence to complain about the cost. At one time he could recover them neither from public funds nor from the prosecutor, and his only remedy was the costly and uncertain one of suing the prosecutor for the tort of malicious prosecution. Over the years various powers to order payment of defence costs in criminal cases were created piecemeal. From 1971 the position was that all criminal courts could order defence costs to be paid out of central funds, and in 1973 a practice direction instructed courts to exercise this power unless there were unusual circumstances: for example, that the prosecutor had misbehaved justifying an order for costs against him rather than against central funds, that the acquittal was on a technicality and against the merits, or that the accused had behaved suspiciously and thereby brought the prosecution on himself.[1] But this power only applied at trials for indictable or either-way offences, and if the accused was acquitted of a summary offence he could get nothing from central funds. By then there was (and still is) a general power to order any prosecutor to pay defence costs, but the courts were (and still are) reluctant to exercise it unless they feel the prosecutor was at fault in bringing the case. So defendants acquitted of summary offences usually had to pay their own costs. This was a sore point for many years. The unfairness was eventually put right when, thanks to an opposition amendment to the Bill which the government reluctantly accepted, the Prosecution of Offences Act 1985 extended to the power to order costs from central funds to trials for summary offences.

The cost of legal aid, whether in the Crown Court or in magistrates' courts, is paid out of central funds less a small amount paid by aided persons. Police forces are paid for out of local funds with a grant of about 50 per cent from central funds, so that the cost of police attending courts does impose a charge on the tax-payer as well as the rate-payer. With so many different items and with the complication of central funds and local funds and grants at varying percentages, it is a difficult matter to give any accurate figures for the real cost of our criminal courts. But in future the introduction of the Crown Prosecution Service should make this daunting task easier than it was.[2]

In the civil courts a litigant has to pay for three main items: (a) the court fees, (b) the expense of collecting evidence and bringing witnesses to court, and (c) the charges of solicitors and counsel if briefed. It is as if a person rents a house: the court fees represent the rent, whilst items (b) and (c) are the expenses of occupying it, and they may vary from the irreducible minimum to riotous extravagance. The cost of the services given by the courts is made up of the salaries and pensions of the judges, the salaries, wages and pensions of the court staff, and the provision and maintenance of buildings and equipment. The principle adopted is that in the Supreme Court, the cost of the judges should fall upon public funds and that all other expenses of the courts should fall upon the suitors. The Supreme Court fees are fixed by the Lord Chancellor and a committee of judges, with the concurrence of the Treasury. The schedule of fees fixed in accordance with the above-mentioned principle in 1884 (and subsequently varied a little) resulted in the receipts exceeding the expenditure (after deducting judges' salaries paid by the State) by a considerable sum. By 1910 the 'profit' amounted to well over a million pounds. The Treasury view was that the 'profit' should be off-set against the capital cost of building the law courts. The

[1] [1973] 1 WLR 718; revised (1981) 74 Cr. Ap. R 48. Thus in the celebrated trial of Mr Jeremy Thorpe in 1979, the judge refused the acquitted defendant his costs because he thought his behaviour had been suspicious.

[2] The National Association for the Care and Resettlement of Offenders (NACRO) estimated the total cost of the criminal justice process, including the cost of the prisons and of the police, to be rather over £5 billion in 1985–86.

445

increased cost of administration due to the war of 1914 led to a distinct 'loss' on the Supreme Court, and the fees were accordingly increased after a committee had considered the matter.[1]

From 1922, there was in most years a surplus over the whole of the expenditure including the judges, and in every year except during the war the receipts were substantially more than the expenditure other than the judges. Put another way, litigants were supposed to get the judge free and to pay for the other services at cost price, but they were generally paying more than the services actually cost. In 1951 a Committee reported 'that there is scope for some reduction in court fees without injustice to the general body of taxpayers'.[2] Since then the position has changed and there are no longer any surplus receipts.

Since county courts are humbler institutions, their finances have been more favourable to the litigant. The court fees are fixed by the Treasury with the concurrence of the Lord Chancellor: 'in the opinion of the Treasury the balance between expenditure and revenue of the county courts should be adjusted on the basis that the State should bear the cost of the court buildings and the salaries, pensions, and travelling expenses of the judges, and that the rest of the expenditure should be defrayed by the suitors' fees.'[3]

In the earlier years of this century the county courts made a modest 'profit' of about £30,000 a year from the suitors on the Treasury theory of fees. From 1915 there was a deficit, becoming so substantial that votes of £200,000 or £300,000 a year were required. The fees were increased and economies made so that by 1925 they became self-sufficient again, with only a token vote from Parliament. In 1937 the total cost was put at £1,045,383 and the receipts at £800,000, the balance of £245,383 consisting of £98,000 for judges' salaries and pensions and various sums for the other items that are paid for by the State. For 1971–72 the net cost was £5,460,500, which included £1,071,000 for the judges.

Following the Courts Act 1971, the annual published figures for public spending lump the High Court and the county courts together and it is no longer possible to study separately the financial performance of each. However, when it comes to planning the future public spending the policy for civil justice is as before: 'For the civil courts the plans take account of the agreed policy of recovering full costs less judicial costs through court fees'.[4] The figures in table 11, taken from the *Estimates* for 1987–88, show how this policy is being carried out.[5]

These figures show that the litigant is indeed being made to pay for most of the cost of civil justice, other than the salary of the judge; in the words of the Civil

[1] (1922) Cmd 1565.
[2] Committee on Supreme Court Practice and Procedure, Second Interim Report, (1951) Cmd 8176, para. 156.
[3] (1923) Cmd 1856, p. 5.
[4] *The Government's Expenditure Plans 1987–88 to 1989–90*, Vol. II; Cm 56–II (January 1987). (Note that in figure 8 on page 484 the figures are for 1986–87.)
[5] *Supply Estimates 1987–88*, Class XI; HC 227–XI (Treasury, March 1987).

Table 11. *The cost of the courts*

Judicial salaries (paid out of the Consolidated Fund)		£32,046,000
Cost of the Lord Chancellor's Office and central administration		£18,237,000
Court services: the major items		
circuit administration	£6,197,000	
civil courts	£96,582,000	
Crown Court	£52,613,000	
jurors (mainly in the Crown Court)	£27,702,000	
Total		£209,642,000
Less 'appropriations in aid':		
court fees	£132,832,000	
VAT refunds	£622,000	
other receipts	£120,000	
	£133,574,000	
Total (excluding judicial salaries)		£76,068,000

Justice Review, 'apart from judicial salaries and legal aid, the cost to the State of conducting civil business was virtually nil'[1] – which no doubt satisfies somebody somewhere, although as an exercise in controlling public spending it is rather illusory, since so many civil litigants are legally aided, and a large percentage of the court fees which they notionally pay are really being taken out of one pocket in the public purse and put back into another.

It has often been argued that the services of the courts should be 'free', which means that everyone by indirect or direct taxes pays the bill; but it is difficult to say what 'ought' to be done except in relation to some definite theory of social structure. A theory at the opposite end of the political spectrum is that litigants should be expected to pay the full cost of the civil court system in so far as they can afford it, and should be subsidised in so far as they cannot. Speaking in 1984, Sir John Donaldson, Master of the Rolls, said this:

The true view is surely that civil justice should be available to every citizen at a price which he can reasonably afford. On that basis, the present system is generous to a fault. Take a simple High Court action. The daily cost has been estimated at about £1,400, of which £800 represents the cost of publicly provided services and £600 the costs of the parties. Why do we meet the public costs in full, but make no contribution towards private costs, other than through legal aid? Why do we not put the whole of the costs on to the litigants and apply legal aid to the public as well as to the private costs? The result of the present system in one particular case was that the public purse subsidised two major oil companies to the tune of £50,000 when they litigated their rights to £3 million for 60 days. Would it not have been better to have charged them the full economic cost, or indeed at a

[1] General Issues Paper (1987), p. 12.

commercial rate, which would have been much higher, and used the money to supplement the legal aid fund? The solution is to charge everyone the full economic or, better still, a commercial rate for the services of the court, including the judges, and to apply an improved and more just legal aid system to these true court costs as well as to the parties' costs.[1]

[1] Address to the Law Society's Annual Conference, 1984; see (1984) 81 Law Soc. Gaz. 2985.

39

'COSTS'

Solicitors have never had the freedom enjoyed in other professions of fixing the amount of their fees. From early times a person presented with a solicitor's bill has been able to get it 'taxed', that is, to have it examined by an official of the court who has power to disallow it or reduce the amount charged for the various items. The position today is regulated by statute. Section 87 of the Solicitors Act 1974 empowers a Committee headed by the Lord Chancellor to make rules governing how much solicitors may charge, and these rules are enforced by the method of taxation as laid down in later sections of the Act.[1]

A bill is made up of disbursements and profit costs. Disbursements are payments made by the solicitor on behalf of his client such as court fees, stamp duties, counsel's fees, payments to witnesses, and so on. 'Profit costs' is the technical term for the solicitor's charges for his own work. It dates from the days when solicitors commonly had no offices and did their work personally from their homes, often meeting their clients in inns,[2] but nowadays of course the solicitor has to meet his business expenses (the rent of his office, salaries and wages of his staff, and so on) before arriving at the net figure that is his real profit. The traditional method of charging was by a string of items. It was most misleading because it suggested that a solicitor could not do anything without noting it down and charging 3s 4d, or 6s 8d or some multiple of such fractions of a pound. There was often no item at all for doing the important part of the work. It was as if a surgeon made up a bill for making an appointment with the patient, inspecting the patient, attending the hospital, supplying swabs and so forth, and omitted to mention his performance of the operation. New methods of charging for particular categories of solicitor's work have been introduced at different dates.

A distinction used for purposes of costs is the division into contentious, which means work done in or for the purpose of proceedings begun before a court or before an arbitrator, and non-contentious, which means everything else. Within the category of non-contentious costs there used to be a further division between costs for conveyancing and costs for other types of work. In 1883 a system of 'scale fees' was introduced for conveyancing, under which the fee charged

---

[1] Useful guides are two booklets published and regularly updated by the Law Society: *Contentious costs and Solicitors Act taxations*, and *An approach to non-contentious costs*.
[2] See Michael Birks, *Gentlemen of the law* (1960).

depended on the amount of the purchase price. As was explained in the previous chapter, scale fees were criticised in a report by the Prices and Incomes Board, and were abolished with effect from 1 January 1973 by the Solicitors Remuneration Order 1972, which now governs payment for all non-contentious work. Under section 2 of this Order:

A solicitor's remuneration for non-contentious business . . . shall be such sum as may be fair and reasonable having regard to all the circumstances of the case and in particular to –
(i)   the complexity of the matter or the difficulty or novelty of the questions raised;
(ii)   the skill, labour, specialised knowledge and responsibility involved;
(iii)   the time spent on the business;
(iv)   the number and importance of the documents prepared or perused, without regard to length;
(v)   the place where and the circumstances in which the business or any part thereof was transacted;
(vi)   the amount or value of any money or property involved;
(vii) whether any land involved is registered land within the meaning of the Land Registration Act 1925;[1] and
(viii) the importance of the matter to the client.

Thus solicitors' charges for non-contentious work consist, broadly speaking, of two kinds of element. There is what solicitors call the 'A' element, which is the time spent on the work multiplied by a given rate per hour, this rate being calculated to see that overheads are covered. And there is a 'B' element to cover 'extras' like the difficulty of the work, the fact that the solicitor dropped everything else to give it his immediate attention, and the sum of money at stake (which is a measure of the possible financial liability of the solicitor if he makes a mistake). It is the 'B' element upon which the firm will usually reckon to make its profit. If the client thinks he has been overcharged he can of course ask the solicitor to reconsider his bill. Failing this, the disgruntled client has two possible courses open to him. He can either have the bill taxed by the court officials, or he can apply to the Law Society, which, after consideration, certifies either that the sum charged is fair and reasonable or that some lesser figure is the proper amount. Thus solicitors, unlike other professionals, are able to establish that their charge was reasonable by a more civilised means than suing their clients for their fees, and arguing the charge was fair in an ordinary contested court case. It is possible for an agreement to be made between solicitor and client fixing the remuneration for the solicitor, though to be valid it must be in writing and be signed by the client. Such formal agreements used to be uncommon, but things have changed in recent years with the abolition of scale fees for conveyancing and the growth of a more commercial and competitive spirit within the profession, as shown by its decision to allow solicitors to advertise. It is no longer unusual for

[1] When scale fees applied to conveyancing there were different scales according to whether it was registered or unregistered land; this provision is there to remind solicitors that they are still expected to convey registered land more cheaply.

solicitors to work to fixed charges, and very common for them to give informal estimates of what the work will cost.

For contentious costs, Rules are made by the Supreme Court Rule Committee (see chapter 7 above) and the County Court Rule Committee (see chapter 7 above) and form part of the rules governing procedure in those courts; for matrimonial cases, rules applicable to both courts are made by a separate Matrimonial Causes Rule Committee. Costs in contentious matters, in which neither party is assisted under the Legal Aid Scheme, are affected by the principle that costs normally 'follow the event', that is to say that the court will order the losing party to pay 'the costs' of the winning party.[1]

But we have to distinguish between different kinds of costs. Any party, whether he wins or loses, is liable to pay his own solicitor all the solicitor's proper charges and disbursements for conducting the litigation in the way that the client authorised, whether expressly or impliedly. These are called 'solicitor and own client costs'. If the client considers the bill to be excessive his remedy is to have it taxed, and when he does this the taxing officer must apply various rules laid down by statute. The main provision is a basic rule that 'all costs shall be allowed except insofar as they are of an unreasonable amount or have been unreasonably incurred and any doubts which the taxing officer may have as to whether the costs were reasonably incurred or were reasonable in amount shall be resolved in favour of the receiving party' – i.e. the solicitor.[2]

The costs that must be paid by the loser to the winner have always been calculated upon a different basis which is less generous. For many years the winner got costs on what was called a 'party and party basis', which meant that he recovered no more than the costs 'necessarily and properly incurred'. This formula usually meant that he recovered between a third and a quarter less than the costs he had actually incurred. Following a revision in 1986, the winner now gets costs on what is called 'the standard basis', which means that 'there shall be allowed a reasonable amount in respect of all costs *reasonably* incurred and any doubts which the taxing officer may have as to whether the costs were reasonably incurred or were reasonable in amount shall be resolved in favour of the paying party'.[3] The new formula is intended to be more generous to the winner. A further complication is that for some types of contentious proceedings which are more or less routine, the Rules lay down charges which are either a flat rate, or leave the charge to be settled between a prescribed maximum and minimum.

[1] The court always has a wide discretion as to costs, but this is a judicial discretion exercised according to principles. If an action is won on a legal technicality, but is an utterly unreasonable and frivolous action, the winning party may get no costs awarded, or even have to pay the loser's costs. Costs can also be apportioned when each party wins on some issue. In some proceedings, particularly in the Chancery Division where the subject-matter of the action is a fund or estate, the court may order all the proper costs of all the parties to be paid out of the fund or estate: the cost of an application to the court is regarded as being part of the expense of administering the estate.

[2] Supreme Court Rules, Order 62 rule 7 paras. 12(2) and 15. These are applied to county court proceedings by the County Court Rules, Order 38.

[3] Supreme Court Rules, Order 62 rule 7 para. 12(1).

These fixed costs are all that the winner can recover from the loser; but the winner must pay his solicitor for his work on the normal basis. The justification for fixed costs is that they save time and trouble in taxation. The main area in which they operate are actions for debt, where the debtor does not dispute the claim and there is no issue before the court on liability. As was mentioned earlier, there is a rule in the county court that the winner can generally claim no legal costs in an action involving less than £25, or less than £500 where the claim is defended and is dealt with under the arbitration procedure for small claims; in these cases the winner can make his opponent pay the court fees and his out-of-pocket expenses only. This is to encourage litigants in small claims to sue in person, usually under the informal arbitration procedure (see chapter 5).

Since 1968 fixed costs have applied in undefended divorce cases in county courts. Under Rules made in 1979, a solicitor receives £73.75 if counsel is briefed, or £87.75 if he takes the case himself. There are further fees relating to consent orders for maintenance, and in relation to arrangements for children and other matters that may arise. Counsel's fees are also fixed. (These rates have fallen badly behind with inflation, and are at present in the course of revision.) These are the costs payable by the respondent to the petitioner or to the Legal Aid Fund if the petitioner is legally aided. In fact it is very largely in the interest of the Exchequer, which carries much of the cost of legal aid, that lies behind these arrangements. Fixed costs are simpler and cheaper to work than are costs which have to be taxed. At the time of writing, there is a move to extend the system of fixed costs to the work done by solicitors on criminal legal aid.

In a High Court action, such as an action for personal injuries or for libel which has ended in a judgment with costs against the loser, the winner's solicitor prepares a bill. For routine matters he puts in charges that are fixed by Rules. On matters where the Rules prescribe a maximum and minimum and where the amount is 'discretionary' he will apply his experience: he knows that he will have to justify these charges on lines akin to those used for non-contentious costs and that his bill is going to receive professional scrutiny. The winner's solicitor then sends the bill to the loser's solicitor; this bill may be agreed to, in which case the loser simply pays the agreed sum. If the loser's solicitor disputes the amount claimed, and a compromise cannot be made, the solicitors 'tax' the bill. In the High Court there are taxing masters assigned for this work, whilst in county courts the work is done by the registrar. Both solicitors or members of their staff attend before the taxing master, and go through the bill item by item, arguing for and against it. The taxing master, applying the principles described on the previous page, disallows any item he thinks is unjustifiable, and reduces the sums that he thinks excessive. Thus if the winner has briefed a leading counsel as well as a junior, the taxing master may say that there was no need for a leading counsel and allow merely an appropriate fee for the junior. This method ensures that a party who has conducted his case on extravagant lines cannot make the losing party pay for that extravagance. When taxation is completed, the sum allowed is known as 'party and party costs'. The party and party costs are rarely as high as the solicitor and own client costs: the client must pay for every disbursement properly made by his solicitor and for all the solicitor's proper charges, so that if he wins and gets costs, the amount that he is liable to pay his solicitor is his 'solicitor and own client costs' less the amount that he receives as 'party and party costs'. There are cases in which a solicitor may be content with the costs recovered from the other side, but that depends on the circumstances and the amount involved. It has already been mentioned that if the client considers that the solicitor and own client costs are too high, he can have these costs taxed. These taxations, which are not common, involve the element of the instructions given by the client; the point here is not the figure at which the work could have been done, but whether the solicitor has charged properly for the work he was instructed to do; work done by way of precautionary measures, and the securing of expensive counsel, must be paid for by the client if he expressly or impliedly authorised it. The actual taxation of a bill costs money, and this must be paid for according to the rule that if less than one-sixth of the bill is disallowed, the costs of taxation, including the obtaining of the order to tax, fall on the person who challenges the bill, whereas if the bill is reduced by more than one-sixth the party putting forward the bill pays for the taxation.

The rules as to costs are commonly explained as if the parties to litigation are able to meet the charges they incur and the amount of any costs ordered against them. Of course in practice a solicitor has to consider the means of his client and explain the position to him. If one of the parties is poor, the other party may be at a great disadvantage. Ordinarily there is little use in suing a poor defendant; if a person has no money there is no sense in trying to make him pay out that which he does not have. In an action for recovery of possession of property, it may of course be worth suing a poor defendant, for getting possession of a house or valuable goods may be worthwhile even when the plaintiff can get nothing in costs from the defendant. A poor plaintiff raises other questions. There are various means by which a poor plaintiff can sue, and these are explained in the next section. Suppose that X, a person without means, complains that he has been libelled in a newspaper and threatens to commence an action. The solicitors to the newspaper will advise that the action will have to be a High Court action, and that if the newspaper defends the action, the solicitor and own client costs will not be less than say £5,000 and will almost certainly be very much greater, and that as X is a person without means there is little chance of recovering any party and party costs from X if the newspaper wins the case. Similar problems come before insurance companies every day. It is obviously cheaper to buy off such complainants with sums of £500 or £1,000 than to defend unsubstantial claims and pay still larger sums to lawyers. Many companies pay out yearly considerable sums in settlement of claims that could be successfully resisted, simply because of the costs that would otherwise be incurred.

On the other hand, a wealthy litigant has a great advantage. As will be explained later, one party can to some extent set the pace in running up costs.

There is also the matter of appeals. One may win in the High Court and be given costs, be taken to the Court of Appeal and win again and be given costs, and then be taken to the House of Lords and lose and have to pay costs not only of the appeal in the House of Lords but also the costs in the courts below. A number of appeals are little more than gambling on the costs.[1]

It must also be remembered that litigants have to pay for the mistakes of judges. If a judge misdirects a jury, or conducts a case in some irregular fashion, the Court of Appeal may order a new trial. A litigant who has spent a large sum is surely suffering from a grievance when he is told that he must now begin all over again because the original trial judge made a mistake.

Many appeals are due to uncertainty in the law. The settling of some rules of common law, and the interpretation of some statutes have cost litigants vast fortunes. Whenever a new trial or an appeal is due to error, a judge or uncertainty in the law, the litigant who suffers should not have to bear the cost. In the first edition of this book in 1940, Professor Jackson put forward the idea of a Suitors' Fund financed by a levy on every proceeding commenced in the High Court. This has since been adopted in various other common law countries, including New South Wales in 1951 and Western Australia in 1964. In England various law reform bodies have pressed the idea, the most recent being the Royal Commission on Legal Services (Benson Commission) in 1979. Presumably it is apathy, plus the fear that it might cost money, which ensures that nothing is done.[2]

Counsel's fees are not fixed by law except in a few matters, notably the fixed fee system in undefended divorce in county courts.[3] There are, however, standard fees for conferences with the solicitor in a case, and for interlocutory matters in the High Court such as drawing a statement of claim, drawing a defence, advising on evidence and steps other than the actual hearing of the case. These scales are settled by discussion between the Bar Council and the taxing masters after consultation with the Lord Chancellor's Office; the significance of these scales is that they are an agreed rate for the job and that if a bill is taxed, counsel's fees on these scales will be allowed.[4]

---

[1] The old case of *Sutherland Publishing Co.* v. *Caxton Publishing Co.* [1936] Ch. 323, [1937] Ch. 294, and [1938] 4 All ER 389 provides an extreme example. In the Court of Appeal Mackinnon LJ spoke of winning or losing 'the costs game', and observed that 'the spice of a gamble may now be added to the joys of litigation'.

[2] The Evershed Committee in their Final Report, (1953) Cmd 8878 p. 217, thought the idea was outside their terms of reference but worth considering in future. *Justice* produced a report, *Proposals for a Suitors' Fund* in 1972. A memorandum by the Law Society in 1973 reviewed the *Justice* report and was broadly in favour. For the Royal Commission on Legal Services see (1979) Cmnd 7648, para. 16.16–16.21.

[3] Counsel's fees used to be in guineas, with an addition for the barrister's clerk, so that 2 guineas was £2.4s. 6d., the rate of commission for the clerk becoming lower for the higher fees. Now all fees are in pounds and clerks' fees have been abolished.

[4] If on a taxation of costs counsel's fees are not allowed in full, counsel must still be paid the full brief fees. The liability to pay counsel is on the solicitor. A solicitor always has to consider whether he can rely on his client to pay all the costs that may be incurred or whether he should obtain some advance payment so that he will not find himself saddled with payments that he cannot recover. Counsel are in a happier position though they may have to wait for payment.

For taking cases in court, brief fees depend on the length and complexity of the case and the standing of counsel who are briefed: the solicitor generally knows what is an acceptable fee or he may discuss it with the barrister's clerk. It is difficult to say whether brief fees are 'reasonable' because cases vary from simple and short to heavy and long, and counsel vary from the barely competent to people of very great ability. The barristers at the top are much in demand, and the service they give must be done personally, as with an actor or a portrait painter; leading counsel have some support from others but not so much as that received by a surgeon, and they cannot delegate work as may be done in business. The most brilliant performance does not produce any subsequent income from the making of records, royalties, performing rights and so on. Hence a busy counsel must look to high fees for a good income, for he cannot take on any more cases than he is doing already. What appears to have happened to the incomes of barristers with established practices is that over the years they have kept pace with the professions generally, though a small proportion of barristers earn a good deal more than the most successful solicitors or medical practitioners. The fees of the most successful can be enormous. For representing Mr Jeffrey Archer in his triumphantly successful three-week libel action against *The Star*,[1] Robert Alexander QC was allegedly paid £150,000, and Michael Hill QC for the newspaper paid £100,000; their junior counsel had a mere £10,000 each.

The Bar, like the solicitors' profession, is becoming increasingly specialised, and in some cases it is the scarcity of a particular barrister's deep knowledge that enables him to charge high fees. In other cases he is expensive mainly because he has 'got a name'. Modern conditions of publicity enable this to happen; a barrister must not of course seek for this, but it may come upon him. Clients like to feel that their affairs are in the hands of well-known barristers, and may feel a sense of importance in having Sir Somebody Something to represent them. If one party briefs expensive counsel, then the other party may feel that they should do the same. In most cases it is a vicious circle. Solicitors sometimes feel that they can escape responsibility by suggesting a fashionable leader. Solicitors do not always think the fashionable barristers of the day are really much better than many others who take more modest fees. But if the expensive leader wins the case, then people say: 'It was worth the fee; nobody else could have done it.' If the case is lost, they say: 'If that great barrister lost the case, then nobody could have won it.'

Litigation is unquestionably expensive, at any rate when the defendant contests the case. Public attention usually focusses on the cost of libel actions, which can swallow astronomical sums. In Mr Archer's libel action, the total costs are said to have come to £670,000: £270,000 in fees to counsel, £150,000 to the plaintiff's solicitors and £75,000 for the defence solicitors, £70,000 in the costs of witnesses (including the plaintiff and his wife), and £105,000 for daily transcripts

---

[1] In which he won a record £500,000 damages against the newspaper for saying that he had sexual intercourse with a prostitute – despite the apparent difficulty from his point of view of having admittedly paid her £2,000 to leave the country. See *The Times* 25 July 1987.

of the evidence, and other documentation.[1] In 1985 a libel action which a doctor brought against the BBC and which was eventually settled, is said to have cost the BBC some £1.2 million in their own and their opponent's costs. Libel actions are rare, however, and various factors put them in a cost-bracket of their own: they can only be brought in the High Court, juries are routinely used (which slows down the pace of trial), the law is complex and they are the happy hunting ground of fashionable counsel. It is the cost of personal injury actions that is more worrying, because these form the bulk of contested litigation, and unlike defamation actions they are not something which it is relatively easy to avoid getting mixed up in. There have been a number of studies of personal injury actions over the years, particularly by the Pearson Commission in 1978,[2] the Cantley Committee in 1979,[3] and the Centre for Socio-Legal Studies at Oxford in 1984.[4]

The most recent study is one by a firm of international consultants, INBUCON, which was undertaken for the Lord Chancellor's Civil Justice Review and was published in 1986.[5] This looked at several hundred cases in which proceedings had been started in county courts, High Court provincial centres, and the High Court in London; most of the cases were settled, but a small percentage were fought to the finish. The plaintiffs' costs averaged out as follows: £1,347 for county court cases which were settled, £2,044 when they were tried; £2,547 for High Court cases in provincial centres which were settled, £4,011 when they were tried; £4,388 for cases in the High Court in London which were settled, £7,298 if they were tried. These figures represent the plaintiffs' costs only, and to get the average total cost it is necessary to add on those of the defendants, which would range from three-quarters of the plaintiffs' costs to the same sum over again. The INBUCON study also brought out the fact that litigation gets proportionately more costly as the sum at issue is reduced. In the High Court the total costs averaged out at 71p per pound recovered in London and 50p per pound in the provinces; but in the county court they exceeded what was recovered, working out at £1.28 per pound. These costs must obviously deter private litigants, except for those who have considerable wealth, legal aid, insurance cover, or the backing of a trade union.

Table 12, which comes from an INBUCON study of 50 cases in which costs were taxed, shows how costs in personal injury litigation are made up. The biggest item is 'preparation for trial', and this represents what the solicitor is paid for what he does. The work he has done will consist of interviewing his client, interviewing witnesses and taking proofs of evidence, writing letters to the defendant's solicitors or insurers, negotiating on the telephone, issuing proceed-

[1] *The Independent* 25 July 1987.
[2] The Royal Commission on Civil Liability and Compensation for Personal Injury, Cmnd 7054.
[3] Report of the Personal Injuries Litigation Procedure Working Party, Cmnd 7476.
[4] D. Harris and others, 'Compensation and Support for Illness and Injury'. For earlier studies readers are referred to previous editions of this book.
[5] INBUCON Study of Personal Injury Litigation. Published by the Lord Chancellor's Department in January 1986. For the Civil Justice Review see chapter 8 above, and Appendix A.

Table 12. *Costs in personal injury cases*

	County court	High Court provinces	High Court London
Number of bills analysed	10	19[a]	20
	%	%	%
Preparation of documents	4.3	2.4	1.5
Preparation for trial	46.1	48.4	49.9
Counsel's fees	14.1	14.3	18.5
Disbursements	10.3	12.9	10.7
Attendances	3.9	3.7	2.9
Taxation	3.1	2.2	1.3
Miscellaneous	0.4	0.8	1.6
Court and taxation fees	7.2	5.8	4.0
VAT	10.6	9.5	9.5
Total	100	100	100

[a]Excluding one bill which contained an exceptionally large figure for disbursements, and which would have distorted the picture.
Source: Survey by INBUCON, International Consultants, printed in the Lord Chancellor's Department's Civil Justice Review Working Paper on Personal Injuries Litigation (1986).

ings, and generally occupying his time with the matter. The second largest sum is fees to counsel: a sizeable proportion, but much less than the solicitors' fees, and tiny compared with counsel's fees in libel cases. Disbursements are made up of payments for medical and other reports, and the expenses of witnesses. The remaining substantial items are court fees, and VAT.

There is no section of the community that is satisfied with the present cost of litigation. A few lawyers find that it is to their advantage, but lawyers as a whole do not gain by it. High costs frighten away clients. Most solicitors regard fighting an action as a misfortune from which they may save their client; a good settlement is better than a victory in the courts, and a solicitor who ignored this would not be doing his duty to his client. But the real effect is that many just and proper claims are compromised because a verdict of the courts is too expensive. The high cost of litigation has led to a number of investigations and proposals designed to lower the cost. These can be divided into two streams: one stream regards the high costs as being due to lawyers being overpaid, whereas another stream seeks reduction of costs through reform in procedure and organisation.

There have been complaints about lawyers and their fees down the ages. Traditionally landlords and wealthy men have opposed peasants and the poor, and used lawyers to do their work. When Jack Cade led the peasants' revolt in 1450 and marched on London, one of the cries was, 'The first thing we do, let's kill all the lawyers.'[1]

[1] This is thoroughly in keeping with that revolt, but the wording comes from Shakespeare, *2 Henry VI,* IV. ii.86.

That lawyers grossly overcharge is still an impression which is widely held: if they knew that the burgee of the Law Society's Yacht Club is a yellow shark on a blue background most members of the public would probably think it was a piece of flagrant cynicism rather than a joke. Where solicitors' fees are concerned, the main controversy in modern times has been fees for conveyancing rather than what they charge for contentious work. The profits solicitors were making out of conveyancing under this system were said to be excessive in three reports by the Prices and Incomes Board in 1968, 1969 and 1971,[1] and as has already been explained this led to the abolition of scale fees in 1973: the controversy about solicitors and conveyancing is now whether other agencies which might be able to do it cheaper should be allowed to do the work in competition rather than whether solicitors charge exorbitantly for it (see chapter 27 above). The Prices and Incomes Board did not say that solicitors were grossly overpaid by comparison with other professionals when one considers the total of what they earn. Indeed, it said that for some litigation at the bottom end of the market they were considerably underpaid. The Royal Commission on Legal Services carefully examined the remuneration of lawyers in 1979, comparing what they earned with various other professions, and this body also thought their pay was generally fair.[2]

Solicitors' firms have sizeable overheads. The staff who are salaried solicitors have to be paid; their salaries, which at the time of writing range from around £12,000 to around £20,000 a year, depending on age, experience, and where they are, are not huge by the standards of other professions. Typists and other supporting staff must be paid the going rate for the area, and there are rents, rates and other office outgoings to pay. All this means that in a firm in the south or east of England time must be costed at £40 an hour before there are any profits for the partners; in London, of course, the rate will be considerably higher. Adding to this perhaps £10 per hour for partners' profits, the firm would charge £50 an hour. Thus even if a case takes considerably less than two days of a solicitor's time to prepare, a bill for £500 would certainly not be excessive.

The fees of different barristers vary widely, which makes it difficult to say that the fees the Bar extracts from civil litigation are in general either too high or too low. In the past, however, and to some extent today, the Bar operates various restrictive practices that undoubtedly put up the costs. An old one concerned the 'circuit system'. Under the old system of Assizes (see chapter 1; chapter 19(i) above) there were seven Circuits, each with its own Bar of barristers who had joined the Circuit and were elected members of the Circuit Mess.[3] A barrister could not belong to more than one Circuit, and only Circuit members could do

---

[1] Report No. 54, (1968) Cmnd 3529, Report No. 134, (1969) Cmnd 4217 and Report No. 164, (1971) Cmnd 4624. There is a fuller account of these reports and the controversies surrounding them in the previous edition of this book.

[2] Cmnd 7648.

[3] Nowadays there are only six Circuits, corresponding with the organisation of courts under the Courts Act 1971.

the Circuit cases for the normal rates. If an 'outsider' appeared, he had to be paid a special fee which at Assizes was 100 guineas for a QC and 50 guineas for a junior; and if both QC and junior had these special fees a further 'kite fee' had to be paid to a member of the Circuit. These rules prevented a client from having the barrister of his choice except at a high cost. They were abandoned in 1964 after a large majority of the Bar had voted to get rid of them. The other restrictive practice was the requirement that a QC may not appear without a junior. At one time the rule was that the junior usually had to be paid a fee from three-fifths to two-thirds of the leader's fee, but in 1966 it was relaxed so that the junior could be paid a fee equal to that which he would have received if he had conducted the case alone. Under the Fair Trading Act 1973 the Director-General of Fair Trading may refer matters to the Monopolies and Mergers Commission for investigation and report, and following a reference in 1974 the Commission in 1976 condemned the 'two counsel' rule as a restrictive practice.[1] After this the Bar abandoned the rule in 1977. Although not now obliged to appear with a junior, a QC may nevertheless stipulate for one, and the rules of conduct for the Bar say that a QC is entitled to expect that he will have one; so although the rule is dead, its soul, like that of John Brown, goes marching on. But of course the litigant can avoid encountering the spectre by briefing junior counsel.

There is still one matter affecting barristers' fees which many people regard as unjustified, and this is that once counsel has been briefed to appear in a case the full brief fee is normally payable to him even if the case is settled and he does not have to appear. The etiquette of the Bar permits him to take less than the agreed fee if this happens, but he is not obliged to do so. The brief fee is what counsel charges for arguing the case in court, and as most cases are eventually settled, this means that clients routinely have to pay for services that counsel have not rendered. The usual justification for this is that if a case is settled at a late stage, counsel has still 'got up' the case, avoided other commitments and cannot usually make profitable use of the time that becomes unexpectedly available: but the brief fee has to be paid whether the case is settled early or late, whether or not counsel has read the papers yet, and even if he is able to make profitable use of the time. This is not quite as outrageous as it sounds. Counsel is only 'briefed' quite late in the course of the solicitor's preparations for trial. At an earlier stage in the preparation counsel will probably have been called on for advice and he may have had to draft pleadings and do other paper-work in connection with the case. The rates of pay for this sort of work are poor, brief fees are high by comparison, and if counsel is overpaid when he pockets some brief fees without having to work for them this in a sense makes up for the paper-work for which he is underpaid. But if it all works out fairly from counsel's point of view, from the client's perspective it looks different: it may well be client A whose wasted brief-fee makes up for the paper-work for which client B underpaid counsel in a case which never got as far as a brief.

[1] *Barristers' service; A report on the supply by Her Majesty's counsel alone of their services* HMSO (1976).

The fact that barristers have exclusive rights of audience in the higher courts undoubtedly puts up the cost of criminal work. It probably has less direct effect on the cost of civil litigation because solicitors have rights of audience in the county courts, which probably means they can appear in most of the contested civil trials in which they would find it economical to do so. But the separation of the two professions may put up the costs indirectly. A report by *Justice* makes this point:

our way of litigation is such that, once a decision to fight has been made, considerations of economy go to the wall. Counsel rarely has any contact with the lay client until shortly before the trial. Counsel does not have to cope with the client's financial position, and concentrates upon the task of winning the case, leaving all financial questions to the solicitor. It is uncommon for counsel to be expert on questions of costs. The solicitor generally follows the advice of counsel; it would be unusual for a solicitor to take it upon himself to say that the expense does not warrant a step advised by counsel.[1]

It is very doubtful, however, if the largest conceivable reduction in lawyers' charges would bring the cost of litigation within the reach of ordinary people. The cost of litigation is broadly speaking made up of (1) court fees, (2) the cost of witnesses and (3) lawyers' fees. If cases are to continue to be heard in the way that they are conducted at present, the expenses under (2), that is the cost of witnesses, cannot be reduced unless witnesses are to be compelled to attend and foot their own expenses and loss of earnings, which would be very unfair to witnesses and make it even harder to get the necessary evidence. As for (3), lawyers' charges, there is no ground for saying that these are generally excessive *for the work that is done*. Lawyers' time and their overheads can be costed, and when that has been done a process of simple accounting can show the relation between the time spent on processes in litigation and what they are paid. On such calculations lawyers are certainly not in general overpaid.[2]

If the cost of litigation is to be substantially reduced, the only possible course is to restructure litigation. The present processes are geared to the oral presentation of cases: the facts of the case must be presented orally by one side, witnesses must be present and be examined, cross-examined and re-examined: and then the other side may go through a similar process; legal arguments must be presented orally, and the judge must deliver himself orally whether in summing up to a jury or in delivering his judgment. This is not the method that is used in any other kind of decision-making, whether in industry or in central or local government. The legal process is in fact a product of the days when the mass of the population were illiterate. We could reduce the length of our hearings by

---

[1] *The trial of motor accident cases* (1966).

[2] Although the Civil Justice Review makes the point that lawyers might be able to provide a more economical service if they quoted for the costs of litigation and there was competition between them: General Issues Paper (1987) p. 83. For the Civil Justice Review see chapter 8 above, and Appendix A.

letting the court call the evidence and letting the judge examine the witnesses,[1] or by cutting out the personal appearance and examination of witnesses and substituting written statements. Most of the arguments of counsel could also be submitted in writing. The argument against all such proposals is that none of them would be as good as the present system. That may be true, but it ignores the point that consumers have no choice: there is no alternative procedure available that is serviceable and cheaper. Hence, if our present system is to be maintained we must look to legal aid and to associations of people (trades unions, employers' associations, consumers' associations and so on, and to insurers standing behind individuals and groups and companies) to meet the costs of their members.

For small claims in the county court, the need for a different method of determining cases was recognised when the 'arbitration procedure' was introduced in 1973.[2] The idea was to provide a private, informal hearing for small claims, with the normal rules of courtroom procedure relaxed so that the parties could present and defend the cases themselves. As explained earlier in this book it has been quite successful. In February 1986 the Lord Chancellor's Department Civil Justice Review produced a working paper on personal injuries cases which was written in the light of the INBUCON survey mentioned above. For the larger personal injury claims, it thought that some sizeable economies could be made under what would still be in essence the present method of trial if the rules of civil procedure were altered to give the court greater control over the progress of the case. This, the Review says, would reduce delay, and delay is a major factor in excessive costs. For the smaller cases the Review accepts the fact that the present method of adjudication will be disproportionately expensive whatever modifications are made to the rules of procedure. It looks at the small claims arbitration procedure, but thinks this is not really suitable to the smaller personal injury claims. 'Experience of handling personal injury cases under that system has shown, however, that unless the matters in dispute are very straightforward and the court itself substantially assists the parties to cross-examine witnesses, arbitration hearings are not well adapted to this business'.[3]

As a possible alternative model it considered something along the lines of the Criminal Injuries Compensation Board (see chapter 23(iii)), which, with a team of 23 part-time members, manages to handle some 30,000 cases a year. Claimants apply to the Board by submitting a written application and supporting documentation. In 90 per cent of all cases it is able to deal with the application on the papers only; in the remaining 10 per cent of cases the applicant is interviewed by a panel of three members.

---

[1] As is done in Germany, with resulting economy of time: see J. H. Langbein, 'The German advantage in civil procedure', (1985) 52 *U. of Chicago LR* 823–66. Professor Jackson used to recall that he was secretary to a judicial inquiry conducted by Lord Goddard, where by dint of the judge calling the witnesses and examining them he got through in a day a mass of evidence which would have taken at least three days under the adversarial method.

[2] See chapters 5 and 7 above for the background and further details.

[3] Civil Justice Review, Personal Injuries Litigation, February 1986, para. 93.

An even more radical suggestion is to lift a category of cases out of the realm of legal obligations enforced through the ordinary law courts and to make it part of public administration. The principal instance in our legal system is the change from Workmen's Compensation, which used the ordinary courts for adjudication, to an Industrial Injuries system working on national insurance and administrative tribunals (see chapter 15(i) above). A key question in personal injury cases is whether obtaining compensation should depend on establishing the injury was caused by someone's fault, or whether injured persons should receive compensation irrespective of whether it was their own fault or someone else's, or an accident for which no one can be blamed. If it is accepted that compensation should be paid whether or not anyone is at fault, there is no doubt that the cheapest way of providing the compensation would be through a state compensation scheme like the industrial injuries scheme, directly financed by the taxpayer; see chapter 8 above.

40

LEGAL AID

It is obvious that a large section of the community cannot possibly afford the costs that have been mentioned in the preceding section, any more than they could afford to pay for private schooling or medical treatment. An extensive system of legal aid and advice is therefore made available to help them.[1] At the time of writing this system is in a state of flux: a Government White Paper in March 1987[2] was followed by a Legal Aid Bill which was introduced in December 1987, and which is before Parliament at the time of writing. A section at the end of this chapter attempts to predict the future pattern.

At present there are four distinct systems of legal aid to contend with:

(1) Legal advice and assistance (generally known as the 'Green Form Scheme'), and its off-shoot 'assistance by way of representation' (generally known as 'ABWOR');
(2) legal aid for civil proceedings;
(3) legal aid for criminal proceedings; and
(4) advice and representation provided by a duty solicitor at a magistrates' court or police station under the Legal Aid (Duty Solicitor) Scheme 1985.

The statutory basis for all of these is two Acts of Parliament – the Legal Aid Act 1974 and the Legal Aid Act 1982 – and a mass of Statutory Instruments made by the Lord Chancellor under powers which those Acts confer on him.[3] Although the Lord Chancellor's Department is ultimately responsible for all of them, they are administered by different agencies. This creates a confusing pattern, and the division of responsibilities is thought to lead to inefficiency. Thus the main proposal in the Legal Aid Bill is the creation of a single Legal Aid Board with overall responsibility.

---

[1] The standard book is the annually produced *Legal aid handbook*, prepared by the Law Society and published by HMSO. An excellent short account is Ole Hansen and Howard Levenson, *Legal aid and how to use it* (1985). The Legal Action Group (LAG), which was formed in 1971, publishes a regular *Bulletin* which is largely concerned with legal aid matters. The Lord Chancellor's Advisory Committee on Legal Aid produces an annual Report, which has hitherto been published together with the annual Report of the Law Society Legal Aid Committee.
[2] *Legal aid in England and Wales: a new framework*, Cm 118.
[3] Most of this legislation is set out in the *Legal aid handbook*, note 1 above.

i Legal advice and assistance

Broadly speaking, this is concerned with giving people who have legal problems advice and help which stops short of representing them in court proceedings; but the possibility of ABWOR (see below) blurs the edges of the definition.

The main system for legal advice and assistance at present is the 'Green Form Scheme'. This was created by the Legal Advice and Assistance Act 1972, and the details are now contained in the Legal Aid Act 1974 and the Legal Advice and Assistance Regulations 1980.[1] This enables a member of the public to have free or subsidised legal help up to a specified value by going to a solicitor who does legal aid work and filling in the appropriate form, which needless to say is coloured green. (At the time of writing the value is £50 (or £90 in cases leading to the preparation of an undefended divorce or judicial separation petition); as a solicitor's time is unlikely to be charged at much less than £50 an hour the scheme does not buy a very large amount of advice.) The solicitor checks that the client is financially eligible, after which advice or help up to the £50 or £90 limit is given without further formality. Further work can be done under the scheme where necessary, but an extension must then be obtained from local Area Legal Aid Committee (see section ii below). Eligibility is determined by a simple means test, which the solicitor administers with the help of a 'key card' containing the relevant figures. The test is based on 'disposable income' and 'disposable capital': that is to say, what income and capital is notionally left over after deductions have been made for dependants and various specified outgoings. The figures are varied at intervals, and new 'key cards' issued accordingly. On the figures issued in March 1987 the client's disposable capital must not exceed £825, and his weekly disposable income must not exceed £118; if his disposable income is between £118 and £56 he is eligible, but is liable to pay a contribution; and if it is less than £56 he gets the service free.

The mechanism for payment is that the solicitor does the work up to the specified limit, calculates the client's contribution (if any), deducts this from the £50 or £90, and then claims the balance from the legal aid fund. The client's contribution he collects directly from the client, and keeps (or decides to forget about it if it is small and he thinks it is not worth the fuss of collecting). The scheme is therefore quick and simple to operate, because there is the minimum amount of correspondence to be done in arranging for the advice to be given and in collecting the payment. But things may become more complicated in either of two situations. The first is where it becomes necessary to apply to the Area Legal Aid Committee for permission to do work in excess of the £50 or £90 limits. The second is where as a result of the solicitor's activities the client recovers money or property. In this case the solicitor has what is known as a 'statutory charge' over the proceeds. Instead of being able to claim payment from the legal aid fund he

---

[1] For details of the schemes that it replaced see previous editions of this book.

must take what the fund would otherwise have paid him out of the proceeds, and the balance is all the client receives.

The Green Form Scheme is available to finance any of the work that a solicitor (or a barrister) normally does. Thus it covers giving general advice to people who are involved in civil or criminal proceedings, and doing things like making wills or writing letters on their behalf. There are two main limits, however. First, the matter must concern English law; thus it is not available for matters of foreign law, or on the application of the European Convention on Human Rights;[1] but it *is* available on a question of EEC law, because EEC law is technically part of English law. Secondly, subject to what is said below, the Green Form Scheme does not cover the work of a solicitor in representing his client in litigation, or taking formal steps in litigation on his behalf.

The Green Form Scheme is quick and simple, particularly when compared with the Legal Aid Scheme which provides finance for those who are involved in civil litigation. Under that scheme, the Department of Health and Social Security must assess the client's means, whereas under the Green Form Scheme the solicitor does it himself with the help of the 'Key Card'. Hence when in 1979 it was decided that state aid should pay for legal representation in certain types of tribunal for which representation was not available under the Legal Aid Scheme, this was done by extending the Green Form Scheme rather than by stretching legal aid. This extension of the Green Form Scheme is known as 'Assistance by Way of Representation', or ABWOR. This is available in three main types of proceedings: domestic proceedings in the magistrates' courts (see chapter 26); applications to Mental Health Tribunals (see chapter 15(iii)); and for representation in disciplinary proceedings before prison boards of visitors. ABWOR is also available, in certain limited situations, as a fall-back to criminal or civil legal aid in county courts and magistrates' courts. ABWOR is obtained in the same way as legal advice and assistance under the Green Form Scheme, except that the solicitor cannot simply go ahead and do the work, but must obtain the permission of the local Area Legal Aid Committee before he represents his client in the proceedings. Eligibility for ABWOR is wider than for advice or assistance in that the amount of disposable capital which disqualifies is £3,000 instead of £825, and the amount of work which may be done is not limited to the £50 or £90 limits that apply to ordinary advice or assistance under the Green Form Scheme.

There are obvious drawbacks to using solicitors in private practice to distribute state-funded legal advice and assistance to the poor. First, it depends on the willingness of solicitors to take on this type of work. Some firms do not wish to do legal aid work at all because they find it does not pay a good enough return, and those that do may have no one who has specialist knowledge in some of the problems which legally aided clients are typically likely to have: difficulties with claiming welfare benefits, for example. Secondly, the work has to be done

---

[1] See chapter 35. But the European Commission has its own legal aid scheme.

through ordinary solicitors' offices. Unlike post-offices and primary schools, these are not evenly distributed around the areas where people live, but tend to be concentrated in the commercial centres of towns, with few to be found in poor residential areas; and they are generally shut when most wage-earners are free to visit them. Thirdly, there was until recently the problem of telling the public that the service is available; as was explained in chapter 27, solicitors were formerly not permitted to advertise. Fourthly, there is the difficulty that many of the poor seem to regard solicitors as beyond their social range and are daunted at the idea of going to see one. All these considerations have often led people to suggest an alternative method: a special salaried service, with a network of offices in poor areas, specialising solely in advising the poor about their kinds of legal problem – housing, welfare benefits, employment, and so forth.

The idea of lawyers attending at certain centres and giving free legal advice first arose in connection with University Settlements in the East End of London in the early years of this century. The work spread to other organisations of a charitable, religious or social nature. Political parties also made provision for this service at some centres. These schemes were originally known as *poor man's lawyers*; where these schemes exist today they are usually called *legal advice centres* or *law surgeries*. They are unofficial and are not affiliated with any local law society and do not have to be approved or noticed by any public body. A centre may flourish without its existence being known outside its immediate locality. The usual arrangement is that a voluntary rota of solicitors and barristers provides for lawyers to attend the centre on one or more evenings in the week. Useful as these centres are there are some inherent disadvantages. If solicitors attend by rota it is difficult to ensure continuity; if the client comes back he usually finds he is going over the same ground again with someone else. It is also difficult for a scheme which depends on a rota of volunteers to do much more than offer advice; writing letters on behalf of clients, and taking other steps, is much harder to arrange. Many of these centres work an arrangement so that when it appears to a solicitor advising at the centre that a client needs work done for him, the case is transferred to his own office and it is done there under the Green Form Scheme.

Neighbourhood law centres, by contrast, are offices where at least part of the staff are lawyers who work there full-time and are paid. They can therefore open during normal office hours as well as offering an evening service and they are able to offer a much more comprehensive service. The first of these in England was the North Kensington Law Centre which opened in 1970.[1] By 1976 the number had risen to fifteen[2] and in 1985 there were some 55, which had linked themselves together with a Law Centres Federation. Most centres are in areas

[1] Much of the impetus came from the USA, where 'neighbourhood law firms' had been in existence for some time. See L. A. Albert and J. Weiss, 'Neighbourhood lawyers – An American experiment', (1968) 118 NLJ 667; R. T. Oerton, 'Solicitors and social need', (1968) 118 NLJ 1108 shows their impact. See also the pamphlet by the Society of Labour Lawyers, *Justice for all* (1968).
[2] See 'Law centres survey', by M. Zander and P. Russell, (1976) 73 Law Soc. Gaz. 208.

where there are few local solicitors. The aim is to provide a comprehensive legal service including court representation, but they do not normally take on the sort of work which local solicitors undertake: if this sort of work is brought to them they usually refer it to a local firm. Centres operate an informal means test and provide what is normally a free service, but some of the work may be done under the Green Form Scheme and then a contribution may be required. Although neighbourhood law centres provide a valuable legal service for many thousands of poor people, their number remains fairly small. This is partly because setting up such a centre depends on local initiative and pressure, and because of finance. Whilst they generate a certain amount of income from the Green Form Scheme, this is not sufficient to cover their outgoings and there is need for further funds. There is no regular government grant. Some money has been found from charitable trusts, and some from various government departments, but the main source up to now has been grants from the local authority. This source is precarious, and a number of neighbourhood law centres have had to close when the local authority has failed to renew the grant, usually following a change in political control at the local town hall, or sometimes because the law centre has made itself unpopular with councillors or officials by taking up the cause of local council tenants or by resisting the council's plans for redevelopment. The Greater London Council (GLC) supported a number of centres in parts of London where the local borough was not willing to provide any money, and these faced closure when the GLC was abolished in April 1986. In the 1970s the Lord Chancellor's Department began to provide finance for seven of the worst-off centres, and this support has continued; but it has not been extended, and in recent years it was said that the Lord Hailsham, who was Lord Chancellor from 1979 to 1987, was opposed to them.

The idea of a centrally-funded national network of offices of the neighbourhood law centre type was first put forward in 1945 by the Rushcliffe Committee,[1] the Departmental Committee whose recommendations gave rise to the Legal Aid Scheme for civil litigation which is discussed in the next section of this book. The proposal was for an area office, branch offices in each centre of population, and 'an itinerant poor man's lawyer' for smaller places. It reached the statute book as section 7 of the Legal Aid and Advice Act 1949, but for reasons of economy this section was never brought into force (although it was re-enacted in the Legal Aid Act 1974).

Across the country there is a network of 910 Citizens' Advice Bureaux. These were founded at the outbreak of the Second World War to give information on urgent wartime matters, but they have continued to flourish since. At a local level they are financed by local authorities and run by local management committees. There is also a central organisation which receives a grant from the Department of Trade and Industry. Many of the enquiries that the Citizens' Advice Bureaux

---

[1] Report of the Committee on Legal Aid and Advice, (1945) Cmd 6641 paras 174–78.

receive nowadays are broadly legal. Over half the bureaux operate rota schemes where local solicitors take turns to run free legal advice sessions at the bureau, and these solicitors can take the enquirers as clients to their firms if further work is needed. Where there is no rota scheme, the bureau staff will refer legal questions beyond their own competence to answer to law surgeries, neighbourhood law centres, and solicitors who operate the Green Form Scheme. Proposals have been made at various times to make the Citizens' Advice Bureaux the main distribution point for free or state subsidised legal advice. The latest of these is discussed at the end of this chapter. The main disadvantage with this idea is that Citizens' Advice Bureaux tend to be concentrated in the larger towns, and if they became the only source of free legal advice this would be difficult for those who live in country areas.

ii Legal aid for proceedings in civil courts

Before the Second World War official provisions for legal aid in civil cases was through what called *poor persons' procedure*. The Law Society had local committees to which a would-be litigant applied. If the committee were satisfied that he had a case, he would be assigned a solicitor and counsel free of charge (other than out-of-pocket expenses). The lawyers were selected from a panel of those who had agreed to provide their services gratuitously, and no fee was payable by the litigant. The service was available only in the High Court, and was subject to a stringent means test. The principal disadvantages were the dependence on the generosity of a section of the legal profession, a means test which excluded even some of those living below subsistence levels, and the complete exclusion of proceedings in the county court – which meant no assistance at all was available for landlord and tenant disputes under the Rent Acts, and certain other types of dispute where one of the parties was particularly likely to be poor. This was obviously most unsatisfactory, yet proposals to make legal aid more widely available were resisted by those in authority, whose argument was that it would 'encourage' litigation. Rejecting the analogy with Health Insurance, a Committee in 1928 said that 'it is manifestly in the interests of the State that its citizens should be healthy, not that they should be litigious':[1] an extraordinary argument, because it fails to notice that a poor person who has been wronged may need a law-suit to put the matter right just as much as a poor person who has been physically injured may need a surgical operation.

Attitudes changed after the war. In 1945 a Departmental Committee chaired by Lord Rushcliffe[2] made a number of radical recommendations: legal aid should be provided by the state paying for it, not by public-spirited lawyers giving their services free; it should be available for civil proceedings in all courts; it should be available not only free to the very poor, but on payment of part of the

[1] Report of the Committee on Legal Aid for the Poor, (1928) Cmd 3016 para. 17.
[2] Report of the Committee on Legal Aid and Advice, Cmd 6641.

cost to anyone who was not rich; and that like the previous scheme it should be administered by the Law Society. The main features of this proposal were brought about by the Legal Aid and Advice Act 1949, which delegated to the Law Society the responsibility of drawing up the regulations for a detailed scheme which the Lord Chancellor and the Treasury had then to approve. The civil Legal Aid Scheme that we have today is in essence the same as the one introduced then; but its statutory basis is now the Legal Aid Act 1974 and the current detailed rules are the Legal Aid Scheme 1985.[1]

The Law Society administers the scheme through a series of committees. In overall charge is a Legal Aid Committee which decides general policy questions. This consists of nine members of the Council of the Law Society, three persons nominated by the Bar, one person nominated by the Lord Chancellor and two laymen nominated by the Council of the Law Society. Below this committee are 15 Area Committees covering different areas of England and Wales. These are composed of practising solicitors and practising barristers, in a ratio of four solicitors to every one barrister; the number of members is laid down by the Legal Aid Committee and can be anything between 16 and 120 members. The Area Committees are served by a secretary and a substantial number of other full-time staff who are employees of the Law Society. The secretary has power to perform a number of acts on behalf of the Area Committee, including granting and (since 1986) refusing a legal aid certificate; in practice he in turn delegates much of the work to members of his staff.

Legal aid is available for most types of proceedings in most civil courts, but there are some important exceptions to this. It is not available for proceedings in coroners' courts, nor for proceedings in most tribunals, including industrial tribunals (although it is available on appeals to the Employment Appeal Tribunal). In the ordinary courts legal aid is not available for various kinds of work, the most important of which are defamation actions and undefended divorces. Undefended divorces were removed from the scope of legal aid in 1977 on the ground that it was now so simple to obtain one that there was no need for either party to be represented at the 'hearing' (see chapter 6(iii)), and it was enough that the parties could obtain advice and help to fill out the necessary forms under the Green Form Scheme; where the divorce is defended, or there are disputes about the custody of children or other ancillary matters (such as financial provision) legal aid may still be granted – and is extensively used for these purposes. Defamation actions have never been within the scope of legal aid, despite the strong recommendation of the Faulks Committee in 1975 that they should be.[2]

The reason they are excluded is partly that defamation actions are very expensive and their inclusion would cost too much public money, and partly that

---

[1] The Legal Aid Scheme 1985 is printed in the *Legal aid handbook*, HMSO. The best account of the origin and development of the scheme is Seton Pollock, *Legal aid: The first 25 years* (1975).
[2] Report of the Committee on Defamation, (1975) Cmnd 5909.

it is widely felt that the law of defamation, if enforced to the limit by everyone who could in theory make use of it, would exercise too great a restraint on freedom of speech. The proper thing to do, of course, would be to reform the law and procedure governing defamation actions to make it cheaper and to limit the overbreadth of the substantive law so that it trenches less upon free speech: but no one is prepared to do this, so we keep a system whereby the rich have too much protection for their good names and the poor have none at all.

The principles for determining whether a person is financially eligible for civil legal aid are broadly the same as for determining whether he is eligible for advice and assistance under the Green Form Scheme, only the figures are slightly different, rather more people qualifying for legal aid than for advice and assistance. The basis once again is 'disposable income' and 'disposable capital'. 'Disposable income' is a person's net income, less permitted deductions for expenses in connection with employment, housing, and the maintenance of spouses and dependants. Disposable capital is all capital resources, but disregarding the value of the house the applicant lives in and its furnishings, and any capital that is the subject of the intended lawsuit. Taking the 1986 figures, a person qualifies for free legal aid if his disposable income is under £2,325 per annum: which in the case of a man with a wife and two small children is possible if his income is under around £7,300 per annum. He is ineligible for any legal aid if his disposable income exceeds £5,585: which for a man with a wife and two small children is probably the case if he is earning more than £12,900. If his disposable income is between £2,325 and £5,585 he is eligible for legal aid, but will be liable to make a contribution of up to one quarter of the amount by which his disposable income exceeds £2,325. This payment is made during one 'contribution period', which is one year; at present, he does not have to make further contributions out of income where the case drags on for longer than a year. Where disposable capital is less than £3,000 no contribution from capital is payable. Where it is over £3,000 but under £4,850 he is eligible, but subject to a contribution of the amount by which his capital exceeds £3,000 (in addition to any contribution from income). And disposable capital over £4,850 normally disqualifies him from legal aid altogether. These financial limits are adjusted at intervals to take account of inflation. In the 1960s and 1970s the increases were regularly less than the rate of inflation, with the result that the proportion of the population eligible for legal aid gradually fell from about 80 per cent of the population to in the region of 40 per cent. In 1978 the limits were raised and since then some 70 per cent of households have been eligible for some legal aid. In 1986, however, there was an ominous move when the Lord Chancellor reduced the amounts that applicants can off-set for dependants when calculating their disposable income, and thereby introduced a concealed cut – and one which discriminated against those who had a number of dependants to care for. For the 30 per cent or so of the population who are above the limits, there is nothing to be had from the Legal Aid Scheme, which is hard because plenty of these will not be in a position to pay the huge costs of High Court litigation. For legal aid in criminal cases there is no upper limit which formally disqualifies a person from state help, although where a rich person is granted criminal legal aid he will be assessed for a large contribution. This seems fairer than the civil legal aid system, which imposes what amounts to a middle-class 'poverty trap'.

When applying for legal aid the procedure is that the applicant fills up a form, usually with the help of a solicitor under the Green Form Scheme (see above), and sends it to the secretary of the Area Committee. To succeed, an application for legal aid must get over two hurdles: the applicant must be within the financial limits, and the claim (or defence) must have some merits. The applicant's financial position is investigated by the Department of Health and Social Security (DHSS); the applicant may have to send the DHSS officials papers, or even attend for an interview. The question of merits is determined by the Area Committee. In all cases the applicant must show that he has reasonable grounds for asserting or disputing a claim, or for being a party to proceedings, and he may be refused assistance if it appears unreasonable that he should receive it in the particular circumstances of the case. The principle which has been adopted for deciding this is for the Committee, who are themselves lawyers in private practice, to ask themselves a hypothetical question: 'What advice would I give to the applicant if he were a private client possessed of sufficient but not superabundant means to pay his own costs?' Legal aid should as a rule be available to the extent to which it is necessary to enable that hypothetical advice to be acted upon. Where an application for legal aid is refused because the DHSS say the applicant is too rich, there is no right of appeal against their assessment of his finances (although the officials may be persuaded to look at the case again). Where it fails because the Area Committee thinks the claim is not worth pursuing or defending, the applicant has a right of appeal which lies back to the Area Committee. This is not so meaningless as it sounds, because in the first place the application will probably have been dealt with either by the secretary or one of his staff in the name of the committee, or by a sub-committee, and on appeal the papers will be read by a fresh set of eyes. All this takes time; indeed, it will often take several months, and in recent years the time taken to process applications has been getting longer as public spending cuts have reduced the number of staff available to deal with applications. But there is a special procedure for urgent applications, which can if necessary be granted by telephone.

Where the application succeeds the applicant is made an offer of legal aid, either free or subject to a stated contribution. If the contribution seems high in the light of what the costs of the action are expected to be, the applicant will usually wish to accept it nevertheless, because the contribution is the maximum that he will have to fork out in respect of his own costs if things go wrong: if he loses the action, or wins but the defendant cannot be persuaded to pay up. But the contribution does not settle the largest amount that he can be made to pay for his own costs where he wins and recovers money or property, because the Law

Society usually has a statutory charge over the winnings from which it is obliged by law to recover the total amount of costs incurred and not recovered from the other side, even where these greatly exceed the contribution. To this extent the statutory charge puts an assisted person into the same position as that of a paying litigant: it is not worth fighting small cases because anything gained will be swallowed up in costs.[1]

If an assisted person is the defendant and he loses, he must like any other defendant satisfy the judgment against him. Whether plaintiff or defendant, if he loses he may also incur liability for his successful opponent's costs: but here he is in a stronger position than someone who is litigating without legal aid, because section 8(1)(e) of the Legal Aid Act 1974 provides that 'his liability . . . shall not exceed the amount (if any) which is a reasonable one for him to pay having regard to all the circumstances, including the means of all the parties and their conduct in connection with the dispute'. As assisted persons are by definition comparatively poor, this frequently means that their successful opponents get little or nothing awarded against them for costs. There is usually no need for tears on their behalf: the defendants in most personal injury claims, for example, are covered by insurance. Sometimes, however, the result could be very unjust. The Legal Aid Act 1974 provides some consolation here, because by section 13 there is power to award costs against the legal aid fund where it is 'just and equitable'. But the amount of consolation is small, because the statute also states that such an order can only be made where the unassisted party would 'suffer severe financial hardship' unless the order was made. The Area Legal Aid Committee may have put the assisted party in a position to conduct a piece of outrageous litigation which should have been strangled at birth, but if the successful defendant is well off he must bear the loss.[2] For this reason it has been suggested that the

---

[1] The statutory charge leads to many difficult questions, particularly in relation to matrimonial or former matrimonial homes. A different one arose in *Davies* v. *Eli Lilly & Co.* [1987] 1 WLR 428. A group of some 1,500 plaintiffs brought a negligence action against a drug company over illness suffered by taking the drug Opren. The costs of establishing liability promised to be enormous, so a legally aided plaintiff with a nil contribution was selected to go first. But this posed the problem for him that if he won damages and costs, there would probably be a huge slice of his costs not covered by the order for costs payable by the defendants, and by operation of the statutory charge this would swallow up all he was likely to win. The courts got around the problem as far as the plaintiff was concerned by making an order that his costs should be split between all the plaintiffs who were hoping to follow in his footsteps if he won – but this solution put the non-legally aided plaintiffs at risk.

[2] See *Orchard* v. *SEE Board* [1987] 2 WLR 102, where the plaintiff obtained legal aid to sue the electricity board on the ground that their supply cables were mysteriously making his house damp. This theory required the plaintiff to show 'that water ran uphill under his cottage, leaving the footings dry, through a layer of bitumen, and in some cases also through a damp proof membrane, and then through a layer of thermoplastic tiles leaving them undisturbed. He would also have to explain this phenomenon in the face of evidence that his experience was unique in the 65-year history of the electricity supply industry and why the other semidetached cottage was not also similarly affected.' In some circumstances – although not in that case – the solicitor acting for the assisted party may be made to pay the costs: see *Kelly* v. *London Transport Executive* [1982] 1 WLR 1055.

defendant-to-be should have an opportunity to argue against the grant of legal aid.

Legal aid cases are conducted in the same way as cases in which parties are not legally assisted, except for costs, which are generally paid out of the legal aid fund. In some situations these are assessed by the Area Legal Aid Committee, but in substantial matters the solicitor's bill is usually taxed by a Taxing Master.[1] Here there are some peculiarities. Briefs to counsel are not marked with any fee, but marked 'Legal Aid' so that the taxing master allows what he regards as a proper fee for the work done. For claims in magistrates' court and county court proceedings, solicitors and counsel are paid out of the legal aid fund the full amount allowed on taxation, but for work in the higher courts counsel receive only 90 per cent of the amount allowed on taxation and solicitors receive disbursements in full and 90 per cent of the amount allowed as profit costs. The 10 per cent deduction stems from a recommendation of the Rushcliffe Committee in 1945.[2] A deduction looked reasonable enough at the time because lawyers had previously done High Court work for poor persons free, and it was a great advance for them that they were to be paid at all. Forty years on the deduction has become a bitter grievance to the legal profession, and is likely to be abolished in the changes to legal aid that are ahead.

iii Legal aid in criminal proceedings

In the nineteenth century there was no public assistance for poor persons in summary trials. For trials on indictment a limited amount of help was provided by the system of 'dock briefs'. By an ancient custom of the Bar, any prisoner who could produce £1.3s.6d. was entitled to select any of the counsel robed and present in court and the counsel was bound to conduct the defence. It was a bad system in as much as it gave little time for the preparation of the case, and because in the old days even this fee would have been beyond the means of any poor prisoners: but it was better than nothing. The possibility of a dock brief survived long after legal aid became generally available in criminal cases, the fee finally rising to a princely £2.23p.[3] Dock briefs were finally abolished by a decision of the Bar Council in 1980. The judge might also 'invite' any counsel present to help the accused – the invitation being one of the sort that can hardly be refused. Unlike the dock brief, this possibility still exists.

The first systematic provision for legal aid in criminal cases was the Poor Prisoners' Defence Act 1903 which was limited to trials on indictment. In 1926 a Committee reported in favour of extending legal aid to preliminary inquiries and to summary trial, though there can be few Reports in which recommendations

---

[1] On taxing bills of costs, see chapter 39 above.
[2] Cmd 6641 p. 35. The deductions were originally greater.
[3] The celebrated case of *Rondel* v. *Worsley* [1969] AC 191, which established that a barrister was not liable in negligence for his manner of conducting a case in court, began with a dock brief.

have been put forward so half-heartedly.[1] The Poor Prisoners' Defence Act 1930 incorporated the Committee's recommendations and provided a comprehensive system for summary trial, preliminary inquiry and trial on indictment. The main problems thereafter were that magistrates, who had the job of deciding whether or not legal aid should be granted, were often reluctant to do so, and that lawyers were poorly paid. The Legal Aid and Advice Act 1949 amended the 1930 Act to cope with these matters, but the changes would have cost money, and on grounds of national economy they were not brought into force until 1960 and 1963.

By now it was felt that it was time for a review of the whole system of criminal legal aid, and for that purpose a Committee was appointed in 1964 with Mr Justice (later Lord Chief Justice) Widgery as chairman.[2] The main recommendations of this Committee were enacted in 1967 and form the basis of the system now in force. The relevant statute is now Part II of the Legal Aid Act 1974, supplemented by the Legal Aid Act 1982.

In criminal cases the decision to grant or withhold legal aid is a matter for the court. Thus magistrates' courts grant legal aid for summary trials and for committal proceedings; legal aid for trial on indictment can be granted either by the committing magistrates or by the Crown Court to which the accused is committed. In the same way legal aid can be given for appeals either by the court that originally heard the case or by the court to which the appeal is directed.[3] This is different from what happens with civil legal aid, where as we have seen the decision is made by a committee of lawyers, who are able to form a judgment on the merits of the case, and decide in the light of these whether legal aid is justified. Where legal aid is granted by a criminal court there can be no real inquiry into 'merits' because the court cannot interrogate an accused person about an offence with which he is charged; that would be contrary to the conception of adversary proceedings and it might be a real prejudice to the fairness of the trial. If we take as an example a person who is accused of a minor theft, it may not seem at all obvious that he should be granted legal aid. But the facts may be that he has previous convictions which make it likely he will be sent to prison on this occasion. These circumstances are obviously relevant to whether he should be granted legal aid, but a magistrates' court cannot be told about such matters when they are about to try him. For this reason it has sometimes been suggested that the granting of criminal legal aid should be taken

[1] Cmd 2638. 'The substance of our view upon the whole question is that in criminal cases the present system works satisfactorily and that no alterations are urgently or imperatively required. But in the course of the exhaustive evidence to which we have listened matters have emerged which we think show that, satisfactory as the system is, it is not incapable of improvement.' (para. 22)
[2] Report of the Departmental Committee on Legal Aid in Criminal Proceedings (1966) Cmnd 2934.
[3] A curious anomaly concerns appeals from magistrates' courts to the Divisional Court by way of case stated or applications for judicial review (see above chapter 21), for which legal aid must be obtained under the civil legal aid scheme, the reason being that the Divisional Court is part of the Queen's Bench Division of the High Court, which is a civil court.

away from the courts and done, like civil legal aid, by an independent committee. The Widgery Committee rejected this idea, however, mainly because they thought that it would result in delay. They also pointed out that the issues are not quite the same. In a civil case the question is whether or not the applicant has good grounds for bringing or defending proceedings, whilst in criminal cases the accused is a party, whether he likes it or not, and the question is whether 'the interests of justice' require that he should be legally represented. This view was accepted by Parliament and the courts remain the authority for deciding upon applications for legal aid.

An application for legal aid may be made orally to the court but in practice most are made to the clerk of the court by filling up the prescribed forms. As the first stages of a prosecution necessarily take place in the magistrates' court even where the case is eventually tried on indictment, this means that in practice most applications for legal aid are made to magistrates' courts. In a magistrates' court the decision to grant or refuse legal aid may be made by a bench of magistrates, a single magistrate or – most frequently – the justices' clerk; although where the clerk refuses legal aid his decision is subject to review, sometimes by the magistrates themselves and sometimes by the Criminal Legal Aid Committee (see below). Where the magistrates have refused legal aid they can sometimes be persuaded to reconsider their refusal; and failing this their refusal can be formally challenged in various several ways. Where the case goes on to the Crown Court, that court has power to grant legal aid even where the magistrates refused it. The magistrates' refusal to grant legal aid is subject to judicial review.[1] This is a complicated and expensive procedure, however, and the Legal Aid Act 1982 therefore added a further possibility in some cases: review by a 'criminal legal aid committee'. These committees are appointed by the Law Society, and in practice they consist of the same persons as the Area Legal Aid Committee that handles applications for legal aid in civil cases.

Section 29(1) of the Legal Aid Act 1974 says 'the power to make a legal aid order shall be exercisable by a court . . . where it appears to the court desirable to do so in the interests of justice . . .' Thus in principle criminal legal aid is available for any proceedings in the criminal courts, and there are no excepted categories of cases as there are with civil legal aid. In certain cases the court is actually obliged to grant legal aid to someone who cannot afford representation. The Legal Aid Act 1974 imposes an obligation in some bail applications where a magistrates' court has to decide whether to remand a person in custody, in cases where the Court of Appeal has quashed a conviction or sentence and the

---

[1] A refusal of legal aid by the Crown Court may also be judicially reviewed where the defendant is appealing to the Crown Court from conviction or sentence in the magistrates' court, or when he has been committed to the Crown Court for sentence; but there is no judicial review where the Crown Court refuses legal aid to someone who is tried there on indictment, because there is a general ban on judicial review of Crown Court decisions made in the course of trial by indictment (see page 209 above).

prosecutor takes a further appeal to the House of Lords, and where a person is committed for trial on a charge of murder.[1]

In some other cases a statute indirectly obliges the court to grant legal aid by forbidding it to do something to a defendant unless he is represented – so forcing the court to grant legal aid to someone who is unrepresented because he is too poor. Thus a court in effect must grant legal aid to someone whom they want to send to prison for the first time in his life, and also to anyone they are thinking to commit for trial by way of a 'new-style' or 'paper' committal (see chapter 22(iv)).

In cases where the court is not legally obliged to grant legal aid, it has a discretion to do so wherever it considers it would be in the interests of justice. In exercising their discretion the courts generally follow the guidance which the Widgery Committee set out in its report, although this has not so far been enacted in a statute. The Committee recommended that legal aid should as a general practice be given to anyone whom the magistrates commit to the Crown Court for trial or sentence if he wants to be legally represented and is financially eligible. For summary trial the Committee set out various circumstances which magistrates should regard as indicating a prima facie case for the grant of legal aid, which have become known as the 'Widgery criteria'. They include the gravity of the consequences which might result from a conviction, such as a real risk of imprisonment; a real risk that conviction would result in loss of employment; that the disgrace resulting from a conviction would be as serious as loss of liberty or livelihood; that the charge clearly raises a substantial question of law; that the nature of the defence involves the tracing and interviewing of witnesses; that there is need for skilled cross-examination of prosecution witnesses or that the person is accused of a sexual offence against a child (which makes it highly desirable that he should cross-examine the witness himself). The Widgery Committee said that legal aid should be granted for committal proceedings where the offence is one triable only on indictment; where the offence can be tried either summarily or on indictment the same tests should be applied as in the case of summary trial. Where the court is in doubt as to whether or not to grant a person legal aid, section 29(6) of the Legal Aid Act 1974 requires the doubt to be resolved in that person's favour.

The guidance that the Widgery Committee gave concerning Crown Court cases was much clearer than the guidance it gave concerning trials in magistrates' courts. The consequence is that in the Crown Court virtually everyone who wants to be legally represented but cannot afford it gets legal aid, and the unrepresented defendant (whether pleading guilty or not guilty) has become a character from the past; but in the magistrates' courts the extent to which legal

---

[1] Another case where legal aid is required under the Legal Aid Act 1974 is where a child in local authority care is brought before a juvenile court at the instance of the local authority, in order to get the court's permission to keep him in secure accommodation. Although the proceedings are civil, they take place in the juvenile court, which is a criminal court, and hence the proceedings are covered by criminal legal aid.

aid is given varies very widely from court to court. Behind this variation lies a very real difference of opinion on the desirability of legal representation in general, and on pleas of guilty in particular. The old-fashioned point of view is that it is a waste of public time and money for a defendant to be legally represented where the case is hopeless or where he is pleading guilty; where the case is hopeless he deserves no help, and where he pleads guilty the only thing to be done is to make a speech saying he is sorry and asking for mercy, which the defendant can do perfectly well for himself. In 1951 this view was forcibly expressed by Lord Chief Justice Goddard in a statement he made in court;[1] this had the predictable result of reducing for a time the extent to which magistrates were granting legal aid. The more modern view, expressed by his successor Lord Parker ten years later, is that 'There are of course occasions when a prisoner can conduct his defence or make a plea in mitigation more effectively in person and without legal representation. But such a case is of course rare. In almost every case the interests of the prisoner can only be safeguarded by legal representation.'[2]

Even when there is really nothing to be said in mitigation which the defendant could not equally well have said for himself, and when the effect of having a lawyer is merely to force the bench to listen to someone with an educated accent taking fifteen minutes to say what the defendant would have said in two minutes before it passes the same sentence it would have passed anyway, there is still a case to be made for legal representation, at public expense if necessary. The prosecution have had a highly trained and articulate expert to put their case. Because the defendant has had one too, he and everyone in court can see that he had as good a chance to put forward his side as the prosecution had when it was their turn. Most defendants are far too inarticulate themselves to put forward a coherent plea in mitigation, especially at a time of great stress.

There is no upper financial limit for the grant of criminal legal aid as there is for legal aid in civil cases; but section 29(2) of the Legal Aid Act 1974 forbids a court to make an order except where a defendant actually needs assistance in meeting the costs of representation. At one time the defendant either got all his costs paid, or none of them. Since 1967 there has been a more flexible system similar to the civil legal aid scheme under which poor defendants have all their costs paid and those who are better off must pay a contribution. As with civil legal aid, his contribution (if any) depends on his 'disposable income' and his 'disposable capital'; in principle these are calculated in the same way as for civil legal aid, but the DHSS is not involved, a different set of regulations apply and the details are not quite the same. Taking the 1987 figures, if the defendant's disposable capital exceeds £3,000, he must contribute the whole excess (and

---

[1] *The Times* 2 October 1951.
[2] His address was attached to a Home Office circular to courts in May 1961; it is reproduced in the First Report of the Working Party on Legal Aid in Criminal Proceedings (1962) HMSO. Lord Parker also pointed out that legal aid is the proper procedure; asking counsel in court to conduct the defence should only be used when it is too late to arrange legal aid.

must usually put the money up at once if it is in a form in which he can get his hands on it). If his disposable income exceeds £48 per week (£2,496 per annum) he must contribute for a period of six months a weekly sum which varies according to a statutory table from £1 per week upwards, depending on the size of his disposable income. If at the end of the case the defendant is convicted and is sent to prison, or otherwise loses his ability to pay any further weekly contributions, the court may let him off his liability to pay the rest. Where he is acquitted the court may remit any contribution due in future, and also order the refund of any contributions already paid; but it is not bound to do so, and might refuse if he was acquitted not on the merits but on a technicality. If, as is unlikely, the contribution paid eventually exceeds the costs of the defence the balance is of course refunded. In practice most of those who come before the criminal courts are quite poor, and contribution orders are only made in some 3 per cent of all cases. It has been argued that the good they do the public purse is not justified by the trouble they cause, particularly in the collection of small weekly amounts.

The amount that a lawyer receives for criminal legal aid work is calculated by officials. For magistrates' court work the Law Society, through its Area Committees established for civil legal aid, tax or assess the solicitor's bills, and sums due are paid out of the Legal Aid Fund.[1] For legal aid for trials on indictment, the costs due to solicitors and counsel are taxed or assessed by the clerk of the trial court. The rates of pay according to which the fees are calculated are laid down by the Lord Chancellor under statutory powers and are usually updated each year. In recent years the level of pay and the method by which it is fixed has generated a lot of heated controversy. Ten years ago there was a widespread public impression that lawyers were doing too well out of the criminal legal aid scheme.[2] Since then there has been a growing complaint from the lawyers doing criminal legal aid work that subsequent increases in legal aid rates have failed to keep up with inflation. In 1986 a number of solicitors' firms that had previously done a lot of criminal aid legal work announced that it was now losing them money and they were giving it up. Section 39(3) of the Legal Aid Act 1974 requires the Lord Chancellor when fixing the rates to 'have regard to the principle of allowing fair remuneration according to the work actually and reasonably done' – a provision intended to make sure that criminal aid legal work no longer had to be done on a semi-charitable basis, as had been the case under earlier versions of the criminal legal aid scheme. In 1986 the Bar, armed with the results of a study by a firm of management consultants which compared the income which could be derived from doing criminal legal aid work with what was obtainable from other types of legal practice, started legal proceedings for judicial review of the decision of the Lord Chancellor, Lord Hailsham, to increase the rates of pay by no more than 5

---

[1] 'Taxing' is explained in chapter 39 above.

[2] This was alleged by M. Zander in 'Costs in Crown Courts – A study of lawyers' fees paid out of public funds', [1976] Crim. LR 5. It drew a fierce counter-attack from Sir Peter Rawlinson, Chairman of the Bar (*ibid.* p. 42).

per cent. Faced with the prospect of the action possibly succeeding,[1] Lord Hailsham retreated, began negotiations, and awarded a larger increase. In these increases solicitors did better than barristers. Sympathy for the Bar over this must be tempered by a feeling although unlucky over pay, the Bar has been lucky to keep its monopoly over rights of audience in the Crown Court; and that the job-sharing which the monopoly causes is one of the reasons why criminal legal aid costs the country so dear and efforts must be made to keep the total bill down. Furthermore, since it was Lord Hailsham who was largely responsible for protecting the Bar's monopoly it is more than a little ironic that he was the Lord Chancellor the Bar took to court. The long-running dispute about rates of pay for criminal legal aid was one of the matters that led to the government scrutiny of legal aid and the big proposals for change that are discussed at the end of this chapter.

A rather unsatisfactory part of the criminal legal aid scheme concerns legal aid for appeals. Where a legally aided defendant is convicted in the Crown Court, his legal aid for the trial will also cover advice on appeal. This may provide him with help in drafting grounds of appeal for submission to the Court of Appeal, but that is all. Once his application for leave to appeal is made the case is handled by the Registrar of Criminal Appeals, whose job it is to sift the papers, obtain the necessary transcripts, and prepare a file for the single judge who grants or refuses leave to appeal. Whether or not legal aid is granted to pursue the appeal is a decision for the single judge; if he refuses leave to appeal he will obviously not grant legal aid. This puts the legally aided defendant in a weaker position than one who can pay his way. If the defendant can afford to pay his own lawyer he is likely to make a better case for leave to appeal; his lawyer can be seeking new evidence and generally making preparations for the appeal whilst leave to appeal is pending; and the appellant is also in a strong position for pursuing the case further if leave to appeal is refused.[2]

iv The duty solicitor scheme

The weakest point in the criminal legal aid scheme always used to be when the defendant first appeared in the magistrates' court. A person may come before the court after he has been arrested by the police, charged, kept in police cells, and then produced from custody directly to the court. This may well happen so quickly that he has no opportunity to get hold of a solicitor even if he wishes to do so. Alternatively he may be arrested, charged, and bailed by the police to appear at court later, or the police may procure his attendance by the issue of a summons. In either of these cases the defendant has the opportunity to consult a lawyer, and

---

[1] See *The Times* 22 and 27 March 1986.
[2] In arguing for a Public Defender, *Justice* made the point that such an official could look after the interests of would-be appellants, and thereby fill a gap in the legal aid system. For the Public Defender, see chapter 22(iv) above.

he will usually have seen a notice in the police station or received a leaflet with his summons telling him how to go about finding one. But even so there seem to be a good many people who do not readily absorb information from notices and forms and so fail to appreciate the facilities that are available. The result is that many people make their first appearance in the magistrates' court without having received any legal advice at all, even where they do not make their entry directly from the cells. A magistrates' court is a confusing place for anyone who is not used to it. Again and again one sees in those courts a defendant who is obviously confused and badly in need of a helping hand.[1]

In 1971 a report by *Justice* examined this need for legal aid and concluded that the best solution would be a duty solicitor on the model of schemes operating in Scotland and Ontario.[2] The duty solicitor is someone who is there at court and available to give immediate advice as and when people need it. In 1972 a duty solicitor scheme was launched in Bristol and it proved successful. The Law Society and the Lord Chancellor gave the scheme their blessing. It was rapidly copied in other areas and by 1975 some thirty schemes were operating. These early schemes were arranged informally by local Law Societies after consultation with the local bench. A few years later the idea was taken up as official government policy, and in the Legal Aid Act 1982 the Law Society was given express statutory power to make regulations, subject to the Lord Chancellor's approval, setting up and governing a nation-wide duty solicitor scheme. The first national scheme was made in 1983, and the scheme at present in operation is that set out in the Legal Aid (Duty Solicitor) Scheme 1985.[3] For the purposes of this scheme the country is divided into 14 regions, with a three-tier structure of committees. In London there is a Legal Aid (Duty Solicitor) Committee which is in overall command; this consists of the Law Society's Legal Aid Committee, fortified by other persons nominated by the Lord Chancellor. For each region there is a Regional Duty Solicitor Committee of between 10 and 35 members; the members include representative solicitors, magistrates, justices' clerks, policemen, probation officers, Crown Prosecutors, and laymen; in addition there are representative duty solicitors and representatives from the local committee (see below). The main function of the Regional Committees is to identify the courts in the area where duty solicitors are needed, and there to establish Local Duty Solicitor Committees. The Local Committees must have at least three members, all solicitors; they may be as large as 15, and include magistrates, justices' clerks, Crown Prosecutors and others. It is the job of the Local Committee to appoint enough duty solicitors to ensure that any defendant who

[1] Keith Devlin, *Sentencing offenders in magistrates' courts* (1970) writes about 'an apparently endless procession of bewildered people being taken in and out of court without any clear idea of what is happening to them or why'. (p. 56)
[2] *Unrepresented defendant in magistrates' courts.*
[3] This is printed in the *Legal aid handbook.*

needs the services of one can obtain it. The duty solicitors are solicitors in practice locally; they do the duty solicitor job as part of a rota. They are paid out of the legal aid fund for their attendance: money is paid to them for the time they spend at court, whether or not their services are called upon.

The duty solicitor in the magistrates' court is meant to be a 'long stop', not something to replace the ordinary criminal legal aid scheme. Thus there are strict limits on what a duty solicitor is allowed to do. He may give general advice. He may represent his client to the extent of making an application for criminal legal aid, or applying for bail on his behalf, or making a swift plea in mitigation for a client who wishes to plead guilty and get the case over and done with then and there. But he is specifically forbidden to fight a case on a plea of not guilty, or to represent a defendant in committal proceedings. And he is not generally permitted to advise or act for a defendant who has his own solicitor, or who has previously obtained legal advice about the case under the Green Form Scheme.

When the Police and Criminal Evidence Act 1984 – see chapter 22(i) – sought to extend the right of a suspect to legal advice when arrested and held at a police station, the government was faced with the problem of seeing legal advice was actually available. The method adopted was to try to extend the duty solicitor scheme. It is now the function of the Local Duty Solicitor Committees to attempt to arrange a rota of duty solicitors willing to be called out at short notice to give advice and assistance to suspects at police stations. As mentioned earlier, this is proving extremely difficult, because the rates of pay which the Lord Chancellor has fixed for this work are subject to upper limits. No matter how anti-social the hour at which the solicitor was called out, and no matter how much work the solicitor had to put in, he was not to be paid more than £90 for advising someone charged with an arrestable offence unless the Law Society gave retrospective permission, and never did he get more than £50 if the matter in issue does not amount to an arrestable offence. These rates did not prove enough to tempt every solicitor out of bed at 3 a.m. – notwithstanding a stick as well as a carrot in the form of a requirement that a solicitor who wishes to be a duty solicitor in the magistrates' courts must make himself available for duties at the police station as well. Consequently not enough solicitors joined the scheme to make it possible for the Local Committees to fill up their rotas, and the scheme is in something of a crisis.

The duty solicitor scheme is neither means-tested nor contributory. A person who needs the services of a duty solicitor, and can find one, is entitled to use the service free of charge. A suspect who has his own solicitor may send for him rather than the duty solicitor if he wishes, and he will be paid for under the scheme; but for the privilege of having a suspected criminal as a regular client, the solicitor is rewarded by a lower rate of pay than the ordinary duty solicitor would have earned.

41

FUTURE PROSPECTS FOR LEGAL AID

Compared with the dismal arrangements that existed when the first edition of this book appeared in 1940, the schemes for legal aid that we have today represent a magnificent achievement. However, the system is beset by problems on all sides and few people are satisfied with it. From the consumer's point of view the provision for legal aid is inadequate in a number of important respects. The schemes are centred firmly on the law courts, and there is little help for cases in tribunals, important as these are. For civil cases in the law courts there is the notorious 'middle-class poverty trap' already mentioned, which puts High Court proceedings out of the reach of many people who are too rich to qualify for civil legal aid but too poor to pay for litigation. For these reasons, one of the few radical proposals to come from the Benson Commission was that there should be a great increase in the scope of legal aid.[1] From the point of view of the government, which has to find the money to pay for legal aid, the problem is that it is expensive, and the cost of it all has been rising rapidly. The total legal aid bill, which for England and Wales was some £100 million in the year 1979/80, is likely to be around £400 million for 1986/7. Whilst this is small in the sense that it is less than half of 1 per cent of total public spending, it is big money nevertheless, and the rate of increase shows that it is likely to get much bigger. The reasons for the rising costs, which far outstrip the rate of inflation, are complicated. Part of it is simply explained by increasing work going through the courts, much of it concerned with the relatively poor. The rising crime rate has been followed by a very great increase in the work-load of the criminal courts (see chapter 19(i) above), and for most criminal defendants legal representation means legal aid. On a smaller scale the rising divorce rate has a similar effect on civil legal aid (see chapter 6(iii)). Another major part of the increase is accounted for by new projects, notably the duty solicitor schemes: duty solicitors in police stations, for example, cost the legal aid fund an extra £20 to £30 million a year. But there seems to be no doubt that the cost per case has been rising as well as the volume of work. Part of the reason for this is to do with social change. For example, the more people who own cars, the more litigation there is against those who sell bad ones, or carry out defective repairs; and the more people who own the house they

---

[1] Royal Commission on Legal Services, (1979) Cmnd 7648.

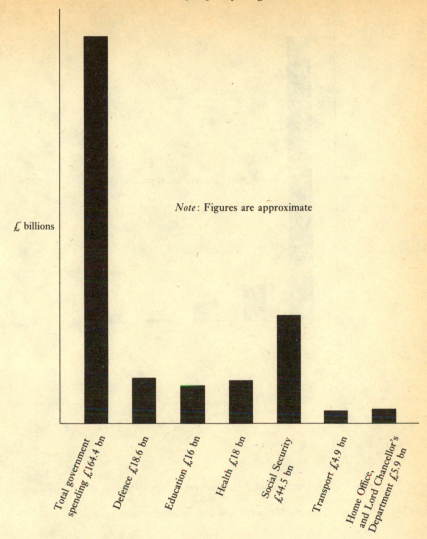

Figure 7 Public spending in perspective: major heads of central government spending as estimated for 1986–87

From *The Government's Expenditure Plans 1987–88 to 1989–90*, Cm 56-I, 1987.

live in, the more people there are with a capital asset to litigate about in the event of divorce. Part of the increased cost per case is a consequence of the increase in work, because increased workload means court delays, and delays inevitably lead to an increased bill for costs.[1]

[1] These matters are interestingly analysed by David Edwards, the Law Society official responsible for legal aid, in (1986) 83 Law Soc. Gaz. 1850.

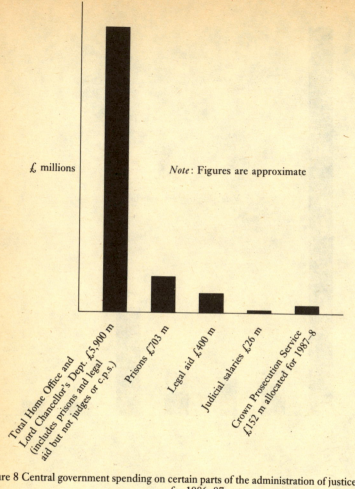

£ millions   *Note*: Figures are approximate

Total Home Office and
Lord Chancellor's Dept. £5,900 m
(includes prisons and legal
aid but not judges or c.p.s.)

Prisons £703 m

Legal aid £400 m

Judicial salaries £26 m

Crown Prosecution Service
£152 m allocated for 1987–8

Figure 8 Central government spending on certain parts of the administration of justice as estimated
for 1986–87
From *The Government's Expenditure Plans 1987–88 to 1989–90*, Cm 56-I, 1987.

Whatever the reasons, the increasing cost makes legal aid expenditure very unpopular with a government which is opposed on principle to increases in public spending. While government officials have described legal aid as 'the fastest-growing social service', Lord Hailsham, the Lord Chancellor, spoke luridly of criminal legal aid 'cascading out of control'. Within the present legal framework, the government's ability to control legal aid expenditure is limited. At present, legal aid is 'demand led' in the sense that everyone who comes along and proves he is within the prescribed criteria has a right to legal aid. The government is not at present able to say, as it does to universities and British Rail, 'here is all you are getting this year, make do with it as best you can'. For some years, as we saw earlier in this chapter, the government tried to keep the costs down where it could. Hence the alteration in the rules for calculating 'disposable income' for civil legal aid, the under-funding of the duty solicitor scheme, and the depression of criminal legal aid rates. By early 1986 it was obvious that measures of this sort were not keeping the legal aid bill down effectively, but were seriously undermining the effectiveness of the service. Hence in January 1986 the government set up a four-month study into the efficiency of legal aid. The Report of the Legal Aid Scrutiny was published in June 1986.[1]

The concern of this report was ways and means of controlling the cost, but it also put forward proposals to expand the scope of legal aid and to increase the value the public receives from the money that is spent. Broadly speaking, the government White Paper that followed[2] warmly embraced the cost-cutting proposals but rejected those which would redirect any of the money saved to expand the scope of legal aid. The current Legal Aid Bill contains some of the proposals contained in the White Paper, and others are expected to be enacted in Regulations under rule-making powers contained in the Bill.

The major proposal to be adopted concerns the administration of legal aid. At one time, civil legal aid was a matter for the Lord Chancellor, but criminal legal aid was a Home Office responsibility. Since 1980 the Lord Chancellor has been the minister with overall responsibility, and since 1949 he has had the help of an Advisory Committee. But it is still the case that the actual administration of the scheme is split between the Law Society and the criminal courts, with the DHSS and the officials of the civil courts doing the odd bit here and there. The Review thought that even if each of these bodies always performed with perfect efficiency, lack of any central administration was bound to be a source of inefficiency, muddle and waste. It therefore proposed the creation of a Legal Aid Board to administer all aspects of legal aid, and this proposal is now contained in the Legal Aid Bill. Some commentators, remembering the fate of some neighbourhood law centres, whose grants from the local council dried up when they were too active in helping the citizens to sue the local council, oppose this on the ground that a Legal Aid Board might be subservient to the government to the extent of trying to cut off legal aid for litigation which the government found embarrassing. But as long as statute continues to lay down who is to qualify for legal aid, the chance of this happening seems small. The main exercise of governmental control is likely to be over the total cost, which is surely quite legitimate, since the government has to find the money.

In the matter of legal advice and assistance, the Review made the controversial suggestion that the Green Form Scheme be scrapped, and the provision of free or subsidised legal advice should be transferred to Citizens' Advice Bureaux (who could then pass on to solicitors those cases they could not handle). They felt this would be substantially cheaper than encouraging solicitors in private practice

---

[1] Report of the Legal Aid Scrutiny (1986), published by the Lord Chancellor's Department.
[2] Legal Aid in England and Wales: A New Framework, (1987) Cm 118.

to give free or subsidised advice, and then to pass the bill on to the public. From the Treasury's point of view, this change is a very attractive idea, because the method of payment would be by making the Citizens' Advice Bureaux annual grants, the size of which the Treasury would control. But there was considerable public opposition to this proposal. The White Paper proposes a watered-down version, with the Green Form Scheme being retained, but advice on all sorts of matters being excluded from it. The likely pattern for the future is that the Green Form Scheme will no longer cover advice on things like welfare benefits, housing problems and employment law, and that 'other agencies' – such as Citizens' Advice Bureaux or neighbourhood law centres – will be invited to tender for providing an advice service to the public in these matters for a fixed cost.

On the subject of legal aid for civil cases, the main Scrutiny recommendation is that the administration should be taken out of the hands of the Law Society and be placed under the Legal Aid Board; this will almost certainly be done, although the system of Area Legal Aid Committees is likely to continue, and their supporting staff will continue to do the same job as officials of the Legal Aid Board rather than the Law Society. The Review thought that costs could be cut if the DHSS no longer assessed the applicants' means, and this was done by the staff of the Area Committee. This idea the government rejected. Predictably, the government has also rejected the recommendation of the Review that the income limits for eligibility for legal aid should go, so removing the 'middle-class poverty trap'. Equally predictably, perhaps, the government enthusiastically accepted the idea that the applicant's contribution out of income should continue for the duration of the case, and should not be limited to one year as now. The government also accepts the idea of the other party being able to make representations against the grant of legal aid in what would obviously be seen as a hopeless case if the Area Committee was in possession of all the facts.

For criminal legal aid, the proposal is that the courts will continue to decide who gets it and who does not. The Review thought that the system of contributions did not justify the complications caused by its existence, and recommended a flat rate contribution of £10 from everyone granted criminal legal aid instead. This idea is rejected in the White Paper. For the present, the government has set its hopes of controlling the cost of criminal legal aid on altering the basis upon which the remuneration of lawyers is calculated, so that more of it is piece-work and less of it is payment by the hour – something which is intended to encourage lawyers to save time and words rather than to use as much of both as possible. The Review suggested that there would be a substantial saving of Crown Court costs if solicitors were granted right of audience; this is rejected in the White Paper, the only reason given being that the Benson Commission rejected it in 1979. The Bar, once again, can heave a sigh of relief.

At present we have a legal aid system which is very costly, despite the fact that the cover it provides has a number of significant gaps. This situation presents the government with a choice of three courses. The first is to do what the Benson

Commission recommended, and pour much more money into legal aid in order to fill the gaps, with the present system of courts and trials remaining much as it is. With a Conservative government committed to cuts in public spending, this is obviously not the choice that will be made. The second is to alter the legal system in a number of cost-cutting ways, so that the gaps can be filled without spending more money. There have been attempts to do this in the past, as when undefended divorce was made so simple that it did not need a court hearing and hence no lawyers were needed to represent the parties, and when the present small claims system was devised in an attempt to enable the parties to manage the procedure as litigants in person. But the scope for more of this is limited, particularly in criminal cases, which is the biggest item in the legal aid budget. It is true that originally trial on indictment was something that took place almost without the help of lawyers, and that summary trial was an informal and largely lawyer-free process until quite modern times. But it would involve a complete reversal of modern thinking about criminal procedure to devise a system of trial in which lawyers are not heavily involved, and if lawyers are involved in criminal cases there must be extensive criminal legal aid. The government's refusal to accept the recommendation of the Scrutiny that solicitors should be given right of audience in the Crown Court suggests that it is not at present very enthusiastic about the make-trials-cheaper approach to the problem. The third course open to the government is to harden its heart, taking the line that legal aid must compete with other forms of public spending, that some gaps in provision are inevitable, and that it is not the business of the government to iron out all the advantages and disadvantages in life that result from differences in wealth. The White Paper suggests that this is government thinking on the matter.

If the government is unlikely to fill the gaps in legal aid provision either by rebuilding the machinery of justice so that it runs more economically or by giving the legal aid fund more fuel in the form of money, is there anything else that can be done about the problem?

One possibility is for the insurance market to provide cover against legal expenses. Such cover is available in various shapes and forms, although as yet it is little used: the INBUCON study for the Civil Justice Review in 1986[1] indicated that such schemes at present finance at the most 2 per cent of all cases. There is probably room for considerable growth in this area, particularly among the 30 per cent of society who are too prosperous to fall within the present limits for civil legal aid. It is unlikely that this could ever be of much use to the genuinely poor, insofar as the present legal aid arrangements fail to help them. (But working people do already have quite a lot of help from a similar source, since membership of a trade union or professional association generally carries entitlement to the services of the union's legal department when help is needed for litigation arising out of employment.)

[1] See chapter 39 above, and Appendix A.

Another way of dealing with the costs of litigation is by allowing contingency fee arrangements. That is a common method in most parts of the United States; a lawyer takes on a case for a plaintiff on the terms that if no damages are obtained the client will not have to pay anything (except perhaps some out-of-pocket expenses) and that if damages are obtained the lawyer will receive a percentage of the amount, varying from a quarter to a half. In England an agreement to support litigation for a share of the proceeds was the criminal offence of *champerty*. The Criminal Law Act 1967 abolished the offence of champerty (along with eavesdropping and a few other obsolete offences) but a champertous agreement continues to be unlawful as being contrary to public policy. It is also professional misconduct for a solicitor to enter into a contingency fee agreement involving the institution of legal proceedings. In the period between the wars there were a few solicitors and barristers who made practice of conducting personal injury cases on a contingency fee basis: it was illegal and unprofessional, but the process did give a remedy to many people who would otherwise have had none. The growth of legal aid has virtually, if not wholly, got rid of those who were known as 'speculative lawyers' or 'ambulance chasers'. There is, however, nothing to prevent anyone offering to help an injured person to obtain damages. Such people use various terms to describe themselves, a common one being 'claims assessor'. The claims assessor, having got in touch with an injured person, explains that he works on a 'no cure, no pay' basis but is to receive a percentage of any sums received. If the injured person agrees, the claims assessor starts negotiations with the insurance company which stands behind the alleged wrongdoer. That is lawful, for anyone may assert a claim on behalf of another on an agreement for a share of the money received; champerty does not arise unless there is litigation. If the claims assessor cannot get any offer from the insurance company that the injured person will accept, there is nothing more that he can do: solicitors are the only people who can start actions on behalf of others. A solicitor who takes over such a case may find some difficulty because the claims assessor may have reckoned on getting a settlement and so have neglected to take steps, such as interviewing witnesses, which ought to have been done at an early stage.

The Law Society considered and rejected the possibility of contingency fees in 1970[1] and again in 1987;[2] it was also considered by the Royal Commission on Legal Services (Benson Commission) in 1979 and firmly rejected.[3]

Outside the USA – and even to some extent within it – informed opinion is that contingency fees work badly for the client, although lawyers thrive on them. Obviously lawyers are happy to take on cases that are likely to succeed, but a person who has a claim that may fail may be unable to find a lawyer who will take it up on a contingent fee. If a lawyer does take the case on a contingency fee basis

---

[1] Memorandum on Maintenance and Champerty: Claims Assessors and Contingency Fees.
[2] Improving Access to Civil Justice.
[3] Cmnd 7648 p. 177.

there are other drawbacks for the client. In so many accident cases there is a stage at which the plaintiff must decide whether to accept a quick settlement or to go on with the case in the hope of getting a larger sum in the end, and the client wants disinterested advice; it is better if a lawyer is not put into a position where he has a direct personal interest in the outcome. If the client wins, he receives less than he ought to since his lawyer takes a large slice of the winnings (though it is possible that damages are fixed specially high in the knowledge that the plaintiff will receive only part of them). Furthermore, a contingency fee system only works where it is expected that a sum of money will be recovered. It cannot apply to a defendant, or to either side in a dispute about the custody of children or any other kind of legal dispute which does not turn on money.

In July 1987 the Law Society produced a document called *Improving access to civil justice* which contained two ingenious ideas. The first of these is the contingency fee scheme, but cleansed and disinfected. The client would pay contingency fees, but these would go to a special contingency legal aid fund, out of which the lawyer would be paid at the normal rates, win or lose. Provided the contingency fees were set at the right level, the fund would be able to pay the plaintiff's lawyer when he loses. This scheme would share some of the disadvantages of the ordinary contingency fee. In particular it could only help plaintiffs, and plaintiffs who are suing for money, and if the plaintiff wins he only gets part of what he deserves. On the other hand it would avoid the conflict of interest between solicitor and client which is such a bad feature of the contingency fee schemes in the USA. This particular scheme was recommended by *Justice* to the Royal Commission on Legal Services in 1978, and has actually been implemented in Hong Kong. A practical problem is that a large sum of money is needed to get it started. In Hong Kong the government conveniently provided an interest-free loan.

The second scheme, which the Law Society calls the 'Fixed Costs Scheme', would work on the same principle as a lucky dip, bottle-stall or tombola: someone buys a ticket at a fixed price, and receives in exchange a prize which may be worth more or less than the sum he paid. Once again there would be a general fund administered either by the government or by the Law Society. The fund would sell the potential litigant a 'ticket' at a fixed price which would be related to the estimated cost of the kind of action he was proposing. His prize would be the payment of his own costs out of the fund if he won the action, and the payment of both his own and his successful opponent's costs if the lawsuit was lost. If he won his opponent would be liable to pay him his actual costs, which might be more or less than what he had originally paid for his ticket, so the ticket might or might not turn out to have been a good buy; but he would be relieved of the worry of an enormous bill for his own and his opponent's costs if everything went wrong. This would obviously not help the litigant who could not afford to contemplate the cost of the ticket, which would hardly be cheap. However, it would be a

489

considerable help for many people who could afford to risk paying their own costs, but not those of their opponent as well if they are unlucky enough to lose.

For the present, any expansion of legal aid is likely to come from some such scheme as these rather than from larger sums provided by the government.

VIII

LAW REFORM

42

THE PROCESS OF LAW
REFORM

There are several aspects of law reform. At the most obvious level, the law may need reforming because it produces results which are contrary to common sense or unfair. This may arise from defects in the substantive law, or defects in procedural law, or both. Substantive law is concerned with rights and wrongs and with the remedies for their violation. Procedural law is concerned with the process by which remedies are made available. Sometimes there is no very clear distinguishing line between substantive and procedural law: thus the definition of a criminal offence, including the maximum punishment prescribed, is substantive law, but whether it is triable summarily or on indictment is procedural. Further, if we consider legal aid, the part of the law that governs eligibility is substantive, yet since the whole purpose is ancillary to bringing or defending cases we think of it as being procedural. However, we must continue to make a distinction because when a part of the law is working badly, different authorities may be responsible depending on whether substantive law or procedure is identified as the source of the trouble. If, for example, some regulations concerning motor vehicles do not seem to be enforced, inquiry may show that the regulations need amending, which is a matter for the Minister of Transport. If the trouble lies in procedure in magistrates' courts, that is nominally for the Lord Chancellor and practically for the Home Office; or enforcement may be tied up with the respective roles of ministry inspectors, police and traffic wardens, which is administrative and not a matter for law reform except insofar as the organisation and procedure of courts is concerned.

At a less obvious level part of the law may be in need of reform because it is in an inconvenient shape rather than because it produces unfair results. Reformers have said over the years that the law ought to be simple, intelligible, certain, well arranged, adequately indexed and put into a physical form that will allow copies to be made available in public libraries as well as in courts and offices. At present the law is to be found in several hundred volumes of law reports and a lesser number of volumes of statutes and subordinate legislation, and lawyers need many textbooks and a considerable apparatus of periodicals, digests and so forth to find their way through so much material and to keep themselves up-to-date. To take a simple example, in this country we have no Penal Code. Thus there is no official book which the citizen may consult to discover even in the vaguest outline what behaviour is and is not a criminal offence, and even for the trained expert the task will sometimes be a difficult one. It is too much to expect that all the law that is required to regulate all the activities and relationships in a complex society could be made simple, but there is a great deal that can be done to improve the form of the law.

Whatever aspect of law reform we are considering, we cannot expect any really substantial contribution from case-law. Judges cannot repeal or amend statutes, so the only way to get an improved statute book is by statute, and that is also the only way to get any codification. Nor can judges make major procedural reforms which involve things like creating new courts or suppressing or amalgamating old ones, or altering the rules that govern the appointment and retirement of judges. It is true that much of our substantive law, common law and equity, was fashioned by the judges through the mechanism of precedent recorded in law reports, but times have changed. The judiciary which functions in a society with an active Parliament accustomed to deal with all manner of social and economic situations has a very different position from that which it had in the days of bold judicial innovation. In any case, a court is subject to severe limitations. To begin with, the kind of case that may offer scope for judicial zeal for reform may not arise at an appropriate time: litigants and appellants cannot be relied upon to produce precedent-fodder when it is needed. Further, a court rarely has a clear field; often there are statutory provisions (which no court can abrogate) and an existing body of reported cases which cannot be ignored. An example may be taken which is now a little dated, but is still of interest because it shows the influence of a member of the judiciary who was undoubtedly a reforming influence. *Ghani* v. *Jones*[1] dealt with police searches. The main point was whether documents seized as the result of a search could be retained or should be returned forthwith, but wider issues came to be considered. There was a tiresome precedent in an earlier case which said that if the police had lawful authority to search premises where someone was arrested, material relevant for *any* crime committed by *any* person could be seized. In *Ghani* v. *Jones* Lord Denning made an attempt to put the law into better shape: after making an admirable summary of the problem he formulated five requisites for police taking articles for use as evidence. The third requisite was that: 'The police officers must have reasonable grounds to believe that the person in possession of it has himself committed the crime, or is implicated in it, or is accessory to it.' But that did not cover the case of the innocent possessor. Suppose your car is driven away without your permission and the police have now recovered it and want to examine it for finger-prints, blood-stains and so on: can you insist on having your car back at once? Another tiresome earlier case suggested that an innocent owner could refuse to allow his car to be inspected. In his original oral judgment Lord Denning expressed 'some misgiving' over that decision, but did not deal with the point further; then in the later

---

[1] [1970] 1 QB 693; see casenote by R. M. Jackson [1970] *Cambridge Law Journal* 1.

written version of his judgment he added a suggestion that the police could inspect the car against the innocent owner's wishes if the owner's refusal was 'quite unreasonable'. This is hardly a tolerable way to reform the law. The first point about the case was that it showed up a shocking gap in the law in that there was no provision allowing a search warrant to be obtained to look for evidence of murder or other serious offences, however obvious it was that relevant evidence was likely to be found on the premises: but it was beyond the competence of the Court of Appeal to deal with that, because the power to issue search warrants is regulated by statute, and it was a case for legislation. As things stood, all the court could do was to lay down rules about what the police could and could not do once they had managed to get access. The second point is that no judge, not even one so well equipped as Lord Denning, can formulate principles or rules to govern police action simply as a result of hearing submissions in court. The higher courts in the USA have the practice of *amicus* briefs filed by persons who are not actual parties to the litigation, and the European Court at Luxembourg invariably has a report from an Advocate General representing the public interest. We have no such system and the court hears no more than what the parties see fit to put forward: there may be many points and considerations that are relevant but which are not put before the court. It is almost inevitable that rulings arrived at through the courts operating in this way will be insufficient and they may be positively detrimental to the public interest. But in the case of something as important as the scope of police powers it is not realistic to expect the courts to do a satisfactory job even with this kind of help, and the only process that ought to be acceptable to a civilised system is that a draft of any proposed change in the law should be available for examination and discussion. This of course is what eventually happened over police powers to search and seize evidence. As was explained earlier (chapter 22(i)) the government eventually set up a Royal Commission, which carried out research and heard evidence from anyone who wished to give it, and after a large amount of public debate the fruits of its labours were the Police and Criminal Evidence Act 1984. This enables the police to obtain search warrants to look for evidence of murder and other serious crimes, regulates clearly what property they may seize in addition to evidence of the crime for which the warrant was issued, and makes it plain that if they seize the property of innocent third parties they may retain it where they need it for forensic tests or to use as evidence at a subsequent trial.

The conclusion that major reforms are a job for Parliament leads us to consider the process of legislation. A bill introduced into Parliament by a private member[1] is not likely to reach the statute book. The government makes such heavy demands upon the time of the House of Commons that a private member's bill usually dies for lack of attention unless an adequate measure of government support is given. In addition to finding time, it is generally necessary to arrange

---

[1] P. A. Bromhead, *Private members' bills in the British Parliament* (1956), examines the role that these bills play in the modern political system.

for the private member to have the assistance of certain officials and particularly of parliamentary counsel on the drafting. A notable example of law reform by a private member's bill was the Matrimonial Causes Act 1937 due to the valiant efforts of A. P. Herbert. There are usually one or two Acts a year that begin in this way, but too much must not be expected from that source. Where there are obvious abuses or gaps the private member may be able to draw a bill and present a satisfactory case in its support; but to find an apt remedy for a legal ill typically needs the sort of complicated and expensive investigation that only the government can afford. Furthermore, where the machinery of justice is concerned it is not easy to make proposals that do not involve the expenditure of public money, and a bill involving expenditure may not be introduced by a private member. So most changes in the machinery of justice must in practice come from the government.

Government bills are proposed by a minister, but under our system of cabinet government no minister may introduce a bill, or even announce that a bill will be introduced, without the sanction of the cabinet. The purpose of cabinet control is twofold. In the first place, all proposals for legislation must be examined to see that they are consistent with government policy, and also to consider the sort of public reception that the bill is likely to have. In the second place, the legislative programme of the government must be arranged with regard to the time available in the House of Commons, for there is more call for legislation than the House can handle by its present procedure. The cabinet exercises these controls largely through committees.[1]

Sessions of Parliament now last a year, beginning in late October or in November, and the programme for a session must be considered several months in advance. It is not customary to disclose the government's programme although there may be a public announcement and the major items will in any case be mentioned in the Queen's Speech on the opening of the next session. The legislative programme must include the annual legislation which governs the raising and spending of money, the maintenance of the army and other matters which require annual authority. There will also be bills to carry out the policy of the government; these, with much of the financial legislation, are the measures particularly associated with the government of the day and are pre-eminently the field of party politics. The remaining bills are not really party measures, though of course politically a government may be called to account for everything its members do, and virtually anything may become a party issue. Sometimes a minister has a project of the non-party kind in which he is personally interested, but the majority of these bills come from the civil servants in government departments. All departments find in the course of their work that some changes

---

[1] The process of producing a bill is described by Sir Granville Ram in a paper 'The improvement of the statute book', (1951) 1 Journal SPIL 442. Further sources are Sir Noel Hutton, 'Mechanics of law reform', (1961) 24 Mod. LR 18, and The Preparation of Legislation (Report of the Renton Committee) (1975) Cmnd 6053.

in the law are needed either to facilitate or extend the department's own work or in matters for which the department has a general responsibility.[1]

Even when a minister has a personal interest in the matter, as with Lord Birkenhead's well-known desire to reform the land laws, he is likely to find that much work has already been done: government is team work, of ministers and of a minister and his department, though the minister has the power and takes the glory. Some bills are designed to carry out the recommendations of commissions and committees. The inquiry will usually have been set up at the instance of the department, but the report must be accepted by the minister before it can be carried out. A minister with no ideas of his own will never be at a loss for projects if he thirsts for action. However they may have originated, the various legislative projects must compete for a place in the programme. A minister who puts forward a project must satisfy his colleagues that it ought to be included. Applying this to measures for law reform, we can examine the situation in this order: first the minister who must move; second, the process of deciding what provisions are needed, which includes any prior investigation that may be required; and third, the arguments which affect whether a proposal is assigned a place in the legislative programme.

i The minister responsible

There is no single minister who has responsibility[2] for law in general or for the machinery of justice. The Home Secretary and the Lord Chancellor share the responsibility, and it is hard to lay down any exact dividing line. The broad division is that the Home Office is concerned with the criminal law, preventing offences, catching offenders, part of the process of trying them, and virtually the whole of the treatment of offenders. The Lord Chancellor is concerned with the composition of all courts, criminal and civil, parts of criminal procedure, and everything relating to civil law and its administration. In addition, other departments have responsibility for parts of the law which relate to their operations, but this does not affect the general responsibility of the Home Secretary and the Lord Chancellor.

The Home Office has a bewildering variety of matters in its care.[3] There is direct responsibility for the metropolitan police and a general responsibility for provincial police. The Home Secretary has various powers concerning criminal

[1] The content and precise form of this kind of legislation is usually discussed between the department and the interests concerned: there is also extensive discussion during the formulation of most statutory instruments: this is well described by S. A. Walkland, *The legislative process in Great Britain* (1968).
[2] In strict use of terms a minister cannot be responsible for that which he has no power to control. No minister is responsible for any particular magistrate or judge or court, or rule of common law or of statute, for he has no power to control them, but the state of the judiciary and the law is a matter for which there is a general responsibility in the appropriate ministers.
[3] See Sir Frank Newsam, *The Home Office* (1954).

procedure, costs in criminal matters, and the organisation and finance of magistrates' courts. Prisons and other institutions for the custody of delinquents are in the care of the Prison Department of the Home Office. There is a close association with the probation system. The care of Broadmoor patients (originally called criminal lunatics) is under the Minister of Health, but the Home Office retains some responsibility for releases (see chapter 15(iii) above). The prerogative of mercy, which includes pardons, commutations and reductions of sentences, is exercised on the advice of the Home Secretary. Race relations and immigration have become major matters with which the Home Office is concerned. The Home Office sends many circulars to magistrates' courts for their information and guidance, particularly when new legislation is coming in. The Home Office has responsibility, in a wide sense, for general policy in penal affairs and for introducing new penal legislation and the revision of existing law.

It was formerly one of the duties of the Home Secretary to appoint the Director of Public Prosecutions. This was rather odd, because the minister to whom the Director was responsible, and who answered for his acts in Parliament, was not the Home Secretary but the Attorney-General. The Prosecution of Offences Act 1985 makes the Director appointable by the Attorney-General as well as responsible to him. It was this Act which created a new department of the civil service, namely the Crown Prosecution Service (see chapter 22 above), of which the Director is the administrative head. The Attorney-General is technically the head of the Crown Prosecution Service, and the minister who is responsible to Parliament for it: this is an office he has to reconcile with his sometimes competing duties as legal advisor to the government, and head of the Bar.

The duties of the Lord Chancellor are many and onerous.[1]

(1) He is Speaker of the House of Lords, which involves his attendance upon the Woolsack when the House is sitting as a legislative body.

(2) He is a member of the government, and is normally in the cabinet. As most heads of departments are in the Commons, it may fall to the Lord Chancellor to present the government's view in the House of Lords on matters that are outside his special knowledge; this may be a heavy burden at times.

(3) He may preside over the sittings of the House of Lords in its judicial capacity. In the years after the Second World War, successive Lord Chancellors were able to find less and less time for this, but Lord Hailsham regarded it as an important part of his duties and during his lengthy tenure of office he did his best to revive the practice.

(4) When he is able to do so, the Lord Chancellor presides over sittings of the Judicial Committee of the Privy Council.

(5) He is head of the Chancery Division of the High Court and *ex officio* a member of the Court of Appeal. He does not in practice sit in either court, and there is normally little work connected with this part of this office.

(6) He is president of the Supreme Court. This involves a considerable amount of work. He makes recommendations for the appointment of High Court Judges and

[1] A convenient summary is given in the Report of the Machinery of Government Committee, (1918) Cd 9230. See also Lord Schuster, 'The office of the Lord Chancellor', (1949) 10 Camb. LJ 175.

in practice advises the Prime Minister as to other judicial appointments. The higher officials of the courts are appointed by him. He must also devote some time to the work of the Rule Committee.

(7) He is responsible for the county court system, which includes the appointment of registrars and other staff. In some matters the control is in the Treasury with the concurrence of the Lord Chancellor.

(8) He makes recommendations for the appointment of Circuit Judges and Recorders under the Courts Act 1971. The appointment and removal of justices of the peace (other than in the Duchy of Lancaster), and of the stipendiary magistrates, is exercised by the Lord Chancellor; the institution of Advisory Committees has not prevented the Lord Chancellor from having to give a fair amount of personal attention to the questions that arise.

(9) He has a substantial amount of work in connection with special tribunals. Normally the appointment of legally qualified chairmen is made by him. The appointment of other members, or of panels, is also made his job by various statutes, particularly by the Tribunals and Inquiries Act 1958. He appoints the Council on Tribunals under that Act, and, as the Council has no executive powers, its recommendations must come before the Lord Chancellor and be approved by him before they can be brought into operation.

(10) He is ultimately responsible for legal aid, both civil and criminal.

(11) He has considerable ecclesiastical patronage, amounting to about one appointment a week; this is about three times the patronage of the two archbishops put together.

(12) There are also duties in connection with the Land Registry, the office of the Public Trustees, and the care of the insane.

It is not surprising that 'Successive holders of the office have testified that it is beyond the strength of any one man to perform the work that ought to be done.'[1]

ii Deciding what needs to be done

The Home Office and the Lord Chancellor's Department have their own legal staff, and so on a smaller scale do the other government departments. But the departmental lawyers could not do all the investigation that is needed for the formulation of new legislation. The work is done either by *ad hoc* committees and Royal Commissions, or by one of several standing committees, or by the Law Commission.

Most of the principal measures of law reform passed in the last hundred years were based on the reports of Royal Commissions or official committees. If law reform is to be successful it must be carefully considered by a wide range of people, many of them experts or concerned with the matters in question; it must command general approval, so that as far as possible it must be outside the sphere of party politics. These things can best be secured more easily from an independent inquiry than from the work of the staff of a department. The evidence that is put before these commissions and committees contains the views

[1] (1918) Cd 9230 ch. x, para. 3.

of those who are specially concerned: organisations, such as professional bodies, trade unions, associations of local authorities and innumerable other bodies often take great care in preparing their statements so that they may be taken as fully representative opinion. The proposals that come from one quarter are commonly put to other witnesses, and as the inquiry progresses there emerges a clear realisation of the measure of agreement and the nature of the opposition that should be expected if a particular course is followed. Suggestions get a critical examination, and the atmosphere of these inquiries is inimical to ill-prepared and vague propositions. Where the government makes funds available, the committee or commission may even commission a research project to find out more than it can discover from listening to witnesses. The James Committee[1] conducted a consumer survey among defendants awaiting trial, and a series of research projects were commissioned by the Royal Commission on Criminal Procedure.[2]

The process of commission and committee builds up a reliable body of information and the solutions produced are commonly practical and workable. The recommendations that are made must of course be considered by the minister concerned, and if he and his colleagues feel able to accept the Report, it is then relatively easy for the minister to put the proposals before Parliament, for it is a great commendation of a measure to be able to say that it is founded on the recommendations of an independent body which has made a full inquiry; the proposals may be attacked, but not on the ground that they come from the politics of the minister or from the machinations of civil servants.

Commissions and committees do not usually draft the legislative changes that they recommend, as virtually all the drafting of government bills is now done in the office of Parliamentary Counsel. Sometimes a committee is expected to produce a draft bill to accompany its Report, and then the practice is to assign one of Parliamentary Counsel to the committee. Drafting is a difficult matter and very much one for experts, and it has its own problems, not the least of which is to know how the consumer controls the expert.

A Royal Commission is the best way of getting a high-level overhaul of a substantial field of law and its administration. But it is slow because the members are busy people who can meet only at intervals; there is no permanent secretariat, and the machinery has to be built up for each inquiry. This is only worth the effort where there is a major problem to deal with, and in the past this sometimes meant that lesser problems were never addressed at all.

One response to this difficulty has been to create standing committees to which a series of smaller problems in a particular area can be referred. In 1934 the Lord Chancellor set up a standing Law Revision Committee to consider difficult questions of 'lawyer's law' which he would refer to them from time to time. This Committee was reconstituted in 1952 and given the more daring title of the Law

---

[1] Report of the Interdepartmental Committee on the Distribution of Criminal Business between the Crown Court and Magistrates' Courts, (1975) Cmnd 6323.
[2] (1981) Cmnd 8092 (The Philips Committee).

Reform Committee. This body dealt with matters of civil law only. In 1959 the Home Secretary set up a criminal equivalent, called the Criminal Law Revision Committee, to examine such aspects of the criminal law as he should refer to them from time to time. Its first major reference was the law of larceny and kindred offences and as a result of its Report we have the Theft Act 1968.[1] It has usually been possible to arrange the Law Commission's programme in harmony with theirs, but matters are more complicated with the Criminal Law Revision Committee, because that is answerable to the Home Office; the other committees are responsible to the Lord Chancellor's Department, as is the Law Commission itself.

These standing committees are there for the using and do not have to be created afresh every time there is a problem, but in other respects they share the drawbacks of *ad hoc* committees. They depend on busy people working in their spare time, they lack regular research facilities, and above all they are purely reactive: it is not their job to look for problems, only to consider those matters which the relevant minister has identified as a problem and handed over to them. In 1963 the idea of a Law Commission was put forward by Mr Gerald Gardiner, later Lord Gardiner and Lord Chancellor, and Mr Andrew Martin, later a Law Commissioner, in a book called *Law reform now* (1963). The idea was for a permanent body of full-time law reformers, equipped with research facilities, whose job it would be to keep the law actively under review. Their idea was taken up by the Labour government, and the Law Commissions Act 1965 created the Law Commission for England and the Scottish Law Commission for Scotland.

The Law Commission consists of a Chairman and four other Law Commissioners, with a supporting staff of around 50. The Commissioners are appointed for a period of five years and may be barristers, solicitors, academic lawyers or judges; if they are judges then by statute they retain their judicial office but are relieved from judicial duties whilst they are at the Law Commission. The Law Commissioners are appointed by the Lord Chancellor, and originally he simply chose people, much as he fills judicial office; more recently the posts other than those to be filled by judges have been advertised and applicants have been interviewed. The first chairman was a judge, Mr Justice Scarman – now Lord Scarman – and all subsequent chairmen have also been judges. Just over half the support staff are civil service lawyers, technically employed in the Lord Chancellor's Department, and the rest are typists, secretaries and so forth.

The least spectacular, but by no means the least useful part of the Law Commission's work is to do with consolidating and revising the statute book. It is customary to speak of 'the statute book' as meaning all of our statutes that are extant. There has been for many years a volume of statutes each year, and in busy

[1] There have been other less famous standing committees concerned with particular areas of law, the work of which has now been taken over by the Law Commission: the Committee on Private International Law (now defunct), and the Statute Law Committee (which still exists, but has so few functions that it meets only once a year).

years more than one volume is produced. There is no rule whereby statutes are automatically removed from the statute book on account of disuse or changed circumstances: the rule is that a statute continues to be in force until it is repealed, in whole or in part, by a subsequent statute. The result has been that the statute book has been cluttered up with statutes or parts of statutes that have not been specifically repealed, including provisions that are inconsistent with later legislation and so repealed by implication (with a possibility of doubt in some instances), provisions that are spent (such as a requirement for claims to be registered within twelve months of a statute coming into force when that time limit has expired), or obsolete because they deal with conditions that no longer exist. The process of getting rid of this clutter is known as *statute law revision* which thus means revision of the statute book and not revision of the law contained in statutes.

Consolidation must not be confused with either statute law revision, or with codification, or reforming, or even reviewing the law. Consolidation is to take all the statutory provisions relating to a subject and to re-arrange them to form a single enactment. This requires far more than the method of scissors-and-paste, for new clauses must often be drafted, language must be harmonised and the bearing of one part upon another has constantly to be checked. When a serious beginning was made last century in the work of improving the statute book[1] a convention grew up that consolidation bills should be referred to a joint select committee of both Houses, and that bills should then go through each House without debate. It is in practice virtually impossible to consolidate without making some amendments to meet inconsistencies or to resolve doubts that have arisen, and there was difficulty over this: if it was accepted that the amendment was minor then both Houses could accept the Bill after the joint committee and spend no time on it, but if the amendments were of substance there was a debate. New provision was made by the Consolidation of Enactments (Procedure) Act 1949. Under this statute the Lord Chancellor lays before Parliament a memorandum about corrections and minor improvements that he thinks should be made in connection with a particular consolidation Bill. People interested may make written representations about these. The Bill and any representations are then referred to a joint committee of both Houses, who must refer their conclusions on these points to the Lord Chancellor and the Speaker. The result is that any corrections or minor improvements that are brought forward must have the approval of the joint committee, the Lord Chancellor and the Speaker, and that they must all be satisfied that the proposals are not such that they ought to be enacted by the usual legislative method. When this has been done neither House can amend the Bill, though the power to reject it is preserved. This Act made the process of consolidation very much easier.

At one time the Lord Chancellor had a Statute Law Committee (a standing

---

[1] See Lord Jowitt, *Statute revision and consolidation* (1951), published by the Holdsworth Club of the University of Birmingham.

committee like the Law Reform Committee) to advise him on the consolidation and revision of statutes. When the Law Commission was created in 1965 this took these matters over, leaving the Statute Law Committee responsible only for superintending the publication and indexing of legislation. Since then the Law Commission has carried out a series of programmes of work in this area. A problem which has sometimes arisen is that in preparing Consolidation Bills the Commission finds that amendments are needed that are not sufficiently minor to come under the procedure described in the last paragraph, but not substantial enough to justify the full process of legislation. This problem has been met by the Law Commission publishing their proposals for the minor and the not-so-minor points, and both go to the Joint Committee of both Houses: if they get through the Joint Committee, neither House will examine the minor points but may re-examine the not-so-minor. A similar arrangement has been made for statute law revision bills. By these means our statute book is being subjected to a thorough and continuing purge.

Codification consists of recasting a body of case-law – usually complicated by some statutes which tinker with minor aspects of it – into the form of a single statute which states it all from first principles. When properly done, it results in the law being both clearer and more readily accessible: when Sir M. D. Chalmers drafted the Bills of Exchange Act in 1882 he reduced a body of some 2,500 cases and 17 statutes into a bill of 100 sections, and the result was an excellent Act. This is a much more exacting process than revision or consolidation, because the case-law nearly always leaves important doubts which have to be resolved, and in resolving them important points of principle must be faced. It is also more complicated to get a codifying statute enacted than one which is only to consolidate or revise, because the resulting codification bill must be passed by the usual legislative process, and inevitably there will be members of either or both Houses of Parliament who think they know better than the codifiers and object to the way in which the points of principle have been resolved. The Law Commission has been responsible for one well-known piece of codification, namely the Animals Act 1971, which codifies the law on liability for animals. At present it is labouring mightily to produce a Criminal Code. Few people doubt that such a code would be an enormous improvement over the present messy and incomprehensible state of much of our criminal law, but the number of contentious points of principle that are raised by drafting such a code are enormous, and it is questionable whether any government will think the political value of the project worth the parliamentary battles likely to be involved in getting it passed.

Reforming the law means attempting to change it for the better, and this is a matter much more exciting and more important than codification, statute law revision or consolidation. Law reform is what everyone had in mind when the Law Commission was created, and it is what people mainly have in mind when they think of it today. In its early days the Law Commission pioneered a new method of approach to law reform: the use of *working papers*. The traditional method of collecting information as used by Departmental Committees and Royal Commissions was for invitations to be sent to all the appropriate organisations and bodies asking them to submit memoranda of evidence, and for there to be an open invitation for anyone else to submit memoranda. The organisations would take stock of a wide range of matters and go to much trouble to produce comprehensive memoranda, a process that took a lot of time; later each organisation would be invited to give oral evidence. The Law Commission consults with government departments and others who are interested and able to help, and then produces a working paper showing the aspects that are seen to be of special concern, the principles or courses that might be followed and the Commission's provisional conclusions. The working papers are made available to anyone interested and they are invited to send in their comments. This directs views on to the areas that really need examining. The Commission then considers the matters again in the light of the comment it has received, comes to a firm conclusion and presents a Report for the Lord Chancellor to lay before Parliament.

Over the years the Law Commission has been responsible for proposing many useful changes which have then been enacted by Parliament. In recent years, however, the process has slowed down considerably. To generalise broadly, the projects the Law Commission has been examining have been less interesting and important, and fewer of their proposals have been reaching the statute book. 'In the period 1965–1982 the Commission produced 59 reports proposing law reform legislation, of which nearly 80 per cent have been implemented by legislation. However, whereas only 15 per cent (6 out of a total of 41) from the period up to 1976 remain unimplemented, over half of the law reform reports in the five years 1977–1982 remain substantially unimplemented.'[1] Things have now reached the point where some people have begun to question whether it performs a useful function any more.[2] In a recent book, R. T. Oerton, who was a lawyer working for the Law Commission for twelve years, gloomily analyses what the troubles have been.[3] The main problem as he sees it is that it is tied hand and foot to the Lord Chancellor and the Lord Chancellor's Department. The Law Commission's functions as laid down in the Law Commissions Act 1965 look impressive – but close attention should be given to the phrases which are printed in italic type in the quotation that follows:

3(1) It shall be the duty of each of the Commissions to take and keep under review all the law *with which they are respectively concerned* with a view to its systematic development and reform, and including in particular the codification of such law, the elimination of anomalies, the repeal of obsolete and unnecessary enactments, the reduction of the number of separate enactments and generally the simplification and modernisation of the law, and for that purpose –

---

[1] See Cretney, 'The politics of law reform – A view from the Inside' (1985) 48 Mod. LR 493.
[2] See Alec Samuels, (1986) 136 NLJ 747; reply by R. T. Oerton, p. 1071.
[3] *A lament for the Law Commission* (1987).

(a)   to receive and consider any proposals for the reform of the law *which may be made or referred to them*;

(b)   to prepare *and submit to the Minister* [i.e. the Lord Chancellor] from time to time programmes for the examination of different branches of the law with a view to reform, including *recommendations* as to the agency (whether the Commission or another body) by which any such examination should be carried out;

(c)   to undertake, *pursuant to any such recommendations approved by the Minister*, the examination of particular branches of the law and the formulation, by means of draft Bills or otherwise, of proposals for reform therein

(d)   to prepare from time to time *at the request of the Minister* comprehensive programmes of consolidation and statute law revision, and to undertake the preparation of draft Bills pursuant to any such programme *approved by the Minister*;

(e)   to provide advice and information to government departments and other authorities *concerned at the instance of the Government* with proposals for the reform or amendment of any branch of the law;

(f)   to obtain such information as to the legal system of other countries as appears to the Commissioners likely to facilitate *the performance of any of their functions*.

(2) The Minister shall lay before Parliament any programmes prepared by the Commission *and approved by him* and any proposals for reform formulated by the Commission pursuant to such programmes.

(3) Each of the Commissions shall make an annual report to the Minister on their proceedings, and the Minister shall lay the report before Parliament *with such comments (if any) as he thinks fit.*

What this means is that the Law Commission looks at nothing except what the Lord Chancellor tells it to look at, and that nothing happens in response to one of its Reports except what the Lord Chancellor is prepared to allow. The Law Commission is independent only in the very limited sense that nobody can tell it what to say about a problem if it is permitted to say anything at all. In its early days the Lord Chancellor was Lord Gardiner, who believed in it; he gave it plenty of important work to do and saw that its work resulted in legislation. But later Lord Chancellors, and Lord Hailsham in particular, clearly did not think much of it, referred less to it, and let more of its reports gather dust upon the shelf. Nor is this all. Other government departments are very territorial and like to keep control over changes in the law affecting what they see as their patch of grass, and in recent years they have usually been able to persuade the Lord Chancellor to keep the Law Commission off it.[1]

The Department of the Environment has successfully put its spanner in the works of various Law Commission reports on matters of land law. The Home Office, too, is sensitive where matters of criminal procedure are concerned, and has usually been successful at keeping these matters to itself. Thus at the time of

---

[1] 'The existence of the Law Commission, an "independent" agency of law reform inserted in the body politic like grit in an oyster, has always been a source of irritation to government departments, but its activities would, if pursued with full-blooded vigour, be particularly uncongenial to a government such as the present one.' (Oerton, *A lament for the Law Commission* p. 26.)

writing we have the strange position that the Scottish Law Commission is looking at the position of children as witnesses, but in England this matter is reserved for the opaque processes of the Home Office. In recent years there has been the added problem of government spending cuts. Following a staff review in 1983 the Law Commission had nearly all its top-grade and therefore most expensive legal staff taken away as an economy measure. This was done on the basis that there would be adequate funding to enable it to recruit staff on short-term contracts – an arrangement that was said to be more flexible and economical. Some of these short-term contract people would be youngsters, and others established lawyers of talent on secondment from the universities and elsewhere; but the latest Annual Report[1] begins with a complaint that the money it is now to receive will not make this possible. The Law Commission was conceived on a grand scale as a body that would take its own panoramic view of the law, identify the parts that are working badly, and propose sensible reforms. Now it looks increasingly as if it is being reduced to a kind of government research institute existing to provide specific answers to narrow legal problems as and when a minister desires one – or wishes to forget a problem whilst appearing to do something about it. Instead of being the architect of the new law it could become the jobbing-builder of the old.

iii Getting the proposals enacted

However sensible and well thought out a report may be, it will almost inevitably gather dust upon the library shelf for ever unless the government can be persuaded to make it part of its legislative programme. As indicated earlier, this means that the relevant minister must be persuaded that the matter is important enough to justify legislation, and he must then convince his ministerial colleagues, all of whom are also pressing the claims of their department for legislative time. Finally, the cabinet must accept that the proposal is politically acceptable within the framework of general policy. We have already seen that one of the reasons why a law reform problem never reaches the stage of any solutions being proposed is that rival departments may be involved and block one another's efforts. The same problem may operate when proposals are in existence, stopping the proposals that have been formulated getting as far as the government's legislative programme. As things stand, reform of the law is an aspect of the work of several government departments, but is central to the work of none. The result can be that law reform proposals are always so far down each one's priority list that time is never found for them. It is often said that the course of law reform would be much smoother if there was a single Ministry of Justice which was responsible for all legal matters, as in many other countries. When nobody is responsible for a thing, the usual result is that there is consistent neglect and therefore there should be a single minister who is definitely responsible.

[1] 21st Report, for the year 1985–86 (May 1987).

Proposals to create a Ministry of Justice were brought before Parliament on various occasions during the last century. The long story of corruption and inefficiency in the officials of the law courts (see below) provided the chief argument. At the time of the Judicature Act of 1873 the worst abuses had been removed, but the framers of that Act found that further changes were needed in the appointment and control of court officials. A Commission was set up to report upon the Administrative Departments of the Courts of Justice. This Commission was primarily concerned with methods of recruiting the officials, but, in discussing the general problems of staffing the departments, the conclusion was that a Minister of Justice should be established. Details were outside their scope, but they made the suggestion that a reorganised Home Office might be the solution. In the absence of any larger scheme it was suggested that the Lord Chancellor should be responsible for the organisation of the courts.[1] When the topic of court officials came before the Royal Commission on the Civil Service forty years later, a Minister of Justice was advocated by Lord Haldane in the evidence he gave to the Commission.[2]

The Machinery of Government Committee, under the chairmanship of Lord Haldane, reviewed the whole position of the administrative side of the legal system.[3] This Committee broke fresh ground in pointing out 'the difficulty of getting the attention of the Government to law reform', and added this argument to that of 'the total inadequacy of the organisation which controls the general administration of the very large staffs' to produce a most impressive case for the establishment of a Minister of Justice. The Committee proposed that the Home Secretary should become Minister of Justice, by the process of transferring some of the work of the Home Office to other departments, leaving the Home Office with its present duties connected with legal administration, and transferring to the Home Office the general work of administration in connection with justice that is now vested in the Lord Chancellor. This would leave the Lord Chancellor free to devote his energies to judicial work and to his position as principal legal adviser to the government. The proposals were not limited to a mere shuffle of existing duties. 'The Minister of Justice would probably sit in the House of Commons and he ought to be accessible to those who have suggestions to make. Besides his administration of the staffs of the various Courts in England, his Department should contain experts charged with the duty of watching over the necessities of law reform, and of studying the development of the subject at home and abroad.'

It is unfortunate that the name Minister of Justice has a sinister sound to many English ears, despite the fact that such a minister is commonly found in most respectable countries. The fear is that 'justice' would then come under his 'control'. In 1986, when the idea was again put forward by the Liberal–SDP

[1] (1874) C 949. [2] (1915) Cd 8130.
[3] (1918) Cd 9230, pt. II, ch. X. See Drewry, 'Lord Haldane's Ministry of Justice – Stillborn or strangled at birth?', (1983) 61 *Public Administration* 396–414.

Alliance, Lord Hailsham told the Bar that it would be 'a menace to the independence of the courts and the judiciary'.[1]

This argument is difficult to dispel because no critic ever explains exactly what it is that he thinks would happen. In some countries with a Ministry of Justice, the appointment and promotion of judges is in the hands of the Minister of Justice. In England the question of a Ministry of Justice need not be complicated by this problem, for there is no reason why this power has to be given to the Minister of Justice, and it could be retained by the Lord Chancellor: indeed, this is what the Machinery of Government Committee of 1918 recommended. It is difficult to see how giving a Minister of Justice control over the administrative arrangements of all the law courts, and the appointment of all the supporting staff, could interfere with the independence of the judges or the integrity of the process of trial. Over many years the Lord Chancellor's Department has been taking over the administrative side of the law courts by a piecemeal process, and nowadays it is only the magistrates' courts which remain largely outside his control. It has not been suggested that any judge has a scrap less independence as a result of this (although it has meant that judges have lost their power to appoint relatives to jobs as court officials without there being any opportunity for public criticism). If the anticipated evil is a Minister of Justice who might sit in the House of Commons and so be an ordinary political minister, without the legal standing and conventional aloofness of the Lord Chancellor, it must be remembered that the Home Secretary already performs many of the duties of a Minister of Justice, and that he no more controls or seeks to control criminal courts than the Lord Chancellor controls or seeks to control civil courts. Lord Birkenhead, who was Lord Chancellor from 1919 to 1922, expressed strong views against a Ministry of Justice. But his best point was only that there is great merit in the position of the Lord Chancellor, who forms a link between the judiciary and the executive, in the absence of which 'the judiciary and the executive are likely enough to drift asunder to the point of a violent separation, followed by a still more violent and disastrous collision'.[2]

There are two points that can be made in answer to this. The first is that it is difficult to see why with the creation of a Minister of Justice this link need be broken: the proposal is to create a Minister of Justice, not to abolish the Lord Chancellor. The second is that if the judiciary need a means of making their views known to the government, there are better ways of doing this than through a Lord Chancellor who has a kind of hybrid office. If he is a judge-cum-politician, and able in that capacity to force the government to take notice of the views of the judges, he can also be a politician-cum-judge, and suppress or ignore them if they are inconvenient. At the end of Lord Hailsham's period as Lord Chancellor he seems to have been severely at odds with much of the judiciary, who were busily telling anyone who would listen about the iniquities of his Civil Justice

---

[1] In a speech to the first annual Bar Conference: see *The Times* 28 May 1986.
[2] Viscount Birkenhead, *Points of view* (1922), I,92.

Review, and he also seems to have fallen out with some of them over his refusal to permit them to make public comments. What the judges need is some sort of collegiate body through which their views can be publicly expressed in the knowledge that the message will be heard in the form in which it is sent, even if the government then decides to overrule them.

In the years since Lord Birkenhead wrote there have been many important changes. One of these has been a big alteration in the constitution and powers of the Lord Chancellor's Department. When Lord Haldane took it over in 1912 it was not far removed from an interesting little museum, and since then it has become a substantial department which has acquired administrative control over most of the court system. Another has been the creation of the Law Commission. This was followed by a period under a Lord Chancellor who was sympathetic to the Law Commission, and for a time the cause of law reform seemed to be doing well despite the absence of a Ministry of Justice. Professor Jackson was originally a strong supporter of the idea of a Ministry of Justice when he wrote the first edition of this book in 1940, but in his last edition he said this:

Many people who are anxious for law reform have continued to regard a Ministry of Justice as being most desirable, and think that such a ministry would resolve their difficulties. I was of that opinion when I first wrote this book, but I have since come to the conclusion that a ministry is not a matter of such great importance. There is often some gain in rearranging departments. In the last few years the ministries responsible for health and housing have been rearranged, but that does not of itself ensure better health or more houses. I do not know of any project for law reform that has failed to progress for lack of a minister. The fact that some suggested reform has not been taken up either by the Lord Chancellor or the Home Secretary does not show that a sound project has fallen between two stools, for who can say that a Minister of Justice would have been more receptive? The original proposal in *Law Reform Now* was that a Law Commission should have a Vice-Chancellor as its head and that he should sit in the House of Commons. That would have made him a minister and a politician. The course actually followed was to create an independent Law Commission and the fact that the Commission's proposals appear to find their way to the statute book without undue difficulty or delay weakens the case for having a Minister of Justice.

Since this was written we have been through a period dominated by an increasingly idiosyncratic Lord Chancellor who was plainly little interested in the Law Commission. When anxious to reform civil procedure, as he was, he set up his own Civil Justice Review (see chapter 8 above) – which he managed to do with such little tact that he seems to have antagonised many of those whose co-operation would be needed if any of the reforms were actually to be carried out. Meanwhile a number of careful and sensible reports from the Law Commission have been permitted to languish unattended to, not because there were any real objections of principle to what they contained, but because other departments besides the Lord Chancellor's Department were involved and could not be bothered with them, and the Lord Chancellor's Department lacked either the muscle or the interest to conquer their apathy. Speaking of the influence of the Department of the Environment on various reports on the law of landlord and tenant, Oerton writes 'It was not that any of our Reports was itself political or biased: no one suggested that. It was simply that any Bill dealing with landlord and tenant law might (so it was said) be made a bone of political contention and so be difficult to pilot through Parliament. And the Department was not prepared to make the necessary sacrifice of time and energy for Bills designed, not to win votes for the Government of the day nor to further Government policies, but merely to improve the law.'[1]

A former Law Commissioner, Stephen Cretney, is less bitter and more optimistic about what has been happening to the Law Commission's proposals than is Oerton; but concludes a review by saying 'I personally doubt whether much more can be achieved short of a major restructuring of departmental responsibilities – involving, for example, a transfer of responsibility for reform of the criminal law from the Home Office to the Lord Chancellor/Minister of Justice.'[2] If Professor Jackson were still alive he might now be returning to his original views on the subject.

[1] *A lament for the Law Commission* (1987) p. 92.
[2] S. Cretney, 'The politics of law reform' (1985) 48 Mod. LR 493 at 513.

Appendix A

◆ ─── ◆

The Final Report of the Civil Justice Review, and the Report of the Marre Committee

The Civil Justice Review (see pages 83–85 above) produced its 181–page Final Report in June 1988.[1] In paragraph 48 the main problems of civil justice are said to involve 'delay, cost, complexity and access to justice'.

As a major source of cost and delay in civil justice the Review identifies the inefficient distribution of business between the High Court and the county court. As explained in chapter 6 of this book, a large amount of the business of the High Court consists of cases which fall within the limits for county court jurisdiction, and which need not have been brought in the High Court at all. It is partly because of this type of work that the High Court is continually overloaded, and hence subject to delay. Delay is bad, not only in itself, but because it invariably means an increase in costs. By comparison with the High Court the county courts are not heavily overloaded. Hence the Civil Justice Review thinks the sensible solution to much of the problem of cost and delay is to send to the county court much of the work which at present is handled by the High Court. As things stand it is theoretically possible for the High Court to transfer work to the county courts – but in practice it does not do so very often. That it is not much done seems to be largely because the High Court and the county courts are two separate systems, and this makes the procedure for transfer a complicated one. Thus once cases are begun in the High Court they are inclined to stay there.

In a Consultative Paper the Civil Justice Review floated the idea of uniting the High Court and the county court within a single system as the obvious solution to this problem.[2] This was not an original suggestion. Professor Jackson strongly pressed the idea in the first edition of this book in 1940, and it was originally proposed in the Second Report of the Judicature Commission in 1872.[3]

In paragraph 104 of its Final Report the Civil Justice Review says this:

The leading argument for a single unified civil court is that it would enable judge power to be allocated to cases on an ideally flexible basis. In a single court with two tiers of judges it would be possible to identify three bands of work, defined in terms of comparative importance, complexity and substance. The top band would go direct to upper tier judges and the bottom band to the lower tier, while a broad middle band would be eligible for trial by either. This band would reflect the overlapping competence of the two tiers of judges rather than assuming a clear dividing line between them, and would enable middle band case allocation to be made by reference to the availability of

---

[1] Report of the Review Body on Civil Justice, Cm 394.
[2] Consultative Paper on General Issues (1987).
[3] Second Report of the Judicature Commission, (1872) xx 217, p. 13.

judicial resources rather than being dominated by rigid financial limits. Specialist cases requiring to be dealt with by High Court judges alone could be sent direct to that tier.

These arguments are strong, and convincing to many lawyers. The Law Society, for example, has come out strongly in favour of the proposal for a single civil court. But such arguments do not impress the Bar, which is hostile to the proposal. Nor did they impress the superior judges, some 40 of whom gave evidence to the Civil Justice Review, and all of whom seem to have been bitterly opposed to the idea. The judges' main objection seems to have been that this would undermine the status of High Court Judges. In paragraph 115 of its Report the Civil Justice Review says this:

There remains one important but less tangible set of arguments against the establishment of a single civil court, taking the form of three perceived risks. The first of these is that public respect for the High Court judiciary may be reduced if the High Court ceases to exist. The second is that it may prove more difficult to recruit High Court level judges to a single court. The third is that the creation of a single court would tend to undermine the independence of the High Court Judges as perceived by Government and the public.

It is tempting to say that these three arguments are merely three different ways of saying that High Court Judges have an over-inflated view of their own status and importance. But the Civil Justice Review took them seriously – or at any rate, took seriously the important political fact that a highly influential body of people believed in them – and in the face of these arguments decided that a single civil court was not a practicable proposition. So in its Final Report the Civil Justice Review dropped the idea, accepted the continued existence of a separate High Court and county court, and concentrated on finding ways in which civil justice could be more effectively distributed between them.

The scheme which the Civil Justice Review eventually devised involves a reversal of the existing pattern under which the High Court has unlimited jurisdiction and county court jurisdiction is restricted. Under the present system of jurisdiction the county court may only hear claims within certain financial limits, and the High Court can try any claim however large or small. The Civil Justice Review proposes giving the county courts a jurisdiction free from any financial limits, and restricting the jurisdiction of the High Court to certain specified types of case, and claims for damages *above* a certain size. In paragraph 124 it says:

(i)   The High Court should handle and try:
    (a) public law cases;
    (b) other specialist cases; and
    (c) general list cases of importance, complexity and substance.
(ii)   Cases of substance means those where the amount in issue exceeds £25,000.
(iii)   There should be a flexible financial band between £25,000 and £50,000 within which cases may be tried in the County Court or the High Court.

As was explained in chapter 6 of this book, the bulk of the time of the High Court is at present taken up with trying claims for damages for personal injury. (The great majority of actions begun in the High Court, as in the county court, are for the recovery of debts; but most of these cases are undefended, and hence take up little judicial time.) The Civil Justice Review is particularly anxious to see that the High Court is relieved of most of its personal injuries work, and that these cases are diverted to the county courts wherever possible. To this end it proposes that all personal injury claims should enter the system via the county court – even where the plaintiff is claiming a sum well within the proposed lower limit for High Court jurisdiction. If these claims start there they will mainly stay there – or so it is thought.

The major transfer of work from the High Court to the county courts would have a significant effect on the nature of the work done in the county courts, and the Review concludes that some changes in the organisation and practices of county courts would be needed if they are to be able to cope. Among the proposals that Civil Justice Review puts forward in this context are: a major revision of the Supreme Court Rules and of the County Court Rules so that both courts should operate under the same procedural rules as far as possible; the creation of an upper tier of Circuit Judges, so that the county courts have a body of more experienced (and better-paid) judges to deal with the heavier cases; and that a senior Circuit Judge should be nominated to take charge of every busy county court, or a group of county courts in areas where there is less business.

Most public comment on these proposals to alter the jurisdiction of the High Court and the county courts has been favourable. But the point has been made, quite validly, that the Civil Justice Review did not ask itself why it is that so many litigants at present choose to use the High Court in cases where the county court is open to them. In most cases litigants will have done this because their lawyers have advised them to do it, and the reason their lawyers so advised them is likely to be that they believe the High Court, notwithstanding the greater cost and delay, offers a superior quality of justice. One barrister has commented as follows:

The High Court is congested because litigants want their disputes before His Lordship in the Strand and not before His Honour in Slough. The High Court judge is a constitutional figure in his own right, whilst the county court is a necessary administrative convenience. The response to the increased demand should be to appoint another 20 or so puisne judges. To put up a NO ENTRY sign to most litigants at the door of the High Court is to sever a vital link between the people and Her Majesty's judges. The constitutional implications of restricting those judges to the service of public companies and to public law disputes are profound.[1]

Removing a large slice of work from the High Court and giving it to the county court will clearly be a satisfactory solution to the problems of cost and delay only insofar as the county courts prove themselves able to provide an acceptable level of service.

The Civil Justice Review tackles the problems of cost and delay by proposing not only changes in the jurisdiction of the courts, but also changes in the way in which litigation is conducted. Here they have put forward three main proposals, all of which were foreshadowed in the Consultation Paper on General Issues (see page 83 above). The first is that the court administration should in future take an active part in controlling the progress of litigation. At present, rules of court lay down in theory the time within which various procedural steps have to be taken, but nothing is done to enforce compliance with these rules unless one party to the lawsuit complains that his opponent is in breach of them. The Civil Justice Review proposes that it should be the job of the court officials to keep an eye on the progress of each case, and to enforce compliance with the rules whether or not one of the parties complains of their breach. The second suggestion is to simplify the interlocutory stages. As was explained earlier in this book (see page 71 above), a number of preliminary decisions about the conduct of a lawsuit are made by court officials,

---

[1] Julian Malins, 'A signal failure' (1988) 138 NLJ 419.

before whom the parties must appear and ask for what they want. These appearances involve the use of lawyers, taking time and costing money. The proposal is to avoid the need for many of these appearances by providing for 'automatic directions': that is to say that a prescribed and pre-packaged collection of procedural steps will automatically be ordained for every case, and there will be no need for a hearing unless one of the parties specifically asks for something different. A third proposal is to change the rules about pre-trial disclosure. At present a litigant is obliged in his pleadings to tell his opponent what his arguments will be, but in general he need not disclose the evidence he will use to support it, and can wait to reveal this at the trial. It is great fun and very exciting for a litigant to be able to spring an unpleasant surprise on his opponent in court with the evidence he unexpectedly calls. But it does not really further the cause of justice if justice is thought to consist partly of getting to the truth, and it wastes court time insofar as it means that it is often unclear in advance of the trial what matters are seriously in dispute. Thus the Civil Justice Review proposes that the parties should be required to disclose to each other in advance of the trial not only the nature of the case they propose to put forward, but also the evidence they will use to support it. Additional proposals to speed and cheapen the path of litigation include a new look at the rules of evidence in civil cases, and a set of professional standards for the conduct of litigation to be issued to solicitors and to barristers by the Law Society and the General Council of the Bar.

In its Final Report the Civil Justice Review also looks at the accessibility of justice, particularly to litigants of small means. The small claims procedure (see pages 34 and 77 above) it considers to have been a great success, in that it enables justice to be obtained in small cases at a cost which bears some sensible relationship to the value of the size of the claim. It recommends that the financial limit for using the procedure should be raised to £1,000. It also proposes that the registrars who handle these cases should be instructed to take an active, inquisitorial approach, and that court staff should be trained and encouraged to give help and advice to litigants. For small claims, debt cases and cases arising out of housing matters, it also proposes that litigants in the county court should be given a statutory right to be represented by a lay person of their choice, subject to the discretion of the court. Despite its general concern about access to justice, the Review carefully avoids getting involved in current disputes about the availability of legal aid. But it does make two mildly controversial proposals. One is that contingency fees should be given further consideration. The other is that the Lord Chancellor should consider the feasibility of a no-fault compensation scheme, financed by private insurance, to supplement or replace tortious liability arising out of the less serious kind of traffic accident.

In general the public response to the Report of the Civil Justice Review has been very favourable. Soon after it was published the Lord Chancellor, Lord Mackay, pronounced himself well pleased with the recommendations, and hinted that there would probably be an Administration of Justice Bill to enact them before long.

As was mentioned earlier in this book (page 354 above), the Marre Committee was set up by the General Council of the Bar and the Law Society to resolve an acrimonious demarcation dispute between the two professions, principally over rights of audience. Its chairman, Lady Marre, was a prominent social worker who was a former chairman of the central appeals advisory committee for the BBC and the IBA. The committee members were six barristers, six solicitors and six persons independent of either profession (one of whom was professor of law at Cambridge). Surprisingly, perhaps, the real reason for setting up the Marre Committee was not stated in the committee's terms of reference, which were wide in the extreme:

(1) To review generally the extent to which the services offered by the legal profession meet the needs and demands of the public for legal services;
(2) to consider how the services of the profession could be made readily available to meet such needs and demands;
(3) to identify those areas where changes in the present education of the legal profession, and in the structure and practices of the profession, might be in the public interest;
(4) to report back to the Bar Council and to the Law Society with recommendations as to how and by whom such areas might be examined further in order to consider such changes as may be required; and
(5) for the purpose of (1), (2) and (3) to consult both inside and outside the profession as thought fit.

These terms of reference are as wide as those of the Royal Commission on Legal Services (Benson Commission) ten years earlier,[1] and inevitably the Committee covered a lot of the same ground. Its 221-page report was published in July 1988.[2] Thus the Marre Committee report deals with much more than rights of audience.

Part I of the report sets out the background to the study. Most of this consists of up-to-date information about the shape and size of the legal profession and how it has changed in the decade since the Benson Commission reported in 1979. It shows how the number of lawyers has steadily grown, and how a rising crime and divorce rate, coupled with a period of economic growth, has caused a steady increase in demand for their services. At the same time public funds have become steadily less available to pay for legal services, and public feeling has become ever less sympathetic to restrictive practices that keep up the price of providing them. In paragraph 4.23 the Marre Committee concludes that 'if the legal profession, and the professions generally, do not initiate appropriate change then it will be forced upon them'.

Part II of the report covers access to legal services. A number of areas of 'unmet need' are described, particularly in the area of social security, welfare and immigration law. It argues the case for more rather than less legal aid. (This of course runs contrary to government thinking on the matter, which is to restrict the cost of legal aid – see chapter 41 above – and it is unlikely that the Marre Committee will persuade the government to change its mind.) The Committee examines contingency fees and the various other current suggestions for financing litigation that were discussed in chapter 41 of this book. It neither opposes them nor supports them, but recommends them for further exploration and discussion. It does oppose, predictably enough, the idea of a 'public defender' as an alternative to legal aid in criminal cases (see page 243 above). The Committee accepts that the problem of 'unmet need' is not simply a question of poor people being unable to afford the fees of lawyers, and says that part of the problem is that people are unwilling to seek legal advice because they are afraid of lawyers, or because they do not trust them. As a partial cure for these matters the Committee recommends that lawyers revise their business practices to make themselves less forbidding and more readily accessible to the public. They praise the increasing trend for solicitors to have 'shop front' offices with attractive decoration and receptionists who are, or at least appear to be welcoming, and

[1] (1979) Cmnd 7648 (see page 361 above).
[2] A Time for Change, Report of the Committee on the Future of the Legal Profession (July 1988). Published by the General Council of the Bar and the Law Society.

they recommend the Bar to revise the rules of practice that at present generally require solicitors and clients to call on barristers when they want to see them, and forbid barristers to do the visiting, even where this would be more convenient to all concerned. On public distrust of lawyers the Marre Committee notes that for barristers and solicitors an adequate system for handling complaints 'is being developed', with the implication that a satisfactory system does not yet exist.

Part III of the Marre Committee report is concerned with legal education. The Committee is in favour of a largely graduate entry to the legal profession, but notes with pain the poor quality of some law graduates, and urges the universities to train them better. It thinks the two professions should share a common academic stage of training, and therefore approves of the proposal to make the Common Profession Examination (see page 350 above) truly common to both branches of the profession, so that graduates in subjects other than law take the same law examination whether they intend to become solicitors or go to the Bar. The Committee also examines the arguments for and against barristers and solicitors sharing a common vocational stage of training. As presented by the Committee the arguments for a common vocational stage and a single Bar-cum-solicitors' Final Examination looks quite overwhelming, but nevertheless it felt it 'imprudent to make any positive recommendation for immediate change'. It strongly recommends that public finance be made available to pay for the courses leading to the barristers' and solicitors' final examinations – something which no government is likely to concede, and least of all the present one. And the Committee approves of continuing education for qualified lawyers, and notes with pleasure that the Bar now looks like adopting the idea. (Solicitors began on this road several years ago: see page 352 above.) Since the report of the Ormerod Committee (see page 346 above) there has existed a Lord Chancellor's Advisory Committee on Legal Education, which seems to have been both sterile and moribund. The Marre Committee proposes this should be replaced by a Joint Legal Education Council to be set up by the Bar and the Law Society, and hopes that this would be fertile and lively.

It was for Part IV, 'The Structures and Practices of the Profession', that the legal world was waiting. The Marre Committee's proposals in this area promised to be particularly important, because here the Bar and the Law Society, which invited the Marre Committee to make proposals, are actually in a position to see that some of the proposals are carried out. Sadly, however, the Marre Committee split on the main point of difficulty, namely the question of rights of audience for solicitors in the courts. The chairman, the six solicitor members and five of the independent members came out in favour of extending rights of audience for solicitors, whilst the six barrister members, together with the one remaining independent member, disagreed and tabled a note of dissent.

There were a number of important matters upon which the whole Committee did reach agreement. These included two important positive proposals: that solicitors should be eligible for appointment as High Court Judges, and that the rule of Bar etiquette forbidding barristers to deal directly with clients should be modified to enable barristers to deal directly with such of their clients as are members of other professions. This proposal for a limited amount of direct access satisfied the barrister members of the Committee; the General Council of the Bar is at present opposed to unlimited direct access bacause of the upheaval this would cause in the way in which barristers' chambers are run.

The Committee was also unanimous on two negative proposals. The first was that there should be no change in the rules on the right of audience in any of the courts apart from the

516

Crown Court. There is a certain lack of logic here. The majority of the Committee thought that solicitors should be given the right of audience in the Crown Court, and if solicitors are thought fit to be trusted with advocacy in serious criminal cases why are they thought unfit for advocacy in serious civil cases? The explanation for this attitude can only be a political one: that there is greater public pressure for solicitors to be given the right to appear in the Crown Court than there is for them to be given rights of audience in the High Court, because the Crown Court, unlike the High Court, operates in places where solicitors are readily available but barristers are not, and the monopoly for barristers is practically inconvenient. Furthermore, solicitors may not be anxious to fight for the right to appear in the High Court just at present, because if the Civil Justice Review proposals are carried out, a large amount of High Court work will be shifted into the county courts, where solicitors have the right of audience already. The other negative proposal upon which the Marre Committee was unanimous was that the advocacy rights in the Crown Court should not be extended to members of the Crown Prosecution Service. Their argument for this was the compelling need for Crown Court prosecutions to be conducted by a lawyer who is independent: which is strange, because the main reason for creating the Crown Prosecution Service was that it should be independent of those who began the investigation (see chapter 22 above).

The point over which agreement between the barristers and the solicitors on the Marre Committee broke down was solicitors as advocates in the Crown Court. The majority of the Committee thought that the solicitors' present limited rights of advocacy in the Crown Court should be expanded to give them the general right to appear in all types of Crown Court work. They said that restricting the right of advocacy to barristers curtails the defendant's right to choose who he wants to represent him; that it frequently means he is represented by a stranger; and that where the defendant's solicitor has to be present in court while counsel argues the case it often causes needless duplication of effort and expense. The only argument against the proposal that the majority of the Committee found convincing was the risk of incompetent advocacy by solicitors who were insufficiently experienced, and this they thought could be met by a system under which solicitors who want to appear in the Crown Courts obtain a licence from a 'rights of audience advisory board' which checks that they know what they are doing. The barristers and their one independent supporter dissented, for the usual reasons. They said that the Benson Commission opposed the idea ten years ago. They said it is a good thing that a client should have a second opinion (and hence, presumably, he must be forced to have one, whether he wants it or not). They said that solicitors are not competent in jury advocacy because they have no experience of it (and, presumably, they must not be given the chance to become competent by experience). And they said that if solicitors acquired the right to take Crown Court cases this would undermine the financial position of the Bar and make it harder for it to continue in existence as a separate profession – something which would tend to lead to the ultimate bogey: *fusion*.

In this the barristers are probably right, in as much as what they predict probably would happen. Low-grade Crown Court work is the bread and butter for young people starting their careers at the Bar and also for a number of older barristers whose career is less than successful. If this work were taken over by solicitors it would probably result in a Bar purged of its less successful older members, and it might also mean a Bar at which it was no longer possible for people straight from law-school to earn a living – and this would ultimately mean a Bar peopled by those who had started their careers as solicitors and then

517

changed over. The Bar hates the idea of this, because it would fundamentally alter the legal world as they know it and love it; so the fact that it might happen is seen by them as a compelling argument against giving solicitors the right to do Crown Court advocacy. But the question is a broader one: from the point of view of the general public, would this rearrangement of the profession be a good thing or a bad thing; and if it would be a bad thing, would it be a worse thing than the inconveniences that are caused by the present Bar monopoly of Crown Court work? At the very heart of the matter of advocacy rights is the issue of fusion; do we want it at all, and if so, how much of it do we want? This is the really difficult point. At the beginning of its report the Marre Committee tells us that it decided not to get into the issue of fusion. As it did not, it is perhaps inevitable that it was unable to reach a unanimous conclusion on the question of rights of audience.

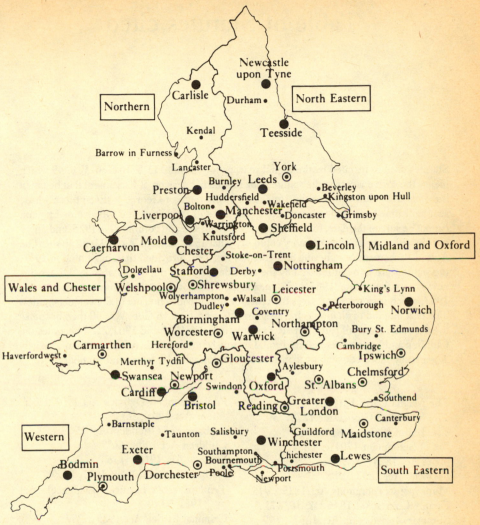

● First Tier (High Court and Crown Court Centres) High Court and Circuit Judges: Civil and Crime

⊙ Second Tier (Crown Court Centres) High Court and Circuit Judges: Crime

• Third Tier (Crown Court Centres) Circuit Judges: Crime

—— Circuit Boundaries

In Greater London the High Court sits at the Royal Courts of Justice and there are Crown Court centres at Acton, Central Criminal Court (Old Bailey), Croydon, Inner London Sesssions House, Isleworth, Kingston upon Thames, Knightsbridge, Snaresbrook, Southwark and Wood Green. *Source: Judicial Statistics*, 1986.

Figure 9 Circuits: High Court and Crown Court centres

519

Table of Statutes cited

Statutes used to be cited by the regnal year, as for example 15 & 16 Geo. V. c. 49 which means the 49th chapter in the statute book passed in a session of Parliament that began in the 15th and continued into the 16th years of the reign of George V. Even those whose accomplishments include remembering the dates of the Kings and Queens of England cannot be sure of the date, for that session began in 1924 and continued in 1925, and only a person with a remarkable memory could say what 15 & 16 Geo. V. c. 49 is all about. The Acts of Parliament Numbering and Citation Act 1962 provided that, beginning in 1963, the statutes are to be numbered by the calendar year and not by the session. Under this new system the statute '1963, c. 37' means the 37th statute in the Volume of Statutes for 1963, which is simpler and gives the year but still provides no clue to the subject-matter. The best method of citation is by the short title, and 15 & 16 Geo. V, c. 49 then becomes the Supreme Court of Judicature (Consolidation) Act 1925 and 1963, c. 37 becomes the Children and Young Persons Act 1963. Obviously the short title (which is actually longer) is generally more convenient than regnal years or calendar years and numbers.

Table of cases cited

Table of Stationery Office publications cited

Official publications can be divided into two broad categories according to whether they come from the activities of Parliament or from other sources. Those arising directly from the work of Parliament include Bills, records of proceedings with reports of debates in each House and in committees, and Acts of Parliament. There are also Select Committees which are appointed each session to inquire into and report on Public Accounts and some other matters, and Select Committees appointed for particular inquiries: their proceedings and reports are published as Parliamentary papers. Powers of delegated legislation give rise to statutory instruments, which are published in a similar form to that used for statutes.

The other types of publication can be subdivided into: (a) Statements on government policy, including material on foreign affairs and other matters; (b) Annual reports from government departments and bodies: (c) Reports from Royal Commissions and Committees of inquiry; (d) Pamphlets and books prepared by or sponsored by government departments on matters with which the department is concerned. Types (a), (b) and (c) are generally presented to Parliament by a minister (nominally by command of the Sovereign) and so are called Command Papers. Before 1870 they carried numbers without any prefix. In 1870 the numbering began again, with the prefix 'C', these running on until the number was over 9000: the process was repeated in 1900 with the prefix 'Cd', again in 1919 with the prefix 'Cmd', again in 1956 with the prefix 'Cmnd', and again in December 1986 with the prefix Cm. These prefixes are often confused, and it is better to include the date as part of the reference. Eventually these papers form part of the volumes of Accounts and Papers for the year, and they may then be cited by the volume in which they are included, but it is not convenient to adopt that as the general system of reference because it cannot be known until some time after a paper has been published.

Sometimes a report is published without being presented to Parliament, as for example a Report in 1937 on the Courts of Summary Jurisdiction in the Metropolitan Area, but that is not a matter of any importance. Royal Commissions and Committees are sometimes referred to by the name of the chairman, as for example the Peel Commission and the Donoughmore Committee, which is not really convenient because there is nothing to link the name with the subject-matter.

On the format of these papers, those in type (a) are often short and have no cover except that on which they are printed, and so they get called 'White Papers'. Those in types (b) and (c) are apt to be longer, and traditionally appeared in covers of stouter blue paper, and so are 'Blue Books'. These are colloquial terms and often all manner of official publications are called blue books. Apart from legislation, the most valuable sources for the administration of justice are to be found in types (b), (c) and (d). The relevant annual reports are listed at the end of this Table. The reports of Royal Commissions, official Committees and Advisory bodies represent the result of independent expert inquiries; a Royal Commission has more dignity and standing than a Committee, but there is no essential difference. It used to be the practice to publish the Minutes of Evidence of these inquiries, but since the First World War this has generally been restricted to Royal Commissions, though reports of Committees often have substantial appendices containing data that otherwise would not be available. Type (d) is akin to ordinary book publishing; the pamphlets and books vary from somewhat slight and popular expositions to the severest kind of technical guide. The principal use of the publications on, for example, probation, prisons and borstals and approved schools, is the provision of an account that is shorter and simpler than that contained in specialist studies. There is no special method of reference to these publications, and they are best referred to by their title and date. A more modern development is the issue of Green Papers, as for example *How Fast* (1968) on speed limits. The object of these papers in green covers is not to set out Government policy but 'to provide the material for a full public debate'.

1872 Second Report of the Judicature Commission (1872) xx 217

1874 Report of the Commission on the Administrative Departments of the Courts of Justice C 949 *507*

1910 Royal Commission on Selection of Justices of the Peace Cd 5250 *404*

1913 Royal Commission on Delay in the Kings Bench Division Cd 6791 (1914) Cd 7177 *82*

1915 Sixth Report of the Royal Commission on the Civil Service Cd 7832 *421, 422, 507*; Minutes of Evidence Cd 8130 *422*

1918 Report of the Machinery of Government Committee Cd 9230 *498, 507, 508*

1920 Royal Commission on the Civil Service Cmd 1049 *423*

1922 Report of the Supreme Court Fees Committee Cmd 1565 *446*

1923 First Report of the County Court Fees Committee Cmd 1856 *446*

1926 First Report of the Committee on Legal Aid for the Poor Cmd 2638 *474*

1927 Report of the Committee on the Treatment of Young Offenders (Maloney Committee) Cmd 2831 *306*

1928 Report of the Committee on Legal Aid for the Poor Cmd 3016 *468*

1932 Report of the Committee on Ministers' Powers (Donoughmore Committee) Cmd 4060 *112*

1933 First Interim Report of the Business of the Courts Committee (Hanworth Committee) Cmd 4625 *82, 362*

1933 Second Interim Report of the Business of the Courts Committee (Hanworth Committee) Cmd 4471 *38, 82, 362*

1934 Committee on Imprisonment in Default of Payment of Fines Cmd 4649 *415*

1936 Final Report of the Business of the Courts Committee (Hanworth Committee) Cmd 5066 *82, 362*

1936 Royal Commission on the Despatch of Business at Common Law Cmd 5065 *82, 362, 363, 371*

1944 Report of the Committee on Justices' Clerks (Roche Committee) Cmd 6507 *185, 403, 415, 416*

1945   Report of the Committee on Legal Aid and Advice (Rushcliffe Committee)
       Cmd 6641   *468, 473*

1945   Report of the Interdepartmental Committee on Rent Control (Ridley
       Committee) Cmd 6621   *135*

1946   Committee on Procedure in Matrimonial Causes; First Interim Report Cmd
       6881 Second Interim Report (1946) Cmd 6945   *60*

1947   Final Report of the Committee on Procedure in Matrimonial Causes Cmd
       7024   *60*

1948   Royal Commission on Justices of the Peace Cmd 7463   *290, 403, 406, 408,
       410, 419*

1949   First Interim Report of the Committee on Supreme Court Practice and
       Procedure (Evershed Committee) Cmd 7764   *82*

1951   Second Interim Report of the Committee on Supreme Court Practice and
       Procedure (Evershed Committee) Cmd 8176   *38, 82, 446*

1952   Third Interim Report of the Committee on Supreme Court Practice and
       Procedure (Evershed Committee) Cmd 8617   *38, 82*

1953   Final Report of the Committee on Supreme Court Practice and Procedure
       (Evershed Committee) Cmd 8878   *82, 92, 104, 454*

1954   Report of the Public Inquiry into the Disposal of Land at Crichel Down
       Cmd 9176   *112*

1954   Report of Inquiries related to the Crichel Down and the Transfer of certain
       Civil Servants Cmd 9220   *112*

1955   Report of the Monopolies Commission on Collective Discrimination Cmd
       9504   *139*

1957   Report of the Committee on Administrative Tribunals and Enquiries (Franks
       Committee) Cmnd 218   *112, 142, 152, 160*

1960   Report of the Committee on Children and Young Persons (Ingleby
       Committee) Cmnd 1191   *310*

1960   Report of the Committee on the Powers of Subpoena of Disciplinary
       Tribunals Cmnd 1033   *138*

1961   Report of the Committee on the Business of the Criminal Courts (Streathfield
       Committee) Cmnd 1289   *174, 179, 180, 295*

1962   First Report of the Working Party on Legal Aid in Criminal Proceedings
       HMSO   *477*

1962   Report of the Departmental Committee on the Probation Service Cmnd
       1650   *284*

1962   Report of the Departmental Committee on the Probation Service, Second
       Report Cmnd 1800   *284*

1962   Report of the Royal Commission on the Police Cmnd 1728   *226*

1963   Report by Lord Denning on the Profumo affair Cmnd 2152   *143*

1964   Report on Children and Young Persons: Scotland (Kilbrandon Committee)
       Cmnd 2306   *309*

1965   Report of Inquiry by Mr A. E. James (Challenor Report) Cmnd 2735   *24*

1965   Report of the Departmental Committee on Jury Service Cmnd 2627   *384*

1965   Report of the Interdepartmental Committee on the Court of Criminal Appeal
       (Donovan Committee) Cmnd 2755   *201, 207*

1965   The Training of Justices of the Peace in England and Wales
        Cmnd 2856   *409*

1965   White Paper on the Parliamentary Commissioner for Administration,
        Cmnd 2767   *165*

1965   White Paper *The Child and the Family and the Young Offender* Cmnd
        2742   *310*

1966   Reform of the Grounds of Divorce; The Field of Choice; Law Commission
        Cmnd 3123   *61*

1966   Reports of the Departmental Committee on Legal Aid in Criminal
        Proceedings (Widgery Committee) Cmnd 2934   *474, 475, 476*

1966   Law Commission Report on Powers of Appeal Courts to Sit in Private and
        the Restriction upon Publicity in Domestic Proceedings Cmnd 3149   *22*

1966   Report of the Royal Commission on Tribunals of Inquiry Cmnd 3121   *143*

1966   Report on the Work of the Probation and After-care Department 1962–1965
        Cmnd 1307   *284*

1967   Report of the Committee on Immigration Appeals (Wilson Committee)
        Cmnd 3387   *132*

1967   Report of the Committee on the Age of Majority (Latey Committee)
        Cmnd 3342   *38*

1967   Report of the Tribunal to Inquire into the Disaster at Aberfan,
        HC 553   *142*

1968   Report of the Committee on Personal Injuries Litigation (Winn Committee)
        Cmnd 3691   *74, 80, 84*

1968   Report No. 54 of the Prices and Incomes Board Cmnd 3529   *458*

1968   White Paper, *Children in Trouble* Cmnd 3601   310

1969   Report of the Royal Commission on Assizes and Quarter Sessions (Beeching
        Commission) Cmnd 4153   *42, 83, 95, 175, 179, 180, 354*

1969   Report of the Committee on the Enforcement of Judgment Debts (Payne
        Committee) Cmnd 3909   *87*

1969   Report on the Work of the Probation and After-care Department 1966–1968
        Cmnd 4223   *284*

1969   Report No. 134 of the Prices and Incomes Board Cmnd 4217   *458*

1970   Report of the Advisory Council on the Penal System, *Reparation by the
        Offender* HMSO (1970)   *281*

1971   Report of the Committee of Death Certification and Coroners (Broderick
        Committee) Cmnd 4810   *195*

1971   Report of the Committee on Legal Education (Ormond Committee)
        Cmnd 4595   *345, 346, 348, 349, 350, 351*

1971   Report No. 164 of the Prices and Incomes Board Cmnd 4624   *458*

1972   Eleven Report of the Criminal Law Revision Committee; Evidence (General)
        Cmnd 4991   *220, 268*

1972   Report of the Tribunal appointed to Inquire into the events of Sunday
        January 30th 1972, which led to loss of life in connection with the procession
        in Londonderry on that day; HL 101, HC 220   *142*

1972   Report of the Tribunal appointed to Inquire into certain issues related to the
        circumstances leading up to cessation of trading by the Vehicle and General
        Insurance Co. Ltd.; HL 80, HC 133   *143*

Table of Stationery Office publications cited

ANNUAL PUBLICATIONS

Civil Judicial Statistics (down to 1974)[1]
Judicial Statistics (for 1975 onwards)
Report of the Law Society on Legal Aid and Advice
Report of the Council on Tribunals
Report of the Law Commission
Report of the Parliamentary Commissioner for Administration
Criminal Statistics
Offences relating to Motor Vehicles
Report of the Prison Department
Report of the Chief Inspector of Constabulary
Report of the Commissioner of Police of the Metropolis
Report of the Criminal Injuries Compensation Board
Report of the Lord Chancellor's Advisory Committee on Legal Aid
Report of the Crown Prosecution Service

[1] To meet the changes made by the Courts Act 1971 *Statistics on Judicial Administration* were published for 1972, 1973, 1974. For 1975 onwards that series has been amalgamated with *Civil Judicial Statistics*, and the amalgam appears as *Judicial Statistics*.

Index

540